MW00584017

WORLDING THE SOUTH

Manchester University Press

Series editors: Anna Barton, Andrew Smith

Editorial board: David Amigoni, Isobel Armstrong, Philip Holden, Jerome McGann, Joanne Wilkes, Julia M. Wright

Interventions: Rethinking the Nineteenth Century seeks to make a significant intervention into the critical narratives that dominate conventional and established understandings of nineteenth-century literature. Informed by the latest developments in criticism and theory the series provides a focus for how texts from the long nineteenth century, and more recent adaptations of them, revitalise our knowledge of and engagement with the period. It explores the radical possibilities offered by new methods, unexplored contexts and neglected authors and texts to re-map the literary-cultural landscape of the period and rigorously re-imagine its geographical and historical parameters. The series includes monographs, edited collections, and scholarly sourcebooks.

Already published

Engine of modernity: The omnibus and urban culture in nineteenth-century Paris
Masha Belenky

Spectral Dickens: The uncanny forms of novelistic characterization   Alexander Bove

Pasts at play: Childhood encounters with history in British culture, 1750–1914
Rachel Bryant Davies and Barbara Gribling (eds)

The Case of the Initial Letter: Charles Dickens and the politics of the dual alphabet
Gavin Edwards

Spain in the nineteenth century: New essays on experiences of culture and society
Andrew Ginger and Geraldine Lawless

 Instead of modernity: The Western canon and the incorporation of the Hispanic (c. 1850–75)   Andrew Ginger

The Victorian aquarium: Literary discussions on nature, culture, and science   Silvia Granata

Marie Duval: Maverick Victorian cartoonist   Simon Grennan, Roger Sabin and Julian Waite

Creating character: Theories of nature and nurture in Victorian sensation fiction   Helena Ifill

Margaret Harkness: Writing social engagement 1880–1921   Flore Janssen and Lisa C. Robertson (eds)

Richard Marsh, popular fiction and literary culture, 1890–1915: Re-reading the fin de siècle   Victoria Margree, Daniel Orrells and Minna Vuohelainen (eds)

Charlotte Brontë: Legacies and afterlives   Amber K. Regis and Deborah Wynne (eds)

The Great Exhibition, 1851: A sourcebook   Jonathon Shears (ed.)

Interventions: Rethinking the nineteenth century   Andrew Smith and Anna Barton (eds)

Counterfactual Romanticism   Damian Walford Davies (ed.)

The poems of Elizabeth Siddal in context   Anne Woolley

Worlding the south

Nineteenth-century literary culture and the southern settler colonies

Edited by Sarah Comyn and
Porscha Fermanis

MANCHESTER UNIVERSITY PRESS

Copyright © Manchester University Press 2021

While copyright in the volume as a whole is vested in
Manchester University Press, copyright in individual chapters
belongs to their respective authors.

An electronic version of this book is also available under a
Creative Commons (CC-BY-NC-ND) licence, thanks to the
support of the European Research Council, which permits
non-commercial use, distribution and reproduction provided
the editor(s), chapter author(s) and Manchester University
Press are fully cited and no modifications or adaptations
are made. Details of the licence can be viewed at
https://creativecommons.org/licenses/by-nc-nd/4.0/.

Published by Manchester University Press
Altrincham Street, Manchester M1 7JA

www.manchesteruniversitypress.co.uk

British Library Cataloguing-in-Publication Data
A catalogue record for this book is available from the British
Library

ISBN 978 1 5261 5288 6 hardback

First published 2021

The publisher has no responsibility for the persistence or
accuracy of URLs for any external or third-party internet
websites referred to in this book, and does not guarantee that
any content on such websites is, or will remain, accurate or
appropriate.

Typeset
by Sunrise Setting Ltd, Brixham

Contents

List of figures   vii
Notes on contributors   x
Acknowledgements   xv

Introduction: southern worlds, globes, and
spheres – *Sarah Comyn and Porscha Fermanis*   1

Part I World/Globe

1   Making, mapping, and unmaking worlds: globes,
    panoramas, fictions, and oceans – *Peter Otto*   39

2   Southern doubles: antipodean life as a comparative
    exercise – *Sarah Comyn*   58

3   Lag fever, flash men, and late fashionable worlds –
    Clara Tuite   78

4   Spatial synchronicities: settler emigration, the voyage out,
    and shipboard literary production – *Fariha Shaikh*   103

5   Augustus Earle's pedestrian tour in New Zealand: or,
    get off the beach – *Ingrid Horrocks*   120

6   Australia to Paraguay: race, class, and poetry in a South
    American colony – *Jason Rudy, Aaron Bartlett,*
    Lindsey O'Neil, and Justin Thompson   139

Part II Acculturation/Transculturation

7   'The renowned Crusoe in the native costume of our
    adopted country': reading *Robinson Crusoe* in colonial
    New Zealand – *Jane Stafford*   161

8   The transnational kangaroo hunt – *Ken Gelder and
     Rachael Weaver*   177

9   'Then came the high unpromising forests, and miles of
     loneliness': Louisa Atkinson's recasting of the
     Australian landscape – *Grace Moore*   196

10   Mapping the way forward: Thomas Baines on expedition
     to the coronation of Cetshwayo kaMpande,
     Zululand, 1873 – *Lindy Stiebel*   215

11   'Wild, desert and lawless countries': William Burchell's
     Travels in the Interior of Southern Africa – *Matthew Shum*   236

12   Short stories of the southern seas: the island as collective
     in the works of Louis Becke – *Jennifer Fuller*   253

                    Part III Indigenous/Diasporic

13   'That's white fellow's talk you know, missis': wordlists,
     songs, and knowledge production on the colonial
     Australian frontier – *Anna Johnston*   273

14   Kiro's thoughts about England: an unexpected text in
     an unexpected place – *Michelle Elleray*   294

15   Mokena and Macaulay: cultural geographies of
     poetry in colonial Aotearoa – *Nikki Hessell*   312

16   Vigilance: petitions, politics, and the African Christian
     converts of the nineteenth century – *Hlonipha Mokoena*   327

17   Reading indigeneity in nineteenth-century British
     Guiana – *Manu Samriti Chander*   346

18   'Some Genuine Chinese Authors': literary appreciation,
     comparatism, and universalism in the *Straits Chinese
     Magazine* – *Porscha Fermanis*   358

The south in the world – *Elleke Boehmer*   378

Bibliography   392
Index   421

Figures

1.1 Robert Burford, 'Panorama of Sydney, N.S.W., in the year
     1829 as painted by Robert Burford and exhibited in Leicester
     Square' (London: Printed and published by Lake & Sons Pty.
     Ltd., n.d.), reproduced from the 'Explanation of a view of the
     town of Sydney', 1829 [DG XV1A/2, Dixson Galleries, State
     Library of New South Wales]   44

1.2 William Heath, 'New Panorama – A Startling Interogation',
     hand-coloured satirical etching, April 1829 [SV/71, State Library
     of New South Wales]   54

2.1 Beato de Liebana Burgo de Osma, 1086 [Wikimedia Commons,
     https://commons.wikimedia.org/wiki/File:Beato_de_
     Liebana_Burgo_de_Osma_1086.jpg]   61

2.2 'The Antipodes', *Melbourne Punch* (28 October 1858), 108
     [Trove, National Library of Australia]   62

2.3 'The Birth of the New Year', *Illustrated Sydney News and
     New South Wales Agriculturalist and Grazier* (12 January
     1876), 12–13 [Trove, National Library of Australia]   64

2.4 John Leech, 'Topsy Turvey – or, our Antipodes', 1854 [H40165,
     State Library of Victoria, http://search.slv.vic.gov.au/
     permalink/f/1cl35st/SLV_VOYAGER1664769]   66

2.5 'Punch's Summary for Europe', *Melbourne Punch*
     (25 April 1861), 52–3 [Trove, National Library of Australia]   67

2.6 'The Metamorphosis of Travel', *Melbourne Punch*
     (19 July 1883), 23 [Trove, National Library of Australia]   73

3.1 Daniel Maclise, 'Alfred, Count D'Orsay', lithograph, 1834
     [NGP D7813, © National Portrait Gallery, London]   79

3.2 Count Alfred D'Orsay, 'Lord Byron', ink and gilt silhouette,
     1823? [NA 338, Newstead Abbey, City of Nottingham
     Museums]   80

3.3 Count Alfred D'Orsay, 'Byron at Genoa', pencil sketch, 1823
     (published 1832) [F. 60, Forster Bequest, © Victoria and
     Albert Museum, London]   81

3.4 Artist unknown, 'Portrait of James Hardy Vaux', originally
     published in Knapp and Baldwin's *New Newgate Calendar*,
     c. 1825 [PXA 2100/Box 36/62, Mitchell Library, State Library
     of New South Wales]   87
3.5 William Romaine Govett, copy of Daniel Maclise, 'Alfred,
     Count D'Orsay', 1834, pen and ink, 1843? [National Library
     of Australia, https://nla.gov.au/nla.obj-138935883]   91
3.6 William Fernyhough, 'Sir Thomas Mitchell', in *Album of
     Portraits, Mainly of New South Wales Officials*, lithograph,
     1836 [442796/3, Mitchell Library, State Library of New
     South Wales, http://archival.sl.nsw.gov.au/Details/archive/
     110327021]   93
3.7 William Fernyhough, 'Piper, the native who accompanied
     Major Mitchell in his expedition to the interior', in *A Series
     of Twelve Profile Portraits of the Aborigines of New South
     Wales*, lithograph, 1836 [National Library of Australia,
     http://nla.gov.au/nla.obj-140394833]   95
5.1 Augustus Earle, 'New Zealand, the entrance of the
     E.O.K. Angha [i.e. Hokianga] River, view taken from
     the bar', 1827 [National Library of Australia,
     http://nla.gov.au/nla.obj-134515122]   124
5.2 Samuel Charles Brees, 'The Hutt Road taken at the Gorge
     looking towards Wellington', 1847 [Alexander Turnbull
     Library, Wellington, New Zealand, https://natlib.govt.nz/
     records/22510170]   130
5.3 Augustus Earle, 'Distant view of the Bay of Islands,
     New Zealand', watercolour, 1827? [National Library of
     Australia, http://nla.gov.au/nla.obj-134504171]   131
5.4 Augustus Earle, 'From the Summit of Cacavada [Corcovado]
     Mountains, near Rio de Janeiro, 1822', watercolour, 1822
     [National Library of Australia, https://nla.gov.au/nla.obj-
     134508248]   133
5.5 Augustus Earle, 'South Head Light, New South Wales',
     watercolour, 1825? [National Library of Australia,
     http://nla.gov.au/nla.obj-134502410]   133
6.1 *Cosme Monthly* (November 1894), n.p. [MS A565, Mitchell
     Library, State Library of New South Wales]   144
6.2 Reading 'Cosme Evening Notes', Lane family photograph
     album [RB030, Cosme Colony Collection, Rare Books and
     Special Collections, University of Sydney Library,
     https://digital.library.sydney.edu.au/nodes/view/6861]   145

8.1 John Skinner Prout, 'The Kangaroo Hunt', in Sarah Bowdich Lee, *Adventures in Australia; or, the Wanderings of Captain Spencer in the Bush and the Wilds* (London: Grant and Griffith, 1851), n.p. 183

8.2 W. Gunston, 'Sport!', in Emilia Marryat Norris, *Jack Stanley; or, the Young Adventurers* (London: Frederick Warne & Co., 1882), n.p. 185

8.3 A. H. Irby, 'Death of the Kangaroo', in Edward Wilson Landor, *The Bushman; or, Life in a New Country* (London: Richard Bentley, 1847), n.p. 189

8.4 A. H. Irby, 'The Bivouac', in Edward Wilson Landor, *The Bushman; or, Life in a New Country* (London: Richard Bentley, 1847), n.p. 190

8.5 Artist unknown, 'Fight with the Kangaroo', in Anne Bowman, *The Kangaroo Hunters* (London: Porter and Coates, 1858), n.p. 192

10.1 Thomas Baines, 'Sketch of the Victoria Mounted Rifles, escort to Theophilus Shepstone, at Rendezvous Camp, Thukela River', 1873 [Robarts family collection] 219

10.2 Thomas Baines, 'Route of the Hon T Shepstone – Ambassador to Zululand and his Natal Volunteer Escort July, Aug & Sept 1873. Observed and drawn by T Baines FRGS Geographer and Artist, Durban Volunteer Artillery' [CU18-AFS-ZAF-S701, Royal Geographical Society Map Room] 220

10.3 Thomas Baines, 'Route of the Hon T Shepstone – Ambassador to Zululand and his Natal Volunteer Escort July, Aug & Sept 1873. Observed and drawn by T Baines FRGS Geographer and Artist, Durban Volunteer Artillery assisted by information from Major Durnford RE, Bishop Schreuder of the Norwegian Mission, Mr Taylor of Tongaat and sketches of surveyors kindly lent by PC Sutherland MD Surveyor General of Natal' [CU18-AFS-ZAF-S70.1, Royal Geographical Society Map Room] 222

10.4 'The Coronation of Cetewayo [sic]', in W. Meynell Whittemore (ed.), *Sunshine for 1883: For the Home, the School and the World* (London: George Stoneman, 1883), p. 160, engraving based on a photograph of 1873, loose sheet [KC PAM 968.3 CET/WMW, Killie Campbell Collections, University of KwaZulu-Natal] 227

14.1 'Kiro, a Native of Rarotonga, Now in England', 'Kiro's Thoughts about England', *Juvenile Missionary Magazine*, 7 (1850), 184 303

16.1 Richard Woodman, 'Jan or Dyani Tzatzoe (Tshatshu); Andries Stoffles; James Read Sr; James Read Jr; John Philip', published by Fisher Son & Co, after Henry Room, line and stipple engraving, 1844 [NPG D8773, © National Portrait Gallery, London] 337

Contributors

Aaron Bartlett is a PhD candidate in English at the University of Maryland. His research focuses on nineteenth-century British poetry and textual culture.

Elleke Boehmer is Professor of World Literature in English at the University of Oxford. Among numerous works on colonial and postcolonial studies, her most recent monographs include *Indian Arrivals 1870–1915: Networks of British Empire* (2015) and *Postcolonial Poetics: 21st-Century Critical Readings* (2018). She is also a novelist and short-story writer, most recently of *The Shouting in the Dark* (2015) and *To the Volcano* (2019). In 2020, she held a British Academy Senior Research Fellowship for the project 'Southern Imagining'.

Manu Samriti Chander is Associate Professor of English at Rutgers University, Newark. He has edited a collection of the short fiction of Egbert Martin (2014), and a special issue of *European Romantic Review* on 'Abolitionist Interruptions' (2017, ed. with Patricia A. Matthew). His monograph *Brown Romantics: Poetry and Nationalism in the Global Nineteenth Century* was published in 2017.

Sarah Comyn is Assistant Professor and Ad Astra Fellow at University College Dublin. She has most recently published *Political Economy and the Novel: A Literary History of 'Homo Economicus'* (2018) and *Early Public Libraries and Colonial Citizenship in the British Southern Hemisphere* (2019, with Lara Atkin et al.). She is currently working on a monograph entitled *A New Reading Public: The Mechanics' Institute on the Goldfields of Victoria, 1851–1901*.

Michelle Elleray is Associate Professor of English at the University of Guelph. She has published extensively on queer film, settler literature, and Victorian literature of empire. Her recent book *Victorian Coral Islands* (2020) examines the intersections of missionary culture and empire in mid-Victorian adventure fiction.

Porscha Fermanis is Professor of Romantic Literature at University College Dublin. Her most recent books are *Early Public Libraries and Colonial Citizenship in the British Southern Hemisphere* (2019, with Lara Atkin et al.) and *Romantic Pasts: History, Fiction, and Feeling in Britain and Ireland, 1790–1850* (forthcoming 2021). She is currently the Principal Investigator of the European Research Council project, 'SouthHem', and is working on a monograph entitled *The Transcolonial Imaginary in Southern Settler Fiction, 1820–1890*.

Jennifer Fuller is Assistant Professor at Jackson State University. Along with a number of recent articles on nineteenth-century writing on the Pacific by R. M. Ballantyne, Louis Becke, and others, she has published *Dark Paradise: Pacific Islands in the Nineteenth-Century British Imagination* (2016), which explores how British authors used depictions of the Pacific to interrogate British identity. She is currently working on a book that explores views of islands in popular culture.

Ken Gelder is Professor of English at the University of Melbourne. His books include *Popular Fiction: The Logics and Practices of a Literary Field* (2004), *Subcultures: Cultural Histories and Social Practice* (2007), *After the Celebration: Australian Fiction 1989–2007* (2009, with Paul Salzman), *The Colonial Journals and the Emergence of Australian Literary Culture* (2014, with Rachael Weaver), *Colonial Australian Fiction: Character Types, Social Formations and the Colonial Economy* (2017, with Rachael Weaver), and *The Colonial Kangaroo Hunt* (2020, with Rachael Weaver).

Nikki Hessell is Associate Professor of English at Victoria University of Wellington. Her books include *Literary Authors, Parliamentary Reporters: Johnson, Coleridge, Hazlitt, Dickens* (2012) and *Romantic Literature and the Colonised World: Lessons from Indigenous Translations* (2018). Her current project is 'Sensitive Negotiations: Indigenous Diplomacy and British Romantic Poetry', funded by the Royal Society of New Zealand.

Ingrid Horrocks is Associate Professor in English and Creative Writing at Massey University. She is the author of *Women Wanderers and the Writing of Mobility, 1784–1814* (2017) and scholarly editions of works by Mary Wollstonecraft and Charlotte Smith, as well as co-editor of the creative-critical collection *Extraordinary Anywhere: Essays on Place from Aotearoa New Zealand* (2016). She is also a travel writer and poet. Her latest book of narrative nonfiction is *Where We Swim* (2021).

Anna Johnston is Associate Professor in English Literature and Deputy Director of the Institute for Advanced Studies in the Humanities at the

University of Queensland. Her books include *Missionary Writing and Empire, 1800–1860* (2003), *The Paper War: Morality, Print Culture, and Power in Colonial New South Wales* (2011), and *Travelling Home, 'Walkabout' Magazine and Mid-Twentieth-Century Australia* (2016, with Mitchell Rolls). *Eliza Hamilton Dunlop: Writing from the Colonial Frontier* (ed. with Elizabeth Webby) is forthcoming from University of Sydney Press.

Hlonipha Mokoena is Associate Professor at the Wits Institute for Social and Economic Research, University of the Witwatersrand, Johannesburg (WiSER). She has published extensively on South African intellectual history, including the monograph *Magema Fuze: The Making of a Kholwa Intellectual* (2011).

Grace Moore is Senior Lecturer in Victorian Studies at the University of Otago. Her books include *Dickens and Empire: Discourses of Class, Race and Colonialism in the Works of Charles Dickens* (2004), *Pirates and Mutineers of the Nineteenth-Century: Swashbucklers and Swindlers* (2011), *The Victorian Novel in Context* (2012), and *Victorian Environments: Acclimatizing to Change in British Domestic and Colonial Culture* (2018, ed. with Michelle J. Smith). Her current book project, *Arcady in Flames*, is a study of the representation of bushfires in nineteenth-century Australian settler literature.

Lindsey O'Neil is a PhD candidate in English at the University of Maryland. Her dissertation-in-progress is entitled 'Reparative Forms: Poetry and Psychology from the Fin de Siècle to WWI'.

Peter Otto is Redmond Barry Distinguished Professor of Literature at the University of Melbourne, Director of the Research Unit in Enlightenment, Romanticism, and Contemporary Culture, and a member of the Australian Academy of the Humanities. His recent publications include *Multiplying Worlds: Romanticism, Modernity, and the Emergence of Virtual Reality* (2011) and *William Blake: 21st-Century Oxford Authors* (2018). He is currently completing a book on 'William Blake, Secularisation, and the History of Imagination', while also working on a project, funded by the Australian Research Council, on 'Architectures of Imagination: Bodies, Buildings, Fictions, and Worlds'.

Jason Rudy is Professor of English at the University of Maryland. His books include *Electric Meters: Victorian Physiological Poetics* (2009) and *Imagined Homelands: British Poetry in the Colonies* (2017). Along with a special issue on *Victorian Cosmopolitanisms* (2010, ed. with Tanya Agathocleous), he has published widely on Romantic and Victorian poetry.

Fariha Shaikh is Lecturer in Victorian Literature at the University of Birmingham. Her publications include *Nineteenth-Century Settler Emigration in British Literature and Art* (2018). She is currently working on a monograph on the nineteenth-century opium wars.

Matthew Shum is a Research Associate in the English Department at the University of Stellenbosch. He has published extensively on imperial culture in colonial South Africa, most recently a monograph entitled *Improvisations of Empire: Thomas Pringle in Scotland, the Cape Colony and London, 1789–1834* (2020).

Jane Stafford is Professor of English at Victoria University of Wellington. Recent books include *Maoriland: New Zealand Literature, 1872–1914* (2006, with Mark Williams), *The Oxford History of the Novel in English, Vol. 9: The World Novel to 1950* (2016, ed. with Ralph Crane and Mark Williams), and *Colonial Literature and the Native Author: Indigeneity and Empire* (2017).

Lindy Stiebel is Professor Emeritus of English Studies at the University of KwaZulu-Natal. She is the author of *Imagining Africa: Landscape in H. Rider Haggard's African Romances* (2001), *Thomas Baines and the Great Map* (2001, ed.), *Still Beating the Drum: Critical Perspectives on Lewis Nkosi* (2005/6, ed. with Liz Gunner), *Henry Rider Haggard* (2009), *Thomas Baines: Exploring Tropical Australia 1855 to 1857* (2012, ed. with Jane Carruthers), and *A Literary Guide to KwaZulu-Natal* (2017, with Niall McNulty).

Justin Thompson is a PhD candidate in English at the University of Maryland. His dissertation-in-progress is entitled 'Women Write the Empire: Genre, Gender, and Governance in the Age of High Imperialism'.

Clara Tuite is Professor of English at the University of Melbourne, where she is also a Co-Director of the Research Unit in Enlightenment, Romanticism and Contemporary Culture. Her most recent books are *Lord Byron and Scandalous Celebrity* (2015), *Byron in Context* (2020, ed.), and, with Claudia L. Johnson, *30 Great Myths about Jane Austen* (2020). She is currently working on an Australian Research Council-funded project, with Gillian Russell, on Regency Romanticism and flash culture in Britain, Ireland, and Australia.

Rachael Weaver is an Australian Research Council Senior Research Fellow in the Australian Centre at the University of Melbourne. She is the author of

The Criminal of the Century (2006) and, with Ken Gelder, *The Colonial Journals and the Emergence of Australian Literary Culture* (2014), *Colonial Australian Fiction: Character Types, Social Formations and the Colonial Economy* (2017), and *The Colonial Kangaroo Hunt* (2020).

Acknowledgements

The Open Access fee for this collection was funded by the European Research Council (ERC) under the Horizon 2020 research and innovation programme (grant agreement no. 679436), and we would like to acknowledge our great debt to the ERC for its generosity. We would also like to thank the ERC and the Irish Research Council (IRC) for contributions towards the cost of illustrations and permissions. We must likewise acknowledge our debt to the ERC for funding the 'Cultural Geographies of the Colonial Southern Hemisphere' conference at University College Dublin in 2017. The conference provided the ideal first airing for many of the chapters in this collection, and we are grateful to all participants and interlocutors for their conversations and contributions.

At Manchester University Press, we would like to thank Matthew Frost, our two anonymous peer reviewers, and our series editors, Andrew Smith and Anna Barton. We are delighted to be among such distinguished company in the 'Interventions: Rethinking the Nineteenth Century' series. We would also like to thank colleagues at University College Dublin for their ongoing support and goodwill, in particular: John Brannigan, Danielle Clarke, Lucy Cogan, Nick Daly, Fionnuala Dillane, Margaret Kelleher, Kathryn Milligan, and Michelle O'Connell. For stimulating conversations and/or advice at various stages, special thanks must go to Sharae Deckard, Alan Lester, Amanda Nettelbeck, Hussein Omar, and Meg Samuelson, as well as to our collaborators in the SouthHem research team, past and present: Lara Atkin, Megan Kuster, Sarah Galletly, Nathan Garvey, Susan Leavy, Sarah Sharp, and Karen Wade-Wilson. Our most substantial and pressing debt of gratitude, however, is to the contributors to this volume, who have made this experience such an intellectually rewarding and happy one.

Finally, we must include a brief note on the uses of language in this collection. We have not italicised words in Indigenous and non-European languages on the basis that they are not 'foreign' to the peoples, cultures, and communities being discussed by contributors. We have capitalised the word 'Indigenous' because this is now standard practice among Indigenous studies scholars. We have, however, declined to standardise the capitalisation (or otherwise) of the racial categories 'black' and 'white' on the basis that the capitalisation of these terms is contested. In the absence of consensus on this issue, we have trusted in the judgement of our contributors in the particular contexts in which they work and write.

Sarah Comyn and Porscha Fermanis
University College Dublin

There is a great difference, in short, between looking *to* a place and looking *from* it.
Edward Gibbon Wakefield, *Letter from Sydney* (1829)

Our people have the whole hemisphere to themselves.
Sydney Smith, *Whether to Go and Whither?* (1849)

All times are important to us. No time has ended and all worlds are possible.
Alexis Wright, 'Politics of Writing' (2002)

thanks for making the South
an erogenous zone
corporeal and sexual
emotive and natural
waiting in the shadows
of dark feminine instinct
Selena Tusitala Marsh, 'Guys like Gauguin' (2007)

To world is to enclose, but also to exclude.
Eric Hayot, *On Literary Worlds* (2012)

Introduction: southern worlds, globes, and spheres

Sarah Comyn and Porscha Fermanis

Linked by the histories, geographies, and legacies of 'imperial desire', the countries and peoples of the southern hemisphere have long been shaped by their approximate otherness.[1] Defined and redefined by shifting European cartographic visions of unknown and unknowable lands inspiring exploration, discovery, conquest, and colonisation from at least the sixteenth century onwards, the qualities of distance and difference ascribed to those southern topographies by a northern gaze have more recently been remapped on to the south as an 'indexical category' and conceptual space.[2] No longer characterised solely or necessarily by hemispheric location, this south is perceived as the antithesis or antimony to the north's modernity, as belated, inverted, nugatory, and even pathological in its relation to the time/space coordinates exported by Euro-American capital and territorial expansion.[3] Whether the American South, the Mediterranean South, or the Global South, the south is nearly always an 'uncanny temporal figure', implying a vertical hierarchy of 'above and below' and 'centrality and marginality' based on the apparently normative qualities of 'free-market democracy, modernity and its absence'.[4] As Harry Harootunian reminds us, this unevenness within the global field is not an incidental or temporary condition but rather a functional outcome of a long history of imperialist and/or neo-imperialist capitalist accumulation, requiring us to reinstate the 'mixed temporalities' and 'historical uncanny' that have been 'written over' by histories of nation statehood, modernity, and globalisation.[5]

Nowhere have these progressive, familiarising strategies been more apparent than in the literary histories and national canons of the historically 'British' southern settler colonies of Australia, New Zealand, and South Africa, where enduring myths of Anglo-Saxon cultural exceptionalism and national self-containment have persistently overwritten the uncomfortable legacies and enduring realities of settler colonialism.[6] Driven by the rise of Black Consciousness, Indigenous activism, and anti-racism movements, revisionary scholarship in multiple disciplines over the last fifty years has

penetrated these colonial amnesias and national characterologies in ways
that have brought to the fore the speculative nature of settler colonies as sites
of 'uneasy emergent' modernities, as well as foregrounding the histories,
genealogies, and cultures of Indigenous, Black, and other non-European
peoples.[7] In the literary field, a number of studies have contested foundational settler myths and reinstated racialised silences within national historiographies and canons. Yet aside from pioneering works by African nationalist,
Black Consciousness, and Indigenous studies scholars, few have radically
questioned the periodisations and conceptualisations of long-standing literary
histories of the 'British world', or sought to move outside either distinctive
national paradigms or a transnational turn limited primarily to dialectical
or comparative relations with Britain and/or America.[8] Despite some significant new work resituating extra- and non-European southern geographies,
temporalities, and histories, the literary histories of the southern hemisphere
remain largely nation-centred and globally marginal.[9]

Beginning with the premise that our current literary histories and conceptual paradigms must take into account neglected histories of southern cultural
estrangement and marginalisation, this collection focuses on the literary cultures of the British-controlled settler colonies in the southern hemisphere
from 1780 to 1920. While our emphasis is primarily on the periods, practices, and ideologies traditionally designated 'Romantic' and 'Victorian' in
British literary studies, we extend our timeframe to the first two decades of
the twentieth century in order to test the relevance, longevity, and/or belatedness of these periodisations and paradigms in a number of extra-European
contexts and cultures. More specifically, the collection encompasses the
English-language, transliterated, and translated literatures of Indigenous,
Black, mixed-race, and European communities in British colonies and settlements in Australia, New Zealand, South Africa, South America, the South
Pacific Islands, and the Straits Settlements, as well as the diasporic and migra-
tory cultures of the Indian, South Atlantic, South Pacific, and Southern Oceans,
including those of Malay, Chinese, and Indian diasporas. Although a single
edited collection cannot hope to adequately cover the richness of émigré,
diasporic, settler, mixed-race, and Indigenous literary traditions over such a
wide geographical space and historical time, we offer eighteen intra- and/or
inter-colonial chapters that reflect the demographics, size, and scale of cultural production in various southern colonies and settlements: eight on (or
partly on) the Australian colonies, three on New Zealand, three on South
Africa, two on the Pacific Islands, one on British Guiana, and one on the
Straits Settlements. In each case, these chapters serve as gestures towards
the various literary cultures of the southern colonies while nonetheless seeing both colony and nation as emergent, permeable, and hybrid, rather than
natural or normative, categories in the nineteenth century.[10] As Christopher

Bayly has pointed out, 'nations' are 'not originary elements to be "transcended"' by transnational forces but rather the complex (and often late) products of those very forces.[11]

Without attempting anything close to complete hemispheric coverage or suggesting that these chapters have any kind of representative status, our aims are, first, to bring under a synoptic framework new scholarship on the literatures and cultures of the southern colonies and to consider methodologies, from worlding to hemispheric analysis, that might allow us to decentre nation-based accounts of literary scholarship in favour of more permeable oceanic and place-based ones; second, to reflect on the southern colonies' interconnected histories of imperialism, settler and mercantile colonialism, and structural inequality; and, third, to collectively elucidate a set of shared thematic concerns, literary forms and tropes, and aesthetic and stylistic practices that are distinctive (although not always exclusive) to the region. The collection's focus on the British southern colonies as an analytical field is not, therefore, intended primarily in the 'possessive sense' – as in, the colonies belonging to Britain – or even in the 'adjectival mode' as a means of describing 'elective, hyphenated forms of belonging', but rather as a way of illuminating complex sets of historical and cultural relationships or correspondences, including shared histories of estrangement, violence, indenture and unfree labour, and the frictions of ethnological encounter, as well as more positive qualities of interconnection, relationality, mobility, syncretism, and circuitry engendered by relative geographic proximity, transnational and transcultural processes, and shared cultural attitudes.[12] This methodological position revises current approaches to British world studies by uncoupling the southern settler and island colonies from studies of settler colonialism in North America, while simultaneously de-prioritising imperial orientations and identities in favour of southern perspectives and south–south relations across a complex of southern oceanic and terracentric spaces.[13]

Although we acknowledge the linguistic and other diversities of the southern colonies, our emphasis on literature in English reflects, as Tamara Wagner has put it, 'the beginning of a global spread of "Anglophone" writing … that "the nineteenth century literary world took for granted"' but that we can now see involved a range of 'suppressions, substitutions, and coercions' that turned English literature into an 'increasingly global phenomenon'.[14] Concerned as much with these suppressions and coercions as with the opportunity to consider literary history and genre formation on a hemispheric scale, our goal is to 'open up wider questions about the definition and status of literature in English' and to consider the ways in which the foundation of English-language national canons silenced other languages and cultural forms.[15] Although the collection primarily explores Anglophone writing and thereby risks reproducing 'the very dominance of English culture and imperial power [it] sets out to question', we understand such writing as existing within a multilinguistic field. We also take seriously Sharon Marcus' call for a truly transnational (as opposed to a merely comparative) approach to literary studies: 'when used rigorously [transnational] refers to countries whose power relations are asymmetrical' and explores 'how those asymmetries "become the conditions of possibility of new subjects"'.[16]

While not all the individual chapters collected here are transnational in their coverage or scope, we see the collection – when taken as a whole – as addressing the asymmetries inherent to Marcus' rethinking of transnationalism. This kind of transnationalism rests not so much on comparative studies concerned with 'national distinctiveness', even ones that study 'variations and interactions among national literatures', or on new imperial histories that see imperial and colonial histories as 'interdependent' and 'mutually constitutive', but rather on recent offerings from postcolonial, world-literary, and Indigenous studies that think 'in less imperialist terms' and resist 're-inforc[ing] the old imperial hegemony, subsuming all history within the boundaries of the imperial relationship' to which comparative accounts can still be susceptible.[17] While acknowledging the importance of pioneering work on cross-cultural, transnational, and lateral literary exchanges within empire by Elleke Boehmer and others, we primarily focus in this collection on southern subjectivities, orientations, and perspectives – what we call 'worldings' – rather than on south–south exchange, seeing the collection as the first step towards a more fully integrated hemispheric account of southern literary history – one that must take into account epistemic specificity as much as it does regional connection.[18]

The primary significance of the collection therefore lies in its attempt to rethink British or metropolitan perspectives and to reorient the literary history and canons of the nineteenth-century British world in order to better account for the varied and sometimes competing perspectives and literary cultures of the southern colonies and their peoples. Conceptualising a shared history of English-language and translated writing from this part of the southern hemisphere has the 'heuristic potential' to challenge both the cohesion of national literary histories of Australia, New Zealand, and South Africa (themselves often seen as secondary to a 'primary framework' of 'English literature') and the 'homogenizations of overarching categories' such as British world and Anglosphere.[19] It also has the potential to reassess critical constructions and periodisations such as Romantic and Victorian by showing how minor, marginal, neglected, and/or non-canonical writers can be central to a different kind of canon – one that is predicated less on metropolitan literary histories and their turning points, or even on the idea of a global 'imperial commons', and more on southern cultural productions in multiple regional centres from Cape Town to Dunedin.[20]

How, we ask, can we construct a new and collective literary history of the southern colonies over the long nineteenth century and why should we want to do so? What is to be gained by thinking collectively about the literatures and cultures of the colonial south? And what can a more regionally specific study of the southern colonies add to British world perspectives that generally include Canada and the United States within their frames of reference? How, too, does our view of literatures traditionally seen within national contexts change when we view them from a regional and/or hemispheric perspective? How do transnational or comparative studies focused on an east–west or north–south perspective alter when seen from south–south perspectives? How might such a literary history challenge our current literary periodisations and conceptualisations of the nineteenth-century British world? And how can we learn from Indigenous and diasporic perspectives in ways that are both intertwined with and independent of what has been called the 'settler aesthetic'?[21]

The impetus behind these questions lies in the recent interest in the legacies of colonial knowledge production and related understandings of southness as part of an ethical 're-territorialising of global intellectual production'.[22] Contemporary theory, scholarship, and activism across multiple disciplines has used the south as a powerful way of writing against Eurocentric and transatlantic ideas of knowledge production and the economic dominance of the north, rejecting in particular 'imperial framings that disavow thinking in and from those areas being studied and compared' and/or that view the south primarily as an abstraction, reflection, or projection of European imaginaries.[23] In attempting to understand what Boaventura de Sousa Santos calls the 'epistemologies of the south' as part of both a larger critique of Eurocentric modernity and a longer, unfinished history of emigration, imperialism, and settler and other colonialisms, this collection looks back to the nineteenth century as a way of understanding the genesis of today's uneven world field and the Global South's 'entangled political geographies of dispossession and repossession'.[24]

A recurring argument in many of our chapters is that the south as we know it today was to a large extent produced at the intersection of nineteenth-century literary, cartographic, political, legal, and economic discourses rather than being a pre-defined spatial, ontological, and/or conceptual category.[25] From the outright fictions of Edward Gibbon Wakefield's 'insider' positioning in *A Letter from Sydney* (1829) to the 'speculative geographies' of James Vetch and Thomas J. Maslen, imperial cartographies and other mutually informing discursive fields began to fill ostensibly 'blank' or 'absent' southern spaces, making southern toponymy 'a vehicle of ... collective wish-fulfilment' where 'names verbalized images of geographical pathos, bridging physical space with imagined communities'.[26] As John Eperjesi has shown in his study of the American Pacific, the 'imperialist imaginary' played a crucial role in producing culturally constructed zones that later become classified geographies.[27] Oceania, for example, was successively imagined and reimagined as the gendered, racialised, and erogenous site of what the Samoan-New Zealand poet and scholar Selina Tusitala Marsh's poem in our epigraph calls 'dark feminine instinct' (stanza II, line 31), where 'skin colour and physical organization' not only elaborated 'region-wide racial taxonomies' but also encouraged an 'interest in racial plasticity, environmental adaptation, mixing or miscegenation, and blurring of racial boundaries'.[28]

This constructed south and its emerging regionalisms and interregionalisms (Oceania, Australasia, Indian Ocean, Malay Archipelago, Pacific Islands, etc.) was itself never unitary or self-contained but existed alongside, and was contingent upon, the other southern worlds lived and imagined by Indigenous and diasporic peoples, which form part of what Anne Salmond has called 'cosmo-diversity' or what James Clifford has described, in an argument against absolutist and rigid oppositions in defining Indigenous experiences, as 'composite "worlds" that share the planet with others overlapping and translating'.[29] Yet as David Chandler and Julian Reid have argued in their trenchant critique of ontopolitics in the neoliberal context, taking alterity seriously means acknowledging not just that there are multiple ontologies or that Indigenous communities constitute different (albeit relational) worlds, but also that they 'world' or enact those worlds in different ways. This requires, as the Aboriginal activist and scholar Mary Graham and the Aboriginal anthropologist Deborah Bird Rose have noted, the extension of 'ontopolitical ethics' into 'the realm of the more-than-human' and the collapse of nature/culture and subject/object divides.[30] Moreover, as Ivan Lacy has pointed out, both world-building and place-making are fundamentally tied to the dynamic and emergent processes of subjectivity and identity formation: 'as places change, so too do identities'.[31]

Following Lacy, Clifford, and others, we understand the various peoples and communities of the southern colonies as existing on a 'continuum' and/or as occupying a 'sometimes fraught borderland' between 'mutually constitutive' Indigenous and diasporic affiliations and identities, as well as between European and non-European ones.[32] The chapters in this collection therefore aim to unsettle 'the analytical metaphor of ... cross-cultural collision' by considering experiences of acculturation and transculturation, looking at the ways in which complex processes of 'adjustment' and 'recreation' can 'allow for new, vital, and viable configurations to arise out of the clash of cultures and violence of colonial and neo-colonial appropriations'. We nonetheless remain alert to the asymmetries of those configurations, and to the ongoing necessity for non-European and Indigenous-centred perspectives that emerge from within local communities.[33]

Southern latitudes, hemispheric methods, and Indigenous reworlding

Drawing on north–south hemispheric approaches that have decentred the United States as a field of analysis in American studies, the collection focuses on what Isabel Hofmeyr has called a 'southern latitude', primarily creating ways of seeing parallels and lines of connection across the southern hemisphere.[34] It therefore involves a way of rethinking the contours of literary production by replacing the 'dominant circuit of cultural production, running from north to south' and west to east with south–north routes, as well as with 'horizontal programmes' that include south–south routes.[35] In particular, we move away from considering 'the relations of new-world cultures to their old-world counterparts' towards an emphasis on the literatures and cultures of the new world.[36] If our approach is more focused on southern perspectives than on southern comparisons or exchanges, it nonetheless shares with American hemispheric studies an analogous desire to reconfigure, or at least to seriously question, the privileged place of Britain in British world studies, as well as similarly arguing for affinities and parallels between the literatures and experiences of the peoples of the colonial south. It therefore moves away from 'nationalist claims for the endogamous production of cultural forms' into a cultural understanding defined by a 'regional logic'.[37]

In encouraging a rethinking of a shared and interregional literary history *from* South Africa, Australia, New Zealand, South America, Southeast Asia, and the Pacific islands, and as well as *from* Indigenous and diasporic spaces, our aim is not just to challenge western and northern conceptions of knowledge production that tend to see literary forms and ideas as radiating outwards from the metropolitan cores of empires to its peripheries, but also to multiply the loci, platforms, and multi-directional circuits on which alternative worldviews might emerge. We aim, too, to produce a more 'geographically inclusive' literary model of the nineteenth century, with 'proof-texts' drawn from so-called 'minor' and 'minority' writers from Australia, South Africa, New Zealand, South America, and the Pacific Islands, and from Māori, Pasifika, Aboriginal, African, Indian, Chinese, and mixed-race writers.[38] While the collection remains interested in intercultural transfers and cultural retentions between old world and new – that is, in how European genres and forms were read, transplanted, circulated, modified, and adapted in the southern colonies, as well as with how the south and its peoples were represented from within European metropoles – its primary focus is on those texts and cultures produced by the experience of travelling, living, and being in the south, emphasising southern locations, southern audiences and modes of addressivity, and south–south interactions.

In making a virtue of a southern perspective from 'below', we seek to counter those literary histories that are nearly always written from 'above', but we do not wish to replicate supra-planetary views of the south as itself a monolithic entity or framework. We have no desire to argue for a single south or for a pan-southern literary culture that is universal in its scope and reach; nor we do we seek to study the literary history of the southern colonies solely from within the history of globalisation – even of the counter-hegemonic kind.[39] The chapters within this collection do not propose a single ideological perspective or methodological approach, just as the southern colonies and settlements we consider do not share a single language, law, literature, demographic, or ethnic base: it is as possible to argue for an Aboriginal south, a Māori south, a Pasifika south, a Khoisan south, and a Boer south as it is to argue for a Black, Green, or Red Atlantic.[40] It is also possible to imagine the south in ways that invoke more explicitly its ongoing epistemological resistance to northern objectification and its lived, sensory experience of 'southern affinity' or 'mutual recognition' – the south in the world – as Boehmer suggests in her concluding chapter in this collection.

Allowing for these perspectives and for the varying critical views of settler colonial, decolonial, postcolonial, and Indigenous studies is not an either/or proposition, but rather the necessary result of bringing together or collocating chapters that cover a wide geographical space and that require us to look across cultures, peoples, and places, including what Clifford has called the practices of Indigenous and 'subaltern region-making', and what Chadwick Allen has called 'trans-Indigenous' methodologies.[41] While it is essential to rethink nineteenth-century settler colonialism and its legacies, to focus *only* on settler colonial paradigms or the space/time coordinates of colonial-modernity is to continue to privilege the universality of Euro-American forms of knowledge and their truth claims.[42] As Shino Konishi has pointed out in an exceptionally even-handed discussion of the relationship between settler colonial studies and Indigenous history, the fear among some Indigenous studies scholars is that settler colonial studies undermines Indigenous theory and agency, and reifies and replicates the 'structural inevitability' of colonial power and/or forces Indigenous peoples into what Alissa Macoun and Elizabeth Strakosch deem a 'false binary between resistance/sovereignty and co-option in the colonizing process', requiring the intervention of alternative methodological positions.[43]

The idea that settler colonial studies is '"primarily a settler framework" for thinking through colonial relations' also finds expression in an ongoing distrust among Indigenous studies scholars towards literary criticism and theory.[44] Literature, as the Goori poet and scholar Evelyn Araluen argues, 'is a term we apply to the textual products of the West, or those texts that reinforce accepted narratives of the other', while literary theory is either

'unconcerned with our material realities and processes of cultural production, or it has seized upon our creations for its tropes and metaphors'.[45] If
for postcolonial scholars such as Gayatri Spivak, there is no lost origin
before colonialism, no 'ontological purity' whereby we can escape the imperial worlding that defines both the coloniser and the colonised, some Indigenous scholars see decolonial studies as offering a better way of attending to
what the Māori scholar Linda Tuhiwai Smith calls 'a long-term process
involving the bureaucratic, cultural, linguistic and psychological divesting of
colonial power'.[46]

Acknowledging our own editorial position as white Europeans outside of
the Global South, working and operating within a Eurocentric institutional
and conceptual framework, requires us simultaneously to draw on a western
vocabulary of literary, cultural, and aesthetic scholarship, and to recognise
the ways in which the apparent universality of such scholarship has been
contested, as well as to acknowledge the ways in which western understandings of literature marginalise alternative traditions of creative expression
and identity formation. Decolonial movements within and outside academia
demand that we recognise the complicity of literary studies in the erasure of
Black, Indigenous, and Asian voices from literary histories, and work to
recover and highlight these literary cultures insofar as we can do so. All of
the chapters in this collection are therefore attentive to the violent racial
histories and cultures of settler colonialism, with at least five chapters centring Black, Indigenous, and/or Asian voices and texts. While this is by no
means a sufficient representation of a southern colonial world that was
never demographically very white or very British, we attempt to denatu-
ralise 'whiteness' throughout the collection, positioning it as a contested,
malleable, and unstable category as we navigate the boundaries of what can
be appropriately known or addressed by non-Indigenous scholars. Our aim
is to come to a more nuanced and ethical position in relation to Indigenous
epistemologies and the worlds they construct, and to consider western and
Indigenous forms of knowledge within a relational ontology, while simultaneously avoiding any investment in what the Unangax̂ scholar Eve Tuck
and K. Wayne Yang have called 'settler moves to innocence': that is, a range
of 'intellectual evasions of settler complicity' in the colonisation of Indigenous peoples.[47]

Recognising that it is not enough to attempt to 'transform settler ontologies',
this collection therefore hopes to learn from the insights of Indigenous studies scholars in ways that are not appropriative and to contribute, however
modestly, to the 'interpenetration of indigenous and exogenous knowledge'.[48]
In particular, it recognises the insights of studies of Indigenous knowledge,
genealogies, and kinships as a way of countering histories of globalisation
that obscure different temporalities, inequalities, and asymmetries of power.

This risks the neglect of disconnected groups, which are seen 'at best as sup-plementary and at worst as irrelevant', as well as obscuring those 'non-cosmopolitan' literary cultures and texts that lie outside the 'global literary paradigm'.[49] As Sanjay Krishnan has pointed out, the prevailing definition of the global – that is, the 'comprehension of the world as single bounded and interconnected entity developing in common time and space' – finds its first systematic expression in the nineteenth century during the rise of European territorial and commercial imperialism. This way of thematising the world resulted in the naturalisation of a homogenising 'global as perspective', securing for itself 'the reification[s] of the global as thing'. For Krishnan, the global does not point to the world as such but rather 'at the conditions and effects attendant upon institutionally validated modes of making legible within a single frame the diverse terrains and peoples of the world'.[50]

In distinguishing the 'globe' and its spatialising methodologies of net-worked globalisation from the 'world' and its temporalising methodologies of mondialisation, this collection draws on an ontological tradition that stretches from Martin Heidegger and Erich Auerbach to Henri Lefebvre, Jacques Derrida, and Jean-Luc Nancy of seeing the world as a spatio-temporal way of inhabiting – as a life-world or a world-picture – rather than as a place on a map or a product of 'globalising assumptions of totality, transition, and transcendence'.[51] While this turn to ontology may seem odd for a collection committed to the spatial or geographic expansion of its field and proof-texts, like Krishnan we seek to decouple the 'representational structures through which the world is objectively given for sight' from the world-as-object.[52] In thinking about 'the prestige and power' of an art work's 'metaphoric capture of totality', one of the central challenges this collection confronts is how better to understand the complex, dialectical relationship between the real world, in which a literary text or art object exists, circulates, and is actuated by readers, and the symbolic or conceptual world (or the idea of a world) it shows or creates: in other words, as Eric Hayot puts it, to demonstrate the ways in which 'a material understanding of the actual world situation' can function as 'a compliment to and subtend-ing force of the world's apprehension as a philosophical concept'.[53]

A second challenge is to think through how our own approaches can enable or disenable the processes of worlding and therefore to understand worlding as a critical sensibility as well as a literary or artistic practice. Christian Moraru has deftly pointed to the key question: 'What does it mean to know our world and lay out this knowledge in our research, to deploy this *geo-epistemology* – the *system* this knowledge implies, one way or the other – so as to aggregate cultural production, to describe its *poiēsis* and agents, and to frame its reading?'[54] Our proposal is not a rejection of the insights enabled by the methodologies of critical global thinking, world-systems theory, and/or world literature, but rather their fusion with a more explicit focus on the ontological dimensions of worlding so as to better appreciate the world-making capabilities of aesthetic objects.[55] To ignore the temporal and spatial constructions of a text's own world and its 'unspoken, world-oriented ideological normativity' is, we argue, to risk replicating 'the presuppositions by which perspectives that cannot find institutional validation within the framework established by the global are occluded or suppressed'.[56]

Conscious of the extent to which worlding is both a process of 'enclosing' and 'excluding', the 'worlding' of our title draws on critical iterations and explications of Heidegger's term by postcolonial, comparative, and world-literary scholars such as Gayatri Spivak, Edward Said, Homi K. Bhabha, Dipesh Chakrabarty, Eric Hayot, Sanjay Krishnan, and John Muthyala to refer to the ways in which imperialist discourse both projects and conceals the world of the colonised other as it absorbs peoples and spaces into 'the consolidation of Europe as sovereign subject' – a universalising 'form of epistemic violence' that continues to play a role in how colonised subjects see themselves long after decolonisation, as well as marking out the 'continuing success of the imperialist project, displaced and dispersed into more modern' (i.e. neoliberal) forms.[57] For Spivak, imperialism is a worlding process that attempts to disguise its own workings, codings, or value-making so as to naturalise western dominance.[58] For Krishnan, too, the point of worlding is not so much to study the world-picture itself (i.e. *what* is seen) but rather to consider the ways in which seeing takes place and 'how that world is coded in value terms and the forms through which the world is brought into view', and therefore to expose its conditional, non-universal status.[59] This kind of worlding, Krishnan argues, is a critical exercise that 'not only illuminates how we might think about the past' but 'may also shed light on a way of productively making strange or unfamiliar our naturalized sight' in a way that involves the kind of engaged, contrapunctal reading that Said advocates when he suggests that we must 'reread' the 'cultural archive' 'with a simultaneous awareness both of the metropolitan history that is narrated and of those histories against which and together with the dominating discourse acts'.[60]

In this formulation, the history of artistic production in sites of colonisation is best understood as what Muthyala calls a 'double movement' – one that gives hegemonic force to white settler identities and ideologies while simultaneously illuminating the existence of alternative worlds that are often only differently accessible – and must be supplemented by the 'dialectical movement' of 'worlding' and 'reworlding', or what Ralph Bauer terms 'the European imperial inscription of a hemispheric terra incognita and a critical (or literary) practice that would unsettle this Eurocentric inscription'.[61]

This dialectical movement perhaps finds its neatest analogy in the idea of 'mapping' and 'remapping' or the cartographic exchanges between Indigenous peoples and foreign European explorers, which created 'double visions' of space and place.[62] If imperial cartography can ultimately be seen as an abstractive 'flattening' of the world via the form of the empirical map, substituting space for place and encouraging a view that is objective and natural, Indigenous mapping enables a 'stereoscopic' blurring of the imperial map's construction of territory as an 'object of rule'.[63] In her discussion of 'Tuki's Universe' (the map, and Māori world, drawn by Tuki Tahua for Philip King in 1793), for example, Judith Binney shows how Tuki 'drew a land, which was, in one map, both actual and mythological', revealing both 'a knowledge of the physical world, and an imaginative attachment to it', and ultimately demanding the restoration of a lost 'indigenous view', that Margaret Jolly ascribes to 'Tupaia's Map', of 'lying low in a canoe, looking up at the heavens'.[64]

Vicente M. Diaz and J. Kehaulani Kauanui's study of *etak*, the form of seafaring navigation through triangulation developed by Carolinian Islanders, outlines just such an Indigenous projection – one that views the canoe as stationary while the islands move in a 'fluidic pathway', allowing for 'a clear and unambiguous sense of one's place at all times'.[65] The Tongan-Fijian scholar Epeli Hau'ofa too suggests a similar reorientation, dismissing land-based 'views of the Pacific' as 'islands in a far sea' in favour of 'a sea of islands', where Oceania 'is huge and growing bigger every day'.[66] Using Hau'ofa's reworlding of Oceania to adjust our viewpoint of southern ports, islands, and land masses allows us to consider them not only from the perspectival approach of the exploratory or mercantile ship, but from the 'perspective of those who gaze out towards the oceans', thereby paying closer attention to the south's 'littoral condition', while also reconsidering the multivalency of its literary, cartographic, political, and imaginative representations, especially when contact between Indigenous peoples, European settlers, and diasporic peoples creates 'double visions' that ask us to challenge Eurocentric worlds.[67]

Southern periodicity, forms, canons, and genres

Evaluating the 'imperial', 'Anglophone', 'geopolitical', 'worldly', and 'global' methodologies currently invigorating Victorian studies, Tanya Agathocleous argues that adopting a 'geographically expansive conception' of the field can produce both a 'heightened sense of the artifice of boundaries' and a 'powerful and empowering' 'disorientation' that encourages us as scholars to embrace 'new vantage points'.[68] The 'global turn' in Romantic and Victorian studies has certainly stimulated a critical reappraisal of both fields over the last two decades, with scholars exploring the relationship between aesthetics, scientific exploration, and colonial expansion, as well as considering the ways in which globalism, cosmopolitanism, and transnationalism, among other concepts, promise to 'transform what we mean by "British" literature'.[69] Taking full account of Romantic and Victorian globalism can reveal the surprising longevity or afterlife of western conceptual and literary frameworks in non-European contexts, as well as offering new critical readings of British texts and their reception. As Nikki Hessell notes, the 'Romantic period, as a unit of literary history, lasts well into the twentieth century in indigenous thought and intellectual activity, and ... such a radical reinscribing of the boundaries of the Romantic period might be essential to comprehending British texts of c. 1789–1832 themselves'.[70]

While the globalising efforts of these important works inform many of the collected chapters that follow, this volume does not primarily define itself as an example of 'Global Romantic' or 'Global Victorian' studies, aiming instead to test the application and meanings of these terms in extra-European contexts, and thereby to decentre and detach 'British', at least to some degree, from its causal attachment to the region's literature. Adopting the rhetoric of 'suspicion' that postcolonial studies mobilises so effectively in its engagement with literary discourses, we 'situate formal concerns' and 'the evolution of genres and styles' in their 'intersection' with specifically southern 'materialist issues and ideological/historical context[s]'.[71] One of the most productive and necessary disorientations of southern literary culture relates to traditional forms of periodisation, which, we argue, fail to take adequate account of southern dates of political, economic, and cultural significance, from the 'foundation' of white Australia in 1788 to the Treaty of Waitangi in New Zealand in 1840 to the Union of South Africa in 1910. We therefore favour a more 'flexible formulation' – the 'long nineteenth century' – that can 'be calibrated to the specifics of individual colonial histories',[72] while also acknowledging that these sorts of colonial-specific narratives retain white foundation myths and are susceptible to what Marilyn Lake identifies as the 'tyranny of the national narrative in Australian history', belying the 'conflict in the encounter between diversity and the incitement to national uniformity'.[73] The teleological march towards nationhood that structures many of the literary histories of the southern colonies can lead, as Mark Williams and Alice Te Punga Somerville argue of New Zealand, to a 'foreshortening' and truncation of literary periods where 'beginnings' are chosen or invented 'rather than simply discover[ed]'.[74]

While we retain the expansionary term 'long nineteenth century', some chapters in this collection aim to 'cross periods' in a methodology that Hayot refers to as 'trans-periodising', both in order to avoid the 'logics of totality' that traditional periodisation can invoke, and because periods organised around key European dates or philosophical concepts cannot adequately address the ways in which literary genres and forms were transformed by settlers and Indigenous peoples in the southern hemisphere.[75] Such an approach has the added value of allowing us to question the ideas of derivativeness and belatedness that all too often accompany studies of non-European literary culture. Manu Samriti Chander argues, for example, that we must rethink and renegotiate claims of originality and derivativeness as 'they open up the possibilities of revising our aesthetic sensibilities and updating our critical conversations', while Alex Watson and Laurence Williams rightly note that there is a tendency both to 'draw a line between "European tradition"' and its 'reception' elsewhere, and to focus on European representations of 'other' places rather than on their own self-constructions.[76]

Hessell's study of Indigenous translations of Romantic works in New Zealand, Hawai'i, and India provides one example of a critical method that disrupts linear periodicity, arguing that 'European notions of period' can be 'meaningless' for Indigenous people and 'distorting' for Indigenous histories, which stress the 'simultaneity of the past and present in ways that European temporality struggles to comprehend'.[77] Walter Mignolo extends Hessell's critique of Eurochronology and Eurocentric literary periodicity to the very term 'literature' itself, instead offering 'languaging' as a decolonial concept that resists literature's universalising tendencies.[78] Attending to Mignolo's criticism of literature's European 'self-referential[ity]', we use the term 'literary culture' in this collection in preference to 'literature' with its weighted imperial connotations.[79] While 'culture' too is Eurocentric in its origins and orientations, it provides us with a more encompassing terminology, asking us to consider what literary histories of Australian Aboriginal, Māori, Malay, or Xhosa culture 'would look like if we moved beyond Eurocentric concepts of authorship, included genres other than fiction and poetry, and situated reading and writing in specific cultural contexts' – for example, persistent 'oral habits' or the political agency cultivated through acts of citation and intertextuality that mark genres such as correspondence and petitions.[80]

At the same time, English-language literacy offered many opportunities for agency, resistance, and reappraisal. While literacy and literary study were undoubtedly 'essential to ... processes of sociopolitical control', Vanessa Smith has shown that Indigenous 'appropriation and interrogation' undermines the belief that 'with the transmission of literacy, the prerogative of interpretation has been surrendered'.[81] Penny van Toorn has revealed the strong disciplinary impulses of educational literacy practices and the connections between the promotion of literacy and the stolen generation in Australia, but she too stresses the need to recognise the arrival of the British in Australia as the 'beginning of an entanglement between two sets of reading and writing practices'.[82] This sense of literary and cultural entanglement is perhaps best captured by Simon Gikandi's characterisation of colonialism as a 'culture of mutual imbrication and contamination' – for example, in Africa where the missionary press is, as Ntongela Masilela and Mbulelo Vizikhungo Mzamane argue, intricately connected to the rise of vernacular presses, 'a new tradition of politically committed writing', and 'modern' African literature.[83]

Our focus on the varying material conditions and forms of co-existing southern cultures provides an opportunity to trace these moments of entanglement and thereby complicate Franco Moretti's study of world literature as 'foreign form' and 'local material': that is, as literature related to a core culture that is largely unmodified by non-canonical authors from a variety of geographic locations. Jahan Ramazani has shown us how mobile or travelling poetic forms contest the traditional view that foreign literary genres and forms were simply imported from metropole to periphery.[84] Spivak too questions Moretti's 'ambition to create authoritative totalizing patterns depending on untested statements by small groups of people treated as native informants', which, as Katherine Bode notes, are then 'amassed at the Anglophone centre'.[85] Lauren Goodlad's revision of Fredric Jameson's concept of the 'geopolitical aesthetic' proves generative here, as it allows us to recognise nineteenth-century literary culture 'not only as structure or process, but also as form' and to situate it within Moretti's formulation of world literature while rejecting his repetition of the 'Jamesonian tic of viewing the classical metropole as an autochthonous structure' that is capable of being modularised elsewhere.[86]

Recent studies of colonial genre and form have further revised Moretti's formula by rejecting his understanding of the novel as the exemplary or paradigmatic mobile form. Jason Rudy, for example, builds on Ramazani's work to emphasise the portability of the poetic form in anthologies, commonplace books, periodicals, and newspapers, which meant that it could 'adapt more quickly to colonial spaces' than 'printed and bound texts', thereby 'allowing for more local forms of expression'.[87] Periodicals and newspapers were of special importance in the colonial context, often providing venues of first publication for poets now considered part of the 'settler canon' in Australia and elsewhere, such as Eliza Hamilton Dunlop, Charles Harpur, Banjo Patterson, and Henry Lawson. Bode's examination of reprint and serialisation culture in nineteenth-century Australian newspapers rightly refutes the idea that British fiction dominated the colonial market, revealing the 'consistent presence of local writing'.[88] Embedded within a material world of circulating goods, poems, short stories, and serialised fiction often appeared earlier and more frequently than novels in the colonies, with their 'formal qualities' potentially more revealing of the 'contradictions of bourgeois national thought', as well as more readily enabling the iteration of local and/or regional identities and reading publics within global print media and communication networks.[89]

The frequent authorial anonymity or pseudonymity of periodical fiction also provides a means of testing assumptions about the 'literary canon and continuing influence of a romantic conception of authorship' in settler colonial states.[90] While we embrace the idea of a global imperial commons where 'reading depended on comparison and circulation', our interest in questions of canonicity in this collection recognises that these 'interdiscursive' imperial cultures co-existed with 'originatory' and proto-nationalist settler myth-making, 'dying race' narratives, and racialised accounts of *terra nullius*.[91] 'Foundational' Australian settler colonial texts, such as Barron Field's *First Fruits of Australian Poetry* (1819), represent Australia as an empty 'waste land' effaced of Indigenous inhabitants, with pastoral 'cultivation' acting as a synecdoche for imperial 'civilisation'. As David Higgins notes, 'the white settlement of Australia was rhetorical as well as physical, involving what Paul Carter has termed the "process of transforming space into place"', with Australian settler literature presenting 'flickers of … nativeness' that Philip Mead detects, for example, in 'William Charles Wentworth's dream-vision of an Australian civilization in his long poem of 1822, *Australasia*, [and] in Charles Harpur's topographic Romanticism'.[92] Similarly, Andrew McCann argues that later works, such as William Lane's *The Workingman's Paradise* (1892) and Henry Lawson's poems, envision 'a white Australian autochthony in which settlers themselves appear as, in Lawson's words, "natives of the land"'.[93]

Te Punga Somerville reminds us that '[c]anons do not produce themselves: they are produced by people': 'certain texts (re)produce certain worlds'.[94] Unsettling the canon is therefore both an additive/substitutive process and a subtractive process, adding or seeking to recover new texts and worlds while also acknowledging how much has been lost or altered by the superimposition of European cultural forms. Emphasising both the power of *terra nullius* and the writing of 'unsettlement' in the history of Australian poetics, Michael Farrell notes that 'admit[ting] the erasure' of Aboriginal people and history from Australia does not mean we can 'pretend to know what has been erased'.[95] Maria Nugent's analysis of the testimony by Wonnarua man and guide Galmarra (known as 'Jacky') of E. B. Kennedy's death in Cape York in 1848 provides an apt example of the difficulty of determining when 'the white editorial hand' enters the script and poses, as Jonathan Dunk points out, an 'epistemological crisis' that marks many Indigenous texts within the colonial archive.[96] This collection recognises that 'literary settlement … is an endless project' while also aiming to *un*settle 'the reigning semantic paradigms that attempt to uphold nation and settlement'.[97] Yet whereas Farrell argues for the reconceptualisaton of national literary history to include the poetics of unsettlement, we suggest a more radical departure from the national paradigm by both looking across and drawing parallels between the literary cultures of southern settler colonies in order to uncover shared genres, forms, and themes, from the unsettling and atavistic drama of the colonial gothic, to the female *bildungsroman* and its rejection of 'happy resolutions' and 'meritocratic drives', to the 'stablising' tradition of the South African 'farm novel' or *plaasroman*.[98] The latter points to the popularity and appeal of settler narratives describing the domestication of landscapes that often silence 'the place of the black man in the pastoral idyll' while simultaneously underscoring the inherent alienation experienced by settlers on these landscapes in ways that are replicated in countless settler novels of enclosure from Australia and New Zealand.[99]

Yet if some literary texts present the settler experience as one of stabilising enclosure, others register acknowledged and/or disavowed violence via disruptions within a text's chosen form, or via complex and formative modes of representation such as bricolage or the hybrid text that amalgamates numerous generic influences. Tracey Banivanua Mar's study of the Australian-Pacific indentured labour trade asks us to consider how real and imagined processes of violence both mimicked and brought the colonial frontier into being. The 'literary conventions of Melanesian discourses', for example, defined by their 'savagery' and 'bloodthirstiness', created a 'self-defensive imagination' that informed pre-emptive attacks against Islanders.[100] South Africa too was a key investigative site for racial taxonomists and ethnographers, figuring heavily in the 'construction of racial stereotypes' through ethnographic displays of Khoisan people and the racialised writings of Robert Knox.[101] The implications of these ethnographic investigations are demonstrable in the peculiarly racialised nature of South African literature evident in works such as H. Rider Haggard's *King Solomon's Mines* (1885). Yet the imperial adventure genre also provided opportunities for the 'reappropriation of Zulu historiography' by John Langalibalele Dube in the 1930s as well as providing a framework for *Mhudi* (1930) by Sol Plaatjie, who 'adopted the style, and linguistic register' of Haggard's imperial romances, but nonetheless 'adapted it for his own purposes, undermining and challenging many of [the genre's] tenets'.[102]

The ideas of adoption and adaptation are suggestive of the plasticity of genres in the southern colonies as well as offering an opportunity to politicise colonial literacy and literature for decolonial purposes. Plaatjie and Thomas Mofolo, for example, mobilised the imperial romance aesthetic while at the same time questioning the 'language of a literary canon closely associated with the culture of colonialism'.[103] On the other hand, the unsettling of genre could also be a sign of the unsettling of colonial notions of civility and respectability, so that 'racist taxonomies [were] forced to become flexible, and thereby [began] to come undone, especially for the imperial reader'.[104] Indeed, it is this unravelling of European literary taxonomies of form, genre, content, and chronology – and its relationship to the 'ideological tensions' within imperialism – that we seek to foreground in this collection, emphasising an unsettling, disorientating literary culture of hybrid genres and forms; an aesthetics of violence, displacement, and resistance; texts that struggle for closure and coherence (with narrative fulfilment frequently underscoring colonial desires for settlement and belonging); and visual, oral, and performance cultures that disrupt Eurocentric literary chronologies.[105]

These kinds of unsettling, hyphenated, and hybrid texts also speak to hybrid forms of belonging, especially in relation to multi-ethnic communities such as the Cape Colony, where, as Archie L. Dick has shown, Cape Muslims 'created an independent world view' with their stories 'recall[ing]', 'recreat[ing]', and 'blend[ing]' the 'folklore worlds of East Asia and Africa'.[106] As the ultimate composite genre, travel writing underscores the processual nature of genre in the southern colonies and its relation to acts of encounter and performances of belonging, 'facilitat[ing] an intersection between a distant culture and a present enterprise' while simultaneously expressing and 'delineating a geography of power', with literacy frequently, and mistakenly, characterised as the 'ticket to travel'.[107] The chapters collected here do not all focus on travel writing but they all respond, in various ways, to Clifford's call to examine the multiple ways in which people, texts, and ideas can travel and the 'kinds of knowledges, stories and theories … they produce' through their travel, challenging the notion that 'non-literate cultures can only ever be the objects' of travelling narratives and exposing the world-making capacities of peoples and cultures too often mischaracterised as minor or marginal.[108]

Towards a worlding of the south

Responding to the many (and sometimes competing) problematics raised in this introduction, the collection is organised thematically around three key structuring ideas or paradigms: Globe/World, Acculturation/Transculturation, and Indigenous/Diasporic. Far from being binary constructs or discrete, closed entities, these paradigms exemplify the ways in which literary cultures often participate in the hybrid and liminal spaces in between the real and the imaginary, mythography and cartography, settlement and dispossession, and theory and practice. The first set of chapters, Globe/World, reflects on the complex relationships between world and globe, temporalisation and spatialisation, and globalisation and mondialisation. Peter Otto's opening chapter, for example, considers how the 1828 panorama 'A View of the Town of Sydney' 'conjured an *Umwelt*' rather than just a view or prospect. Unlike the globe, the panorama did not attempt to 'englobe' or 'bring a disorganised mass into an ordered whole' but rather foregrounded a 'multiplicity of worlds', with its 'virtual' or 'hyper-realistic illusion' arousing 'audience interest in how it had been constructed'. Part of the rise of optical media technologies that materialised the 'movement between mind and world', the panorama is a world-making form which offers, as Otto demonstrates, layered hybrid spaces and plural ontologies that, in this case, both represent a 'modernising' or 'civilising' process and unsettle the very processes of settlement it depicts.[109]

Otto's examination of the fictions shaping the virtual worlds of the colonial panorama resonates in Sarah Comyn's discussion of northern constructions of the southern hemisphere as antipodal. One of the most potent of the European fictions or myths surrounding the south, the Antipodes was imagined as upside down or back to front with feet facing the wrong direction. Examining poetry, fiction, letters, and illustrated articles in a range of newspapers from nineteenth-century Australia, Comyn demonstrates the extent to which the cartographic, corporeal, and metaphoric inversion associated with the Antipodes not only shaped a 'heightened form of comparative consciousness' in the southern colonies but was also reinscribed in newspaper depictions of settlers' lived worlds and experiences.[110] Repurposing the tropes of doubling and antipodality, these portrayals challenge Eurocentric ideas of cultural superiority, colonial belatedness, and hemispheric difference in favour of spatial and cultural reorientations between north and south, as well as anticipating discourses of Australian nationhood and federation.

Clara Tuite's chapter on 'flash' culture and 'lag fever' also reconsiders the idea of colonial belatedness but this time through the lens of linguistic mobility, arguing that the flash and cant languages of thieves and convicts can be understood as a demotic kind of world language that connects underclasses with upper classes within and across metropolitan Regency London and the convict spaces of colonial Australia. Linking transnational genealogies of masculine self-fashioning and print-visual form with the social arenas of fashionability, convictism, penal transportation, and settler culture across Britain, Ireland, Europe, and Australia, Tuite's chapter argues for the 'transformative elements of [cultural] lag', with flash language 'bristling against spatial and geographical backwardness, and highlighting the transformative elements of disjunction'. As language moves or circulates across the globe, Tuite argues, it enables new forms of world-making that both realise 'the Regency as a model of global modernity' and register the 'energy and dynamism of the colonial peripheries'.

Continuing the themes of self-fashioning and sociability evident in Comyn and Tuite's chapters, Fariha Shaikh's examination of ephemeral shipboard periodicals produced en route to Australia considers their role in transforming emigrants on board ships into colonists, through an anticipatory language and logic that imagined (often violent) encounters with Indigenous peoples. Drawing on methodologies from the 'blue humanities', Shaikh considers the ship not simply as a self-enclosed floating world, but 'also as a piece of travelling communication' that enabled transfers of 'cultural norms' across oceanic spaces. The shipboard periodical, as Shaikh shows, emphasises the mobility of genres such as travelogues, tales, and theatrical performances as they adjust to the littoral aspects of the southern hemisphere, but it also demonstrates the extent to which such genres were already fully embedded in settler discourses of race and power.

Ingrid Horrocks' chapter on Augustus Earle returns us to the visual arts raised in Otto's chapter (Earle was one of the painters whose work inspired 'A View of the Town of Sydney') as it considers the multiple worldings and, in this case, reworldings that can emerge from imperial-era travel books and paintings. Earle's *Narrative of a Residence in New Zealand* (1832) features that key trope of white imperial travel writing, the prospect view, which in his case is frequently accompanied by visual depictions. Arguing that a scholarly focus on arrival, prospects, and moments of encounter produces readings that highlight the emergence of a magisterial European eye, Horrocks moves us away from 'the global movements of oceanic travel' to scrutinise more fully the mundane activities within Earle's texts and paintings, such as walking, guiding, and toiling. Using a mobilities studies lens in combination with ecocritical studies, Horrocks argues for the importance of a methodological approach to the imperial travel genre that takes into account the unstable and shifting double visions of Pākehā and Māori relations.

Utopian worlds across Australia, North America, and South America are the subject of Jason Rudy, Aaron Bartlett, Lindsey O'Neil, and Justin Thompson's chapter on William Lane's socialist community in Paraguay – 'Nueva Australia' (est. 1893) – a new south that sought to preserve the colour line and was open only to English-speaking Anglo-Saxons. Despite its overt racism, Lane's vexed utopian project suggests a sense of radical disenchantment with a colonial capitalist system driven by labour shortages, scarcity, and capital accumulation. Examining how race and labour are intertwined in Lane's periodical, the *Cosme Monthly*, the authors demonstrate how poetry, song, and, in particular, minstrelsy were used to romanticise enslavement in the service of the white working classes and to 'situate the Cosmans in relation to other white-supremacist movements' across Australia and North America, while at the same time constructing a 'racial and political isolation' that was undermined by the reality of their dependence on Indigenous Guaraní.

The second set of chapters in this collection, Acculturation/Transculturation, focuses on the aesthetics of settlement, the uneasy and unsettling processes of acculturating to a new world, and the 'affects of belonging', or what Terry Goldie calls 'the impossible necessity of becoming indigenous', as well as on examples (violent and non-violent) of cultural encounter, colonial blending, and transculturation.[111] Attentive to what Leilani Nishima and Kim D. Hester Williams term 'racial ecologies', some chapters also consider the relationship between settler colonialism, indigeneity, and radically changing/changed environments, recognising that 'nature and environment are relational sites' in which 'embodied racial identities and ecological space and place' are 'navigat[ed]'.[112]

The section opens with Jane Stafford's analysis of the reading of *Robinson Crusoe* in colonial New Zealand, which considers Defoe's novel not just as an exemplum of the challenges and hardships of settlement, but also as a 'shared language', 'measure', or metaphor, an adaptable trope about the English capacity for industry, economic self-sufficiency, and 'natural' authority. These qualities, it was felt, underwrote the work's suitability as the first novel to be translated into te reo Māori. In exploring settler and Indigenous responses to *Robinson Crusoe*, Stafford considers wider questions relating to the English literary canon and its role in the project of nation-building and 'civilising' missions. 'Modelled', 'refigured', and 'translated' in New Zealand, *Robinson Crusoe*, Stafford argues, was a symbol of 'cultural memory' and 'continuity' integral to the imperial project of improvement and to the still ongoing practices of settlement and land dispossession, albeit one that demonstrates the limitations of this project in the face of Indigenous agency and activism.

Ken Gelder and Rachael Weaver's chapter investigates a similarly global narrative of masculine adventure, exploration, and attempted subjugation: the kangaroo hunt. Surveying the genre in a wide range of textual and visual representations, Gelder and Weaver demonstrate the significance of the kangaroo as a species both to scientific programmes of acclimatisation and to heroic accounts of settler dominance. As a transnational figure circulating within a global imperial commons and networks of colonial science, the kangaroo became its own generic device with symbolic investments ranging from anti-slavery narratives to explorations of global biodiversity. The kangaroo hunter, on the other hand, could be portrayed either as a settler or as a wandering explorer, frequently refracting the violence of the hunt on to Indigenous peoples on colonial frontiers. As Gelder and Weaver demonstrate, the kangaroo hunt narrative, while often seen simply as an account of masculine individualism and homosociality, is demonstrative of the extent to which 'sites of colonial conquest and imperial trade' had a 'profound impact on how ecologies were recognized and imagined'.[113]

Grace Moore's chapter on Louisa Atkinson is also concerned with the relationship between settler acculturation, acclimatisation, and environmental adaptation. Focusing on Atkinson's bushfire stories, the chapter argues that her depictions of fire-setting and fire-fighting are distinct from those of her contemporaries in that they seek to promote respect for the bush. In Atkinson's stories the bushfire becomes an 'emblem of settler discomfort', while the forests subjected to land clearances by settlers frequently come to represent Indigenous Australians in ways that point to the 'deep connection between the land and its traditional owners', but also to the violent dispossession of Indigenous peoples by settler farming and land-management practices that equate to 'ecological vandalism'. Atkinson's work, Moore argues, also 'recasts the role of the settler woman in relation to the land', demonstrating the resourcefulness and capability of Australian settler women in the face of disaster, and resisting the already formulaic story of 'female endangerment' and rescue in the bush.

Taking as its case study Thomas Baines' expedition to Zululand for Cetshwayo kaMpande's coronation, Lindy Stiebel's chapter considers the significance of settler mappings of British/African geo-political interests. Examining Baines' accounts of the expedition, including newspaper reports, journal entries, maps, and illustrations, Stiebel demonstrates his complex and ambivalent engagement with the Zulu kingdom, landscape, and people. As 'Special Correspondent' for the *Natal Mercury*, Baines is jovial and jocular, but his maps approach the topography of Zululand with a 'scientific seriousness': unlike previous maps of the region, Baines' colonial cartography provides a record that instantiates the Zulu king's possessions, 'mark[ing] the territory as populated' and recording Zulu place names, while nonetheless anticipating and depicting settler expansion, invasion, and violence. While Baines' primary concern is to promote British political and economic interests, his maps nonetheless chart the intrusion of a colonial order into the heart of Zululand, capturing a key moment in the political history of British and Zulu relations.

Matthew Shum's chapter considers a very different African expedition and travelogue: William Burchell's two-volume *Travels in the Interior of Southern Africa*, published in London in 1822 and 1824. Arguing that Burchell 'does not provide an easy fit for the default postcolonial judgment of the European naturalist explorer as the advance agent or epistemological vanguard' of empire, Shum suggests that Burchell's botanical and geological writings are infused with what Pierre Hadot has described as an 'Orphic' sense of the phenomena of the world, one that gives primary emphasis to the numinous rather than the instrumental or 'Promethean' aspects of science. In his representations of Indigenous Africans, too, Burchell's writings move away from standard ethnographic accounts and towards sympathetic and affective registers that nonetheless maintain 'categorical distinctions' between human races. Recognising the ambivalent impact of his own 'immersion in "uncivilized" societies', Burchell demonstrates the extent to which the European in colonial sites can be an imperilled or 'stressed figure', unable to 'modulate' his own emotions and functioning as 'a limit case for the exercise of metropolitan sentiment'.

Moving from travel narratives to the genre of the short story, this section ends with Jennifer Fuller's chapter on Louie Becke's Pacific stories in *By Reef and Palm* (1894). Seeing Becke's stories as a 'colonial experiment in archipelagic writing', Fuller offers a relational reading of each of the stories in the volume, arguing that Becke's stories represent a 'networked vision of a collective region' defined by 'continual circulation, transformation, and exchange'. If Becke redefines the genre of the short story to coincide with the colonial perception of islands as places of violence, sexual transgression, and transactionalism, portraying the 'calculative logic' of Pacific cross-cultural and interracial relations, he nonetheless also provides examples of European and Islander agency that resist Eurocentric moral judgement. Fuller's reading of Becke's collection allows us to see it both as a means of 'aggregating' literary worlds and as a commentary on the increasing invisibility of islands in the face of western globalisation, 'suggesting that violent intimacies are small scale echoes of the larger problem of cultural erasure in the Pacific'.

Following on from Fuller's consideration of interracial intimacy, the collection's final section, Indigenous/Diasporic, considers the Anglophone and/or translated literary cultures of Indigenous populations and non-European diasporas, looking in particular at questions of Indigenous agency, resilience, and resistance; diasporic movement and identities; and imperial literacy, subjecthood, and citizenship. The chapters in this section aim to de-emphasise white settler experience as normative and white writing as archetypal of literary cultures in the southern hemisphere, and instead foreground Indigenous, Black, Creole, and Southeast Asian voices. Focusing on the genres of the petition and on vernacular periodical cultures, many of its chapters attempt to problematise European liberalism's ideal of a 'universal subject' by paying attention to what Tim Rowse characterises as the redemptive potential of 'Indigenous liberal universalism'.[114] As numerous scholars have shown, '[t]he presumptive universalism of abstract liberal principles is compromised when these principles encounter the actuality of the colonial other', challenging ideas of cosmopolitanism and demonstrating liberalism's inherent provinciality.[115]

The section begins with Anna Johnston's chapter, which considers the long and complicated history of linguistic collection in Australia and its contribution to cross-cultural processes of colonial knowledge production. Using the archival traces left by two nineteenth-century women – Eliza Hamilton Dunlop at Wollombi in New South Wales, Darkinyung country and a meeting place between Darkinyung, Awabakal, and Wonnaruah people, and Harriet [Harriott] Barlow in the Maranoa District south of Charleville, Queensland, originally home to the dispossessed Mandandanji people – Johnston analyses wordlists, vocabularies, transcriptions of Indigenous songs, and records of Aboriginal language groups as intimate forms of exchange on (often violent) Australian colonial frontiers. In so doing, Johnston reveals 'the imbrication of language collection, knowledge production, Indigenous engagement, and settler advocacy', as well as reflecting both on the ongoing nature of a 'dispossessive colonialism' and on the possibility of using linguistic sources for language reclamation and revitalisation projects in the present day.

Also considering the racialised nature of the colonial archive, Michelle Elleray's chapter examines the often 'fraught borderline' between Indigenous writing and European editorial practices in the 1850 publication of translated and abridged instalments from the travel journal of Kiro, a Cook Islander who lived in England from 1847–50. While originally intended for a Cook Islands readership, 'Kiro's Thoughts about England' was published as a text for British children that conformed with the 'disciplinary structures of Christianity' and missionary expectations of the 'newly converted'. 'Kiro's Thoughts about England' thus raises the issue of 'how we are to read recovered literary texts by peoples disempowered through imperial processes' when these texts are often entangled with or made to conform to dominant structures of power. Reading Kiro's writing in transhemispheric terms, Elleray considers how we might reframe both his writing and Indigenous status within the context of South Pacific values, genealogies, and belief systems, thereby recognising the 'Islanders' agency in suturing the new to the old' and resituating their past and future in relation to the new 'technology of alphabetic literacy'.

Moving from the appropriation and rewriting of Kiro's journal by missionaries to the reappropriation of Thomas Babington Macaulay's verse in petitions written by Te Whānau a Rerewa to secure their lands from the 1860s onwards, Nikki Hessell's chapter is concerned with questions of imperial literacy or the ways in which circulating European concepts, including universalism, could be repurposed to create 'a resurgent Māori identity from within a European tradition and aesthetic'. Hessell's chapter centres around the Ngāti Porou rangatira (chief) Mokena Kōhere and the ways in which his grandson Rēweti Kōhere framed his grandfather's legacy via lines from Macaulay's poems. If Macaulay famously 'placed a "New Zealander" at the centre of a reimagined metropolis', Hessell argues that in Rēweti Kōhere's appropriation of Macaulay's lines it is Macaulay and not Māori 'who is figured as mobile and exotic, his texts reaching Aotearoa and undergoing various translations, appropriations, and reinterpretations'. Hessell's chapter demonstrates not only that poetry and its strategic citation was a key element of Māori rhetoric, political diplomacy, and petitioning, but also that its repurposing was central to Māori land claims and their relevant legal instruments in the early decades of the twentieth century.

Similarly looking at the petition as a genre of political writing and as protest literature, Hlonipha Mokoena considers the often 'forgotten history of [African] liberalism' in the longer context of the end of apartheid and the establishment of a constitutional democracy. Distinguishing between 'minor' and 'major' liberal traditions, Mokoena demonstrates the extent to which the printed word became 'an expression of political subjecthood', encouraging 'vigilance' or 'watchfulness over the actions and policies of successive colonial governments' even as a major liberalism, 'dependent on missionaries for its spread and justification', failed to produce its desired results. As Mokoena shows, the petition was itself 'a reproduction of the ideological foundations of mission stations' and their particular form of rhetorical tutelage, but, when liberated from 'the stranglehold of the mission station', it was also a powerful form of protest that later prompted the idea of a 'native congress' such as the South African Native National Congress and its 'reformist parleys with white politicians and white capitalist interests'.

Focusing on the Afro-Creole poet Egbert Martin, Manu Samriti Chander's analysis of the complex othering of Indigenous peoples by Guianese literati argues that the rise of periodical culture in British Guiana from the late 1830s 'came to ground ideas of humanity in the capacity to read and thereby participate fully in the social life of the colony'. Examining the close relationship between 'literacy and cultural legitimacy' in a range of periodicals and missionary writing, as well as in Egbert's poetry, Chander argues that Indigenous Guianese peoples, or Amerindians, were 'understood as essentially illiterate' and 'always in danger of falling back into a pre-civilised' and pre-Christian state, thereby becoming the 'cultural field's abject other'. Drawing on the idea of Creole indigeneity, 'whereby Creole claims to belonging erase those of Indigenous peoples', Chander understands Egbert's poetry as complicit in a wider imperial process of erasing Indigenous peoples from the cultural field in a bid to 'appeal for recognition … to centres of imperial power'. Decolonising cultural recognition, then, involves refusing 'recognition from the Global North' and instead 'offer[ing] recognition to Amerindian communities'.

Similar questions of cultural recognition are taken up in Porscha Fermanis' chapter on the ways in which Straits Chinese elites in Singapore strategically used discourses of comparatism and universalism both to marginalise 'native' Malays and 'sojourning' Chinese diasporas, and to point to colonialism's inherent contradictions. Examining the political stakes of comparatism and its relationship to anticolonial, postcolonial, and ethnic nationalism in the context of Nanyang South Sea and Indian Ocean spaces, Fermanis reads the *Straits Chinese Magazine* (est. 1897) as an anticolonial project. Despite its apparent investment in the logic and rhetoric of imperial liberalism, Straits Chinese contributors to the magazine ultimately turn European comparatism on its head, encouraging a reversal of the comparative gaze and an exposition of the defective use of Enlightenment methodologies by European comparatists. If Straits Chinese authors often fall back on arguments for the universality of human experience, the *Straits Chinese Magazine* demonstrates the extent to which competing Sinocentric and Islamocentric civilisational accounts could disrupt European modes of seeing, destabilising what is considered natural and self-reflexively exposing the Eurocentric grounds on which comparisons are made.

Notes

1 Paul Carter, 'Australindia: The Geography of Imperial Desire', *Postcolonial Studies*, 18 (2015), 222–33. On the difference between 'otherness' and 'approximate otherness', see Jonathan Z. Smith, 'What a Difference a Difference Makes', in Jacob Neusner and Ernest S. Frerichs (eds), *To See Ourselves as Others See Us: Christians, Jews, 'Others' in Late Antiquity* (Chico: Scholars Press, 1985), pp. 3–48.

2 For an overview of this cartographic history, see Avan Judd Stallard, *Antipodes: In Search of the Southern Continent* (Melbourne: Monash University Publishing, 2016). For the term 'indexical category', see Jean Comaroff and John Comaroff, 'Theory from the South: A Rejoinder', *Cultural Anthropology Online*, 25 February 2012, n.p., https://culanth.org/fieldsights/theory-from-the-south-a-rejoinder (accessed 24 June 2019). On the Global South as a 'conceptual space', see Stephen Muecke, 'Cultural Studies' Networking Strategies in the South', *Australian Humanities Review*, 44 (2008), 39–51.

3 A useful definition of Global South can be found in Mathew Sparke, 'Everywhere but Always Somewhere: Critical Geographies of the Global South', *The Global South*, 1:1 (2007), 124. For a critique of the Global South as term/concept, see Walter Mignolo, 'The Global South and World Dis/Order', *Journal of Anthropological Research*, 67:2 (2011), 165–88.

4 Comaroff and Comaroff, 'Theory from the South', n.p.; Kevin Murray, 'Keys to the South', *Australian Humanities Review*, 44 (2008), 24; Harry Harootunian, 'Remembering the Historical Present', *Critical Inquiry*, 33:3 (2007), 486. On the ways in which the European global imperial imaginary marginalised its own south, see, e.g., Roberto M. Dainotto, *Europe (In Theory)* (Durham: Duke University Press, 2007); and Franco Cassano, *Southern Thought and Other Essays on the Mediterranean*, ed. and trans. Norma Bouchard and Valerio Ferme (New York: Fordham University Press, 2012).

5 Harootunian, 'Historical Present', 474.

6 On the performance and re-enactment of settler possession, see Bain Atwood, *Possession: Batman's Treaty and the Matter of History* (Melbourne: Melbourne University Press, 2009).

7 Penelope Edmonds, "'I followed England round the world": The Rise of Trans-Imperial Anglo-Saxon Exceptionalism and the Spatial Narratives of Nineteenth-Century British Settler Colonies of the Pacific Rim', in Leigh Boucher, Jane Carey, and Katherine Ellinghaus (eds), *Reorienting Whiteness* (Basingstoke: Palgrave Macmillan, 2009), p. 109. On settler colonial studies, see, e.g., Patrick Wolfe, *Settler Colonialism and the Transformation of Anthropology: The Politics and Poetics of an Ethnographic Event* (London and New York: Cassell, 1998); and Lorenzo Veracini, 'Introducing Settler Colonial Studies', *Settler Colonial Studies*, 1:1 (2011), 1–12. On Black Consciousness and the role of Steve Biko, Njabulo Ndebele, and others, see, e.g., Tendayi Sithole, *Steve Biko: Decolonial Meditations of Black Consciousness* (Lanham: Lexington Books, 2016); and Ian M. Macqueen, *Black Consciousness and Progressive Movements under Apartheid* (Pietermaritzburg: University of KwaZulu-Natal Press, 2018). On the interpenetration of Black Power and Indigenous oppositional politics in the Māori and Pasifika context, see Robbie Shilliam, *Black Pacific: Anti-Colonial Struggles and Oceanic Connections* (London: Bloomsbury Academic Press, 2015).

8 For excellent literary histories that nonetheless primarily retain the national paradigm, see, e.g., Peter Pierce (ed.), *The Cambridge History of Australian Literature* (Cambridge: Cambridge University Press, 2009); David Atwell and Derek Attridge (eds), *The Cambridge History of South African Literature* (Cambridge: Cambridge University Press, 2012); and Mark Williams (ed.), *A History of New Zealand Literature* (Cambridge: Cambridge University Press, 2016). On the transnational turn, see, e.g., Robert Dixon, 'Australian Literature–International Contexts', *Southerly*, 67:1/2 (2007), 15–27; and David Carter, 'After Postcolonialism', *Meanjin*, 66:2 (2007), 114–19. For Indigenous studies scholarship from the southern hemisphere that has decentred western literary histories, see, e.g., Alice Te Punga Somerville, *Once Were Pacific: Māori Connections to Oceania* (Minneapolis: University of Minnesota Press, 2012). For the African and/or pan-African perspective, see, e.g., Victoria J. Collis-Buthelezi, 'Caribbean Regionalism, South Africa, and Mapping New World Studies', *Small Axe*, 19:1 (2015), 37–54, and 'Under the Aegis of Empire: Cape Town, Victorianism, and Early-Twentieth-Century Black Thought', *Callaloo*, 39:1 (2016), 115–32; and Khwezi Mkhize, 'Empire Unbound: Imperial Liberalism, Race and Diaspora in the Making of South Africa' (PhD dissertation, University of Pennsylvania, 2015).

9 Isabel Hofmeyr's work has been pioneering in its decentralising efforts. See, e.g., 'Universalizing the Indian Ocean', *PMLA*, 125:3 (2010), 721–9. See also Manu Samriti Chander, *Brown Romantics: Poetry and Nationalism in the Global Nineteenth Century* (Lewisburg: Bucknell University Press, 2017); Jason Rudy, *Imagined Homelands: British Poetry in the Colonies* (Baltimore: Johns Hopkins University Press, 2017); Nikki Hessell, *Romantic Literature and the Colonised World: Lessons from Indigenous Translations* (Basingstoke: Palgrave Macmillan, 2018); Fariha Shaikh, *Nineteenth-Century Settler Emigration in British Literature and Art* (Edinburgh: Edinburgh University Press, 2018); and Philip Steer, *Settler Colonialism in Victorian Literature: Economics and*

Political Identity in the Networks of Empire (Cambridge: Cambridge University Press, 2020).

10 Tony Ballantyne, 'Putting the Nation in its Place? World History and C. A. Bayly's *The Birth of the Modern World*', in Anne Curthoys and Marilyn Lake (eds), *Connected Worlds: History in Transnational Perspective* (Canberra: ANU Press, 2005), p. 24.

11 C. A. Bayly et al., 'AHR Conversation: On Transnational History', *The American Historical Review*, 111:5 (2006), 1449.

12 Saul Dubow, 'How British Was the British World? The Case of South Africa', *The Journal of Imperial and Commonwealth History*, 37:1 (2009), 2–3. On mobilities studies, see, e.g., Tony Ballantyne, 'Mobility, Empire, Colonisation', *History Australia*, 11:2 (2014), 7–37.

13 For an elaboration of this position, see Sarah Comyn and Porscha Fermanis, 'Rethinking Nineteenth-Century Literary Culture: British Worlds, Southern Latitudes and Hemispheric Methods', *Journal of Commonwealth Literature* (2021), n.p., https://doi.org/10.1177/0021989420982013 (accessed 1 February 2021).

14 Tamara S. Wagner, 'Introduction: Narrating Domestic Portability: Emigration, Domesticity, and Genre Formation', in Tamara S. Wagner (ed.), *Victorian Settler Narratives: Emigrants, Cosmopolitans and Returnees in Nineteenth-Century Literature* (London: Pickering & Chatto, 2011), pp. 1, 2.

15 Paul Giles, *Virtual Americas: Transnational Fictions and the Transatlantic Imaginary* (Durham and London: Duke University Press, 2002), p. 5.

16 Sharon Marcus, 'Same Difference? Transnationalism, Comparative Literature, and Victorian Studies', *Victorian Studies*, 45:4 (2003), 679, 681.

17 Marilyn Lake, 'White Man's Country: The Trans-national History of a National Project', *Australian Historical Studies*, 34:122 (2003), 348, 349; Marcus, 'Same Difference', 680, 682.

18 For studies of interdiscursive, intertextual, and lateral relations between peripheries within empire, see, e.g., Elleke Boehmer, *Empire, the National and the Postcolonial: Resistance in Interaction* (Oxford: Oxford University Press, 2002); Françoise Lionnet and Shu-mei Shih (eds), *Minor Transnationalism* (Durham: Duke University Press, 2005); and Neil Lazarus, *The Postcolonial Unconscious* (Cambridge: Cambridge University Press, 2011). On Indigenous mobility and transnationalism, see, e.g., Lynette Russell, *Roving Mariners: Australian Aboriginal Whalers and Sealers in the Southern Oceans, 1790–1870* (New York: State University of New York Press, 2012); and Rachel Stanfield (ed.), *Indigenous Mobilities: Across and beyond the Antipodes* (Canberra: ANU Press, 2018). On the Global South and lateral relations, see Elena Fiddian-Qasmiyeh and Patricia Daley (eds), *Handbook of South–South Relations* (Oxford: Routledge, 2018). On the balance required between tribal epistemic specificity and 'relational regionality', see Tol Foster, 'Of One Blood: An Argument for Relations and Regionality in Native American Literary Studies', in Janice Acoose, Daniel Heath Justice, Christopher B. Teuton, and Craig Womack (eds), *Reasoning Together: The Native Critical Collective* (Norman: University of Oklahoma Press, 2008), pp. 265–302.

19 Philip J. Holden, 'Between Modernization and Modernism: Community and Contradiction in the Paracolonial Short Story', *Philippine Studies*, 55:3 (2007), 321; Nicholas Jose, 'Introduction', in Nicholas Jose (ed.), *Macquarie PEN Anthology of Australian Literature* (Sydney: Allen & Unwin, 2009), p. 1.

20 On a global imperial commons, see Antoinette Burton and Isabel Hofmeyr, 'Introduction', in Antoinette Burton and Isabel Hofmeyr (eds), *Ten Books that Shaped the British Empire: Creating an Imperial Commons* (Durham: Duke University Press, 2014), p. 1.

21 See Marcia Langton, *Well, I Heard It on the Radio and Saw It on the Television* (North Sydney: Australian Film Commission, 1993), cited in Evelyn Araluen, 'Resisting the Institution', *Overland*, 227 (2017), n.p., https://overland.org.au/previous-issues/issue-227/feature-evelyn-araluen/ (accessed 26 June 2019).

22 Johannesburg Workshop in Theory and Criticism, www.jwtc.org.za (accessed 26 June 2019).

23 Walter D. Mignolo, 'On Comparison: Who Is Comparing What and Why?', in Rita Felski and Susan Stanford Friedman (eds), *Comparison: Theories, Approaches, Uses* (Baltimore: Johns Hopkins University Press, 2013), p. 115. See also, e.g., Raewyn Connell, *Southern Theory: The Global Dynamics of Knowledge in Social Science (Sydney: Allen & Unwin,* 2007); Boaventura de Sousa Santos, *Another Knowledge Is Possible: Beyond Northern Epistemologies* (London and New York: Verso, 2008); and Jean Comaroff and John L. Comaroff, *Theory from the South: Or, How Euro-America Is Evolving toward Africa (*Boulder: Paradigm Publishers, 2011).

24 Boaventura de Sousa Santos, *The End of the Cognitive Empire: The Coming of Age of Epistemologies of the South* (Durham: Duke University Press, 2018), p. 1; Sparke, 'Everywhere but Always Somewhere', 117.

25 Comaroff and Comaroff, *Theory from the South*, p. 47.

26 Carter, 'Australindia', 225, 224; Paul Giles, *Antipodean America: Australasia and the Constitution of U.S. Literature* (Oxford: Oxford University Press, 2014), p. 14.

27 John Eperjesi, *The Imperialist Imaginary: Visions of Asia and the Pacific in American Culture* (Hanover: University Press of New England, 2005), p. 3.

28 Selina Tusitala Marsh, 'Guys Like Gauguin', in *Fast Talking PI* (2009; Auckland: Auckland University Press, 2012), pp. 37–8; Bronwen Douglas, 'Foreign Bodies in Oceania', in Bronwen Douglas and Chris Ballard (eds), *Foreign Bodies: Oceania and the Science of Race, 1750–1940* (Canberra: Australian National University Press, 2008), p. 8; Warwick Anderson, 'Racial Conceptions in the Global South', *ISIS*, 15:4 (2014), 782, 783.

29 Sugata Bose, *A Hundred Horizons: The Indian Ocean in the Age of Global Empire* (Cambridge, MA: Harvard University Press, 2006), p. 6; Anne Salmond, *Tears of Rangi: Experiments across Worlds* (Auckland: Auckland University Press, 2017), p. 2; James Clifford, *Returns: Becoming Indigenous in the Twenty-First Century* (Cambridge, MA: Harvard University Press, 2013), p. 64.

30 David Chandler and Julian Reid, '"Being in Being": Contesting the Ontopolitics of Indigeneity', *The European Legacy*, 23:3 (2018), 257, 260; Mary

Graham, 'Some Thoughts about the Philosophical Underpinnings of Aboriginal Worldviews', *Australian Humanities Review*, 45 (2008), 181–94; Deborah Bird Rose, 'An Indigenous Philosophical Ecology: Situating the Human', *The Australian Journal of Anthropology*, 16:3 (2005), 294–305. See also Mario Blaser, 'Ontology and Indigeneity: On the Political Ontology of Heterogeneous Assemblages', *Cultural Geographies*, 2:1 (2014), 49–58.

31 Ivan Tacey, 'Tropes of Fear: The Impact of Globalization on Batek Religious Landscapes', *Religions*, 4 (2013), 250.

32 James Clifford, 'Indigenous Articulations', in Rob Wilson and Christopher Leigh Connery (eds), *The Worlding Project: Doing Cultural Studies in the Era of Globalization* (Berkeley: New Pacific Press, 2007), p. 15. On articulation theory as opposed to threshold or authenticity approaches to indigeneity, see Stuart Hall, 'Gramsci's Relevance for the Study of Race and Ethnicity', *Journal of Communication Inquiry*, 10:2 (1986), 5–27.

33 Ingrid Horrocks, 'A World of Waters: Imagining, Voyaging, Entanglement', in Mark Williams (ed.), *A History of New Zealand Literature* (Cambridge: Cambridge University Press, 2016), p. 26; Silvia Spitta, *Between Two Waters: Narratives of Transculturation in Latin America* (Houston: Rice University Press, 1995), p. 2.

34 Isabel Hofmeyr, 'Southern by Degrees: Islands and Empires in the South Atlantic, the Indian Ocean, and the Subantartic World', in Kerry Bystrom and Joseph R. Slaughter (eds), *The Global South Atlantic* (New York: Fordham University Press, 2018), p. 82. On American hemispheric studies, see, e.g., the classic Gustavo Pérez Firmat (ed.), *Do the Americas Have a Common Literature?* (Durham: Duke University Press, 1990); and Bianet Castellanos, Lourdes Gutiérrez Nájera, and Arturo Aldama (eds), *Comparative Indigeneities of the Américas: Toward a Hemispheric Approach* (Tucson: University of Arizona Press, 2012).

35 Southern Conceptualisms Network, www.museoreinasofia.es/en/southern-conceptualisms-network (accessed 26 June 2019).

36 Ralph Bauer, 'Hemispheric Studies', *PMLA*, 124:1 (2009), 234–50.

37 Stephen Shapiro, *The Culture and Commerce of the Early American Novel: Reading the Atlantic World-System* (University Park: Penn State University Press, 2008), p. 4.

38 Alex Watson and Laurence Williams, 'British Romanticism in Asia, 1820–1950: Modernity, Tradition, and Transformation in India and East Asia', in Alex **Watson** and Laurence **Williams** (eds), *British Romanticism in Asia: The Reception, Translation, and Transformation of Romantic Literature in India and East Asia* (Basingstoke: Palgrave Macmillan, 2019), p. 20; Philip Steer, 'The Historians, the Literary Critics, and the Victorian Settler Empire', *Literature Compass*, 15:5 (2018), 4.

39 ALICE, http://alice.ces.uc.pt/en/ (accessed 26 June 2019).

40 See, e.g., Paul Gilroy, *The Black Atlantic: Modernity and Double Consciousness* (Cambridge, MA: Harvard University Press, 1993).

41 Clifford, *Returns*, p. 58; Chadwick Allen, *Trans-Indigenous: Methodologies for Global Native Literary Studies* (Minneapolis: University of Minnesota Press, 2012) and 'A Trans*national* Native American Studies?', n.p., https://escholarship.

org/uc/item/82m5j3f5 (accessed 26 June 2019). On Indigenous mobility, see, e.g., Tracey Banivanua Mar, 'Shadowing Imperial Networks: Indigenous Mobility and Australia's Pacific Past', *Australian Historical Studies*, 46:3 (2015), 340–55.

42 See, e.g., Walter D. Mignolo, *Local Histories/Global Designs: Coloniality, Subaltern Knowledges, and Border Designs* (Princeton: Princeton University Press, 2000); and David Slater, *Geopolitics and the Post-Colonial: Rethinking North–South Relations* (Oxford: Blackwell, 2004).

43 Shino Konishi, 'First Nations Scholars, Settler Colonial Studies, and Indigenous History', *Australian Historical Studies*, 50 (2019), 1–20; Alissa Macoun and Elizabeth Strakosch, 'The Ethical Demands of Settler Colonial Theory', *Settler Colonial Studies*, 3:4 (2013), 426, 436. For an overview of critical Indigenous studies, see Aileen Moreton-Robinson (ed.), *Critical Indigenous Studies: Engagements in First World Locations* (Tucson: University of Arizona Press, 2016).

44 Konishi, 'First Nations Scholars', 291.

45 Araluen, 'Resisting the Institution', n.p.

46 Linda Tuhiwai Smith, *Decolonising Methodologies: Research and Indigenous Peoples* (Auckland: Zed, 1999), p. 98. More recently, see Jo-Ann Archibald, Jenny Lee-Morgan, and Jason De Santolo (eds), *Decolonizing Research: Indigenous Storywork as Methodology* (London: Zed, 2019). On Spivak's position, see R. Radhakrishnan, *Theory in an Uneven World* (Malden: Blackwell, 2003), p. 157.

47 Eve Tuck and K. Wayne Yang, 'Decolonization Is Not a Metaphor', *Decolonization: Indigeneity, Education & Society*, 1:1 (2012), 1–40, cited in Araluen, 'Resisting the Institution', n.p.

48 Araluen, 'Resisting the Institution', n.p.; Margaret Jolly, 'The South in Southern Theory: Antipodean Reflections on the Pacific', *Australian Humanities Review*, 44 (2008), n.p., http://australianhumanitiesreview.org/2008/03/01/the-south-in-southern-theory-antipodean-reflections-on-the-pacific/ (accessed 26 June 2019).

49 Jonathan Saha, 'No, You're Peripheral', 18 July 2013, n.p., https://colonizing-animals.blog/2013/07/18/no-youre-peripheral/ (accessed 5 April 2019), cited in Gareth Curless, Stacey Hynd, Temilola Alanamu, and Katherine Roscoe, 'Editor's Introduction: Networks in Imperial History', *Journal of World History*, 26:4 (2016), 705–32; Michael Allan, '"Reading with one Eye, Speaking with One Tongue": On the Problem of Address in World Literature', *Comparative Literature Studies*, 44:1–2 (2007), 16–17.

50 Sanjay Krishnan, 'Reading Globalization from the Margin: The Case of Abdullah Munshi', *Representations*, 99:1 (2007), 40–41, 41.

51 Mei Zhan, *Other-Worldly: Making Chinese Medicine through Transnational Frames* (Durham: Duke University Press: 2009), p. 23. See also Martin Heidegger, 'On the Origin of the Work of Art', in *Basic Writings*, ed. David Farrell Krell (New York: Harper Collins, 2008), esp. pp. 168, 171–2, and 'The Age of the World Picture', in *Off the Beaten Track*, ed. and trans. Julian Young and Kenneth Hayes (Cambridge: Cambridge University Press, 2002), esp. p. 60.

52 Krishnan, 'Abdullah Munshi', 41.

53 Eric Hayot, *On Literary Worlds* (Oxford: Oxford University Press, 2012), pp. 40, 28.

54 Christian Moraru, '"World", "Globe", "Planet": Comparative Literature, Planetary Studies, and Cultural Debt after the Global Turn', n.p., https:// stateofthediscipline.acla.org/entry/"world"-"globe"-"planet"-comparative-literature-planetary-studies-and-cultural-debt-after (accessed 2 March 2020).

55 For the macrosociological approach of world-system units and scales of analysis, see, e.g., Immanuel Wallerstein, *The Modern World-System* (New York: Academic Press, 1964), esp. p. 98; and Peter Hitchcock, *The Long Space: Transnationalism and Postcolonial Form* (Stanford: Stanford University Press, 2010), esp. p. 35.

56 Hayot, *On Literary Worlds*, p. 7; Krishnan, 'Abdullah Munshi', 41.

57 Gayatri Chakravorty Spivak, 'Three Women's Texts and a Critique of Imperialism', *Critical Inquiry,* 12:1 (1985), 243–5, 243. See also 'The Rani of Sirmur: An Essay in Reading the Archives', *History and Theory*, 24:3 (1985), 254, 247. For another engagement with Heidegger's idea of worlding in the context of subaltern studies, see Dipesh Chakrabarty, *Provincializing Europe: Postcolonial Thought and Historical Difference* (Princeton: Princeton University Press, 2000), esp. pp. 95, 241.

58 For this characterisation of Spivak's position, see Sue Thomas, *Imperialism, Reform, and the Making of Englishness in Jane Eyre* (Basingstoke: Palgrave Macmillan, 2008), p. 2.

59 Krishnan, 'Abdullah Munshi', 50.

60 Krishnan, 'Abdullah Munshi', 54; Edward Said, *The World, the Text, and the Critic* (Cambridge, MA: Harvard University Press, 1984), p. 51.

61 John Muthyala, *Reworlding America: Myth, History and Narrative* (Athens: Ohio University Press, 2006), p. 2; Bauer, 'Hemispheric Studies', 241–2.

62 Margaret Jolly, 'Imagining Oceania: Indigenous and Foreign Representations of a Sea of Islands', *The Contemporary Pacific*, 19:2 (2007), 508–45.

63 Patrick D. Joyce, *The Rule of Freedom: Liberalism and the Modern City* (London and New York: Verso, 2003), pp. 36, 37.

64 Judith Binney, 'Tuki's Universe', *New Zealand Journal of History*, 38:2 (2004), 215; Jolly, 'Imagined Oceania', 509.

65 Vicente M. Diaz and J. Kehaulani Kauanui, 'Native Pacific Cultural Studies on the Edge', *The Contemporary Pacific*, 13:2 (2001), 317. Diaz is Filipino-Pohnpeian and Kauanui is Kānaka Maoli.

66 Epeli Hauʻofa, 'Our Sea of Islands', in Eric Waddell, Vijay Naidu, and Epeli Hauʻofa (eds), *A New Oceania: Rediscovering Our Sea of Islands* (Suva: University of the South Pacific, 1993), pp. 6–7.

67 Meg Samuelson, 'Rendering the Cape-as-Port: Sea-Mountain, Cape of Storms/Good Hope, Adamastor and Local-World Literary Formations', *Journal of South African Studies*, 42:3 (2016), 524. For an examination of the 'littoral condition' of the southern hemisphere, see, e.g., Meg Samuelson and Charne Lavery, 'The Oceanic South', *English Language Notes*, 57:1 (2019), 37–50.

68 Tanya Agathocleous, 'Imperial, Anglophone, Geopolitical, Worldly: Evaluating the "Global" in Victorian Studies', *Victorian Literature and Culture*, 43 (2015), 657.

69 Tanya Agathocleous and Jason R. Rudy, 'Victorian Cosmopolitanisms', *Victorian Literature and Culture*, 38 (2010), 390. See also, e.g., Alan Bewell, *Romanticism and Colonial Disease* (Baltimore and London: Johns Hopkins University Press, 2003), and *Natures in Translation: Romanticism and Colonial Natural History* (Baltimore and London: Johns Hopkins University Press, 2017); Deirdre Coleman, *Romantic Colonization and British Anti-Slavery* (Cambridge: Cambridge University Press, 2005); Tim Fulford, Debbie Lee, and Peter J. Kitson (eds), *Literature, Science and Exploration in the Romantic Era* (Cambridge: Cambridge University Press, 2004); Evan Gottlieb, *Romantic Globalism: British Literature and the Modern World Order, 1750–1830* (Columbus: Ohio State University Press, 2014); Lauren M. E. Goodlad, 'Cosmopolitanism's Actually Existing Beyond; Toward a Victorian Geopolitical Aesthetic', *Victorian Literature and Culture*, 38 (2010), 399–411, and *The Victorian Geopolitical Aesthetic* (Oxford: Oxford University Press, 2015); Upamanyu Pablo Mukherjee, 'Introduction: Victorian World Literature', *The Yearbook of English Studies*, 41:2 (2011), 1–19.

70 Hessell, *Romantic Literature and the Colonised World*, p. 7.

71 Charles Forsdick and Jennifer Yee, 'Towards a Postcolonial Nineteenth-Century', *French Studies*, 72:2 (2018), 172, 174. See also Elleke Boehmer, *Colonial and Postcolonial Literature: Migrant Metaphors* (Oxford: Oxford University Press, 1995).

72 Margaret Harris, 'The Antipodean Anatomy of Victorian Studies', *AUMLA: Journal of the Australasian Universities Modern Language Association*, 100 (2003), 68; Maggie Tonkin, Mandy Treagus, Madeleine Seys, and Sharon Crozier-De Rosa, 'Re-Visiting the Victorian Subject', in Maggie Tonkin, Mandy Treagus, Madeleine Seys, and Sharon Crozier-De Rosa (eds), *Changing the Victorian Subject* (Adelaide: University of Adelaide Press, 2014), p. 3.

73 Marilyn Lake, 'White Man's Country', 347; Patricia Grimshaw, Marilyn Lake, Ann Mcgrath, and Marian Quartly, *Creating a Nation, 1788–1900* (Ringwood: Penguin Book Australia, 1994), p. 2.

74 Mark Williams, citing the work of Alice Te Punga Somerville, 'Introduction', in Mark Williams (ed.), *A History of New Zealand Literature* (Cambridge: Cambridge University Press, 2016), pp. 3, 2.

75 Hayot, *On Literary Worlds*, pp. 149, 156.

76 Chander, *Brown Romantics*, p. 101; Watson and Williams, 'British Romanticism in Asia', p. 2.

77 Hessell, *Romantic Literature and the Colonised World*, pp. 229, 230, 5–6. See also Mark Rifkin, *Beyond Settler Time: Temporal Sovereignty and Indigenous Self-Determination* (Durham: Duke University Press, 2017).

78 Mignolo, 'On Comparison', pp. 100, 106.

79 Mignolo, 'On Comparison', pp. 104–5.

80 Penny van Toorn, *Writing Never Arrives Naked: Early Aboriginal Cultures of Writing in Australia* (Canberra: Aboriginal Studies Press, 2006), p. 2; Jeff Opland, 'Nineteenth-Century Xhosa Literature', *Kronos*, 30 (2004), 22; Mbulelo Vizikhungo Mzamane, 'Colonial and Imperial Themes in South African Literature, 1820–1930', *The Yearbook of English Studies*, 13 (1983), 181–95; Amin Sweeney, *A Full Hearing: Orality and Literacy in the Malay World* (Berkeley: University of California Press, 1987), p. 1; Horrocks, 'A World of Waters: Imagining, Voyaging, Entanglement', pp. 18, 25; Arini Loader, 'Early Māori Literature: The Writing of Hajaraia Kiharoa', in Mark Williams (ed.), *A History of New Zealand Literature* (Cambridge: Cambridge University Press, 2016), pp. 31, 33.

81 Gauri Viswanathan, *Masks of Conquest: Literary Studies and British Rule in India* (New York: Columbia University Press, 1989), pp. 3, 10; Vanessa Smith, *Literary Culture and the Pacific: Nineteenth-Century Textual Encounters* (Cambridge: Cambridge University Press, 1998) pp. 109, 5, 116.

82 Van Toorn, *Writing Never Arrives Naked*, p. 20.

83 Simon Gikandi, *Maps of Englishness: Writing Identity in the Culture of Colonialism* (New York: Columbia University Press, 1996), p. xviii; Anna Johnston, *Missionary Writing and Empire, 1800–1860* (Cambridge: Cambridge University Press, 2003), p. 29; Ntongela Masilela, 'Vernacular Press', in Simon Gikandi (ed.), *Encyclopedia of African Literature* (London: Routledge, 2003), pp. 547–54; Mzamane, 'Colonial and Imperial Themes in South African Literature, 1820–1930', 183.

84 Jahan Ramazani, *A Transnational Poetics* (Chicago: Chicago University Press, 2009).

85 Gayatri Chakravorty Spivak, *Death of a Discipline* (New York: Columbia University Press, 2003), pp. 107–8; Katherine Bode, *Reading by Numbers: Recalibrating the Literary Field* (London: Anthem Press, 2012), p. 11.

86 Franco Moretti, 'Conjectures on World Literature', *New Left Review*, 1 (2000), 65; Goodlad, 'Cosmopolitanism's Actually Existing Beyond', 404, 406.

87 Rudy, *Imagined Homelands*, p. 7.

88 Katherine Bode, 'Fictional Systems: Mass-Digitization, Network Analysis, and Nineteenth-Century Australian Newspapers', *Victorian Periodicals Review*, 50:1 (2017), 101, and '"Sidelines" and Trade Lines: Publishing the Australian Novel, 1860–1899', *Book History*, 15 (2012), 115.

89 Holden, 'Between Modernization and Modernism', 319, 326.

90 Katherine Bode, 'Thousands of Titles without Authors: Digitized Newspapers, Serial Fiction, and the Challenges of Anonymity', *Book History*, 19 (2016), 298.

91 Burton and Hofmeyr, 'Introduction', pp. 1, 2, 5; Julie F. Codell, 'Introduction: Imperial Co-Histories and the British and Colonial Press', in Julie F. Codell (ed.), *Imperial Co-Histories: National Identities and the British and Colonial Press* (Danvers: Rosemount Publishing, 2003), p. 16.

92 David Higgins, 'Writing to Colonial Australia: Barron Field and Charles Lamb', *Nineteenth-Century Contexts*, 32:3 (2010), 219; Philip Mead, 'Nation,

Literature, Location', in Peter Pierce (ed.), *The Cambridge History of Australian Literature* (Cambridge: Cambridge University Press, 2011), p. 549. For an overview of legal understandings of the term *terra nullius*, see Thomas H. Ford and Justin Clemens, 'Barron Field's *Terra Nullius* Operation', *Australian Humanities Review*, 65 (2019), 1–19.

93 Andrew McCann, 'Romanticism, Nationalism and the Myth of the Popular in William Lane's *The Workingman's Paradise*', *Journal of Australian Studies*, 25:70 (2001), 2.

94 Alice Te Punga Somerville, 'Canons: Damned If You Do and Damned If You Don't: A Response to Adam Kostsko', *Australian Humanities Review*, 60 (2016), 189.

95 Michael Farrell, *Writing Australian Unsettlement: Modes of Poetic Invention 1796–1945* (New York: Palgrave Macmillan, 2015), p. 2.

96 Maria Nugent, 'Jacky Jacky and the Politics of Aboriginal Testimony', in Shino Konishi, Maria Nugent, and Tiffany Shelam (eds), *Indigenous Intermediaries* (Canberra: Australian National University Press, 2015), p. 72; Jonathan Dunk, 'Reading the Tracker: The Antimonies of Aboriginal Ventriloquism', *JASAL: Journal of the Association for the Study of Australian Literature*, 17:1 (2017), 3.

97 Farrell, *Writing Australian Unsettlement*, p. 4, and 'The Colonial Baroque in Australia: On Drover Boab Texts, Wiradjuri Clubs, and Charlie Flannigan's Drawings', *Criticism*, 58:3 (2016), 428.

98 Patrick Brantlinger, *Dark Vanishings: Discourse on the Extinction of Primitive Races, 1800–1930* (Ithaca: Cornell University Press, 2003), p. 230; Ken Gelder, 'The Postcolonial Gothic', in Jerrold E. Hogle (ed.), *The Cambridge Companion to the Modern Gothic* (Cambridge: Cambridge University Press, 2014), pp. 191–207; Mandy Treagus, *Empire Girls: The Colonial Heroine Comes of Age* (Adelaide: University of Adelaide Press, 2014), pp. 247, 250; J. M. Coetzee, 'Farm Novel and "Plaasroman" in South Africa', *English in Africa*, 13:2 (1986), 1–19.

99 Coetzee, 'Farm Novel and "Plaasroman" in South Africa', 17. For a revisionist account, see Sam Naidu, 'The Emergence of the South African Farm Crime Novel: Socio-Historical Crimes, Personal Crimes, and the Figure of the Dog', *English in Africa*, 43:2 (August 2016), 9–38. On settler novels of enclosure, see Steer, *Settler Colonialism in Victorian Literature*.

100 Tracey Banivanua Mar, *Violence and Colonial Dialogue: The Australian-Pacific Indentured Labor Trade* (Honolulu: University of Hawai'i Press, 2007), pp. 24, 29.

101 Saul Dubow, *Scientific Racism in Modern South Africa* (Cambridge: Cambridge University Press, 1995), p. 24.

102 Kathryn Simpson, 'H. Rider Haggard, Theophilus Shepstone and the Zikali Trilogy: A Revisionist Approach to Haggard's African Fiction' (PhD dissertation, Edinburgh Napier University, 2016), pp. 24–5; Brian Willan, 'What "Other Devils"? The Texts of Sol T. Plaatje's *Mhudi* Revisited', *Journal of Southern African Studies*, 41:6 (2015), 1343.

103 Simon Gikandi, 'Realism, Romance, and the Problem of African Literature', *Modern Language Quarterly*, 73:3 (2012), 311–12.

104 Jonathan Lamb, Vanessa Smith, and Nicholas Thomas, 'Introduction', in Jonathan Lamb, Vanessa Smith, and Nicholas Thomas (eds), *Exploration and Exchange: A South Seas Anthology, 1680–1900* (Chicago: University of Chicago Press, 2000), p. xviii; Mandy Treagus, 'Crossing "The Beach": Samoa, Stevenson and the "Beach at Falesä"', *Literature Compass*, 11:5 (2014), 316.

105 On colonial anxieties and the ways in which these anxieties figure as forms of resistance to imperial infrastructures, see Dominic Davies, *Imperial Infrastructure and Spatial Resistance in Colonial Literature, 1880–1930* (Oxford: Peter Lang 2017), esp. p. 35.

106 Archie L. Dick, *The Hidden History of South Africa's Book and Reading Cultures* (Toronto and London: University of Toronto Press, 2012), p. 27.

107 Lydia Wevers, *Country of Writing: Travel Writing and New Zealand, 1809–1900* (Auckland: Auckland University Press, 2002), n.p.; Smith, *Literary Culture and the Pacific*, p. 116.

108 James Clifford, 'Notes on Travel and Theory', *Centre for Cultural Studies Inscriptions*, 5 (1989), n.p., https://culturalstudies.ucsc.edu/inscriptions/volume-5/james-clifford/ (accessed 5 July 2019); Smith, *Literary Culture and the Pacific*, p. 116.

109 Helen Groth, 'Mediating Popular Fictions: From the Magic Lantern to the Cinematograph', in Ken Gelder (ed.), *New Directions in Popular Fiction: Genre, Distribution, Reproduction* (London: Palgrave Macmillan, 2016), p. 288.

110 Giles, *Antipodean America*, p. 24.

111 Terry Goldie, *Fear and Temptation: The Image of the Indigene in Canadian, Australian, and New Zealand Literatures* (Montreal and Kingston: McGill-Queens University Press, 1989), p. 13.

112 Leilani Nishime and Kim D. Hester Williams, 'Introduction: Why Racial Ecologies?', in Leilani Nishime and Kim D. Hester Williams (eds), *Racial Ecologies* (Washington: University of Washington Press, 2018), p. 4.

113 Devin Griffiths and Deanna Kriesel, 'Introduction: Open Ecologies', *Victorian Literature and Culture*, 48:1 (2020), 6.

114 Tim Rowse, 'The Indigenous Redemption of Liberal Universalism', *Modern Intellectual History*, 12:3 (2015), 583.

115 Theodore Koditschek, *Liberalism, Imperialism, and the Historical Imagination: Nineteenth-Century Visions of a Greater Britain* (Cambridge: Cambridge University Press, 2011), p. 5; Duncan Ivison, 'Non-Cosmopolitan Universalism: On Armitage's Foundations of International Political Thought', *History of European Ideas*, 41:1 (2015), 80.

Part I

World/Globe

1

Making, mapping, and unmaking worlds: globes, panoramas, fictions, and oceans

Peter Otto

[Jakob von Uexküll] was taking the step from monological meta-physics, which interprets the world as mono context and projects it on to a single eye, to a pluralistic ontology that estimates as many worlds as there are eye types and other sensors to see and feel them, without resorting to the hypostasis of an eye of all eyes (or a sensor of all sensors).

Peter Sloterdijk, *Spheres: Plural Spherology* (2013)

This chapter's primary focus is on 'A View of the Town of Sydney', a panorama exhibited in the upper viewing-circle of Robert Burford's Leicester Square Panorama from December 1828 until at least March 1831.[1] It was based on eight overlapping views of Sydney, as seen from Palmer's Hill in the Government Domain, which were drawn by the artist and adventurer Augustus Earle under the supervision of Governor Darling's brother-in-law, Colonel Dumaresq, who carried the drawings to London.[2] This was not the first panoramic view of Sydney to be shown in London. It was preceded by Major James Taylor's 'sketches for a "panorama of Port Jackson and of the Town of Sydney"', engravings of which were exhibited in 1824 at the Leicester Square Panorama, perhaps in the foyer of that building. But it was the first full-scale panorama of Sydney and as such played an important part in shaping popular perceptions of the Antipodes and, to that extent, also of the southern hemisphere. It was so successful that when 'A View of the Town of Sydney' closed, Burford almost immediately offered a second full-scale panoramic view of the Antipodes, this time 'A View of Hobart Town, Van Diemen's Land, and the Surrounding Country', based again on drawings by Earle.

The word 'panorama' can refer to a 360-degree painting intended to be viewed from a central position *and* to the circular building (a panorama rotunda) designed to display it. The latter includes a central viewing platform; intercepts, which hide the upper and lower edges of the painting that covers its inside walls; and a concealed source of light, which streams down from above. The word also names the panorama's optical environment as a whole, patented by Robert Barker in 1787, which is complete only when spectators are added to the viewing platform of a panorama rotunda in which a circular painting has been hung. In this environment, spectators bring the panoramic illusion to life, as they half-perceive and half-create a hyper-realistic virtual reality 'that extends in a complete circle around [them], to an imagined horizon (and then to an implied beyond)'.[3] This collocation of convincing illusion and amazing verisimilitude is why, as suggested by the titles of the two most important books on Australian panoramas – *Canvas Documentaries* (1998) by Mimi Colligan, and *Capturing Time* (2012) by Edwin Barnard – panorama paintings are routinely treated as realistic records of places and times. And this in turn underwrites the belief that panoramic entertainments appealed to nineteenth-century audiences because they recalled the global/panoptic views previously reserved for the powerful.[4]

These claims are true, as far as they go. And yet it is important to recall that the panorama was a place of sociability as much as careful observation; it conjured an *Umwelt*, rather than a conventional prospect, which could be viewed from numerous points of view; and, perhaps most importantly, its hyper-realistic illusion aroused audience interest in how it had been constructed, which in turn suggested that the actual world, like the panorama's virtual world, is 'an appearance within psychological and cultural systems of perception'.[5] With regard to all these remarks, 'A View of the Town of Sydney' is a case in point. For those inside its apparently objective virtual world, the fictions shaping it are everywhere apparent – in the patterns it makes visible, the myths it invokes, the traces it retains of the cultures it attempts to efface or redeem, and in the variety of responses it rouses in, and the number of ways it is construed by, viewers. In this hybrid space, the real and the imaginary, the objective and the mythological, settler and colonised, even settlement and unsettlement move into surprising proximity with each other.

As this suggests, 'A View of the Town of Sydney' both resists and comes to display what Peter Sloterdijk describes as 'the spatial law of the Modern Age ... namely that one can no longer interpret one's own place of origin as the hub of the existent and the world as its concentrically arranged environment'.[6] And as such, it offers a vehicle for thinking through the challenges that emerge when we turn our attention from the north to the south, from a hemisphere dominated by land to one dominated by the ocean – or, more abstractly, from a fixed to a shifting world, structured primarily by time, place, and agency rather than unity, purity, and order. In the following pages, my argument unfolds in five stages: Globes, Panoramic Realism, Regeneration, Fictions, and Oceans. The first, second, and third trace the democratisation, as represented by the panorama, of the all-encompassing view normally associated with gods, kings, and (for the eighteenth century) towering natural philosophers like Isaac Newton. This ought to be a moment of enlightenment, in which the view from on high becomes visible to anyone willing to pay the price of admission. And yet, as the fourth and fifth stages will suggest, it brings with it the seeds of its own demise, by making it equally apparent that the 'whole' seen from on high is a fiction designed to manage unruly multiplicities, each of which is able to constitute itself as the 'hub of the existent and [of] the world as its concentrically arranged environment'. For those standing in Burford's panorama, I want to suggest, this realisation is coincident with the moment when their virtual journey from the northern to the southern hemisphere begins.

Globes

In the nearly 500 years since the Magellan expedition circumnavigated the earth (1519–22) and Nicolaus Copernicus published *On the Revolutions of the Heavenly Spheres* (1543), the globe has been a ubiquitous presence in the western imagination. It is not difficult to see why. The former provided tangible proof that the earth is a globe and, in so doing, opened the possibility that the world could be viewed, by a human observer, as a single self-contained form – a possibility realised on 12 April 1961, when Yuri Gargarin became the first person to orbit the earth. The latter marks the emergence of the 'New Science', developed by Johannes Kepler and Galileo Galilei in the sixteenth and seventeenth centuries, which culminates in the work of Isaac Newton. For the eighteenth century, Newton's discovery of the laws of motion and of universal gravitation, and description of the paths followed by celestial and terrestrial globes in absolute time and space, placed him (metaphorically) at an altitude still greater than the one implied by Magellan or attained by Gargarin.

These giddy heights and the global view they make possible are powerfully evoked by Edmund Halley's 'Ode to Newton', included in the prefatory material accompanying the first edition of *Philosophiae Naturalis Principia Mathematica* (1687). According to Halley, Newton's 'sublime intelligence has made it possible for us', following in Newton's footsteps, 'to climb the heights of heaven' and from this eminence to see the 'pattern of the heavens', 'the immovable order of the world / And the things that were concealed from generations of the past'.[7] In the eighteenth century, versions of this trope were a staple of popular accounts of Newton's genius. In 'The Ecstasy. An Ode' (1720), for example, John Hughes represents Newton as '[t]he great *Columbus* of the Skies', whose 'Soul . . . daily travels here / In Search of Knowledge for Mankind below'.[8] Similarly, Albrecht von Haller writes in

Gedanken über Vernunft, Aberglauben und Unglauben ('Thoughts on Reason, Superstition and Incredulity' [1729]) that 'Newton, overleaping the bounds prescribed to created spirits, traces the vast plan of the universe'.[9] And Alexander Pope in his *Essay on Man* (1733–34) urges Newton to 'Go, wondrous creature! mount where science guides ... Go, soar with Plato to th'empyreal sphere, / To the first good, first perfect, and first fair'.[10]

All-encompassing views (and powers) such as these were traditionally reserved for God and, in less expansive form, for kings, as his representatives on earth. The extent of the former is suggested by images of the 'Salvator Mundi' ('Saviour of the World'), in which Jesus is seen holding a globe (the world) in his left hand, while raising his right hand in blessing. And the latter is symbolised by cartographic globes, such as those made by Vincenzo Corinelli for Louis XIV in 1683, which evoke the king's (supposed) panoptic gaze and global power. As Christian Jacob explains: 'The symbolic grasp of the world, held in the open palm, is coupled with a panoptic gaze – on the miniaturized representation, grasping at the same time the whole of terrestrial form and the infinite details of its places.'[11] In both contexts, the globe also represents the power to 'englobe', to bring a disorganised mass into an ordered whole, which is exercised by gods in the creation of worlds and by kings in the creation of empires. It follows therefore that for some, such as John Desaguliers, Newton's philosophy is 'the only true *Philosophy*' and, the law-abiding universe it describes, the '*perfect Model*' of good government.[12]

One assumes that gods are able easily to grasp 'at the same time the whole of terrestrial form and the infinite details of its places'; but, notwithstanding the optimistic conclusion of Desaguliers' poem, when kings attempt the same feat they run into difficulties. The terrestrial and celestial globes made by Coronelli for Louis XIV, for example, were each four metres in diameter, much too large to be held in the palm of even a royal hand and for many of the details inscribed on their surfaces to be read by anyone. Louis solved the second of these problems by ordering special glasses to be ground, which reconciled 'the contemplative gaze from above with the close-up view belonging to the myopic reader'.[13] The glasses therefore become somewhat comic emblems both of his real power and its obvious limitations.

By the middle of the eighteenth century, Newton was often depicted as ignorant of an analogous difficulty. In Pope's *Essay on Man*, for example, the lines quoted above are followed by a volte-face in which ascent is troped as a loss of sense that makes Newton, once he returns to earth, no more than a fool.[14] Much the same about-face occurs in Haller's *Die Falschheit menschlicher Tugenden* ('The Falseness of Human Virtues' [1730]), published just one year after *Gedanken*. In this later poem, Haller again tropes Newton as a 'transcendent genius', whose mind 'passing the bounds of visible space, travels in worlds unknown'; but he nevertheless concludes that 'all [his] painful and incessant labours have served no purpose but to shew ... the weakness and ignorance of man'.[15] The regularity, harmony, and stability of things when seen from on high only throws into relief the unpredictability, complexity, contingency, and multiplicity of the worlds in which we are immersed.

These ambivalent assessments of Newton's achievements are informed by Enlightenment thought, which regards the senses as 'the source of all human knowledge' and, consequently, no longer identifies the natural 'with the mathematical or metaphysical'.[16] They become still more negative in the wake of the discovery, by Romantic writers, of the roles played by desire, imagination, language, and perspective in the construction of experience, and therefore also of knowledge and of the world in which we live. And this in turn means that the relation between distance and immersion, which in early modern cultures can still be presented as a contrast between substance and surface, becomes an oscillation between competing demands, reflected in Romantic distinctions between mathematical and living form or, in more contemporary idiom, between geometrical and anthropological space (Maurice Merleau-Ponty), analytical and processual space (Michel Serres), and so on.[17] In the late eighteenth and early nineteenth century, the tension between these poles becomes commonly visible in the panorama, where an all-encompassing view becomes available not just to Newton but to anyone who pays the price of entry.

Panoramic realism

Like most large-scale panoramas painted in the nineteenth century, 'A View of the Town of Sydney' has not survived; and, in this case, even the drawings on which it was based have been lost. All that remains is the guidebook, entitled *Description of a View of the Town of Sydney, New South Wales; The Harbour of Port Jackson, and Surrounding Country*, which provides a visual and a verbal description of the scene. The former, a rough sketch printed on a folding plate, entitled 'Explanation of a View of the Town of Sydney' and, when extracted from that volume and treated as a stand-alone engraving, 'Panorama of Sydney N.S.W' (Figure 1.1), singles out for attention sixty of its most important landmarks.[18] The latter, drawing on information provided by Dumaresq, includes a brief history of the colony and of the European discovery of Australasia, to which it appends a short explanatory paragraph for each of the sites flagged by the explanatory design. Although this might not seem much to go on, it is enough to conjure, in broad outline, the view encountered by Burford's customers.

As previously noted, 'A View of the Town of Sydney' was taken from the top of Palmer's Hill in the Government Domain (a site near the present-day Statue of Governor Phillip in Sydney's Botanic Gardens).[19] From this vantage point, the view arranges itself into four unequal, roughly horizontal layers. In the first, the foreground of the painting, the Domain, slopes gently down and

Figure 1.1 Robert Burford, 'Panorama of Sydney, N.S.W., in the year 1829 as painted by Robert Burford and exhibited in Leicester Square' (London: Printed and published by Lake & Sons Pty. Ltd., n.d.), reproduced from the 'Explanation of a view of the town of Sydney', 1829

away from the viewing platform on all sides, creating the impression that we are standing in the middle of a gentleman's park. Up close to the spectators are three scenes centred on Australia's Indigenous inhabitants, entitled *Natives* (No. 16), *Native climbing a Gum* (No. 60), and *King Boongaree* (No. 19). Boongaree, who is the only Aboriginal person named in the panorama, was given the fictitious title of 'King' by Governor Lachlan Macquarie. He was 'a Garigal man, probably from the Broken Bay–West Head group to the north of Port Jackson',[20] who in 1801–2 had sailed with Matthew Flinders on *H.M.S. Investigator*, becoming the first Aborigine to circumnavigate Australia.[21] As the most important intermediary between black and white worlds, he is shown with his cocked hat raised in greeting, as *Genl. Darling*, the Governor of the Colony, and *Co^l. Dumaresq*, Darling's private secretary, approach on horseback (No. 18). The colony's military administration, the proximate world to which Darling and Dumaresq belong, is represented a little further away from the viewing platform by the *Governor[']s House* (No. 40), *Government Stables* (No. 48), *Entrance to Government Gardens* (No. 17), and *Entrance to Government Domain* (No. 4).

The second layer, which begins just beyond the border of the Government Domain, includes the town of Sydney and the waters of Port Jackson. The former, which stretches in an arc from the south to the north-west, occupies almost 'the whole neck of land which separates Sydney [Cove] from Cockle Bay', while the vast expanse of the latter, edged by numerous coves and bays, runs from the north-west to the east.[22] As one gazes at the panorama, albeit in imagination, these contrasting ribbons of stone and water seem almost to be intertwined with each other, with the harbour glimpsed at various points behind the city, and buildings such as the Governor's House, the Government Stables, and the *residence of M^r. Fraser* (No. 59), the Colonial Botanist, scattered along the southern coast of Port Jackson.

The third layer, which forms the backdrop to the scene, is composed of three elements. First, the 'bold and precipitous shore' opposite Sydney Cove, which, as one follows it to the east, becomes a long 'chain of commanding and almost barren cliffs'.[23] Next, the low hills, rising from this shoreline, which join with others to encircle the colony, and which are made still more prominent by the windmills perched, like tutelary gods, on top of them. And third, the expanse that extends in all directions outwards from this circle of hills, to the distant horizon and, implicitly, to the beyond, which is indirectly presented by the *North Head* and *South Head* (Nos 53 and 54), beyond which lies the Pacific Ocean; the *Blue Mountains* (No. 35), which until 1813 were an unpassable barrier to western expansion of the colony; *Botany Bay* (No. 9), where Captain Cook in 1770 and the First Fleet in 1788 first landed on the East Coast of Australia; and, finally, the road leading inland to Paramatta (No. 11), the second European settlement in Australia.

The sky composes the fourth layer of the painting, which covers nearly 40% of the canvas. Because the upper and lower edges of the painting are hidden by intercepts, it seems to reach up and over the viewing platform and outwards to an infinite aerial world. High above the spectators, light floods through the skylight into the panorama, uncovering 'golden clouds of dazzling brightness, which are ... floating in the blue sky' and bringing the illusion as a whole almost to life. [24]

Regeneration

Those who flocked to see 'A View of the Town of Sydney' had probably experienced on other occasions the panorama's ability to give birth, as if from nothing, to an almost-real double of the world. But in this particular panorama, each time Sydney rises before the eyes of its audience, it echoes the subject matter of the painting, namely the creation (apparently ex nihilo) of an antipodean colony, which seemed likely to become an 'Albion reborn'.[25] In Burford's *Description of a View of the Town of Sydney*, these parallels between panoramic illusion, fledgling colony, and regenerated Albion are foregrounded by the poem he chose as epigraph – 'Visit of Hope to Sydney-Cove, Near Botany-Bay', by Erasmus Darwin.

Darwin's poem first appeared as epigraph to *The Voyage of Governor Phillip to Botany Bay, with an Account of the Establishment of the Colonies of Port Jackson & Norfolk Island*,[26] the first 'official' account of the founding of the new colony.[27] In a letter to Josiah Wedgwood, Darwin suggested that Hope's speech be extended by adding lines such as 'Here future Newtons shall explore the skies / Here future Priestlys, future Wedgewoods rise'.[28] But even without these additions, from her position 'High on a rock amid the troubled air', Hope's voice exerts a power that repeats in miniature God's creation of the world:

> 'Hear me,' she cried, 'ye rising realms! record
> Time's opening scenes, and truth's unerring word,
> There shall broad streets their stately walls extend,
> The circus widen, and the crescent bend;
> There ray'd from cities o'er the cultur'd land,
> Shall bright canals and solid roads expand.
> There the proud arch, colossus like, bestride,
> Yon glittering streams, and bound the chafing tide;
> Embellished villas crown the landscape scene,
> Farms wave with gold, and orchards blush between;
> There shall tall spires, and dome-capt towers ascend,
> And piers and quays their massy structures blend;
> While with each breeze approaching vessels glide,
> And northern treasures dance on every tide!'[29]

In 'A View of the Town of Sydney', this vision of miraculous emergence/ regeneration is conjured by constellations of buildings that together take shape as a modern (colonial/European) city, centred on local/global networks of landed wealth, commerce, communication, religion, moral improvement, and so on. The picture is thrown sharply into relief through contrast: Sydney is contrasted with Indigenous cultures, radically different from anything previously encountered by the settlers; a landscape completely unlike those found in Britain; and the presence of a military government and penal colony, represented by the *Military Barracks* (No. 21), *Military Hospital* (No. 33), and *Phoenix Hulk* (No. 45), among others. And it seems about to detach itself from these contexts, in a moment of miraculous rebirth, because they are represented as fading away. But this last remark takes us too quickly to the next stage of our argument. Here we must pause long enough to map the contours of this emerging world.

In the early years of the colony, its economy was centred on the *Commis-sariat Store* (No. 41), which was an arm of the colonial administration. But during the 1820s, its work was eclipsed by the emergence of a modern market economy, represented in Burford's panorama by the *Bank of Australia* (No. 37), the *Bank of New South Wales* (No. 20), and a host of business enterprises, made visible through allusions to retailers, shipbuilders, sealers, merchants, and so on.[30] Alongside these developments, a fledgling aristocracy has begun to emerge, raised by landed wealth, which is indexed by the town house of Sir John Jamieson (No. 23), one of the richest men in the colony, the *Land Board Office* (No. 22), and the *Australian Agricultural Company*[']s [Offices] (No. 39), which managed 'one million acres of land'.[31]

These developments proceed hand in hand with religion, which appears as a network of 'friendly' differences, with its primary nodes marked by the town's two Anglican churches – *St James*[']s *Church* (No. 8), with its 46-metre spire rising high above the horizon, and *St Phillip*[']s (No. 27), high on Church Hill, with its equally tall clock tower. Their 'competitors' include the *Catholic Chapel* (No. 3), the Methodist *Wesleyan Chapel* (No. 7), and the Presbyterian *Scotch Kirk* (No. 25). And, stitching church, commerce, and landed wealth together, the colony's philanthropic institutions, the hallmarks of an enlightened society, are represented by, for example, the *Orphan School* (No. 31), *School of Industry* (No. 15), and 'National School for the children of the lower orders'.[32]

The primary communication system that supports this activity is evoked by the *Sydney Gazette* (No. 32), one of 'eight newspapers ... published in the colony'; the *Road to Paramatta*, which connects coastal to inland parts of the colony; and the ships on the waters of Port Jackson, which link Sydney to other parts of Australia, the United Kingdom, and the larger world.[33] The most important of the system's switching points include the *Light House* (No. 55), which guides ships in and out of the Harbour, and the busy *King's Wharf & Dock*, where goods move in and out of the colony.

This multi-media assemblage supports a wide range of second-order communication systems, such as those associated with religion, commerce, natural science, and the military. The extent of the first is suggested by Burford's remark that the colony's Archdeacon, Thomas Hobbs Scott, is under the jurisdiction of the Archbishop of Calcutta; and the second by the sailors seen on the streets of Sydney, who include 'Chinese, Otahetians, South Sea Islanders, Zealanders, &c.'.[34] The colony's *Botanic Gardens* and its superintendent, M[r]. *Fraser*, are part of a global network of collectors and natural scientists. And so too are the naval ships singled out by Burford as worthy of mention, such as *H.M.S. Warspite* (No. 56), which arrived in Sydney in 1826, from Trimcomalee in Sri Lanka (Ceylon), carrying the Commander-in-Chief in the East Indies, Commodore Sir James Brisbane, and bringing news of the end of First Anglo-Burmese War (1824–26).

The most obvious cultural institution is the building, owned by Barnet Levey, which is described as 'intended for a theatre', but things look less sparse if we add the forms of sociability found in the colony: 'dinner and evening parties'; balls and assemblies; fraternal organisations, such as 'the Sons of St. George, St. Patrick, St. Andrew, and [the] Bachelors of Sydney'; and hotels, such as the *Sydney* (No. 28), the 'Australian', and 'Hill's', which 'vie with the best establishments of the same kind in England . . . as may the common pot houses with the lowest in St. Giles'.[35] And, of course, if we relax our definition still further, cultural institutions are everywhere apparent: in the fledgling civilian legal system, represented by the *New Court House* (No. 12); the religious, philanthropic, military, and scientific cultures mentioned above; and, still more broadly, the culture of discovery/settlement, to which much of what I have described above belongs. This last aspect is foregrounded by *H.M.S. Fly* (No. 50), which left Sydney in December 1826 to help establish a settlement at Western Port, in Southern Victoria, and *H.M.S. Success* (No. 46), which set off on 17 January 1827 to explore the Swan river on Australia's western coast, where in 1829 the Swan River Colony was established (renamed in 1832 the Colony of Western Australia).

Sydney, the city at the centre of Burford's panorama, is impressive – so much so that if we allow the contexts mentioned earlier to fade, one might be ready to conclude with Joseph Banks that, thanks to its foundations, 'the future prospect of empire and dominion ... cannot be disappointed' and that 'England may revive in New South Wales when it has sunk in Europe'.[36]

Fictions

At this point in my argument, 'A View of the Town of Sydney' might still seem a work of realism, even if tinged with idealism; but it is, of course, much more *and* much less than that. Indeed, even when attempting dispassionately to describe its contents, as I have been doing, it is difficult to ignore the narratives stitching its parts into a whole recognisable-as-reality by European audiences. The most important of these narratives is that of discovery, which weaves together journeys already completed (from Botany Bay to Sydney, from Sydney across the Blue Mountains, and so on) with those about to be attempted by *H.M.S. Voltage* and *H.M.S. Success*. Discovery is, of course, a chapter in the story of Australian settlement, which belongs to the story of the British Empire. In all these contexts, discovery/settlement sets in motion stories of material and of moral improvement. While standing in Burford's panorama, the first can be heard through the contrasts drawn between imprisonment and convivial assembly, modest early and magnificent later buildings, and so on; and the second in contrasts between the machinery of incarceration, such as *Phoenix Hulk* and *Pinchgut Island* (No. 51), and the engines of moral regeneration, such as *St. James[']s Church* (No. 8) and the *School of Industry*. And all these narratives underwrite the story, mentioned earlier, of 'Albion reborn'.

One need not dispute the data interpreted by these narratives in order to see that what are experienced by some as facts (discovery, settlement, improvement, rebirth) seem to others to function as fictions, deployed to mask unpalatable realities, such as the belated discovery of Australia by Europeans (they arrived 60,000 years late); the convict experience of exile, cruelty, and injustice; the Aboriginal experience of dispossession, displacement, and genocide; and so on. Inside the panorama these realities are kept from sight by yet another story, this time of the transition from nature to civilisation, which is exemplified (supposedly) by the transition from black to white worlds. 'The aboriginal inhabitants of New South Wales,' Burford tells us, 'are … the very lowest of the human species … having neither huts or clothes … and, being totally unacquainted with any kind of agriculture, they exist on fish, fruit, worms, grubs, &c. and, occasionally, on human flesh.'[37] Ignoring the mishmash of falsehoods paraded in this sentence, much the same picture is conjured by the panorama, where the primary Aboriginal figures, apparently without 'huts or clothes', are clustered in the foreground of the illusion, close to the viewing platform. This is a locale aligned with nature, as suggested by the kangaroo, emu, and horses also found there. And it is for that reason also a space of paternalism, firmly under the control of the Government, where the work of civilisation must begin.

Like it or not, to stand on Burford's viewing platform and look out over the panoramic illusion is to become entangled with this story of civilisation: the viewer's gaze is drawn from Aboriginal nature, close to where we are standing, to the present represented in the middle ground by Sydney, where the work of rearticulating Aboriginal 'nature' is underway, and from there to the future, evoked by the still unexplored realms beyond the horizon. Towards the east, the peripatetic labour of hunting and gathering, represented by *Native climbing a Gum*, is dismissed by the cultivated fields of the Botanic Gardens. To the south, behind the scene entitled *Natives*, which portrays Aboriginal justice as payback, we can see *St. James[']s* and the *New Court House*.[38] Here, the first scene (*Natives*) recalls the Old Testament dictum of 'an eye for an eye', which is dismissed by buildings that represent respectively a New Testament that proclaims and a judicial system (supposedly) based on Christian love and forgiveness. To the south-west, Governor Darling and Colonel Dumaresq, both on horseback, having left the city behind them, approach 'King Bongaree [sic]'. At first glance, this reverses the trajectories we have been mapping – but in fact the Governor and his private secretary have come to proclaim what the other narratives enact, namely the imposition of colonial forms of government on Aboriginal Australia, in which 'King Bongaree' stands beneath Colonel Dumaresq, who answers to General Darling, the governor of the colony, who serves the 'real' King in London.

One of the many striking features of this painting is that Aboriginal figures are represented without reference to families or clans, whereas prominent settlers are normally introduced through their domestic establishments: Mr J. Mac Arthur's 'magnificent residence', 'the residence of Francis Forbes', the 'elegant . . . residence of Mr. Underwood', and so on.[39] In the early nineteenth century, bourgeois domestic establishments like these were commonly aligned with the paternal family, centred on the wife/mother, whose sensibility and consequent proximity to nature makes her a source of empathy, benevolence, and, therefore, philanthropy. During the journey from nature to civilisation, this suggests, Aboriginal social systems are displaced by the paternal-family structures characteristic of western modernity.

The point is economically made in the contrast between, on the one hand, the solitary Boongaree and, on the other hand, Darling and Dumaresq, connected to each other by the marriage in 1817 of the former, who was then forty-six, to the sister of the latter, the nineteen-year-old Eliza Dumaresq. Boongaree, in fact, had several wives, but that is beyond the grasp of this panorama, whereas the Darlings' domestic establishment, *Governor[']s House*, can be seen to the west, where Eliza's labours as a woman of sensibility are represented by the [Female] *School of Industry* and [Female] *Orphan School*.[40] Without dismissing her achievements, the switch this implies, from Indigenous inhabitant to female settler as representative of 'nature', adds yet one more layer to the apparatus of dispossession.

When seen as a whole, the bundle of narratives I have been describing map in surprising detail a 'civilising' process, which functions as a mode of initiation into western modernity. And this draws our attention to one more contrast, this time between Sydney, with its Botanic Gardens, the locale where this process assumes cohesive form, and, on the other hand, the initiation taking place to the east, labelled *Kangaroo & Dog Dance* (No. 58), which assumes a form very different from the first. Because *Kangaroo & Dog Dance* is on lower ground than Sydney and the Aboriginal figures we have been discussing, it seems much further away, almost to the point of vanishing. It therefore seems to fit neatly into the narrative of settlement/progress mapped by the panorama as a whole, in which Aboriginal/aboriginal 'nature' is both pushed to the margins of the colony and, in the paternal family, differently imagined. And yet, at the same time, it is important to note that it is here that we glimpse for the first time a conjunction of convict/settler and Aboriginal worlds, rather than a passage from the second to the first. The linear, predominantly rectangular and/or vertical forms of the colony, which rise without obvious reference to their surroundings, except as resource, are radically different from the curved lines of the *Dance*, which echo the landscape surrounding them. Further, dance implies modes of embodiment and engagement radically different from those underwriting the work of Sir John Jamieson, Thomas Hobbs Scott, or Charles Fraser. And while the civilising process draws the human apart from its others, during the *Kangaroo & Dog Dance* the domains of animal, land, and human overlap with each other.

As this second world takes shape, it is possible to experience a sudden volte-face, in which spectators find themselves gazing not at the future-Albion projected by the panorama but at what that vision sets aside. From this point of view, the colony is an alien body, immersed in a world it does not understand, growing through extension and duplication of itself, and this in turn evokes a sense of catastrophe. In 'Theses on the Philosophy of History', Walter Benjamin writes of 'the angel of history' as caught by 'a storm [that] is blowing from Paradise', which 'propels him into the future to which his back is turned, while the pile of debris before him grows skyward'. Although 'The Angel would like to stay … and make whole what has been smashed', he cannot while the storm that 'we call progress' rages.[41] But in Burford's panorama only the windmills' Cyclopean eyes are looking backwards, and these multi-winged angels of history show no sign of wanting to mend 'what has been smashed'.[42]

Oceans

The contrast between colonial and Aboriginal *worlds* throws into relief the work of exhibition, everywhere apparent in Enlightenment cultures, which draws objects, places, and peoples away from discourses deemed local, so that they can be rearticulated by those thought to be universal. Inside 'A View of the Town of Sydney', the Botanic Gardens is an obvious part of the colony's exhibition system, which disentangles plant specimens from merely local knowledges of them so they can be rearticulated by a 'universal' system of classification able to place them within the global kingdom of plants. But so too is the 'New Gaol', a complex 'loosely based on Bentham's panopticon', in which prisoners (it was proposed), after being sorted into types, would be placed in buildings, one for each type, that could be monitored from a central viewing platform.[43] The prison's position on a hill overlooking the colony performs an analogous role, reminding settlers and convicts that their actions are likely to be visible by those above. Sydney's military institutions and hospitals also depend on categorisation/exhibition to bring wayward bodies into accord with respectively the overarching narratives of power and health. And so too do institutions such as the 'National School for the children of the lower orders', the 'school for the education and civilization of the Aborigines', the school for 'female children of the lower classes', and so on, which remove certain 'types' of people from their homes, in order to house them in institutions where behaviour, now visible to their custodians, can be reformed.[44]

Most significantly for the argument of this chapter, exhibition is the organising principle of the panorama itself. Inside the panoramic illusion, spectators are immersed in a milieu crowded with virtual entities detached from the cultural contexts to which their 'real' doubles belong. This is at first experienced as a disordered, unmanageable whole (a sublime object) that stops audiences in their tracks. But this same milieu, precisely because it attenuates the links that normally bind perceptions and things, makes it possible for the visible to be rearticulated in relation to a fundamental ground (progress, rebirth, empire, and so on). For those willing to be prompted by the panorama's guidebook and/or its spatial narratives, the panoramic experience therefore follows the path of the sublime, which concludes with spectators, now confident of their place in the whole, moved by feelings of 'admiration, reverence and respect'.[45]

In all the cases we have mentioned, the art of exhibition depends on estrangement (distanciation). Superintendents of the institutions I have mentioned adopt positions and play roles that lift them above the worlds where the objects of their work are found, so that the work of abstraction, classification, and rearticulation/reformation can begin. Similarly, the restorative work of the sublime depends on distance – if we come too close to a sublime object the experience is terrifying rather than delightful.[46] And with regard to the panorama, the viewing platform, the categories presented by Burford's guidebook, and the painting's visual narratives keep spectators at a distance from the disordered, unmanageable world that it exhibits, so that they can be uplifted rather than overwhelmed. It is hardly surprising, therefore, that those unwilling or unable to distance themselves from one or more of the entities it displays will be moved in ways not countenanced by the guidebook.

The volte-face mentioned earlier, prompted by the *Kangaroo & Dog Dance*, is a case in point, which is intensified if, for example, one moves closer to the event depicted by reading the first-hand account of the virtual *Dance*'s real double, found in *An Account of the English Colony in New South Wales* (1798) by David Collins, which was illustrated by engravings based on drawings by Thomas Watling, who also witnessed the event. And one imagines that for those able in memory or imagination to actually step inside the Dance, the consequent reversal of perspective will reframe the logic of the panorama as a whole, unleashing a flood of quite different emotions.

A second example can be found in the last chapter of 'Tales of the Early Days' (1894), by Price Warung, the pseudonym of William Astley, which describes a visit to Burford's 'A View of the Town of Sydney'. On this occasion, it is a human guide, rather than a printed one, who re-presents the panoramic illusion in glowing terms. His lecture begins smoothly enough, but before long the accuracy of the painting is disputed by a member of the audience, who gradually becomes more and more disruptive, while the guide, who seems never to have been to the colony, becomes more and more embarrassed. The tables are turned, however, when the guide turns to the Phoenix Hulk, no more than a spot on the horizon, and his interlocutor becomes flustered and then falls silent. This is the prison from which the latter has escaped and to which he will be returned.[47] At this moment, as Graeme Davison remarks, 'The glittering harbour suddenly takes on a new aspect, as a landscape of punishment, as well as civilisation. The dark spot on the horizon becomes a window into a gothic tale of forgery, extortion, betrayal and murder.'[48]

But even for those without first-hand experience of Sydney, the pictorial elements that draw their eye and the worlds they consequently construe are dependent on their point of view. Although something similar might be claimed about responses to any work of art, in full-scale panoramas the contingency of perception is heightened because, as previously remarked, it establishes a milieu rather than a prospect – 'a field of open causality, each determination of which is an enactment by the spectator of only one of the possibilities it contains'.[49] Just as importantly, the frames through which the painting is viewed are more mobile than those used to frame conventional paintings. It is often remarked, of course, that panorama paintings have no (visible) edge or frame; but this lack foregrounds a quite different kind of frame, one produced by interactions and conversations between spectators, which function as a mobile (rather than static) frame through which the painting is seen. Further, at the Leicester Square panorama visitors were treated to not one but two full-circle panoramas, joined to each other by darkened corridors and winding staircases, with each playing a role in framing the other. With regard to these matters, the panorama we are considering is once again a case in point.

Figure 1.2 William Heath, 'New Panorama – A Startling Interogation',
hand-coloured satirical etching, April 1829

Soon after 'A View of the Town of Sydney' had opened in the upper circle
of the Leicester Square Panorama, it was joined by a 'View of Pandemonium',
the mythical home of Satan and his crew, which was shown in the Panorama's lower circle. This conjunction of an idealised real city, raised by Hope's
voice, and a realistically presented fictional palace, which according to John
Milton came into existence 'like an exhalation' from the earth, offers audiences a wealth of possible frames with which to explain, contrast, or valorise
one or other of the locales.[50] But even this wealth seems like poverty when
an audience arrives, as depicted by William Heath in his satirical print 'New
Panorama – A Startling Interogation' (Figure 1.2). To the question posed by
the man selling tickets, 'Do you wish to go to Hell? / or Botany-Bay?', 'Sir,'
a young man replies, 'I wonts to got to Bottomybay.' Overhearing them
both, a young girl confides to her mother that she would 'like to see the
Naughty Place'. The pair's desired destinations play with the parallels
between Sydney and Pandemonium, the virtual and the actual, and with the
crossovers between manifest and latent desire, which the assembled crowd
develops further through contrasts between startled men and concerned
women, flamboyant hats and almost bare feet, heavy clothing and hidden
bodies, and so on. The hubbub makes clear that, once inside the panorama,
each will encounter a virtual reality different from that seen by the others.

Although this kind of multiplication of realities is often described as heralding the loss of a centre, there is in fact no shortage of centres in modernity, which now spring up everywhere, only a shortage of peripheries.[51] For those inside the shifting world this produces, geography becomes a kind of autogeography, in which what is seen is inflected by one's history and experience; locality becomes a kind of translocality, in which the familiar exists alongside the strange; and politics becomes 'artful' in the sense that it depends on the story being told. Seen in this light, 'A View of the Town of Sydney' pushes us to think once again about the analytical tools needed to describe the formation, in the late eighteenth and early nineteenth century, of this oceanic world: how best to live in a world where what was taken 'to be the eternal order of things is no more than a local context of immanence that carries us';[52] and how the forms of permanence found in the southern hemisphere, such as those developed by Indigenous peoples, might open ways of dwelling in and engaging with the world and its two hemispheres. Topics like these turn our gaze, one more time, from the northern hemisphere, the host to the centres in modern times of global power, to the more fluid worlds of the southern hemisphere. And from this perspective, when we look once again at 'A View of the Town of Sydney', it suddenly dawns on me that Boongaree is waving goodbye rather than hello to Darling and Dumaresq, and that the pair, leaving at long last the symbolic centre of the illusion, might be about to join the crowd on the viewing platform, who will soon step forward into the world of multiple centres outside.

Notes

1 Sibylle Erle et al. (eds), *Panoramas, 1787–1900: Texts and Contexts*, 5 vols (London: Pickering and Chatto, 2013), 1:249. The argument in this chapter belongs to a project on 'Architectures of Imagination' (DP180102604), funded by the Australian Research Council.

2 For details of Earle's career, see Jocelyn Hackforth-Jones, *Augustus Earle: Travel Artist* (Canberra: National Library of Australia, 1980), p. 8.

3 Peter Otto, *Multiplying Worlds: Romanticism, Modernity, and the Emergence of Virtual Reality* (Oxford: Oxford University Press, 2011), p. 24.

4 See, for example, Bernard Comment, *The Panorama* (London: Reaktion Books, 1999), pp. 136, 138.

5 Otto, *Multiplying Worlds*, p. 44.

6 Peter Sloterdijk, *In the World Interior of Capital: For a Philosophical Theory of Globalization*, trans. Wieland Hoban (Cambridge: Polity, 2013), pp. 29–30.

7 I am quoting from the translation of Edmund Halley's 'Ode on This Splendid Ornament of Our Time and Our Nation, the Mathematico-Physical Treatise by the Eminent Isaac Newton' published in *The Principia: Mathematical Principles*

of Natural Philosophy, trans. I. Bernard Cohen and Anne Whitman (London: University of California Press, 1999), pp. 379–80.

8 John Hughes, *The Ecstasy. An Ode* (London: Printed by J. Roberts, 1720), p. 7.

9 Quoted in Simone De Angelis, 'Newton in Poetry', in Helmut Pulte and Scott Mandelbrote (eds), *The Reception of Isaac Newton in Europe*, 3 vols (London: Bloomsbury Academic, 2019), 1:575.

10 Alexander Pope, *An Essay on Man*, in *Alexander Pope: The Major Works*, ed. Pat Rodgers (Oxford: Oxford University Press, 2008), p. 281 (Epistle II, ll. 19, 23–4).

11 Christian Jacob, *The Sovereign Map: Theoretical Approaches in Cartography throughout History*, trans. Tom Conley (Chicago: University of Chicago Press, 2006), p. 323.

12 John Theophilus Desaguliers, *The Newtonian System of the World, the Best Model of Government* (Westminster: Printed by A. Campbell for J. Roberts, 1728), p. 32.

13 Jacob, *The Sovereign Map*, pp. 323–4.

14 Pope, *Essay on Man*, p. 282 (Epistle II, l. 30).

15 Quoted in De Angelis, 'Newton in Poetry', pp. 576–7.

16 De Angelis, 'Newton in Poetry', p. 569.

17 Michel Serres, *The Parasite*, trans. Lawrence R. Schehr (Baltimore: Johns Hopkins University Press, 1982); Maurice Merleau-Ponty, *Phenomenology of Perception*, trans. Colin Smith (London: Routledge and Kegan Paul, 1962).

18 Figure 1.1 reproduces 'Panorama of Sydney' rather than 'Explanation of a View' owing to the greater clarity of the former. However, in order to avoid ambiguity, and to emphasise the design's role in *Description*, I will refer to both images indiscriminately as 'Explanation of a View'.

19 J. P. McGuanne, 'Old Government House', *Journal of the Royal Australian Historical Society*, 1 (1902), 73.

20 Maria Nugent, 'Mediating Encounters through Body and Talk', in Shino Konishi, Maria Nugent, and Tiffany Shellam (eds), *Indigenous Intermediaries: New Perspectives on Exploration Archives* (Acton: Australian National University Press, 2015), p. 88.

21 Nugent, 'Mediating Encounters', p. 88.

22 Robert Burford, *Description of a View of the Town of Sydney, New South Wales; The Harbour of Port Jackson, and Surrounding Country* (1829; North Sydney: Library of Australian History, 1978), p. 1.

23 Burford, *Description of a View of the Town of Sydney*, p. 4.

24 Anonymous, 'Panorama of Sydney', *Sydney Monitor* (19 September 1829), p. 1.

25 John White, *Journal of a Voyage to New South Wales*, ed. A. H. Chisholm (Sydney: Angus and Robinson, 1962), p. 140; Daniel Southwell, 'Journal and Letters of Daniel Southwell', Appendix D, in *Historical Records of New South Wales, Vol. II*, ed. F. M. Bladen (Sydney: Charles Potter, 1893), p. 692. I was drawn to both sources by Deirdre Coleman's important chapter on '"New Albion": The camp at Port Jackson', in *Romantic Colonization and British Anti-Slavery* (Cambridge: Cambridge University Press, 2005), pp. 141–63.

26 Arthur Phillip, *The Voyage of Governor Phillip to Botany Bay; with an Account of the Establishment of the Colonies of Port Jackson & Norfolk Island*, annot. James J. Auchmuty (1789; Sydney: Angus and Robertson, 1970), p. xxiii.

27 Phillip, *The Voyage of Governor Phillip to Botany Bay*, t.p.

28 Erasmus Darwin, 'To Josiah Wedgwood, June 1789', in *The Letters of Erasmus Darwin*, ed. Desmond King-Hele (Cambridge: Cambridge University Press, 1981), p. 190.

29 Burford, *Description of a View of the Town of Sydney*, p. 3.

30 Gordon Beckett, *The Colonial Economy of NSW: A Retrospective between 1788 and 1835* (Singapore: Trafford, 2012), pp. 83–4.

31 Burford, *Description of a View of the Town of Sydney*, pp. 10–11.

32 Burford, *Description of a View of the Town of Sydney*, p. 8.

33 Burford, *Description of a View of the Town of Sydney*, pp. 8, 10.

34 Burford, *Description of a View of the Town of Sydney*, p. 6.

35 Burford, *Description of a View of the Town of Sydney*, pp. 8, 6. 10.

36 Quoted in Coleman, *Romantic Colonization*, p. 141.

37 Burford, *Description of a View of the Town of Sydney*, p. 8.

38 Burford, *Description of a View of the Town of Sydney*, pp. 8–9.

39 Burford, *Description of a View of the Town of Sydney*, pp. 9, 10.

40 Anita Selzer, *Governors' Wives in Colonial Australia* (Canberra: National Library of Australia, 2002), pp. 89–92; Noeline J. Kyle, '"Delicate Health … Interesting Condition …": Eliza Darling, Pregnancy and Philanthropy in Early New South Wales', *History of Education*, 24 (1995), 32.

41 Walter Benjamin, 'Theses on the Philosophy of History', in *Illuminations*, ed. Hannah Arendt, trans. Harry Zorn (London: Pimlico, 1999), p. 249.

42 Benjamin, 'Theses on the Philosophy of History', p. 249.

43 Tanya Evans, *Fractured Families: Life on the Margins in Colonial New South Wales* (Sydney: University of New South Wales Press, 2015), p. 128.

44 Burford, *Description of a View of the Town of Sydney*, pp. 8, 7–8, 8.

45 Edmund Burke, *A Philosophical Enquiry into the Origin of our Ideas of the Sublime and Beautiful* (London: Printed for R. and J. Dodsley, 1757), p. 42.

46 Burke, *Philosophical Enquiry*, pp. 13–14.

47 Price Warung, 'At Burford's Panorama', in Bruce Bennett and Robert Dixon (eds), *Tales of the Early Days* (Sydney: Sydney University Press, 2009), pp. 172–83.

48 Graeme Davidson, *City Dreamers: The Urban Imagination in Australia* (Sydney: NewSouth, 2016), p. 23.

49 Otto, *Multiplying Worlds*, pp. 30–1.

50 John Milton, *Paradise Lost*, in *The Poems of John Milton*, ed. John Carey and Alastair Fowler (London: Longmans, Green & Co., 1968), p. 503 (Bk I. l. 710).

51 Sloterdijk, *Into the World Interior*, p. 29.

52 Sloterdijk, *Into the World Interior*, p. 29.

2

Southern doubles: antipodean life as a comparative exercise

Sarah Comyn

In the prologue to a series of squibs titled 'Australian Doubles' in 1856, *Melbourne Punch* describes the 'startling' discovery 'that the physical equipoise which exists between the two hemispheres of the world extends to the moral and mental qualities of the inhabitants' such that *'every man in the Northern hemisphere has his double in the Southern'*.[1] Beginning with 'The History of Victoria' by a 'Thomas B. Camawley' (clearly parodying Thomas Babington Macaulay's *History of England* [1848]), the series of 'Australian Doubles' articles features satirical accounts of the colony of Victoria's history that lampoon both the imitative qualities of colonial writers and the works of popular authors and poets such as Thomas Carlyle, Charles Dickens, R. H. Horne, Henry Wadsworth Longfellow, and Alfred Tennyson among others.[2] *Melbourne Punch*'s parody of the tendency of colonial Australian authors to model themselves on their northern counterparts enacts what Paul Giles describes in *Antipodean America* (2013) as 'a heightened version of comparative consciousness', one that defines 'the antipodean imagination' as a state in which the 'phenomenological selfhood of any given culture is refracted through alternative perspectives'.[3] Invoking both *Terra Australis* (the southern continent) and its geographic northern antipode through its reference to hemispheric 'equipoise', the 'Australian Doubles' series imagines antipodean duplicates that simultaneously reproduce *and* upset, mirror *and* refract, the 'original' northern writer, artist, politician, and/or artefact.[4]

Melbourne Punch's 'comparative consciousness' forms the starting point of this chapter's analysis of the implications the 'antipodean imagination' and its southern 'doubles' had for how the southern hemisphere was imagined, conceived, mocked, and celebrated by the poetry, fiction, parodies, letters, and illustrated articles published by Australian newspapers in the second half of the nineteenth century. While Giles uses the perspective offered by a 'comparative consciousness' to frame his analysis of how American literature adopts and adapts an 'antipodean aspect' from Australasia, this chapter will instead focus its attention on how this 'antipodean aspect' animated discussions concerning the social, political, and economic formations of the Australian colonies in the nineteenth century.[5] Examining newspaper representations of settler colonial life in Australia, it reveals the surprising and imaginative ways that settlers both identified with and rejected the antipodean mythologies of the southern hemisphere. With a focus on the three decades following the discovery of gold in Australia (1851), the passing of the *Australian Constitutions Act* (1850), and the achievement of responsible government (1855–56), the chapter's analysis of newspaper accounts will also demonstrate how these depictions mobilised the trope of antipodal inversion to portray a growing economic and colonial independence that provided a means of addressing the north and destabilising Eurocentric hierarchies.[6]

Imagined cartographies and geographies of the Antipodes

The imaginative pull of a 'south' in opposition to a European 'north' is not unique to the nineteenth century. William Eisler traces the 'invention of the concept of a southern continent' to Pythagoras; and numerous medieval maps abound with images of this continent that both await its discovery and reject its existence as a possibility.[7] In his examination of the cosmographies, cartographies, and geographies – both 'real and imagined' – that defined the 'search for the southern continent' by Europeans in the early modern period, Avan Judd Stallard demonstrates the explorative and creative appeal of the imagined south. A place of legend and mythography, the 'imagined geography' of this southern region nonetheless contained the reifying power of 'verisimilitude': 'the way these entities appear real; the way an imagined geography is drawn or described to approximate reality, with all the hallmarks of a place that is known or knowable'. The 'more verisimilitude', argues Stallard, 'the more potent its legend' and 'the more fervent[ly]' people 'promote its existence'.[8]

Arguably one of the most potent and indeterminate of the European legends surrounding the south is that of the Antipodes, whose mythological inhabitants could have feet that face in the opposite direction. The Antipodes could also be an upturned world with inhabitants walking upside down so that 'their opposite feet will touch the bottoms of our feet in a bodily and uncanny fashion', generating, according to Alfred Hiatt, a process of self-reflection.[9] Hiatt identifies the 'ancient antipodal trope of the world turned upside down' as a stimulus for the philosophising that accompanied imaginings of *Terra Australis*, such that the Antipodes becomes 'a place of reflection, isolation and self-discovery, a blank space, and so a mirror for humanity'.[10] If the existence of *Terra Australis* was necessary to 'balance the

weight of land in the northern hemisphere' – a product, Hiatt argues, 'not
simply of speculation but of calculation' – the idea of the Antipodes as a
world upside down, back to front, or topsy-turvy could provide its own
balancing force of inversion.[11] This antipodean force of opposition is always,
however, suggestively unstable, with the meaning and region of the Antipodes ambiguous, indeterminate, 'fantastical', and 'changeable'.[12] A 'trigger for
self-examination', the topsy-turvyness of the Antipodes and its inversive
potential could manifest itself cartographically, corporeally, and/or metaphorically.[13] Examining representations of life in the southern hemisphere in
colonial Australian newspapers demonstrates how the cartographic inversion of the Antipodes moves from the map and is, in turn, remapped on to
the routines and domesticities as well as the culture and politics of settler
life, through the portrayal of corporeal ('touching our feet in a bodily and
uncanny fashion') and metaphorical inversions. Such inversions involve a
way of living and forming identities in negatives rather than positives, but
these negatives are themselves increasingly transformed into the positives of
colonial political assertiveness and increasing economic independence in the
wake of the Australian gold rushes.

Antipodean corporeality

Although the region signified by the Antipodes remained necessarily ambiguous throughout the history of the concept, Matthew Boyd Goldie notes
that by the eighteenth century 'the idea of the antipodes comes to designate an
area in Oceania', and by the twentieth century the Antipodes is frequently,
though not always, aligned with Australia and New Zealand, sometimes
together, occasionally apart.[14] This association of Australia with the Antipodes would prove captivating for those portraying Australia in the nineteenth
century, both from outside and within the Australian colonies. As Bernard Smith
has famously argued, 'the antipodes are not a place, but a relationship ... a
spatial and cultural relationship between north and south', and specifically
for the purposes of this chapter, between colonial Australia and Britain.[15]
Smith's 'antipodean point of view', like Giles' 'comparative consciousness',
emphasises the relational nature of the antipodean perspective which calls
upon its opposite even as it rejects it as myth.[16]

In considering what she describes as the 'embodiments of Australia in
world literature', Vilashini Cooppan lingers on the figure of the 'antipodean
foot' (which she terms a 'species of continental fetishism') best represented
in the Osma Beatus map of 1086 (Figure 2.1), where the mythological figure
of a Skiapod shields itself from the red-hot southern sun.[17] 'A proxy substi-
tute' for the southern continent, the antipodean foot evokes a corporeal

Figure 2.1 Beato de Liebana Burgo de Osma, 1086

inversion that promotes 'displacement and disavowal': 'the order of the aus-
tral map' is 'that it confirms disbelief in the southern continent even as it
directs its gaze toward it'.[18]

Contemplating the corporeality of antipodality, Goldie similarly argues
that the concept of the Antipodes can be embodied and performed. Using
Eve Kosofsky Sedgwick's term 'beside', Goldie considers how the encounters
between 'British and Pacific cultures' in the nineteenth century can perform
a 'wide range of desiring, identifying, representing, repelling, paralleling, dif-
ferentiating, rivalling, leaning, twisting, mimicking, withdrawing, attracting,
aggressing, warping, and other relations'.[19] Goldie's sense of the antipodean
'beside' shares an epistemological space with Stallard's 'verisimilitude',
alongside what Goldie terms the 'continuum of disorientation' created by
those in the north who attempt to 'address the south'.[20] This 'disorientation'
provides an opportunity, however, for the south to instead reorient antipodean inversions, which in turn can be used to discredit the north's preconceptions of the south as 'topsy-turvy'. The 'antipodean figures of Australasia
have often involved', Giles argues, 'a more playful sense of topsy-turvy as
both a ludic and ontological condition'.[21]

Figure 2.2 'The Antipodes', *Melbourne Punch* (28 October 1858), 108

These playful qualities lend themselves to a practice of antipodean reorientation in newspapers, where the potential slippage between the real and imagined antipodean worlds of Australia complicates a perfect inversion and instead suggests a potential correspondence, a collapsible duality, which can playfully raise inversive doubles, only to erase them.[22] Like the 'Australian Doubles' of *Melbourne Punch*'s parodic imagination, these southern doubles are both like and unlike their northern peers. In an 1858 engraving titled 'The Antipodes' (Figure 2.2), for example, *Melbourne Punch* draws on the drama and theatrics of the hippodrome to playfully allude to and upset the expectations of corporeal inversion in Australia. While Mrs Wilkins is repelled by the young men surrounding her, having 'never expected' to encounter 'people walking on their heads' in Australia, these figures in fact perfectly capture the Eurocentric expectations of antipodal habitation. Performing corporeal inversion, *Melbourne Punch*'s illustration raises European assumptions about the Antipodes only to dispute them through Mrs Wilkins' disavowal. In doing so, Mrs Wilkins performs and embodies the full range of Goldie's antipodean 'beside' from 'desiring' to 'warping'. *Punch*'s mention of Mrs Wilkins having gained her knowledge from 'read[ing] in some book or other' teasingly reflects the fact that European assumptions about Australia were frequently dependent on unverifiable accounts and descriptions in newspapers and books. This concern with antipodean representations of

Australia, and in particular their unwieldy nature (as represented by the figures walking on their hands), is one that would preoccupy colonial newspapers' engagement with the trope of antipodality.

A poem simply titled 'The Antipodes' published by *Sydney Punch* in 1869 similarly captures Goldie's sense of the 'bodily and uncanny' as it reinscribes and embodies the antipodean feet of cartographic inversion, imagining the people of the north and south walking on top of one another:

> Things on the whole don't look askew:
>   It's all serene somehow or other;
> And yet 'tis veritably true
>   That I am treading on my mother.
> Oh mother, dear! forgive the act,
>   Great Nature's laws my steps control;
> Love leaps o'erall. We are in fact,
>   Now more than ever sole to sole. (lines 9–16)[23]

With Goldie, we can recognise the appeal of Sedgwick's 'beside' as offering an understanding of the Antipodes that appreciates and complicates inversion as simultaneously 'withdrawing' and 'attracting', 'repelling' and 'paralleling'. The poem's speaker and mother are not just opposite one another but connected, touching 'sole to sole', and inhabiting a space of 'beside'.

The north/south comparative exercise was nonetheless frequently used by colonial newspapers and was perhaps most readily deployed in their depictions of Christmas and New Year celebrations in the south as the reverse of the north in climate, mood, and fashion. In a lengthy illustrated account of 'How We Spend Our Christmas Holidays', the *Illustrated Australian News for Home Readers* depicts various forms of activity, including fishing, hiking, hunting, and playing cricket.[24] Playing cricket at Christmas time, the article declares, is 'decidedly un-English but thoroughly Australian'.[25] Reprinting the illustration from the article, the *Illustrated Sydney News and New South Wales Agriculturalist and Grazier* used the depictions of summer holiday activities to accompany a poem called 'How We Spend Our New Year's Holidays', which celebrates:

> Boating on the river,
>   Cricket in the park,
> Blazing at the wild birds
>   From daylight until dark
> Fishing where the shadows
>   O'er the waters play;
> That's how we contrive to spend
>   The New Year's Holiday. (lines 1–8)[26]

NORTH.   SOUTH.

Figure 2.3 'The Birth of the New Year', *Illustrated Sydney News and New South Wales Agriculturalist and Grazier* (12 January 1876), 12–13

The theme of energetic activity, youthful vigour, and colonial abundance is also emphasised in an illustrated article titled 'The Birth of the New Year' from the same issue of *Illustrated Sydney News* (Figure 2.3), which states: 'North of the line the New Year is a subject of hearty welcome, but also of affectionate care. South he is a lusty Infant, capable of looking after himself at a very early period of his career.'[27] Here the infants' bodies perform hemispheric difference and corporeal inversion, with the colonial infant's independence and resilience emphasised in contrast to the swaddled and helpless infant of the north.[28]

The 'conceit of inversion', as Giles argues, 'works to illuminate areas of conflict or crossover that are implicit within, but repressed by, the power of hegemonic English cultural forms, with the specific geographical consciousness of the antipodes morphing implicitly into a much broader critique of Anglocentric customs'.[29] The Antipodes as a concept – and how it is visually and textually represented – has the potential to reorient perspectives, with these antipodean accounts providing a means for the south to address and potentially critique the north.

Metaphorical inversion: 'The Mirror Upside Down'

As we have seen, the Antipodes was recognised as a powerful metaphor by settlers in Australia and, as such, was frequently employed to criticise the political establishment. A letter to the editor of the *Courier* in 1857, fittingly titled 'Topsy Turvy', uses, for example, the metaphor of the Antipodes to lament the protectionist economic policies in operation in Tasmania, stating that: 'Tasmania in geographical position is the antipodes of Great Britain. She is also likely to become the antipodes in many other considerations.' After listing the numerous instances of antipodal thinking and government in the colony of Tasmania, the letter concludes: 'Thus the antipodes of geographical position – the world upside down – are politically maintained.'[30]

Depicting Australia as a site of economic and political inversion to that of England was also a trope frequently used by English publications, possibly the most famous illustration of this being John Leech's frontispiece to *Punch*'s 'Pocket Book' in 1854. 'Topsy Turvey – or, our Antipodes' (Figure 2.4) portrays a Regent Street relocated to the canvas town of the goldfields, where ladies and gentlemen now serve the crude and dissolute diggers. The shouted orders of the diggers emphasise the education and thereby the social 'fall' and disgrace of their new colonial servants. Mocking and patronising these intellectuals, one card-playing digger instructs: 'Now, then, you Master of Arts! Look sharp with that Pale Ale'; while another digger shouts from his tent: 'Hollo There, you Intellectual Being Where the Doose are My Highlows?'. As Anthony Trollope would observe during his tour of Australia in 1871–72, '[p]robably the class of miners which as a class does best is that of experienced men who work for wages', while the 'class of miners' who 'does worst is that composed of young gentlemen who go to the diggings, led away, as the fancy, by a spirit of adventure, but more generally, perhaps, by a dislike of homely work at home'.[31] The potential for the gold rush to disturb class distinctions and boundaries is also noted by an emigrant to the gold diggings of Bendigo, John Green, who writes in an 1853 letter to his sister in England: 'Every one here is met and meets another on an equality, lawyers, doctors, prigs and parsons, magistrates and housebreakers, all fraternise, addressing one another as "mate".'[32] Leech's etching uses the antipodean trope of inversion to highlight the disruptive social and economic power of the gold rushes and thereby upends British class relations with the working and upper classes inhabiting the same social sphere but with a reversal in status and power.

Published a year earlier, a poem in the *Courier* titled 'Topsy-Turvy' uses both the theme of the goldfields' wealth and the legacy of convict transportation to imagine a 'Bill Sykes at the antipodes' (line 109) alongside a world

Figure 2.4 John Leech, 'Topsy Turvey – or, our Antipodes', 1854

that rewards criminality and punishes hard work.[33] Subtitled 'Being Verses by a Poor Man Puzzled', the poem juxtaposes the criminal Sykes with the 'hard-working, honest Giles Jolter' (line 45). Sykes gets 'free' passage to Australia through transportation:

> And then, when arrived in Botany Bay,
> > With his ticket-of-leave, of grub he lands full–
> If he chooses to hire, it's ten shilling' a day,
> > If he chooses to dig, it's gold in handsfull. (lines 34–7)

Giles Jolter, in contrast, on learning 'how there were lands / Where on the other side the ocean, / Work was more plentiful than hands' (lines 78–80) has to apply to the 'Commissioners of Emigration' (line 88) only to be told six weeks later that '"No more labourers were wanted!"' (line 106). While the poem is clearly critical of the bureaucracy surrounding emigration, like Leech's frontispiece, it also strikes an anxious note about the economic, class, and moral topsy-turvyness increasingly associated with Australia following the gold rush. The poem also signals Australia's potential to surpass Britain's opportunities for wealth, with Jolter, his 'wife and little ones pining' (line 108), while Sykes 'His pouch with virgin gold is lining' (line 110).[34]

Melbourne Punch, in turn, plays with this idea of economic inversion in a startling image titled 'Punch's Summary for Europe' (Figure 2.5), published

Figure 2.5 'Punch's Summary for Europe', *Melbourne Punch* (25 April 1861), 52–3

in 1861.[35] Over two pages, the illustration juxtaposes the economic promise of the colony of Victoria with the image of a starving England. The image is inscribed: 'Showing what a man may suffer in Victoria and in England' and 'Respectfully dedicated to the old folks at home'. Shu-Chuan Yan has rightly argued that *Melbourne Punch*'s 'diptych promotes the Arcadian myth of the New World that motivates exploration and conquest', thereby acting as a form of imperial propaganda that encourages colonial expansion with 'the southern hemisphere offer[ing] the space lacking in a crowded homeland'.[36] This myth-making of Australia as a land of boundless space returns us to Hiatt's notion of the Antipodes as a 'blank' and ties the idea of the Antipodes to that of *terra nullius*.[37] *Punch*'s participation, here, in the legacy of booster literature to the goldfields nonetheless also hints at the potential reversal of pecuniary and political power between colony and metropole, with a sense of the growing colonial economic and political independence following the discovery of gold and the achievement of responsible government by the colony of Victoria in 1855. The 'comparative consciousness' that the Antipodes inspires could, therefore, view the 'topsy-turvy land' not as backwards or back-to-front, but instead as a place of progress and opportunity.

Recognising the tendency of the British press to misrepresent the facts and realities of the Australian colonies, the *Adelaide Times* complained in an article titled 'Holding the Mirror Upside Down' that '[n]ever does an English newspaper come to hand but we tremble to open it, lest, like the savage who possessed a cracked looking-glass, we should be frightened to death at our own disfigurement. Everything is antipodean – facts, figures, and fancies, all upside down.' The discovery of gold is noted as being the particular cause of misinformation: 'Does a South Australian find a grain of gold at Stony Creek, forthwith it is transformed into an immense nugget, discovered by a Victorian, at Rocky Gully.' The association of Australia with criminality is also emphasised as a topic subjected to antipodean fantasies (similar to those animating 'Bill Sykes at the antipodes'): 'Does one man pick another's pocket, it is "a fearful increase of crime in the colony of Adelaide," and so forth.'[38]

In contrast to *Melbourne Punch*'s 'Summary for Europe', the *Adelaide Times* evokes the trope of antipodean inversion to assert control over the narrative and depiction of their colony. This anxiety about antipodean representations of the Australian colonies is also evident in a poem addressed to Anthony Trollope by *Sydney Punch*. Eagerly anticipating Trollope's visit to the colonies in 1871, the paper nonetheless hopes for an 'accurate' account of the visit:

> And only hope you brought across this way
> Impartial eyes, and really mean to see with them,
> Not like some writers that before to-day
> Have turned facts 'topsy-turvey' – Satan *be* with them! (lines 19–24)[39]

Such accounts demonstrate the imaginative hold the topsy-turvy antipodean trope could exert and the concerns about misrepresentation that shaped many of the responses adopting an antipodean mode. They also reveal the malleability and adaptability of these metaphoric inversions: while *Sydney Punch* acknowledges that Australia is a 'strange new-fangled [place]' and that those 'used to slippered ease / Prefer old England's home to the antipodes', it still insists upon verisimilitude and invokes antipodean mythology to simultaneously demonstrate and erase negative differences.[40]

As the illustrations and articles above suggest, hemispheric contrasts became a useful trope for imaginative works. The two hemispheres are frequently appealed to as a sign not only of difference but also of distance (the consequence, of course, of emigration), with titles such as 'Home at Last: A Tale of Both Hemispheres' (serial fiction by 'Kelp' published weekly in the newspaper *The Record* in 1869), 'Christmas in the Two Hemispheres' (a satirical illustration for *Melbourne Punch*), and 'The Antipodes: Both Sides' (a poem) demonstrating the popularity of the theme.[41] Published in 1869, 'The Antipodes: Both Sides' imagines a 'Willie in Sydney' writing and receiving a response from a 'Jane in England'.[42] William writes several stanzas to his beloved, beginning:

Come, dearest, come! I have won you a home.
   And my Eden awaits my Eve!
My heart beats 'Come!' and my pen writes 'Come!'
   And with joy you may England leave.

We'll live where the skies are blue all day,
   And the summer's long and bright;
Where the 'Southern Cross' and the 'Milky Way'
   Flame out through the azure night! (lines 1–8)

While Jane intends to join her dearest, she is not entirely convinced by the image he paints, responding:

Yes, William, I leave this dear, dear land,
   But yet my kindred tell,
That roses have thorns to the gathering-hand
   In the bright land where you dwell.

They say that dreadful monsters prowl
   Port Jackson's glorious bay;
And that squalls burst down, and tempests growl,
   From the blue of your brightest day.

They say both your shores and seas have sharks,
   That your wild birds have no song;
That night has no nightingales, morn no larks,
   Your screeching woods among. (lines 41–52)

Mirroring Willie's account and inhabiting a 'comparative consciousness', Jane's response transforms his descriptions from positive into negative portrayals of her potential new homeland. Like the *Adelaide Times* (but from the opposite perspective), Jane fears Willie is holding the mirror upside down.

In 1882, *Sydney Punch* used the theme and title of 'The Antipodes' in a poem that parodies both the lies of booster literature and the exoticism and easy abundance associated with emigration to the Antipodes:[43]

A good old honest country pair,
   Who'd made a little money,
And thought that they would like to live
   Where all was bright and sunny;
They longed to reach that glorious land
   Where cloud and fog are never
And where the gentle breezes fan
   And sunshine reigneth ever. (lines 1–8)

The poem proceeds to describe all the quaint and contrasting elements of the Antipodes the couple have been assured they will encounter, including: 'Where cherries are inside their stones / Or stones outside their cherries' (lines 15–16). They hope 'To watch the folk walk on their heads / As in that land they do it' (lines 17–18), and to 'see the bright cross in the sky / With some one pointing to it' (lines 19–20). Unsurprisingly the couple are disappointed when the booster myths of the gold rush (the same the *Adelaide Times* complained painted the colonies antipodean) prove a 'falsehood plainly!': 'They peered about them vainly / No speck of gold could either see' (lines 33, 31–2). The couple continue to be disenchanted by antipodean realities when two street urchins enter the scene:

> But just in time two little lads,
>   The one, his whistle playing,
> The other *standing on his head*
>   Came up, for pennies praying.
> 'Oh! look ye, John,' old Betsy cried,
>   'They have not wholly sold us;
> The folk are walking on their heads –
>   There's *one* thing true they've told us.' (lines 42–49)

The antipodal figure of the child walking on its hands and begging both confirms and upsets the couple's antipodean expectations. Playing to the stereotype of the upside-down, topsy-turvy south, the begging child nonetheless unsettles and upturns the view of the gold-rush wealth associated with Australia. Dispelling metropolitan delusions, the poem resituates the Antipodes the right-way-up in a similar fashion to *Sydney Punch*'s earlier request of Trollope not to 'turn facts topsy-turvy'. Like *Melbourne Punch*'s depiction of Mrs Wilkins' encounter with corporeal inversion outside the hippodrome, this poem both fulfils and displaces northern preconceptions regarding antipodean Australia. The poem raises the binaries of north/south only to complicate and collapse them by satisfying only some but not all the antipodean categories. Performing an antipodes of 'beside', the poem demonstrates Goldie's argument that 'the ways that the Antipodes have corresponded and failed to correspond with European conceptions of the space and its peoples are more complex and challenging than clear oppositionality'.[44]

The Antipodes writes back

A short story printed in the *Australasian* in 1870 again draws on the topsy-turvy theme of contrasts to reorient north/south economic, class, and moral hierarchies. Entitled 'A Tale of Two Hemispheres', it begins: 'It is not long since the world received from one of its greatest fiction-writers a tale of two cities. I now propose to narrate a tale of two hemispheres.'[45] With its explicit reference to Charles Dickens' novel, the story registers itself as a tale of difference and opposites. *A Tale of Two Cities* (1859) famously begins:

> It was the best of times, it was the worst of times, it was the age of wisdom, it was the age of foolishness, it was the epoch of belief, it was the epoch of incredulity, it was the season of Light, it was the season of Darkness, it was the spring of hope, it was the winter of despair.[46]

Building on this theme of contrasts, 'A Tale of Two Hemispheres' is set in an 'upturned' world that resembles Leech's goldfields illustration: 'when Jack and Gill were as good as their quondam master and mistress, and a great deal better; and people who had travelled from one side of the world to the other found that it was really and truly turned upside down'.[47]

'A Tale of Two Hemispheres' narrates the story of Frank Hungercash, who is disowned by his 'self-made' and wealthy merchant father, Solomon, when he falls in love with the penniless Laura. Assuming an 'aristocratic title in a spirit of bitter irony at his fallen fortunes', Frank flees to the Australian colonies as one 'Algernon Fortescue' to find his fortune in order to marry Laura. After some false-starts, first in goldmining and then in an attempt to be one of the Australian 'squatocracy', Frank finally manages to make enough money as a store owner to secure Laura's travel to the colonies and their subsequent marriage and settlement in Melbourne.[48] Adopting an 'antipodal orientation', the story ends with an inversion of the parable of the prodigal son.[49] The repentant father, Solomon, goes in search of his son to find that Frank has become a self-made man of the colonies: 'the fatted calf was killed, not by the father in welcome of his prodigal son, but by the prodigal son in honour of his vagabond parent, and ... the three generations of the Hungercashes are at this moment the happiest people in Her Majesty's dominions'.[50] While the story begins with the rejection of his father's wealth, Frank nonetheless repeats his father's economic journey in becoming a wealthy merchant. Relocating this journey to the Australian colonies, however, allows Frank to maintain his moral code and forces his father to abandon his hypocritical ways so that the 'taciturn mammon worshipper' is 'transformed into a kindly and somewhat garrulous sexagenarian'.[51] Rather than a place of degeneration that celebrates criminality, the Antipodes instead becomes a place of moral regeneration.

An opposite journey to that of Frank Hungercash can be found in the satire 'The Metamorphosis of Travel', published in *Melbourne Punch* in 1883, which traces the journey of a couple, the Lilleys, as they undertake the grand tour of 'Yurrup'.[52] Having seen the great sights of England and continental Europe, the Lilleys return to the colonies deeply discontented. In a comic inversion of the European grand tour, they now visit the cultural sights of Melbourne only to rate them on a scale from 'commonplace' to 'terribly commonplace' to 'dreadfully commonplace', and finally to 'exceedingly commonplace'. Performing what Giles identifies as the Eurocentric forms of cultural hegemony often implicit in antipodean representations, the Lilleys are even unimpressed by the Old Masters when they are transposed to the colonies (Figure 2.6).[53] Described as 'jaundiced eyed', the Lilleys, while unable to 'dispute their genuineness', are still happy to 'disparage' the 'merit' of the Old Masters as the 'art deteriorated and became commonplace in the vitiating climate of the colonies'.[54]

Even nature's wonders are dismissed as 'commonplace' and inadequate reproductions of European art. During a viewing of the Aurora Australis (Figure 2.6), described as 'a beautiful specimen of the Southern Light', everyone 'save the Lilleys' is impressed:

> 'Pooh' said the Lilleys, 'after walking through a splendid art gallery in company with a noble lord and gazing upon a sunset by Turner, I can assure you the tints of this Aurora are exceedingly commonplace.'[55]

For the Lilleys, nothing based in the southern hemisphere has any value: 'In the southern hemisphere, all, all was terribly commonplace.' *Melbourne Punch*, however, ultimately undermines this Eurocentric vision of cultural superiority by having the Lilleys roundly rejected by their colonial companions. Having undergone the 'metamorphosis of travel' and lost their antipodean footing, the Lilleys live as exiles in their colonial home, their spectral existence tainted by the 'spectacles of foreign travel'.[56]

This survey of fictional and parodic representations of the southern hemisphere in colonial Australian newspapers demonstrates the power of the Antipodes as a metaphor of inversion that may encourage a 'comparative consciousness' but does not necessarily always paint the southern hemisphere as the negative of the north; rather, the south is just as often the north's contrasting positive. The south could, as in the case of Frank Hungercash, be imagined as the prodigal son who saves his vagabond father, the north. The Antipodes' inversive potential is, moreover, frequently used to collapse rather than maintain dualities. By mobilising the trope of antipodality, Australian newspapers could reorient the Australian colonies and allow the south to address the north as it moved steadily from 'below' to 'besides', anticipating and animating the move from a discourse of colonial self-governance to one of Australian nationhood and federation that began to seriously emerge in the 1880s.[57]

THE METAMORPHOSIS OF TRAVEL.

Before they went to Yurrup.

It would have been difficult to find in Victoria two more estimable people than Mr. and Mrs. P. K. Lilley before they went on the grand tour to "Yurrup." They were decent matter-of-fact people, neither better nor worse than their neighbours. They were satisfied with their lot, enjoyed their simple pleasures, and were, on the whole, a very happy couple. When, however, Mr. Lilley's savings had grown to a good amount, he and his wife decided to take a trip to Europe—and thereby hangs this brief but truthful tale.

The Lilleys went to Europe, saw the sights of England and the Continent, and then returned to Victoria. Why they came back is to this day an unsolved mystery, for they were so pleased with everything European, and so disgusted with everything colonial, that their friends marvelled at their return, and marvelled still more that they should continue to remain in this out-of-the-way one-horse place.

Travel had made the once homely contented Mr. and Mrs. Lilley æsthetic, aristocratic, supercilious, and inclined to look down upon the poor Colonials whom a year before they considered their equals. The atmosphere of "Yurrup," and the privilege of breathing the same air as English nobles and foreign consuls, had saturated the Lilleys with the quintessence of the *nil admirari* spirit, at least so far as anything in "the colonies" was concerned. Their discontent naturally bred disgust in their former friends.

To these much-travelled people everything in Victoria was "commonplace"—dreadfully commonplace, and nothing like what they had been accustomed to at London, Parry, or Firenze.

"Dreadfully commonplace."

One day Mr. and Mrs. Lilley were invited to what was considered in colonial circles rather an aristocratic ball. Some friends asked them afterwards what they thought of the affair.

"Well meant, no doubt, well meant," replied Mr. Lilley ; "but to my fancy, decidedly commonplace—uncommonly commonplace"

"You see," chipped in Mrs. Lilley," after moving in the highest circles of London and the continong, and seeing the true ar'stocracy, one is not satisfied with mere commonplace society."

They condescended occasionally to go to some of the Melbourne theatres, but they sat through the pieces with the wearied air of superior persons, who had made up their minds to be resigned. When the audience—a commonplace one, of course—applauded, the Lilleys gazed upon the theatre-goers with a supreme pity for the people who could be entertained by such commonplace acting.

"Look at that supernumary bearing the banner," said Mrs. Lilley, "is he not quite too—"

"He is replied her husband ;" then turning to one of the party with them," he added, " Ah, you should have seen Henry Irving. A commonplace supernumerary like that is intolerable after Irving. There is no comparison between the two."

Nobody ever dreamt of hinting that there was, but Mr. Lilley glared round the house as fiercely as if each person there had asserted that the banner-bearing super. was immensely superior to the Apostle of the spasmodic in Art.

"Ah, you should see Irving."

In the jaundiced eyes of the metamorphosed Lilleys, even imported works of art deteriorated and became commonplace in the vitiating climate of the colonies. They went to see some "old masters" now in the possession of a colonist. Mr. Lilley couldn't very well dispute their genuineness, but he could at any rate disparage their merit.

"Ah, you should have seen the 'old masters' at Rome," said he ; "they were far superior to these. There was an absence of anything commonplace about them, was there not, my dear ?"

"Oh yes," answered the better half of the Lilley echo. "At Rome we did indeed see glorious old masters. After the Roman old masters, I should say that these were old journeymen."

"Terribly commonplace."

Viewed through the spectacles of foreign travel, everything and everybody in this Little Pedlington appeared to the Lilleys "dull, flat, stale, and unprofitable." The sky was less blue, the air less invigorating, the grass less green, and the sun less bright than those of the great old world. Colonial meat had not the exquisite flavour of the English article—colonial religion was not as pious as the foreign goods, and colonial men and women were not as good, as well-educated, as refined, or as cultured as the people with whom the Lilleys had associated during their travels. In the southern hemisphere, all, all was terribly commonplace. The travellers talked so of the lords and dukes whom they had met that there could be no doubt when the Lilleys shuffled off their mortal coil, they would prefer to be

"Genteelly damned beside a lord
Than saved in vulgar company."

Their acquaintances bore their airs with meekness or a long time. But at length one man rebelled. The Lilleys were with others gazing at a beautiful *Aurora Australis*. It was a magnificent specimen of the Southern light and all—save the Lilleys—were enthusiastic.

"Pooh," said the Lilleys, "after walking through a splendid art gallery in company with a noble lord and gazing upon a sunset by Turner, "I can assure you the tints of this Aurora are exceedingly commonplace."

This was too much for the rebel colonial.

"Look here," said he, "since everything in this colony is so dreadfully commonplace, how is it that you ever came back here? If you and the noble lords and dukes and counts were such great chums as you make out, how was it that you and they managed to tear yourselves away from each other ? You left England as quietly as you went there, I believe, and I haven't heard that before you tore yourself away, any weeping deputations of a sorrowing and uncommonplace nobility waited upon you and besought you to remain in their kindred circles. If we are all so commonplace, why remain here ? Tell us, we pray, will you ever go home again ?"

The Lilleys vouchsafed no reply to this rude man.

"He is one of the vulgar *canaille*," said Mr. Lilley, with lofty contempt, "uncultured and unawayed by those gentlemanly instincts which characterised the nobility with whom we mingled during our tour through 'Yurrup.'"

"Quite so," acquiesced Mrs. Lilley. "He is really the most commonplace man we have met since our return to this commonplace colony."

The months are passing by and the aristocracies of Europe appear to be surviving the loss of the society of the Lilleys. To the astonishment of their colonial acquaintances in general and the rude rebel in particular, no cable message has yet arrived from the crowned heads of Europe praying the Lilleys to soon return and leave us commonplace people to our fate. 'Tis passing strange.

COULTAS BROTHERS, 8 SWANSTON STREET, have opened the above premises with a Large and Well-Selected Stock of Woollens. Gentlemen may rely on getting a Really First-class Article.

Figure 2.6 'The Metamorphosis of Travel', *Melbourne Punch* (19 July 1883), 23

Acknowledgement

This research was funded by the Irish Research Council.

Notes

1 'Australian Doubles', *Melbourne Punch* (3 April 1856), p. 65, emphasis in original.
2 Examples of the satirical pieces produced by *Melbourne Punch* include: 'Latter-Day Civilization by Thomas Larcyle' (10 April 1856), p. 73; 'The Song of Lah Lah Troba by Henry W. Strongfellow' (22 May 1856), p. 124; and 'The Dream of Gold. The Squatting Era by Alfred Pennyson' (29 May 1856), p. 135.
3 Paul Giles, *Antipodean America: Australasia and the Constitution of U. S. Literature* (Oxford: Oxford University Press, 2013), pp. 24, 41.
4 For an account of the historical and philosophical relationship between *Terra Australis* and the Antipodes, and for the significance of hemispheric balance to both concepts, see Alfred Hiatt, '*Terra Australis* and the Idea of the Antipodes', in Anne M. Scott, Alfred Hiatt, Claire McIlroy, and Christopher Wortham (eds), *European Perceptions of Terra Australis* (London and New York: Routledge, 2016), pp. 9–44.
5 Giles, *Antipodean America*, p. 25.
6 These are the years covering the conferral of responsible government for the colonies which are the primary focus of this chapter: New South Wales, South Australia, Victoria, and Tasmania (previously Van Diemen's Land). South Australia's responsible government was conferred in 1856, but its 'first responsible parliament' only sat in 1857, while Queensland achieved separation from New South Wales and responsible government in 1859. The passing of the *Australian Constitutions Act* in 1850 'enabled', according to André Brett, 'the separation of Victoria from NSW and foreshadowed fully representative legislatures in all the Australian colonies except Western Australia' ('a small and marginal settlement, it did not receive the privilege until 1890'). See André Brett, 'Colonial and Provincial Separation Movements in Australia and New Zealand, 1856–1865', *The Journal of Imperial and Commonwealth History*, 47:1 (2019), 55, 51.
7 William Eisler, *The Furthest Shore: Images of Terra Australis from the Middle Ages to Captain Cook* (Cambridge: Cambridge University Press, 1995), p. 9. See also Matthew Boyd Goldie, *The Idea of the Antipodes: Place, People and Voices* (London and New York: Routledge, 2010); Alfred Hiatt, *Terra Incognita: Mapping the Antipodes before 1600* (Chicago: University of Chicago Press, 2008); and Avan Judd Stallard, *Antipodes: In Search of the Southern Continent* (Melbourne: Monash University Publishing, 2016).
8 Stallard, *Antipodes*, pp. 6, 188, 47.
9 Goldie, *The Idea of the Antipodes*, p. 3; Hiatt, '*Terra Australis* and the Idea of the Antipodes', p. 19.
10 Hiatt, '*Terra Australis* and the Idea of the Antipodes', p. 14.
11 Hiatt, '*Terra Australis* and the Idea of the Antipodes', p. 10.

12 Kate Fullagar, 'Introduction: The Atlantic World in the Antipodes', in Kate Fullagar (ed.), *The Atlantic World in the Antipodes: Effects and Transformations since the Eighteenth Century* (Newcastle upon Tyne: Cambridge Scholars Publishing, 2012), p. xiv. For the indeterminacy of the antipodean region and the instability of the term, see also Goldie, *The Idea of the Antipodes*, p. 3.

13 Hiatt, '*Terra Australis* and the Idea of the Antipodes', p. 19. For an excellent account of the Antipodes' association with these three types of inversions, see Giles, *Antipodean America*, esp. pp. 25–38. The cartographic version of Giles' 'comparative consciousness' is perhaps best represented by Pierre Desceliers' map of 1550 where the upside-down, back-to-front nature traditionally associated with the antipodean south is shared equally by the northern and southern hemispheres: whether reading from the south or the north of this map, the opposite hemisphere's titles are upside down.

14 Goldie, *The Idea of the Antipodes*, p. 165.

15 Bernard Smith, *Modernism's History: A Study in Twentieth-Century Art and Ideas* (Sydney: University of New South Wales Press, 1998), p. 7.

16 Smith, *Modernism's History*, p. 7.

17 For a history of the Osma Beatus Map, see John Williams, 'Isidore, Orosius and the Beatus Map', *Imago Mundi*, 49 (1997), 7–32.

18 Vilashini Cooppan, 'The Corpus of a Continent: Embodiments of Australia in World Literature', *JASAL: Journal of the Association for the Study of Australian Literature*, 15:3 (2015), 7–8.

19 Goldie, *The Idea of the Antipodes*, pp. 4–5. For Sedgwick's original account of 'beside', see *Touching Feeling: Affect, Pedagogy, Performativity* (Durham and London: Duke University Press, 2003), pp. 8–9.

20 Goldie, *The Idea of the Antipodes*, p. 1.

21 Giles, *Antipodean America*, p. 25.

22 Goldie, *The Idea of the Antipodes*, pp. 4, 5.

23 *Sydney Punch* (13 March 1869), p. 129. This poem was also reprinted in the *Wagga Wagga Advertiser and Riverine Reporter* (17 March 1869), p. 4, and the *Mount Barker Courier and Onkaparinga and Gumeracha Advertiser* (7 December 1883), p. 196. Published over a decade later, the *Mount Barker Courier*'s reprint included an attribution to the Scottish-born Australian poet, James Brunton Stephens. For the prevalence of reprinting in Australian newspapers and periodicals, and the relationship between metropolitan and provincial publications, see, e.g., Katherine Bode, 'Fictional Systems: Mass-Digitization, Network Analysis, and Nineteenth-Century Australian Newspapers', *Victorian Periodicals Review*, 50:1 (2017), 100–38; and Elizabeth Webby, 'Australia', in J. Don Vann and Rosemary T. VanArsdel (eds), *Periodicals of Queen Victoria's Empire: An Exploration* (Toronto and Buffalo: University of Toronto Press, 1996), pp. 19–60.

24 'How We Spend Our Christmas Holidays', *Illustrated Australian News for Home Readers* (29 December 1875), p. 209. Reprinted from the *Illustrated Adelaide News* (20 December 1875), pp. 7–8.

25 'How We Spend Our Christmas Holidays', p. 211.

26 'How We Spend Our New Year's Holiday', *Illustrated Sydney News and New South Wales Agriculturalist and Grazier* (12 January 1876), p. 11.

27 'The Birth of the New Year', *Illustrated Sydney News and New South Wales Agriculturalist and Grazier* (12 January 1876), p. 11.

28 For an analysis of the popularity and significance of representing the Australian colonies as youth in newspapers and periodicals, see Richard Scully, 'Britain in the *Melbourne Punch*', *Visual Culture in Britain*, 20:2 (2019), 158; and Simon Sleight, 'Wavering between Virtue and Vice: Constructions of Youth in Australian Cartoons of the Late-Victorian Era', in Richard Scully and Marian Quartly (eds), *Drawing the Line: Using Cartoons as Historical Evidence* (Clayton: Monash University ePress, 2009), pp. 194–239.

29 Giles, *Antipodean America*, p. 26.

30 'Topsy-Turvy', *Courier* (24 January 1857), p. 2.

31 Anthony Trollope, *Australia*, eds P. D. Edwards and R. B. Joyce (St Lucia: University of Queensland Press, 1967), p. 123.

32 John Green, 'Letter: Bendigo gold fields, to Eliza Green, England, 1853 July 22', cited in Lorinda Cramer, 'Diggers' Dress and Identity on the Victorian Goldfields, Australia, 1851–1870', *Fashion Theory*, 22:1 (2018), 89.

33 'Topsy-Turvy', *Courier* (29 January 1853), p. 3. This poem was first published in the *Courier*, a newspaper from Hobart, Tasmania. The colony's history as a penal colony (Van Diemen's Land) from 1800–53 may explain the fascination with the convict class and the ticket-of-leave system, but the poem proved popular and was reprinted in at least five other newspapers, including newspapers in the colonies of New South Wales (also a former penal colony until 1850) and Victoria (which had no official transportation policy, but still received and relied upon a convict labour force). For an account of Australia's early European settler and convict history, see Alan Atkinson, *The Europeans in Australia: A History, Vol. 1, The Beginning* (Oxford: Oxford University Press, 1997).

34 'Topsy-Turvy', *Courier* (29 January 1853), p. 3.

35 'Punch's Summary for Europe', *Melbourne Punch* (25 April 1861), pp. 52–3.

36 Shu-Chuan Yan, '"Kangaroo Politics, Kangaroo Ideas, and Kangaroo Society": The Early Years of *Melbourne Punch* in Colonial Australia', *Victorian Periodicals Review*, 52:1 (2019), 90.

37 For a recent summary of the legal and political understandings of *terra nullius* and its association with Australia, see Thomas H. Ford and Justin Clemens, 'Barron Field's *Terra Nullius* Operation', *Australian Humanities Review*, 65 (2019), 1–19.

38 'Holding the Mirror Upside Down', *Adelaide Times* (4 March 1856), p. 214.

39 'A Welcome to Anthony Trollope', *Sydney Punch* (7 October 1871), p. 171.

40 'A Welcome to Anthony Trollope', p. 171.

41 The first chapter of 'Home at Last: Both Sides' was published in the *Record* (11 February 1869), p. 7, and the final chapter was published in the *Record* (6 May 1869), p. 7; 'Christmas in the Two Hemispheres', *Melbourne Punch* (26 December 1861), pp. 322–3; 'The Antipodes: Both Sides' was first published in the *Sydney Morning Herald* (19 June 1869), p. 4, and reprinted in the sister newspaper, *Sydney Mail* (26 June 1869), p. 11 (both part of the *Sydney Morning Herald* group), and the *Toowoomba Chronicle and Queensland Advertiser* (30 June 1869), p. 4. For the popularity and significance of serialised fiction and the frequency of

pseudonymous and anonymous publications in Australian newspapers, see Katherine Bode, 'Thousands of Titles without Authors: Digitized Newspapers, Serial Fiction, and the Challenges of Anonymity', *Book History*, 19 (2016), 284–316. For the relationship between the *Sydney Mail* and the *Sydney Morning Herald*, see Elizabeth Webby, 'Australia', pp. 45–6.

42 *Sydney Morning Herald* (19 June 1869), p. 4.
43 'The Antipodes', *Sydney Punch* (8 April 1882), p. 134.
44 Goldie, *The Idea of the Antipodes*, p. 5.
45 'A Tale of Two Hemispheres', *Australasian* (9 July 1870), pp. 37–8.
46 Charles Dickens, *A Tale of Two Cities*, ed. Richard Maxwell (London: Penguin Books, 2000), p. 5.
47 'A Tale of Two Hemispheres', p. 37.
48 'A Tale of Two Hemispheres', p. 37.
49 Goldie, *The Idea of the Antipodes*, p. 9.
50 'A Tale of Two Hemispheres', p. 38.
51 'A Tale of Two Hemispheres', p. 38.
52 'The Metamorphosis of Travel', *Melbourne Punch* (19 July 1883), p. 23.
53 Giles, *Antipodean America*, p. 26.
54 'The Metamorphosis of Travel', p. 23.
55 'The Metamorphosis of Travel', p. 23.
56 'The Metamorphosis of Travel', p. 23.
57 For a discussion of these debates, see John Hirst, 'Empire, State, Nation', in Deryck M. Schreuder and Stuart Ward (eds), *Australia's Empire* (Oxford: Oxford University Press, 2008), pp. 141–62.

3

Lag fever, flash men, and late fashionable worlds

Clara Tuite

Our story starts not in the southern colonies but with a canonical scene of literary expatriation and scandalous celebrity: Lord Byron in Genoa, spending the spring of 1823 with the so-called 'Blessington circus', a tight little entourage of idler-adventurers who cast their web across Ireland, England, and continental Europe. The 'circus' was named for the Irish author and literary hostess Marguerite Gardiner, Countess of Blessington, and her second husband, Charles John Gardiner, the Earl of Blessington. It also included Blessington's daughter, Lady Harriet Gardiner, and Alfred, Count D'Orsay – Marguerite's companion, supposed lover, and surrogate son, supposedly the Earl's lover as well, and Harriet's husband for a few years. It was a tangled web they wove.

Lady Blessington had a shadowy past. Born Margaret Power in Tipperary, she had been married off young by her father, an abusive minor landowner. Having left her drunken husband, she later became, as she put it, 'that despised thing, a kept mistress', excluded from respectable London society even after her marriage to Blessington in 1818.[1] In autumn 1821, she met twenty-year-old Alfred, the second son of a general in Napoleon's *Grand Armée*. Alfred had taken up a position in the army of the restored Bourbon monarchy, but in 1823 resigned his commission to travel with the Blessingtons in Italy and France. A spectacularly beautiful Regency Adonis, D'Orsay was known as 'the king of dandies', with all the ambiguity that entails: 'mannish rather than manly', he was 'resplendent like a beetle' and 'like some gorgeous dragonfly skimming through the air'.[2] Representations of D'Orsay often featured him on horseback, as in the background of the 1834 lithograph by the Irish artist Daniel Maclise, published in *Fraser's Magazine* (Figure 3.1).

The story goes that the Blessington circus turned up on Byron's doorstep one afternoon, accidentally on purpose in the rain. At first, Byron avoided meeting them; thereafter, he was punctiliously effusive with Lady Blessington but far more interested in D'Orsay, of whom he said, 'having lived so long out of the world, it was rather an amusement to see what sort of an animal

Figure 3.1 Daniel Maclise, 'Alfred, Count D'Orsay', lithograph, 1834

a dandy of the present day is'. He later described D'Orsay as re-fashioning 'an ideal of a Frenchman *before* the Revolution' – that is, an ornamented style of dandy, not the impeccably restrained kind invented by Beau Brummell in Mayfair in the 1790s.[3] D'Orsay himself produced several well-known images of Byron during his association with the Blessington circus, including an ink and gilt silhouette (Figure 3.2) and a pencil sketch, reworked in 1832 (Figure 3.3) to illustrate Blessington's *Conversations of Lord Byron*, which was serialised in the *New Monthly Magazine* in 1832–33 and published in one volume in 1834.[4] Career exiles all, Blessington, Byron, and D'Orsay embodied new possibilities of upward social mobility forged through glamorous scandalous celebrity.

My chapter traces the relationship between this celebrity European self-exile and the enforced mobility associated with penal transportation to

Figure 3.2 Count Alfred D'Orsay, 'Lord Byron', ink and gilt silhouette, 1823?

Figure 3.3 Count Alfred D'Orsay, 'Byron at Genoa', pencil sketch, 1823
(published 1832)

Australia and the settler culture that oversaw it. I explore circuits of scandalous celebrity, unrespectability, exile, expatriation, convictism, and settler culture; careers of upward and downward mobility; and the interpenetrations of colonial Australian and London metropolitan life. I examine the transportation and transformation of the social identity of the dandy, and of what we might call the dandy silhouette, which may be as precise as what Christopher Breward calls the 'Londonate' look of Beau Brummell in the

Regency period.[5] Here, D'Orsay's portrait of Byron functions as a 'silhouette' in the symbolic sense of a prototype of the Regency dandy that travelled across London and Europe to Botany Bay, Newcastle, and Van Diemen's Land.

Dandyism is usually regarded as a European phenomenon; but as Jessica Feldman argues, 'displacement' and 'international proliferation' are crucial to 'placing' it. Dandyism, she writes, 'exists in its purest form always at the periphery of one's vision, often in a foreign language or a text requiring decipherment'.[6] A vital form of dandyism as a coded language is 'the flash', a 'foreign' language of thieves and gypsies, also known as 'St. Giles' Greek' after the London district associated with vagrancy.[7]

During the Regency, the flash language of the London criminal class was made over into a fashionable language and sociable style that linked it with the 'ton' and 'the world'. It took on new and intriguing infusions when it travelled to an antipodean setting from the late 1780s. As the colonial surgeon Peter Miller Cunningham wrote in *Two Years in New South Wales* (1827):

> A number of the slang phrases current in St Giles's *Greek* bid fair to become legitimised in the dictionary of this colony: plant, swag, pulling up, and other epithets of the Tom and Jerry school … In our police-offices, the slang words are regularly taken down in examinations … Among the lower classes, these terms form a part of every common conversation; and the children consequently catch them. In addition to this, the London mode of *pronunciation* has been duly ingrafted on the colloquial dialect of our Currency youths![8]

The flash mediated between elite culture and the underworld as a kind of classless language, equally fascinating to an elite worldly subject such as Lord Byron, the popular antiquarian Francis Grose in his *Classical Dictionary of the Vulgar Tongue* (1785, 1811, 1823), and the transported convict James Hardy Vaux, whose *Vocabulary of the Flash Language* (1819) has the distinction of being the first Australian dictionary. Grose and Vaux were primary sources for Byron's 'flash' Canto XI of *Don Juan*. My chapter engages the 'flash' as an exotic hybrid, a kind of world language of the underworld that connects Regency London to glamorous-scandalous European exile, late grand-tourism, and the enforced mobility of penal transportation, mediating transnational circuits of masculine social identity and connecting convict culture to fashion and to new worlds of social mobility.

Another social identity that the flash language commemorates is the lag, variously defined as 'a man transported', 'a convict under sentence of transportation', a returned transport or ticket-of-leave convict, or someone avoiding the enforced mobility of penal transportation.[9] A potent coinage of the flash language is 'lag fever': 'A term of ridicule applied to men who being under sentence of transportation, pretend illness, to avoid being sent from the gaol to the hulks.'[10] This idea of 'lag fever' speaks to the stigma of convictism and to the sense of the colonial south as a world of backwardness, regression, and delay.

The 'lag ship' was 'a transport chartered by Government for the conveyance of convicts to New South Wales; also, a hulk, or floating prison, in which, to the disgrace of humanity, many hundreds of these unhappy persons are confined, and suffer every complication of human misery'.[11] The hulks were rightly feared. In 1776, after American independence halted transportation to America, convicts sentenced to hard labour were crowded into decommissioned warships, which were used as floating prisons. After a 1778 inquiry exposed the horrendous conditions on the hulks, the authorities decided that 'Australia provided a possibility for the resumption of transportation, which no longer seemed so bad now that the alternatives had been explored'.[12] The hulks now became the first stage of transportation. Convicts were then moved to the ships that would take them on the long journey to Australia, where they would remain until they were released. The first convicts to Australia arrived in Botany Bay in 1788.

After the flash coves moved south from the London hulks, St Giles' Greek became 'ingrafted' on the tongue of the local Australian dialect and vice versa. One such ingrafting, as though lugubriously commemorating the long sea journey, or perhaps just the stasis of the hulks, is the flash word for spectacles, 'BARNACLES', after the marine crustaceans that cling to the bottom of ships, or the human attendants that cannot be easily shaken off.[13] Flash glasses are laggers too, it seems, as are flash shoes, 'crabshells', another crustacean form, fashioned to fit the sideways movement from one place to another.[14]

In the original 1785 Grose's *Classical Dictionary*, 'lag' meant 'to lag, to drop behind, to keep back', and the lag as a subject was 'the last of a company'.[15] By 1811, it took on the extra meanings associated with transportation to New South Wales. In using the flash coinage 'lag fever' to revisit conceptions of colonial belatedness, I highlight the transformative elements of lag and seek to illuminate the flash as a form of popular Romantic retrospective avant-gardism. I read the flash language, then, as the index of a late fashionable world of expatriated Regency dandyism. I read it, too, for its agential power, as a random collection of 'late fashionable words' (as Grose called it) that is also world-*making*: anachronistically sustaining, moving in and out of 'the world' of elite Regency London, travelling south in 'crabshells' in subversive refractions of the world-system of the British Empire, and celebrating the powers of ancient slang in a new time and place.[16]

The convict lagger is a kind of idler, too, but different from the glamorous idlers of Lord Byron's *Hours of Idleness* (1807) or Lady Blessington's *The Idler in Italy* (1839–40) and *The Idler in France* (1841). Indeed, the colonial lag was often both a labourer *and* a dandy, with claims to social respectability. Penal transportation and punitive convict mobility were a world apart from free settler movement or Byronic self-exile. But the culture of the flash, mediating Mayfair and cockney dandyism in expatriated and colonial convict forms, suggests that the convict lag has surprising connections to the European idler.

'Gentlemen of the shade': Byronic flash and transportation

In April 1823, when Byron was in Genoa, going out for morning rides with the Blessington circus, he was also revising Canto XI of *Don Juan*, the so-called 'flash' canto, and revisiting London in the company of Juan. When Juan arrives, he comes through Shooter's Hill on the outskirts of London, with its gallows at the foot and its gibbet at the summit, framing the vision of London as the capital of the British Empire through its sites and implements of punishment, part of *Don Juan's* wide-ranging critique of Tory England: 'Alas! Could She but fully, truly, know / How her great name is now throughout abhorred ... How all the nations deem her their worst foe, / That worse than *worst of foes*, the once adored / False friend, who held out freedom to mankind, / And now would chain them, to the very mind' (*DJ* X, st. 67, lines 529–36).[17]

Accompanying this critique is a picaresque narrative of Juan's adventures in London. After his arrival, Juan is waylaid by Tom, the highwayman, or 'footpad' robber, who holds him up with a knife. Juan pulls out his gun and shoots Tom dead, while he is in 'Full flash' (*DJ* XI, st. 17, line 135), and then regrets it. Speaking as Juan in an intimate piece of indirect discourse, Byron's narrator notes:

> Juan, who saw the Moon's late minion bleed
> As if his veins would pour out his existence,
> Stood calling out for bandages and lint,
> And wished he had been less hasty with his flint.
> (*DJ* XI, st. 14, lines 109–12)

Canto XI deploys flash vocabulary with its rich strain of demotic bravura, linguistic wit, and inventiveness, while reworking the Shakespearean intertext of Falstaff's appeal to Hal (in *Henry IV, Part I*): 'Marry, then, sweet wag, when thou art king ... let us be Diana's / foresters, gentlemen of the shade, minions of the / moon' (I. ii. lines 23–7).

Thieves had already been renamed with honorifics in William Harrison's *Description of England* (1577), which is part of Holinshed's *Chronicles*, a source for *Henry IV*. Grose's *Classical Dictionary*, the Bible of flash, invokes Falstaff to justify its use of rude words: 'with great truth [I] make the same defence that Falstaff ludicrously urges in behalf of one engaged in rebellion, viz. that he did not seek them, but that, like rebellion … they lay in his way, and he found them'.[18] *Don Juan* reworks the Shakespearean scene into a contemporary picaresque. As Tom dies, Juan sees 'the Moon's late minion bleed / As if his veins would pour out his existence'. To be a late minion is to be recently deceased, but also a lag. Saluting the fallen flash man, this passage recirculates an earlier form of thief's language that Shakespeare honours; and, like Shakespeare, it exalts the thieves, lyricises their work, and pays tribute to their aspirations to gentility. These 'gentlemen of the shade' are shadowy characters – secret, subversive, poetically associated with the night and the queen of the moon, Diana, and also with 'moon men' and link boys, as Grose defines them: 'link boys are said to curse the moon, because it renders their assistance unnecessary: these gentry, frequently under colour of lighting passengers over kennels, or through dark passages, assist in robbing them'.[19]

Social elevation through disguise is a vital element of flash culture. Indeed, the elevation of thieves is a primary story of Australian colonial history, marking the transformation of convict into settler, at first stealing silk handkerchiefs, then purchasing them. With the institution of transportation, the language of thieves became the language of convicts, transported to a place where everything is 'Opposite to England & … even the Moon is Top side Turvy your summer our winter'.[20] Transplanting the customary heroic association between banditry and moonlight, the late-nineteenth-century Victorian bushranger Captain Moonlite continues this tradition of Diana's foresters as a flash 'minion of the moon'.

Captain Francis Grose was familiar with the colonies through his son, Francis, who was Lieutenant Governor of New South Wales from 1792 to 1794, succeeding the first governor, Arthur Phillip. Francis Grose was a lax and indolent governor who abolished civil courts and established military rule, winding back the public farming that was a primary mode of convict labour and colonial development. He made generous land grants to his officers, including John Macarthur, whom he appointed the inaugural inspector of public works; and his own substantial reserve, Grose Farm, eventually became the grounds of the University of Sydney.[21]

The Regency moment of flash language and style hosted an abundance of new styles of masculine self-fashioning, cosmopolitan and colonial modes of fashionability, and new social types. Many flash coinages are not just new words but new social identities: a 'FLASH [is] a person who affects any peculiar habit, as swearing, dressing in a particular manner, taking snuff, &c., merely to be taken notice of, is said to do it *out of flash*'; a 'NEEDY-MIZZLER [is] a poor ragged object of either sex; a shabby-looking person'; a 'SHARP [is] a gambler, or person, professed in all the arts of play; a cheat, or swindler';

a 'RAG-GORGY [is] a rich or monied man, but generally used in conversation when a particular gentleman, or person in high office, is hinted at; instead of mentioning his name, they say, the *Rag-gorgy*, knowing themselves to be understood by those they are addressing'. Another kind of flash man is the 'fancy-man', a pimp; the 'scamp' is a thief; then there is the 'beau-nasty', or 'slovenly fop'; the 'Duke of limbs' is 'a tall, awkward, ill-made fellow', while the '*real* swell' (*DJ* XI, st. 17, line 134) is both a gentleman and a man of fashion.[22] These flash men had their consorts – the 'blowing' (*DJ* XI, st. 19, line 151) or 'blowen' was a 'mistress of a gentleman of the scamp' – and queer sisters, the 'flash mob' inmates of the Female Factory who in 1840 rioted and staged witchy cabals in the hills outside Hobart.[23]

Another key source of flash language is Pierce Egan's *Life in London* (1821), which features the escapades of the well-heeled Tom and Jerry slumming it in the poorer districts. Using the language of racing, Egan produces a mock stud pedigree of 'a Dandy in 1820. The Dandy was got by vanity out of Affectation – his dam, Petit-Maitre or Maccaroni, – his grand dam, Fribble – his great grand dam – Bronze – his great great grand dam, Coxcomb – and his earliest ancestor Fop.'[24] The parodic genealogy suggests that the dandy is a little tired, a little antiquated, not entirely flash. The dandy was then superseded by the flash man or 'Corinthian', which Grose's *Dictionary* defines as 'a frequenter of brothels'. The flash man and other relatives of the Londonate dandy are all commemorated in the new popular antiquarian genre of the urban lexicon, including Grose's *Classical Dictionary* and Vaux's *A New Vocabulary of the Flash Language*.

Flash returns and lag fever

James Hardy Vaux (1782–1841) was a professional thief, lag, and recidivist, who was transported three times to New South Wales (Figure 3.4). Originally a clerk, he was arrested in April 1800 for pilfering from his employers. He was acquitted on that charge, but soon after was sentenced to seven years' transportation for stealing a handkerchief. His father, a butler and house steward to an MP, seems to have used his contacts to arrange for his son to avoid the hulks and go straight to the transportation ship.

Vaux's *Memoirs* detail his pre-criminal career as a copying clerk – a member of London's new semi-professional class. His narrative celebrates the transformative power of reading as a means of self-improvement, describing how

> during the course of a wild and dissipated life … a portion of my time was always devoted to the perusal of books, and a part of my money, however hardly or dishonestly obtained, to the purchase of them: and to this moment I still consider them the most valuable property a man of my disposition can possess.[25]

Figure 3.4 Artist unknown, 'Portrait of James Hardy Vaux', originally published in Knapp and Baldwin's *New Newgate Calendar*, c. 1825

The *Memoirs* were recognised as highly literate and literary. The *London Magazine* in 1827 described the book as 'one of the most singular that ever issued from the press'.[26] Vaux's fascination with language also produced his *Vocabulary of the Flash*, which was published with the *Memoirs*. The *Vocabulary* was dedicated to Vaux's former jailer, Thomas Skottowe, with the suggestion that it 'will afford you some amusement from its novelty; and that from the correctness of its definitions, you may occasionally find it useful in your magisterial capacity'.[27]

The flash language combined the new (slang) with the old (cant), and claimed ancient customary usage. Marilyn Butler observes that 'Grose's whimsical preface ... makes play with the idea of classicality', hence the reference to 'St. Giles' Greek'.[28] As William Moncrieff writes in *Tom and Jerry* (1821), the stage adaptation of *Life in London*, 'FLASH, my young friend, or slang, as others call it, is the classical language of the Holy Land; in other words St. Giles' Greek'.[29]

Flash lexicons drew authority from flash's relationship to earlier slang languages. John Camden Hotten's *Dictionary of Modern Slang, Cant, and*

Vulgar Words (1859) traces how during the Regency, 'Slang ... received numerous additions from pugilism, horse-racing, and "fast" life generally', and observes that it 'was generally termed FLASH language'. Hotten's *Dictionary* actively recirculates words used by rebels and revolutionaries as far back as the sixteenth century, taking as its epigraph a quote from Charles II's chaplain Robert South: 'Rabble-charming words, which carry so much wild-fire wrapt up in them'.[30] This linguistic retrofitting can be seen as activating a kind of lag fever, a popular retrospective avant-gardism charged with demotic bravura and the power of anachronism. This retroactivity makes the flash a peculiarly dynamic – even dialectical – vehicle of cultural lag, bristling against spatial and geographical backwardness, and highlighting the transformative elements of disjunction.

This term 'lag fever' figures in one sense the belatedness of the colonial world; it confirms the experience of penal transportation as a backward movement of space and time, bestowing the social identity of 'lags' and their backward state.[31] But it can run both ways; its multiple uses show that the colonial lag can outrun the imperial centre, reflecting the metropole back in a less flattering light. Even Byron fantasised about being a settler in Van Diemen's Land, as he wrote to his agent: 'I have long had a notion of emigration from your worn out Europe – but am undecided as to the *where* – South America – The United States – or even van Diemen's land – of which I hear much as a good place to settle in.'[32] Byron was then completing the draft of Canto XI, which he would send to John Murray in October 1822.

That the lag could charge the transformative elements of colonial disjunction is amply demonstrated by Vaux, whose convict career sees a pattern of release, relapse, and re-transportation. (He seems to have been the only prisoner transported to Australia as many as three times.) Vaux's story of transportation is one of departures and returns, with ongoing contact and cultural interpenetration between London and the colony. Vaux wrote his *Memoirs* and flash *Vocabulary* in Newcastle, known as 'the Hell of New South Wales', a place of secondary punishment where the most dangerous convicts were sent to dig in the coal mines. Military rule in Newcastle ended in 1823, shortly after Vaux's time there, and the area was opened up to farming.

Vaux's repeat offending consolidated a circuit between metropolis and colony. When he first published his *Memoirs* in 1819, he was connected to influential colonial figures such as Samuel Marsden and Barron Field, the author of the first Australian book of poetry, *First Fruits* (1819). Indeed, Field arranged for the manuscript to be published in London by John Murray. This flow between the metropole and the colony transformed Vaux into a recognisable literary icon and Australian type of rebel.

In a stage adaptation of Vaux's *Memoirs* by William Moncrieff, entitled *Van Diemen's Land! Or Settlers and Natives* (1830), Vaux features in the character list as 'a pupil of the Barrington School' (named after the pick-pocket George Barrington),[33] and compares the transported convicts' situation with that of 'our masters, the settlers':

> we're transported here with more justice than they are; we come here for our sins, and they for their misfortunes; – they come here at their own expence, we at the government's; – they run all the risk – we share all the profit. I never worked so hard for my dinner as when I was obliged to steal it.[34]

The flash was by definition alert to structural injustice: 'to be flash to any matter or meaning, is to understand or comprehend it ... to *put* a person *flash* to any thing, is to put him on his guard, to explain or inform him of what he was before unacquainted with'.[35]

Vaux's iconic status is registered when his name appears in the 'Invocation' that opens Pierce Egan's *Life in London* (1821; originally serialised in 1820), a roll-call of literary influences and patrons, including John Murray:

> But thou, O, MURRAY, whose classic front defies, with terrific awe, ill-starred, pale, wan, and *shabbily* clad GENIUS from approaching thy splendid threshold ... open thy doors, and take the unsophisticated JERRY HAWTHORN by the hand: and although not a CHILDE HAROLD in birth, a CORSAIR bold, or a HARDY VAUX, *wretched* exile; yet let me solicit thee to introduce him to thy numerous acquaintance.[36]

Here, Vaux's convict memoir, the narrative of the career criminal, is invoked as a source of authority on a par with the poetry of Lord Byron. The 'Invocation' reverses the flow of the lag and '*wretched* exile' – not from metropolis to colony but the other way around, chiming with Byron's desire to leave 'worn out Europe'. Chiming here too is Byron's imagined transportation in *Don Juan* Canto III of the Lake Poets Robert Southey, William Wordsworth, and Samuel Taylor Coleridge, whose late political conservatism reneged on youthful Pantisocratic idealism: 'Such names at present cut a convict figure, / The very Botany Bay in moral geography' (*DJ* III, st. 94, lines 841–2).[37] This was written in September 1819 (published in August 1821), possibly with Vaux's recently published convict memoir and flash *Vocabulary* at hand. By claiming Vaux's colonial memoir as an influence and inspiration for his account of London metropolitan life, Egan honours picaresque criminality. 'HARDY VAUX' rubs shoulders with CHILDE HAROLD and the CORSAIR – the brooding traveller and the pirate, who put into circulation the powerful form of Byronic scandalous celebrity. Egan's *Life in London* creates a specific intertextual relationship between the fabled Byronic mode of celebrity self-exile and the enforced mobility of penal transportation to colonial Australia.

Egan's *Life in London* is usually identified as the great sensation that popularised flash language and introduced this dynamic currency of common social life to the upper classes; but as its 'Invocation' demonstrates, Egan's version in fact followed Vaux's *colonial* deployment of the flash, as did Byron's flash canto of *Don Juan*. There was a significant interpenetration between metropole and periphery. Egan figures publishing as a form of social patronage, invoking the doors of Murray's publishing house to effect an introduction: of the unsophisticated Jerry to his 'numerous acquaintance' by the powerful Murray, the epicentre of worldly London contacts.

Despite Egan's figure of Murray taking literary newcomers by the hand, the publisher's relationships with Vaux and Byron were not a tireless flow of bonhomie. Murray published Vaux's *Memoirs* on 12 January 1819, six months before the first two cantos of Byron's *Don Juan*. He published both books with a sense of ambivalence; tellingly, both were later published by the radical John Hunt. Murray put his name to the first edition of Vaux's memoir, but quickly dropped the connection.[38] He was similarly awkward about the first two cantos of *Don Juan*, which he published without his name (thereby giving pirates carte blanche). In April 1829, Vaux absconded and went to Ireland. The next year he was convicted of passing forged bank notes, or 'queer screens'. His death sentence was commuted to transportation for seven years, and he returned to Sydney. In 1841, he disappeared from the record, but his *Memoirs* and *Vocabulary of the Flash* had far-reaching influence.

Dandified silhouettes and sartorialised violence

The D'Orsay–Byron dandy silhouette has another afterlife in colonial Australia through the colonial functionary William Romaine Govett (1808–48), a surveyor in New South Wales. A sketchbook album belonging to Govett, held at the National Library of Australia, includes a pen and ink copy of Maclise's 1834 sketch of D'Orsay, together with copies of other literary identities – Blessington, Thomas Egerton (Jane Austen's first publisher), Leigh Hunt, William Bowles, and Laetitia Landon. They seem to be original handdrawn copies of the Maclise illustrations, but they also suggest in places a process of tracing, with the intermediation of print and pen, making it difficult to determine whether they are manuscript or print. The image of D'Orsay has a caption added: 'THE OBSERVED OF ALL OBSERVERS' (Figure 3.5).[39] There are sketches and watercolours of Australian flora and fauna, including kangaroos and the 'Head of an eagle shot by me on the banks of the Wollondilly River, New South Wales, 8th April 1828'. In Govett's sketchbook, the literary lions of Regency London share the stage with the stars of the Australian animal kingdom, and the Regency metropolis is interpenetrated by the colonial peripheries. Govett uses flash words, such as 'Spanker' (the flash name for horse) for his dog, which was bitten by a snake.[40]

Figure 3.5 William Romaine Govett, copy of Daniel Maclise, 'Alfred, Count D'Orsay', 1834, pen and ink, 1843?

Govett was an assistant to the New South Wales Surveyor, Sir Thomas Mitchell. Govett's Leap, a waterfall with a 1,000-metre drop in the Blue Mountains, outside Sydney, was named by Mitchell, who referred to Govett as 'a wild young man who needed control'.[41] He was such a wild young man that popular legend confused him with a local bushranger; as late as 1871, the *Sydney Mail* described Govett as 'a queer card', a 'Swell', and 'a convicted felon', who was 'lagged for robbery', and who had taken his own life by throwing himself down a gorge.[42] In fact, Govett was made redundant in

1834 and returned to England, where he died in 1848 apparently of natural causes. Nevertheless, this legend of the 'wild young man' has an added resonance when read against an entry by Govett in a notebook and sketchbook detailing the discovery of the cataract:

> It was an amusement with me always when I approached the edge of these precipices, to loosen large masses of rock, and by the assistance of the men lying on their backs, and pushing with their feet, to upset them into the abyss below – and one could form a tolerable judgement of the frightful depth they had to fall before they came in contact with any thing, from observing the time of silence, from the instant of their dislodgement, until they struck, and reechoing thundered from rock to rock and valley to valley, resounding again and against the more distant walls of the gully.[43]

Govett's 'amusement' suggests a particular experience of space, configured by temporal effects of lag, delay, and deferral, where lag is experienced as a form of vertiginous sublimity. This curious temporal experience of 'observing the time of silence' includes the vicarious thrill of experiencing 'the frightful depth' *at* a distance, as Govett hears the rock striking *in* the distance, experienced as a physical sensation: lag as exhilaration.

As the colonial 'wild young man', Govett both copies and displaces the late Regency dandy type, D'Orsay – that iconic silhouette of modern urban masculinity inaugurated in 1790s Mayfair, transformed into other dandy kinds (buck, swell, flash man, or fancy man), and then expatriated or transported to the colonies. When Govett returned to England in 1834, he wrote twenty articles on Australia for the *Saturday Magazine*, including accounts of Indigenous–settler contact that commented on white brutality, and a description of a corroboree attuned to masculine gesture, dress, and ritual.

Govett's superior in New South Wales thereafter became the highly decorated Major Thomas Mitchell, after whom the Major Mitchell Cockatoo was named: 'Few birds,' Mitchell wrote, 'more enliven the monotonous hues of the Australian forest than this beautiful species whose pink-coloured wings and flowing crest might have embellished the air of a more voluptuous region.'[44] Mitchell embodied another form of dandy: the military man. He had been a general in the Peninsular Wars (against Napoleon) under the Duke of Wellington, who became the nineteenth century's most famous military celebrity. Recalling his career under Wellington, Mitchell made it a practice to name colonial sites after battle sites in Spain.[45] He also had a problematic relationship with Indigenous Australians, which is commemorated in a controversial portrait, a silhouette lithograph by William Fernyhough (Figure 3.6).[46]

In this portrait, which echoes a famous silhouette of the Duke of Wellington, Mitchell is presented with a riding crop and spurs. Most strikingly, he is looking at a portrait of the Wiradjuri man John Piper, his guide and

Figure 3.6 William Fernyhough, 'Portrait of Sir Thomas Mitchell',
in *Album of Portraits, Mainly of New South
Wales Officials*, lithograph, 1836

interpreter on his third expedition into the interior. This portrait within a
portrait reproduces Fernyhough's original portrait of Piper, 'the native who
accompanied Major Mitchell in his expedition to the interior' (Figure 3.7).[47]
In it, Piper is 'posing proudly with the accoutrements of settler regard that
had been given to him by Mitchell', of which Mitchell wrote:[48] 'I clothed
him in my own red coat, and I gave him also a cocked hat and feather, which
had once belonged to Governor Darling' – a ritual gifting that suggests
something more complex than the passing on of cast-offs.[49]

But the plot thickens. In December 1836, the executive council investigated Mitchell for the killing of seven Aboriginal people at Dispersion

Mountain. In his defence, Mitchell claimed that Piper had warned him of an impending Aboriginal attack. David Hansen suggests that the print may have been intended 'as a reminder … of Piper's responsibility and Mitchell's innocence'.[50] So the image mediates a contemporary controversy around frontier violence. It suggests how polite colonial settler culture is allied with state-sanctioned violence through rituals of 'decoration', patronage, and intimate recognition as a form of social control. Complex, ambivalent, and powerful, this mass-produced silhouette takes on the symbolic and didactic functions of more elevated forms of portraiture. In staging an intimate reciprocity between Mitchell and Piper (similarly featured in the frontispiece to Mitchell's *Expeditions*), it simultaneously salutes a traditional martial form of homosocial friendship and inscribes the tensions that marked that relationship, which culminated with Piper's betrayal by Mitchell. And while in the investigation Mitchell's defence made much of having been reluctant to shoot, in his *Expeditions into the Interior* (2nd edn 1839) he openly glorifies the violence, recalling how he named the hill in commemoration of the events.[51]

This curious double portrait may be no less exploitative for being intimate, but it also functions as a vehicle of Indigenous self-assertion. As Grace Karskens argues, in early colonial Australia, some Aboriginal men, like Piper, embraced European military clothing to signify their identification with white men and their superior social status.[52] The jackets they wore were important emblems of masculine power. Mitchell also rewarded Piper with the gift of a breastplate, and the moniker 'King'; but Piper pointedly declared that he did not want to be known as a 'King' but as the 'Conqueror' of the inland.[53] Nevertheless, it is telling that in Fernyhough's image, the 'Conqueror' appears in miniature, held in the palm of Mitchell's hand. After his fame, when people gave him money, Piper 'purchased silk handkerchiefs, and wore them in his breast', as Mitchell notes approvingly: 'to his great credit, he abstained from any indulgence in intoxication, looking down, apparently with contempt, on those wretched specimens of his race, who led a gipsy life about Sydney'.[54]

These portraits demonstrate clothing's potent agency; as Linda Colley writes of the Napoleonic Wars: 'Never before or since have British military uniforms been so impractically gorgeous … And the more exclusive a regiment an officer belonged to, and the higher his rank, the more dazzling his uniform was likely to be. In every sense he was dressed to kill.'[55] The dazzling red coat is an enactment – and an enigmatic conjunction – of power and violence, resonating in the colonies like the echo of Mitchell's naming practices. The red coat and its sartorial power is a key protagonist in the history of colonial Australia, where, in Margaret Maynard's words, 'what was at first virtually a military prison was to be transformed, within a single generation, into a fully organised capitalist society'.[56] The dandy military man and the colonial functionary had a significant role in this transformation, as did the

THE NATIVE WHO ACCOMPANIED MAJOR MITCHELL
IN HIS EXPEDITION TO THE INTERIOR

Figure 3.7 William Fernyhough, 'Piper, the native who accompanied Major Mitchell in his expedition to the interior', in *A Series of Twelve Profile Portraits of the Aborigines of New South Wales*, lithograph, 1836

convict dandy and his Indigenous guide and interpreter. 'Gentlemen convicts mixed freely in elite social circles and often lived like men of fashion', spending their earnings freely, as Jane Elliott notes.[57]

This relationship between labour and self-fashioning is documented in the journal of the labourer Evan Evans, who records that on 18 October 1803 he received '1 Handkerchief in payment for felling straggling trees at the lagoon'; he also purchased silk handkerchiefs, black silk and ribbon,

duck trousers, and a dimity petticoat for his wife. As Elliott writes, 'labourers in New South Wales chose to spend large amounts of their earnings not
merely on clothing but on good quality things, which would normally have
been considered the prerogative of members of the classes above them'.[58]
Men's shirts were made of the finest muslin made in India 'even in the very
early days, when it seemed that the colony was nothing more than a prison'.[59]

Such items of dandy apparel embody what Arjun Appadurai termed 'the
long-distance journey of commodities' that marked the Euro-colonial world-
system, in which the colonies became stalled as the metropolises' past.[60]
Nevertheless, as part of this journey, new worlds of the future refract the
imperial centre. The convict's new-found ability to purchase silk and self-
fashion as a dandy marks his escape from impoverishment, filling his stomach
and his 'flesh-bag' – the evocative flash word for shirt.

'A total smash': scandalous celebrity and Regency modernity

A sensational case study of criminal celebrity and upward convict social
mobility is offered by the genteel criminal Thomas Griffiths Wainewright
(1794–1847), an English artist, suspected poisoner, and convicted forger,
who in 1837 was transported to Van Diemen's Land, where he was eventually granted a ticket of leave in 1845 and became a noted society portrait
painter. His trial papers described him as a 'gentlemanly man', 'wearing
moustaches'.[61] In a self-portrait entitled 'Head of a Convict', Wainewright
openly models the figure of the convict dandy, with his 'jacket turned up in
a slightly Byronic fashion'.[62]

In her fine study of colonial Australian portrait drawings, Joanna Gilmour refers to Wainewright as 'the best trained, best connected and most
accomplished' of 'Australia's convict artists'.[63] In his 1844 petition for a
ticket of leave, Wainewright 'submits, with great diffidence … A Descent,
deduc'd thro Family Tradition & Edmonstone's Heraldry, from a stock not
the least honoured in Cambria – Nurtured with all appliances of ease and
comfort'. His 'modest competence' in 'pen & brush' had brought him 'to the
notice & friendship of men whose fame is European'.[64] Indeed, his grandfather Ralph Griffiths founded the *Monthly Review*, and Wainewright himself
wrote for the *London Magazine*, producing art reviews under the pseudonym
Janus Weathercock, in the character of a leisured dandified connoisseur. He
claimed to have enjoyed the friendship of Charles Lamb and the acquaintance
of William Hazlitt and Thomas Carlyle. Trained by the fashionable London
portrait painter Thomas Phillips, who painted Byron in his Albanian dress,
Wainewright was apprenticed to Phillips' studio, where he made a copy of
Phillips' iconic 'cloak' portrait of Byron, *Portrait of a Nobleman* (1814).

Wainewright's petition makes much of the colony's bad language: 'Take pity, Your Excellency! and grant me the power to shelter ... my ears from a jargon of filth & blasphemy that would outrage the cynism [sic] of Parny himself.' The reference is to Éveriste de Parny, author of *Les Poésies érotiques* (1778), which was banned by the French government in 1827.[65] Granted his ticket of leave in 1845, Wainewright established himself as a portrait painter and was commissioned by a number of prominent families in Van Diemen's Land. As Gilmour notes, he associated with settler colonials, 'middling public servants or those of less-elevated social origins ... more anxious to present themselves as gentrified'.[66] Through his portraits, which he signed TGW, Wainewright documented and collaborated in this process of colonial making and remaking.

One of his clients was Major Robert Power, Lady Blessington's brother, who had arrived in 1840 and became Surveyor General of Van Diemen's Land. Power commissioned a portrait of his daughter, Margaret, who shared her aunt's maiden name. By February 1847, this portrait had found its way to London, where Lady Blessington showed it to her guests at Gore House (apparently including Charles Dickens, who was fascinated by Wainewright and later based a story on him, *Hunted Down*).[67] Gore House was Blessington's last London home before she was forced to flee to escape her creditors after the Irish potato disease ate up her remaining jointure; she and D'Orsay went into exile in France, where they lived until their deaths.

Wainewright's portrait of Blessington's niece in Blessington's home embodies the interpenetration of the liminal yet transformative Regency cultures of scandalous celebrity, exile, colonial settlerdom, and convictism. It may have been one of the portraits sold in 1849 in the break-up of Gore House (the Royal Albert Hall now occupies the site). As her contemporary biographer wrote: 'here was a total smash, a crash on a grand scale of ruin, a compulsory sale in the house of a noble lady, a sweeping clearance of all its treasures'.[68] In *The Idler in France*, Blessington herself romanced the auction as a genre of ruins. Doing the rounds of the curiosity shops on the Quai D'Orsay, she purchased an amber vase said to have belonged to the Empress Josephine: 'When I see beautiful objects collected together in these shops, I often think of their probable histories, and of those to whom they belonged ... the *gages d'amour* are scattered all around. But the givers and receivers, where are they? Mouldering in the grave, long years ago.'[69] The same fate awaited her own possessions: 'the rare and beautiful *bijouterie* which I have collected with such pains, and looked on with such pleasure, will probably be scattered abroad, and find their resting place not in gilded salons, but in the dingy coffers of the wily *brocanteur*'.[70]

In this chapter, I have sought to highlight the transformative elements of colonial lag in the work of scattering abroad. Like the shadow art of the silhouette medium – proleptic of the new media of photography, cinema, and screen projection, but nostalgic and retrospective – this eerie gentleman of the shade, Wainewright, models simultaneously a 'real time' Regency dandyism that conjures its own belated forms and a newly transformed dandy that transports the shadowy pasts and arriviste careers of scandalous success into a new arena of global modernity, hosting a complex traffic between metropolis and colony, respectability and unrespectability, fame and notoriety, settler colonialism and convictism.

The story of new Regency masculine social identities – European rentier expatriates, respectable men, swells, flash men, wild colonial men, gentlemen of the shade, convicts broken or remade anew through tickets of leave, and their Indigenous guides and brokers, who then became their own self-made colonial men – is not a simple story of supersession; it is one of intermediation and interpenetration. In this sense, rather than being the Regency's distant other – at the far remove of an irreversible lag – Botany Bay, Newcastle, and Van Diemen's Land can be seen as realising the Regency as a model of global modernity. If the transported flash language, like the lag fever it indexes, figures the belatedness of the colonial world, it does so with a twist: registering an energy and dynamism of the colonial peripheries, as a charged capacity for influencing, transforming, and outrunning Britain's imperial metropolitan centre, and possibly even providing the refracting lenses – barnacles, or queer screens – through which to see it more clearly.

Acknowledgements

The research and writing of this chapter were supported by the Australian Research Council. I also thank Jenny Lee, Caitlyn Lehmann, Gillian Russell, and the editors of this volume, Sarah Comyn and Porscha Fermanis.

Notes

1 Quoted in Terence Allan Hoagwood and Kathryn Ledbetter, *'Colour'd Shadows'*: *Contexts in Publishing, Printing, and Reading Nineteenth-Century British Women Writers* (Basingstoke: Palgrave Macmillan, 2005), p. 54.

2 Mrs Carlyle, quoted in Michael Sadleir, *Blessington-D'Orsay: A Masquerade* (London: Constable, 1947) p. 280; Mrs Newton Crosland, quoted in Sadleir, *Blessington-D'Orsay*, p. 268; Mrs Carlyle, quoted in Sadleir, *Blessington-D'Orsay*, p. 279; Gronow, quoted in Sadleir, *Blessington-D'Orsay*, p. 278.

3 Lord Byron, *Byron's Letters and Journals,* ed. Leslie Marchand, 12 vols (London: John Murray, 1980), 10:136–7.

4 For details of the Byron drawings traditionally attributed to D'Orsay, see Annette Peach, *Portraits of Byron* (London: The Walpole Society, 2000), pp. 117–20.

5 Christopher Breward, *Fashioning London: Clothing and the Modern Metropolis* (Oxford: Berg, 2004), p. 28.

6 Jessica R. Feldman, *Gender on the Divide: The Dandy in Modernist Literature* (Ithaca: Cornell University Press, 1993), p. 2.

7 Gregory Dart observes that the 'thick verbal texture' of the flash language created 'a kind of classless language, a polyglot vocabulary that was not tied down to any particular social milieu'. 'Flash Style: Pierce Egan and the Literary Culture of the 1820s', *History Workshop Journal*, 51 (2001), 191.

8 Peter Cunningham, *Two Years in New South Wales*, ed. David S. Macmillan (1827; Sydney: Angus & Robertson, 1966), p. 209.

9 Francis Grose, *Classical Dictionary of the Vulgar Tongue* (London, 1811), n.p.; James Hardy Vaux, *A New and Comprehensive Vocabulary of the Flash Language* (London: Printed by W. Clowes, 1819), p. 185.

10 Grose, *Classical Dictionary* (1811), n.p. Grose also lists 'Bay Fever' as an illness shammed to avoid being sent to Botany Bay.

11 Vaux, *Vocabulary*, p. 185.

12 Julie Coleman, *A History of Cant and Slang Dictionaries: Volume 2: 1785–1858* (Oxford: Oxford University Press, 2004), p. 139.

13 Vaux, *Vocabulary*, p. 155.

14 See Vaux, *Vocabulary*, p. 165, and Grose, *Classical Dictionary* (1811), n.p., given as an Irish term.

15 Francis Grose, *A Classical Dictionary of the Vulgar Tongue* (London: Printed for S. Hooper, 1785), n.p.

16 See Grose's reference to 'those late fashionable words, a Bore and a Twaddle, among the great vulgar, Maccaroni and the Barber, among the small'; *Classical Dictionary* (1811), p. ii.

17 All in-text references are to Lord Byron, *Don Juan, The Complete Poetical Works*, ed. Jerome J. McGann (Oxford University Press, 1986).

18 Grose, *Classical Dictionary* (1785), pp. iii, viii.

19 The 1785 edition of Grose's *Classical Dictionary* has an entry for 'MOON MEN', defined as 'gypsies'.

20 William Noah, quoted in Grace Karskens, *The Colony: A History of Early Sydney* (Sydney: Allen & Unwin, 2009), p. 17.

21 Grose, biographical note at http://adb.anu.edu.au/biography/grose-francis-2130 (accessed 12 February 2020). See also Karskens, *The Colony*, pp. 87, 90, 118–21, 138.

22 Vaux, *Vocabulary*, pp. 174, 191, 205, 200–1, 241.

23 See Kay Daniels, 'Feminism and Social History', *Australian Feminist Studies*, 1 (1985), 9.

24 Pierce Egan, *Life in London* (1821; Cambridge: Cambridge University Press, 2011), p. 42.

25 *Memoirs of James Hardy Vaux. Written by himself. In two volumes* (London: Printed by W. Clowes, 1819), pp. 15–16.

26 'Memoirs of James Hardy Vaux', *London Literary Magazine*, 19 (September 1827), 55.

27 Vaux, *Memoirs*, p. 152.

28 Marilyn Butler, *Mapping Mythologies: Counter-Currents in Eighteenth-Century British Poetry and Cultural History* (Cambridge: Cambridge University Press, 2015), p. 135.

29 W. T. Moncrieff, *Tom and Jerry* (1821). Moncrieff also wrote a burletta called *The Dandy Family and the Ascot Jockies* (1818). See advertisement, *Morning Post* (15 June 1818), n.p.

30 John Camden Hotten, *Dictionary of Modern Slang, Cant, and Vulgar Words* (London: John Camden Hotten, 1859), p. 50.

31 In his seminal analysis, Frantz Fanon critiques the status of the postcolonial black man as always 'too late': *Black Skin, White Masks* (1952; London: Pluto Press, 1986), pp. 1, 91, 92.

32 *Byron's Letters and Journals*, 9:215.

33 On Barrington's fame, see Nathan Garvey, *The Celebrated George Barrington: A Spurious Author, the Book Trade, and Botany Bay* (Potts Point: Hordern House, 2008).

34 W. T. Moncrieff, *Van Diemen's Land: An Operatic Drama in Three Acts* (London: John Cumberland, n.d. [1831]), p. 22.

35 Vaux, *Memoirs*, p. 174.

36 Egan, *Life in London*, p. 8.

37 Byron's 'Botany Bay in moral geography' seems to refer to *A New Moral System of Geography, Containing an Account of the Different Nations Ancient and Modern* (Bath: Printed for G. Riley, 1790), which features an outline of Botany Bay for children (pp. 181–7). The Hordern House website refers to it as 'the first educational work to refer to settled Australia', www.hordern.com/pages/books/3506031/new-moral-system/a-new-moral-system-of-geography-containing-an-account-of-the-different-nations-ancient-and-modern (accessed 14 April 2020).

38 Noel McLachlan notes that there is 'virtually no trace left of the original edition bearing Murray's name': *The Memoirs of James Hardy Vaux* (London: Heinemann, 1964), p. xxi. As the *Australian Dictionary of National Biography* entry on Vaux notes, Barron Field 'arranged for its publication in London by John Murray, along with the slang dictionary, but Murray's imprint does not appear on most extant copies'.

39 ANL Rex Nan Kivell Collection, PIC T2306 NK5991/2 LOC NL Shel. The sketchbook has been digitised and is catalogued as though a printed item; but the images appear to be a series of original pen and ink copies of the lithograph etchings from *Fraser's*, all initialled WRG on the bottom right-hand side.

40 According to the 1859 *Dictionary of Modern Slang*, 'Cant is old; Slang is always modern and changing. To illustrate the difference: a thief in *Cant* language would term a horse a PRANCER or a PRAD, — while in *slang*, a man of fashion would speak of it as a BIT OF BLOOD, or a SPANKER.'

41 Thomas Mitchell, 'Report of Surveyor General', ML, A2146, 1832, NSW State Archives and Records.

42 *Sydney Mail and New South Wales Advertiser* (11 March 1871), p. 40; (18 March 1871), p. 87; (11 March 1871), p. 40.

43 William Romaine Govett, notebook and sketchbook, http://acms.sl.nsw.gov.au/_transcript/2012/D14753/a5504.html (accessed 7 March 2020).

44 Mitchell quoted in John Gould, *Handbook to the Birds of Australia*, vol. 2 (London: John Gould, 1865), p. 6.

45 See Paul Carter, *The Road to Botany Bay* (London: Faber, 1987), p. 118. See also Christine Wright, *Wellington's Men in Australia: Peninsular War Veterans and the Making of Empire c. 1820–40* (Basingstoke: Palgrave Macmillan, 2011).

46 William Fernyhough, *Album of Portraits, Mainly of New South Wales Officials* (1836).

47 William Fernyhough, *A Series of Twelve Portraits of Aborigines of New South Wales* (Sydney: J. G. Austin, 1836).

48 David Hansen, '"Another Man's Understanding": Settler Images of Aboriginal People', in Cathy Leahy and Judith Ryan (eds), *Colony: Australia 1770–1861 / Frontier Wars* (Melbourne: National Gallery of Victoria, 2018), pp. 108–19.

49 On Piper's clothes as 'cast off', see Elisabeth Findlay, 'Peddling Prejudice: A Series of Twelve Profile Portraits', *Postcolonial Studies*, 16:1 (2013), 2–27.

50 Hansen, '"Another Man's Understanding"', p. 319 n.23.

51 Thomas Mitchell, *Three Expeditions into the Interior of Eastern Australia, Second edition, Carefully Revised*, 2 vols (London: T. & W. Boone, 1839), 2:1104.

52 See Grace Karskens, 'Red Coat, Blue Jacket, Black Skin: Aboriginal Men and Clothing in Early New South Wales', *Aboriginal History*, 35 (2011), 1–36.

53 In the same series by Fernyhough, Bungaree is referred to explicitly as 'King', appearing with a 'King Bungaree' breastplate around his neck.

54 Mitchell, *Three Expeditions*, 2:338.

55 Linda Colley, *Britons: Forging the Nation 1707–1837* (New Haven: Yale University Press, 1992), p. 19.

56 Margaret Maynard, *Fashioned from Penury: Dress as Cultural Practice in Colonial Australia* (Cambridge: Cambridge University Press, 1994), p. 9.

57 Maynard, *Fashioned from Penury*, p. 18; Jane Elliott, 'Was There a Convict Dandy? Convict Consumer Interests in Sydney, 1788–1815', *Australian Historical Studies*, 26 (1994), 373–92.

58 Elliott, 'Was There a Convict Dandy?', 385.

59 Elliott, 'Was There a Convict Dandy?', 387.

60 Arjun Appadurai, 'Disjuncture and Difference in the Global Cultural Economy', in Bruce Robbins (ed.), *The Phantom Public Sphere* (Minneapolis: University of Minnesota Press, 1993), p. 269.

61 Quoted in Andrew Motion, *Wainewright the Poisoner* (New York: Alfred A. Knopf, 2000), p. 182.

62 Annette Peach, 'Wainewright, Thomas Griffiths [pseuds. Janus Weathercock, Cornelius van Vinkbooms]', n.p., https://doi.org/10.1093/ref:odnb/28403 (accessed 7 March 2020).

63 Joanna Gilmour, *Elegance in Exile: Portrait Drawings from Colonial Australia* (Canberra: National Portrait Gallery, 2012), p. 153.

64 Thomas Griffiths Wainewright, petition for ticket of leave to Governor Wilmot, 16 May 1844, State Library of NSW Aw 15, p. 2.

65 Wainewright, petition for ticket of leave, p. 3.

66 Gilmour, *Elegance in Exile*, p. 156.

67 See Jonathan Curling, *Janus Weathercock: The Life of Thomas Griffiths Waine-wright* (London: Nelson, 1938).

68 R. R. Madden, *The Literary Life and Correspondence of the Countess of Blessington*, 3 vols (London: T. C. Newby, 1855), vol. 1, pp. 203, 205.

69 Madden quoting the Countess of Blessington, *The Idler in France*, 2nd edn, 2 vols (London: Henry Colburn, 1842), vol. 2, pp. 202–3.

70 *The Idler in France*, pp. 59, 57 for '*gages d'amour*'.

4

Spatial synchronicities: settler emigration, the voyage out, and shipboard literary production

Fariha Shaikh

This chapter explores the spatialising methodologies of shipboard periodicals produced on three ships as they voyaged between Britain and Australia across the oceanic expanses of the southern hemisphere in the mid-nineteenth century: the *Sobraon*, the *Somersetshire*, and the *True Briton*. By the 1860s, newspapers produced on board the ship by passengers between Britain and the Antipodes were a regular affair: fair copies of newspapers were produced by hand and distributed around the ship, or, if the ship carried a printing press, newspapers were produced at sea. A critical body of work within the fields of settler colonial studies and the blue humanities has slowly begun to develop around this genre, with attention being drawn to the pivotal role that they played in shaping settler colonial aspirations and the broader contours of maritime literary culture.[1] Shipboard periodicals are an ephemeral and marginal genre, in that they were an almost ubiquitous presence on voyages and held an important function and value at the time of their production, but are often characterised as being without 'enduring literary value'.[2] In contradistinction to this view, this chapter embeds maritime literary culture and the production of shipboard periodicals firmly within some of the key ideological frameworks of settler colonial discourse. It argues that if the production of shipboard periodicals produced sociability at sea, then this sociability was also embedded in settler discourses of race and power.

Bringing the blue humanities into conversation with settler colonial studies through the lens of shipboard periodicals allows us to interrogate the ways in which the seemingly ephemeral genre of shipboard periodicals participated in creating 'the persistent legacies of settler colonialism in the Global South'.[3] In 'The Ship, The Media, and the World', Roland Wenzlhuemer argues that '[w]hen people, things, or ideas move, [they] create a connection – sometimes fragile, sometimes more stable – between their origin(s) and their destination'.[4] Thinking of the ship not only as a floating piece of 'home' but also as a piece of travelling communication which carries with it a certain set of people and ideologies allows us to interrogate more fully the colonising work that it does and disperses. The ship journey, as David Armitage, Alison Bashford, and Sujit Sivasundaram astutely argue, is not just an 'experiment in habitation': when 'it transfers materials, ideas, nature and people across locales', it also raises questions of how 'to create, distil or transform cultural norms', and 'how to proclaim and dramatize from a culture from the deck and "across the beach" to a newfoundland'.[5] Shipboard periodicals are a distinct example of this 'transfer' of a 'cultural norm': produced quite literally on the move, they are shaped by the spatial, temporal, and material limitations of the voyage. As they move across the globe, they disseminate not only news of what happens on a particular voyage, but also the cultural form of the periodical.[6]

As Jude Piesse has argued, land-based periodicals in this period are marked by a mobile subjectivity: they circulate widely throughout the British Empire, and within a settler colonial context they 'not only reflected mobility, but were actively involved in *producing* it'.[7] Shipboard periodicals might be said to go one step further: not only do they reflect and actively produce mobility, they are also produced out of the conditions of being mobile. Written or printed on board the ship, many shipboard periodicals, including the ones discussed in this chapter, were reprinted and circulated after the voyage as souvenirs, or to encourage chain migration. The editors of the *Dover Castle*, for example, write that while they are 'aware' that the newspaper 'will prove of but little interest to our fellow passengers' as they are all 'so well acquainted with it', they hope that it will be 'looked upon in quite a contrary light' by 'those who have never travelled round the world'.[8] Ships travelling on return journeys to England often carried with them emigrants going back home to see their family and friends, who were able to contribute pieces offering advice on how and where to settle. As well as acting as a 'record' of 'anything of interest occurring during the voyage' so that 'the ways and doings of so illustrious a community may not be lost to posterity',[9] the shipboard periodical also functions as an emigrant guidebook. 'There are many on board who have had long and varied experiences of colonial life, habits and customs', writes the *Somersetshire Gazette*, and it is hoped that their contributions outlining their 'former trials' and 'difficulties overcome' may be 'a means of forewarning, and therefore forearming novices'.[10]

In *Imperial Boredom* (2018), Jeffrey Auerbach writes that 'as ships grew in size and safety, navigation improved, and the routes to India and Australia became more frequently traversed during the first half of the nineteenth century, ocean travel became normalized'.[11] As one writer for the *Eclectic Review* commented in 1865, whereas travelling around the world 'fifty years ago would have made our fortune', 'everybody travels now, everyone sees everything and goes everywhere'.[12] Tracing a change across the centuries in how voyages were experienced, Auerbach concludes that '[i]f a seventeenth-century voyage to the East was a perilous journey into the unknown, by the mid-nineteenth century it had become a cheerless interlude'.[13] Comments on the monotony of the voyage are rife in passenger diaries and in shipboard newspapers. One disgruntled emigrant, Alexander Mackay, commented that: 'Happy is he who, under such circumstances, has a resource against ennui in his own reflections.'[14] While boredom and monotony can be traced across the imperial archive, appearing as it does in countless diaries, letters, and journals, shipboard newspapers demonstrate that this boredom can also be a site of literary productivity. The *Sobraon Occasional*, for example, announces that it 'wishes to encourage the fine arts of sea-life – arts of killing time, of grumbling, of chaffing'.[15]

As this chapter shows, the ship and its journey is a site of more complicated emotions and connections than just those of bringing people from one point to another across empire. Ships and the periodicals that were produced to and from the southern hemisphere are shaped by overlapping geographies of imperial desire: 'home' is a confused and ambiguous space in these periodicals, and, as they track the voyage across the waters on their pages, the journey becomes a space of both imagined and real connections. In demonstrating how shipboard periodicals 'figuratively map the real-and-imagined spaces of their worlds, both within the text and with reference to a space outside of the text', this chapter will show how colonial anxieties and aspirations shaped the spatial logic of shipboard periodicals.[16] In particular, it draws upon specific examples of travelogues, tales, and shipboard theatre to show that while representations of space within each of these genres is marked by an 'anticipatory' moment, it is an anticipation not so much of a sense of 'home' as it is for a sense of what forms encounters with Indigenous peoples will take.

Ships on the emigrant run

The *Sobraon*, the *Somersetshire*, and the *True Briton* were regulars on the Australia run, but of the three, only the *Sobraon* was purpose-built as an emigrant ship. It served the Australia run for twenty-five years, between 1866 and 1891. Designed to carry only ninety first-class passengers and forty second-class passengers, and built to complete the journey in as little as seventy-five days, the *Sobraon* signalled to all prospective travellers that she served a particular clientele. This chapter examines shipboard periodicals from three of the voyages made by the *Sobraon*: *Our Voyage: Extracts from the Sobraon Gossip* (1875), the *Sobraon Occasional* (1875), and the

Sobraon Mercury (1877). While *Our Voyage* was produced as a manuscript periodical on board the ship en route from Melbourne to London, the copy that exists today is a miscellany of the original issues that was reprinted in London.[17] The *Occasional* was printed on board the ship from London to Melbourne, and the *Mercury* was printed on board the ship from Melbourne to London. Of all three of the ships discussed here, the *Sobraon* was the one that enjoyed the most continuity between voyages: for twenty-four years, from 1867 until 1891, the ship sailed under Captain James Elmslie, whose reputation for generosity and conviviality was an attractive draw for many travellers.[18] He was fondly remembered as a 'genial commander' and for the 'great care he always took in looking after the comfort of his passengers',[19] while *Our Voyage* includes a note of 'gratitude' to Elmslie at the end of the voyage for 'his generous and considerate kindness on several occasions'.[20]

Unlike the *Sobraon*, which was built as a luxury emigrant ship, the *Somersetshire*'s maiden voyage carried convicts to Hobart Town as early as 1814 and then again in the 1840s. However, from the 1860s onwards, the ship started making regular voyages between London and Melbourne.[21] This chapter examines the *Somersetshire Argus* (1868), the *Somersetshire Sea Pie* (1870), and the *Somersetshire Gazette* (1872). Both the *Argus* and the *Sea Pie* were produced on the journey coming back to London, where they were printed, and the *Gazette* was written on the outward journey and printed at Melbourne.[22]

Of the three ships, the least amount of information is available on the *True Briton*. The two newspapers that were produced on board the ship are the manuscript shipboard periodical *Open Sea* (1868), which was made during the journey to Melbourne, and *True Briton Observer* (1870), which was printed when it arrived in Melbourne from Plymouth.[23]

At first glance, this brief overview of the ships, their periodicals, and their routes suggests a focus on only two strands in a rich interconnected network of travel and trade across the southern hemisphere that is already in place by, but consolidates itself during, the nineteenth century: that between Plymouth or London and Melbourne. I would argue, however, that this shows that settler colonial migration did not simply produce a mono-directional flow from Britain to the Antipodes: it also set into play a multitude of other journeys which criss-crossed the oceans in the southern hemisphere. Some of these were return journeys for emigrants who were either going back to visit their friends and family in England or were leaving the colonies. Even journeys to the Antipodes contained not just first-time emigrants but settlers, too. The *Sobraon Occasional* remarks that among its passengers are:

> Australians returning with their families from pleasure or business trips to
> Europe; young folks from the old country going out to the colonies either as

visitors or settlers; pale invalids seeking in the healthy sea breeze, and under the clear skies of Australia, the health and spirits they had lost by over-work or exposure to our own fickle climate.[24]

Another periodical points to the plurality of nationalities on board the ship: 'Of course "Britishers" were in the majority; but besides them were Greeks, Americans, Nova Scotians, Poles, Italians, Germans, and a few Asiatics; almost all languages and sects, mingling in sweet disharmony.'[25] We might reconsider, then, the notion of a singular 'voyage out': on the same voyage, for some, the outward route to Australia was a familiar return to home, while for others it was leaving home behind.

This entanglement of connections is further exemplified when we take into account the materiality of the ships themselves. As Nilanjana Deb argues, ships are more than the sum total of the journeys they take: attending to the materials of which they are comprised, the cargo that they carry, and the labour required to make them and that they transport are often just as important in untangling the colonial connections they embody.[26] Despite their 'centrality' to '"global" history', 'ships as arenas in their own right have often remained beyond the global historian's gaze'.[27] In the nineteenth-century cultural imagination, however, they were an embodiment of an 'imperial maritime rhetoric' which symbolised power, where the ship's 'alleged capacity to overawe and intimidate indigenous coastal peoples was very much part of that rhetoric'.[28] The three ships under discussion here are also the product of various kinds of colonial connections. Despite being purpose-built for the Australia run as a luxury emigrant ship, for example, the *Sobraon* takes its name from the first Sikh-Anglo war, specifically the Battle of Sobraon (1846), in which the East India Company defeated the Sikh Khalsa Army. The *True Briton* was a Blackwall frigate, a type of trading sail ship built at Blackwall for the purposes of trading with India following the collapse of the East India Company's charter in 1833, when the market for trade in India opened up. Many frigates were built from and carried teak from Mawlamyine in Burma, as well as carrying cargo from country to country through the southern hemisphere. After the Suez Canal opened, in 1869, which made it easier for other ships to travel to and from India, Blackwall frigates were used in the wool trade between Britain and Australia. Both the *Somersetshire* and *True Briton* were made by the shipbuilders Money Wigram & Sons, a firm with key colonial interests in shipbuilding for trade with Australia. Focusing on the ships themselves as objects which are materially implicated in the processes of colonialism, rather than mere carriers of people across the oceans, brings to the surface the ways in which the dyadic relationship between metropole and colony is inflected – and even structured by – lateral south–south connections.

Shipboard periodicals and maritime literary culture

Examining shipboard periodicals that were produced on different voyages made by the same ship highlights that, as a genre, shipboard periodicals are not discrete entities. Although each run was limited by the duration of the voyage, the travellers often signalled that they were aware that the practice of producing shipboard periodicals was a commonplace one. For example, the *Somersetshire Gazette* writes that now that the 'good ship' has 'once more started on her long voyage from the shores of merrie England to the Antipodes', the passengers who by now 'have so far recovered from the effects of a closer acquaintance with old Neptune's domain than they have been accustomed to' might 'wish at least to emulate their predecessors, and keep up good old customs':

> On the last outward-bound passage of this vessel a paper was started, and published regularly every seventh day ... We, the editors of the Somersetshire Gazette ... shall endeavour to follow the example of prior journalists, and ... hope to prove that the present numerous and mixed assemblage are in nowise behind their predecessors.[29]

The passengers on the *Somersetshire* were clearly aware that they were travelling on a ship on which former travellers had produced periodicals before – the *Somersetshire Sea Pie* and the *Somersetshire Argus* – and were keen to continue this sea-based tradition. While the periodicals produced on the *Sobraon* do not make such an overt acknowledgement of previous periodicals, there are close parallels between them. For example, the collected editions of the *Sobraon Mercury* and *Sobraon Occasional* both start with a 'List of Officers, Crew, and Passengers', and each individual issue of both periodicals contains an update on 'Notes on the Voyage'. *Our Voyage* also starts with a note on the ship, containing information such as the ship's dimensions, which shipping company built it, and what type of ship it is. Such close similarity in formal composition suggests that passengers on each voyage were aware that they were continuing a tradition started on previous voyages. The 'imagined community' thus stretches across maritime space and time to connect each voyage, such that the ship becomes a vessel that transports people *and* has an identity of its own.

In addition to referencing the periodicals made on the *Somersetshire*'s previous voyages, the *Somersetshire Gazette*'s nod to 'prior journalists' could also refer to the wider culture of producing shipboard periodicals. Indeed, it is not the only periodical to acknowledge this wider culture. The *Dover Castle*, for example, argues that its passengers 'will not look upon our attempt at the establishment of a weekly paper as one without precedent, but will remember the success nearly always attending such a step', and points to the example of SS *Great Britain* where 'lately, a printing press was kept and a very neat and useful paper issued weekly', which was 'liberally distributed at a nominal charge to all her passengers' upon the 'termination of the voyage'.[30] Thus, passengers on the voyage between Britain and Australia were well aware that they were participating in a wider maritime culture when they produced their periodicals. In both the *Dover Castle* and the *Somersetshire Gazette*, there is a clear sense of pleasure that they are following a specifically *maritime* literary tradition. However, as Philip Steinberg argues, 'ocean-space typically is represented as a "special" space that lacks the paradigmatic attributes of "regular" space'; in particular, the ocean is constructed as 'empty' space.[31] Steinberg's argument helps frame the genre of shipboard periodicals in two important ways: first, it helps us to understand the ways in which cultural production continues to happen at sea (and in this sense, the sea is 'regular' space); second, it allows us to understand the complexity of the ways in which shipboard periodicals imagined themselves as part of maritime culture: one that is not just produced 'out there' on the 'empty spaces' of the ocean, but is part of more complicated circuits of exchange.

As mentioned previously, shipboard periodicals self-consciously drew upon a familiar vocabulary of home, villages, and towns to describe the space of the ship; fair copies were often printed at the port of arrival as souvenirs of the voyage. A skit entitled 'Newspaper Boys' from the *True Briton* engages in a virtual conversation with land-based periodicals:

> Do you know why the Newspaper Boy is the happiest of mortals? No! Then I will tell you! He can always get the 'Latest News' from all the papers, and by means of the 'Telegraph' he can 'Despatch' the 'Daily News' to his friends ... he can shelter himself under 'Temple Bar,' but generally prefers the neighbourhood of 'Belgravia' to that of 'Cornhill.' He always goes with the 'Times,' and enlists under any 'Standard' that promises him the greatest advantage ... he takes in 'Punch' 'Once a Week,' and is happy 'All the Year Round'.[32]

In addition to drawing on a land-based spatial imagination, excerpts from shipboard periodicals also circulated in land-based periodicals, such as in the *Eclectic Review* and *Chambers's Journal*. In 1867, for example, an article appeared in the *Eclectic Review*, bringing to the attention of its 'land-loving readers' the 'establishment of a weekly newspaper' as 'one of the new phases of ship-board life in large ocean steamers'.[33] The *Somersetshire Sea Pie* writes that '[s]hip newspapers have now become such a recognised institution, that ... it is unnecessary to do more on this occasion than simply to announce the fact of the publication of the present one'.[34] In the same year, an article in *Chambers's Journal* wrote that while many of its 'stay-at-home' readers may not have heard of them, in actual fact, 'in not a few of our large, long-voyaging clipper-ships, it is customary ... to publish a weekly newspaper'.[35]

In drawing out the popularity of shipboard newspapers for its land-based readers, the *Eclectic Review* and *Chambers's Journal* both suggest a dichotomy between the literature produced and read at sea and that produced and read on land. Yet the practice of producing shipboard periodicals did not just happen in the supposedly contained spaces of the oceans and seas. The production and circulation of shipboard newspapers dismantled, rather than upheld, a dichotomy between land- and sea-based reading practices. This raises the question of how literature that is produced at sea is embedded in the histories of racial and gender inequalities engendered by settler colonialism. How might we read shipboard periodicals not as a document of a journey but, like the ships on which they were produced, as deeply implicated in colonial structures of dispossession?

Racial encounters in shipboard periodicals

Much attention has been paid to the role that poetry has played in settler colonial formations of 'home'. Jason Rudy argues that one of the reasons for the spread of poetry through the colonies is that 'poems adapted more quickly to colonial spaces, allowing for more local forms of expression', and that they could 'circulate with ease through Britain's colonies, spaces that at first were not equipped to publish longer works'.[36] As Rudy rightly argues, shipboard poetry produced on the voyage out was 'anticipatory': it looked forward to 'home' in the colonies.[37] Poetry, however, was not the only genre that circulated in these periodicals: it shared the pages of the shipboard periodical with plays, short fiction, and descriptive accounts of the places through which the ship was moving.[38] These cultural outputs were more than a means of just relieving 'imperial boredom': shipboard theatre, as Aaron Jaffer has noted in another context, often played a pivotal and 'symbolic' role in articulating political sensibilities and national identities, and the same can be said of the short fiction and travel writing that appeared in shipboard periodicals.[39]

As the ship travelled through the waters, each weekly instalment of many, if not all, of its periodicals offered a daily record of latitude and longitude to allow interested passengers to keep track of the ship's journey. Narrative description, where the journey allowed something of interest, was another way in which the passengers engaged with the spaces through which they travelled. One particularly noteworthy account is in the *Sobraon Mercury*, when the ship stopped at St Helena:

> Early accounts of the island all describe it as being covered with vegetation, as having in many places dense forests of ebony and other trees. It is generally believed that the destruction of these forests was chiefly caused by goats, which

were introduced by the first Portuguese settlers in 1513. This is much regretted by botanists, for the indigenous flora of the island was one of the most singular in the whole world. Since the island has been denuded of its forests the soil which must have covered the rocks has been blown and washed away, for now most of the hills are quite bare.[40]

Here, the description of the present land as being 'denuded', 'washed away', and 'bare' is contrasted with an earlier, precolonial moment when the island was 'covered with vegetation' and 'dense forests of ebony and other trees'. A sense of loss that Indigenous plants have been wiped out is indicated through the botanists' 'regret', but rather than also seeing the act of the *Sobraon* stopping over at St Helena as part of colonisation *in the present moment*, the passage pushes the moment of colonisation back to the sixteenth century and the 'early accounts' of the Portuguese.[41] Furthermore, there is no recognition of the fact that British colonisation of Australia, to where their ship was heading, was having precisely the same effects on the Indigenous people and environment. The passengers of the *Sobraon Mercury* recognise the loss that settler colonialism entails, but they fail to recognise themselves as the cause of that loss.

As a short story called 'A Night of Terror' in the *Sobraon Occasional* shows, the encounter between settlers and Indigenous peoples was often imagined as violent.[42] The story follows Alice, a girl in 'one of the country districts of Tasmania', and her younger brother, Abel, who live with their father in an 'uncouth dwelling, built of wooden slabs with a shingle roof'. At the start of the story, Alice and Abel are sat 'in the rude verandah in front of their house': the roughness of their house indicates both the poverty of the small family but also the relative newness of the settlement. A sense of foreboding lies over both of them – they are the only two alone in the settlement, with their father having 'gone away' and 'Morris and his wife' the 'only people but ourselves on the place to-night'. Alice asks uneasily what advice their neighbour M'Coy had given 'about blacks when he came over on Monday?'. Abel is 'not quite sure' but remembers that it is '[s]omething about "mischief and black devils, that was all"'. Alice moves through her chores as night sets, but she cannot rid herself of the 'vague foreboding of impending danger', or 'shake off an unwonted feeling of depression and uneasiness'.

The first sign of supposed danger is 'a low prolonged howl, not a dog's moan, or the wail of the wind': 'only human beings could produce that strange peculiar note', but to Abel and Alice's ears 'there was something unearthly' about it too. The wail is followed by a 'succession of sharp hard taps on the window-pane at the back, resembling the sound of sticks or stones rattling against it'. Reminded of 'all the tales of horror one has heard of mutilation and slaughter', Alice snatched up the gun, with the powder and shot, from the mantel-piece, and bidding Abel, in low-measured tones, get the pistol from her father's room, that they might each fire alternately from the back-window, she proceeded to load, with much nerve and self-control. Parley was useless; any attempt at it would have lost them irretrievably.

Alice fires through the 'volley of spears [that] came rattling on, smashing the panes, falling into the room, and tearing the blinds to ribands'. During the 'desperate encounter', 'Alice and her brother loaded and fired in turn, amid the howls and fierce imprecations of the blacks, who had now come to close quarters'. Eventually wounded, Alice takes up Abel, who has cut his hand, and 'clasped him to her breast, determined to defend him with her last gasp': such valiance, however, is not required in the end, as a 'stranger' chases off the attack and saves them both. Ending in a moralistic tone, the narrator highlights to readers that 'it certainly behoves all pioneers to take warning by her terrible adventure, and spare their wives and daughters such experiences as cannot fail to darken their future lives'.

Unlike in the account of St Helena, here the colonial violence is foregrounded, rather than being pushed to an earlier historical moment. Domesticity is fragile and made secure not through the domestic labour of settler colonial women, but through their ability to take up arms and participate in violence against Indigenous people. Within the periodical press, the 'question of empire' was brought together with the 'woman question' to debate and frame the role that women might or should play in Britain and the colonies.[43] As the voyage out was often seen as a preparatory stage for life in the colonies, the journey was an apt space for reimagining the role that women might play in them. The gender imbalance between Australia and England meant that women were often seen as a civilising influence. Interestingly, however, while Alice 'shores up domestic norms' by protecting her home, she does so through an 'erosion of gender norms', as she represents a double inversion of stereotypical gender roles: not only does she protect her brother but she also participates in the violence that usually marked boys' adventure fiction.[44]

In the first two issues of the *Somersetshire Gazette*, a short play was published with the title *The Row, the Wreck, and the Reconciliation*.[45] The dramatis personae lists Julius Caesar Hannibal Smith who has 'just ... lost some twenty thousand pounds', his daughter Zerlina, her lover and Smith's clerk, Lorenzo Jones, and an old and rich merchant, Alonzo de Robinson, who Julius has decided to marry Zerlina off to because he is 'only sixty ... and such a swell'. The plot is fairly predictable: upon hearing that Lorenzo and Zerlina are in love, Julius orders that she shall marry Alonzo. Zerlina and Lorenzo both escape on a ship that is bound for China, a ship on which Alonzo also happens to be travelling out on for business. The ship is shipwrecked, and the company find themselves on a strange 'desert island'. Here, they are met by the 'King of the Cannibal Islands', who orders his troupe of followers to '[s]eize the barbarians' and:

> skin them carefully:
> The girl is young and tender, her we'll roast –
> The man is tougher, cut him up in bits
> And make of him a currie, hash, or stew.

His attention is diverted, however, when he catches sight of one of Zerlina's 'thirteen bonnet boxes', and his entire demeanour is transformed:

> A bonnet, as I live. How very chaste!
> I'll try it on. Let's see, which is the front?
> There! Does it suit me?

Lorenzo offers him the bonnet as a gift, and the King 'to express my sense of gratitude' promises: 'We will not eat you – that is – not to-day.' Out of nowhere, Julius appears: he has also been shipwrecked and had been cast adrift until he arrived at the island. He comes bearing good news: Lorenzo, it turns out, is in fact a 'nobleman of high degree' and, as a result, he blesses the wedding between Lorenzo and Zerlina.

The desert island they find themselves on is surrounded by '[p]alm trees, sago, canoes, yams, tomahawks, chutnee, etc'. Rather than pointing to any one specific region of the world, the island is a colonial nowhere, abstracted from any real sense of place to stand in for any colony at all. In this, the play is marked by a very different sense of place to either that in the account of St Helena or in 'A Night of Terror'. Within its colonial nowhere, women are seen to have a civilising influence. On the one hand, Zerlina is a caricature of a female figure, who has brought with her 'thirteen boxes and five trunks' and yet still considers herself to have come aboard with 'nothing' to wear. Yet it is her bonnet box that saves the day, and the play therefore emphasises the civilising influence of women in the colonies – something that settler colonial narratives frequently stressed as well.[46]

Like so many of the short stories and poems that were written for ship-board periodicals, the play relies on familiar narrative conventions for its comedy and plot. When Julius is asked at the end of the play how it can possibly be that Lorenzo is a noble gentleman, he airily replies: 'The usual thing – / A wicked uncle and a treacherous nurse, Changeling at birth, forged wills, a strawberry mark / Upon the arm, and all the rest of it.' Rather than incorporating them into a narrative flow, Julius merely lists these familiar genre markers by way of an explanation; it is the genre, rather than content, that is stressed here. Much of the comedic effect of the play derives from the breaking of the fourth wall, as characters openly exploit the limited resources on board the ship, such as when Lorenzo vows to 'do my all to make him [Alonzo] miserable; Strange substances he'll find between his sheets, / Crumbs, nutshells, boot-jacks, hair-brushes, etcetera'. Stage directions in the play, such as setting the scene 'somewhere near the main brace', and the instruction to 'revive' a fainting Zerlina with 'the contents of the inkstand' (which stands in for a bottle of smelling salts), indicate that the play was written and performed on board the ship by its passengers. When the captain announces 'we've sprung a leak / And run upon a rock', he jokingly reassures his ship, 'but what of that / There's lots of time for dinner 'ere we sink'. Lorenzo's response, similarly, is entirely at odds with the gravity of the situation: 'How very awkward, I object to this; / My feet will get so very damp.' The slapstick comedy of the play, which is produced by a continual undercutting of the audience's expectations, hides a nascent anxiety about staging a shipwreck on board a floating ship.

The account of St Helena, 'A Night of Terror', and *The Row, the Wreck, and the Reconciliation* are all examples of what Renaud Morieux has called 'vernacular … experiences of the sea': they are representations of the ways in which everyday colonisers experienced the sea and voyage.[47] This vernacular experience, however, is embedded within a colonial ideology. As Patrick Brantlinger has argued, it was only 'as white settlement expanded and met with increasing Aboriginal resistance' that the discourse of cannibalism was invoked to justify settler violence.[48] If Zerlina's feminine charm, embodied by her bonnet, is portrayed as the civilising influence in the shipboard play, 'A Night of Terror' imagines a very different role for women in the colonies, where the domestic space is protected by a woman through violence. Humour is used to contain the double threat of shipwreck and being devoured by cannibalism in the play, as it is used elsewhere to contain the threat of 'going native': the *Sobraon Mercury* notes the 'great merriment [which was] caused by the dressing up of Master G. Lindley and Miss May Elmslie in native costume'.[49]

Most studies of shipboard newspapers have focused on the ways in which their production contributed to the formation of a sense of place and a community at sea, with lines often drawn distinctly between who was included in this community and who was not.[50] Joanna de Schmidt, for example, argues that 'a ship's newspaper was simultaneously a space for social exchange and a means of establishing social boundaries at sea in an age of increasing global shipboard travel'.[51] Attending lectures, putting on plays, and reading out short stories were certainly an important part of this 'social exchange'. Yet, as these examples show, shipboard sociability was deeply implicated in reproducing settler racisms and discourses of power. The 'worlds' that are imagined in these shipboard periodicals are thus marked by considerations of the forms that racial encounters can take: the black body is variously rendered invisible, violent, and an object of mockery on the periodical's pages. Similarly, colonial spaces take a range of spatial representations, from the supposedly violent outback of Tasmania to an imaginary colonial nowhere, but all of these 'worlds' nonetheless operate within racialised discourses of power.

Shipboard periodicals and the Global South

'Water,' argues Clare Anderson, 'is not just an empty space, but *the* canvas on which history is enacted.'[52] Shipboard periodicals are an important, albeit small, part of this history: being produced at sea does not exempt them from being an integral part of the cultural outputs of settler emigration. Indeed, uncovering the porous nature of their mobility, as they move between water and shore, demonstrates the ways in which they are framed by, and transport, colonial hierarchies of race. The maritime culture that shipboard periodicals are a part of is thus not separate from land – the periodicals' content and circulation is shaped by the real and imagined spaces that they move through.

Drawing attention to the problematic ways in which different spatial imaginaries of land and sea, and of ship and colony, are synchronic with, and map on to, each other through the pages of the shipboard periodical is part of an 'intentionally complex strategy of speaking back' that characterises the methodological imperative of both 'southern theory' and criticism from the Global South.[53] 'No longer characterised solely or necessarily by geographic location',[54] the Global South is instead an 'ideological concept highlighting the economic, political and epistemic dependency and unequal relations in the global world order, from a subaltern perspective' and a 'tool aimed at problematizing the hegemonic world order'.[55] If it is a location at all, then it is a 'location where new visions of the future are emerging and where the global political and decolonial society is at work'.[56] Michelle Tusan has already written of the difficulties of 'reading British colonial periodicals against the grain', 'given the inaccessibility of source material and the difficulty of uncovering the views of indigenous peoples due to the mediating influence of print and the colonial archive'.[57] As this chapter has shown, however, reading against the grain allows us to hold shipboard periodicals to account as part of the ongoing legacy of the imperial order, rather than to see them straightforwardly as a celebration of sociability or community formation at sea. While it is true that the 'very act of critique, or more accurately what can seem like acts of repetitive critique' can 'sometimes keep European geographies and histories centre-stage', it is also true that sometimes it is precisely this 'repetitive act of critique' that is needed.[58] Such critique encourages us to look for the ways in which the ship, and the cultural forms it transports, are implicated in discourses of racialised power.

Notes

1 For an example of the former, see 'Emigrant Shipboard Newspapers: Provisional Settlement at Sea', in Fariha Shaikh, *Nineteenth-Century Settler Emigration in British Literature and Art* (Edinburgh: Edinburgh University Press, 2018), chapter 2, pp. 63–94. On the term 'blue humanities', see John R. Gillis, 'The Blue Humanities', *Humanities*, 34:3 (2013), www.neh.gov/humanities/2013/mayjune/feature/the-blue-humanities (accessed 25 January 2020).

2 Kevin Murphy and Sally O'Driscoll, *Studies in Ephemera: Text and Image in Eighteenth-Century Print* (Lewisburg: Bucknell University Press, 2013), http://ebookcentral.proquest.com/lib/bham/detail.action?docID=1117172 (accessed 25 January 2020).

3 Meg Samuelson and Charne Lavery, 'The Oceanic South', *English Language Notes*, 57:1 (2019), 37.

4 Roland Wenzlhuemer, 'The Ship, the Media, and the World: Conceptualizing Connections in Global History', *Journal of Global History*, 11:2 (2016), 164, https://doi.org/10.1017/S1740022816000048 (accessed 25 January 2020).

5 David Armitage, Alison Bashford, and Sujit Sivasundaram, 'Introduction: Writing World Oceanic Histories', in David Armitage, Alison Bashford, and Sujit Sivasundaram (eds), *Oceanic Histories* (Cambridge: Cambridge University Press, 2018), p. 9.

6 It is also worth bearing in mind that the dispersal of the periodical form into the countries of the colonial south often superseded older forms of communication. See, e.g., Sally Young, *Paper Emperors: The Rise of Australia's Newspaper Empires* (Sydney: University of New South Wales Press, 2019); Isabel Hofmeyr, *Gandhi's Printing Press: Experiments in Slow Reading* (Cambridge, MA: Harvard University Press, 2013); J. Don Vann and Rosemary VanArsdel (eds), *Periodicals of Queen Victoria's Empire: An Exploration* (Toronto: University of Toronto Press, 1996); and Chandrika Kaul, *Reporting the Raj: The British Press and India, c. 1880–1922* (Manchester: Manchester University Press, 2003).

7 Jude Piesse, *British Settler Emigration in Print, 1832–1877* (Oxford: Oxford University Press, 2016), p. 1.

8 John G. Horsey, *A Voyage from Australia to England: An Interesting Account of Incidents Occuring on Board the Blackwall Liner 'Dover Castle' Published on Board That Ship as a Weekly Newspaper under the Title of the 'Dover Castle News'* (London: Steam Press, 1867), p. 20.

9 *The Sobraon Mercury: An Occasional Journal Published at Sea during the Voyage of the Ship 'Sobraon' from Melbourne to London* (Published at Sea, 1877), p. 9.

10 *The Somersetshire Gazette: A Ship Newspaper Issued on Board the S. S. 'Somersetshire', on Her Passage from Plymouth to Melbourne* (Melbourne: Sands & McDougall, 1872), p. 1.

11 Jeffrey Auerbach, *Imperial Boredom: Monotony and the British Empire* (Oxford: Oxford University Press, 2018), p. 12.

12 'The Newspaper on Board an Ocean Steamer', *Eclectic Review* (8 January 1865), p. 40.

13 Auerbach, *Imperial Boredom*, pp. 12–13.

14 Alexander Mackay, 'An Emigrant Afloat', *Household Words* (31 August 1850), p. 537.

15 *The Sobraon Occasional: Published on Board the 'Sobraon' during Her Outward Voyage to Melbourne, from October 7th to December 26th* (1875), n.p.

16 Robert T. Tally, Jr, *The Routledge Handbook of Literature and Space* (London: Taylor & Francis, 2017), p. 3.

17 The introduction to the periodical acknowledges 'Mrs Price and Mr Powell, whose services as "printing presses" were invaluable' (p. vi).

18 After the ship stopped sailing the seas, it was used as a reformatory school in Sydney Harbour.

19 'Death of Captain Elmslie', *Evening News* (15 July 1908), p. 5; 'The Late Captain Elmslie: A Sailor's Appreciation', *Daily Telegraph* (27 August 1908), p. 4.

20 *Our Voyage: Extracts from the Sobraon Gossip: A Weekly Newspaper Published on Board the Sobraon during the Passage from Melbourne to London, Feby. 13th to June 12th, 1875* (London: Printed by T. Pettitt, 1875), p. 60. A newspaper called the *Homeward Bound* was also published in 1882 on the *Sobraon*.

21 Ian Hawkins Nicholson, *Log of Logs: A Catalogue of Logs, Journals, Shipboard Diaries, Letters, and All Forms of Voyage Narratives, 1788 to 1988, for Australia and New Zealand and Surrounding Oceans* (Nambour: The Author jointly with the Australian Association for Maritime History, 1990), p. 252.

22 Like the *Sobraon*, the *Somersetshire* attracted travellers with a literary sensibility; other newspapers such as the *Somersetshire News* (1869) and the *Somersetshire Times* (1878) were also produced on other voyages.

23 On the *Open Sea*, see Shaikh, *Nineteenth-Century Settler Emigration*, pp. 63–94.

24 *Sobraon Occasional*, p. 4.

25 'The Newspaper on Board an Ocean Steamer', p. 39.

26 Nilanjana Deb, '(Re)moving Bodies: People, Ships and Other Commodities in the Coolie Trade from Calcutta', in Supriya Chaudhuri, Josephine McDonagh, Brian Murray, and Rajeswari Sunder Rajan (eds), *Commodities and Culture in the Colonial World* (London: Routledge, 2018), pp. 115–28.

27 Martin Dusinberre and Roland Wenzlhuemer, 'Editorial – Being in Transit: Ships and Global Incompatibilities', *Journal of Global History*, 11:2 (2016), 155–6.

28 John M. Mackenzie, 'Lakes, Rivers and Oceans: Technology, Ethnicity and the Shipping of Empire in the Late Nineteenth Century', in David Killingray, Margarette Lincoln, and Nigel Rigby (eds), *Maritime Empires: British Imperial Maritime Trade in the Nineteenth Century* (Woodbridge: Boydell in association with National Maritime Museum, 2004), pp. 117–18.

29 *Somersetshire Gazette*, p. 1.

30 *Dover Castle*, p. 1.

31 Philip E. Steinberg, *The Social Construction of the Ocean* (Cambridge: Cambridge University Press, 2001), p. 34.

32 *The True Briton Observer: A Newspaper Published on Board the Ship, 'True Briton', on Her Passage from Plymouth to Melbourne, Victoria* (Melbourne: R. M. Abbott, 1871), p. 9.

33 'The Newspaper on Board an Ocean Steamer', p. 39.

34 *The 'Somersetshire' Sea Pie. A Weekly Newspaper Written on Board the S. S. Somersetshire ... 28th April to 9th July, 1870*, ed. by J. William Sewell (London: J. Tuck & Co, 1870), p. 2.

35 'The Press at Sea', *Chambers's Journal of Popular Literature, Science and Arts* (3 August 1867), p. 488.

36 Jason Rudy, *Imagined Homelands: British Poetry in the Colonies* (Baltimore: Johns Hopkins University Press, 2017), p. 7. For a discussion of poetry circulating in periodical elsewhere in the southern hemisphere, see Lara Atkin, 'The South African "Children of the Mist": The Bushman, the Highlander and the Making of Colonial Identities in Thomas Pringle's South African Poetry (1825–1834)', *The Yearbook of English Studies*, 48 (2018), 199–215. For a discussion of how the short story developed in British and Australian periodicals, see Graham Law, 'Savouring of the Australian Soil? On the Sources and Affiliations of Colonial Newspaper Fiction', *Victorian Periodicals Review*, 37:4 (2004), 75–97.

37 Rudy, *Imagined Homelands*, p. 38.

38 Indeed, the shipboard periodical was a veritable miscellany of advertisements, letters to editors, lost and found notices, and requests for paper and contributions, as well as poetry, short fiction, and plays. I have chosen to focus on travelogue, theatre, and short fiction as these have received the least attention in current scholarship on the cultural work of shipboard periodicals.

39 Aaron Jaffer, *Lascars and Indian Ocean Seafaring, 1780–1860: Shipboard Life, Unrest and Mutiny* (Woodbridge: Boydell, 2015), p. 82.

40 *Sobraon Mercury*, p. 36. The correct year of Portuguese arrival is in fact 1502.

41 Trevor Boult, *St Helena: A Maritime History* (Stroud: Amberley, 2016).

42 *Sobraon Occasional*, pp. 38–41.

43 Hilary Fraser, Stephanie Green, and Judith Johnston, *Gender and the Victorian Periodical* (Cambridge: Cambridge University Press, 2003), p. 121.

44 Janet C. Myers, *Antipodal England: Emigration and Portable Domesticity in the Victorian Imagination* (New York: State University of New York Press, 2009), pp. 45, 47.

45 *Somersetshire Gazette*, pp. 2–3, 6.

46 Myers, *Antipodal England*; Rita S. Kranidis, *The Victorian Spinster and Colonial Emigration: Contested Subjects* (Basingstoke: Macmillan, 1999).

47 Renaud Morieux, Clare Anderson, Jonathan Lamb, David Armitage, Alison Bashford, and Sujit Suvasundaram, 'Oceanic Histories: A Roundtable', *Journal of Colonialism and Colonial History*, 19:2 (2018), n.p., https://muse.jhu.edu/article/700167 (accessed 1 February 2020).

48 Patrick Brantlinger, *Taming Cannibals: Victorians and Race* (Ithaca: Cornell University Press, 2011), p. 29. Brantlinger is drawing upon the work of Kay Schaffer, *In the Wake of First Contact: The Eliza Fraser Stories* (Cambridge: Cambridge University Press, 1995).

49 'Abstract of a Lecture Delivered by Rev. G. Daniel, On the South Sea Islands and Islanders', *Sobraon Mercury*, p. 27.

50 See, for example, Bill Bell, 'Bound for Australia: Shipboard Reading in the Nineteenth Century', *Journal of Australian Studies*, 25 (2001), 5–18.

51 Johanna de Schmidt, '"This Strange Little Floating World of Ours": Shipboard Periodicals and Community-Building in the "Global" Nineteenth Century', *Journal of Global History*, 11 (2016), 230.

52 Morieux et al., 'Oceanic Histories', n.p.

53 Mehita Iqani and Fernando Resende, *Media and the Global South: Narrative Territorialities, Cross-Cultural Currents* (London: Routledge, 2019).

54 Fermanis and Comyn, 'Introduction', *Worlding the South*, p. 1.

55 Walter D. Mignolo, 'The Global South and World Dis/order', *Journal of Anthropological Research*, 67 (2011), 166; Gesine Müller, Jorge J. Locane, and Benjamin Loy, 'Introduction', in Gesine Müller, Jorge J. Locane, and Benjamin Loy (eds), *Re-Mapping World Literature: Writing, Book Markets and Epistemologies between Latin America and the Global South* (Boston: De Gruyter, 2018), p. 3.

56 Caroline Levander and Walter Mignolo, 'Introduction: The Global South and World Dis/Order', *The Global South*, 5:1 (2011), 3.

57 Michelle Tusan, 'Empire and the Periodical Press', in Andrew King, Alexis Easley, and John Morton (eds), *The Routledge Handbook to Nineteenth-Century British Periodicals and Newspapers* (London: Routledge, 2016), p. 159.

58 Morieux et al., 'Oceanic Histories', n.p.

5

Augustus Earle's pedestrian tour in New Zealand: or, get off the beach

Ingrid Horrocks

Dubbed the 'wandering artist', Augustus Earle briefly studied at the Royal Academy in London before, in the words of the *Quarterly Review* of 1832, he

> perambulated America, North and South, from Canada to Paraguay: he has passed the Alleghanies and the Andes, and made sketches of numberless cities and harbours, which subsequently, being transferred to the panorama-limners, have enlightened most of us either in Leicester Fields or the Strand. He has wandered all over India in like fashion, and brought home the materials for panoramas of Madras, Bombay, and we know not how many more places in our Eastern empire.[1]

During this life of global mobility, Earle also lived in New South Wales, Australia, and, most pertinently for this chapter, in Aotearoa New Zealand, writing the travel book *A Narrative of Nine Months' Residence in New Zealand, in 1827* (1832).[2] Although Earle's works were originally produced primarily for a metropolitan audience in London, they have since made him one of the most important European visual artists of Aotearoa New Zealand working immediately prior to formal colonisation, as well as a key figure in early colonial Australian art. Earle's many sketches, watercolours, oil paintings, and hand-coloured lithographs of New Zealand scenes and of Māori people have become instantly recognisable to those with even a casual interest in the history of New Zealand, even if they could not attribute them to Earle. His prose narrative, too, was republished in the 1960s as an early contribution to New Zealand literary culture in English.

In this chapter, I want to suggest ways by which we might go about re-reading the various 'worldings' that emerge from imperial-era travel books such as Earle's by applying greater scrutiny to how movement is figured within them. This mobilities studies approach calls for a range of scales to be treated alongside one another, from the global movements of transoceanic travel such as that evoked above, to mundane 'embedded material practices' such as a day's walk in the bush in company.[3] Here I heed recent calls made in fields as diverse as mobilities studies and postcolonial ecocriticism to pay attention to competing epistemologies of nature and place, and of different possible relations not only between peoples, but between peoples moving in place.[4] My contention is that the methods of postcolonial ecocritical literary humanities can be enriched by being brought into closer relation with work on mobilities that treats the minute alongside the global. I am particularly interested in what happens when we read mobilities within prose travel texts alongside – and to an extent against – the perhaps more dominant worldings evoked by the visual art of precolonial and early colonial periods.[5]

What I hope to do in this chapter, more specifically, is to outline a model for approaching European-authored travel texts of the nineteenth century (and potentially travel writing more generally) that helps to move beyond an approach to their aesthetics shaped by moments of arrival and meeting, and prospect views. A scholarly focus on arrival and prospects in relation to European-authored travel writing about the southern hemisphere, and in particular about the Pacific, still leans towards producing readings that highlight explicit moments of cultural encounter. This in turn lends itself to a focus on the development in these texts of what Mary Louise Pratt and others term the 'imperial eye'[6] – that is, a European eye and accompanying discourse that works to organise and process information for 'a society intent on both territorial and epistemological mastery of new lands'.[7] Using the example of Earle, I am interested in what happens when we approach texts such as these, instead, by pushing beyond moments of explicit encounter to pay attention to more mundane, local, and embodied movements within them – movements of *both* the European traveller(s) in the text and of Indigenous peoples, in this case Māori.

Writing on the middle ground

Earle's work is especially relevant to those concerned with the 'contact zone' as evoked in travel writing because it was composed when the geo-political balance of power had not yet shifted in New Zealand, and organised European colonisation was not a certain outcome. I approach this work as a Pākehā New Zealander of British descent, a position of culpability that makes the continued consideration of this moment especially important. In the 1820s, New Zealand was among the places in the Pacific still least known to Europeans.[8] Even the first Anglican mission was not established until 1814, and the ship on which Earle arrived in 1827 was bringing to Aotearoa New Zealand one of the first groups of Wesleyan missionaries and their wives. There were small communities of Europeans living in the north of New Zealand by this stage, such that Earle's account of the early days of his visit reads like so many house calls. At one point, he is pleased to come across a 'snug little colony of our own country'.[9] However, Europeans had no jurisdictional authority in New Zealand in 1827 and were exponentially outnumbered. The estimated population of 100,000–160,000 Māori when James Cook's *Endeavour* first made landfall in 1769 had dropped to 70,000–90,000 by 1814, mostly due to the new diseases Europeans brought with them. Even by the later date, however, the resident European population in Aotearoa New Zealand, consisting of sealers, shore whalers, traders, escaped convicts, and missionaries, is estimated to have been only in the vicinity of 1,200.[10] It cannot be understated, then, 'the degree to which this world peculiarly, and predominantly, belonged to and was controlled by Tangata Whenua [people of the land]'.[11]

In part as a result of such demographics, Earle's text is not saturated by the sense of an 'Old New Zealand' (read: Māori culture) strategically evoked as *already* being lost that tends to mark even very early colonial-period texts of subsequent decades. Large-scale land seizures leading to Māori dispossession were still to come, while the rapid and violent transformation of New Zealand's nonhuman environments by the 'ecological imperialism' of forestry and pastoral agriculture was only just beginning.[12] Written in the late 1820s, Earle's *Narrative of a Residence in New Zealand* can be seen as inhabiting what has been called in other contexts 'the middle ground', a phrase drawing on the model of American historian Richard White. This model has been applied to a very specific phase in the contact and encounter (and invasion) process, which historian Vincent O'Malley argues in New Zealand ran from around 1814 to 1840 and, at its best, was characterised by efforts towards mutual accommodation and understanding.[13] It is a space that ideally allowed for the creation of diverse, hybrid, and mobile practices and understandings.

Given this context, it is unsurprising that leisure travellers to New Zealand such as Earle were a new and still rare, although not unknown, phenomenon in the 1820s. In not having an explicit aim for his visit, Earle as author is distinct from the majority of his predecessors and near contemporaries. Unlike James Cook, for example, he had no letter from the Admiralty instructing him to assess possible new territory for the Empire, nor was he an official voyage artist like William Hodges. He was not an evangelical missionary like William Yate and William Wade, who wrote books based on their experiences in New Zealand in the 1830s. Nor was he travelling for clear financial reasons like Richard Cruise, who wrote a book about his ten months in New Zealand in 1820 in charge of the military detachment on a convict ship from Australia commissioned to replace its human freight with a cargo of spars for the return journey to England.[14] Nor was Earle a naturalist like his friend Charles Darwin, who visited in 1835, or Joseph Banks or the Forsters before Darwin, in New Zealand to collect botanical specimens.

The original introduction to Earle's work presents him, instead, as someone driven by '"a love of roving and adventure"'.[15] He stayed for such a length of time in New Zealand, for the most part living with local Māori, because he was effectively stranded when his ship was commissioned for other work. His New Zealand narrative was published alongside his shorter work of travel about his time shipwrecked on Tristan da Cunha. This framing of Earle as adventurer, artist, and travel writer, combined with the particular historical moment in which he visited, by no means removes his narrative from the discourses of imperialism or mercantile capitalism. In fact, as Elizabeth DeLoughrey reminds us, the accidental arrival is a 'powerful and repeated trope of empire building and British literature' in this moment, so should be treated with scepticism.[16] It does, nonetheless, when combined with the historical moment of his visit, subtly shift the emphasis of Earle's narrative nonfiction text and thereby the kinds of 'apprehensions', to use Rob Nixon's term, that prove possible within his narrative.[17]

Arrival and first encounter

Although I will ultimately argue that we need to move beyond it, the arrival scene in such texts remains the obvious place to start, both because it is such a marked feature of travel texts of this sort, and because it has underpinned so much conceptual thinking about the history of encounter and colonial history. Since Mary Louise Pratt's influential work on the 'contact zone' and the rhetoric of travel texts, the arrival scene has rightly been understood as a key trope in travel writing (particularly nineteenth-century travel writing), and an important place to look for how such texts work.[18] In relation to the Pacific in particular, the Australian historian Greg Dening's related metaphor of the beach as a zone of transcultural contact, and of encounter and exchange, emerged from the 1990s as a useful analytical tool for understanding the complexity of early European texts about the Pacific and the histories they have influenced.[19] To complete a triumvirate of influential conceptual imaginings, the 'two worlds' metaphor for examining New Zealand history, exemplified by historian and anthropologist Anne Salmond's work, is also structured by attention to arrivals and explicit moments of encounter between two peoples.[20] Earle's own work has in fact provided useful visual representations for this historiographical imagining. Emblematically, his canonical oil painting and related lithograph, 'The Meeting of the Artist and Wounded Chief, Hongi [Hika], Bay of Islands, November 1827', depicting a meeting with the powerful Ngāpuhi Rangatira (chief) and members of his iwi (tribe) on a beach near Kororāreka, appears on the cover of Salmond's *Tears of Rangi: Experiments across Worlds* (2017).[21] Earle's

Figure 5.1 Augustus Earle, 'New Zealand, the entrance of the E.O.K. Angha
[i.e. Hokianga] River, view taken from the bar', 1827

narrative account of his arrival in the Hokianga area, depicted visually in
Figure 5.1, in October 1827 works in a similar way, as a touchstone, to
readings of his *A Narrative of Nine Months' Residence*.[22] I want to look at
this account of arrival, in order to, on the one hand, suggest the kinds of
understandings that emerge from this critical approach and, on the other,
briefly to suggest its potential limitations.

Earle's account of the moment his ship arrives in New Zealand neatly exemplifies the structure of what we have become attuned to find in such textual
representations. He presents his readers with the kind of utopian arrival scene
troped repeatedly in literature about the Pacific (in particular Tahiti) in which
European visitors are greeted not with any suspicion or potential resistance,
but are enthusiastically welcomed:[23]

> As the arrival of a ship is always a profitable occurrence, great exertions are
> made to be the first on board. ... others very soon coming up with us, our
> decks were crowded with them, some boarding us at the gangway, others
> climbing up the chains and bows, and finding entrances where they could. All
> were in perfect good humour, and pleasure beamed in all their countenances.[24]

Earle presents a scene of sympathy and commercial exchange ('profitable
occurrence') and carefully positions himself as a controlling eye/I observing
the scene, beginning (in an often cited passage): 'I examined these savages,
as they crowded round our decks, with the critical eye of an artist.'[25] If science and the discourse of natural history worked as one way to underwrite
claims to disinterested innocence in much of the early voyage literature (as
well as in accounts of interior journeys in Africa and South America), Earle's
claim to being an observer is founded on his role as artist. The message of
the textual scene for readers back home in Britain is clear: there is nothing
to fear in such encounters for either party. The Indigenous people are wel-
coming and the European narrator is in control of the interaction.

Charles Darwin was famously put out when this kind of scene failed to
unfold for him when he visited New Zealand in 1835.[26] In fact, even Earle's

own arrival did not quite work out this way. Having established the friendly terms of the encounter, Earle then reveals (as if incidentally) that he actually experienced the encounter quite differently himself: 'The first thing which struck me forcibly was, that each of these savages was armed with a good musket.'[27] These are armed men climbing aboard. However, by the time the reader is presented with this fact within Earle's text, Māori have already been figuratively *dis*armed. Once we consider this, the rhetorical work being done by scenes of arrival or landfall such as this one becomes clearer, along with the very particular representation of the relationship between the visitors and those in whose land they are arriving. Reading the arrival scene in Earle's text yields, then, roughly what we have come to expect: a naturalising of colonial capitalist discourse, a vision of imperial expansion seemingly welcomed by Indigenous people, an opportunity for a generalising comparison between the 'natives' and the 'Indians' of other nations, as well as, when we look still closer, an undercurrent of unease which belies European claims to comfort and mastery of the situation.

This trope of arrival reinforces one of the most abiding metaphors of the imperial project – the imagining of Indigenous peoples and far-flung lands as static and in place, while the European, transoceanic explorer (a Crusoe-like figure) is mobile, visiting, as it were, from the future. This is part of the sleight of hand by which empire turns geography into history, and space into time.[28] It is also visually repeated in the many images of Māori by Earle, and even more so in the works of more explicitly colonialist artists such as George French Angus, which depict Indigenous people sitting or crouching on the ground, involved in domestic or ceremonial tasks, static and in place, and so waiting to be visited, observed, and eventually colonised by the traveller-artist-anthropologist-colonist.[29] The Enlightenment mode of thought – deeply enmeshed with Whiggish and stadial models of history – that such visual depictions evoke is one that makes it difficult to recognise what Doreen Massey calls 'the real challenge' of the 'radical contemporaneity' of 'coeval others', and the co-presence of simultaneous, diverging narratives.[30] Or to use the terms of this collection, it makes it hard to reinstate a sense of 'mixed temporalities' and the 'historical uncanny' that Sarah Comyn and Porscha Fermanis, quoting Harry Harootunian, call our attention to in their introduction. In essence, arrival can only get us so far.

Pedestrian touring

What different understandings of history and coeval 'life worlds' might emerge when we push beyond arrival scenes and other explicit moments of meeting that recur in European encounter narratives, to seek out and

examine accounts of more quotidian activities such as walking? In the
example of Earle, this takes us most directly to an extended prose depiction
of a pedestrian tour taken in company early in his time in New Zealand.
This is the first and most structured of many accounts Earle gives of having
'rambled' 'about the country', mostly in peaceful circumstances, but at one
point fleeing from a situation of local warfare in worn-out shoes.[31] In the
account of his first tour, he narrates a three-day journey he and his Scottish
companion Mr Shand took with an unnamed local rangatira (chief), who
also provides two men to carry their baggage. Along the way, a number of
other Māori men join them, to guide and 'bear us company'.[32] The walk
takes the group across the top of the North Island from the Hokianga on the
west coast to Keri-keri on the east.

This part of Earle's text is different in tone from his opening examination
of a new people and place with 'critical eye'. Despite the domesticating
phrase 'pedestrian tour', which suggests a pleasant walk in the Lake District
more than an imperial adventure narrative, once this companionable group
reach the head of the Hokianga river and switch from canoe to foot, Earle
quickly becomes unable to frame the scene with any authority:

> We travelled through a wood so thick that the light of heaven could not pene-
> trate the trees that composed it. They were so large, and so close together, that
> in many places we had some difficulty to squeeze ourselves through them. To
> add to our perplexities, innumerable streams intersected this forest, which
> always brought us Europeans to a complete stand-still.[33]

These passages of difficult movement through a landscape present an
embodied account of a terrain and nature that the European traveller is
almost unable to traverse. They must 'squeeze' themselves to pass, contract-
ing in space rather than observing and expanding as happens with the arrival
scene and prospect eye; and they are often brought to a 'complete' halt. At
times during this first walk the European travellers are passively 'seated' on
top of the Māori men's loads. They are carried across 'such places', Earle
writes, 'as I dared scarcely venture to look down upon'.[34] Earle's narrative
voice moves in and out of what seems to be self-parody in such moments. In
this instance, the vision and bravery suggested by the verb 'venture' is
reduced to a kind of fearful peering, and the narrating traveller hardly dares
even do that. Notably, such passages do not amount to the kind of visual set
pieces or 'word pictures' for which Earle's text is noted and which scholars
have read as linguistic versions of his paintings.[35] In these moments (parody
or not), Earle's visual perspective is rendered unworkable by the difficulty of
navigating this new, immersive situation.

Paying attention to how the narrative develops reveals that in such passages two different ways of being in a particular nonhuman ecology emerge.

The contrast between the tentative, limited capacity of the European visitor in this space and that of familiar Māori mobile inhabitation materialises most strongly in Earle's account of the second day's journey. After a night in which the group is hosted by local Māori en route, Earle writes that at day-break, they

> proceeded on our journey; we had eight miles more of this thick forest to scramble through, and this part we found considerably worse than that we had traversed yesterday. The roots of the trees covered the path in all directions, rendering it necessary to watch every step we took, in order to prevent being thrown down; the supple jacks, suspended and twining from tree to tree, mak-ing in many places a complete net-work; and while we were toiling with the greatest difficulty through this miserable road, our natives were jogging on as comfortably as possible: use had so completely accustomed them to it, that they sprung over the roots, and dived under the supple jacks and branches, with perfect ease, while we were panting after them in vain. The whole way was mountainous. The climbing up, and then descending, was truly frightful; not a gleam of sky was to be seen, all was a mass of gigantic trees, straight and lofty, their wide spreading branches mingling over head, and producing throughout the forest an endless darkness and unbroken gloom.[36]

Here, the 'toiling' Europeans are in constant danger of being 'thrown down' and the experience as a whole is characterised by a lack of light and an inability to get a sense of the space. For Earle's narrator it is a 'truly frightful' experience of 'endless darkness' and 'unbroken gloom'. In contrast, how-ever, Māori are depicted as 'comfortably' negotiating and traversing this space, 'jogging on', springing and diving with 'perfect ease', 'accustomed' to this kind of movement.

The effect of the scene is that the experience of the sublime evoked – a discourse in which Earle's paintings show he was well versed – is explicitly isolated to the Europeans.[37] In the process the European experience of place is rendered subjective and even comical. Earle's text in such moments pres-ents the reader with two simultaneous experiences of the same landscape: cutting through the 'frightful' European experience, which may have been hyped up to fit the survival strand of travel writing popular in Earle's day, is Māori familiarity, and their sense of ease and being at home in this ecology. This familiarity is reinforced by the many chance encounters Earle describes with Māori, even in the densest parts of the bush. At one point, 'in the midst of this wood', they meet a man and his family busy planting a cleared patch of land. This is likely an area to which the family have ancestral rights and use through the practice of ahi kā (burning fires of occupation). At other points they meet 'groups of naked men' moving through the bush with whom the Māori members of their own party exchange what Earle calls 'barbarous songs of recognition'.[38] Again, Māori familiarity – here 'recognition' – emerges, while 'barbarous' only serves to underscore the European literal lack of comprehension.[39] Although Earle was in New Zealand during a period of increased tension between different tribal groups in the north, in general the 1820s was a period of peace and prosperity among northern Māori, allowing them to move safely and freely, as seen here, around the complex networks of pathways within their overlapping territories.[40]

What emerges from paying attention to a textual moment such as this 'pedestrian tour' in Earle's narrative, then, is a vision of a space almost untraversable to Europeans – and certainly so without guidance – and at the same time fully inhabited (and inhabitable), in use, and familiar to local Māori. At one point Earle describes a 'beaten footpath' 'worn so deep as to resemble a gutter more than a road'.[41] The same physical space in the text is uncannily and simultaneously depicted as dense forest (as experienced by the European visitors) and as familiar garden (as experienced by Māori). Māori are not fused with wilderness or nature here but rather an ecology is glimpsed to which they are integral, genealogically and literally at home. Two experiences of this ecology, two simultaneous realities, in some sense partially co-exist at points like this in Earle's text (if always at one remove from Indigenous experience). They exist not as a face-to-face encounter (as in a scene of meeting) but implicitly and in parallel. Or to use other terms, Te Ao Pākehā (the world of strangers) and Te Ao Māori (the familiar, every-day world) are both partially present in the text, not as explicit, verbalised 'world views' but as coeval states of existence in place. The pedestrian tour in Earle might be understood to work as an embodied, narrativised gesture towards the kind of cartographic exchange between Indigenous people and European explorers discussed by Comyn and Fermanis, coming close to Margaret Jolly's notion of 'double vision'.[42]

Such scenes, which seem to be relatively rare in travel texts from contact zones, are especially worth seeking out because of the generic conventions of the travel writing of exploration, which frequently create what Pratt calls 'textual apartheid', either in the form of a separation of people from land-scapes or via ethnographic accounts of inhabitants abstracted from the spaces they inhabit.[43] This occurs most explicitly in the way in which travel books, including early books about New Zealand, are most often structured by separating the 'narrative' from ethnographical accounts with titles such as 'Inhabitants' or 'Manners and Customs', and then again from sections on 'Geography'. Such generic conventions make the representation of mobility textually difficult, as well as failing to account for the mobilities of the various peoples who inhabit both land and text.

It is interesting to note in the case of Earle that even though he produces a prose narrative account of walking in the bush, there seem to be no available visual depictions by him of such moments. The closest thing to a pedestrian tour in his wider oeuvre, in fact, is the narrative series of four watercolours he did of an overnight camping trip in the Cabbage Tree Forest in the Illawarra, south of Sydney.[44] However, in this case, the European figure in the depicted scenes is evidently travelling by horse, a mode of movement that makes a significant difference to how place is experienced, while the Indigenous peoples depicted, here the Indigenous people of the Illawarra region, are stationary, predominantly represented, once again, as seated on the ground. These are scenes in the bush, but they are scenes of meeting more than of movement.

In the evolution of representations of a single or particular moment within the work of George French Angus, the artist who most closely followed Earle in producing a substantial body of work featuring New Zealand, we find an example of the visual-art equivalent of 'textual apartheid' in the process of being actioned. Angus spent time in New Zealand in the years immediately following the 1840 Treaty of Waitangi, and so the formal beginning of colonisation, and he produced an illustrated account of his travels, *Savage Life and Scenes in Australia and New Zealand: Being an Artist's Impressions of Countries and People at the Antipodes* (1847). At one point in his text, Angus, like Earle, gives an account of a walk, this one from what was by then a European settlement in Wellington to Porirua harbour. Like Earle, Angus had a local guide (the nephew to the chief Te Rauparaha), but unlike Earle he makes no mention of whether this man traverses the 'mountainous' 'narrow track' or 'Maori footway', in 'some places knee-deep with mud', with any more ease than the European members of the party do. In fact, Angus' written account of the walk is pure description of 'scenery' that is 'exceedingly picturesque'.[45] These pages of Angus' book contain an engraving based on his drawings of the walk, 'Scene in a New Zealand Forest', a rare forest image in his oeuvre. However, as in all Angus' images, Māori represented in the scene appear posed and still, one figure seated in the foreground, with another two figures standing further back along what may or may not be a path. They sit and stand awkwardly in the bush rather than seeming to inhabit, much less own, or be of it, so that it is more like a staged photograph than a scene of action. More tellingly still, when a hand-coloured lithograph of the image appeared in the accompanying large and expensive pictorial work, *New Zealanders Illustrated* (1846), the actual New Zealanders were removed into separate images altogether, sectioned off from what became merely picturesque scenery, both aesthetically and materially available for habitation by Europeans.[46]

A strikingly similar hand-coloured engraving, 'The Hutt Road taken at the Gorge looking towards Wellington', appeared in the lush large-scale illustrated travel book of Angus' direct contemporary Samuel Brees, a surveyor for the New Zealand Company in the more explicitly conflictual later nineteenth-century moment (Figure 5.2).

THE HUTT ROAD TAKEN AT THE GORGE LOOKING TOWARDS WELLINGTON

Figure 5.2 Samuel Charles Brees, 'The Hutt Road taken at the Gorge
looking towards Wellington', 1847

Again, this is almost a stand-alone depiction of figures in the bush in the
artist's oeuvre. And, again, Māori are posed and stationary, here standing
outside a small whare (dwelling). However, in this case there is also a European figure in the image, depicted in action, cutting down a tree. As if the
message were not clear enough, the engraving appears on a page of Brees'
book along with two idealised engravings of colonial houses and farms,
with Indigenous humans and Indigenous nature equally absent.[47] This context of Indigenous removal makes Earle's distinctive textual representation
of Māori in motion all the more poignant.

The prospect

Finally, I want to turn to the prospect view, while keeping mobilities still in frame. As with the arrival scene, understandings of the dynamics of travel narratives such as Earle's have been shaped by the critical attention paid to prospect views, as well as by how we have been taught to read the authority of the prospect within British imperial discourse.[48] Earle's work provides us with an example of what happens when visual images shape what receives most attention within written texts rather than vice-versa. Arrivals and prospect views within the discourses of imperial and colonial travel are in some ways the same: both invoke a moment of stasis and consideration enacted within the movements of the mobile European traveller. Their corollary is that the Indigenous people encountered, viewed, or overseen are conceived of as static.

Earle's watercolour 'Distant view of the Bay of Islands, New Zealand' (Figure 5.3) depicts the moment in which his party emerged from the bush above the Bay of Islands near the end of their pedestrian tour. As often happens in Earle's paintings, a figure that seems to be identified with the artist is depicted as a 'spectator figure'.[49] Here he seems to be the only figure actually looking out across the landscape.

One reading of the posture of his guides/companions is that they are bent under their loads, in some way still involved in the act of walking and so not taking in the wider prospect which only the white man views. Most starkly, Francis Pound reads the Māori figures in this painting as 'European's beasts

Figure 5.3 Augustus Earle, 'Distant view of the Bay of Islands, New Zealand', watercolour, 1827?

of burden', their movement opposed to the single European figure's stillness as a sign of their lack of aesthetic sensibility. At first glance, then, this could be seen to be a quintessential representation of Pratt's '"seeing-man" … the white male subject of European landscape discourse – he whose imperial eyes passively look out and possess'.[50]

However, this seems to greatly oversimplify this puzzling image. While scholars such as Pound have seen Earle's many visual representations as simplistically mapping the European picturesque on to Aotearoa New Zealand (and adding imperial power structures to the power dynamics already inherent to the picturesque), others have seen a more nuanced artistic practice, in particular one that works, to quote W. J. T. Mitchell's brief but brilliant reading of this painting, to 'represent the Maori gaze as a presence in the landscape' in a way that enacts 'an encounter that leaves us in an odd, disturbing, liminal space'.[51] Mitchell and Alex Calder both draw attention to the Māori carving in the image and the way in which this introduces another viewpoint, ultimately creating an allusion within the image to a space, and a way of seeing, that seems *unseen* by the European figure within Earle's image: a kind of double prospect.[52]

Art historian Leonard Bell has observed that the 'halted traveller' and the 'back-to-the viewer' figure is a leitmotif in Earle's travel art in general, paralleling (and possibly predating) the use of this figure as a trope of experience in the work of the German painter Caspar David Friedrich. Moreover, Bell notes how often this figure in Earle's images is distinctively off-balance, suggesting not, Bell argues, an omniscient eye, but rather a figure encountering and seeking some way into the new. Bell suggests that in Earle's travel art the prospect is an inherently unstable position: the prospect viewer depicted taking in the view frequently looks almost preposterously out of place in the environment in which he finds himself.[53]

Earle's Brazilian prospect viewer, shown in Figure 5.4, looks quite close to a direct satire on Friedrich's most iconic image, 'Wanderer above the Sea of Fog' (1818), painted four years earlier. The prospect viewer appears even more off-balance in two of Earle's New South Wales paintings. In one, he is literally kneeling, looking fearfully down over the sea; in another, the tiny prospect figure stands on a rocky outcrop so extreme it looks about to break off (Figure 5.5).[54] Rather than enacting dominance or ownership, the *unstable* prospect viewer, we might say, highlights the contingency of subjectivity in Earle's work.

Shifting mobilities

Paying attention to the figure of the 'toiling' mobile subject within Earle's *written narrative*, as well as to the movements of his Indigenous mobile counterparts, allows us to build on and further complicate understandings of the

Figure 5.4 Augustus Earle, 'From the Summit of Cacavada [Corcovado] Mountains, near Rio de Janeiro, 1822', watercolour, 1822

Figure 5.5 Augustus Earle, 'South Head Light, New South Wales', watercolour, 1825?

'halted traveller' in his visual art. Earle's verbal description of the view captured in his 'Distant view of the Bay of Islands' (Figure 5.3) consists only of the words: 'Having at length attained the summit of a hill, we beheld the Bay of Islands, stretching out in the distance.' This description, however, comes at the

end of the paragraph beginning '[a]fter three or four hours of laborious struggling', and containing his account of the deep worn footpaths 'most painful'
for a European to walk, but which pose 'no inconvenience' to Māori members
of the party. Earle describes his Māori companions singing as they walk.[55]
Coming at the end of this paragraph, Earle's brief allusion to reaching the
'summit of the hill' seems more a gesture of exhaustion than what could rightly
be called a linguistic prospect view with its associated claims to mastery or
ownership. It is as though all that embodiment, all that traversing of the landscape, all that hybridity of experience, has exhausted the travelling narrator.

The narrative framing of the prospect in Earle's written text, represented not
only by the embodied labour of the subject-in-motion within a dense and difficult landscape but also by depictions of the European subject as off-centre and
uncomfortable in his journey, works to unsettle claims to vision or mastery that
in other circumstances such prospective moments might be expected to signify.
So too does the co-presence of Māori on the hilltop alongside the European
traveller, neither the subjects of his gaze, nor following where he looks, but
seemingly involved in their own trajectory, views, thoughts, and stories-so-far.

It seems no coincidence, then, that two Earle paintings painted close in time
to his 'Distant view of the Bay of Islands' are unusual for him, neither fitting his
practice of depicting Māori sitting, either at rest at the end of the day or
involved in ceremonial or domestic chores. In one, 'Entrance to the Bay of
Islands New Zealand', two Māori figures are seen walking, seemingly on their
way between places – a rare sight in such work. The other is a prospect, looked
down over by a single Māori man, while another man sits resting nearby.[56]
Given my re-reading of Earle, it is not entirely surprising that in the 'Distant
view' watercolour the European figure may appear to be standing still but is in
fact on a path distinctly curved to form the shape of a Māori waka (canoe).

If Earle's Māori companions do not pause in their movements (and are not
brought to a 'complete standstill'), then maybe this can be read as evoking a
sense in which this is their narrative – a narrative that is ongoing and at this
point in history fully in possession of the meaning-making and stories of this
particular place. Colonialism and ecological imperialism, to use Alfred Crosby's term, are not yet fully in play.[57] A mobility-focused critical approach
allows us to see Māori members of the party as the more successful travellers
in this text, inscribing their landscape step-by-step through the material practices of their everyday movements. This is *their* pedestrian tour. As Pacific
historian Nicholas Thomas observes of voyage literature, if we can see these
early moments of representation as 'replete with contradictions and contradictory possibilities, if their uncertainties meant that other things easily could
have happened, it is perhaps easier to imagine that other things can happen
now'.[58] One way to help us see the 'other things' that can happen now is the
further development of conceptual models such as that of mobility. Part of

what attention to mobility offers is a reminder of the different ways in which it is possible to imagine – and to enact – relationships between peoples and peoples in place: another small gesture towards decolonising our histories.

Acknowledgements

I would like to acknowledge my students at Massey University who discussed Earle with me; the audiences at Princeton University, the University of York, University College Dublin, and Victoria University, who gave me useful comments on early drafts; and Philip Steer, Nikki Hessell, and Sarah Ross for reading.

Notes

1 'Review of *A Narrative of Nine Months' Residence in New Zealand*', *Quarterly Review*, 48 (October 1832), 133.

2 Augustus Earle, *Narrative of a Residence in New Zealand, in 1827; Journal of a Residence in Tristan Da Cunha*, ed. E. H. McCormick (1832; Oxford: Clarendon, 1966). Like many nineteenth-century travel texts this prose work has predominantly been treated as a historical source (in Earle's case, as a somewhat unreliable one) rather than as an aesthetic work in its own right. Notable exceptions to this appear in Lydia Wevers, *Country of Writing: Travel Writing and New Zealand 1809–1900* (Auckland: Auckland University Press, 2002), still the best book on nineteenth-century European-authored travel writing about New Zealand; and Alex Calder, *The Settler's Plot: How Stories Take Place in New Zealand* (Auckland: Auckland University Press, 2011). The widest contemporary dissemination of Earle's visual depictions of New Zealand took the form of a series of ten hand-coloured lithographs published as *Sketches Illustrative of the Native Inhabitants and Islands of New Zealand* (London: New Zealand Association, 1838), in which 'The Wounded Chief Hongi and His Family' appeared as the second plate.

3 Doreen Massey, *For Space* (London: Sage, 2005), p. 9. For an overview of the mobilities framework, see James Faulconbridge and Allison Hui, 'Traces of a Mobile Field: Ten Years of Mobilities Research', *Mobilities*, 11 (2016), 1–14.

4 Elizabeth DeLoughrey, Jill Didur, and Anthony Carrigan, 'Introduction: A Postcolonial Environmental Humanities,' in Elizabeth DeLoughrey, Jill Didur, and Anthony Carrigan (eds), *Global Ecologies and the Environmental Humanities* (London and New York: Routledge, 2015), pp. 2–3.

5 This is not so much in relation to visual works published within the *Narrative* itself, which number only six and are crude engravings by J. Stewart after Earle, but rather Earle's wider oeuvre, in particular his watercolours.

6 Mary Louise Pratt, *Imperial Eyes: Travel Writing and Transculturation*, 2nd edn (New York: Routledge, 2008).

7 Wevers, *Country of Writing*, p. 86. In relation to Earle, this is to an extent the case even in work such as Wevers', which is attuned to Earle's 'humanism' and sympathy for Māori and to the ways in which his uncertainties emerge as he works 'constantly to understand what has happened, what border he has crossed, and what the meaning of his territorial journey is' (pp. 85–6).

8 Earle addresses himself to an audience imagined, much like himself, as being familiar with New Zealand through the literature surrounding James Cook's voyages of the eighteenth century, but little beyond that (see, e.g., p. 58). The extended review of Earle's narrative in the *Quarterly Review* in 1832 was still referencing the 'Boyd incident' of 1809 in Whangaroa and referring to New Zealand as 'the land of bloodshed' (p. 135).

9 Earle, *Narrative*, p. 66.

10 Damon Ieremia Salesa, *Racial Crossings: Race, Intermarriage, and the Victorian British Empire* (Oxford: Oxford University Press, 2011), pp. 54, 66.

11 Salesa, *Racial Crossings*, p. 88.

12 Alfred Crosby, *Ecological Imperialism: The Biological Expansion of Europe, 900–1900* (Cambridge: Cambridge University Press, 1986); Eric Pawson and Tom Brooking (eds), *Making a New Land: Environmental Histories of New Zealand*, new edn (Dunedin: Otago University Press, 2013).

13 Vincent O'Malley, *The Meeting Place: Māori and Pākehā Encounters, 1642–1840* (Auckland: Auckland University Press, 2012), pp. 7–8; Paul Monin, 'Maori Encounters and Colonial Capitalism', in Giselle Byrnes (ed.), *The New Oxford History of New Zealand* (Melbourne: Oxford University Press, 2009), pp. 125–46.

14 Ingrid Horrocks, 'A World of Waters: Imagining, Voyaging, Entanglement', in Mark Williams (ed.), *A History of New Zealand Literature* (Cambridge: Cambridge University Press, 2016), pp. 17–30.

15 Earle, *Narrative*, p. 49.

16 Elizabeth DeLoughrey, *Routes and Roots: Navigating Caribbean and Pacific Island Literatures* (Honolulu: University of Hawai'i Press, 2010), p. 13.

17 Rob Nixon, *Slow Violence and the Environmentalism of the Poor* (Cambridge, MA: Harvard University Press, 2011), p. 15. In using Nixon's term 'apprehension' here, I by no means put forward Earle as a 'writer-activist'. However, I do mean to activate Nixon's sense that narrative nonfiction is capable of carrying creative perceptions not easily explained directly.

18 Mary Louise Pratt, 'Fieldwork in Common Places', in James Clifford and George E. Marcus (eds), *Writing Culture: The Poetics and Politics of Ethnography* (Berkeley: University of Berkeley Press, 1986), pp. 33–7.

19 Greg Dening, *Mr Bligh's Bad Language: Passion, Power, and Theatre on the Bounty* (Cambridge: Cambridge University Press, 1992).

20 Anne Salmond, *Two Worlds: First Meetings between Maori and Europeans, 1642–1772* (Auckland: Viking Press, 1991), and *Tears of Rangi: Experiments across Worlds* (Auckland: Auckland University Press, 2017), p. 54.

21 On Earle's shaping of depictions of this encounter and others, see Leonard Bell, 'Augustus Earle's *The Meeting of the Artist and the Wounded Chief Hongi, Bay of Islands, New Zealand, 1827,* and His Depictions of Other New Zealand Encounters', in Alex Calder, Jonathan Lamb, and Bridget Orr (eds), *Voyages and*

Beaches: Pacific Encounters, 1769–1840 (Honolulu: University of Hawai'i Press, 1999), pp. 241–63.

22 Wevers, *Country of Writing*, pp. 80–1.

23 Pratt, 'Fieldwork', pp. 35–7. See also Vanessa Smith, *Intimate Strangers: Friendship, Exchange and Pacific Encounters* (Cambridge: Cambridge University Press, 2010). This can be seen as part of what DeLoughrey has written about as 'repeating islands' (*Routes and Roots,* pp. 11–12).

24 Earle, *Narrative*, p. 57.

25 Earle, *Narrative*, p. 57.

26 Charles Darwin, *Charles Darwin's Beagle Diary*, ed. Richard Darwin Keynes (Cambridge: Cambridge University Press, 1988), p. 381.

27 Earle, *Narrative*, p. 58.

28 Massey, *For Space*, pp. 7–11; DeLoughrey, *Routes and Roots*, p. 16.

29 George French Angus wrote that in his writing and painting his 'aim has been to describe faithfully impressions of savage life and scenes in countries only now emerging from a primitive state of barbarism; but which the energy and enterprise of the British colonists, and the benign influence of Christianity combined, will eventually render the peaceful abodes of civilized and prosperous communities'. *Savage Life and Scenes in Australia and New Zealand: Being an Artist's Impressions of Countries and People at the Antipodes*, 2 vols (London: Smith, Elder, and Co., 1847), I:vi–vii.

30 Massey, *For Space*, pp. 6–9.

31 Earle, *Narrative*, pp. 122, 172.

32 Earle, *Narrative*, pp. 67–8.

33 Earl, *Narrative*, p. 69.

34 Earl, *Narrative*, p. 69.

35 E. H. McCormick, 'Introduction', in *Narrative of a Residence in New Zealand*, p. vi.

36 Earle, *Narrative*, p. 72.

37 The presence of the sublime in Earle's imagination at this point in his writing up of his journey is demonstrated by the explicit reference to Salvator Rosa in his account of the previous night in a hut in a Māori village. However, in the hut, surrounded by curious men (described as 'savage spectators' [p. 70]), Earle is careful to reassert mastery, much as he does in the arrival scene: 'All my fears had by this time subsided, and being master of myself, I had leisure to study and enjoy the scene' (p. 71).

38 Earle, *Narrative*, pp. 69, 73.

39 Although Earle does seem to have eventually acquired some knowledge of the Māori language, he would have had little at this point.

40 Salmond, *Tears of Rangi*, pp. 321–2. Later in his narrative Earle does tell of having to escape back across the island after the chief who had given him protection was defeated and the missionaries refused him sanctuary (p. 168).

41 Earle, *Narrative*, p. 72.

42 Margaret Jolly, 'Imagining Oceania: Indigenous and Foreign Representations of a Sea of Islands', *The Contemporary Pacific,* 19 (2007), 532.

43 Pratt, *Imperial Eyes*, p. 60.

44 The series consists of two watercolours inscribed 'Cabbage Tree Forest, Ilawarra [Illawara] New South Wales, 1827', and two watercolours inscribed 'A Bivouack,

day break, on the Illawara Mountains, 1827', Solander Box A33 #T75–78 NK12/37–40, National Library of Australia, https://nla.gov.au/nla.obj-134498890/view; https://nla.gov.au/nla.obj-134499059/view; http://nla.gov.au/nla.obj-134499210/view; https://nla.gov.au/nla.obj-134499370/view (accessed 20 October 2019). To see the works in context, see Jocelyn Hackforth-Jones, *Augustus Earle: Travel Artist: Paintings and Drawings in the Rex Nan Kivell Collection National Library of Australia* (Martinborough: Alister Taylor, 1980), pp. 18, 105–6.

45 Angus, *Savage Life*, pp. 244–6.

46 'Scene in a New Zealand Forest near Porirua', *New Zealanders: Illustrated by George French Angas* (London: Published for the Proprietor by Thomas Mclean, 1846), plate 7, n.p.

47 'Residence of the Honourable Major Richmond at Wellington' and 'Residence of the Honorable Frances Molesworth at the Hutt', in Samuel Charles Brees, *Pictorial Illustrations of New Zealand* (London: John Williams, 1847), n.p.

48 John Barrell, *English Literature in History, 1730–80: An Equal, Wide Survey* (London: Hutchinson, 1983), p. 35; Pratt, *Imperial Eyes*.

49 Francis Pound, 'Spectator Figures in Some New Zealand Paintings & Prints', *Art New Zealand*, 23 (1982), 40–5. There is also a possibility that this is not a stand-in for the artist at all, but a depiction of his rather taciturn and endlessly disappointed travelling companion, Mr Shand.

50 Pratt, *Imperial Eyes*, p. 9.

51 W. J. T. Mitchell, 'Imperial Landscapes', in *Landscape and Power* (Chicago: University of Chicago Press, 2002), p. 27.

52 Calder, *Settler's Plot*, pp. 45–7.

53 Bell, 'Not Quite Darwin's Artist', p. 65. See also Bell, 'To See or Not to See: Conflicting Eyes in the Travel Art of Augustus Earle', in Julie F. Codell and Dianne Sachko Macleod (eds), *Orientalism Transposed; The Impacts of the Colonies on British Culture* (Aldershot and Brookfield: Ashgate, 1998), pp. 117–39.

54 Augustus Earle, 'Near Sidney [Sydney], from the Summit of the South Head close to the light house, used as a blacksmiths shop, N. S. Wales', c. 1825, PIC Solander Box A33 #T74 NK12/36; South Head Light, New South Wales [1825?], PIC Solander Box A35 #T97 NK12/59, National Library of Australia, https://nla.gov.au/nla.obj-134498735/view; https://nla.gov.au/nla.obj-134502410/view (accessed 20 October 2019).

55 Earle, *Narrative*, pp. 73, 72.

56 'Entrance to the Bay of Islands New Zealand' (1827), NK12/66; 'Ranghe Hue [Rangihoua] a Fortified Village New Zealand' (1827), NK 12/141, National Library of Australia, https://nla.gov.au/nla.obj-134515969/view; https://nla.gov.au/nla.obj-134503539/view (accessed 20 October 2019).

57 See Crosby, *Ecological Imperialism*.

58 Nicholas Thomas, 'Liberty and License: The Forsters' Accounts of New Zealand Sociality', in Alex Calder, Jonathan Lamb, and Bridget Orr (eds), *Voyages and Beaches: Pacific Encounters, 1769–1840* (Honolulu: University of Hawai'i Press, 1999), p. 134.

6

Australia to Paraguay: race, class, and poetry in a South American colony

Jason Rudy, Aaron Bartlett, Lindsey O'Neil,
and Justin Thompson

In 1893, Queenslander William Lane embarked with 234 white Australian immigrants for Paraguay, where they were to establish a utopian socialist community. Hundreds more Australians would follow, drawn to what was promised as a worker's paradise in South America. According to the *New Australia*, a newspaper published in New South Wales prior to the emigrants' departure, in Paraguay 'the means of working, including land and capital, should belong to the workers, who, by co-operative working, could then produce to supply all their wants, and need not produce for the profit of anybody else'.[1] Lane was a notorious racist, and his motivation for the Paraguayan colony was in part a response to the influx of Asian immigrants to Australia in the later decades of the nineteenth century. Our interest in Colonia Cosme, the town eventually established and maintained in the Paraguayan jungle, centres around its newspaper, the *Cosme Monthly*, and its accounting of minstrel performances there. We read Cosme's poetry and song, and its engagement with the form of minstrelsy, as part of a larger effort by Lane and his fellow émigrés to situate the colony in relation to Australia, the United States, and Great Britain, specifically in racialised terms. Our chapter begins with an overview of Australia's late-century labour crisis, which precipitated Lane's migration scheme. We turn then to the *Cosme Monthly* and its complex negotiations of race and class via poetry and song.

Australian labour and the vision of Paraguay

William Lane was an English-born immigrant to Australia, arriving in Brisbane in 1885. Among the few possessions he brought with him to the southern hemisphere were copies of Marx's *Capital* (1867) and Adam Smith's *Wealth of Nations* (1776).[2] Two years later he founded the *Boomerang*, a newspaper that advocated for the Workers' Party and expressed deeply racist arguments against Asian immigrants who were at that time settling in

Queensland as agricultural labourers.[3] According to the *Brisbane Courier*, 30,000 Chinese had emigrated to Queensland in the decade leading up to 1887, inspiring a manifesto by the Australian Anti-Chinese League that called for severe restrictions on Asian immigration.[4] This was the context for Lane's 1888 'Asian invasion' novel, *White or Yellow: The Coming Race War of 1908 AD*, serialised in the *Boomerang*. By the early 1890s Lane had determined that Australia would never be the utopian white socialist colony he wanted it to be.

This conclusion reflected both racial animus and class unease. Australia in the closing decades of the nineteenth century was in a state of economic crisis, resulting in what Thomas Keneally has labelled 'a savage class battle'.[5] Labour historian Humphrey McQueen writes that '[e]conomic fears and pure racism were', throughout this period, 'inextricable, with each feeding the flames of the other's fire'.[6] Most significant for Lane was the Australian Maritime Strike that erupted in 1890 from a local disagreement between dock workers and management, eventually turning into an international labour strike. According to Bruce Scates, the strike 'was phenomenally large by nineteenth century standards; 50,000 Australian workers were involved and perhaps as many as 10,000 New Zealanders', and though generally known as a maritime strike, it quickly 'spread to include shearers, miners, labourers, counters, storemen and railwaymen'.[7] In the pages of the *Worker*, a Brisbane newspaper Lane founded in 1890 with the subtitle 'Journal of the Associated Workers of Queensland', Lane attempted to articulate the demands of a labour movement that he envisioned as both international (or, at least, Anglophone) and particularly Australian.[8] '[U]nionism must be made so broad', he argued in November 1890, 'that everybody can stand under it and none need be against it'.[9] In trying to resist the natural capitalist tendency towards lower wages and higher productivity, Lane identified capitalists and non-white immigrants to Australia as equal obstacles. As in the American West, where 'public anxieties over major shifts in the American industrial landscape and class relations became displaced onto the racialised figure of the male Chinese labor migrant', as Edlie Wong has shown, so too Chinese workers in Australia were targeted with especial vehemence.[10] According to McQueen: 'Once the Chinese [in Australia] were perceived as an economic threat the belief in Anglo-Saxon superiority quickly turned Chinese customs into conclusive proof of [Asian] infamy.'[11]

As the strike built momentum in the summer of 1890, the secretary of the Amalgamated Shearers' Union asked his members to co-operate with the striking wharf labourers so as to 'draw such a cordon of unionism around the Australian continent as will effectually prevent a bale of wool leaving unless shorn by union shearers'.[12] No single union could withstand the power and the pressure of the capitalists, but perhaps together they could.

The language of solidarity and mutual aid did not extend across racial lines, however. Lane's editorials in the *Worker* advocated the exclusion of Chinese workers from membership of the unions. Other progressive policies in the *Worker* were similarly intertwined with Sinophobic resentment. A letter in June 1890 proposes opening a co-operative clothing store to save workers money, and then adds 'this system would go a long way to banish Chinese out of the colony'.[13] Presumably, these proposed co-ops would sell only to white members, compelling Chinese workers to pay higher prices elsewhere.

An editorial in the very first issue of the *Worker* is aghast at the Chinese-friendly policies of labour unions in New South Wales, warning against letting unions 'touch the leprous agony': 'No Chinese need apply where the [Queensland Shearer's Union] is about, and the southerners ought to make the same regulation.'[14] In the next issue, representatives of the New South Wales labour unions dispute this fact and, by June, the newspaper's 'Editorial Mill' wants to settle 'the unfortunate misunderstanding that existed previously' when the *Worker* alleged that the Shearers' Union had Chinese members.[15] While Lane continued to attack Chinese workers, all non-white workers qualified as a threat. 'It is very evident,' he laments in a July 1890 editorial, 'that there is a determination on the part of a section of the employing class to keep kanakas, Javanese, coolies, Chinese or some other sort of cheap and nasty labour in the country by hook or crook.'[16] Later in the same issue, he threatens lynch-like violence: 'If the Charters Towers cooks' union doesn't let the Chinamen understand that from the kitchen he must go, its members will cut off his pigtail and hang themselves with it in carrier-like rotation, heaviest first.'[17]

Brisbane's position in northern Australia might help explain why the white Queensland unions were so vehement in their Sinophobia. More than Sydney or Melbourne, nineteenth-century Brisbane embodied Homi Bhabha's sense of Australia as a place where 'the nations of Europe and Asia meet'.[18] Between 1863 and 1904, according to Penelope Edmonds and Amanda Nettelbeck, 62,000 Pacific Islanders were imported to work 'in Queensland sugarcane plantations, the pastoral sector and colonial households'.[19] Queensland enacted the first limit on Chinese immigration in 1877, decades before the official 'White Australia' policy that would restrict Australian immigration through most of the twentieth century. Phil Griffiths notes that 'politicians in Queensland railed against a "Chinese invasion", fearing that their control over the minimally colonised north and over the process of colonisation was threatened'.[20]

Indigenous Australians were not as much of a concern for the *Worker*, but the editors nonetheless positioned them as impediments to land ownership. An editorial in the inaugural issue demands that the Australian government follow the example of some South American countries in settling areas of

Indigenous land, asking: 'Are we going to let Spanish-Americans do more to keep back Indians than Anglo-Australians do to keep back poverty?'[21] The *Worker* thus positions poverty and Indigenous land claims as intertwined. Only by forcibly dispossessing Indigenous peoples, the editors argue, can poor Anglo-Australian workers find suitable work. These issues only intensified in urgency as the strikes crumbled in late 1890; by early 1891, dock workers and shearers returned to work without employers meeting their demands. Attempting to turn a regional labour dispute into an international strike had been a huge risk for Australian workers and, as Scates describes, they lost nearly everything that Australian workers had gained through previous actions: 'The Maritime Strike reversed a generation's achievements: unions collapsed, federations failed, strikes fell prey to the "terror" of victimization.'[22] Lane saw in this not just the failure of the Australian labour movement but 'the elimination from the political parties of the enthusiasm of courage and sacrifice'.[23]

These economic and political frustrations form the context in which Lane committed to establishing a socialist, whites-only colony in the Paraguayan jungle, a moment in Australian colonial history in which working-class whites felt increasingly estranged from the southern continent's future. Among other things, Lane was drawn to Paraguay's isolation from neighbouring countries, and the local government's promise that immigrants there would be left to their own devices. South America in the nineteenth century had earned a reputation as a space of greater freedom. As Jessie Reeder notes, 'Latin America powerfully, principally, and uniquely entered the British imagination as a symbol of freedom, a standard-bearer of anti-colonial liberation.' Insofar as Lane saw himself and his fellow émigrés as economic and cultural refugees (rather than part of a broader colonial apparatus), he would have been drawn to 'the perception that Latin America had deservedly won its liberty from European imperialism'.[24] According to Theodore Child, author of *The South American Republics* (1891), Paraguay specifically 'offer[ed] the two economical conditions essential to the success of useful European immigration, namely, facility of cultivation and salubrity of climate'.[25] Moreover, the Paraguayan government encouraged immigration from abroad following the disastrous War of the Triple Alliance (1864–70), which had left Paraguay as 'a land stripped of crops and cattle' with a decimated population numbering under 250,000.[26] According to Natalicio González, who was born near Cosme and briefly served as Paraguayan president (1948–49), the postwar government readily sold off land to foreign investors: 'The peasantry was dispossessed of the lands of its ancestors; state lands became the property of bankers from London; foreign companies took control of the press and the natural wealth of the nation.'[27]

The history of Lane's 1893 journey to Paraguay and the establishment of his first settlement there, Nueva Australia, has been well documented in

Gavin Souter's *A Peculiar People* (1968) and Anne Whitehead's *Paradise Mislaid: In Search of the Australian Tribe of Paraguay* (1998).[28] That colony fractured in less than a year, with sixty-four of Lane's hardliners – those who insisted on teetotalism and strict adherence to the 'colour line' – breaking off in May 1894 to form a new community, Colonia Cosme, forty-six miles to the south.[29] By the *Cosme Monthly*'s earliest tally, among these first Cosmans were thirty-nine men (of whom thirty-two were single), nine women, and twelve children.[30] Only two of the nine women were single, a disparity that at first proved socially awkward. Single women had both the right to vote and the freedom to remain unmarried, even as the *Monthly* praised 'the ancient and wholesome customs of our people ... that for ages have gathered together under one roof-tree, husband, wife and children in one family'.[31]

The *Cosme Monthly* began publication some six months after the colonists' fractious departure from Nueva Australia, in November 1894. At a time when colonists were one bad harvest away from starvation, $100,000 in debt, and living in grass huts (a perceived inconvenience that immigrants from Europe as well as Australia would continue to find unpalatable), William's brother John Lane began to publish the *Cosme Monthly* by hand (Figure 6.1).

In a neat script on vertically ruled paper, he sketched out three maps that accompany the paper's first article, a detailed description about 'Getting to Cosme'. This was a process that involved not just an eighteen-mile overland trek, but numerous administrative obstacles most likely compounded by the language barrier between the Spanish-speaking government of Paraguay and Lane's desired population of 'English-speaking Whites'.[32] If Cosme's first printed issue is optimistic in imagining that anyone would bother to 'get' to Cosme at this early moment, it is only because pessimism was one of the many luxuries the colony could not afford; as the *Cosme Monthly* betrays throughout its run, recruiting new members was seen as vital to the success of the colony.

The *Monthly*, eventually distributed to North America, Europe, New Zealand, and Australia, seems to have been regarded as key to the colony's growth. Its audience was decidedly not Cosmans – they had their own paper, the *Cosme Evening Notes*, which was distributed by voice at the nightly social gathering (Figure 6.2). The *Monthly*'s contents were at times overtly propagandistic, leading the New Zealand *Oamaru Mail* (est. 1876), for example, to share in 1897 that the Paraguayan colony had 'settled the food question by growing all they need for their own consumption'.[33]

This impulse to broadcast success was tempered by the colonists' conviction that their lifestyle was not for everyone. New colonists were of little value to Cosme if they abandoned Paraguay upon finding the conditions unacceptable. While manifesto and persuasion abound, the bulk of the *Cosme Monthly* is devoted to a fairly pragmatic ongoing account of life in

Figure 6.1 *Cosme Monthly* (November 1894), n.p.

the colony. The same principal sections appear for much of the paper: 'Weather', 'Health', 'Food', 'Crops', 'Stock', 'Work Done', 'Arrivals', 'School', 'Social Life'. These sections function just as much to tamp down the expectations of newcomers as to inform loved ones or interested parties oversees

Figure 6.2 Reading 'Cosme Evening Notes', Lane family photograph album

about ongoing life in the colony. Of course, other factors than an aversion to a meatless diet or inadequate housing might disqualify would-be colonists, a fact of which Lane was keenly aware. The following becomes the closing refrain of the paper for much of its life: 'To save needless enquiries everybody should understand that: COSME is (1) a common-hold not a common-wealth; (2) For English-speaking Whites – who accept – (3) The Life-Marriage. (4) The Colour-Line. (5) and Teetotalism among their principles, and who realise in their hearts that (6) COMMUNISM IS RIGHT.'[34]

Beginning with the January 1897 issue, the *Cosme Monthly* also included poetry in its pages, much of which was reprinted from the *Cosme Evening Notes*. In what follows, we examine how the poetic genres of the newspaper reflect the colony's mingling of political aspiration and racial animus. Lane's distorted vision of racial and political isolation manifested in regular minstrel performances, even as that isolation was in no way real: the newspaper inadvertently shows the degree to which Cosme depended on its Guaraní neighbours for its continued survival. Our method takes a cue from Simon Gikandi, who finds in *Slavery and the Culture of Taste* (2011) that 'the construction of the ideals of modern civilization demanded the repression of what it … had unconsciously assimilated'. Gikandi argues that in eighteenth-century Europe, enslavement needed to be 'quarantined' from the emerging 'culture of modernity', even as that culture depended on enslavement for its economic well-being.[35] Inspired by Gikandi, we examine what gets left out of the narratives Cosme writes for itself, and how poetry and minstrel performance in effect quarantined Cosme's culture from the Indigenous Guaraní on whose knowledge and support it depended. We see through Cosme's minstrel performances the continuation in Paraguay of the racism and xenophobia on which Lane founded his original contributions to the Australian labour movement. The firm lines minstrelsy helped draw around race and class enabled Cosme to define itself distinctly in relation to those not permitted within the community.

Cosme poetry

'The Free-Built Homes of Cosme', published in the August 1897 *Cosme Monthly* (reprinted from the *Cosme Evening Notes*), offers a clear example of how poetry, and specifically poetic rewriting, contributed to political ideology in the Paraguayan colony:

> The free-built homes of Cosme,–
>   With their bare mud-plastered walls,
> And hard mud floors all carpetless
>   Where damp the footstep falls,–
> Are dearer far to hearts that beat
>   In brotherly accord,
> Than the richest palace ever built
>   For millionaire or lord.[36] (lines 1–8)

Readers of the *Cosme Monthly* would likely have known the original poem to which this makes reference: Felicia Hemans' 1827 'The Homes of England', the final stanza of which addresses

> The free, fair Homes of England!
> Long, long in hut and hall,
> May hearts of native proof be rear'd
> To guard each hallowed wall!
> And green forever be the groves,
> And bright the flowery sod,
> Where first the child's glad spirit loves
> Its country and its God.[37] (lines 33–40)

Each stanza of Hemans' poem opens by addressing a different kind of home: 'The stately homes', 'merry homes', and 'cottage homes'. Each of the Cosme stanzas begins instead with the same line: 'The free-built homes of Cosme'. The distinction is crucial, marking a significant political difference between the two poems. Tricia Lootens has pointed out that Hemans links the English dwellings of her poem 'within a harmonious national hierarchy' in a way that stands out in retrospect as deeply politically suspect. Lootens rightly calls the poem a 'sentimental, reactionary pastoral fantasy at its crudest', insofar as it suggests that those in extreme poverty live as happily as aristocrats in stately manor homes.[38]

Across the nineteenth century, rewritings of this specific poem proliferated in British colonial spaces, a phenomenon traced in *Imagined Homelands: British Poetry in the Colonies* (2017). For example, an 1845 Chartist revision published in Adelaide, South Australia, laments 'The happy homes of England, alas! where have they gone?' In Saint John, New Brunswick, in 1868, the 'pleasant homes of England' are a nostalgic memory willingly left behind to make room for possibilities enabled by the Canadian colony, including upward mobility and westward expansion.[39] The Australian and Canadian revisions are politically motivated, highlighting differences between Britain and its colonies, specifically with respect to class. Something more radical still is at work in the Cosme poem. 'The free-built homes of Cosme' point to the egalitarianism at the heart of Cosme's communist ideal. The *Cosme Monthly* articulates these political views explicitly in an essay published in the same issue as the poem: 'Human society, by its very nature, is strong or weak as the ties which bind it are strong or weak. The competition in modern society, makes it a house divided against itself, which cannot stand.'[40] Cosme represents itself as a classless society. The gesture to Hemans highlights not just the politics of the colony, but how those politics were understood to distinguish it from both Hemans' 'sentimental, reactionary pastoral fantasy' and the politics of other Anglo colonial spaces, Australia in particular, which had so disappointed Lane and his compatriots.

'The Free-Built Homes of Cosme' also echoes Banjo Paterson's well-known 1889 'Clancy of the Overflow', originally published in Sydney's *Bulletin* (est. 1880), in its critique of what the Cosme poet calls 'the cramped and stifling cities / Where the sound of strife ne'er cease'. Paterson's poem longs for life outside the newly industrial city:

> I am sitting in my dingy little office, where a stingy
> Ray of sunlight struggles feebly down between the houses tall,
> And the foetid air and gritty of the dusty, dirty city
> Through the open window floating, spreads its foulness over all.[41] (lines 17–20)

Cosme residents, like the idealised Clancy of Paterson's poem, live instead beneath 'open skies, / Where man with man can live, and feel / The Good within him rise'. In echoing one of the key poems of Australian nationalism, the Cosme poet frames the Paraguayan colony as exactly the kind of free, pastoral space many urban Australians romanticised. The dual negotiation of Hemans (among the foremost female poets of the nineteenth century) and Paterson (celebrant of Australian masculinity) also points to the colony's gender politics, which residents likely considered modestly progressive. Not only were single women allowed to vote, widows were apportioned the same share in the Colony as married women.[42] That said, women 'resign[ed] on marriage' their voting rights, and Lane's priorities unquestionably privileged communism over women's rights: economic concerns consistently took precedence over matters of gender.[43]

A less enthusiastic framing of Cosme emerges in a rewriting of a Henry Lawson poem originally published in the *Cosme Evening Notes*, the 'Dying Cosman'. The poem implicitly connects the Paraguayan colony to the Australian nationalist movement. Lawson, whose nationalist poetry was published in Sydney's *Bulletin*, had worked for the *Boomerang* with Lane in the early 1890s, and he was at the wharf in Sydney to watch Lane's ship, *The Royal Tar*, set out for Paraguay in 1893.[44] The Cosme poem, published in 1898, reflects unease at the state of Lane's settlement:

> My pals they are good chaps and hearty,
>   True and staunch to the very last gasp:
> They have stuck to their leader and party,
>   'Tis a pleasure their hard hands to clasp.
>
> But there's one fearful thing though that frights me,
>   Now they're har up and cannot get meat,
> 'Tis the dread when I'm dead, if they sights me,
>   That my corpse they will cut up and eat.
>
> Roll me up in my shirt and my blanket
>   And bury me far down below,
> Where no cannibals ere shall molest me,
>   In a place where my mates never go.[45] (lines 1–12)

The original poem is quite different. Like many of Lawson's publications, 'The Dying Stockman' celebrates the rough and tumble life of Australia's working men, seen as constitutive of the emerging Australian nation:

> A strapping young stockman lay dying,
> His saddle supporting his head;
> His two mates around him were crying,
> As he rose on his pillow and said:
>
> 'Wrap me up with my stockwhip and blanket,
> And bury me deep down below,
> Where the dingoes and crows can't molest me,
> In the shade where the coolibahs grow'.[46] (lines 1–8)

Lawson here helps concretise the idea of Australian 'mateship': white male homosocial bonding most powerful among working-class labourers and agriculturalists. With obvious humour, the Cosme poet transforms Lawson's stockman into a settler anxious his peers will eat him after his death. The colony liked to highlight its connections to Australian working-class culture: 'Cosme men,' the October 1896 issue informs its readers, 'are as rough in their ways and speech as most Australian bushmen are.'[47] Similarly, the Cosme colony was meant to celebrate community in ways akin to Lawson's poem. The parody hints that perhaps the trust did not go so deep. Cannibalism itself may be read as a gross enlargement or parody of the communist ideal, a recognition that the circumstances of the colony were not self-sustaining, and a fear of having to offer a final sacrifice to the community in death.

The long and mistaken history of associating Indigenous peoples with cannibalism additionally suggests an anxiety about the communist project fixing the settlers in a state similar to that of the Guaraní. Cosme at the time was eating an almost entirely vegetarian diet, and the colonists' material conditions must have looked similar to or worse even than their Indigenous neighbours. That the Cosmans were living in grass huts looms large in the paper's early pages. The tongue-in-cheek humour of 'The Dying Cosman' thus suggests a more serious set of underlying concerns: that the Cosme venture was regressive rather than utopian; that the experiences of the colony gave the lie to the supposed strengths of the 'industrious' Anglo-Saxon; and that it might have been better had Lane's compatriots remained in Australia to fight for better lives there. Our point is both political and generic. 'The Free-Build Homes of Cosme' and 'The Dying Cosman' begin to suggest how Cosmans used poetry and poetic rewriting to contemplate their precarious state. Minstrelsy, to which we now turn, ratchets up even further the *Cosme Monthly*'s political and cultural stakes.

Minstrelsy in the colony

'America,' according to Adam Lifshey, 'was forged by an ongoing production of absence: the lives that disappeared, the societies and ecologies that vanished, the dynamics of disembodiment that were constituent of the Conquest in all its variegated forms.'[48] In the case of Cosme, what Lifshey calls the 'production of absence' took rhetorical shape as tenacious disregard: few references to Paraguay's Indigenous Guaraní appear in the *Cosme Monthly* even as the Australian settlers were living among and trading with the local people, learning from them how to navigate a new climate and terrain, and using their traditional lands as sites for their 'free-built homes'. The remaining pages of this chapter consider how Cosme minstrel performances take the place of explicit engagement with the Guaraní, situating the Cosmans in relation to other white-supremacist movements, in particular the defeated American Confederacy and the emerging policies of White Australia.

Just below the 'Dying Cosman' is another rewriting of a popular poem, but in a very different register. 'I Wish I Was Back in Cosme' turns to the United States, echoing the song considered to be the de facto anthem of the Confederacy, 'I Wish I Was in Dixie':

> I wish I was back in Cosme ahuskin' of the corn,
> A chaffin' an' a laughin' an' awaitin' for the horn:
> For it's huskin' time in Cosme, but me, I'm sittin' here
> A wondrin' how they're getting' on in Cosme now this year.[49] (lines 1–4)

The poem is in keeping with a worldwide Anglo-American phenomenon that had especial strength in Australia, where minstrel shows were popular throughout the nineteenth century. American minstrel troupes toured Australia, and home-grown Australian minstrel companies such as the Australian Railroad Minstrels in turn toured the United States, supporting Richard Waterhouse's claim that minstrelsy in the closing decades of the nineteenth century 'became less of a specifically American phenomenon and more of an Anglo-American institution'.[50] Cosme's minstrelsy reflects this global circulation, and specifically its work in establishing what came to be perceived as working-class white culture.

Historians have addressed in some detail the nineteenth-century emergence of what David Roediger calls 'an ersatz whiteness' that developed in direct contrast to the stereotyped blackness of minstrelsy.[51] Eric Lott finds that Black minstrelsy in the American context 'made possible the formation of a self-consciously white working class', specifically in the 1830s and 1840s: 'It was through "blackness" that class was staged.'[52] Minstrel performances found humour not only in racist caricature but in 'mocking the arrogance, imitativeness, and dim-wittedness of the [white] upper classes in "permissible" ways, as in a kind of carnival', as Sean Wilentz has shown.[53] The mid-century blackface minstrel show was thus the domain of the white working classes, a space carved out through vicious humour directed at both people of colour and more privileged whites. A similar dynamic was at work in the context of Cosme. We suggest minstrelsy functioned in the Paraguayan colony in both racial and class registers, working to promote both Lane's racism and Cosme's communist ideals.

To situate on the same page references to both Henry Lawson's 'Sick Stockman' and 'I Wish I Was in Dixie' in effect triangulates Cosme in relation to both the emerging White Australia movement and the Jim Crow policies developing in the American South. After its 1859 premiere in New York City, 'Dixie' was on the London stage by 1860, and it became one of the most popular shanties for British sailors.[54] 'Dixie' emerged at a pivotal time in race relations and economic hardship that ultimately turned the United States towards war.[55] The enslaved person portrayed in the text of 'Dixie' longs to return to his birthplace in the South because of the failure of his romance with the North:

> I wish I was in de land ob' cotton,
> Old times dar are not forgotten;
> Look away! Look away! Look away, Dixie Land!
> In Dixie's Land whar I was born in,
> Early on one frosty mornin',
> Look away! Look away! Look away, Dixie Land![56] (lines 1–6)

Like many minstrel songs, 'Dixie' aims to assuage the guilt of Northern audiences with humour. Hans Nathan argues that 'Dixie' both 'sharply focused the main cause of the political turmoil while affording relief in laughter from its tensions'.[57] The historic appeal of the song is apparent in an 1861 *New York Commercial Advertiser* article:

> 'Dixie' has become an institution, an irrepressible institution in this section of the country … whenever 'Dixie' is produced, the pen drops from the fingers of the plodding clerk, spectacles from the nose and the paper from the hands of the merchant, the needle from the nimble digits of the maid or matron, and all hands go hobbling, hobbling in time with the magical music of 'Dixie'.[58]

The systemic racism embodied in the 'institution' of 'Dixie' functions as a vehicle for affiliation among members of the working and lower-middle classes: the clerk, the merchant, the maid, and the matron. In this way, minstrelsy demonstrated what Lott calls a 'mixed erotic economy of celebration and exploitation' that ultimately unsettled boundaries both physical, through the medium of blackface, and cultural, through the appropriation of Black culture.[59]

In the context of Cosme, the 'Dixie' rewriting suggests nostalgia for the affiliations of the colony's working community. The corn huskings referenced in the song were called 'husking bees', large social gatherings following a harvest during which all fit Cosmans would pause their normal work and husk as much grain as possible in a single day. The July 1897 *Cosme Monthly*, for example, recounts that '[o]n June 17th, a very merry cornhusking bee was held and about a ton and a half of corn was husked'.[60] Though the rewriting of 'Dixie' has the surprising effect of putting Cosme workers in the labouring position of enslaved Americans, the poem makes political sense in its celebration of working-class community. Moreover, the evident industriousness of the husking Cosmans suggests pride in their labour. This realignment from the enslaved labour of 'Dixie' to the free labour of Cosme reflects what Lott calls 'the complex racial negotiations that took place in the everyday lives of working people' throughout the nineteenth century, negotiations that minstrel performances made explicit.[61]

At least two pieces labelled minstrel songs appear in the pages of the *Cosme Monthly*, in April and September 1899. Given the newspaper's regular mention of minstrel performances, these are likely representative of many others. For example, in September 1896, the newspaper reports: 'A minstrel performance on the Saturday night proved very successful. J. Dias interlocutor, W. Mabbot and W. Lawrence cornermen. A few songs, harmonised choruses, Cosme jokes. A farce came after, followed by usual Saturday "Interval" and dancing.'[62] The minstrel song of the September 1899 issue appears directly after a prose description of the work of 'hoeing and stumping', the latter being a process of removing tree stumps to prepare for ploughing. Throughout the nineteenth century, Anglo colonists represented stumping as a key stage in domesticating new colonial space. In Catherine Parr Traill's 1839 memoir, *The Backwoods of Canada*, for example, Traill's husband tells her that their 'Canadian farm will seem ... a perfect paradise by the time it is under cultivation; and you will look upon it with the more pleasure and pride from the consciousness that it was once a forest wild'.[63]

In Cosme, hoeing and stumping land originally belonging to the Guaraní, the Australian settlers represent their labour through the frame of minstrelsy:

> Hoeing weeds on Cosme land,
>   Chip, chip, chipping all the day.
> Bending back and blist'ring hand,
>   Chip, chip, chipping all the day.
> But hoes grow blunt and weeds grow strong,
>   And strokes grow short and hours grow long,
> While distant seems the dinner gong,
>   Chip, chip, chipping all the day.[64] (lines 1–8)

Like 'Dixie', this song works ambiguously. Both poems signal a fantasy of Cosme as a space where socialised labour allows all residents an equal share in work and resources, and where white colonialists have made a foreign space their own. Through recycling the tropes of minstrelsy, Cosme joins the American South as a region constructed by longing for what must have seemed at times an unattainable ideal: Lane's fantasy of a self-sufficient and racially homogenous community.

Nostalgia and longing are key features of traditional minstrel songs. For example, in a 1910 anthology of minstrel songs, 'The Old Home Ain't What It Used to Be' appears directly before a version of 'Dixie':

In the fields I've worked when I tho't 'twas hard,
But night bro't its pleasures and rest,
In the old house down by the riverside,
The place of all the world best;
Oh where are the children that once used to play
In the lane by the old cabin door?
They are scattered now, and o'er the world they roam,
The old man ne'er will see them more.[65] (lines 13–20)

Similarly, from the same collection, 'The Little Old·Cabin in the Lane' contemplates a property where 'de fences are all going to decay… / An' de creek is all dried up where we used to go to mill, / De time has turned its course an-odder way'.[66] These minstrel songs, including 'Hoeing and Stumping', foreground both places of rest (the cabin, the dinner gong calling workers back from the fields) and places of work (the farm, the mill). Minstrel songs repeatedly emphasise the contrast between a nostalgic present and a convivial, familial past, all to romanticise enslavement for predominantly white audiences.

By using this same imagery and structure, 'Hoeing and Stumping' effectively puts Cosme workers in the labouring position of enslaved Black Americans in a way similar to the article on the cornhusking bee. However, the Cosme poem replaces overrun cabins and fallow plantations with active labour working against nature's encroachment. 'Hoeing and Stumping' is still a song of longing but in a future-looking, proleptic form, anticipating the colony's economic autonomy. The particular appeal of minstrelsy seems to develop from the desire for solidarity among the Cosmans. In Roediger's assessment of American minstrelsy, 'blackfaced whites derived their consciousness by measuring themselves against a group they defined as largely worthless and ineffectual'.[67] For Cosme's inhabitants, those other groups would have included the Asian immigrants to Australia against whom Lane had railed in the *Boomerang* and the *Worker*, Australia's Indigenous populations, and Cosme's neighbouring Guaraní, whom the *Cosme Monthly* framed in adversarial terms:

> The Guarani clings stubbornly to the Guarani customs. This is irritating to the European, but who shall say that the Guarani is not right? Our exchange difficulties are among those which make settlement in Paraguay so exceptionally difficult to all Europeans, such difficulty naturally increasing the more outside exchange has to be relied upon. And European settlement cannot but be fatal to the Guarani, however profitable it may be to landowning and mercantile classes.[68]

The performance of minstrel songs in Paraguay thus allows the Australian emigrants to lay claim to working-class pride while simultaneously marking their sense of difference from their Indigenous neighbours. The success imagined in 'Hoeing and Stumping', the newspaper argues, will come at the direct expense of the Guaraní, for whom the Australian settlement will ultimately prove 'fatal'. Ironically, the need to mark a sense of difference with the Guaraní proved fatal to Lane's project itself. As in Nueva Australia before it, Lane was unable to prevent the Cosme colonists from crossing the colour line that he had made foundational to his communitarian project. On August 12, 1909, the remaining Cosme settlers divided what was left of the colony's assets, bringing a formal death to a project whose founding members, William Lane first among them, had long since returned to Australia.[69]

The poetry and song of the *Cosme Monthly* offer significant insight into the politics of the struggling colony, a place generally not accounted for in discussions of 'Greater Britain' or the global Anglo world. As a colony of the southern hemisphere, Cosme's backward glance would always be towards Australia, even as it worked thoroughly to distance itself from the southern continent by creating a new 'south' in Paraguay. Through its retrograde celebration of minstrelsy, Cosme also imagined itself in relation to the defeated Confederate states, yet another 'south' whose politics took disturbing new shape in South America. That actual Confederate loyalists had settled in Brazil following the Civil War – the 'Confederados', as they were called – could only have strengthened the perception in Cosme that Paraguay offered future possibilities to the white working classes that had become unavailable elsewhere in the English-speaking world.[70] This regressive utopianism signals the colony's divergence from more progressive nineteenth-century social movements. For example, whereas Engels and Marx want to abolish class-based hierarchies, Lane and his fellow émigrés aim to establish in Cosme a new, white plantocracy that is, as the *Communist Manifesto* scathingly writes of French 'bourgeois socialism', 'both reactionary and Utopian'.[71] Ultimately, Cosme's political and cultural framework was governed by the colony's racial and class grievances, its sense of having suffered 'industrial slavery' in Australia.[72] Cosme's attempted isolation, a 'quarantine' in Gikandi's terms, offers an extreme example of how race and labour intertwined disturbingly across English-speaking spaces at the end of the nineteenth century.

Notes

1 'Lecture by the Chairman', *New Australia* (17 December 1892), p. 3; *New Australia Co-operative Settlement Association Papers, 1889–1927*, State Library of New South Wales, Sydney, MS A1563.

2 Lloyd Ross, *William Lane and the Australian Labor Movement* (1935; Sydney: Hale & Iremonger, 1980), p. 30.

3 The newspaper announced in May 1888 that it had sold 250,000 copies '[a]cross six months and twenty six issues'. Though unquestionably popular within the labour movement, David Crouch notes that '[t]he ultimate reach of the weekly newspaper is difficult to measure'. *Colonial Psychosocial: Reading William Lane* (Newcastle upon Tyne: Cambridge Scholars Publishing, 2015), p. 20.

4 'Anti-Chinese League Manifesto', *Brisbane Courier* (15 November 1887), p. 7.

5 Thomas Keneally, *Australians: Eureka to the Diggers* (Sydney: Allen & Unwin, 2011), p. 141.

6 Humphrey McQueen, *A New Britannia: An Argument Concerning the Social Origins of Australian Radicalism and Nationalism* (1970; New York: Penguin, 1980), p. 46.

7 Bruce Scates, 'Gender, Household and Community Politics: The 1890 Maritime Strike in Australia and New Zealand', *Labour History*, 61 (1991), 70.

8 The first issue of the *Worker* (1 March 1890) announces itself as a monthly with a circulation of 14,000. One year later (7 March 1891), the newspaper is a fortnightly reaching 20,000. The *Worker* became a weekly as of 2 April 1892.

9 John Miller [William Lane], 'The Editorial Mill', *Worker* [Brisbane] (1 November 1890), p. 1.

10 Edlie Wong, *Racial Reconstruction: Black Inclusion, Chinese Exclusion, and the Fictions of Citizenship* (New York: New York University Press, 2015), p. 124.

11 McQueen, *A New Britannia*, p. 47.

12 Quoted in Arthur Duckworth, 'The Australian Strike, 1890', *Economic Journal*, 2:7 (1892), 432–3.

13 J. W., 'Another Co-operative Proposal', *Worker* (4 June 1890), p. 6.

14 [Untitled], *Worker* (1 March 1890), p. 4.

15 John Miller [William Lane], 'The Editorial Mill', *Worker* (4 June 1890), p. 2.

16 John Miller [William Lane], 'The Editorial Mill', *Worker* (1 July 1890), p. 3. 'Kanakas' referred to Polynesian or Melanesian workers, often at Queensland plantations, according to the *Oxford English Dictionary*.

17 Willian Lane, 'Central Queensland Labourers', *Worker* (1 July 1890), p. 11.

18 Homi K. Bhabha, 'Introduction' to *Nation and Narration*, ed. Homi K. Bhabha (London and New York: Routledge 1990), p. 6.

19 Penelope Edmonds and Amanda Nettelbeck, 'Precarious Intimacies: Cross-Cultural Violence and Proximity in Settler Colonial Economies of the Pacific Rim', in Penelope Edmonds and Amanda Nettelbeck (eds), *Intimacies of Violence in the Settler Colony: Economies of Dispossession around the Pacific Rim* (New York: Palgrave Macmillan, 2018), p. 11.

20 Phil Griffiths, '"This is a British Colony": The Ruling-Class Politics of the Seafarer's Strike, 1878–79', *Labour History*, 105 (2013), 132.

21 John Miller [William Lane], 'The Editorial Mill', *Worker* (1 March 1890), p. 1.

22 Scates, 'Gender, Household and Community Politics', 70.

23 Ross, *William Lane and the Australian Labor Movement*, p. 162. James Belich writes that 'a new version [of working-class optimism] emerged' in Australia after the 1890s economic crisis, 'emphasiz[ing] quality over quantity, and the welfare state over natural abundance'. *Replenishing the Earth: The Settler*

Revolution and the Rise of the Anglo-World, 1783–1939 (New York and Oxford: Oxford University Press, 2009), p. 363.

24 Jessie Reeder, *The Forms of Informal Empire* (Baltimore: Johns Hopkins University Press, 2020), p. 9.

25 Theodore Child, *The South American Republics* (New York: Harper & Brothers, 1891), p. 368. According to Gavin Souter, Lane read the Paraguay chapter from Child's book in essay form, published in the July 1891 *Harper's*. Souter, *A Peculiar People: The Australians in Paraguay* (Sydney: Sydney University Press, 1968), p. 34. The essay was reprinted across several issues of the *New Australia* in 1893.

26 Philip Raine, *Paraguay* (New Brunswick: Scarecrow Press, 1956), p. 195.

27 Natalicio González, 'The Paraguayan People and Their Natural Tendencies', in Peter Lambert and Andrew Nickson (eds), *The Paraguay Reader: History, Culture, Politics* (Durham: Duke University Press, 2013), p. 182.

28 According to the *New Australia*, the Sydney newspaper published to record Lane's venture, the *Royal Tar* sailed for South America with heads of households and single women numbering as follows: from Queensland (forty-two), New South Wales (fifteen), South Australia (six), and New Zealand (one). 'The wives and families of married members are to be taken as included in the above.' 'Pioneers', *New Australia* (1 August 1893), p. 3.

29 Jan M. G. Kleinpenning, *Rural Paraguay, 1870–1963: A Geography of Progress, Plunder and Poverty*, 2 vols (Madrid: Iberoamericana Vervuert, 2009), 2:245.

30 'Six Monthes Progress of Cosme Colony', *Cosme Monthly* (January 1895), p. 4. State Library of New South Wales, MS A1565. All citations from the *Cosme Monthly* are drawn from this archive.

31 'Women in Cosme', *Cosme Monthly* (May 1897), p. 1. The article notes that being forced into marriage through 'the fear of want, the lust for wealth, and the many other evils of civilization that drag marriage through the mire of the marketplace, have in Cosme no foothold, so that they whom God would join together need never keep asunder'.

32 *Cosme Monthly* (June 1895), p. 4.

33 'A Small Newspaper', *Oamaru Mail* (27 November 1897), p. 1.

34 E.g. *Cosme Monthly* (June 1895), p. 4. It warrants noting that, though Cosme professes to 'communism' in principle, Marx and Engels critique the kind of utopian socialism that Lane advocated.

35 Simon Gikandi, *Slavery and the Culture of Taste* (Princeton: Princeton University Press, 2011), p. xii.

36 'The Free-Built Homes of Cosme', *Cosme Monthly* (September 1897), p. 4.

37 Felicia Hemans, 'The Homes of England', *Blackwood's Magazine*, 21 (1827), 392.

38 Tricia Lootens, 'Hemans and Home: Victorianism, Feminine "Internal Enemies", and the Domestication of National Identity', *PMLA*, 109:2 (1994), 248.

39 Jason Rudy, *Imagined Homelands: British Poetry in the Colonies* (Baltimore: Johns Hopkins University Press, 2017), pp. 59–62.

40 'Brotherhood and Civilisation', *Cosme Monthly* (September 1897), p. 1. The reference to Abraham Lincoln's 16 June 1858 'house divided' speech warrants note.

41 Banjo Paterson, 'Clancy of the Overflow', *Bulletin*, 10 (1889), 17.

42 'Cosmeism', *Cosme Monthly* (February 1900), pp. 1–2.

43 *Cosme Monthly* (February 1900), p. 2.

44 Dorothy Hewett, 'The Journey of Henry Lawson', *Australian Left Review*, 7 (1967), 34.

45 'The Dying Cosman', *Cosme Monthly* (April 1898), p. 4.

46 Henry Lawson, 'The Dying Stockman', *Queenslander* (4 August 1894), p. 212.

47 'Impressions of Life in Cosme', *Cosme Monthly* (October 1896), p. 4.

48 Adam Lifshey, *Specters of Conquest: Indigenous Absence in Transatlantic Literatures* (New York: Fordham University Press, 2010), p. 1.

49 'I Wish I Was Back in Cosme', *Cosme Monthly* (April 1898), p. 4.

50 Richard Waterhouse, 'The Minstrel Show and Australian Culture', *Journal of Popular Culture*, 24 (1990), 158.

51 David Roediger, *The Wages of Whiteness: Race and the Making of the American Working Class*, rev. edn (1991; London: Verso, 2007), p. 118.

52 Eric Lott, *Love and Theft: Blackface Minstrelsy and the American Working Class* (1993; Oxford: Oxford University Press, 2013), pp. 9, 67.

53 Sean Wilentz, *Chants Democratic: New York City and the Rise of the American Working Class, 1788–1850*, 20th anniversary edn (Oxford: Oxford University Press, 2004), p. 259.

54 W. B. Whall (ed.), *Sea Songs and Shanties*, 4th edn (Glasgow: James Brown, 1920), p. 120.

55 See James L. Huston, *The Panic of 1857 and the Coming of the Civil War* (Baton Rouge: Louisiana State University Press, 1987); and Kenneth M. Stampp, *America in 1857: A Nation on the Brink* (New York: Oxford University Press, 1990).

56 Daniel Decateur Emmett, 'I Wish I was in Dixie's Land' (New York: Firth, Pond & Co., 1860), n.p.

57 Hans Nathan, *Dan Emmett and the Rise of Early Negro Minstrelsy* (Norman: University of Oklahoma Press, 1962), p. 259.

58 Quoted in Nathan, *Dan Emmett*, p. 285.

59 Lott, *Love and Theft*, p. 6.

60 'Social Life', *Cosme Monthly* (July 1897), p. 3.

61 Lott, *Love and Theft*, p. 108.

62 'Social Life', *Cosme Monthly* (September 1896), p. 2.

63 Catherine Parr Traill, *The Backwoods of Canada: Being Letters from the Wife of an Emigrant Officer, Illustrative of the Domestic Economy of British North America* (London: Charles Knight, 1836), p. 126. For more on British colonial land clearing, see Rudy, *Imagined Homelands*, pp. 119–24.

64 'Hoeing and Stumping', *Cosme Monthly* (September 1899), p. 3.

65 C. A. White, 'The Old Home Ain't What It Used to Be', in *Minstrel Songs, Old and New: A Collection of World-Wide, Famous Minstrel and Plantation Songs* (Boston: Oliver Ditson, 1910), pp. 168–9.

66 Will S. Hays, 'The Little Old Cabin in the Lane', in *Minstrel Songs, Old and New*, pp. 6–7.

67 Roediger, *The Wages of Whiteness*, p. 118.

68 'A Paraguayan Market', *Cosme Monthly* (November 1898), p. 3.

69 See Souter, *A Peculiar People*, Chapter 13: 'A State of Drift'.

70 See Eugene C. Harter, *The Lost Colony of the Confederacy* (Oxford, MS: University of Mississippi Press, 1985).

71 Karl Marx and Friedrich Engels, 'The Manifesto of the Communist Party', in Terrell Carver and James Farr (eds), *The Cambridge Companion to the Communist Manifesto* (Cambridge: Cambridge University Press, 2015), p. 248. Lane ended up as the pro-war editor of the conservative *New Zealand Herald* (est. 1863), his racism perhaps prefiguring his bourgeois conservatism.

72 'What Cosme Aims At', *Cosme Monthly* (December 1894), p. 2.

Part II

Acculturation/Transculturation

7

'The renowned Crusoe in the native costume of our adopted country': reading *Robinson Crusoe* in colonial New Zealand

Jane Stafford

'Ever since my first acquaintance with Robinson Crusoe I had a wish to live on an island, to feel gloriously independent, and to be monarch of all I surveyed.' So wrote New Zealand colonist Henry Weekes in explanation of his decision in 1845 to purchase Puketutu, a small, volcanic, economically unpromising island in the middle of the Manukau Harbour, near Auckland. This, he conceded, might have been a 'boyish' fancy but 'by a chain of circumstances I afterwards had my desire ... even at this distance memory can vividly recall these pictures to the mind's eye'.[1]

In his essay 'Crusoe's Books: The Scottish Emigrant Reader in the Nineteenth Century', Bill Bell asks:

> How exactly does the act of reading reinforce or challenge the cultural assumptions of the reader far from home? What, in more general terms, is the connection between the circulation of texts and the preservation of cultural identity under strange skies?[2]

This chapter attempts to address these questions by examining the eponymous Crusoe in terms of what Peter Mandler refers to as the 'throw' of his text, 'its dissemination and influence', 'distribution and reception', in a particular reading community, that of mid-nineteenth-century New Zealand.[3]

Crusoe, Bell reminds us, recovers from the wreck of his ship practical objects but also books – 'three very good Bibles', '*Portugueze* books' including 'two or three Popish prayer-books', and 'several other books, all of which I carefully secur'd', along with 'pens, ink, and paper'.[4] His subsequent reading is, by his own account, exclusively of one of the 'three very good Bibles'. The 'several other books', whatever they might be, do not feature. The Bible is initially an inadvertent but efficacious remedy when he is ill; subsequently, reading the scriptures and reflecting on them becomes a central part of a purposeful reading programme.

'Cultural memory,' Bell asserts, 'is in exile contingent on – even reinforced by – the continued practices of reading and writing.'[5] The fictional Crusoe reads the Bible; the voluntary exiles of nineteenth-century emigration certainly brought their Bibles with them, but they also read more widely, and *Robinson Crusoe* was a central text in the production and maintenance of their cultural memory. In colonial New Zealand, the inventories of importers, booksellers, and stationers invariably include, alongside Byron, Scott, Irving's *Catechisms*, and the anthology *Mornings in the Library*, copies of *Crusoe* – the original as well as the juvenile retellings.[6] In ironic contrast to the reading habits of Crusoe himself, a commentator in the Wellington newspaper *The Colonist* observes that 'Robinson Crusoe finds almost as many readers as the Scriptures'.[7]

Gail Lowe emphasises the central role of colonial newspapers in the construction of these complex networks of affiliation and reassurance, and the way in which they 'enabled a local perspective on metropolitan news, politics and trade ... speaking as they did to local concerns, audiences, and readerships' while at the same time 'help[ing] foster a nascent local literary culture'.[8] In colonial New Zealand newspapers, there are repeated references to *Robinson Crusoe*. Paradoxically, while the adjective 'inimitable' is repeatedly applied to Defoe's hero, the message of these various citations was to insist that he be imitated. But at the same time, the malleability of his narrative, its openness to widespread, heterogenous applications, is apparent. Not so much a template for settler life as a variety of templates, models, compacted shorthand allusions, and justifications, Defoe's work was applied widely as a marker of a shared language of culture, literacy, and nostalgia, as well as a measure against which to narrate both the exigencies and the moral values of settlement.

In this, the Empire was replicating the reading habits of the metropole. In 1854, *The New Zealand Spectator and Cook Strait Guardian* reproduced an article from the *Liverpool Journal*, 'What do the people read?', a survey from the Manchester Free Library, which found that Defoe's popularity was exceeded only by that of Scott, and that *Robinson Crusoe* had been borrowed 239 times in the previous year. The author is conscious that reading fiction is still looked at with disapproval, and defends the genre:

> Novels have a never ceasing attraction, for man is fond of the ideal; and those who call novels trash know nothing of the law of mind. The most difficult work in all the range of literature is a good novel, and hence it is that we have hundreds of good histories, thousands of good (brief) poems; but our language cannot boast of thirty good novels.[9]

A novel, he asserts, even one that is 'trashy and foolish' and read only for amusement, excites sympathy, 'and God has so ordained it that sympathy bestows itself exclusively on virtue and goodness'.[10] In the New Zealand setting, the republishing of this article points to an uncertainty – over the reading of fiction and, by extension, other cultural practices – born of distance. Charlotte Macdonald writes that although '[i]n colonial New Zealand, paper, books, carefully fashioned pictures, writing and reading were to be found in even the most incongruous places and circumstances', there was a 'pervading fear … that colonial life might be attended by a loss of culture [which] found reassurance in evidence of reading, writing, an appreciating eye, educated tastes and habits'.[11]

Reading Defoe's work in colonial New Zealand, and, just as importantly, citing the novel in public discourse, were thus affirmations of cultural continuity. And at the same time, these repeated references were part of an exercise in memory and nostalgia – as Bell puts it, 'the preservation of cultural identity under strange skies'. Thomas Bracken's 1884 poem 'A Paper from Home' sets out the relation between memorialisation and emigrant reading:

A digger sat dreaming of times that were fled,
For mem'ry was painting old scenes, and recalling
Dear faces and forms from the realms of the dead.
His fancy renewed the old pictures long faded.
The sheet in his hand seemed a leaf from life's tome,
Its paragraphs bright and its articles shaded –
He smiled and he sighed o'er that paper from home.[12] (lines 1–8)

In evoking *Robinson Crusoe*, the memory of a pleasurable childhood reading experience is recalled; the place where that reading experience occurred – the pre-emigration home – is summoned to mind; while present-day access to the same book, or simply present-day communal referencing of that book, despite distance, imaginatively returns the reader to their childhood. It reassures that, separation notwithstanding, they are still within a cultural orbit which is not just literary but connected by reassuring networks of mutuality and familiarity.

Henry Weekes associates Crusoe with 'boyish fancies'; to the columnist of the *Wellington Independent*, he is the 'hero of our boyish days'.[13] 'How often in our youthful days have we pored over the pages of that inimitable romance, the "Adventures of Robinson Crusoe"', writes a contributor in the *Southern Cross*,[14] while the *Nelson Examiner* remembers 'the romantic though fabulous adventures of Robinson Crusoe [which] so entranced our boyish days'.[15] But *Robinson Crusoe* could also be read and referenced by the adult emigrant reader as a handbook and guide to the challenges of settlement, a text for the future rather than an evocation of the past. Mavis Reimer, Clare Bradford, and Heather Snell suggest it 'stands as the touchstone for the narrative of colonial adventure and conquest';[16] the newspaper

The Colonist puts it more prosaically – in *Crusoe*, 'thoroughly practical lessons of political economy are embellished with the charms of fiction'.[17]

Refiguring Crusoe

In keeping with Miles Ogburn's observation of 'global networks' of reading that are 'local at every point', 'the immortal mariner' is refigured in terms of the needs and aspirations of particular settler societies.[18] In New Zealand newspapers, Crusoe is repeatedly pictured as a lesson in industry and self-sufficiency, an emblem of work, investment, and return. The *Otago Witness* asserts:

> *no colonization can be effected without capital*. It is evident that a man must be supported till he can gather his first crop; and it is a matter of history, from Robinson Crusoe to that of the backwoodsman of America. The former had his food, seed, and implements from a wreck; the latter, generally with a young wife, starts, not only rifle in hand, but with a team and a well-loaded dray.[19]

The experience of the fictional Crusoe and the (presumably) realist backwoodsman are conflated. Character and attitude are presented as crucial settler attributes, with Crusoe emblematic of what is needed in the new colony. *The Colonist* describes Crusoe as

> struggling with an invincible purpose, an indomitable self-reliance to become self-supporting, and compelling success by sheer force of character and inexhaustible fertility of resource. These were commenced when the immortal mariner committed his first seed corn to the prolific earth, and were securely perfected when he gathered the first fruits of his labor. His native good sense told him that there was no investment so safe and reproductive as that of industry in the cultivation of his native soil.[20]

'Self-reliance' and 'force of character' set against an 'inexhaustible fertility of resource' is the mantra of settler economic success, 'safe and reproductive' results of settler 'industry' the expectation. Crusoe is pictured as having both 'native good sense' and cultivating his 'native soil', 'native' in the first sense conveying his Britishness, 'native' in the second sense the appropriative transferral of ownership from Indigenous to coloniser. Defoe's island has become the settler's land claim while Crusoe's character exemplifies not that of the often beset and improvisational castaway but that of the ideal settler, with, according to *The Colonist*, 'the labors, the self-denial, the self-reliance, the perseverance, the cheerful adaptability to the circumstances, the thrift, the forethought, the ingenuity, and patient pluck'.[21] Crusoe models 'the direction to which [the settler's] industrial efforts should naturally tend, both for his present sustentation, and in order to lay the foundations of future wealth'.[22]

In the *Daily Southern Cross*, a lecture by William Gisborne, 'Footprints on the Sands of Time', invites its readers to see the footprint on the beach not, as Crusoe did, as an occasion of fear, but as a metaphor for the New Zealand settler's responsibility to posterity:

> Shall we not then, in our brief journey, try to leave some traces of good behind us? Is there not in this country ample sphere for the effort? Placed in the midst of a semi-barbarous race can we do nothing to promote their civilisation? Have we not a wilderness around us to subdue, a Colony to create, political institutions, in which the humblest can share, to turn to best advantage?[23]

Even Crusoe's ability to 'reanimate his drooping spirits … [to sum] up the good points of his lot' is, in the view of the *Southern Cross*, a salutary lesson to counter the pervading melancholy of colonial society.[24] 'You may be happy on Robinson Crusoe's island,' chimes in the Otago *Witness*, 'you may be miserable in Paris or in London. It must depend on yourself whether you are the one or the other.'[25]

Crusoe is thus the standard against which to measure settler competence and success, both practical and psychological, prescriptive and descriptive. But at the same time, the dangers of inappropriate modelling and of irresponsible reading were also signalled. The novel might contribute to an overly romanticised view of settler life if read without discrimination. The *Otago Witness* warned:

> the gentleman of limited means and a delicate wife, who have pictured to themselves the delights and felicity of the Robinson Crusoe sort of life of a colony, where they may walk hand in hand through lovely meadows and charming groves, is very apt to be disappointed, when the husband has to dig potatoes, and the wife do the ordinary domestic work; the romance of the thing soon wears off.[26]

In a lengthy piece titled 'A New Zealand Robinson Crusoe', published over several issues of the *Otago Daily Times* in 1862, an anonymous clergyman gives an account of being marooned for five months on a small island off the New Zealand coast, and compares, rather resentfully, the challenges of his actual experience against those of his expectations derived from his reading:

> Unlike Robinson Crusoe, I had not even a dog or a cat for my companion, I had no wrecked ship wherefrom to draw any resources. I was totally unarmed. I had no tools wherewith to build, plant, or dig; I had no seeds to plant even if I had tools. I had no books to while away the long tedious hours, no means whereon to write even an account of my sufferings and fate, though perchance they might one day be read in my bones whitening on the beach.[27]

Not just his deprived circumstances but his own innate abilities suffer by comparison with his fictional model: 'I remembered that Robinson Crusoe became swift enough of foot to run [stray goats] down,' he writes glumly. 'I much doubted my capability of doing so.'[28] Vanessa Smith points to the number of autobiographical accounts of Pacific castaways who draw on Crusoe as a model.[29] In this particular re-enactment – or perhaps reverse enactment – the clerical castaway's natives are not Defoe's hostile cannibal hoards or the subservient Friday but efficient and familiar – local Māori out on a fishing trip – one of whom credits the castaway's survival not to the Robinsonesque qualities of an Englishman but to that of a native:

> I proceeded to narrate my adventures of the last few months, in the course of which I was frequently interrupted by his savage ejaculations of astonishment. When I had done he said, 'Ah, well, you would make a good Maori,' that being the very highest compliment he could pay me.[30]

Modelling Crusoe

To return to Henry Weekes and his island: Weekes is a somewhat dilettante settler, largely untouched by the moralising agendas of local newspaper columnists. He preaches no lesson from his Robinsonade, apart from a final warning: 'Moral. The life of early colonists, even under favourable circumstances, is not all *rose-water*.'[31] His account is framed with literary epigraphs from Byron and Samuel Johnson, and he has a classical tag for every occasion. There is no reference whatsoever to any Christian mode of thought or purpose. He has no ethnographical interests. Nor is he shaped by any overt colonising ideology. He shows no awareness of the history of his island – he reports an amicable conversation with its previous Māori owner without comment; the narrative of his friend 'Mr Fairburn' of 'many a thrilling story of native savagery', whose family, under the protection of 'a powerful chief' in Northland 'in a few years ... became lords paramount in that part of New Zealand, acquiring large tracts of land', is recounted with admiration but with no sense of a desire to imitate.[32] Though he describes himself as ambitious to take a part in the founding of a new colony, at the same time he expresses the wish to lead 'a country life'.[33] Actualising his boyhood memories of *Robinson Crusoe* by buying an island, manufacturing his own Crusoe-esqe setting, and casting himself in the leading role, he uses *Robinson Crusoe* as a literary rather than a didactic model. His account exhibits that combination of modest heroism and wry self-deprecation, rueful and humorous, observable in Defoe's text but also common in settler self-reporting and articulated in small narratives of comic ineptitude.

As a counter to the pious editorialising of the newspapers, Weekes offers his audience amusement in narratives of the way his island resists all attempts at domination, cultivation, or domestication. The island is covered with 'edible thistles and other weeds among the universal fern, and a flock of goats fat and frisky'.[34] There is a 'whare', or hut, furnished with 'simple articles of furniture' and 'backed up with a pretty shrubbery growing among basaltic rocks'.[35] But daily life is basic. A chimney has to be built; cooking is 'an open-air affair with camp-oven and gypsy kettles'.[36] And the attempt to transplant both the reality and the atmosphere of home (i.e. England) is not successful: an apple tree brought out from Plymouth 'unfortunately exhausted itself in the excitement of the tropics, and after sending out buds, each time nearer the root, at last gave up in despair'.[37] There is a comic recognition, similar to that of his model Crusoe, of the clash between his idealised notion of control over his environment and the actuality of his island existence: 'our first batch of bread', he writes, 'was a failure, looking very much like those loafs dug out of the ashes of Pompei'; the 'much-loved garden' is destroyed by sheep and cows after Peter the horse demolishes the fence while scratching his back; wild pigs eat the lambs; on a trip across the harbour to visit friends, the boat capsizes. Weekes writes: 'The first object I saw on getting my head above water was my wife encircled by an inflated silk cape which acted as a float.'[38]

The loneliness of Robinson Crusoe is gestured to but not convincingly. Puketutu is, he admits, only barely an island: 'about the time of low water it could be reached from the mainland by a shell bank having at each end a shallow channel with a soft mud bottom, the whole distance being about two miles'.[39] It was in fact in hailing distance of the mainland. And far from being singular as was Crusoe, Weekes is accompanied by his wife. The couple are able to participate in pleasant and decorous social occasions; he writes, 'we occasionally selected a fine day when the tide served for paying visits to our Onehunga and Auckland friends', and the visits are 'returned in the shape of a boating party, or by some sports man with his gun'.[40]

Crusoe's encounter with natives is dramatic and frightening, as he contemplates 'such a pitch of inhuman, hellish brutality, and the horror of the degeneracy of human nature' displayed in 'the shore spread with skulls, hands, feet and other bones of human bodies'.[41] Henry Weekes' is more benign but not without its uncertainties and misreadings. Soon after his arrival on Puketutu, he writes: 'the sound of voices reached me from over the water and very soon a canoe rounded the point of our little landing-place with four or five natives. One Maori jumped out and came towards me with extended hand and a friendly "Tenáqui [Tena koe]"'. The Māori give 'presents in token of their good will, and to show that we Pakehas belonged to and would be protected by the people of Ihumátu [Ihumātao]'.[42] Weekes and his wife are soon enmeshed in a genial and mutually beneficial economy of gift and exchange, both pragmatic and ritualised. They are welcomed, sustained, protected, but also in a sense owned by the people of 'Ihumátu', their pet Pākehā. They are not exactly Pākehā-Māori, that designation from a slightly earlier period for Europeans who lived with Māori tribes, often intermarrying and facilitating trading links.[43] It is difficult to see the economic advantage the amateur Weekes could afford the local Māori community although the relationship may have conferred prestige on the donors.

Weekes' account is without the exotic, romanticised view of Māori characteristic of the later, Maoriland period. There is a sense in his account that he feels himself on the periphery of something not understood, for which he does not have the interpretive intellectual or literary models necessary to effect familiarisation. He chooses not to interpret. He is aware of 'bad feeling' between neighbouring tribes; one night he hears a volley of muskets and is visited by

> an armed party of eighty men under the command of Te Kau on their way to the seat of war. This chief, the original owner of the island, was quite friendly ... most considerate in his manner, and yet he had been an inveterable [sic] old cannibal ... A chaunt used in rowing soon informed us that they were off, and shortly afterwards on ascending the nearest hill we saw two war canoes rounding the point of the island, the paddles glistening in the sun, moving like the legs of a huge centipede.[44]

Though not particularly aware of it, Weekes was observing a period of change. Ihumātao and its associated settlements of Awhitu and Pukekawa were part of the Tainui-Waikato confederation of tribes, at that time under the authority of Te Wherowhero, who later became the Māori king Potātau. Te Wherowhero's presence was seen by the governor Sir George Grey as protection for the recently arrived settlers of Auckland against Ngā Puhi incursions from the north – which may be what Weekes witnesses. Tony Ballantyne points to the fact that 'Indigenous social change was woven into imperial networks and global forces', and certainly the increasing Pākehā presence in the area was met by local Māori with changes in their social organisation and agricultural practices as trade with Pākehā burgeoned. The gardens of Ihumātao, with its rich alluvial soil, had been cultivated since the fourteenth century, and was an important part of the growing Auckland market. Ballantyne writes:

> the consequences of these transformations – increased agricultural surpluses and trade – were valued aspects of rangatiratanga (chieftainship). A central responsibility of leadership in the Māori world was overseeing the production, storage and distribution of food.

Weekes and his wife are the recipients of 'manaakitanga – hospitality that recognises and enhances mana'.[45] Ballantyne has used the terms 'entanglement' and 'strategic intimacies' to convey the complex nature of these links.[46]

Translating Crusoe

Weekes does not claim that his Māori visitors, either neighbourly or passing, are fellow Crusoe enthusiasts. But five years later they could have been. In 1852 Henry Tacy Kemp translated *Robinson Crusoe* and in 1854 Bunyan's *Pilgrim's Progress* into te reo Māori (the Māori language). The governor Sir George Grey considered the works would be 'useful and interesting' to Māori, and Kemp requested that the government printer issue 1,000 copies.

Writing about John Bunyan's *Pilgrim's Progress*, Isabel Hofmeyr identifies 'translatability' as 'an a priori assumption in the Protestant mission world ... Driven by universalistic theories of language and evangelical ardour, mission organizations held that any and every text with the "right" message was translatable.'[47] *Robinson Crusoe* and *Pilgrim's Progress* were obvious choices for colonial translation projects, following their widespread popularity in the metropole, and particularly with working-class readers. Jonathan Rose, in his history of nineteenth-century British working-class reading, writes that 'three books in particular stand out: the Bible, of course, *Pilgrim's Progress*, and *Robinson Crusoe*. In the memoirs of common readers they are frequently discussed together, and men from humble backgrounds ... remembered reading *Pilgrim's Progress* or *Robinson Crusoe* as literal truth'.[48] Describing them as 'the best sellers of Hanoverian Britain', Rose suggests that 'all told essentially the same story ... thrilling tales of adventure, about amazing journeys and terrific struggles, and memorable heroes who, with the help of God, miraculously prevail'.[49]

Kemp's translation was only half the length of the original – no different in this from many English editions in the eighteenth and nineteenth century, where condensation was more the rule than the exception.[50] In Kemp's version, Crusoe's journal and inventories were left out. And there were, perhaps inevitably, places where the official nature of the project and its governmental sponsorship trumped accuracy or literary values. Lani Kavika Hunter discusses a number of these, most intriguingly the transposition of Friday placing his head under Crusoe's foot in the original to Crusoe himself doing so in the te reo version: 'This simple but explicit act of physical subordination installs a strangely bizarre political *stance* which will be reproduced both openly and covertly by Pakeha writers throughout the nineteenth and twentieth centuries.'[51] But it is difficult to discriminate between the two versions as images of colonial power: in the te reo version, Crusoe imposes his will on the subservient Friday; but in Defoe's original, Friday is shown as being if not the initiator then at least collaborative with that act of subordination. In the te reo version, Crusoe then addresses Friday – Hunter states, 'the Maori text adds several lines wholly absent from the Defoe original' – and makes an undertaking that Crusoe will treat Friday with love (aroha).

In return, Friday must be obedient to Crusoe as his master.[52] It is here that the ideological underpinning of the translation projects seem most overt – as the *Colonist* might put it, the transactional 'embellished with the charms of fiction'.

The Pākehā reception of the te reo *Robinson Crusoe* reflected the familiarity and affection in which the original was held. A review in the *Wellington Independent* exclaimed:

> So Robinson Crusoe after having gone through editions innumerable in his native tongue, and been translated into most of the known languages of the world, has at length, by the able assistance of the Native Secretary, Mr Kemp, made his first appearance in the vernacular tongue, on the Maori stage! And right glad we are to greet the renowned Crusoe in the native costume of our adopted country; his new clothes become him well, he is still the hero of our boyish days, the veritable adventurer at whose feet we have often so long and partially sat to listen to his simple, yet wild and wonderous story![53]

The writer may have been partial – the *Independent* was the printer of both *Crusoe* and *Pilgrim's Progress*. But there is sense of confidence and satisfaction that the enjoyment of the original will be shared by Māori readers. *Crusoe* may have been chosen because of its capacity for practical application – to imbue Māori with those qualities of self-reliance and hard work the newspaper commentaries hoped for in the Pākehā settler, a tool of assimilation. This was not necessarily a colonial imposition. As Lachy Paterson points out, such values 'reflected changes Māori were themselves trying to effect or cope with'.[54] But there is also a sense that the imaginative and pleasurable aspects of the text were an incentive for the translators and something that they wished to pass on to their readers. The *Independent* reviewer of Kemp's translation continues, perhaps a little defensively:

> It may be objected that Robinson Crusoe is inferior in point of religious or moral interest to many others which might have been selected for the purpose of promoting the education of the aboriginal population. To which we answer, that we may publish, and distribute book after book, containing the most valuable information, filled with the sublime truths of religion, and adorned with the most beautiful moral precepts, and yet to those who are unable to read, or who have no taste for reading, such books must necessarily remain a dead letter. They will never be read until a taste for reading has been implanted and nurtured.[55]

This end, 'it was thought would be most likely effected by enlisting their sympathies and interest in the pure though exciting narrative of De Foe's inimitable hero'.[56] Reading is conceptualised as pleasure rather than (or as well) as indoctrination. In a later account of his translations, Kemp says that they were intended for 'the benefit and amusement of the Maori people'. He continues, '[t]he dearth of light literature has been a long-felt want with the Maori people. It is true that they have the Bible, Prayer and hymn books, with a few other minor religious publications' and concludes that *Robinson Crusoe* and *Pilgrim's Progress* 'found a ready welcome with the Maoris'.[57]

However, the Māori response to the te reo *Crusoe* is in fact difficult to gauge; there are only second-hand Pākehā accounts of its reception, often written some time after its publication and usually in a self-congratulatory mode. Māori early enthusiasm for literacy and reading is a common observation.[58] Hofmeyr, writing of translation and the nineteenth-century empire generally, claims that 'shared ideas of literacy as a miraculous agent and books as magical objects grew up as a field of discourse between missionary and convert', and this was true to a certain extent with Māori, although the practical, economic aspects of literacy as a tool of modernity were also important.[59] Kemp's preface to the first edition of *Crusoe* and the *Independent* review both claim that one of the guarantees of the translation's success is that 'the manner in which the story is told, corresponds entirely with the manner in which the Maories themselves are in the habit of relating events of any great importance'.[60] But it is difficult to know what is meant by this. In 1900, Thomas Hocken wrote, 'as *Pilgrim's Progress* and *Robinson Crusoe* were exactly suited to native taste they were in high favour, until the inevitable Killjoy made it known that they were allegories, and then all interest ceased'.[61] Again, it is unclear what 'exactly suited to native taste' means, and Hocken's use of the term 'allegories' must refer to *Pilgrim's Progress*, surely, rather than *Crusoe*.

According to William Swainson, again with no supporting evidence, '[t]he story of "Peter the Great," which has been written for them in Maori, is read with avidity; while "Robinson Crusoe" has no charms for them, because it is not true'.[62] But, as noted, it was common for all kinds of readers – Māori and Pākehā, New Zealand and British – to read *Crusoe* as fact rather than fiction. The title of Kemp's te reo translation, *He kōrero tipuna Pākeha no mua, ko Ropitini Kuruho, tona ingoa / na Te Kepa i whakamāori*, means 'A Māori translation of a tale of a historical Pākehā of time gone by whose name is Robinson Crusoe', suggesting that readers were explicitly invited to view the account as nonfiction – and Defoe's original text is certainly complicit in that mode of reading. While the te reo Bible was widely popular and sought after, there is evidence that Māori readers could be as disapproving of fiction in general as Victorian Pākehā.[63] A Māori newspaper complains that 'such tales as that of *Robinson Crusoe* and other trivial things' have edged out political news.[64] In the 1880s, the imprisoned Māori prophets Te Whiti-o-Rongomai and Tohu Kakahi rejected *Robinson Crusoe* in favour of the Bible. Their jailer John Ward wrote:

> As neither of the prisoners have anything to read, I proposed to get them trans-
> lations of *Robinson Crusoe*, and other light literature, but neither of them
> would hear of it. The books I mentioned were fables, they said (*korero nuka*),
> but they would like a Bible (*Paipera*) very much.[65]

For the Māori reader, as for the Pākehā, the Bible supplied a range of literary
forms – history, mythology, genealogy, theology, narrative, poetry, and
polemic – many of which seemed to speak to their own literatures. But this
way of reading was also in keeping with British readers, where, according to
Rose, both 'the Bible and Bunyan ... were both read through the same set of
interchangeable frames: literal, fictional, allegorical, spiritual, political'.[66]

Peter Lineham argues that 'Māori were accustomed to prophetic words,
and the scripture seemed similar, although this was not how the missionaries
explained it. Thus Māori culture became, at least briefly, intensely literal in
its use of the Bible.'[67] Judith Binney, Vincent O'Malley, and Alan Ward
describe Biblical forms as striking 'a rich vein of cultural identification'.[68]
And even Swainson conceded that although 'the modern New Zealanders
[i.e. Māori] are essentially a practical matter-of-fact people', '[t]heir songs
and poems, both ancient and modern, abound, in fact, with poetic imagery'
which is 'occasionally highly figurative, and sometimes so obscurely so as to
be intelligible only to a few'.[69] George Grey wrote in the preface to *Polynesian Mythology*, that Māori

> frequently quoted, in explanation of their view or intentions, fragments of
> ancient poems or proverbs, or made allusions which rested on an ancient sys-
> tem of mythology ... the most important part of their communications were
> embodied in these figurative forms.[70]

In introducing Māori to 'light literature' Kemp and his sponsors were
perhaps engaged in a more complex and lengthy project. In its review of
Kemp's *Crusoe* translation, the *Independent* makes an overt comparison
between potential Māori readers and the generations of British working-
class readers who were 'painfully' aware of 'their want of mental culture',
and 'more highly appreciate the advantages that knowledge confers', but
who for various reasons had not had the opportunity to acquire 'a taste for
reading', whose 'habits and occupations have removed them far away from
communion with books'. The reviewer concludes 'that it is but reasonable to
suppose that the same hindrance to the diffusion of knowledge, at least to
some degree, exists among the native race'.[71]

If none of Henry Weekes' Māori visitors brought with them a copy of
Kemp's translation, then neither did they resemble the Indigenous figures in
Defoe's novel. Weekes' neighbours are confident actors in a complex web of
mutually sustaining, sophisticated economic practices; they exhibit a shared
civility and a sense of host responsibility based on the traditional practices
of Aotearoa, but in concert with the changing circumstances of mid-century

New Zealand. In *Robinson Crusoe*, the natives are bestial cannibal hordes or the grateful and subservient Friday. Weekes' Indigenous are his genial though tough-minded neighbours and the tangential passing war party that pays him no concern. He does not attempt to conscript either group into his Robinsonade fantasy of Puketutu Island.

And yet Puketutu does have a Friday. It is not one of the Māori locals; it is Weekes' white servant Edwards, who is referred to by this name – 'My man "Friday"'.[72] The narrative treats Edwards as a comic turn – a 'lazy fellow' who soon becomes 'practically his own master'. Weekes asserts that 'to a stranger he appeared "half-saved"' – that is, simple-minded – 'yet he would now and then give evidence of much good sense'.[73] The Weekes' social inferior, he is nonetheless efficient, practical, knowledgeable (even of the Māori language in which he is proficient), and indispensable to these frankly amateur Crusoes, who feel lonely when he is absent. He is 'native' – as Weekes' description of him as 'Friday' implies. *The Colonist* describes Crusoe's 'native good sense' and his 'native soil'. Edward may not display much of the former: his negligence burning fern leads to the destruction of the house and Weekes' final decision to sell the island. But in terms of the latter, being in the process of acquiring a 'native soil', Edwards/Friday models the process of settler Indigenisation which looks forward to a time when the Māori inhabitants of the Manakau Harbour will have been displaced.

After the wars of the 1860s, 1.2 million acres of land were confiscated from Waikato-Tainui, including the gardens of Ihumātao. The Waikato-Tainui Raupatu Deed of Settlement, signed by Queen Elizabeth and the Māori Queen Dame Atairangikaahu on 22 May 1995, included $170 million and an apology for past Treaty breaches, 'something which', according to Richard Hill, 'held tremendous significance for the claimants and which created both national and international precedents'.[74] But the principle of private land not being subject to Treaty claims meant that Ihumātao itself remained in the possession of the Pākehā farming family it had been granted to on confiscation. When that family sold it, and despite promises that it would be included in the nearby historic reserve, the land was rezoned as a Special Housing Area and in 2016 was sold to a property developer. A protest, occupation, and negotiations between the government, the Auckland City Council, and the Maori king Tūheitea Paki are continuing.

Notes

1 Memorandum Book, 1855–77; XTS.130.1, Puke Ariki, New Plymouth, New Zealand; Henry Weekes, 'My Island', *The Establishment of the New Plymouth Settlement in New Zealand, 1841–1843*, eds J. Rutherford and W. H. Skinner (New Plymouth: Thomas Avery, 1940), p. 115. In te reo Māori, 'puke' means hill

and 'tutu' a shrub. Although Weekes refers to his island as Puketutu, it was for a period known as Weekes' Island. It is now referred to as either Puketutu or Te Motu a Hiaroa, named for Hiaroa, the sister of the Tainui navigator Rakataura. See James Cowan and Maui Pomare, *Legends of the Maori,* vol. 1 (1930; Papakura: Southern Reprints, 1987), pp. 43–4.

2 Bill Bell, 'Crusoe's Books: The Scottish Emigrant Reader in the Nineteenth Century', in Bill Bell, Philip Bennett, and Jonquil Bevan (eds), *Across Boundaries: The Book in Culture and Commerce* (Winchester: Oak Knoll Press, 2000), p. 116.

3 Peter Mandler, 'The Problem with Cultural History', *Cultural and Social History,* 1 (2004), 96–7.

4 Daniel Defoe, *Robinson Crusoe* (1719; Penguin: London, 2012), p. 61.

5 Defoe, *Crusoe,* p. 61.

6 A. K. [Anne Knight], *Mornings in the Library, Being a Collection of Short Extracts from Various Authors, with Introduction and Poems by Bernard Barton* (London, 1830?).

7 Anon, 'Agriculture – the Basis of Colonial Prosperity', *Colonist* (28 December 1858), p. 3.

8 Gail Lowe, 'Book History', in Ralph Crane, Jane Stafford, and Mark Williams (eds), *The Oxford History of the Novel in English, Volume 9: The World Novel to 1950* (Oxford: Oxford University Press, 2016), p. 15.

9 Anon, 'What Do the People Read?', *New Zealand Spectator and Cook Strait Guardian* (25 March 1854), p. 4.

10 'What Do the People Read?', p. 4.

11 Charlotte Macdonald, 'Beyond the Realm: The Loss of Culture as the Colonial Condition', *Journal of New Zealand Studies,* 12 (2011), 2.

12 Thomas Bracken, 'A Paper from Home', collected in *Lays of the Land of the Maori and the Moa* (London: Sampson, Low, Marston, Searle and Rivington, 1884), p. 148, but published earlier in various New Zealand newspapers.

13 Anon, 'Review', *Wellington Independent* (29 May 1852), p. 3.

14 Anon, [Editorial], *Southern Cross* (13 November 1847), p. 2.

15 Samuel Stephens, 'Sketch of an Excursion from Nelson, through Queen Charlotte Sound and the Waitoi Pass to the Wairau Plain, &c', *Nelson Examiner and New Zealand Chronicle* (29 March 1845), p. 13.

16 Mavis Reimer, Clare Bradford, and Heather Snell, 'Juvenile Fiction', in Crane, Stafford, and Williams (eds), *Oxford History of the Novel in English: Volume 9*, p. 280.

17 Anon, 'Agriculture – the Basis of Colonial Prosperity', *Colonist* (28 December 1858), p. 3.

18 Miles Ogburn, *Indian Ink: Script and Print in the Making of the East India Company* (Chicago: Chicago University Press, 2007), p. 11.

19 William Cargill, 'Dunedin Mechanics Institution: Lecture Delivered by Captain Cargill', *Otago Witness* (30 July 1853), p. 3.

20 Anon, 'Agriculture – the Basis of Colonial Prosperity', *Colonist* (8 December 1858), p. 3.

21 *Colonist* (28 December 1858), p. 3.

22 *Colonist* (28 December 1858), p. 3.
23 William Gisborne, 'Footprints on the Sands of Time: A Lecture', *Daily Southern Cross* (14 August 1857), p. 3.
24 Anon, [Editorial], *Southern Cross* (13 November 1847), p. 2.
25 Archibald Michie, 'Colonists Socially, and their Relation to the Mother Country', *Otago Witness* (24 March 1860), p. 2.
26 Anon, [Editorial], *Otago Witness* (3 January 1857), p. 3.
27 Anon, 'A New Zealand Robinson Crusoe', *Otago Daily Times* (29 August 1862), p. 6.
28 *Otago Daily Times* (29 August 1862), p. 6.
29 Vanessa Smith, 'Crusoe in the South Seas: Beachcombers, Missionaries and the Myth of the Castaway', in Lieve Spaas and Brian Stimpson (eds), *Robinson Crusoe: Myths and Metamorphoses* (London: Macmillan, 1996), pp. 62–77.
30 *Otago Daily Times* (29 August 1862), p. 6.
31 Weekes, 'My Island', p. 131.
32 Weekes, 'My Island', p. 130.
33 Weekes, 'My Island', p. 115.
34 Weekes, 'My Island', p. 116.
35 Weekes, 'My Island', p. 117.
36 Weekes, 'My Island', p. 118.
37 Weekes, 'My Island', p. 121.
38 Weekes, 'My Island', p. 127.
39 Weekes, 'My Island', p. 116.
40 Weekes, 'My Island', p. 122.
41 Defoe, *Crusoe*, p. 160.
42 Weekes, 'My Island', p. 119.
43 See Trevor Bentley, *Pakeha Maori: The Extraordinary Story of the Europeans Who Lived as Maori in Early New Zealand* (Auckland: Penguin, 1999).
44 Bentley, *Pakeha Maori*, p. 125.
45 Tony Ballantyne, 'Christianity, Commerce, and the Remaking of the Māori World', in Kate Fullagar and Michael McDonnell (eds), *Facing Empire: Indigenous Experience in a Revolutionary Age* (Baltimore: Johns Hopkins University Press, 2018), pp. 193, 203, 207.
46 Ballantyne, 'Christianity, Commerce', p. 207; Tony Ballantyne, 'Strategic Intimacies: Knowledge and Colonization in Southern New Zealand', *Journal of New Zealand Studies*, 14 (2013), 4–18.
47 Isabel Hofmeyr, *The Portable Bunyan: A Transnational History of* The Pilgrim's Progress (Princeton: Princeton University Press, 2004), p. 13.
48 Jonathan Rose, *The Intellectual Life of the British Working Classes* (New Haven: Yale University Press, 2001), p. 93.
49 Rose, *The Intellectual Life of the British Working Classes*, p. 94.
50 Rose, *The Intellectual Life of the British Working Classes*, p. 107. For example, an eighteenth-century chapbook version was, according to Rose, eight pages long with Friday appearing in the final paragraph.
51 Lani Kavika Hunter, 'Spirits of New Zealand: Early Pakeha Writers on Maori' (PhD dissertation, Auckland University, 2004), p. 97.

52 Hunter, 'Spirits of New Zealand', p. 98.

53 Anon, 'Review', *Wellington Independent* (29 May 1852), p. 3.

54 Lachy Paterson, *Colonial Discourses: Niupepa Māori, 1855–1863* (Dunedin: Otago University Press, 2006), p. 35.

55 *Wellington Independent* (29 May 1852), p. 3.

56 *Wellington Independent* (29 May 1852), p. 3.

57 Henry Tacy Kemp, *Revised Narrative of Incidents and Events in the Early Colonizing History of New Zealand from 1840 to 1880* (Auckland: Wilson and Horton, 1901), pp. 7, 11.

58 See, for example, Shef Rogers' discussion, 'Crusoe among the Maori: Translation and Colonial Acculturation in Victorian New Zealand', *Book History*, 1 (1998), 183–4.

59 Hofmeyr, *Portable Bunyan*, p .13.

60 Anon, 'Review', *Wellington Independent* (29 May 1852), p. 3.

61 T. M. Hocken, 'Some Account of the Beginnings of Literature in New Zealand: Part I, the Maori Section', *Transactions of the New Zealand Institute*, 33 (1900), 488.

62 William Swainson, *New Zealand and Its Colonization* (London: Smith, Elder, 1859), p. 45.

63 C. J. Parr, 'A Missionary Library: Printed Attempts to Instruct the Maori, 1815–1845', *Journal of the Polynesian Society*, 70 (1961), 436–40.

64 Frith Driver-Burgess, 'Korero Pukapuka, Talking Books: Reading in Reo Māori in the Long Nineteenth Century' (MA dissertation, Victoria University of Wellington, 2015), p. 20.

65 John P. Ward, *Wanderings with the Maori Prophets, Te Whiti and Tohu; Being Reminiscences of a Twelve-Month Companionship with Them, from Their Arrival in Christchurch in April 1882 to Their Return to Parihaka in March 1883* (Nelson: Bond, Finney & Co., 1883), p. 7. 'Nuka' means 'deceptive' or 'trick'.

66 Rose, *The Intellectual Life of the British Working Classes*, p. 160.

67 Peter Lineham, *Sunday Best: How the Church Shaped New Zealand and New Zealand Shaped the Church* (Auckland: Massey University Press, 2017), p. 136.

68 Judith Binney, with Vincent O'Malley and Alan Ward, *Te Ao Hou: The New World, 1820–1920* (Wellington: Bridget Williams Books, 2018), p. 20.

69 Swainson, *New Zealand and Its Colonization*, p. 45.

70 George Grey, *Polynesian Mythology and Ancient Traditional History of the New Zealand Race as Furnished by Their Priests and Chiefs* (Auckland: H. Brett, 1855), p. x.

71 Anon, 'Review', *Wellington Independent* (29 May 1852), p. 3.

72 Weekes, 'My Island', pp. 121, 127.

73 Weekes, 'My Island', p. 131.

74 Richard Hill, *Maori and the State: Crown–Maori Relations in New Zealand/ Aotearoa, 1950–2000* (Wellington: Victoria University Press, 2009), p. 259.

8

The transnational kangaroo hunt

Ken Gelder and Rachael Weaver

The kangaroo hunt narrative genre was invented early on by the appropriately named John Hunter. Hunter was second captain of the HMS *Sirius*,
arriving at Sydney Cove with the First Fleet in 1788. An astronomer and
naturalist, his notebook, *Birds & Flowers of New South Wales Drawn on
the Spot in 1788, 89 & 90* (1790), contained 100 illustrations of native flora
and fauna, including a watercolour of a kangaroo to which Hunter ascribed
an Aboriginal name, *Pa-ta-garang*. His account of the beginnings of settlement, *An Historical Journal of the Transactions of Port Jackson and Norfolk
Island*, was published in London in 1793. Here he writes: 'The animal
described in the voyage of the *Endeavour*, called the kangaroo (but by the
natives *patagorong*) we found in great numbers; one was lately shot which
weighed 140 pounds.'[1] Kangaroo hunting as a practice had already been
described by other First Fleet chroniclers, like John White and Watkin Tench.
But Hunter was the first writer in the colonies to turn the kangaroo hunt
into a narrative that presented the quarry as a fitting adversary, focusing on
its strength and physical characteristics, describing the chase itself and the
methods used for hunting, and detailing the struggle to the death between
the kangaroo and the hunter's dogs:

> The strength this animal has in its hind quarters is very great: in its endeavours
> to escape from us, when surprised, it springs from its hind legs, which are very
> long, and leaps at each bound about six or eight yards ... they have vast
> strength also in their tail; it is, no doubt, a principal part of their defence, when
> attacked; for with it they can strike with prodigious force, I believe with suffi-
> cient power to break the leg of a man ... We for some time considered their tail
> as their chief defence, but having of late hunted them with greyhounds very
> successfully, we have had an opportunity of knowing that they use their claws
> and teeth. The dog is much swifter than the kangaroo: the chase, if in an open
> wood (which is the place most frequented by the animal), is seldom more than
> eight or ten minutes, and if there are more dogs than one, seldom so long. As
> soon as the hound seizes him, he turns, and catching hold with the nails of his
> fore-paws, he springs upon, and strikes at the dog with the claws of his hind

feet which are wonderfully strong, and tears him to such a degree, that we have frequently been under the necessity of carrying the dog home, from the severity of his wounds; few of these animals have ever effected their escape, after being seized by the dog, for they have generally caught them by the throat, and held them until they were assisted, although many of them have very near lost their lives.[2]

The hunting and killing of kangaroos is a direct expression of settler domination over species. A naturalist's naming and classification of a species is one part in a chain of colonising events that includes description, visual representation, killing, dissecting, eating – and significantly, exporting and exhibiting. Kangaroos – and kangaroo body parts – were already being transported back to England for scientific study, general curiosity, and popular entertainment. Markman Ellis notes that 'Botany Bay was a media event in London', generating two key exports: 'preserved kangaroos' and 'information'.[3] Joseph Banks had brought skins and skulls back to London, commissioning one of the most famous artists of the day, George Stubbs, to paint the kangaroo. Stubbs' oil painting was exhibited at the Society of Artists of Great Britain in 1773 under the title *Portrait of the Kongouro from New Holland, 1770*, and was remarkably influential, with the image reproduced by other artists; it also appeared as an engraving in John Hawkesworth's bestselling 1773 journal of Cook's voyage. Penny van Toorn notes that Banks was also given 'a large stuffed kangaroo' by Arthur Phillip.[4] Phillip himself had carried four live kangaroos back to England in 1793 on the HMS *Atlantic*, along with Bennelong and Yemmerrawanne of the Eora nation; Banks later gave two of these kangaroos to Queen Charlotte for her Kew Gardens menagerie. Around this time the entrepreneur Gilbert Pidcock included a live kangaroo in his small travelling circus.[5] Christopher Plumb notes the 'kangaroo mania' in England during this period;[6] while Richard Neville suggests that by 1800 there were so many kangaroos living there 'they were said to be almost naturalised'.[7]

Transnational kangaroos

This is the beginning of the transnationalisation of the kangaroo – which meant, among other things, that kangaroo hunting became a recognised recreational activity outside of Australia. One article appeared in English newspapers in March 1851 titled 'A Kangaroo Hunt in West Surrey'. It reproduces the familiar tropes of an English fox or stag hunting narrative, absorbing the kangaroo into existing traditions while also highlighting the novelty of the species:

Extraordinary as it may appear, there has been a genuine kangaroo hunt in the vicinity of Dorking. One of these animals, some four months ago, escaped from the pen in which it had been confined at Wotton, the seat of Mr W. J. Evelyn, M.P., and has been running wild in the neighbouring woods ever since, bidding defiance to several attempts to effect his capture. On Monday, however, by Mr Evelyn's direction, a regular hunting party was formed to accomplish this object ... Almost immediately the extraordinary animal broke cover, evidently determined to show sport ... the chase got warm, and, dogs and men in close pursuit, he reached the foot of Leith-hill. Here the animal's peculiar mode of progression was exhibited in a style which astonished the field – a singular succession of leaps carrying it over the ground at a rate perfectly startling ... At last, hard pressed, the animal took refuge in a pond on High Ash Farm, Abinger, where a groom succeeded in capturing him, though not without receiving a fraternal embrace, from which his shoulder suffered for some days.[8]

By the 1860s, the acclimatisation society of Paris was making determined efforts to bring kangaroos to France. The Jardin d'Acclimatation was reported to have 'some hundreds of kangaroos, recently arrived from Australia' and introduced 'into several estates' where they were 'hunted in that country like other game. The flesh is sold in the market, and is thought a great dainty.'[9] The Société Zoologique d'Acclimatation in Paris was established in 1854; in 1858 it set up gardens in part of the Bois de Boulogne, with the intention of importing and naturalising species from around the world. The globalisation of the kangaroo was, of course, part of a much larger project of species circulation through similar acclimatisation organisations around the world, including Australia. In fact, Australian acclimatisation societies were themselves actively contributing to the live export of kangaroos: a report of the Victorian branch in 1861 notes that 'Bennett's kangaroo is the most abundant species in Australia, extremely hardy, and much the best calculated for acclimatisation in an English park'.[10] A newspaper report in Australia in 1874 remarked that a French landowner at Beaujardin, near Tours, had 'let loose kangaroos, which are multiplying very abundantly, and give excellent sport, and a good eating'. 'The kangaroo,' it added, 'is destined to become in a few years, quite a French animal.'[11]

The exported kangaroo became a familiar enough figure to generate its *own* narrative. An anonymous article in *Bell's Life in London and Sporting Chronicle* from 9 May 1830 is titled 'Adventures of a Kangaroo'. Here, the author visits one of George Wombwell's popular travelling menageries in England and is 'particularly struck by a very fine kangaroo, whose magnificent proportions proved him to be one of the finest specimens of his species'.[12] But as he watches the kangaroo in its cage, he imagines that it feels the indignity of its imprisonment 'as poignantly as the poor blacks who are daily torn from their homes and their families and put in slavery'.[13] Here, Wombwell the entertainer is read as a slave trader; and the kangaroo is placed in the imperial framework of a growing anti-slavery movement, displaced, imprisoned, and exploited. The author then dreams that the kangaroo is speaking to him, telling its own story firsthand, 'in as good English as if it had been brought up in this country':

> 'I am', said he, 'the son of Boungarie-Bammee, the King of the Kangaroos at Botany Bay. My father was allowed to be the most stately of his race, and had often been marked down as the prey of the "bush-rangers", but luckily escaped their pursuit, and may yet, for aught I know, be enjoying his liberty. My mother was not equally fortunate, for, while pregnant of myself and two little sisters, she fell into the snares of the hunters, was taken alive, and presented to Governor Darling, who, admiring her symmetry, sent her as a present to the King of this country.'[14]

This remarkable narrative – where a kangaroo speaks, possibly for the first time – directly connects the kangaroo hunt to the business of acclimatisation: the mother is captured, not killed, and exported to England (the site of her enslavement). It also links back to Arthur Phillips' 1793 voyage to England with those four kangaroos and two Eora men. In fact, the narrative wants to give this kangaroo its own Indigenous identity and kinship system, tying the kangaroo hunt and its consequences to Aboriginal dispossession and demonstrating a parallel between, for example, Bennelong's experience of expatriation and that of an acclimatised native species.

The kangaroo is also an exhibited 'curiosity'. When she arrives in England the mother is sent to a menagerie, where she is greeted by kangaroos who are already there:

> Her sufferings, on being thus torn from the scene of all her joys, she has often described to me as dreadful, but, bearing up against them with true philosophy, she arrived safe in this country, and was, at last, conveyed to the Royal Menagerie in Windsor Great Park, where, to her surprise, she found several of her old friends, who had, like herself, been transported from Australia, by way of exchange, perhaps, for animals of a more mischievous description who had been transported to her native wilds.[15]

The Windsor Park menagerie was built for George IV in the early 1820s. Jane Roberts notes that by 1828 newspapers were reporting 'there were "no less than a dozen remarkably fine kangaroos in the Royal menagerie at Sandpit Gate"', one of the park's major entrances.[16] Perhaps the best-known imported animal in Windsor Park at this time was a giraffe, a favourite of the king. 'I had the pleasure of being associated with the celebrated Giraffe,' the kangaroo says. George IV died a month after 'Adventures of a Kangaroo' was published, and the animals in the menagerie were moved on to

Regent's Park Zoo. The kangaroo looks back at his time at Windsor Park with some fondness:

> I had nothing to regret; in fact, I enjoyed as much liberty as I wished, had plenty to eat and drink, and became as great a favourite with my keepers as if I had been their own flesh and blood. I had, too, the proud satisfaction of being caressed by his Majesty, the Marchioness of Conyngham [the King's mistress], and all the great Ladies of the Court, who were constantly admiring the increasing dimensions of my tail, which, as you are aware, constitutes a prominent feature in my person.

Along with all the other animals, the kangaroo is moved to Regent's Park Zoo, where – locked in a cage – he befriends a 'samboo [or sambar] deer' that is later 'condemned to death', 'given to feed a lion in the opposite den'. The kangaroo worries about his own possible execution. He is, instead, 'conducted to the Tower of London, where, under a new gaoler, my lot became still harder than before'. When Wombwell buys him, the kangaroo feels relatively free again, travelling 'almost every part of the Kingdom'.[17] But he yearns to return to the menagerie at Windsor Park, where he was born. This is a fully expatriated kangaroo, no longer connected to Australia in any way: born in England, acclimatised to English park life, exhibited by an entrepreneurial English showman, and entangled in a global assemblage of exotic species.

Global kangaroo hunts

The kangaroo hunt was itself part of a global narrative to do with travel, adventure, and hunting as a rite of passage for young men in particular. It could also provide the means for educating readers about species biodiversity in remote places. Sarah Bowdich Lee was well known as the first biographer of the renowned French naturalist Georges Cuvier: her *Memoirs of Baron Cuvier* appeared in 1833, a year after his death. Lee and her husband T. Edward Bowdich had worked with Cuvier in Paris; they also spent some time in west Africa. Lee was a prolific natural historian; her book on taxidermy appeared in 1820 and considers, at one point, the best way of bringing species collected overseas back to menageries and museums in Britain and France. It recognises that menageries provide the naturalist with an opportune way of analysing species, and wonders how acclimatised species from around the world might contribute to the domestic economy: 'The Peruvian sheep, the lama [sic], the kangaroo, the casoary [sic], may, perhaps, one day be very useful.'[18]

In the 1850s Lee published two adventure novels that mirrored each other in plot and circumstances and shared a naturalist's fascination with exotic-species description. *The African Wanderers; or, the Adventures of Carlos and Antonio* (1850) is about an orphaned Spanish boy who is adopted and educated by an English soldier. Later on, he goes away to sea, makes a friend, and ends up in west Africa, hunting genet cats, porcupines, leopards, wild boar, and buffalo. Lee's companion novel was published the following year in London, titled *Adventures in Australia; or, the Wanderings of Captain Spencer in the Bush and the Wilds* (1851). Lee had never visited Australia, so she relied on a range of London-published source material for her species information, some of which she lists in her Preface: for example, Robert Brown's *Prodromus of the Flora of New Holland and Van Diemen's Land* (1810) – Brown had sailed with Matthew Flinders on the *HMS Investigator* and went on to become head of the Botanical Department at the British Museum – the physician-naturalist George Bennett's *Wanderings in New South Wales, Batavia, Pedir Coast, Singapore, and China* (1834), and John Gould's *The Birds of Australia* (1841–48).[19]

Bernhard Gissibl has talked about a 'mobile, transnational class of globe-trotting hunters' in a post-frontier empire, who participate in 'controlled' forms of recreational hunting, like the safari, 'in the wake of conquest'.[20] But in Lee's Australian novel, Captain Spencer precedes this post-frontier moment. He has recently fought in the second Anglo-Sikh War, in 1848–49; to recuperate, he takes a ship to Australia, accompanied by his horse, dog, and a talking parrot. Spencer's journey to Australia is a detour from an ongoing military occupation in the interests of empire that has exhausted him. Shipwrecked on the west Australian coast, he seems to have no sense of purpose other than to kill a kangaroo: 'If I could but shoot a kangaroo,' he tells himself, 'I would go back [to India] directly.'[21] Against his better judgement, Spencer gets involved in frontier conflict. Under attack, he kills an Aboriginal man, an event that deeply troubles him. Later on, he helps a wounded Aboriginal man called Kinchela and they become companions. Lee's novel makes it clear that Spencer is a 'wanderer', not a settler: he is a 'mobile', 'transnational' figure that remains at a distance from the imperatives of dispossession, development, and nation-building. Species information in this novel – and in Lee's African novel, too – gives it a kind of picaresque structure: characters stumble from one species to the next, almost at random. The kangaroo hunt is one of the few things that gives Spencer a specific trajectory, a destination. And with Kinchela to advise him, it also helps him to learn a little about Aboriginal people. At one point, Spencer joins a group of Aboriginal people on a large-scale kangaroo hunt, 'a regular battue' as the novel puts it.[22] The emigrant Tasmanian artist John Skinner Prout illustrated Lee's novel with a series of lithographs, one of which shows Spencer dressed in white and on his white horse charging through the battue and scattering the kangaroos in front of him (Figure 8.1). Interestingly, he is

Figure 8.1 John Skinner Prout, 'The Kangaroo Hunt', in Sarah Bowdich Lee, *Adventures in Australia; or, the Wanderings of Captain Spencer in the Bush and the Wilds* (London: Grant and Griffith, 1851), n.p.

carrying a spear, not a rifle; an enthusiastic participant, he is both integrated into the action here and a kind of counterpoint to it, a stark contrast to the Aboriginal hunters around him.

The global hunting novel often turned to Australia as a site of adventure, even though its authors – like Lee – may never actually have been there. Emilia Marryat Norris was the daughter of the bestselling sea-adventure novelist, Captain Frederick Marryat. She wrote sea-adventure novels herself, some of which were set in the Pacific. Norris never visited Australia; it is not even clear if she visited the Pacific. Her novel *Amongst the Maoris* was published in 1874; it was reprinted in 1882 with the title *Jack Stanley; or, the Young Adventurers*. Jack is a young protagonist who travels to New Zealand to find the man who may have swindled his father. The novel touches on the Māori land wars but they seem remote from the main action. The Māori characters are, however, generally shown to be subjugated, working in the service of European settlers. Stanley meets a seasoned military officer, Colonel Bradshaw, who is now living peacefully in the bush, not far from Wellington. Bradshaw becomes his mentor, telling him stories about Māori customs and practices. Almost out of the blue, he tells Stanley about a kangaroo hunt in Australia. Colonel Bradshaw turns out to be the opposite of Captain Spencer: a military officer in the service of empire who is against hunting as a recreational practice. He tells Jack Stanley about a kangaroo hunt in order to demonstrate 'why I dislike the idea of it'. A hunting party singles out 'one large male kangaroo' and their dogs run it down until it is exhausted. 'I was nearest to him at the time he gave in,' the Colonel says,

> and I saw him rushed upon by the savage brutes, who gnawed and worried him, covering his soft grey fur with blood. He stood impotently beating the air with his forefeet, and the great tears ran from his beautiful eyes and down his cheeks. I was thankful that I was armed with a gun, that I might as soon as possible shoot the poor beast dead; and by the time the others came up, I was standing over him, feeling in my own mind that I had joined in a cowardly, unmanly sport, and vainly regretting that I had been an accessory in any degree to what I now looked upon as unworthy of me.[23]

W. Gunston's illustration in the novel – with the ironic title 'Sport!' – also conveys an impression of melancholy in the wake of the killing (Figure 8.2).

Such moments of regret over the kill are generally rare. Global recreational hunters mostly relished the hunt as an uplifting experience, often underpinned by a fascination with the natural sciences, especially in relation to species classification. French explorer Count Ludovic de Beauvoir's *A Voyage around the World* (1870) chronicles his travels through the Dutch East Indies, Java, China, Japan, Australia, and California in the mid-1860s. De Beauvoir was twenty-one when the trip began; he travelled with the young Prince Pierre d'Orléans and the naturalist Albert-Auguste Fauve, who was only a teenager at the time. In Java they hunted deer, crocodiles, and rhinoceros. They arrived in Australia in July 1866 and soon went kangaroo hunting along the Murray River in Victoria. 'In this short time,' he writes, 'how our feelings as sportsmen have been excited! What lucky shots we have had! What delightful sport! Shall we ever have such again?'[24] De Beauvoir thinks about taxidermy and how best to preserve specimens to take back to Europe: 'in future we may each bring home a perfect museum of natural history'.[25]

At one point de Beauvoir separates from the rest of the kangaroo hunters, overcome with enthusiasm:

> I found myself alone in pursuit, driving in my spurs till I could no longer pull them out of my horse's sides; but the kangaroo still kept more than a hundred yards a-head. At last I gained upon him by degrees, and came up with him. But I had been fool enough not to bring any arms with me, and I dared not approach, for our hosts had warned us that the brute is exceedingly dangerous when he is brought to bay, and can strangle a man in his arms in no time ... Luckily the Prince had come up with me, and he was armed; he put an end to our duel by a ball through the heart of the brute; you may imagine our delight[26]

"SPORT!"—p. 254

Figure 8.2 W. Gunston, 'Sport!', in Emilia Marryat Norris, *Jack Stanley; or, the Young Adventurers* (London: Frederick Warne & Co., 1882), n.p.

This is a kangaroo hunt narrative that exaggerates the violent potential of the quarry: the kangaroo is a threatening 'brute' that must be shot through the heart. Soon afterwards, de Beauvoir chronicles 'a duel with an old kangaroo':

> I was at twenty paces when the kangaroo turned and charged me; still at full gallop, and rather excitedly, I fired my revolver at him; the ball struck him in his fore-paws, he turned, then charged again. My first ball missed him, but

I sent him a second 'warning' which staggered him, and a third which 'suppressed him' altogether. A last ball finished him, and put an end to the frightful convulsions in which he died at my feet. I cannot tell you how exciting this wild chase, pistol in hand, was, and the fantasia round the brute as he charged furiously, after the prolonged anxiety as to which would give in first – horse or kangaroo.[27]

In John Hunter's much earlier kangaroo hunt narrative, the kangaroo kills hunting dogs. But here the kangaroo charges at the mounted hunter. The word 'fantasia' references the work of French artists such as Eugène Delacroix and Eugène Fromentin, both of whom had painted traditional Arab hunting and military scenes (e.g. Delacroix's *Fantasia arabe* [1833]). 'As a simulacrum of Arab military force,' Philip Dine writes, 'the fantasia would become an almost compulsory theme for visiting French artists.'[28] After he kills the kangaroo, de Beauvoir comes 'to fetch my beautiful prize, whose skin we took'. 'I am preserving it carefully,' he writes to his family in France, 'you will see his claws and the marks of my bullets.'[29]

The kangaroo hunt was itself an 'almost compulsory theme' for visiting artists in Australia. One of the earliest was Augustus Earle, 'the first professionally trained freelance travel artist to tour the world'.[30] Earle had sailed with Charles Darwin on the HMS *Beagle*. Before that, he had travelled to the United States and South America; for eight months he was a castaway on the island of Tristan da Cunha, occupying his time by painting and 'organising dangerous hunting expeditions in search of food'.[31] Richard Keynes writes that he gave 'full rein to an ambition to record the scenery in remote places previously unvisited by any artist'.[32] Earle arrived in Sydney in January 1825 and went on to produce the colony's earliest lithographs. His most celebrated Australian oil painting, *A Bivouac of Travellers in Australia in a Cabbage Tree Forest, Day Break* (1827), was set somewhere in the Illawarra subtropical rainforest, south of Wollongong. It presents a detailed scene, with a group of nine settlers and two Aboriginal men around a campfire. Some are half-asleep, others are preparing breakfast and attending the horses. There are two kangaroo dogs, curled up and still sleeping. And in the foreground of the painting, in the shadows, is a dead kangaroo: this is the aftermath of a kangaroo hunt.

Jocelyn Hackforth-Jones notes the significance of the term 'bivouac' in this painting's title, suggesting that it came out of his investment in the Romantic concept of the 'noble frontiersman'.[33] It is also often associated with military camps. The term was routinely adopted in early Australian settler chronicles of exploration, drawing these two things together. Thomas Braidwood Wilson first visited Australia in 1826, around the same time as Augustus Earle. In the late 1820s Wilson went on an expedition along the Swan River and down to King George's Sound, described in his memoir,

Narrative of a Voyage round the World, published in London in 1835. The expedition party is accompanied by an Aboriginal guide named Mokare, who carried 'a fowling-piece, which he would not go without' and who at one point 'succeeded in shooting a large kangaroo'.[34] Soon afterwards, Wilson writes, 'we bivouacked in the vicinity of a lagoon'; the party settles down to camp 'by the golden rays of the departing sun'; a fire is kindled, and 'the kangaroo was speedily cooked in various ways'.[35]

Wilson's *Narrative of a Voyage* is one of many early explorer chronicles that also maps out terrain for future settlement. It works by generating excitement and interest in the colonial project, not least through its investment in the romance of bivouacking and the thrill of the kangaroo hunt. On the other side of the country at around the same time, the agricultural agent Robert Dawson was making a much more overt attempt to promote the colonies and attract entrepreneurial newcomers. His book *The Present State of Australia* (published in London in 1830) is an account of three years spent in New South Wales exploring country on behalf of the Australian Agricultural Company. Like Earle, Dawson arrived in Sydney in 1825; soon afterwards, he took a group of settlers to Port Stephens, north of Newcastle, heading up the Karuah River. His expedition inland brought him into contact with different communities of Aboriginal people. Eager to kill kangaroos, Dawson, like Wilson, shared his guns with the Aboriginal guides: 'They are excellent shots, and I have often lent them a musket to shoot kangaroos, when it has always been taken care of and safely returned.'[36] This is a self-confident colonial racism, certain that Aboriginal people will always dutifully return guns to settlers (rather than, say, use them to shoot them).

On another expedition in November 1826, Dawson's party carries muskets, rifles, 'a brace of pistols', 'two double-barrelled fowling pieces', and 'two brace of kangaroo dogs'.[37] He writes: 'we bivouacked for the night on the banks of the Karuah, in the pleasant country before described'.[38] The description of the camp almost precisely recalls the socially integrated scene in Earle's *A Bivouac of Travellers in Australia*:

> my black friends had squatted themselves around the fire, smoking their pipes, and patiently awaiting their turn to partake of the favourite beverage. Our utensils were not many upon this occasion: they consisted of a tea-kettle, a large saucepan, a frying-pan, a few pewter plates, several tin pannicans, which served us for tea and drinking-cups, a spoon or two, some knives and forks, and a few napkins.[39]

It is worth noting that there is almost always a dead kangaroo beside these campfires: 'And now back to our bivouac,' Dawson writes, '[where] native dogs ... [are] carrying off the remains of kangaroo which the blacks had left about the fire.'[40]

These bivouac scenes are repeated often enough to become generic, working as quintessential expressions of settler colonial experience. Edward Wilson Landor emigrated to Western Australia in 1842, where he worked as a barrister and a journalist, writing on colonial affairs. Landor arrived in Perth with his two brothers, an assortment of dogs – a bloodhound, a mastiff, and a cocker spaniel – and some guns, shot, and gunpowder. He regards the colony as post-frontier, where Aboriginal people are in his view now both 'docile' and 'useful' to the colonial project. Landor was a kind of republican, speaking up for the farming development of the colonies and the 'ardent spirit of adventure' of new immigrants. He did not much like 'young men who are the wastrels of the World' because they 'betake themselves, on their arrival, to the zealous cultivation of field-sports instead of field produce'.[41] Even so, Landor himself enjoys a kangaroo hunt, riding with a party along the Canning River, 'attended by a native on foot, and five kangaroo dogs'.[42] His interest in kangaroos is heightened by the work of what he calls 'the French naturalists'; soon they chase after kangaroos, the dogs outpace the hunters, and one of the dogs later leads them to a spot 'where [a] kangaroo lay dead'.[43] A book illustration by A. H. Irby (a soldier and artist who came to Western Australia in 1840) shows a different kind of scene, with the hunter and his dogs poised to kill a kangaroo at close quarters (Figure 8.3).

That evening, Landor writes, 'we bivouacked near a small pool of water … The horses were tethered out and fed; a good fire was kindled, and with kangaroo steaks, cold fowls and ham, and brandy and water, we managed to make a tolerable supper.'[44] Earlier on, Landor camps again near the Canning River, where a settler and some Aboriginal people in the party have built a small hut 'for our night quarters'.[45] Unable to sleep, Landor thinks about the forests around him, wondering 'what spirits roamed abroad, melancholy and malignant'.[46] The camp provides what he calls 'a little circle of light' that seems 'like a magician's ring, sacred and safe from evil spirits that filled the air around'.[47] The bivouac here works as a kind of protective force field that keeps the frontier – imagined here as Gothic – at a safe distance:

> The appearance of the bivouac, to one viewing it from the surrounding darkness, was very picturesque. Every object was lighted up by the cheerful blaze – the cart with its packages in or about it, the sleepers in their blue or red woollen shirts, under the sloping roof, their guns leaning against the uprights, their shot-belts and pouches hanging in front – the kangaroo-dogs lying round the fire, and as near to it as possible – the surrounding trees and shrubs glittering with a silvery light, their evergreen foliage rustling at the breath of the soft land-breeze – altogether formed a striking and peculiar scene.[48]

In Irby's sketch of this scene, we can see the bivouac; it looks as if there is a kangaroo near the fire, attended by a Chinese cook, and another kangaroo

DEATH OF THE KANGAROO.

Figure 8.3 A. H. Irby, 'Death of the Kangaroo', in Edward Wilson Landor, *The Bushman; or, Life in a New Country* (London: Richard Bentley, 1847), n.p.

is being skinned in the background, with a kangaroo dog looking on (Figure 8.4). The settler – Landor himself, perhaps – is at the centre of the scene, standing with arms folded, smoking a pipe: a dominating figure.

The erotics of the kangaroo hunt

The accounts above confirm that the global hunting (and exchange) of species unfolded in the context of imperialism and empire, military occupation, exploration and settlement, and developments in the natural sciences. Hunting often operated in an aristocratic register of privilege and global mobility, as a recreational activity that would take young men around the world. Horace Wheelwright had practised as a lawyer in England in the mid-1840s; in 1847 he went to Sweden and Norway both to hunt and to pursue his interest in natural history. He emigrated to Australia, probably in 1852, trying to make his fortune on the Victorian goldfields, but without success. He then turned to *professional* hunting: the hunter, he wrote, 'has the satisfaction of knowing that, should all other trades fail, he can at least get his living by his gun if he knows how to use it'.[49] Wheelwright's *Bush Wanderings of a Naturalist: Or, Notes on the Field Sports and Fauna of Australia Felix* was published in London in 1861 and reprinted several times over. We have

THE BIVOUAC

Figure 8.4 A. H. Irby, 'The Bivouac', in Edward Wilson Landor, *The Bushman; or, Life in a New Country* (London: Richard Bentley, 1847), n.p.

already seen the figure of the wanderer in Lee's novel, *Adventures in Australia,* published ten years earlier. The wanderer is distinguished from the settler in these narratives, as someone less tied to the business of nation-building and property accumulation. 'There is very little fore-thought with the shooter,' Wheelwright remarks at one point. The hunter here is a bit like Landor's 'wastrels', emigrants with no plans for the future, including the future of the colonies.[50] 'Six years' rambling over the forests and fells of Northern Europe had totally unfitted me for any settled life,' Wheelwright writes; falling in with another new arrival, he adds: 'The gun had often brought both of us "to grief" in the Old World, so we agreed that for once it should help us out in the New.'[51] Even so, Wheelwright thinks that, compared to other global hunting memoirs – like Mayne Reid's popular *Hunter's Feast* (1860) – his book about hunting in Australia will 'appear dull and devoid of interest'.[52]

The first chapter in *Bush Wanderings of a Naturalist* is devoted to kangaroos. It chronicles the species' various physical attributes and behaviour, their habitats, and so on; finally, it describes the kangaroo as quarry that could indeed rival sought-after game species in other countries:

> Although harmless and inoffensive when unmolested, nature has furnished the kangaroo with a dreadful weapon of defence in the powerful hind claw, with which it can rip up a dog, like the tusk of a boar; and I have seen a large kangaroo take up a powerful dog in its fore claws, bear-fashion, and try to bite it.[53]

Wheelwright was also an amateur naturalist, and pays special tribute to the work of John Gould. What distinguishes the wanderer-naturalist from the traveller or the visitor here is his ability to provide the reader with an immersive sense of place and species-knowledge; he goes wherever experience leads him as opposed to following fixed routes, itineraries, or preconceived ideas, thereby affording a unique insight into the realities of his destination. In his 1865 book *Ten Years in Sweden*, he writes that 'English travellers are exploring every corner of the globe, men now "scamper through" lands, which twenty years ago they knew only on the map'. In response to this, he asks an interestingly modern question: how best can a 'stranger' write about a foreign country?[54] The answer, for Wheelwright, involves careful first-hand observation and prolonged exposure to local conditions.

Wheelwright's chapter on 'The Australian Bush' in a posthumous collection of essays published in 1866, *Sporting Sketches: Home and Abroad*, describes returning to London and coming across a novel about the kangaroo hunt: Anne Bowman's *The Kangaroo Hunters* (1858). Like Sarah Bowdich Lee and Emilia Marryat Norris, Bowman had never visited Australia. Wheelwright initially thinks the book must be a memoir, an accurate account of kangaroo hunting by an old colonial. 'I turned in early that night in order to thoroughly enjoy an anticipated treat,' he writes.[55] But the illustrations alone are enough to disillusion him. One of them, 'Fight with the Kangaroo', shows two boys violently struggling with a kangaroo; one of them is in its grip (Figure 8.5).

'Why, the strongest bushman that ever lived,' Wheelwright complains, 'would have stood no chance whatever if the kangaroo once could *put the hug on him* in the manner he is doing to the lad in the picture.'[56] He is dismayed to discover that the book is a novel written by 'a lady'; in fact, Bowman was the author of a number of global adventure novels, many of which involved big-game hunting. Wheelwright is so appalled by the novel's inaccuracies that he cuts it into pieces: 'It might come in handy,' he notes, 'for wrapping specimens in.'[57] This is a male professional hunter's disdain for a woman's novel about kangaroo hunting which seems utterly remote from its realities. By this time, Wheelwright is himself in London with his career as a kangaroo hunter behind him, except that it continues to inhabit his unconscious: 'I got through my book and fell asleep,, he writes. 'I recollect I dreamt all night of kangaroo, and fancied I was engaged in a deadly struggle with an "old man", which all at once, like the stag of Saint Hubert, assumed a beautiful female form.'[58]

Hubertus was a French courtier from the eighth century who went hunting one day in the Ardennes forest in the north-east of France. A stag suddenly turned to admonish him, and when a crucifix appeared between its horns Hubertus renounced hunting and joined the Catholic Church. Boria

Figure 8.5 Artist unknown, 'Fight with the Kangaroo', in Anne Bowman,
The Kangaroo Hunters (London: Porter and Coates, 1858), n.p.

Sax notes that this event enabled Hubertus to 'reconsider his way of life in a
very intimate way' and comments: 'All animals ... can lead us into other
realms.'[59] Wheelwright has no such conversion, but his unwavering commitment to the masculine authenticity of the hunt finds itself overturned in this
London dream about kangaroos, inspired by a woman's global adventure
novel of empire he had dismissed as inauthentic. We have seen someone
dream about a kangaroo in England before. In this case, Wheelwright's
imaginary struggle with an 'old man' turns into an embrace by a 'beautiful
female form'. This certainly suggests a reconsideration of the business of
kangaroo hunting 'in a very intimate way'. Transported back to London, the
kangaroo hunt is also now transmuted into a kind of erotic feminine fantasy, as if all the things this hunter had rejected while working in the Australian bush return belatedly to haunt him.

Notes

1 John Hunter, *An Historical Journal of the Transactions of Port Jackson and Norfolk Island* (London: John Stockdale, 1793), p. 54.
2 Hunter, *An Historical Journal*, pp. 54–5.
3 Markman Ellis, '"That Singular and Wonderful Quadruped": The Kangaroo as Historical Intangible Natural Heritage in the Eighteenth Century', in Eric Dorfman (ed.), *Intangible Natural Heritage: New Perspectives on Natural Objects* (New York: Routledge, 2012), p. 64.
4 Penny van Toorn, *Writing Never Arrives Naked* (Canberra: Aboriginal Studies Press, 2006), p. 69.
5 John Simons, *Kangaroo* (London: Reaktion, 2013), p. 144.
6 Christopher Plumb, *The Georgian Menagerie: Exotic Animals in Eighteenth-Century London* (London: I. B. Tauris & Co. Ltd., 2015), p. 111.
7 Richard Neville, *Mr J. W. Lewin, Painter and Naturalist* (Sydney: NewSouth and National Library of Australia, 2012), p. 17.
8 Anon, 'A Kangaroo Hunt in West Surrey', *The People's Advocate and New South Wales Vindicator* (15 March 1851), p. 11.
9 James Mason, *The Year-Book of Facts in Science and the Arts for 1876* (London: Ward, Lock, and Tayler, 1877), p. 18.
10 Anon, 'Acclimatisation of Animals', *Argus* (25 February 1861), p. 5.
11 Anon, 'Kangaroos in France', *Hamilton Spectator* (23 May 1874), p. 2.
12 Anon, 'Adventures of a Kangaroo', *Bell's Life in London and Sporting Chronicle* (9 May 1830), p. 1.
13 Anon, 'Adventures of a Kangaroo', p. 1.
14 Anon, 'Adventures of a Kangaroo', p. 1.
15 Anon, 'Adventures of a Kangaroo', p. 1.
16 Jane Roberts, *Royal Landscape: The Gardens and Parks of Windsor* (New Haven and London: Yale University Press, 1997), p. 366.
17 Anon, 'Adventures of a Kangaroo', p. 1.
18 Sarah Bowdich Lee (Mrs R.), *Taxidermy: or, the Art of Collecting, Preparing, and Mounting Objects of Natural History* (London: Longman, Hurst, Rees, Orme, and Brown, 1820), p. 121.
19 Sarah Bowdich Lee (Mrs R.), *Adventures in Australia; or, the Wanderings of Captain Spencer in the Bush and the Wilds* (London: Grant and Griffith, 1851), p. 3.
20 Bernhard Gissibl, 'The Conservation of Luxury: Safari Hunting and the Consumption of Wildlife in Twentieth-Century East Africa', in Bernd-Stefan Grewe and Karin Hofmeester (eds), *Luxury in Global Perspective: Objects and Practices, 1600–2000* (Cambridge: Cambridge University Press), p. 269.
21 Lee, *Adventures in Australia*, p. 30.
22 Lee, *Adventures in Australia*, pp. 259–60.
23 Emilia Marryat Norris, *Jack Stanley; or, the Young Adventurers* (London: Frederick Warne & Co., 1882), p. 252.
24 Ludovic de Beauvoir, *A Voyage around the World* (London: John Murray, 1970), p. 138.

25 De Beauvoir, *A Voyage around the World*, p. 138.
26 De Beauvoir, *A Voyage around the World*, p. 143.
27 De Beauvoir, *A Voyage around the World*, pp. 144–5.
28 Philip Dine, 'Horse Racing in Early Colonial Algeria: From Anglophilia to Arabomania', in Daniel O'Quinn and Alexis Tadié (eds), *Sporting Cultures, 1650–1850* (Toronto: University of Toronto Press, 2018), p. 145.
29 De Beauvoir, *A Voyage around the World*, p. 145.
30 Jocelyn Hackforth-Jones, *Augustus Earle: Travel Artist* (Canberra: National Library of Australia, 1980), p. 1.
31 Hackforth-Jones, *Augustus Earle*, p. 11.
32 Richard Keynes, *The Beagle Record* (Cambridge: Cambridge University Press, 2012), p. 1.
33 Hackforth-Jones, *Augustus Earle*, p. 18.
34 Thomas Braidwood Wilson, *Narrative of a Voyage round the World* (London: Sherwood, Gilbert & Piper, 1835), p. 242.
35 Wilson, *Narrative of a Voyage*, p. 245.
36 Robert Dawson, *The Present State of Australia; a Description of the Country, Its Advantages and Prospects, with Reference to Emigration: And a Particular Account of the Manners, Customs and Conditions of Its Aboriginal Inhabitants* (London: Smith, Elder & Co., 1830), p. 63.
37 Dawson, *The Present State of Australia*, p. 101
38 Dawson, *The Present State of Australia*, p. 104.
39 Dawson, *The Present State of Australia*, p. 101.
40 Dawson, *The Present State of Australia*, p. 178.
41 Edward Wilson Landor, *The Bushman; or, Life in a New Country* (London: Richard Bentley, 1847), p. 5.
42 Landor, *The Bushman*, p. 331.
43 Landor, *The Bushman*, p. 333.
44 Landor, *The Bushman*, p. 334.
45 Landor, *The Bushman*, p. 160.
46 Landor, *The Bushman*, p. 162.
47 Landor, *The Bushman*, p. 162.
48 Landor, *The Bushman*, p. 163.
49 Horace Wheelwright, *Bush Wanderings of a Naturalist: Or, Notes on the Field Sports and Fauna of Australia Felix* (London: Routledge, Warne & Routledge, 1861), p. xii.
50 Wheelwright, *Bush Wanderings*, p. 215.
51 Wheelwright, *Bush Wanderings*, p. x.
52 Wheelwright, *Bush Wanderings*, p. xi.
53 Wheelwright, *Bush Wanderings*, p. 17.
54 Horace Wheelwright, *Ten Years in Sweden: Being a Description of the Landscape, Climate, Domestic Life, Forests, Mines, Agriculture, Field Sports, and Fauna of Scandinavia* (London: Groombridge and Sons, 1865), p. x.
55 Horace Wheelwright, *Sporting Sketches at Home and Abroad* (London: Frederick Warne & Co., 1866), p. 417.

56 Wheelwright, *Sporting Sketches*, p. 418.
57 Wheelwright, *Sporting Sketches*, p. 418.
58 Wheelwright, *Sporting Sketches*, p. 419.
59 Boria Sax, *Imaginary Animals: The Monstrous, the Wondrous and the Human* (London: Reaktion, 2013), p. 31.

9

'Then came the high unpromising forests, and miles of loneliness': Louisa Atkinson's recasting of the Australian landscape

Grace Moore

A botanist, journalist, taxidermist, and fiction-writer, Louisa Atkinson (1834–72) was the first Australian-born woman to publish a novel, and a stern critic of violence in the name of progress. *Gertrude the Emigrant* (1857) appeared when its author was only twenty-three, but by then Atkinson was already an accomplished nature writer and a highly respected botanical illustrator.[1] She had also begun to pen short stories for the local newspapers, and went on to publish five more novels (an additional novel, *Tressa's Resolve*, was published posthumously). Atkinson's works are remarkable for the sensitivity and wonder with which they depict the Australian landscape and its plant-life, while her fiction is closely attentive to European settlement's devastating impact upon the land. She was a prolific columnist who published regularly in the *Sydney Morning Herald* and the *Sydney Mail* from the early 1860s until her death at the age of thirty-eight. In addition to providing rich descriptions of the flora and fauna she encountered on her many excursions into the bush, her columns also – because they ran over such a long period – mapped the changes wrought by settlers on the New South Wales countryside.

Atkinson was a regular contributor to the *Horticultural Magazine*, and her work was admired by botanists including Ferdinand von Mueller and William Woolls. Her name appears regularly in the proceedings of the Horticultural Society of New South Wales as, for instance, on 6 July 1864 when, at its Annual General Meeting, the society's honorary secretary distributed edible tubers supplied by 'Miss Atkinson of the Kurrajong', who was keen for the members to taste them and to understand how Indigenous Australians used them as food.[2] This example typifies Atkinson's immersive and experiential interest in plant-life: she once sent a jar of 'native cranberry' jam to the Sydney Horticultural Society to allow its members to taste a fruit about which she had written.[3] She celebrated native plants and wildlife, learning about them from the Indigenous men and women she knew. She even attempted to introduce a 'Native Arts' column to the *Illustrated Sydney News* in the early 1850s that would deal with Indigenous Australian culture. The feature ran twice before it was discontinued, although Atkinson wrote as though it was to have been a long-term venture.

Reflecting her great passion for Australian flora, Atkinson's writing is notable for its rejection of European aesthetic conventions, offering a corrective to the settler novel's picturesque and sublime framings of the outback as though it were an English vista.[4] That she lived entirely in Australia is of undoubted significance in Atkinson's advocacy for the distinctiveness and importance of Australian wildlife. Her upbringing was highly unconventional, and she spent much more time out of doors, observing plants and animals, than was usual for a middle-class girl.[5] Unlike many of her contemporaries, she strove to capture the extraordinary beauty and difference of New South Wales and Queensland, while at the same time recording the rapidity with which change was being imposed upon the regions. Fascinated by Indigenous culture, Atkinson attempted to promote an understanding of the land's traditional custodians and to highlight their more nuanced and reciprocal relationships with the natural world, although her racial politics oscillated between affectionate respect for the Indigenous men and women she knew personally and what Elizabeth Lawson identifies as 'overt racism'.[6] She also, as this chapter demonstrates, explored the destruction to the human and nonhuman worlds by settlers, whose attempts to make a home away from home failed to respect and understand Australia's carefully balanced ecology and the people who had successfully managed it for many generations.

Louisa Atkinson's country was Kurrajong, north-west of Sydney, which is also the Indigenous name given by the people of the Darug, or Dharug, nation for the types of trees (also known as the bottle tree) that once grew there. In discussing and using the term 'country' in this chapter, I take my definition from Deborah Bird Rose, who beautifully encapsulates the ineffable pervasiveness of country, and the mutual care and cross-species dependency that it envelops:

> Country in Aboriginal English is not only a common noun, but also a proper noun. People talk about country in the same way that they would talk about a person ... People say that country knows, hears, smells, takes notice, takes care, is sorry or happy ... country is a living entity with a yesterday, today and tomorrow, with a consciousness, and a will toward life.[7]

Atkinson's sensibility towards country could not approximate this kind of Indigenous connection, but her location was quite literally defined by woodland, and she embraced that connection in much of her writing, even as she grieved for its violent removal. A keen observer of her surroundings, Atkinson was particularly interested in the failures of settler colonisation, which were frequently associated with violence of one kind or another, including violence against the land.

In this chapter I examine Atkinson's representations of the massive land clearances that became a hallmark of settler interactions with country throughout the nineteenth century and beyond. I also examine Atkinson's use of the bushfire as a trope to critique settler understandings of the Australian natural world. Focusing on her fire stories, I consider how her depictions of fire-setting and fire-fighting are distinct from those of her contemporaries (for instance Mary Theresa Vidal and Ellen Clacy) and how her writings sought to promote respect for the bush, both reconfiguring the forest as an imaginative space in settler culture, and reassessing contemporary debates about land clearance and the bush as a 'resource' to be plundered.

Pastoralism, land clearance, and bushfire stories

Atkinson's position in relation to land clearance is interesting, given her background. Her father, James Atkinson, was a successful pastoralist who, when he died, owned more than 3,000 sheep and 200 cattle. He was a respected civil servant and the author of a prize-winning book, *An Account of the State of Agriculture & Grazing in New South Wales* (1826), which, as T. M. Perry tells us in James' entry in the *Australian Dictionary of National Biography*, 'was an important work', emphasising 'the problems of adapting European plants, animals and farming methods to a strange environment'.[8] James Atkinson's work is not cheerful reading for the modern environmentalist. It is clear that he saw forests as 'obstacles', to use Robert Pogue Harrison's characterisation of them, and much of the book recounts in copious and painful detail the most efficient processes for eradicating trees:[9]

> Some persons have preferred digging a deep hole on one side, and by throwing the stump down into it, have succeeded in burying it out of the reach of the plough; others have taken off a belt of bark all round the tree, and killed it while standing, afterwards clearing the land by grubbing or stump-failing. This is attended with some benefit, as the tree is then ready for burning as soon as it is down, but then the wood gets hard and dry, and is much more difficult to cut up. Some have barked the trees, and set fire to them standing; many will completely burn down, but a great many stumps and fragments will remain, and require as much or more trouble to be got rid of, than the whole tree would in the first instance; and it does not appear that much benefit arises from the system.[10]

There is something quite devastating about reading this volume of apparently endless suggestions for wiping out native forests. With his talk of stump burial, tree and grass burning, ring-barking, and killing trees while standing, this 'management' of the land reads today as nothing short of ecological vandalism. Yet within its context, Atkinson's advocacy of ecocide was regarded as the height of effective land management.

James Atkinson was far from unique in his beliefs. Rose reminds us of the disturbance to the ecological equilibrium caused by settlers to country when she notes that '[s]ettlers laid waste to land as they worked it; their land use practices meant that they were always hungry for more land ... They took with them their disregard for life-support systems.'[11] With their European aesthetic and their sense of Australia as a disorderly space to be ransacked into submission, many settlers were challenged by the uncanny appearance of the twisty, sprawling eucalypt forests. Yet at the same time, they were quick to invest them with pecuniary value, so that often when we look at early histories of colonial 'progress', sections which appear to be devoted to trees are actually accounts of timber prices and market values. John Stephens in his emigrants' guide, *The History of the Rise and Progress of the New British Province of South Australia* (1839), wrote of the stringy bark: 'it is estimated that, if twenty thousand persons emigrated to the Australian shores every year, for the next century, there would be enough for them all'.[12] Trees here are simply resources, and if Stephens is thinking about their expendability, it is only to the degree that he wants there to be enough to go around. His work pays no attention to renewal, or the need to nurture the forest, and it lacks understanding of the careful management needed to promote regrowth and regeneration.

While Louisa Atkinson's background could easily have made her an apologist for pastoralism of this kind, she had an incisive understanding of the damage that land clearance was causing. Her representations of farmers in her novels are notable for the insights she offers into attempts to subdue the arid and unruly land by force. Furthermore, her writing is remarkably prescient in its understanding of the environmental impact of deforestation and the far-reaching legacy of drought with which Australia contends today. As a realist novelist, she recorded the changes that the settler community forced upon the land, often with deep insights into the long-term impact of what she was witnessing, although also with sympathy for migrant farmers who were ill equipped to deal with their new conditions.

Although not approving the culling of trees, Atkinson saw that one solution would be a more sustainable form of planting, whereby fast-growing species such as cedar and walnut might provide the wood that settler society consumed at an increasingly alarming rate. As she wrote in a piece for the *Sydney Morning Herald* in 1870, 'it would seem advisable to plant suitable trees largely year by year; for, while the woodman's axe can fell the growth of a century in an hour, the forest springs up but slowly'.[13] Despite her great love of Australian native plants and creatures, she saw no difficulty in allowing imported varieties of trees. Given her professional friendships with proponents of acclimatisation like Ferdinand von Mueller, it is perhaps unsurprising that Atkinson was able to imagine native and introduced plant-life living happily alongside one another.

Atkinson was alert from an early age to the trouble settlers could wreak in an Australian forest. In a short story, published in 1853, when she was nineteen, 'The Burning Forest: A Sketch of Australian Bush Life', she offered a vivid account of a fire caused by a careless itinerant gold digger, whose refusal to extinguish a campfire leads to the death of several members of a Scottish migrant family.[14] Those who perish are shown to be hard-working and respectful of the landscape. However, the man behind the catastrophe, identified only as 'Tom', conflates the vastness of the bush with expendability. When he is asked to extinguish a campfire he has lit, against the urgings of the more experienced bushmen in his party, he declares: 'you're not so soft as to think I would take the trouble to put out a log when there are a thousand on every acre ... Bother the bush, it is better burned. There's plenty of it.'[15] Here, Atkinson explicitly aligns Tom's carelessness with the pastoralist tree-felling agenda, drawing a connection between clearance and fire. The fact that there *are* a thousand trees on every acre should, in and of itself, be a good reason to be sure that fires are put out. Yet Tom, though new to the bush, approaches it with a confidence akin to that of Stephens' guidebook – a confidence that Atkinson wants her readers to realise is misplaced.[16]

Atkinson does not flinch from showing her reader the consequences of reckless conduct in the bush. She focuses on the terror caused by the flames, or, as her narrator terms them, the 'devouring element', along with the dread of the family as they await their deaths.[17] While an adult daughter survives with her youngest sibling in her arms, the mother of the family watches and prays as her children are showered with burning leaves and then, one by one, drown in the pond to which they have retreated for safety. As the last child succumbs to the water, the narrator says of the mother: 'Then all incentive to exertion was over, and she laid her weary head beside theirs, and the wave rippled over them.'[18] While this scene may be a little sentimental for the taste of today's readers, it offers a confronting reminder of the results of heedless behaviour in the bush. It also demonstrates a much more sophisticated understanding of cause and effect than many of the other settler fire stories that were beginning to appear in the colonial press and becoming a staple of Australian fiction.

One of the earliest literary depictions of a bushfire appeared in Mary Theresa Vidal's 'The Cabramatta Store' (1850).[19] While there are certainly earlier references in settler fiction, Vidal was the first to weave a bushfire into her story's plot, although she lived in Australia for only five years.[20] Fire appears very early on in the work, as a warning of the environment's hostility to migrants. The story features the settlers Grace and John Lester, who have recently emigrated to New South Wales. Grace sees smoke when she is on a shopping trip and asks what it can be, to which the shopkeeper responds quite casually: 'O, it is the bush-fires. Why don't you see them every evening? I heard old Harry say … that he counted as many as nine or ten the night before last. Some say that's what makes it so hot.'[21] Another customer, a schoolmaster, interjects with the suggestion that the fires might be responsible for the warmth of Australia's climate, before adding 'but I suppose it is the heat in the first place which causes the fire, though I heard the gentlemen talking the other night, and some said they thought it might be the blacks, forgetting to put out their fires, and so it spreads'.[22]

The nonchalant tone with which these characters discuss fire points to the fact that the settler community had yet to fully learn its destructive force. The almost throwaway reference to 'the blacks' as responsible for the fire anticipates an anxiety that emerges in some later settler fiction, which imagines scenarios in which Indigenous Australians might turn fire into a weapon against Europeans. Here, the schoolmaster implies an absent-mindedness in relation to fire that is completely at odds with what we know today of its importance to Indigenous land management prior to Invasion.[23] His words reflect a widespread misunderstanding of Indigenous fire practices, while at the same time signalling the casual racism which appears in many settler works, where inexplicable and unfortunate events are attributed to 'the blacks'.

A few pages later, Vidal captures the speed with which flames could take hold, when she moves from a scene with her settler hero John discussing the importance of a campfire on a hot night to keep snakes at bay, to a dramatic bushfire – in the very next paragraph – as John travels home and sees '[t]he tall trees were some of them red hot to the top; the fire seemed to run apace, and every leaf and stack was so dry there was nothing to impede its progress'.[24] As John continues towards his home, he meets two men hurrying to fight the blaze, although they make it clear that there is 'not much mortal hands can do now every thing [sic] is so dry and water so scarce'.[25] Rather than going to assist with the unfolding catastrophe, John continues on his way home, improbably suggesting that there are already too many men rendering assistance. This is the last we hear of the fire – John goes on to eat his supper, showing an almost comic degree of sang-froid. That the fire does not have a lingering narrative presence is partly a consequence of the vignette form in which Vidal was writing, but it also suggests that, for the author, a bushfire was not significantly distinct from the kinds of fires she might have witnessed or read about back in England.[26]

The great fires of Black Thursday (6 February 1851) saw the beginnings of a shift in understandings of the power of the bushfire. Ellen Clacy was among the first to memorialise the day – on which almost a quarter of the colony of Victoria burned – in fiction. Like Vidal, Clacy did not remain permanently in Australia and seems to have spent very little time there, having travelled to the gold diggings with her brother in 1853 before abruptly returning to England after a couple of months.[27] She made the most of her short time in the southern hemisphere, however, by supporting herself through writing articles and stories about her travels, adopting the nom de plume Cycla. Her short story 'The Bush Fire' appeared in *Lights and Shadows of Australian Life* (1854) and is notable for its extreme melodrama. As I have argued elsewhere, Clacy's story uses the bushfire as a plot device to bring about a relationship between two characters of different social classes.[28] The rugged, yet well-read working man, Hugh, rescues the aloof heroine, Julia, and his heroics allow the social distance between them to be effaced. Clacy's story is specific as to its setting, capitalising on the topicality of the Black Thursday fires for its drama: 'Was it a thick black fog approaching? No; horror of horrors, it was smoke! and, as it comes nearer, the red flames are discernible ... the dense dark mass, intermingled with lurid streaks was behind her.'[29] While no doubt thrilling to the Victorian reader, Clacy's depiction of the fire is subordinate to her romance plot. Like Vidal, Clacy reveals little interest in the distinctiveness of the Australian landscape. Furthermore, while her bushfire offered an element of novelty to her story, it might easily have been interchanged with any other calamity from which Hugh could have rescued Julia.

Atkinson's bushfire novels, ecology, and settler discomfort

As an Australian-born naturalist, Atkinson was better attuned to outback ecology than these more mobile women, and as a result her fire scenes are much more than fleeting adventures designed to bring about dramatic rescues. Fire was, for Atkinson, a reality of life in the Australian wilderness, and her attitude towards the bushfire made it much more than a plot contrivance. As 'The Burning Forest' demonstrates, Atkinson resists the settler propensity to contain the landscape by revelling in its difference, rather than attempting to understand it on European terms. She also recognises the need to preserve the 'wilderness' all around her, and is often critical of the pastoralists and their investment in clearing scrub. Moreover, her understanding of Australia's ecology means that she writes with an awareness of fire as a recurring phenomenon, rather than representing it as a one-off catastrophe laden with opportunities for melodrama.

Dale Spender has helpfully distinguished Atkinson's position from that of her English predecessors, observing that Atkinson 'conveyed her deep and enduring commitment to her country' and 'experienced no conflict of loyalties between the old and the new'. If she 'saw in Australia the possibility for the creation of a new egalitarian society' it was one 'based not on exploitation but upon the mutual respect of human beings who had regard for their environment', giving her writing 'a curiously contemporary appeal'.[30] C. A. Cranston and Charles Dawson have similarly noted that 'Atkinson introduced readers to indigenous plants and animals, rather than engaging in agoraphobic distortions that dismissed the local as dangerous or inferior to British biota'.[31] Atkinson's holistic attitude towards her surroundings made her acutely sensitive to, and appreciative of, the uniqueness of the New South Wales landscape. She approached what settler culture often saw as the bush's hostility with curiosity and awe, and used her fiction and her journalism to teach her readers that its otherness was not unruly or vulgar but just fascinatingly different.

While Atkinson's novels were somewhat derivative in their plotting, their attention to environmental detail makes them a valuable resource for understanding the ecological impact of settler encounters with the bush. In addition to being an annual concern for those who made their homes in and around woodland, the bushfire became for Atkinson an emblem of settler discomfort. Building on her early short story, she incorporated bushfires into two of her novels and began to gently challenge ideas of the fire as an enemy, along with the sensationalism that had already begun to surround its representation. She was also a vocal critic of forest clearance. In her first novel, *Gertrude the Emigrant* (1857) – the story of a young orphan, who has recently arrived in Australia – Atkinson made deforestation a backdrop to the novel's action, thus signalling her awareness of the repercussions that could ensue from the wholesale removal of trees:[32]

> It was a dull scene at the best; great stiff stringybark trees all round, or where they had fallen before the axe, the stumps remained, bleached white, or charred, by some bush fire, to a sombre hue; in fact just then Gertrude thought it looked not unlike a graveyard: the grass was brown and dry, and the trees, every hue but green; their scanty branches casting little shade.[33]

For Gertrude and the omniscient storyteller, the cleared ground is a deathscape, and its interweaving of the axe-felled trees with the charred remains of the fire seems to have been deliberate. Atkinson went a step further in her later – and very personal – novel *Tom Hellicar's Children* (1871). The work opens with a description of the villainous embezzler Richard Hellicar's home: 'a red brick house, on a bare mound, with extensive fields spreading around it – bleak open fields cleared of trees'.[34] The narrator draws attention repeatedly to the 'cleared fields' and 'stumpy' terrain, on one level representing the 'improvements' of farmers clearing room for livestock, but on another making a subtle equation between moral bankruptcy and the destruction of native forests.[35]

Elsewhere in *Gertrude the Emigrant*, Atkinson interlaces her delicate heroine's illness with an oppressively hot summer. The unworldly Gertrude has fallen in love with an unsuitable rogue, Charley Inkersole, and her feverish sickness is a psychosomatic response to her inner conflict – she loves Charley deeply, yet she knows, as a virtuous young woman, that she should not. Following the conventions established by earlier fire-writers like Clacy and Vidal, Atkinson uses the fire as an outlet for Gertrude's intense emotional arousal. Fearful at the prospect of being caught in a blaze, she cannot help but think of Charley, and her restlessness as the fire approaches the homestead becomes entangled with her attempts to suppress her desire for him. Having just learned that she is unlikely to see Inkersole for some time, the narrator observes of Gertrude that 'the fire alarmed her, and she found she was repeating aloud "not till after Christmas"'. Readers are left to draw a parallel between the heat of the flames and the intensity of Gertrude's passion.

Atkinson is, however, concerned with the fire not as a mere plot device, but as a recurring challenge of settler life:

> When darkness did come, there were apparent, not one, but five, vast portals of burning red, in a solid mass, like sombre grey masonry, arching over head, from which glared out rays of light, as from a luminous world beyond. The air was still, hot, and close; the tree frogs shrieked by the water, and the grasshopper chirped. The smoke was sensibly thicker, and when Gertrude retired to rest, it was with a troubled heart, which yet was solaced by committing its burdens to Him 'who comforteth us in all our distresses.'[36]

Atkinson's description is attentive, not just to the heat and light, but also to sound. The reference to the shrieking tree frogs and the grasshopper reveal a deep attention to the fire's ramifications beyond the human world. It also offers an interesting contrast to Ellen Clacy's depiction of the Black Thursday fire, in which she imagines only silence: 'Everything was hushed in an awful silence: the noisy birds, the animals, the reptiles, all living things had fled, and the fire came rushing on.'[37] Atkinson's representation of the effects of a bushfire is much more inclusive than those of her immediate literary forebears. For her, a fire is not simply a *human* tragedy, but an event that affects the equilibrium of every aspect of bush life. Moreover, what makes Atkinson's writing distinct is an understanding of fire ecology – her narrators do not treat the approaching flames as a one-off event, but understand that fire is a phenomenon bush-dwellers need to accept and understand as part of their lives. As the fire historian Tom Griffiths notes, fire is 'the genie of the bush': unlike the 'sprites, elves and wood nymphs' that populate 'the forest folklore of the northern hemisphere', the Australian bush 'harboured a rather different creature' – one that required colonies to live alongside it rather than regarding it as a hostile enemy.[38]

Atkinson's characters seem at least partially aware of the importance of remembering fires past, and the need to be prepared for the conflagrations yet to come. As flames appear in the distance, they think back to a bushfire three summers past, referencing its trajectory in relation to land clearance and noting how fires can 'turn' because of factors like running water and gusts of wind. This recollection of a recent fire is prompted by Gertrude's outcry, 'The bush on fire! Oh, what can we do?', yet instead of sparking panic, her words bring forth the reassurance 'Don't be frightened: it's away in the gullies'.[39] Later, the characters seek guidance from Nanny, an Indigenous servant, as to where the fire will go next, and she speaks of how her people's camps will be moved in response to the threat. While she does not develop the parallel, Atkinson sets up an implicit comparison between the flexibility of the land's traditional custodians who decamp in the face of fire, and the vulnerability of the settlers, who must watch and wait.

The farm comes so close to danger that, the narrator informs us,

> As night approached, the sun was shut out from their view, and a thick darkness veiled the earth; the wind rose, and carried up columns of sparks and blazes; then died down to a perfect calm: again arose, each time driving the flames before it with frightful rapidity, till a wall of fire shut in the farm.[40]

Yet the tone remains measured, with the narrator attending to the elemental detail of the experience, rather than the human dimension. When the novel's hero, Edward Tudor, arrives, instead of sweeping Gertrude off her feet, in the manner of Clacy's Hugh Clements, he calmly instructs her on what to do if the fire takes hold: 'Mark the lowest line of fire, dash through [on horseback]; you must wrap wet blankets round you, don't fear … get down to the long swamp, and stay in the water.'[41] The plan turns out to be completely unnecessary, and Gertrude joins the rest of the household – men and women – in keeping the fire away from both the homestead and the harvest.

In resisting both the rescue and escape narrative (which had, by this point, already become somewhat formulaic), Atkinson recasts the role of the settler woman in relation to the land. While Gertrude, as a youthful new migrant must be instructed so that she may learn appropriate responses, the novel shows the other women of the household to be both resourceful and capable in their fire-fighting efforts. Atkinson here resists narratives of female endangerment in the bush, while at the same time rejecting the idea of the fire as a one-off event. The chapter ends with a focus on the changing seasons, and we learn that 'the sweeping destruction of the fire was half-forgotten'.[42] Yet while the prospect of autumn might provide relief, embedded in this reference to the changing seasons is a reminder that summer – and the flames – will return.

Atkinson was not, however, completely consistent in her disdain for those involved in deforestation or in her approval of acclimatisation. In her final, posthumously published serial, *Tressa's Resolve* (1872), she offers a critique of the transposition of European farming techniques to Australia through the figure of Tyrell Love, a would-be gentleman farmer whose sheep station fails through his lack of environmental knowledge. Importantly, this work predates the so-called 'nervous nineties', which, as Susan K. Martin notes, produced works which were 'rife with anxious hauntings ... and stories of drought, flood, failed farming and environmental pests'.[43] Atkinson was attuned to these concerns before they became mainstream anxieties, and in this work she sought to explore them through a lens that the settler community might understand – itself.

Mr Love purchases 40 acres and sets about clearing it almost immediately, romantically figuring the spaces as a 'garden of Eden' and fantasising about bringing the heroine Tressa to live there as a 'sweet Eve'. The narrator describes the metropolitan character's consternation at the vastness of the countryside:

> Trees 200 feet in height and of huge girth: the fall of the first great forest king; felled with such infinite labour – so many strokes of the axe. First the great tree trembled, then a few sharp snaps, then a moaning sound as it slowly overbalanced and crashed to the ground, tearing away branches and smaller trees in its fall. It was a moment of victory for Tyrell, and he would not draw the inference from this first essay that to clear even one acre would be the work of Herculean toil and of time.[44]

Atkinson here effectively combines her knowledge of the toil involved in pastoralising the land with a lament for the fallen tree and the many that will follow. What the narrator describes here is a murder with the gigantic 'forest king' 'trembling' and 'moaning' as its long life is cut short. This scene encapsulates what Rose has termed 'violent unmaking', with its total disregard for the respect, reciprocity, and balance that govern Indigenous interactions with the nonhuman world.[45]

The narrator's invitation to contemplate the 'work of Herculean toil and time' does not simply ask us to think about her hero's labour, but also demands that we consider the indiscriminate destruction ahead, not just on this farm, but on land across Australia. Atkinson's trees are sentient beings and it is not a stretch to suggest that they feel pain, just as she seems to in writing of their plight. In her novel of the previous year, *Tom Hellicar's Children*, she had imagined the sap of a gum tree as blood-like, dripping down on the character Ruth, as she contemplates the removal of her children.[46]

The scene that Atkinson presents in *Tressa's Resolve* is an ecological massacre site, the results of whose destruction reach down the years to the present day. Moreover, in reading it as such, it is important to emphasise that the discourse surrounding the clearing of trees from the land frequently masked settler efforts to clear people from that same space. Atkinson – who was fond of the many Indigenous Australians she knew personally – did not always engage with that concern explicitly. She often reproduced the pervasive 'doomed race' ideology in representing Indigenous people as a less vigorous group, who would slowly die out rather than adapt to the relentless modernity that licenced the felling of both trees and people, thereby eliding settler responsibility for their elimination.[47]

Inevitably, Tyrell Love's sheep farm becomes a money pit and, fearful of being mistaken for a fortune hunter, the novel closes with Tyrell 'suffer[ing] and struggl[ing] in silence', unable to own his love for Tressa, who is condemned to a life of waiting and caring for her sickly aunt.[48] A parallel plot involving Tressa's sister Bessie sees the older girl working as a paid companion for a spoiled young woman named Adeline in Northern Queensland, whose husband, Andrew Murray, is even less able than Tyrell, attempting to run a sheep station in drought conditions. Atkinson draws parallels between Adeline and her environment, afflicting her with a deathly fever which mirrors the sweltering heat of the sun and the aridity of the land so that the bushfire that ignites at the height of Adeline's 'fatigue and alarm' reflects both the intense neurosis that the environment stimulates in the young woman, and the tinder-dry reality of cleared land.[49] Deliberately lit by Indigenous Australians, Atkinson's narrator does not pause to consider why the fire was set, lingering instead over settler tribulations: the unforgiving heat and the difficulty of escape by horseback.[50]

Writing in a journalistic piece of an aborted journey in January 1861 through the Grose Ranges, Atkinson similarly notes the difficulties her party experienced moving through dense vegetation. Eventually, the group gives up, but she adds for her reader's interest: 'Since then the bush fires have swept away the greater part of this forest, charred stems and ashes are all that remain ... when the rain shall have washed them, it may be safe to venture through this standing army of blacks.'[51] Atkinson's expression is fascinating here. As Susan K. Martin reminds us in an analysis of Charles Harpur's poem 'The Bush Fire', ring-barked trees were a pale and ghostly presence on the landscape, frequently imagined as haunting reminders of the white men behind their destruction.[52] With her 'standing army' of burned, blackened trees, Atkinson plays with emerging narrative conventions surrounding the forests which were being deliberately killed. Here, the charred eucalypts appear like sentinels, and there is a dignity to them that is entirely absent from representations of the abject sun-bleached, ring-barked trees to which she implicitly contrasts them. Atkinson was a sufficiently skilled botanist to understand the link between fire and renewal that underpins Australia's ecology, and when equating the trees with Indigenous Australians, she gestures to the deep connection between the land and its traditional custodians.

Environmental journalism, slow violence, and settler ecocide

Atkinson's novels offer fascinating insights into the impact of both fire and clearance upon settlers, Indigenous peoples, and their environments. Yet it is her journalism that truly marks her out as a pioneer conservationist and in which she is much more willing to condemn attempts to turn the land to productivity. While Atkinson's fiction uses scenarios like bushfires to subtly initiate her readers into an understanding of Australia's difference, she is more pointed in her attacks on settler ignorance of country in her journalism, particularly in her work on deforestation. Publishing only under her initials seems to have invested Atkinson with confidence, as her journalistic voice is undoubtedly that of an expert, and her many columns take in native animals and sea-life, plants (particularly ferns), land clearance, and the challenges associated with life in the bush.

Lawson has remarked that Atkinson was 'unusual in noticing with alarm the decline of species in the districts she knows and treasures'.[53] This was at a time when, as Tim Bonyhady notes, artists like Eugene von Guerard elided the settler impact on the land by painting Australian landscapes that were apparently untouched.[54] Atkinson, by contrast, shows a passion in her writing for what the later botanist A. G. Tansley was to term 'wild nature'.[55] Lawson continues to highlight just how unusual Atkinson's voice was by arguing that 'a century and a half before the present crisis of native forests and selecting her words carefully, she blames "the extensive killing of the forests" for the loss of large flocks of birds and the making of deserts'.[56]

The article to which Lawson refers, 'Climatic Influences on the Habits of Birds' (16 June 1870), anticipates the dislocation that we see today as a result of climate change. Atkinson observes 'considerable disturbance[s] in the animal kingdom' following a drought in which '[s]ome birds forsook their usual haunts to wander ... while others from a distance visited us'.[57] These reluctant avian migrants have been displaced from their homes, and Atkinson was keen to make her readers understand their own complicity in their removal (readers of the 1870s were more receptive to discussions of dislocated birds than people). She was very conscious that human agency was accelerating environmental change on an unprecedented scale in Australia. Writing in her regular column for the *Herald* on 24 May 1870, Atkinson noted that on an excursion to Cavan to gather bivalve specimens from the Murrumbidgee river, she was struck by this change and its implications for the future: 'But the scattered trees are evidently rapidly dying, pointing to a time when these ranges will be clear.'[58] Elsewhere, she comments: 'It needs no fertile imagination to foresee that in, say, half a century's time, tracts of hundreds of miles will be treeless.'[59] It is impossible to put a figure on the exact scale of forest damage in the nineteenth century, but modellers suggest that Australia has lost 40% of its trees since European settlement. There were some attempts to slow the onslaught. As early as 1803 Philip Gidley King, the third governor of New South Wales, attempted to legislate against tree felling on the banks of rivers and watercourse to prevent soil erosion, yet '[l]ike many efforts to protect the land, this one was ignored'.[60]

Atkinson wrote a piece which appeared in the *Sydney Morning Herald* on 3 February 1871 that attacks over-farming, and in which she suggests that inexperience and ignorance might explain the relentlessness with which landowners cleared and planted. It is typical of her compassionate approach to landscape and people that she would appeal to good sense and goodwill, earnestly believing that education would bring about change:

> Let us hope that a few good seasons will restore prosperity to the land; but it is very doubtful if the small landholder system can ever be permanent where a drought, or over-wet season, reduces the owner to want, unless a far more careful style of cultivation is pursued ... Some people argue that the earth was made for man and *must* support him, and that his instinct will teach him how to cultivate it. Many a ruined farmer has tried the truth of this hypothesis.[61]

In addition to her dismay at how any man might come to Australia and reinvent himself as a farmer, regardless of his skills and knowledge, Atkinson was highly critical of the entitlement with which settler farmers approached the land. She deplored waste and, in the same article, she hit out at farmers who killed native animals but made no use of their carcasses or skins. Still, the fact that she continued to pen her column, week after week, suggests that Atkinson saw it as her responsibility to educate those around her.

Atkinson discussed some of the catastrophic harm caused by settler ignorance in 'After Shells in the Limestone', where she reveals a landscape that is almost post-apocalyptic in its deadness:

> For some years past the black butts and flooded gums in the vicinity of Berrima have been dying, until now the 'floss' or treeless watersheds of that district are bordered by belts of dead timber. Even the woolly butts are now perishing, while in many localities miles of forest have died – apart from artificial means or ringbarking – that the ultimate consequence will be of a nature materially to affect those districts there can be no doubt.[62]

In the same article, she anticipates today's conversations about forests as the 'lungs of the world' and offers a vision of Australia's future that is uncannily familiar to the modern reader:

> It would seem that the forests have acted as safety valves to carry off the superfluous moisture of the earth, and to attract that of the atmosphere, thus forming a circulating system. The minor vegetation is undergoing a considerable change. Rushes and aquatic plants present themselves in erstwhile dry regions. In time, there is much reason to fear, this excessive humidity will give place to the reverse; and like other treeless countries we shall suffer from an arid climate and soil. But our wide forests render such a catastrophe a misfortune in the distance.[63]

This prophecy of a 'misfortune in the distance' anticipates the ecocritic Rob Nixon's reminder of what he terms the 'slow violence' of the settler community against both the environment and those who had tended it. Arguing that it is always the dispossessed who first experience the adverse effects of reckless environmental policies, Nixon notes that Indigenous Australians dubbed early European settlers '"the future eaters": the newcomers [who] consumed without replacing, devouring the future at a speed bereft of foresight, hollowing out time by living as if the desert were a place of infinite, untended provision'.[64] As early as 1870, Atkinson showed her readers that they were those 'future eaters', who take everything and replenish nothing. Admittedly, she regarded the problem as one that posterity would need to confront, and her scope for activism was limited, but she nonetheless wrote against the grain of a community who saw themselves as improvers, not destroyers.

Reading backwards from a present in which deforestation and global warming are extending the fire season, today's Australians – particularly those in rural and outlying areas – can be certain that this misfortune is no longer in the distance. Gamilaraay and Yuwalaraay elders from Walgett in north-west New South Wales say that they have never seen conditions like today's droughts, and they doubt that the changes can be reversed.[65] That Atkinson was able to foresee today's crisis is a testament to her prescience but also to her incisive understanding of ecological cause and effect. As Lawson has noted, 'Louisa knew that the greatest problem was forest felling',[66] but she also saw the world around her as so much more than 'high unpromising forests and miles of loneliness'.[67] For Atkinson the forest is worthy of preservation, not just because of the sustenance it offers, but because for her it was both a home and a continuing source of amazement even as her homemaking involved the dispossession of Indigenous Australians. The felling of trees became for her the epitome of casual waste and, in both her fiction and her journalism, it was at the root of all harm to the forest.

Acknowledgements

I would like to thank Lyndall Ryan and Angela Wanhalla for the opportunity to discuss some of the ideas in this chapter at their 'Afterlives' symposium (Museum of New Zealand Te Papa Tongarewa), and Richard J. King for discussions of Atkinson and fire.

Notes

1 Atkinson wrote under a variety of guises, sometimes using her own name, but at others writing as L. A. and later L. C. (her initials as a married woman) or 'an Australian Lady'.

2 Patricia Clarke, *Pioneer Writer: The Life of Louisa Atkinson: Novelist, Journalist, Naturalist* (Sydney: Allen & Unwin, 1990), p. 142.

3 Penny Olsen, *Louisa Atkinson's Nature Notes* (Canberra: National Library of Australia, 2015), pp. 89–90.

4 See, e.g., Simon Ryan, *The Cartographic Eye: How Explorers Saw Australia* (Cambridge: Cambridge University Press, 1996).

5 Clarke's biography, *Pioneer Writer*, offers a gripping account of Atkinson's early life, including her mother's flight from an abusive second marriage (p. 28). Atkinson wrote an account of their escape, 'Incidents of Australian Travel' (1863), as well as an account of their new life in a ramshackle outstation at Budong in a series of newspapers articles entitled 'A Voice from the Country: 'Recollections of the Aborigines' (1863).

6 Elizabeth Lawson's 'Louisa Atkinson: The Distant Sound of Native Voices' and 'Louisa Atkinson: Writings on Aboriginal Land Ownership' are, to date, the only sustained studies of Atkinson and indigeneity. Elizabeth Lawson, 'Louisa Atkinson: The Distant Sound of Native Voices', Occasional Paper No. 15, English Department University College, Australian Defence Force Academy, Canberra (1989); 'Louisa Atkinson: Writings on Aboriginal Land Ownership', *Margin*, 21 (1989), 15–20.

7 Deborah Bird Rose, *Nourishing Terrains: Australian Aboriginal Views of Landscape and Wilderness* (Canberra: Australian Heritage Commission, 1996), p. 7.

8 T. M. Perry, 'Atkinson, James: 1795–1834', *The Australian Dictionary of National Biography*, n.p., http://adb.anu.edu.au/biography/atkinson-james-1726 (accessed 30 November 2019).

9 Robert Pogue Harrison, *Forests: The Shadow of Civilization* (Chicago: University of Chicago Press, 1992), p. 51.

10 James Atkinson, *An Account of the State of Agriculture and Grazing in New South Wales*, 2nd edn (1826; London: J. Cross, 1844), p. 128.

11 Rose, *Nourishing Terrains*, p. 77.

12 John Stephens, *The History of the Rise and Progress of the New British Province of South Australia*, 2nd edn (London: Smith, Elder & Co., 1839), pp. 62–3.

13 L. C. [Louisa Atkinson], 'A Voice from the Country: After Shells in the Limestone', *The Sydney Morning Herald* (24 May 1870), p. 5.

14 L. A. [Louisa Atkinson], 'The Burning Forest: A Sketch of Australian Bush Life', *The Illustrated Sydney News* (22 October 1853), p. 4.

15 Atkinson, 'The Burning Forest', p. 4.

16 For an extended discussion of 'The Burning Forest', see Grace Moore, '"Raising High Its Thousand Forked Tongues": Campfires, Bushfires, and Portable Domesticity in Nineteenth-Century Australia', *19: Interdisciplinary Studies in the Long Nineteenth Century*, 26 (2018), n.p., https://doi.org/10.16995/ntn.807 (accessed 19 November 2019).

17 Atkinson, 'The Burning Forest', p. 4.

18 Atkinson, 'The Burning Forest', p. 4.

19 Mrs Francis [Mary Theresa] Vidal, *Cabramatta, and Woodleigh Farm* (London: Francis & John Rivington, 1850).

20 Vidal lived in Penrith, New South Wales from 1840 to 1845, having travelled to Australia with her husband, who was a clergyman.

21 Vidal, *Cabramatta, and Woodleigh Farm*, p. 16.

22 Vidal, *Cabramatta, and Woodleigh Farm*, p. 16.

23 See Bill Gammage, *The Biggest Estate on Earth* (Sydney: Allen & Unwin, 2011) for a detailed account of land management before 1788.

24 Vidal, *Cabramatta, and Woodleigh Farm*, p. 24.

25 Vidal, *Cabramatta, and Woodleigh Farm*, p. 24.

26 Vidal left Australia after a five-year stay, and 'The Cabramatta Store' was published some time after her return home.

27 It is believed that Clacy – a single woman at the time – may either have become pregnant on the voyage to Australia, or have taken the journey to conceal a pregnancy, thus accounting for the haste of her return. See Margaret Anderson, 'Mrs. Charles Clacy, Lola Montez, and Poll the Grogseller: Glimpses of Women on the Early Victorian Goldfields', in Iain McCalman, Alexander Cook, and Andrew Reeves (eds), *Gold: Forgotten Histories and Lost Objects of Australia* (Cambridge and New York: Cambridge University Press, 2001), pp. 225–49.

28 For more detail, see Grace Moore, 'Surviving Black Thursday: The Great Bushfire of 1851', in Tamara S. Wagner (ed.), *Victorian Settler Narratives: Emigrants, Cosmopolitans and Returnees in Nineteenth-Century Literature* (London and New York: Routledge, 2016), pp 129–39.

29 Mrs Charles [Ellen] Clacy, *Lights and Shadows of Australian Life*, vol. 1 (London: Hurst & Blackett, 1854), p. 178.

30 Dale Spender, *Writing a New World: Two Centuries of Australian Women Writers* (London and New York: Pandora, 1988), p. 105.

31 C. A. Cranston and Charles Dawson, 'Climate and Culture in Australia and New Zealand', in John Parham and Louise Westling (eds), *A Global History of Literature and the Environment* (Cambridge: Cambridge University Press, 2016), p. 240.

32 Interestingly, Clacy's narrator in 'A Bush Fire' insists that Julia 'was safe, as precautions had been taken, by cutting down, or burning all the grass, etc, round

and near the dwelling, for the safety of it and its inmates' (p. 178). Later, Hugh takes Julia to a 'large tract of barren land, being prepared for cultivation' (p. 180), pointing to the signs of land clearance, and explicitly aligning it with safety.

33 Louisa Atkinson, *Gertrude the Emigrant: A Tale of Colonial Life* (1857; Sydney: University of Sydney Library, 2000), p. 151.

34 Louisa Atkinson, *Tom Hellicar's Children* (1871; Canberra: Mulini Press, 1983), p. 5.

35 Atkinson, *Tom Hellicar's Children*, pp. 23, 28.

36 Atkinson, *Gertrude the Emigrant*, p. 98.

37 Clacy, *Lights and Shadows of Australian Life*, pp. 178–9.

38 Tom Griffiths, 'Remembering', in Christine Hansen and Tom Griffiths, *Living with Fire: People, Nature and History in Steels Creek* (Collingwood: CSIRO Publishing, 2012), p. 162.

39 Atkinson, *Gertrude the Emigrant*, p. 96.

40 Atkinson, *Gertrude the Emigrant*, p. 98.

41 Atkinson, *Gertrude the Emigrant*, p. 99.

42 Atkinson, *Gertrude the Emigrant*, p. 100.

43 Susan K. Martin '"Tragic Ring-Barked Forests" and the "Wicked Wood"': Haunting Environmental Anxiety in Late Nineteenth-Century Australian Literature', in Laurence W. Mazzeno and Ronald D. Morrison (eds), *Victorian Environmental Nightmares* (London: Palgrave Macmillan, 2019), p. 139.

44 Louisa Atkinson, 'Tressa's Resolve, A Tale by the Late Mrs. Calvert', *The Sydney Mail and New South Wales Advertiser* (2 November 1872), p. 569.

45 Deborah Bird Rose, *Wild Dog Dreaming: Love and Extinction* (Charlottesville and London: University of Virginia Press, 2011), p. 97.

46 Atkinson, *Tom Hellicar's Children*, p. 20.

47 'Poor creatures! with their sins and good qualities; friendships and hatreds, so quickly to have passed away!'. 'The Fitzroy Waterfalls' (1871), in Louisa Atkinson, *Excursions from Berrima and a Trip to Manaro and Molonglo in the 1870s* (Canberra: Mulini Press, 1980), p. 18.

48 Atkinson, 'Tressa's Resolve' (7 December 1872), p. 729.

49 Atkinson, 'Tressa's Resolve', p. 730.

50 Atkinson, 'Tressa's Resolve', p. 730.

51 L[ouisa] A[tkinson], 'A Voice from the Country, the Ranges of the Grose', *Sydney Morning Herald* (30 January 1862), p. 5.

52 Martin, '"Tragic Ring-Barked Forests" and the "Wicked Wood"', pp. 126–7.

53 Elizabeth Lawson, *The Natural Art of Louisa Atkinson* (Sydney: State Library of New South Wales Press, 1995), p. 85.

54 See Tim Bonyhady, *Images in Opposition: Australian Landscape Painting, 1801–1890* (Oxford: Oxford University Press, 1984).

55 Curiously, Atkinson's landscape paintings and drawings are rather more romanticised than her columns. When we see fallen trees in her visual works, they tend to be artistically angled and they do not always convey the scale of the deforestation that she captures so brilliantly in her writing.

56 Lawson, *The Natural Art of Louisa Atkinson*, p. 85.

57 L. C. [Louisa Atkinson], 'Climatic Influences on the Habits of Birds', *Sydney Mail* (16 June 1870), p. 12.

58 L. C. [Louisa Atkinson], 'A Voice from the Country: After Shells in the Limestone', *The Sydney Morning Herald* (24 May 1870), p. 5.

59 Atkinson, 'A Voice from the Country', p. 5.

60 Rose, *Nourishing Terrains*, p. 77.

61 L. C. [Louisa Atkinson], 'Hanging Rock on the Southern Road', *Sydney Morning Herald* (3 February 1871), p. 5.

62 Atkinson, 'A Voice from the Country', p. 5.

63 Atkinson, 'The Fitzroy Waterfalls' (1871), p. 18.

64 Rob Nixon, *Slow Violence and the Environmentalism of the Poor* (Cambridge, MA: Harvard University Press, 2011), p. 96.

65 Michael Slezak, 'The Destruction of Australia's Landscape', *Guardian* (7 March 2018), n.p., www.theguardian.com/environment/2018/mar/07/scorched-country-the-destruction-of-australias-native-landscape (accessed 10 November 2019); Lorena Allam and Carly Earl, 'For Centuries the Rivers Sustained Aboriginal Culture. Now They Are Dry, Elders Despair', *Guardian* (21 January 2019), n.p., www.theguardian.com/australia-news/2019/jan/22/murray-darling-river-aboriginal-culture-dry-elders-despair-walgett (accessed 10 November 2019).

66 Lawson, *The Natural Art of Louisa Atkinson*, pp. 85–6.

67 Atkinson, 'Tressa's Resolve' (2 November 1872), p. 569.

10

Mapping the way forward: Thomas Baines on expedition to the coronation of Cetshwayo kaMpande, Zululand, 1873

Lindy Stiebel

Knowledge about the life and work of artist-explorer John Thomas Baines (1820–75) has become well established in academic circles since J. P. R. Wallis, in 1941, focused a spotlight on Baines' oeuvre and career.[1] Later biographies have added fresh dimensions to Baines scholarship, establishing him as a remarkably talented and versatile artist, explorer, cartographer, and journal writer.[2] Given the volume of attention paid to Baines over the years, it is surprising that there still remains material awaiting discovery. This has nonetheless proved true of Baines' final expedition – a 'last hurrah'[3] – when, in 1873, he offered himself as a 'Special Correspondent' to accompany the retinue of Theophilus Shepstone (1817–93), then the powerful Secretary for Native Affairs in Natal, on an expedition into Zululand to crown Cetshwayo kaMpande, the new incumbent on the Zulu throne. Baines' life had, by then, almost reached its end: he died in May 1875 in Durban at the age of 55. The purpose of this chapter is both to look more closely at Baines on his last expedition as a writer and mapper of settler interests, and to assess the geo-political significance of the unexplored maps and other material discovered upon investigation.

Briefly to situate Baines and the Zululand expedition: by the year 1873 Baines had travelled extensively throughout much of southern Africa and far beyond. Born in King's Lynn, Norfolk, he came to the Cape Colony as a young man and spent more than a decade in South Africa (1842–53). Thereafter, he joined an expedition to explore North Australia (1856–57), then linked up with David Livingstone and traversed part of the Zambezi River from the African east coast (1858–59). This was followed by two years (1862–63) in what is now Namibia, and a few years later, from 1869 to 1872, Baines was employed by a gold-prospecting company in what is now Botswana and Zimbabwe. Although these expeditions were highly productive in terms of art, journal-recording, and, not least, personal adventure and experience, not all ended well for Baines. His involvement in the South African Gold Fields Exploration Company in 1869 exposed his lack of business acumen and nearly bankrupted him. Moreover, in joining this prospecting company, he became an active agent of settler expansion. In his association with the South African Gold Fields Exploration Company, a subsidiary of the Natal Land and Colonisation Company, Baines became an emissary for the colony of Natal. The leitmotif of Baines' life from 1871 to its end in 1875 was his attempt to re-float the company, pay off his debts, and restore his reputation.

It was in this light that Baines volunteered to accompany Shepstone on an expedition into Zululand to crown Cetshwayo as Zulu king in 1873. Some historians have described the event as 'a caricature of a "coronation" ceremony'.[4] But in his biography of Shepstone, Jeff Guy reminds us that behind the ceremonies and posturing were very real considerations of power and position.[5] Charles Ballard summarises the proceedings as follows: 'The events surrounding Cetshwayo's coronation mark a watershed in Anglo-Zulu political and economic relationships.'[6] When Mpande died peacefully towards the end of 1872 and his death was made known early the following year, Shepstone and Cetshwayo, Mpande's son, each contemplated a move that would advance their cause. For his part, Cetshwayo – on the advice of John Dunn and the senior Zulu chiefs – sought the support of Natal for his accession to the throne and sent a delegation to Pietermaritzburg in late February 1873 to solicit it. Formal recognition by the colony was to Cetshwayo's advantage in dealing with rivalry from his royal siblings, acknowledging his right to the throne, avoiding another civil war, and in gaining help in dealing with the encroaching Boers. For Shepstone, the advantages of 'crowning' Cetshwayo would give him (Shepstone) prestige, power over the king as 'kingmaker', and in addition – he hoped – promote unity within the Zulu kingdom, which bordered on the colony of Natal. Moreover, and significantly, by supporting Cetshwayo, Shepstone might secure African labour from the disputed territory or from the Mozambique region. This would assist Natal's expansion and placate settler grievances against the continuing independence of the Zulu kingdom that lay across the Thukela River.

Amid fears of treachery on both sides, on 8 August 1873 the impressive coronation pageant with Shepstone at its head crossed the Thukela River into Zululand. His Natal Volunteer Corps incorporated detachments of the Natal Carbineers, the Richard Rifles, the Weenen Yeomanry Cavalry, the Alexandra Mounted Rifles, the Victoria Mounted Rifles (VMR), and the Durban Volunteer Artillery with two field guns. Some 300 African levies brought up the rear. A 'willing agent in Shepstone's schemes', Baines attached himself to the volunteer corps, an unwitting pawn in a game with important later consequences.[7] It was a chance for a break from the depressing task of fundraising, as well as a chance to experience new landscapes and communities, and to depict them in word and image. Baines maintained a detailed journal which found immediate publication in the *Natal Mercury* (est. 1852), for which he was Special Correspondent. In addition, Baines drew and compiled an important, and little known, map of Zululand at this time.

Mapping the way

Though the emphasis on Baines' output is generally on the drawings and paintings of his travels and adventures, in recent years scholars have paid increasing attention to Baines' manuscript and printed maps. Starting their work in the late 1990s, a combined South African/Australian research team published their first work on Baines-as-cartographer in a ground-breaking format: the CD *Thomas Baines and the Great Map* (2001), which gathers together a digitised and hyperlinked version of the 1872 manuscript map Baines drew of the route the Gold Fields expedition took to Matabeleland, some of the paintings from that expedition, and academic commentary.[8] This was followed by a second group project concerning Baines, this time focusing on the map he drew of the coast of the Gulf of Carpentaria as part of Augustus Gregory's 1855 expedition to North Australia. The book, entitled *Thomas Baines: Exploring Tropical Australia* (2012), included chapters analysing the map and expedition from various points of view: historical, political, cartographical, discursive (given its dense annotation), and artistic.[9]

Of course, other researchers have written about Baines from this perspective – Jeffrey Stone most notably[10] – but finding his maps has not always been straightforward given Baines' peripatetic life on expeditions in far-flung lands.[11] Some, because funded by a body such as the Royal Geographical Society (RGS), were easier to locate. For example, Baines' sketchbooks and numerous paintings, plus a manuscript map from the Gregory expedition to Australia mentioned above, are to be found in the Map Room at the RGS London headquarters. When it came to finding the map discussed in this chapter, the route was less obvious as the coronation expedition had not been funded by the RGS. While Wallis wrote that one of the attractions for Baines in joining the coronation expedition to Zululand in 1873 was that 'mapping an uncharted route was a potent lure' for him,[12] and Stone mentioned the existence of 'extant manuscript cartography by Baines in the RGS Map Room, dated 1873 and the first half of 1874',[13] no particular map of the route had been analysed in any detail or reproduced in any of the biographies of Baines. That such a map existed was clear: Baines recorded drawing the route taken by Shepstone in his daily journal, quizzing locals as to correct place names and giving copies of the map to helpful informants like

Mr Robertson, the missionary, and, most importantly, a sketch to William Emery ('Em') Robarts (1847–1903), a surveyor by profession and a member of the VMR, one of the volunteer corps accompanying Shepstone.

Robarts had asked Baines to make a sketch of the VMR escort while they sat in a tent on the banks of the Thukela River. In a letter to his wife, Liz (nee Povall), dated 5 July 1873 (but subsequently corrected by his grandson also named William Emery ('Bill') Robarts [1921–2002], the family archivist, to the month of August), Em wrote:

> Mr Baines the traveller and artist is with us in his professional capacity. Well last night I spent a very pleasant evening with him & Capt Drake in his tent – songs and jokes – and I then asked him to make a sketch of our tent with all hands sitting round inside, with the breakfast things all used after as we had done – of course the likenesses are not accurate but as a sketch it is very good. We intend to have it photographed when we get back – I keep the sketch and will of course shew it to you. We will have it framed and keep it as a momento [sic] of the trip.[14]

The black-and-white photograph alluded to above has been reproduced in various places but a recent meeting with the Robarts family on their farm in Zululand revealed both the sketch and a section of a map drawn by Baines of the expedition's route. The 'sketch' in real life is a large watercolour whose colours are very well preserved (Figure 10.1).[15]

Bill Robarts documented the names of all ten of the men seated in the sketch in his archive's notes,[16] and added a few corrections to his grandfather's original roll call of those sketched at the back of the framed painting: 'There were 10 persons in the group but only 9 names are given. Robert Plant's name must be inserted between A. Blamey and J. Adams ... Tom Garland was only a trooper (later he became Capt). Em was Sergeant in charge of the party (in the Zulu War he became a Lieutenant).'[17] The painting is given a title and signed by Baines in the bottom right-hand corner: 'Victoria Mounted Rifles at Rendezvous Camp, Tugela River August 1st to 8th 1873 – presented to the Corps by their friend, the artist'. Besides a small water mark top left in the painting, it is undamaged after hanging in the farmhouse for over a century. Accompanying this painting in the Robarts family's collection is a framed section of Baines' map to the coronation site (Figure 10.2).

Em Robarts refers to this gift from Baines in the diary he kept during the coronation expedition, also still well preserved in the Robarts family archive. The diary entry for 20 August 1873 reads: 'Mr Baines gave me this morning a tracing of his map of the road we have come and also a list of the distances.'[18] Bill Robarts, in his unpublished account of the Robarts family, explains why the map would have been an appropriate gift: 'Also accompanying the force was artist and geographer Thomas Baines, an accomplished

Figure 10.1 Thomas Baines, 'Sketch of the Victoria Mounted Rifles, escort to Theophilus Shepstone, at Rendezvous Camp, Thukela River', 1873

navigator and he and my grandfather (a surveyor) worked together to plot the route to Mahlabatini.'[19] This map is framed together with the black-and-white photographic print plus the list of the men's names stuck on to the map sheet on the left-hand side. Baines has formally entitled this map 'Route of the Honble T. Shepstone and his Natal Volunteer Escort to Zululand Sheet 2 – from Rendezvous Camp south of the Tugela ... Observed and drawn by T Baines FRGS, artist and geographer, Durban Volunteer Artillery'. It seems probable that Em (or Bill) Robarts stuck the photo and its description on to the map and had the whole framed for posterity. But if this was Sheet 2, where was Sheet 1? Further research led to the Brenthurst Library that owns Baines' journals from the Zululand expedition. The three notebooks of journal entries contain many calculations of daily distances achieved,[20] a few rough pencil sketches of places to act as aides-memoires, some patchy doggerel verse which Graham Dominy has transcribed and commented upon,[21] a list of athletics events, and the results achieved by the volunteer corps who were bored with waiting for Cetshwayo to appear for his coronation, but little or no mention of the map he was simultaneously compiling.

It was not until a chance request at the RGS that the mystery was solved. Though Stone, as mentioned above, had alerted researchers to the materials relating to Baines and his work in Natal that are lodged at the RGS, a

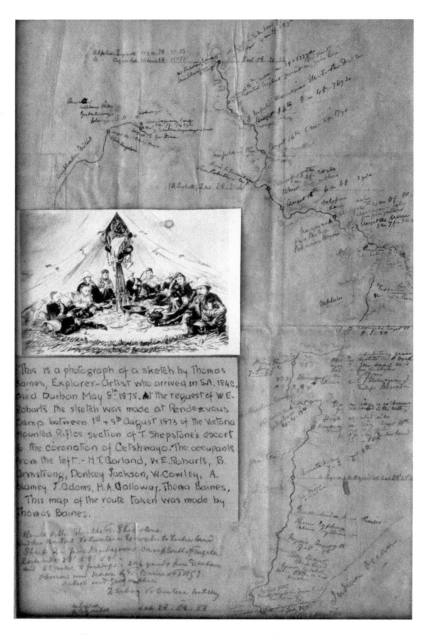

Figure 10.2 Thomas Baines, 'Route of the Hon T Shepstone – Ambassador to Zululand and his Natal Volunteer Escort July, Aug & Sept 1873. Observed and drawn by T Baines FRGS Geographer and Artist, Durban Volunteer Artillery'

preliminary search drew a blank when it came to anything relating to 1873. However, among the many maps filed in the South Africa S.97 folder dated c. 1865 was an anomaly: the official map of the coronation route (Figure 10.3).[22]

At 101cm x 64cm it is considerably bigger than the route map owned by the Robarts family and is, indeed, the entire map (in other words, Sheets 1 and 2, though they comprise just one sheet of paper in the official map). Baines must have worked on sections of the map on separate sheets and then combined his workings into the final product. That it is *the* official map is evidenced by the fact that it is inscribed in Baines' hand – 'Presented to the Royal Geographical Society by the Artist' – and also by the fact that further research showed that it had been sent to the RGS as a separate item by Baines in 1874, and was not part of the donation to the RGS in 1888, post Baines' death, which makes up folder S.97. Baines clearly attached enough importance to his finished map to send it to the RGS immediately. This map, together with the other fine work he had already sent to the RGS as part of the Gregory expedition, would have been the basis of Baines being elected RGS Honorary Fellow for life in 1874. He was also awarded a gold watch with an inscription acknowledging his 'long-continued services to Geography' by the RGS, although as he did not return to England before his death, this was never officially presented to him but was sent to his sister. The significance of the coronation route map has now been acknowledged by the RGS – it has been re-catalogued as a single item with the correct year for ease of reference.[23]

The map itself includes Baines' 1872 route from Utrecht to Pietermaritzburg and Durban on the left-hand 'half' (perhaps Sheet 1 in Baines' terms), while the route of Shepstone (and Baines) from Durban to the coronation kraal in Zululand in 1873 occupies the right-hand side of the map (Sheet 2 owned by the Robarts family correlates to this, although the RGS map is more fully annotated and drawn, plus hand-coloured to show the hills). Meticulous as ever with his observations, Baines is at pains to point out where there are possible inaccuracies. He refers, for example, to the occasional problems encountered in measuring distance with a trocheameter, such as 'fewer revolutions of wheels than ought to be made in the distance travelled' during steep descents. As ever, too, with Baines, he demonstrates complete dedication to the enterprise at hand by not only mapping the route, but sketching, journaling, and writing articles for the *Natal Mercury* newspaper for the coronation expedition. All this work was unpaid except, perhaps, the commissioned work for the newspaper. Wallis recalls that Baines 'submitted a detailed account of the Cetshwayo expedition for Shepstone's approval, but, of the £5000 the Government spent on the "coronation" he received not a penny, not even for the map, a useful piece of public service'.[24]

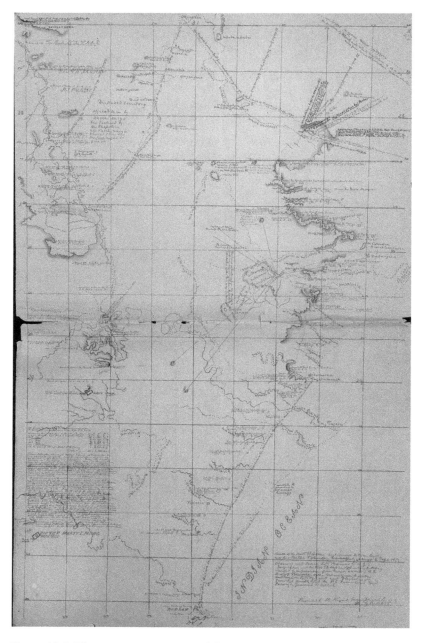

Figure 10.3 Thomas Baines, 'Route of the Hon T Shepstone – Ambassador to Zululand and his Natal Volunteer Escort July, Aug & Sept 1873. Observed and drawn by T Baines FRGS Geographer and Artist, Durban Volunteer Artillery assisted by information from Major Durnford RE, Bishop Schreuder of the Norwegian Mission, Mr Taylor of Tongaat and sketches of surveyors kindly lent by PC Sutherland MD Surveyor General of Natal'

Stone suggests that, as Baines did not discover any major geographical feature as Livingstone, for example, did, he was never considered in his day to be a major explorer or cartographer: 'Without a major geographical discovery, his impact was always likely to be modest … He put no large rivers, lakes or mountains on the map for the first time.'[25] The power of his maps today lies in the insights they provide into historical moments such as Cetshwayo's coronation, especially because they can be read together with his sketches, paintings, diaries, and articles. As part of a larger jigsaw puzzle relating to how settlers mapped and understood British/African geo-political interests, they are invaluable. Thus, one of the important aspects of Baines' Zululand map (together with the accompanying material) is that it configures the Zulu kingdom as a spatial entity and presents this to a western audience in a scientifically acceptable way. While some groups, particularly African communities, were previously wiped off the map by cartographers, in the case of Baines' coronation map, the Zulu become entrenched within their space and are given territorial boundaries, towns, and distinct geographical features. When the Anglo-Zulu War was declared in 1879, there was thus a visible country to be conquered. However, Baines' Zululand map was not a map of land appropriation and, unusually, he does not only give western or English names to features and settlements: he also records Zulu place names such as 'hill of the trees bent by the lions, i.e. the prevalent SE breeze', 'river of the Crocodile named after this regiment', and 'hill of the green stones'. Within Zulu territory he meticulously notes the various trading stores as well as those vanguards of colonialism, the mission stations and their missionaries. In particular, mention is made of Dingane's kraal, where Voortrekker leader Piet Retief and his party were murdered in 1838, the kraal where Mpande died and was buried, and the hill at which many Zulu executions were held.

Baines' map should be seen in conjunction with other maps of the region: Friedrich Heinrich Jeppe's 1868 map showed Zululand as a neighbouring region to the Boer South African Republic, as was the Portuguese territory that abutted Zululand on the north, but which Baines did not include in his map. Rivalry for control of land in the subcontinent grew more urgent in the 1870s, and each enclave was being hemmed in by maps. It is in this respect that Baines' Zululand map is especially relevant. While the trader John Sanderson presented his 1861 map of the region to the RGS with geographical features such as rivers and mountains noted, he gave very few place names or positions of clan settlements. In contrast, though his was not the first map of Zululand, Baines marked the territory as populated, with occupied places clearly shown. This was new: it was difficult to map Zululand because entry required the permission of the Zulu king and certainly no formal survey was possible. Cetshwayo's strategic delays – from 18 August to 1 September – before meeting Shepstone gave Baines time and opportunity over a number of weeks to construct his map and check the accuracy of his coordinates. It was, strategically, the coronation expedition that provided the opportunity for him, and for a large group of military volunteers – many of whom would go on to conquer the Zulu in the war of 1879 – to experience the landscape of the Zulu kingdom at first hand and map it for the west.

Baines' map, then, drawn while on an expedition invited by the Zulu king, shows a place occupied by Zulu kinspeople with isolated missionaries and traders in their midst. It is not 'empty' or there for the taking; the earth is 'marked'.[26] Through his annotation, not only of place names but also the movement of the expedition, Baines charts the intrusion of a colonial order into the heart of Zululand as had not happened before. In this regard, he is an active participant in this process. This expedition allowed a colonial state to 'crown' the king of an independent country, and to present 'demands' to him that would secure some measure of overall authority by Natal over the king's administration of his own country and thus tragically compromise his independence. The importance of Baines' map is that it charts this geo-political intrusion for us all to see today.

A special correspondent

Besides working daily on gathering measurements for his map, Baines was also recording details of life en route to the coronation as part of his appointment as Special Correspondent to the *Natal Mercury*, the Durban-based newspaper, which appeared three times a week in 1873. The newspaper editor proudly advertised the appointment of Baines to colonial readers, who would have been following with intense interest the events in Zululand. He declared his

> pleasure to announce that we have been able to secure the services, as special representative of this journal, of our old and well known friend – artist, traveller and writer – Mr T Baines FRGS. Mr Baines, on receiving our request, at once agreed to waive other engagements, and accept a position offering him such ample scope for the exercise both of his pen and pencil. Our readers, therefore, will be kept apprised of every incident connected with the expedition.[27]

Whether Baines was to be paid for his services to the newspaper is unclear, but what *is* clear is how welcome this offer was to Baines as a way to enable his part in the expedition and escape, if briefly, his ongoing financial wrangles with the Gold Fields company and the accompanying stress referred to earlier. Baines was clearly a Shepstone supporter, according to Norman Etherington, who 'links Thomas Baines with Shepstone's visionary plans for expanding Natal influence to the Zambezi and beyond'.[28] Perhaps Baines was also motivated by a desire to shape through his journalism how readers perceived this important phase of Anglo-Zulu engagement. Jane Carruthers and Marion Arnold suggest that Baines, '[n]ow firmly within the Natal camp and the friend of many locally born political leaders ... undertook many commissions that were highly propagandistic, although not necessarily lucrative'.[29]

Whatever the case, when reading the pieces Baines wrote in 1873, one is struck by the carefree, jocular, and sometimes jingoistic tone he adopted, which sits occasionally uneasily with the scientific seriousness which he also shows when capturing most minutely the daily progress of the expedition and events at camp. Although Baines had shown a similar humorous side to his writing in his *Blue Jacket Journal* (1855), written at sea en route to Australia before the Gregory expedition nearly 20 years previously, this relaxed tone is not one heard from Baines in the years before this expedition, beset as he had been with problems. This is also a Baines surrounded by friends and companions; he is happy in these weeks, as we shall see when analysing the journalistic pieces he wrote. He has many roles to play – newspaper correspondent, cartographer, artist – in an unknown environment which he finds fascinating, amid conducive company. Wallis concurs with this assessment: 'His [Baines'] letters from Injembe to his sister are livelier and more full of quip and jest than usual, while his journal and his articles to the *Natal Mercury* while visiting Zululand show no trace of gloom.'[30] Robarts attests to Baines being 'one of the lads' – Baines had evidently seen a good deal of 'roughing it' in his life[31] – and an interesting travel companion. The two men evidently got along and shared an interest in ascertaining correct measurements for their physical position in Zululand.

Baines mentions Em Robarts in the *Natal Mercury* of 19 August 1873: 'Mr Robarts of the Victoria Mounted Rifles proposed to take a lunar distance for longitude, but the nearly full moon was so bright that it dimmed the only star (Antares) that we could use, and the attempt did not succeed';[32] and again the next day, 10 August: 'Mr Robarts came at night and assisted me in taking a lunar observation, which occupied us til midnight.'[33] Besides Robarts, to whom he gifted the painting of the VMR in the tent plus 'a tracing of his map of the road we have come and also a list of the distances', Baines referred to others, too, as 'friend', which was not the norm for Baines, frequently the loner.[34] From the outset, in his first article for the *Natal Mercury*, Baines notes:

> I had the good fortune to fall in with my friend Captain Drake, formerly of the *Justicia* of Cape Town, now commander of a buck wagon and tent, which he hospitably invited me to share with him. It need hardly be said that I accepted the invitation as freely as it was given ... a friend in need kindly lent me a horse ... and thus relieve[d] Shank's nag of at least twenty miles of the journey.[35]

It seems Baines was hardly well equipped as an independent observer on this trip – no tent and no horse speak to a severe impoverishment – and yet he had an optimistic outlook in relation to the camping trip he was about to make. His optimism was well founded: Baines' report for the *Natal Mercury* written at Flag Staff, Umhlali and published on 29 July records offers to share tents from Captain Escombe and also from Dr Lyle; the same article reports: 'I got out the sextant – kindly lent me by Captain Wilson, and nautical almanac by Captain Airth – and observed the two following stars'; plus a 'social breakfast with my friends Mr and Mrs Hart' in the morning.[36] The third piece published in the *Natal Mercury* confirms that the friendship and cordiality extended further: from Rendezvous Camp near the Thukela River where the escort awaited the arrival of Shepstone, Baines reports that 'Saturday night was duly honoured: "songs all round" was the order of the evening, the canvas walls allowing the songs of one tent to be audible to all the rest.'[37]

While this tent scene speaks to the men's perceived role as kindred 'colonial spirits' tasked to extend British influence over the Zulu nation, the trip was not expected to be without tension and hardship when it came to anticipating how the Zulu king would receive the column moving ever closer towards him, not to mention the occasional difficulties the terrain would offer the wagons, guns, and oxen. In his next episode sent to the *Natal Mercury*, dated 19 August 1873, Baines observed: 'We expect rough country tomorrow and if there were any ideas among us that this escort was to be a mere picnic in uniform, it is likely to be dispelled by the stern teaching of experience.' A little later in this same article, a cautionary note is sounded: 'I believe part of the duty of the corps is to prove to the natives that our intentions are peaceful ... Nevertheless a wise precaution has been taken to order that every man shall be provided with ten rounds of ball cartridge.'[38] In the meantime, however, the mood prior to the coronation for those escorts awaiting further developments was light, even frivolous: in order to pass the time while waiting for Cetshwayo to agree to an exact location for the coronation, a programme of athletic sports was organised – some pages of Baines' diaries are filled with sporting results of one such programme with events such as high jump, sack race, and three-legged race listed.[39] These are, of course, also reported in the *Natal Mercury*: 'As for the four days we are to spend here, a committee of sports is to be formed, and foot and horse races, cricket matches, coast against up-country, and all sorts of amusements are talked of.'[40]

These efforts to relieve boredom were devised by, and for, the white men accompanying Shepstone, settlers in the main. But what do the pieces Baines was writing for the newspaper tell us about the Zulus who were with them as part of their escort, and also of Cetshwayo and his people? As an artist,

Baines seems always to be evaluating the Zulu he sees as potential subjects for his pencil. His diary entry dated 28 August offers a good example:

> I had noticed one fine young man wearing two or three Union Jack handker-chiefs as a shawl and presently some of our friends came and begged me to sketch the handsomest man in Zululand. He was asked to stand for me, the request being put in such a form as to render it a compliment; and as soon as he understood our wishes he threw off his mantle and faced towards me ... He had no head-ring, but his crisp hair was two or three inches long, his forehead large, his eyes large clear and open, his nose aquiline, his mouth especially small and well formed ... his neck massive, his chest full ... Of course my sketch under such circumstances was imperfect, but I think I can correct and develop it.[41]

At the coronation itself, Baines was, of course, terribly keen to sketch the ceremony but 'I did not use my sketchbook folio lest by any possibility I should give cause of offence, but folded small pieces of paper so that I could push them up my left sleeve or hold them in the hollow of my hand.'[42] He reported doing a few sketches where he could: 'the rush of the Zulus' during the ceremony, the 'thrones while they were vacant', but, sadly, none of Cetshwayo himself as Baines could not get close enough to him. Other sources portray Cetshwayo and Shepstone at the coronation (Figure 10.4).

Baines does, however, provide a description of the crowned king: 'Never-theless his majesty looked right regal in his crimson and gold coronet, with

Figure 10.4 'The Coronation of Cetewayo [sic]', in *Sunshine for 1883* (London: George Stoneman, 1883), p. 160

its towering crimson ostrich plumes rising from each pinnacle and curling gracefully backward.'[43] There are many references in the *Natal Mercury* articles to sketching Zulu men from the royal kraal, particularly the northern magnate 'Oham' [Hamu kaNzibe of the Ngenetsheni] and 'Ziweda' [Ziwedu kaMpande], the king's half-brother. Hamu is singled out as a 'really jolly fellow [who] has won all our hearts' and a worthy subject to sketch, 'a splendid specimen of humanity, and would have excited the admiration of our home farmers could he have been transported just as he was to Islington or Smithfield to be exhibited beside our prize cattle'.[44] This demeaning comparison fits into the casually racist and patronising tone with which the Zulu are generally portrayed by Baines, perhaps in an effort to 'fit in' with the settler jargon and assumed views of his readership.

There are a few offensive descriptions of the royal wives, too, by Baines, repeated in the general editorial comments that preceded his pieces. A comparison of one particular set of descriptions is useful in that Baines' observations are slightly softened by levity and an effort at euphemism, as opposed to that of the editor. Baines' entry of 22 August recalls how one of Cetshwayo's wives

> has attained such enviable dimensions that she is valued at no less than a thousand head of cattle. Indeed one of the reasons given by Ketchwayo for wishing us to come down to him, is that he wishes his wives and sisters to see him crowned, and many of them are so beautiful that they could not possibly walk up the hill, and could not be carried without great inconvenience.[45]

In contrast, the editor summarises this entry by Baines baldly as follows: 'some are too fat to climb the hill'.[46] The hearsay description of the wives is intensified once Shepstone's party is allowed to meet the women of the royal household a few days later. Baines' diary entry of 30 August relays the party's impression: 'Of course all were in prime condition, and the *belle* of the nation was so fat that even the calves of her legs hung in folds over her ankles, just as the skin of an Indian rhinoceros does about its body.'[47] How much of this is Baines angling for a smile from his readers in Natal is impossible to say. Although there are vestiges of a similar kind of patronising attitude in a few of his journal entries describing Aboriginal Australians from the North Australia expedition, these derogatory and dismissive attitudes, particularly towards the Zulu women, are of a piece with writing for a 'popular' settler audience and not for the Fellows of the RGS.[48]

One echo from the North Australia expedition recalls the more scientific side of Baines – on that expedition, the grass burning of Aboriginal Australians was misunderstood as an aggressive act rather than the farming practice it indeed was. On this campaign, Baines never feels under the same lonely threat when the Zulu burn grass nearby, understanding that it is a necessary form of communication, involving 'signalling by means of smoke every movement that is made, and runners are employed to carry any messages not provided for in the telegraphic mode'.[49] Unlike the North Australian expedition where there is limited verbal interaction between white and black men, in Zululand much more conversation is possible given the number of available translators and white men who could speak Zulu. Baines is, therefore, able to respond when approached by members of the Zulu royal family with a request for advice as to how to make beards grow – he suggests 'a little fat or marrow or vegetable oil pressed out of the ground-nut as the only thing I would recommend'.[50] Em Robarts corroborates this interchange in his diary, adding that Baines 'gave them the best advice he could and seized the opportunity to get a sketch of them'.[51]

As to the future relations between British and Zulu after the coronation, Baines makes no prediction, save that Mr Dunn is singled out for praise for his 'efforts in the cause of peace and British interests', and Hamu, a rival for the throne at the time, is not judged to be a threat to the king 'as long as his own rights are not invaded'.[52] Praise is deemed fit for the accompanying volunteer escorts and, of course, for Shepstone, the ultimate chief, with whom Baines had 'the honour of dining' a few days after the coronation on Saturday 6 September, '[passing] a very pleasant evening'.[53] Baines' own death was to follow in less than two years and the Anglo-Zulu War a few years after that, but at this moment, brought together for a 'short-lived pageant', as Baines terms the coronation, Zulu and settler slept peacefully each in their respective camps.[54]

Finally – though much more could be said about the pieces Baines wrote for the *Natal Mercury* – we can derive insights into how he viewed the challenging environment of the Natal north coast and Zululand during the weeks he spent charting the expedition's course. That the terrain was arduous and dangerous is well referenced by Baines. Crocodiles were a frequent threat to life when crossing the waterways, while some of their body parts were seen as lethal in Zulu witchcraft practices. The scientist and anthropologist in Baines is eager to record these observations and educate his readers. Of a crocodile caught crossing the Umvoti river, Baines wittily observes 'that he acquires a musty flavour, but a little pepper, salt and hunger make excellent sauce for the tail steaks'.[55] Besides the crocodiles, Baines writes of different kinds of antelope shot for the pot by members of the various escorts and sketched by himself, together with snakes and bird-life. The fascinating wildlife complements the landscape, which Baines describes scientifically but warmly. One such example can suffice to illustrate the confluence of scientific endeavour and aesthetic appreciation in Baines when applied to his Zululand environment:

> Today I completed the plotting down of our track, and at night was fortunate
> enough to get a quiet moment for an altitude of Alpha Lyroc, which gave lati-
> tude 28 deg.21 min.41 sec. ... The country now is less difficult, the ridges are
> broader and more level ... One of these glens we passed today with a little
> waterfall trickling over a rock was a perfect little gem in the wilderness.[56]

This is all of a piece with the contented tone Baines adopts in his submissions
to the *Natal Mercury*: the coronation expedition was a happy one for Baines,
with a united party on expedition, no great privations, and many friendly
companions to assist with any need, as well as enabling a contribution to
science and one's country through the map and observations. For once,
Baines feels an insider, as is evident from his opening sentence addressed to
Natal Mercury readers: 'It would be but a poor compliment to imagine you
so unacquainted with our border policy or with the history of our relations
with the neighbouring tribes as to require enlightenment upon a subject
which ... has for some time engrossed the attention of Natal ... our colony.'[57]

Baines' emphasis on '*our* colony' and '*our* relations with neighbouring
tribes' brings into stark relief the purpose of both the coronation and the
mapping expedition, which was to promote British political and economic
interests and to unite British settlers in a common interest. The same article
a little further on contains a poem by Baines entitled 'Ketchewahyo's Coronation', more evidence of what Dominy describes as Baines' 'doggerel verse'
penned for this trip.[58] One particular verse reinforces the sense Baines projects of being an insider writing for other like-minded readers, assuming a
pro-Shepstone bias for himself and others accompanying the expedition:

> Then at once through all Natal, there rose a mighty voice,
> Sure of Englishmen and colonists Somtseu[59] can have his choice,
> We'll muster thick around him, and make his heart rejoice,
> As he travels to Ketchwaiiyo's coronation.
>
> *Chorus* Hurrah, hurrah, we'll sing the jubilee
> Hurrah, hurrah, we'll have a jolly spree
> More power to the elbow of his Zulu Majesty
> As we march to Ketchwaiiyo's coronation.[60]

From the *Natal Mercury* archive of articles written by Baines, one gathers a
picture of Baines himself on this expedition, ever busy, measuring everything
from animals to distance, writing, drawing, staying up to midnight to copy
his journals to catch the post, filling in names on his map – 'I gave Mr Robertson a tracing of my map, asking him to furnish me with details of the
country around, so that I may afterwards add them in' – talking to local
informants, gleaning information: in short, being the ever diligent servant of
empire that he was.[61]

Cartographic expansion

Stalling the coronation with numerous delays, it is likely that Cetshwayo had second thoughts about the wisdom of his strategy in inviting Shepstone to perform the service. Moreover, unexpectedly as far as Shepstone was concerned, Cetshwayo had already been proclaimed king on 14 August in the traditional manner at the emaKheni kraal in the emaKhosina valley, and all his rivals had bowed to his accession.[62] Shepstone's 'pantomime' coronation was therefore superfluous, except insofar as it might offer support to the king against incursions from Natal settlers and the Boers, as well as some protection from Britain. Dutifully, Cetshwayo acceded to the agreement that Shepstone insisted upon at the coronation, although many of his chiefs did not approve. It was these terms that were later to be misinterpreted by Shepstone as introducing a 'fundamental change' in the relationship between Natal and Zululand.[63] Some of them formed the basis for the invasion of Zululand in 1879 and the subsequent dissolution of the kingdom. R. L. Cope concludes that Cetshwayo and Shepstone were both disappointed, and that neither of them kept to the agreement that had been made.[64] Zululand was annexed by Britain in 1887 and subsequently incorporated into Natal in 1897.

As to Baines' legacy from the expedition, very little remains besides the map, the journals, and the newspaper articles. Single sketches can be found in various archives – for example, in the Killie Campbell Library – but no large 'coronation expedition' archive survives intact, such as is available, for example, for researchers interested in Baines and the North Australian expedition at the RGS. The most probable explanation is that Baines' sudden death relatively soon after the coronation expedition left his papers and paintings unsorted. Carruthers and Arnold list the various effects he left after his death: 'an engine and crushing machine worth £100, artist's materials worth £25, firearms, various tools, a share in a wagon, manuscript maps, stationery, clothing and some mercury, the total value of which was £211'.[65] Ironically, the RGS Baines holdings from the North Australia expedition sold in 2014 for £2.75 million, even then thought an undervaluation.

Reading Baines' various narratives together – his cartography, artworks, and newspaper reports as a Special Correspondent – provides unique insight into the unfolding tale of Cetshwayo's 'coronation', Shepstone's part in it, and the roles of other important members of the Zulu kingdom such as 'Oham' and 'Ziweda'. Mapping, painting, and writing, these accounts together form a narrative – both literal and metaphoric – that not only records Baines' own experiences, but also portrays a crucial moment in the history of British settler colonial and Zulu relationships, when diplomatic missions (however performative) were still being undertaken, and before settler expansion into the Zulu kingdom and the unfolding of the Anglo-Zulu

War. In acknowledging the Zulu kingdom's land names in his colonial cartography, Baines maps the Zulu king's possessions, but he also anticipates and depicts colonial encroachment and the erasure of the Zulu kingdom through settler violence and invasion. While not an official colonial agent on this expedition, as Baines spreads his map, so does he spread the reach of the British Empire.

Notes

1 J. P. R. Wallis, *Thomas Baines: His Life and Explorations in South Africa, Rhodesia and Australia, 1820–1875*, 2nd edn (Cape Town: A. A. Balkema, 1976).

2 See, e.g., Jane Carruthers and Marion Arnold, *The Life and Work of Thomas Baines* (Cape Town: Fernwood Press, 1995); Jane Carruthers, *Thomas Baines: Eastern Cape Sketches, 1848 to 1852* (Johannesburg: The Brenthurst Press, 1990); Russell Braddon, *Thomas Baines and the North Australian Expedition* (Sydney: Collins in association with the Royal Geographical Society, 1986); and Marius and Joy Diemont, *The Brenthurst Baines: A Selection of the Works of Thomas Baines in the Oppenheimer Collection Johannesburg* (Johannesburg: The Brenthurst Press, 1975).

3 This chapter began as an article written by Jane Carruthers and Lindy Stiebel, '"The Last Hurrah": Thomas Baines and the Expedition to the Coronation of Cetshwayo kaMpande, Zululand, 1873', *Southern African Humanities*, 32 (2019), 57–82. Permission to use material from the article has been granted by both *SAH* editor Gavin Whitelaw and article co-author Jane Carruthers.

4 John Laband and John Wright, *King Cetshwayo kaMpande* (Durban and Ulundi: Shuter and Shooter, KwaZulu Monuments Council, 1980), p. 75.

5 Jeff Guy, *Theophilus Shepstone and the Forging of Natal* (Pietermaritzburg: University of KwaZulu-Natal Press, 2013), p. 383.

6 Charles Ballard, *John Dunn: The White Chief of Zululand* (Johannesburg: Ad Donker, 1985), p. 105.

7 Graham Dominy, 'Thomas Baines and the Langalibalele Rebellion: A Critique of an Unrecorded Sketch of the Action at "Bushman's Pass", 1873', *Natal Museum Journal of Humanities*, 3 (1991), 46.

8 Lindy Stiebel, Jane Carruthers, Vivian Forbes, and Norman Etherington, *Thomas Baines: The Great Map* (Durban: Campbell Collections of the University of Natal, 2001), CD format.

9 Lindy Stiebel and Jane Carruthers (eds), *Thomas Baines: Exploring Tropical Australia, 1855 to 1857* (Canberra: National Museum of Australia, 2012).

10 Jeffrey Stone, 'The Cartography of Thomas Baines', in Michael Stevenson (ed.), *Thomas Baines: Artist in Service of Science* (London: Christie's International Media, 1999), pp. 118–29.

11 See Lindy Stiebel, 'A Map to Treasure: The Literary Significance of Thomas Baines's "Map of the Gold Fields of South Eastern Africa" (1875)', *South African Historical Journal*, 39 (1998), 64–9.

12 Wallis, *Thomas Baines: His Life and Explorations*, p. 217.

13 Stone, 'The Cartography of Thomas Baines', p. 120.

14 W. E. [Em] Robarts, Letter to his wife Liz dated 5 July 1873, Robarts family archive, Empangeni.

15 See, e.g., Wallis, *Thomas Baines: His Life and Explorations,* p. 216. The size of the map owned by the Robarts family is 500mm x 380mm and their coloured sketch is 255mm x 395mm.

16 Em Robarts listed nine men: Capt [corrected to Trooper by Bill Robarts] Henry T. Garland, Lieut. [corrected to Sergeant] W. E. Robarts, B. Armstrong, ? Jackson, W. Cowley, A. Blamey, [R. Plant inserted], J. Adams, H. A. Galloway, and Thomas Baines (artist).

17 W. E. [Bill] Robarts, 1995 inscription back of Baines painting 'Victoria Mounted Rifles at Rendezvous Camp, Tugela River August 1st to 8th 1873', Robarts family archive, Empangeni.

18 W. E. [Em] Robarts, fieldbook 27 August 1872 to 9 September 1873, Robarts family archive, Empangeni.

19 W. E. [Bill] Robarts from a talk that Robarts gave to the Zululand History Society on 23 March 1993. One copy was kept by the family and another donated to the Society.

20 See the Brenthurst Library, Baines African Collections, MS049/4; letter book vol. VI, MS49/6 (book no. 6433).

21 Graham Dominy, 'Thomas Baines: The McGonagall of Shepstone's 1873 Zululand Expedition?', *Natalia*, 21 (1991), 75–9.

22 RGS Map Room South Africa, S.97 – Spec Routes of T. Baines and J. Sanderson, c. 1865. Twenty–six MS. Route maps illustrating the journeys of T. Baines, J. Sanderson etc. in Natal, Zululand RGS. Includes 26 sheets in various sizes. MSS c. 1865. Received 19 July 1888.

23 The new call number is CU18-AFS-ZAF-S701.

24 Wallis, *Thomas Baines: His Life and Explorations*, p. 219.

25 Stone, 'The Cartography of Thomas Baines', 128.

26 For a discussion of British late imperial practices when depicting African landscapes through painting, mapping, and writing, see Lindy Stiebel, *Imagining Africa: Landscape in H. Rider Haggard's African Romances* (Westport: Greenwood Press, 2001).

27 'The Coronation of Cetywayo. Mr Shepstone's Embassy', *Natal Mercury* (29 July 1873), p. 2.

28 Cited in Dominy, 'Thomas Baines and the Langalibalele Rebellion', 76.

29 Jane Carruthers and Marion Arnold, *The Life and Work of Thomas Baines* (Cape Town: Fernwood Press, 1995), pp. 74–5.

30 Wallis, *Thomas Baines: His Life and Explorations*, p. 217.

31 Robarts, fieldbook 27 August 1872 to 9 September 1873.

32 'The Coronation of Cetywayo. In Zululand (by Our Special Correspondent)', *Natal Mercury* (9 August 1873), p. 2.

33 'The Coronation of Cetywayo. In Zululand (by Our Special Correspondent)', p. 2.

34 Robarts, fieldbook 27 August 1872 to 9 September 1873.

35 'The Coronation of Cetywayo. En route to Zululand (by Our Special Correspondent) Royal Hotel, Verulam', *Natal Mercury* (28 July 1873), p. 5.

36 'The Coronation of Cetywayo. En route to Zululand (by Our Special Correspondent) Flag Staff, Umhlali', *Natal Mercury* (29 July 1873), p. 5.

37 'The Coronation of Cetywayo. En route to Zululand (by Our Special Correspondent) Rendezvous Camp, near Fort Williamson, Tugela', *Natal Mercury* (12 August 1873), p. 5.

38 'The Coronation of Cetywayo. In Zululand (by Our Special Correspondent)', *Natal Mercury* (19 August 1873), p. 2.

39 Brenthurst Library, Baines African Collections MS049/11/3.

40 'Monthly Summary. The Coronation of Cetywayo. Mr Shepstone's Embassy', *Natal Mercury* (23 August 1873), pp. 7–8.

41 'Monthly Summary. The Coronation of Cetywayo. In Zululand', *Natal Mercury* (23 September 1873), pp. 7–8.

42 'Monthly Summary. The Coronation of Cetywayo. In Zululand', pp. 7–8.

43 'Monthly Summary. The Coronation of Cetywayo. In Zululand', pp. 7–8.

44 *Natal Mercury* (4 September 1873), p. 3.

45 *Natal Mercury* (4 September 1873), p. 3.

46 'Coronation of Cetywayo', *Natal Mercury* (2 September 1873), p. 3.

47 'Monthly Summary. The Coronation of Cetywayo. In Zululand', pp. 7–8.

48 See Lindy Stiebel, '"Cooeing to the Natives": Thomas Baines's Encounters with the Other on the North Australian Expedition of 1855–57', in Carruthers and Stiebel (eds), *Thomas Baines: Exploring Tropical Australia*, pp. 50–69.

49 'The Coronation of Cetywayo. En route to Zululand (by Our Special Correspondent) Rendezvous Camp, near Fort Williamson, Tugela', p. 5.

50 'Monthly Summary. The Coronation of Cetywayo. In Zululand', pp. 7–8.

51 Robarts, fieldbook 27 August 1872 to 9 September 1873.

52 'Monthly Summary. The Coronation of Cetywayo. In Zululand', pp. 7–8.

53 'The Coronation of Cetywayo. Homeward Bound', *Natal Mercury* (23 September 1873), p. 5.

54 'Monthly Summary. The Coronation of Cetywayo. In Zululand', pp. 7–8.

55 'The Coronation of Cetywayo. En route to Zululand', *Natal Mercury* (5 August 1873), p. 5.

56 'The Coronation of Cetywayo. In Zululand', *Natal Mercury* (26 August 1873), p. 5.

57 'The Coronation of Cetywayo. En route to Zululand', *Natal Mercury* (31 July 1873), p. 5.

58 Dominy, 'Thomas Baines and the Langalibalele Rebellion', 77.

59 This was Theophilus Shepstone's Zulu name.

60 'The Coronation of Cetywayo. En route to Zululand', *Natal Mercury* (31 July 1873), p. 5.

61 'The Coronation of Cetywayo. Homeward Bound', p. 5. Mr Robertson was the missionary attached to the Mackenzie Mission at 'Kwama Gwasa'. Baines had met the Robertsons on board the *Basuto* on the voyage from Algoa Bay to Natal.

62 Richard Lidbrook Cope, 'The Origins of the Anglo-Zulu War of 1879' (PhD dissertation, University of the Witwatersrand, 1995), pp. 47–8; John Laband, *The Eight Zulu Kings* (Johannesburg: Jonathan Ball, 2018) pp. 190–3.
63 Cope, 'Origins of the Anglo-Zulu War', p. 44.
64 Cope, 'Origins of the Anglo-Zulu War', p. 54.
65 Carruthers and Arnold, *Life and Work*, p. 75.

11

'Wild, desert and lawless countries': William Burchell's *Travels in the Interior of Southern Africa*

Matthew Shum

William Burchell was an English naturalist who arrived at the Cape Colony in November 1810. After a brief period exploring Cape Town and its environs, he spent four years journeying 7,000 kilometres through remote and often unexplored regions beyond the boundaries of the colony. His original intention had been to traverse the central plains of the country to the furthest known Indigenous settlement at Litakun (present-day Dithakong/Vryburg), before heading towards the Portuguese settlements on the eastern coast. His ambition was to go 'farther into the interior than had been before attempted'.[1] As it happened, Burchell did succeed in doing this, but his plan to reach the Portuguese settlements was thwarted by the refusal of his party of Khoi servants, apprehensive about the dangers they faced, to accompany him any further.[2] Burchell then headed back to Cape Town via a circuitous route along the east coast, but he never recorded this section of his journey. He arrived in Cape Town in April 1815 and sailed for England a few months later, taking with him his journals, over 50,000 plant and animal specimens, and an extensive collection of sketches and paintings. It was seven years before the first account of his travels appeared in 1822, followed by a second volume in 1824. Official recognition of Burchell's endeavours was muted. Although he received an honorary degree from Oxford in 1834, he was, according to one of his contemporaries, 'signally neglected by his government' and never awarded a pension – and this despite Burchell's refusal of an offer by the Prussian government of generous remuneration and residence in Berlin if he donated his collections to their museums.[3] From 1825 to 1830 Burchell travelled in Brazil, again at his own expense, where he was attached to a diplomatic mission. The journals recording this visit have never been found, but his collections and the visual archive of this journey have survived. In the final decades of his life, disappointed by the lack of recognition his work had achieved, he became increasingly reclusive and took his own life in March 1863.

In the Cape Colony, Burchell travelled as a private individual 'not vested with the authority of government'.[4] In the context of the time, this was a significant deviation: people venturing beyond the boundaries of the colony usually did so with the backing either of the government or of some association connected with colonial exploration. This kind of authorisation had benefits for the explorer, in particular the provision of armed men to protect the expedition, a precaution considered indispensable to the safe passage of European travellers. In stark contrast to this practice, Burchell's expedition was self-financed and minimally guarded; it was also undertaken in conditions of secrecy. 'The extent of my plan was known to but few of my friends,' he wrote in early 1811, 'several reasons induced me to keep it secret; of which, one, was the difficulty, and, perhaps, impossibility, which would be found in persuading Hottentots to enter into my service.'[5] But what were the other 'several reasons' he had for concealing his intentions from the colonial public? At least one of these was that, as Burchell puts it: 'My undertaking was generally looked on in Cape Town as an imprudent attempt, after the failure of an expedition, in which, previous to its setting out, every precaution had been taken, and provision made, to ensure its success; and whose numbers and strength so much exceeded mine.'[6] Burchell is referring here to an official expedition led by Dr Cowan and Captain Donovan, accompanied by two other colonists and sponsored by Lord Caledon, the Colonial Secretary. Two years previously this expedition, which also aimed to reach the Portuguese settlements on the east coast, disappeared without trace despite being protected by 'private soldiers in the garrison ... and about fifteen Hottentots'.[7]

The fate of Cowan's expedition did not deter Burchell, even though his own expedition was significantly more vulnerable to the various dangers faced by travellers. Not only did his immediate party never consist of more than ten people, but it was frequently rotated; when they arrived back in Cape Town he was the only person who had set out with the original group. Furthermore, aside from the missionaries with whom Burchell was obliged to travel in the initial stages of his journey, he chose to have no Europeans in his party, thus placing himself in constant proximity to Indigenous peoples. I highlight the hazards of Burchell's journey to underscore the fact that it was undertaken within a climate of risk, a risk that was as much phenomenal as it was physical. For extended periods Burchell placed himself within an environment in which his sense of self was unsettled and he was assailed, as he puts it, by 'daily fatigues and anxieties of the mind'.[8] Although his travels provided useful data for subsequent ventures into the interior with more instrumental intentions, and he was later to compile a report for the Colonial Office on the prospects for the state-sponsored 1820 settlement scheme, Burchell, as we shall see, does not provide an easy fit for the default postcolonial judgement of the European naturalist explorer as the advance agent or epistemological vanguard of the imperial process.

Burchell is best known today as a naturalist and for his landscape paintings and sketches, but little attention has been paid to his observations of, and his interactions with, Indigenous southern African people. In the 'Preface' to the first volume of *Travels in the Interior of Southern Africa* (1822–24), he asserts his intent to extend his 'researches' beyond the natural world or 'the works of the creation' to include 'the investigation of man in an uncivilized state of society'.[9] He adds that this 'will be found to offer ... a picture not altogether undeserving of attention if the writer should be able by words to communicate to others those feelings which he himself experienced, and those impressions which his abode among the natives of Africa has made upon his own mind'.[10] Burchell promises the reader not the standard descriptions of ethnographic customs and manners (although he does in fact offer quite a lot of this), but something different: the evocation of 'feelings', the textures of 'experience[s]' and 'impressions' provoked by his interaction with Indigenous people – precisely that field of affect whose formal domain was the discursive rather than the scientific or the taxonomic. It is on these interactions that this article will concentrate, and in particular those with the San ('Bushmen'), who were represented to him by the colonists as 'a set of beings without reason or intellect' and hence a challenge to the unitary notion of the human.[11] Before doing this, however, I will briefly consider Burchell the naturalist or natural philosopher, since it is in this capacity that he is best known and because his understanding of the natural world bears on his understanding of the human world.

Burchell as natural philosopher

Burchell's parents owned a large nursery on the banks of the Thames, which was 'renowned for containing exotic and hardy plants from all over the world'.[12] Growing up in this intercontinental botanical hub, Burchell developed the preoccupations which were to dominate his adult life. He was privately schooled, fluent in several languages, and had a particular facility for drawing, which was further developed by special tutoring. He did not go to university, however. After a period touring on the continent, he worked for his father and extended his knowledge as an apprentice gardener at Kew Gardens, then the centre of botanical traffic from around the world. In his early twenties his precocious talents were recognised when he was made a member of the prestigious Linnean Society. At this point the trajectory of his hitherto settled life changed. He refused employment in his father's nursery and for reasons that are not clear sailed to the island of St Helena, where he had entered into a commercial contract with a merchant. At that time the volcanic island served mainly as a port on colonial maritime routes, but it was also renowned for its unique geological and natural features. After Burchell's business dealings foundered, he was employed as a schoolteacher before being appointed by the governor as the custodian and superintendent of a new botanical garden. This arrangement eventually came to an end, but during his tenure Burchell began keeping a journal of his experiences, as well as compiling sketches and drawings of the island. After a five-year residence on the island, Burchell sailed to the Cape. One can only conjecture that through contact with people sailing to and from the Cape, Burchell conceived the idea of journeying beyond the boundaries of the colony into the interior of the country. He had no experience whatsoever of expeditionary travel.

Critical understanding of natural science in this early colonial context often takes its academic bearings from Mary Louise Pratt's influential *Imperial Eyes: Travel Writing and Transculturation* (1992). A central argument of the book is that systems of scientific naming and classification – with the binomial Linnean system the major culprit – act to integrate the natural world into a European 'planetary consciousness' shedding it of context and particularity.[13] Drawing on Michel Foucault's analysis of eighteenth-century thought in *The Order of Things* (1966/1970), Pratt argues that the 'systemizing of nature' that the Linnaean taxonomy introduced into natural history 'extracted specimens not only from their organic or ecological relations with each other, but also from their places in other peoples' economies, histories, social and symbolic systems'.[14] In Pratt's understanding, the natural scientist performs the groundwork for the 'global resemanticising' ushered in by imperial expansion, and bears the stigma of complicity in this process.[15] However, the broad claims of Pratt's argument become less persuasive when closely examined in particular contexts. When Pratt discusses eighteenth and early-nineteenth-century southern African travellers and naturalists, for example, she never mentions Burchell, concentrating mainly on John Barrow, who travelled into the interior in his official capacity as the Private Secretary to Lord Macartney, governor of the colony from 1795 to 1798. As it happens, Barrow was Burchell's nemesis and Burchell frequently attacked or mocked Barrow in the pages of his *Travels*. In certain respects, Burchell's *Travels* may even be considered a rejoinder to Barrow, and certainly it is an account of a very different kind. I mention Pratt's book not in order to engage with it in detail, but to clear the way both for a less recriminatory understanding of natural science in this period and for Burchell's practice of it.

In a reappraisal of the Romantic period, Richard Holmes has argued that we should revise, even reverse, the notion that Romanticism as a 'cultural force' was deeply invested in the subjective, and hence hostile to the objectivist empiricism of the sciences.[16] In a richly illustrated argument, Holmes places Romantic science on the same continuum as Romantic poetry, contending that both were united by a magnified sense of the 'wonder' of the world. For Holmes, notions of quest, of venturing, and especially of 'the exploratory voyage, often lonely and perilsome' were central to Romantic science, as it sought to expand the borders of human knowledge.[17] It is not surprising, since wonder is a primary or first-order emotion without an objective calculus, that such a science has an aesthetic as well as an informational dimension, whether this is an expressive aesthetic, a discerning of an aesthetic of formal design in nature itself, or some combination of the two. Also pertinent here, and operating within a wider timeframe, is Pierre Hadot's study of the long durational history of the idea of nature, *The Veil of Isis* (2006). Hadot identifies two central currents animating western thought about nature, or more precisely about unveiling the secrets of nature: the 'Promethean' and the 'Orphic'. The former, as the name suggests, is mechanistic and instrumental, and seeks to 'tear nature's secrets away from her … for utilitarian ends', while the latter seeks a reciprocity with nature, a respect for its mysteries, as Orpheus with his lyre enchanted the natural world.[18] For Hadot, this contemplative-poetic science, for which Plato's *Timaeus* is the prototype, enlists not only the empirical methods of science, but 'the work of art, the discourse or poem, as a means of knowing nature'.[19] Such Orphic science and its sense of aesthetic perception, he claims, reached its peak in the late eighteenth and early nineteenth centuries, particularly in Germany and particularly in the figure of Goethe, 'the model of an approach to nature that was both scientific and aesthetic'.[20] This approach to nature was not confined to Goethe and the poets; one of its exemplary figures was the explorer naturalist Alexander von Humboldt, who knew Goethe well, and who praised him for his attempt to 'renew the bond which at the dawn of mankind united together philosophy, physics and poetry'.[21] It was Humboldt, more than any other naturalist of this period, who worked to integrate the aesthetic into the repertoire of natural science, particularly in his *Views of Nature: or Contemplation of the Sublime Phenomena of Creation* (1808), where he argued that 'the physical world is reflected with truth and animation on the inner susceptible world of the mind'.[22]

It is difficult to estimate the degree of influence Humboldt had on Burchell. The environmental historian Richard Grove finds 'a consciously aesthetic approach to landscape' in Burchell's writing about St Helena which is 'contemporary with … Humboldt on precisely the same theme', but Burchell never cites Humboldt, or other prominent German naturalists such as George Foster.[23] However, the degree of international exchange fostered by the traffic in botanical specimens and exchanges both between individuals and scientific societies, as well as the rapid diffusion of printed material, make it very likely that Burchell was aware of those currents of thought of which Humboldt was the most prominent representative. Although an obvious aestheticism informs Burchell's rendering of the natural world, he also draws on late Enlightenment and early Romantic lineages that are distinctively British. His framing aesthetic concepts, however qualified, are the picturesque, the beautiful, and the sublime, and his notions of human progress and historical teleology are implicitly marked by the four-stages theory of the Scottish Enlightenment. Whatever admixture of influences we might ascribe to Burchell, his writing about nature is infused with an Orphic wonder for what he witnesses in the landscapes of 'a country still in a state of nature and where art has done so little'.[24]

Burchell divides his work into 'scientific and ... literary parts', without specifying how this division actually operates.[25] For the contemporary reader this distinction is certainly not a stable one, as the two categories constantly overlap. Some sense of these differing approaches may be gained by comparing three different descriptions of the Karoo. The first offers a panoramic perspective, where Burchell is standing on an elevated ridge:

> The Great Karoo, stretched out before me, presented, at this distance, no visible object to break the evenness of the plain, or relieve the eye. The rivers and their Thorn-trees were lost in the vast extent, and were not to be distinguished as a feature in the landscape ... In these solitary wilds, no moving being was to be seen, no sound to be heard.[26]

This is Burchell drawing on literary modes of landscape representation current at the time, and there is nothing in this passage to distinguish it from any number of similar descriptions of the Karoo in the nineteenth century, the colonial *locus classicus* of a denuded landscape into which only an abyssal emptiness can be read. But there are occasions, as J. M. Coetzee has observed, where Burchell gestures towards an aesthetic of landscape that is distinctly African in character rather than a recycled version of European categories, particularly the picturesque.[27] While this awareness does not result in a new expressive form, and Burchell reverts to his default settings for landscape description, there is nonetheless a recognition that the southern African interior possesses a 'species of beauty' with which 'European painters ... may not yet be sufficiently acquainted'.[28] In the second description, viewing the sparse landscapes of the interior where hardly anything intervenes between earth and sky and the latter stretches into an infinity of 'boundless aerial space [which] seemed lifted further from the globe', Burchell cryptically remarks: 'The painter who viewed these scenes, might, if he knew it not before, feel a conviction that the truest definition of *Taste*, *Beauty*, the *Picturesque*, may be found in that of the word *Nature*.'[29] He seems to be suggesting here that there is an inner congruence between art and nature, that art achieves its highest form when it imitates, or embodies, the design of nature, and that aesthetic perception, in the Humboldtian manner, is a mode of understanding nature.

In a third passage the understanding of nature as a unified phenomenon rather than nature as landscape becomes evident when Burchell the natural scientist views the Karoo. Two days after the observations cited above, we have the following: 'I took a botanical ramble, and added forty-eight plants to my collection, many of which I have never met with either before or since.'[30] Burchell then provides, in a lengthy footnote, a breakdown of these plants with their binomial Latin names and some further detail about genera and species. Here the scenic aspects of landscape give way to a sense of its rich inner configuration:

> The harmony which pervades every part of the universe, is not less wonderful and beautiful in the distribution of animals and vegetables over the face of the globe than in the planetary system, and in the sublime arrangement of myriads of worlds through the inconceivable infinity of space ... In the wide system of created objects, nothing is superfluous: the smallest weed or insect is indispensably necessary to the general good, as the largest object we behold ... Nothing more bespeaks a littleness of mind, and a narrowness of ideas, than the admiring of a production of Nature, *merely* for its magnitude, or the despising of one, merely for its minuteness: nothing more erroneous than to regard as useless, all that does not visibly tend to the benefit of *man*.[31]

In Hadot's terms, this is a fully Orphic view of material phenomena, in which the design of nature is as inconceivable in its complexity and extent as it is purposive in its dispositions, and in which the 'physics of utilization', or the idea that nature should be the object of utilitarian value, is rejected.[32] Again and again, Burchell will reiterate this point as he passes through the arid interior of the country, where the discerning eye of the naturalist reads a landscape populous with phenomena that are, to European eyes, entirely novel. Yet Burchell cautions against the error of regarding these regions solely in terms of their scale or their prospective utility, a coded warning, perhaps, against a merely acquisitive colonialism. In another passage Burchell declares that his decision to journey into the interior of the country was driven by the desire '[t]o view the admirable perfection of *Nature* in a new light, and not less beautiful in the wilds of Africa, was the irresistible motive which led me on'. This undertaking is not a merely a matter of 'amassing collections of curious objects' or 'the narrow field of nomenclature', but an exploration 'worthy of the philosopher, and of the best talents of a reasonable being'.[33]

Sympathy beyond the jurisdictions of law

If the natural world opens so abundantly before Burchell in his southern African travels, and everywhere reveals purposive design and the 'breath of divinity', what then of the human world?[34] What of its design and its purpose? It is here that Burchell enters into more intractable territory. We recall that he travels, for the most part, without any European familiars and beyond the boundaries of colonial polity. While his small party is armed and the Khoi with whom he travels are in his pay and under his command, there is no security in his position. On a number of occasions his authority is threatened by recalcitrant members of this party, and external dangers, in one form or another, are always imminent. We cannot know the degree to which Burchell retrospectively shaped his journals to edit out or palliate whatever real anxiety he may have felt, but even so there are scattered references throughout the *Travels* which indicate a persistent discomposure: 'In these wild, desert, and lawless countries,' he writes, 'the mind, always ready to feel mistrustful and suspicious of treachery, easily takes alarm at every occurrence which may wear a dubious look.'[35] When Burchell first went beyond the borders of the colony, he left behind 'the jurisdiction and protection of regular laws' and surrendered himself to 'the hostility, or the hospitality, of savage tribes'.[36] This act of social and symbolic divestment, of voluntarily crossing over into lawless and hostile dominions, is, however, anticipated 'with pleasure'. Burchell is convinced that he will find 'virtue' among these tribes, despite his own fears of danger and the colonial consensus, so often expressed to him, that they represent a threat to life. Although the reference to 'savage tribes' is generalised, it is clear that Burchell has a particular interest in the 'Bushmen', or San hunter-gatherers, and he asserts the desire to enter their world not as an armed antagonist but as a sympathetic observer.

Burchell's first brief encounter with the San is marked by relief, as if a burden of anthropological apprehension had been lifted from his shoulders. They were not, as he had been led to believe, 'only a set of beings without reason or intellect' but 'men of lively manners and shrewd understanding'.[37] His second, more extended encounter beyond the boundaries of the colony, occurs when his party is visited by a group of eleven San, including three women. Although at first Burchell discerns 'great mistrust ... and symptoms of much fear', these anxieties are gradually dispelled and, facilitated by gifts of tobacco and beads, a lively exchange between the two groups takes place.[38] Burchell concludes his account of this meeting by regretting his inability to represent the emotions it aroused in him:

> Desirous of transfusing into the minds of others those powerful feelings of interest which I myself on beholding and conversing with this little family of Bushmen experienced ... I never, more than at this moment, longed to possess that command of language, and that talent of descriptive representation which might enable me to impart all those peculiar sensations with which my first interview with this singular nation, inspired me.[39]

Here Burchell presents himself to the reader as a person under the spell of 'powerful feelings' and 'peculiar sensations', which are too overwhelming to describe and thus 'transfuse[d] into the minds of others'. It is as if this encounter with the San has produced a range of emotions that defy any transcription into language. What do we make of this?

We might begin by considering that medium regarded as the most suitable vehicle for 'transfusing' strong emotions to readers: the sentimental novel, and the cluster of cognate categories that it mobilised, such as sensibility, sympathy, and the person of 'feeling'. It is clear that Burchell is conscious of these literary modes. In another passage describing his time spent among the Bachapin (Tswana) people, for example, he writes:

> yet nothing but breathing the air of Africa, and actually walking through it and beholding its living inhabitants in all the peculiarity of their movements and manners, can communicate those gratifying and literally indescribable, sensations, which every European traveller of feeling, will experience on finding himself in the midst of such a scene.[40]

Once again Burchell emphasises both the emotive nature of his experience and his inability to describe it adequately. If, as a natural scientist, Burchell is committed to the observation and recording of natural phenomena, as a 'traveller of *feeling*' he is the embodiment of a strange churn of sensations occasioned by being in the 'midst of' African people, and which is incapable of expression, let alone classification. While Burchell does indeed engage in intensive ethnographic description – of the body, of bodily ornamentation, of dwelling places, of clothing, of hunting, of music, of language, and the list goes on – alongside this there is an anti-ethnography, an emergent archive of 'feeling', of what is shared in sympathetic communication. This precinct of experience is not available for transcription. Referring to time spent watching San nocturnal dancing, he notes:

> I find it impossible to give by means of mere description a correct idea, either of the pleasing impressions received while viewing this scene, or of the kind of effect which the evening's amusement produced upon my mind and feelings. It must be seen; it must be participated in: without which, it would not be easy to imagine its force, or justly to conceive its nature. There was, in this amusement, nothing which can make me ashamed to confess that I derived as much enjoyment from it, as the natives themselves: there was nothing in it which approached to vulgarity; and in this point of view, it would be an injustice to these poor creatures not to place them in a more respectable rank, than that to which the Europeans have generally admitted them ... I sat as if the hut had been my home, and felt in the midst of this horde as though I had been one of them; for some few moments, ceasing to think of sciences or of Europe, and forgetting that I was a lonely stranger in a land of wild untutored men.[41]

Even if Burchell's vocabulary here occasionally displays a reliance on disparaging normative judgements of the San, it is clear that he feels himself akin to them, that he conceives them as part of a human community, and that this feeling of powerful reciprocity belongs to the affective realm of the literary rather than the demonstrable realm of the scientific. Furthermore, Burchell's insistence on the participatory nature of his experiences ('it must be seen, it must be participated in'), and their irreducibility to 'data', acknowledges the autonomy of other forms of social life and how there are occasions when these can only be approached through associative sharing rather than objective or extractive observation.

It is this imprecision, this reliance on subjective mood or feeling, which might, paradoxically, account for the lack of consistency in Burchell's representation of the San, which, contrary to what one might expect, runs across an unstable spectrum from admiration and fellow-feeling to disapprobation and even disgust (emotions which present no barrier to representation). On one occasion, for example, Burchell and his party come across a group of particularly impoverished San, whose only possessions are what they have to hand and who live in the shelter of a mountain cavern: 'Their life, and that of the wild beasts, their fellow inhabitants of the land, were the same. Of both, the only care seemed to be that of feeding themselves and bringing up their young ... Truly, these were the most destitute of beings, and the lowest in the scale of man.'[42] Burchell confesses himself 'distressed to melancholy' by these people, in whom he is able to discern only the barest lineaments of the human. 'While my eyes were fixed in painful observation on their vacant countenances,' he writes, 'I asked myself, What is man? And had almost said; Surely all the inhabitants of the globe never sprang from the same origin!'[43] If Burchell does not quite commit himself to this notion, he does not hold back in continuing to derogate this group as 'the outcast of the Bushman race' and the 'lowest of the human species'.[44] Later he finds corroborating evidence of this view in various aspects of their behavior, such as the 'dog-like voracity' with which they eat some meat that is offered to them.[45] When he learns how they continue to tolerate a man who murdered his brother in order to obtain unimpeded access to his wife, Burchell (even as he admits he cannot be certain of the truth of this tale) denounces the 'horde' for its 'bestial ignorance' and an inability to distinguish between right and wrong.[46] This alleged sliding off the human scale, and the harshness of Burchell's denunciation, becomes even more perplexing when he observes an 'incredible' improvement in their appearance after a few days – a result of being regularly fed. The fact that this group of people might have behaved in the way that they did out of acute hunger (he also notes their listlessness, incuriosity, and apathy) does not elicit a retrospective amendment from the normally even-handed Burchell.

What, we might ask, has happened to the sympathetic amity of his other encounters with the San, and its production of benign but inexpressible feeling? Throughout the *Travels* there is a marked indeterminacy in Burchell's relationship with a range of Indigenous people, and this fluctuation of feeling is in many cases directly linked to the changing nature of his relationship with them, especially when these relationships turn sour. But with the San none of these conditions apply in any substantial way. Paradoxically, it is the San who prove the least vexatious of the Indigenous inhabitants, not least because they are in no position to bargain with Burchell and happily accept what he has to offer them – mainly in the form of tobacco and a share of the game his party shoots. So this passage is an unusual one, and more especially so since Burchell normally invests so much attentive curiosity in this 'race'. Yet in the general tenor of his relationship with the San he is open to their humanity and unique capabilities, despite the fact that he believes their bare lives to be, among all the people he encounters, 'in the lowest degree of human polity and social existence'.[47]

As we have seen, Burchell often has recourse to the vocabulary of the sentimental to convey the texture of his encounters with the San and other Indigenous peoples. Here he describes taking leave of a group of San with whom friendly relations were established:

> As I rode away from their dwellings ... a general salutation was given by the whole assembly; and in a tone so mild and expressive of so much *gratitude*, that a man must have no heart at all, who could witness a scene like this, unmoved. I confess that to my ear the sound was grateful in the highest degree; and while I turned my head to view them for the last time, the pleasure which beamed in their happy countenances, communicated itself to my own feelings, in a manner the most affecting and indelible.[48]

The affective domain of 'the heart' and 'feelings' dominate this exchange. In the absence of a shared language, emotions are semaphored through visual and auditory signs which spontaneously reveal their presence and establish a bond of common humanity between the two parties. By employing the familiar registers of the sentimental, Burchell is repeating a gesture widespread in the colonial literature of the period. As Lynn Festa remarks, sentimentality attained 'dazzling popularity' during that historical moment when European colonialism was beginning to gain momentum and should be understood 'less as a chapter in the history of the freestanding modern individual than as a response to colonial expansion'.[49] In a powerful analysis of the interconnections between ideology and the aesthetic, Festa argues that one of sentimentalism's central functions was not to critique colonial expansion but to enable it, or at least to render it acceptable to the reading public, by endowing colonised subjects with 'the semblance of similitude while maintaining categorical distinctions'.[50] Burchell himself was conscious of such distinctions, which he understood as those between the 'heart' and the 'mind'. 'The *mental powers of Bushmen*,' he maintains, are never to be extolled; for whatever concessions may be made in favour of their heart, nothing can be said in praise of their mind ... The *feelings of the heart* and all its various passions ... are the common property of all mankind, but in the higher faculties of the mind ... the savage claims but little share. It is in the improvement of these faculties and powers, that civilised nations may place their high superiority.[51]

Yet there are occasions, as we shall see, when Burchell wavers in this judgement, or when his own behavior threatens to undermine the very distinctions which he seems elsewhere to uphold.

An aberrant expedition

Burchell's most protracted engagement with the San occurs in the opening section of the second volume where, after having made his way as far north as the missionary station at Klaarwater (Griquatown), his journey stalls because he cannot find local people to join his depleted party. His solution, after first considering a return to Cape Town, is to double back to Graaf Reinet, the nearest colonial town, and attempt to recruit there. This journey is fraught with danger, however, since it requires navigating unknown territory: he must traverse an area known by the colonists as 'Bushmanland', notorious for its hostile inhabitants and never before crossed by a white man. So dangerous is this undertaking perceived to be that the missionaries at Klaarwater, who do everything they can to deter Burchell, request that he sign a declaration indicating that he voluntarily undertook the journey, lest they be accused of colluding in his death. Because of the nature of the terrain he must pass through, Burchell and his party have to travel light, without a wagon; his men ride oxen and Burchell a horse. 'Put[ting] aside the influence of habit and custom, and of those necessities which belong only to civilized society,' he writes, 'I discovered that we might dispense with nearly everything.'[52] This is a journey within a journey, in which everything is stripped down to essentials; even cooking utensils are left behind.

Although he exercises due caution, Burchell's fears are dispelled when he and his party of Khoi establish cordial relations with the local San. This enables Burchell to spend time in situ, observing their habits and interacting with them socially. When danger does come, it comes when his party enters the colony and encounters white people. It later emerges that a rumour had spread throughout the district that a large group of Khoi 'under the command of a white-man, were marching to attack the colony', and that the townspeople had armed themselves and set up watch in expectation of this.[53] Even though these rumours, which Burchell dismisses as 'ignorance and fear combined', are soon dispelled, the notion that wandering through

Bushmanland with minimal protection was suicidal is not so easily banished.[54] His attempt to recruit Khoi to accompany him on his return journey
is met with numerous difficulties, not least of which is the belief among the
townspeople that these recruits will never return alive; for this reason the
members of Burchell's party are referred to as 'the Englishman's *dood volk*
(dead men)'.[55] Burchell's expedition is regarded as aberrant, a flouting of
racial norms that can only end in disaster. The intimation is clear: Burchell
has 'gone native'. And indeed Burchell himself implicitly acknowledges as
much. When he crosses over into the colony and comes into contact with
white people for the first time, he experiences an odd moment of revulsion:

> two men of the family, and several women and children, came and stood round
> me. Their complexion struck me as unpleasantly fair and colorless, their fea-
> tures as disagreeably sharp, and the expression of their countenances as wild
> and senseless ... The women were insipidly fair, and rendered therefore the
> more remarkable by the contrast of strong black eyebrows. To this, both in
> them and the men, was added a very illshaped and protruding nose.[56]

The white face has become the alien face. Burchell, accustomed to the facial
tonalities of Indigenous people, sees the white face as the mark of disjunction
and ugly angularity; whiteness is an 'insipid' evacuation of color. The moment
might be brief – Burchell immediately seeks to qualify if not to cancel it – but
it speaks to the extent to which his immersion in 'uncivilized' societies has
changed him, even altering, at times, his modality of perception.

If this were an isolated event, it might not merit much attention; but there
is a pattern at work in the *Travels*. Consider the following, where he describes
his feelings of reinvigoration when rain relieves a long drought:

> I know not how to account for the great change it produced, not only in my
> bodily feelings, but even in those of my mind ... I fancied that I possessed the
> strength to walk the whole length of Africa. Impatient of inactivity, I longed to
> roam over boundless plains or climb the lofty mountain; all my troubles and
> difficulties retired to the furthest distance, where I viewed them as diminished
> almost to nothing. Rapt in this musing, delightful mood methought a benefi-
> cent deity ... advanced toward me, and whispered softly in my ear, that sweet
> word LIBERTY: which repeating, till it thrilled in every nerve, the celestial
> being seemed to say: *Follow me*. And where indeed could I have obeyed the
> enticing summons, so easily and uncontrolled, as in the wild regions before
> me? By subsequent experience I have learnt that the delightful sensation of
> unshackled experience could never be recalled, after I had re-entered the colo-
> nial boundary. Here the ideas of restraint began to usurp its place; and at Cape
> Town it became completely annihilated. But if society smothered and extin-
> guished it, I became, on the other hand, like one of society, adopting its mode
> of thinking, and enjoying its refinements, and its reasonable pleasures, as a
> compensation for those which I had lost.[57]

In this strange passage Burchell records his imagined mutation into an unrestricted expansion of being as he roams the 'wild regions' beyond the boundaries of convention and polity. He considers this 'delightful sensation of unshackled liberty' to be one in which he is set free of the coordinates of the self required by 'society' – or, to put it another way, he becomes what he himself designates as a 'savage'. For at work in these imaginings is a more concrete reference; in the *Travels* it is the San who occupy the position of liberty in a polarity with civilisation.

In an earlier passage describing a San guide, Burchell writes admiringly of his 'beautiful *symmetrical form*', with a 'gait the most easy and free that I had ever beheld'. He then adds: 'All the limbs, *unshackled* by clothing, moved with a grace never perhaps seen in Europe' (italics mine).[58] This characterisation of the guide as embodying both aesthetic form and uninhibited ease of movement would seem to be the inspiration behind the imagined self ranging freely through the wilderness. In the same passage Burchell also goes on to make a distinction between 'liberty and 'society': 'I envied the Bushmen the uncontrouled [sic] freedom of their lives ... Unfortunate that civilization, and this form of *liberty* cannot, hand in hand, journey through the nations of the world.'[59] In declaring himself, or part of himself, an elective San, Burchell seems aware that he is making a startling claim, in which sympathy is superseded by identification. In the very next paragraph he hastens to assure the reader that he means what he says: 'The picture here given of the remarkable effects of the atmosphere on my feelings,' he writes, 'is neither overdrawn nor over-coloured; and though not easily accounted for, is not, therefore, the less exact and faithful.'[60] But is it not unlikely that a mere effect of the weather should continue to be felt for an extended period before fading as he re-enters the colony and then undergoing 'complete annihilation' when he arrives in Cape Town some three years later? Surely Burchell is being disingenuous here, even rather slyly so?

Burchell was aware that his *Travels* contained 'contradictory ... sentiments' and he ascribed this to the fact that he 'faithfully displayed' the vicissitudes of his journey, in which 'change of circumstance' led to a change of heart or a modification of opinion. He therefore advises the reader that certain sentiments are circumstantial, and belong 'to that date only'; 'more correct ideas', he maintains, can only be formed by the reader considering these expressions of sentiment in their varied contexts, and 'form[ing] his judgements upon natural and unpicked evidence'.[61] Yet even if we take into account the episodic nature of Burchell's travels, and acknowledge the candour ('unpicked') with which his changing sentiments are recorded, this does not result in a balanced aggregation. To the contrary: in Burchell's text the force field of sentiment is subject to considerable volatility. In this setting the 'man of feeling' turns out to be a stressed figure, overwhelmed by his emotions and absolutely unable to modulate them into anything approaching a stable core of responses. It is hard to imagine how it could have been otherwise. Burchell was acutely vulnerable for most of his travels and was obliged to negotiate his passage through the interior rather than enforce it from a position of strength. He often perceived himself to be manipulated by the people he encountered, who were well aware of the relative weakness of his authority and used this to their own advantage. This exasperated Burchell, who complained of 'that deceit, and disregard for truth ... pervading more or less every African tribe', though it is likely that Indigenous people would have understood their own behaviour as a kind of strategic reparation.[62] Nor was he entirely at home with his own party, who at times would ignore his injunctions or refuse his requests. It is little wonder that a degree of misanthropy creeps into his writing. Observing his dogs sleeping around the fire one night, Burchell comments: 'When wandering over pathless deserts, oppressed with vexation and distress ... I have turned to these, as my only friends, and felt how much inferior to them was man when actuated only by selfish views.'[63] Burchell functions as a limit case for the exercise of metropolitan sentiment, with its unstated dependence on hierarchies of race and class. When the European traveller is reliant on the goodwill of those he encounters and does not have the capacity to command obeisance, then the conditions of possibility for sympathetic exchange either disappear or diminish significantly. Burchell's fraught relations with Indigenous people remind us, however, that it was possible to enter zones of contact that were more open and transactional despite their incoherence and their transitory quality.

Notes

1 William J. Burchell, *Travels in the Interior of Southern Africa,* 2 vols (1822–24; London: The Batchworth Press, 1953), vol. 1, p. 40.
2 The terms 'Hottentot' and 'Bushman' are no longer considered acceptable nomenclature. Except where I am quoting directly from Burchell, I use the term 'San' in the place of 'Bushman' and 'Khoi' in place of 'Hottentot'. My understanding is that these are currently considered appropriate designations.
3 Quoted in Edward B. Poulton, *William John Burchell* (London: Spottiswood & Co. Ltd, 1907), p. 45.
4 Burchell, *Travels,* vol. 1, p. 358.
5 Burchell, *Travels,* vol. 1, p. 40.
6 Burchell, *Travels,* vol. 1, p. 111.
7 Burchell, *Travels,* vol. 1, p. 40.
8 Burchell, *Travels,* vol. 1, p. 11.
9 Burchell, *Travels,* vol. 1, p. 5.
10 Burchell, *Travels,* vol. 1, p. 5.
11 Burchell, *Travels,* vol. 1, p. 164.

12 Susan Locher Buchanan, *Burchell's Travels: The Life, Art and Journeys of William John Burchell* (Cape Town: Penguin Books, 2015), p. 9.
13 Mary Louise Pratt, *Imperial Eyes: Travel Writing and Transculturation* (London: Routledge, 1992), p. 15.
14 Pratt, *Imperial Eyes*, pp. 29, 31.
15 Pratt, *Imperial Eyes*, p. 31.
16 Richard Holmes, *The Age of Wonder: How the Romantic Generation Discovered the Beauty and Terror of Science* (London: Harper Press, 2009), p. xvi.
17 Holmes, *Age of Wonder*, p. xvi.
18 Pierre Hadot, *The Veil of Isis: An Essay on the History of the Idea of Nature* (Cambridge, MA: The Belknap Press, 2006), p. 95.
19 Hadot, *Veil of Isis*, p. 156.
20 Hadot, *Veil of Isis*, p. ix.
21 Quoted in Laura Dassow Walls, *The Passage to Cosmos: Alexander Humboldt and the Shaping of America* (Chicago: Chicago University Press, 2009), p. 32.
22 Alexander von Humboldt, *Views of Nature: or Contemplation of the Sublime Phenomena of Creation* (London: Henry G. Bohn, 1810), p. 154.
23 Richard H. Grove, *Green Imperialism: Colonial Expansion in Tropical Island Edens and the Origins of Environmentalism* (Cambridge: Cambridge University Press, 1995), p. 350.
24 Burchell, *Travels*, vol. 1, p. 5.
25 Burchell, *Travels*, vol. 1, p. 3.
26 Burchell, *Travels*, vol. 1, p. 156.
27 J. M. Coetzee, *White Writing: On the Culture of Letters in South Africa* (Sandton: Radix, 1988), pp. 38–41.
28 Burchell, *Travels*, vol. 2, p. 194.
29 Burchell, *Travels*, vol. 1, p. 203.
30 Burchell, *Travels*, vol. 1, p. 161.
31 Burchell, *Travels*, vol. 1, p. 162.
32 Hadot, *Veil of Isis*, p. 95.
33 Burchell, *Travels*, vol. 1, pp. 348, 349.
34 Burchell, *Travels*, vol. 2, p. 233.
35 Burchell, *Travels*, vol. 1, p. 315.
36 Burchell, *Travels*, vol. 1, p. 101.
37 Burchell, *Travels*, vol. 1, p. 164.
38 Burchell, *Travels*, vol. 1, p. 205.
39 Burchell, *Travels*, vol. 1, p. 206.
40 Burchell, *Travels*, vol. 2, p. 314.
41 Burchell, *Travels*, vol. 2, pp. 47–8.
42 Burchell, *Travels*, vol. 1, p. 316.
43 Burchell, *Travels*, vol. 1, p. 316.
44 Burchell, *Travels*, vol. 1, p. 316.
45 Burchell, *Travels*, vol. 1, p. 316.
46 Burchell, *Travels*, vol. 1, p. 319.
47 Burchell, *Travels*, vol. 2, p. 248.
48 Burchell, *Travels*, vol. 2, p. 29.

49 Lynn Festa, *Sentimental Figures of Empire in Eighteenth-Century Britain and France* (Baltimore: Johns Hopkins University Press, 2006), pp. 2, 3.

50 Festa, *Sentimental Figures*, p. 56.

51 Burchell, *Travels,* vol. 2, p. 40.

52 Burchell, *Travels,* vol. 2, p. 11.

53 Burchell, *Travels,* vol. 2, p. 97.

54 Burchell, *Travels,* vol. 2, p. 102.

55 Burchell, *Travels,* vol. 2, p. 113.

56 Burchell, *Travels,* vol. 2, p. 75.

57 Burchell, *Travels,* vol. 1, p. 356.

58 Burchell, *Travels,* vol. 1, p. 293.

59 Burchell, *Travels,* vol. 1, p. 293.

60 Burchell, *Travels,* vol. 1, p. 293.

61 Burchell, *Travels,* vol. 2, p. 217.

62 Burchell, *Travels,* vol. 2, p. 217.

63 Burchell, *Travels,* vol. 1, p. 174.

12

Short stories of the southern seas: the island as collective in the works of Louis Becke

Jennifer Fuller

There is a certain monotony, perhaps, about these stories. To some extent this is inevitable. The interest and passions of South Sea Island life are neither numerous nor complex, and action is apt to be rapid and direct. A novelist of that modern school that fills its volumes … by refining upon the shadowy refinements of civilised thought and feeling, would find it hard to ply his trade in the South Seas Island society. His models would always be cutting short in five minutes the hesitations and subtleties that ought to have lasted them through a quarter of a life-time.[1]

The Earl of Pembroke's introduction to Louis Becke's collection of short stories *By Reef and Palm* (1894) raises important questions about the nature of colonial Pacific fiction and the role of romance in the age of realism. By the late nineteenth century, the novel had established itself as literature's primary popular medium and took for its focus the lives of average, often metropolitan, British citizens. Yet such novels proved inadequate to express the concerns of a growing Empire, which seemed to need genres to evolve overnight to address an ever-changing set of circumstances and explain them to readers back home. Many colonial writers took to the short story as a medium for expression, a journalistic form that allowed them to create sketches of life rather than epochs of experience. Like the literature of islands, the short story has often struggled for a place in the literary canon that rivals or even approximates that of poetry or the novel. Considered too brief for publication outside of a medium like magazines, short stories are almost always presented and reprinted in anthologies or collections. Like their literary counterparts, many Pacific islands are considered too small to be of global interest by themselves – we tend to speak of the Marshall Islands, not of Majuro or Ebeye. And like the short story, these islands seem to only garner attention when grouped or clustered together, an anthologising of geography. By examining the short story in the context of island collectivities, we may be able to glean insights into the connections between literary and geographic networks, as well as between the island politic and the larger geo-political concerns of empire.

Australian-born author Louis Becke seems particularly amenable to a discussion of the connections between (colonial) text and (Pacific) context. Becke once enjoyed a popular reputation among nineteenth-century authors and readers, with works appearing in numerous colonial and metropolitan magazines such as the *Pall Mall Gazette, English Illustrated, Sketch, Illustrated London News,* and *New Review.* Not only did Becke have the sup-port of the 13th Earl of Pembroke (of the same family that was once Shakespeare's patron), but he also counted among his contacts Rudyard Kipling, Sir Arthur Conan Doyle, and Mark Twain. Yet despite his position among the literary elite of his day, Becke's work remains largely out of print. Today, Becke's stories are rarely read or taught in classrooms, appearing only in a few anthologies (usually of 'South Seas Stories'). So why do his contemporaries in the field of short fiction – Joseph Conrad, Rudyard Kipling, and Robert Louis Stevenson – remain a vital part of the English literary canon while Becke has quietly slipped into obscurity?

Part of the answer lies in Becke's medium and his inclination towards what we now might classify as extremely short stories or sketches. As Anne Bradshaw has calculated, 'Becke's short stories are very short – the 14 in *By Reef and Palm* range in length from about 900 words to a maximum of 2,000 words. Conrad's short stories, by contrast, range from a minimum of 5,700 words ("The Lagoon") to 47,000 words ("The End of the Tether").'[2] As modernism gained favour, in many ways transitioning the short story from its nineteenth-century relationship with the oral tale in favour of psychological insight and mood (the 'shadowy refinements' mentioned by Pembroke in his introduction), Becke's narratives began to be labelled as 'magazine-ish' in their focus on romance over realism.[3]

Short fiction had long struggled to find its footing with British readers. The demand for short fiction was largely produced by American periodicals while British magazines continued to focus on the serialised novel.[4] It was not until the very end of the nineteenth century that the short story really began to compete with poetry and the novel for a place in the hearts of British readers. The popularity of the Victorian short story 'was made possible by a powerful concatenation of circumstances ... a broadening of the educational base, mechanization of printing, and the development of mass-circulation periodicals specializing in fiction'.[5] Arising out of the new interest in newspapers and periodicals, the short story filled a niche genre in providing brief fiction for readers inundated by the rapid pace of the modern world. For British readers especially, the short story lent itself particularly well to depictions of the growing Empire. As the borders of the nation grew to include an even wider array of countries and peoples, '[t]he "native" or exotic found its way into English literature as a new arena for fantasy, replacing the romantic medieval *topos* of Morris and Rossetti'.[6] Much of Becke's success came from his ability to capitalise on this growing art form in British, American, and Australian newspapers. Establishing himself as the British authority on the South Seas, Becke initially found a career as a writer for colonial periodicals, 'publishing stories, sketches, and reviews' in the Sydney *Bulletin* and elsewhere, as well as writing '"London Notes" for the *Sydney Evening News*'.[7] Using 'not only his own name, but such pseudonyms as "Ula Tula", "Te Matua", "Papalangi", and "A South Sea Trader"', he self-consciously emphasised his dual role as both 'insider' or spokesperson for the islanders and foreigner living in the islands.[8] As with Kipling, it was Becke's ability to bring the exotic to the world of the domestic that endeared him to readers.

Despite his immense popularity with late-nineteenth-century readers, Becke remains almost invisible in literary criticism. Of the handful of articles that reference him, many focus on comparing Becke's works to those of fellow Pacific writer Joseph Conrad, a comparison which largely works to flatter his better-known counterpart by providing an early template for Conrad to improve and perfect in his fiction.[9] The effect of such critical and canonical moves is neatly outlined by Eric Hayot in his work on the Eurocentric self-enclosure of literary canons. When we focus on 'the vital importance of such notions as originality, novelty, progress – being first, in short – then we are essentially doomed to tell a progressive history of aesthetic innovation in which the contributions of the non-West remain supplemental, or constitute thematic appendixes to form'.[10] While Hayot is primarily referring here to non-western authors, the idea that island narratives are supplementary to the western literary canon is part of a long cultural and material history reflecting the invisibility of islands and their inhabitants. Bringing Becke out of his subsidiary role to Conrad and back into focus requires both a rethinking of our larger critical frameworks and a repositioning of Becke – one which focuses not on the strengths of his individual tales but rather on his collections of stories, and which opens up new ways of looking at colonial literature of the islands.

The subject of the stories in *By Reef and Palm* is largely interracial relationships: 'Of the fourteen stories in the volume all but one have a white man and a native wife or lover either centrally or peripherally in the situation.'[11] While these 'loves' help to drive the narratives and position the collection within a social and cultural space that Anne Stoler has referred to as 'the intimate frontiers of Empire', the other key theme that underlies each of the stories is the necessity of trade and the brutal consequences of colonial systems of exchange.[12] On the one hand, as Sumangala Bhattacharya notes, the stories act as colonial fantasies of exotic paradises where men can live lives removed from the responsibilities of the metropolitan centre:

> The domestic ideal associated with white women was regarded by many men in the 1890s as trammeling the free-spirited masculinity of the nomadic Australian bush-worker, a male figure commonly mythologized as the epitome of Australian nationalism. In contrast, domestic and sexual relations with island women were free of such cultural baggage and could be imagined as unstable and fluid.[13]

On the other hand, despite the cultural fantasy that these relationships were beyond colonial influence, Becke's repeated emphasis on trade, both of goods and of people (specifically women), continually undermines this narrative idealism of 'free love'.

While Becke's stories do not develop the psychological depth of Conrad's, focusing more on events than interiority, these events nonetheless show his deep understanding of the world of the colonial Pacific. Even Becke's critics seemed impressed by the realism provided by his personal experience. As Chris Tiffin notes, '[r]eviewers generally agreed that while Stevenson's portrayals of the South Seas were much richer in both atmosphere and characterisation and therefore more artistic, Becke knew a lot more about actual life there'.[14] This emphasis on Becke's ability to portray 'actual life' is echoed in Pembroke's introduction: 'Every one who knows the South Seas, and, I believe, many who do not, will feel that they have the unmistakable stamp of truth.'[15] If what makes Becke's stories unique among his contemporaries is their sense of authenticity, it behoves us to interrogate what lent them this authority.

As Pembroke notes, Becke's stories have strong similarities, which he calls 'monotony'. Yet it is precisely this retelling of tales that gives Becke's work a unique place among his contemporaries. While other British South Seas writers, notably Conrad and Stevenson, focus primarily on longer stories that centre on a white trader's experience on a single island (usually in Polynesia), Becke's stories roam across islands, repeating a similar tale of love and trade in a myriad of variations. Thus, Becke's collection is uniquely positioned as a colonial experiment in archipelagic writing, with his collection functioning as a 'text that deliberately effects a rewriting of island cartographies ... by remapping insular and archipelagraphic cartographies, highlighting them as symbols of multiplicity, proliferating spaces that each reader interprets according to their desires'.[16] If, as Elaine Stratford has argued, the goal of archipelagic readings is 'to radically recentre positive, mobile, nomadic geopolitical and cultural orderings between and among island(er)s' then literary criticism must move away from presenting a single text as representative of colonial Pacific experience, looking instead for what Jonathon Pugh has termed 'assemblages, networks, filaments, connective tissues, mobilities, and multiplicities'.[17]

As an attempt to provide one look into the complex imperial and Indigenous networks that constituted the 'South Seas', I offer a reading of each of the stories in *By Reef and Palm* in relation to their position in the collection. By reading these stories as a group or collective, we get a sense of the larger world of the South Pacific as viewed through a variety of colonial lenses, as a communal conversation rather than a singular perspective. Becke continues to shift the viewpoint from individual islands and islanders to a larger vision of the Pacific as a whole, presenting island literature not as a static tale of a single place but as a networked vision of a collective region – a region defined not by a single story, but by the movement between stories, a space where our interpretations of events and characters are defined by continual circulation, transformation, and exchange.

Of love and exchange: Becke's island relationships

By Reef and Palm begins with 'Challis the Doubter', a colonial fantasy of island marriage. Challis is an Australian who leaves the mainland, tired of his wife's condemnation of his need for her loyalty. The story skips ahead four years to find Challis reflecting on his former wife while making a new life for himself in the islands: 'She's all right as regards money. I'm glad I've done that. It's a big prop to a man's conscience to feel he hasn't done anything mean; and she likes money – most women do. Of course I'll go back – if she writes. If not – well, then, these sinful islands can claim me for their own; that is, Nalia can.'[18] Becke sets up Challis as an honorable romantic, a 'sentimental imperialist', supporting his first wife even though she is unfaithful.[19] Unlike the insincerity of this wife, who 'really liked Challis in her own small-souled way – principally because his money had given her the social pleasures denied her during her girlhood', Challis' island wife Nalia is beautiful, hard-working, and trustworthy (Becke notes that she has had prior lovers, but none since she has married Challis).[20] However, here, too, the base reality of exchange, debt, and obligation is merely softened rather than completely removed by affective ties. As Nalia tells Challis with uncompromising honesty, 'Am I a fool? Are there not Letia, and Miriami, and Elinĕ, the daughter of old Tiaki, ready to come to this house if I love any but thee? Therefore my love is like the suckers of the *fa'e* (octopus) in its strength.'[21] Upon reflection, Challis realises his good fortune in having an honest wife who sees his material wealth as spousal generosity rather than a necessary qualification, and the narrative ends with the idea that she will bear him a son, a perfect union of colonial desire and island gratitude.

This idealistic view of the coming together of the acculturated 'sentimental agent of imperialism' and the faithful island woman jars with the second story in the collection, "'Tis in the Blood', in which a 'fat German' has paid to have a half-white, half-Samoan girl trained by Sisters to be his educated wife.[22] Becke's narrator emphasises both the gendered embodiment of exchange (in this case, literally an exchange of the female body for money) and the transactional nature of the relationship, noting that 'he's spent over two thousand dollars on her already'.[23] Another of the white traders doubts that this education will have been cost effective: 'Bet a dollar she's been round Vagadace way, where there are some fast Samoan women living. 'Tis in the blood, I tell you.'[24] The doubts of the German trader's friends prove to be justified. Vaega, the young woman, is seduced by the smooth words of 'a stalwart half-caste of Manhiki', Allan the boatswain.[25] Unlike the obedient Nalia, Vaega shows little desire to play by the rules of her sponsored education, escaping with Allan to a ship where she 'sang rowdy songs, and laughed all day, and made fun of the holy Sisters'.[26]

While the idea of 'free love' was an appealing part of the masculine fantasy of island women, Becke is clear that these actions are not without consequences. After just six months, Allan abandons Vaega, who then 'drifted back to Apia, and there, right under the shadow of the Mission Church, she flaunted her beauty', a euphemism for prostitution.[27] Trained from birth to see herself as a commodity, Vaega embraces her role in the island trade, determined to make the most of her situation and ending the story by stating matter-of-factly, 'there's an American man-of-war coming next week, and these other girls will see then. I'll make the *papalagi* officers shell out.'[28] Becke repositions the western fantasy of island women's sexual proclivity as one of economic survival, with island prostitution represented as just another bargain among others. While Becke's title implies that Vaega's disloyalty is 'in the blood', reflecting European stereotypes of the hypersexual island 'Venus', the story's position next to 'Challis' raises questions as to whether 'good' island women are born or made.[29] By placing the two stories in conversation, Becke asks readers to consider whether the islanders' love and loyalty depend on individual temperament or on the realities of island trade, thereby denaturalising the European association of island women with promiscuity.

'The Revenge of Macy O'Shea' pushes the complications of free love even further. Unlike Challis and the German, who work as traders in the islands, Macy O'Shea is a 'sometime member of the chain-gang of Port Arthur, and subsequently runaway convict, beachcomber, cutter-off of whaleships, and Gentleman of Leisure in Eastern Polynesia'.[30] While Becke often made charming anti-heroes of the social outcasts that populated the small islands, in this story O'Shea presents the worst face of the white colonial enterprise.

The friction in the story is caused when O'Shea announces he will be marrying the 'half-caste' daughter of a trader named Malia, a choice which his current wife, Sera, vehemently protests, more on the basis of her dignity and 'white blood' than from sexual jealousy: 'I would sell myself over and over again to the worst whaler's crew that ever sailed the Pacific if it would bring me freedom from this cruel, cold-blooded devil!'[31] However, Sera also knows her options within the island economy are limited to a commodified choice between value, labour, or circulation. Killing her husband means either condemning herself to a life of prostitution or living in servitude on the island: 'I am a stranger here, and if I ran a knife into his fat throat, these natives would make me work in the taro-fields, unless one wanted me for himself.'[32]

Malia is also a pawn in the game of trade defined and driven by the contours of masculine desire: 'The transaction was a perfectly legitimate one, and Malia did not allow any inconvenient feeling of modesty to interfere with such a lucrative arrangement as this whereby her father became possessed of a tun of oil and a bag of Chilian [sic] dollars, and she of much finery.'[33] Readers barely have time to process Malia's arrival before she is murdered by the vengeful Sera, metonymically becoming the oil and dollars that 'gasped out its life upon the matted floor'.[34] Becke ends the story with O'Shea beating Sera to death with the 'serrated tail of the *fai* – the giant stinging-ray of Oceana [sic]', hinting at the repercussions of flouting island law by killing one of its own.[35] Unlike 'Challis' and ''Tis in the Blood', which revolve around the emotional consequences of Pacific relationships, 'The Revenge of Macy O'Shea' reveals the violence inherent in their transactional nature. The 'free-spirited' white man that Bhattacharya identifies as the heart of colonial mythology is revealed to be a cruel and murderous tyrant, unrestrained by law or moral propriety, displacing his lust and sexuality on to the women around him in way that renders the 'excessive' emotions of those women as somehow responsible for rousing the violence of masculine desire.

While these three stories set up an overlapping yet multifaceted way of looking at 'free' love, Becke makes a seemingly sudden departure with 'The Rangers of the Tia Kau', which is the only story in the collection not to feature a romance. Instead, the story centres on a tribal chief, Atupa, who, worried that his deified ancestors are angry at the new 'foreign god', sends his people on a journey to rally nearby islands against visiting missionaries and their religion. On the way, the villagers are overtaken by a terrible storm and attacked by a frenzy of sharks who kill all but two of the voyagers. On first reading, the tale seems to have little connection to the stories that come before, yet it too is an examination of trade and love in the Pacific: instead of an earthly exchange, here Becke investigates a heavenly one. As a trader, Becke was familiar with the other influential group of island visitors: Christian missionaries. Starting with the London Missionary Society in 1796, the

British began a campaign of sending missionaries to the islands, deeply concerned about the narratives of cannibalism, promiscuity, and heathenism popularised by explorers like Captain Cook. While proselytising endeavours were viewed with great favour by their supporters in the colonial metropole, native islanders had varying responses to the spread of the Gospel, ranging from distrust, to accommodation, to Indigenous proselyting.[36]

The representation of the islanders in this story veers between depictions of Indigenous agency and Indigenous gullibility. The final paragraphs of the story are a discussion between one of the survivors and a trader, in which the survivor concludes: 'Had not Atupa been filled with vain fears, he had killed the man who caused him to lose so many of our people.'[37] Unsurprisingly, the trader reacts with shock at the native's desire to kill a missionary, but the survivor calmly relativises the effects of Christ's Gospel in the Pacific:

> Aye, that would I – in those days when I was *po uli uli*. But not now, for I am a Christian. Yet had Atupa killed and buried the stranger, we could have lied and said he died of a sickness ... And then had I now my son Tāgipo with me, he who went into the bellies of the sharks at Tia Kau.[38]

Becke carefully weighs the death of a missionary against the death of a family member in the islands: on the one hand, the converted islander seems to regret his bloody impulses, but on the other, he wishes he could return to his pre-converted state where murdering a follower of the Son of God would save the life of his own son. In this often overlooked tale in the collection, we see Becke question yet another transactional relationship, asking if the promise of a heavenly reward brought by the missionaries is worth the sacrifice – both in the loss of the islanders' children and their way of life.

In light of the islanders' ability to sacrifice family for devotion, 'Pallou's Taloi' also reads as an examination of the cost of love. While visiting a fellow island expat, the narrator meets a trader, Pallou, and his wife, Taloi, who immediately surprises the narrator as 'instead of squatting on a mat in native fashion, she sank into a wide chair, and lying back inquired, with a pleasant smile and in perfect English, whether I was feeling any better. She was very fair, even for a Paumotuan half-caste ... I said to Pallou, "Why, any one would take your wife to be an Englishwoman!".'[39] Taloi's approximation of the white women is a performative display of cross-cultural flexibility that only partly obscures her island blood. In this, as in other ways, Taloi is reminiscent of Vaega, having been sent to school in Sydney where she rebelled against the strict rules (and tore the dress off a student who called her skin 'tallowy') before being brought back to the islands to marry her guardian, a French trader.[40] On the way, Taloi falls for the ship's mate Pallou, who ends up murdering the Frenchman to save his lover from her unwanted fate. Unlike Nalia, who willingly plays a subservient role to Challis, Taloi insists on speaking her own mind when Pallou attempts to silence her: 'Shut up yourself, you brute! Can't I talk to any one I like, you turtle-headed fool? Am I not a good wife to you, you great, over-grown savage?'[41] Yet unlike Macy O'Shea, a brute, Pallou seems to appreciate Taloi's outspokenness: 'It was easy to see that this grim half-white loved, for all her bitter tongue, the bright creature who sat in the big chair.'[42] Charmed by their story, the narrator grants the two a trading station and a place to hide from the French gunships hunting them down. When Taloi dies a few months later, Pallou commits suicide, choosing love over an easy life of trade. Yet, considered in conversation with 'The Rangers of the Tia Kau', readers cannot help but wonder if this love is also a transaction – one of earthly reward bought through eventual suffering, an inversion of the missionaries' promises.

This interrogation of the dangers one undertakes for the love of family continues in 'A Basket of Bread-Fruit'. A white trader in Samoa is lonely and tells the locals that if someone will find him a wife 'unseared by the breath of scandal' he will take her to a nicer village.[43] An old woman offers her granddaughter to the trader in exchange for passage to a western island where she will rejoin her people: 'The girl shall go with thee. Thou canst marry her, if that be to thy mind, in the fashion of the *papalagi*, or take her *fa'a Samoa*. Thus I will keep faith with thee. If the girl be false, her neck is but little and thy fingers strong.'[44] The trader appreciates the good deal, realising he can get a wife without having to provide presents to her family for their approval in a relatively 'cost-free exchange'.[45] Here both parties approve a relationship as a form of equal exchange, quality goods for quality service. However, the trader gets more than he originally bargains for, taken in by the very system he had sought to exploit. When he meets the girl purchased with his gifts, he finds her weeping, not as we might expect for being sold to a stranger, but because her brother and cousin have been killed and beheaded. Looking for food to comfort her, he reaches into the grandmother's container of breadfruit only to discover it contains not fruit, but human heads (those of the girl's murdered kin). Playing on the trader's desire for an island wife, the grandmother has bought passage away from her enemies, saving her granddaughter from those who would kill her.

Once again, Becke complicates the simple love story of the Pacific: here the love is between a grandmother and her granddaughter, and it is only through trade that she can secure a possible safe future, away from their enemies. The narrative hints at the darker realities of coercive island trade, such as blackbirding. As David Northrup notes, the South Pacific entered 'the labour trade in the early 1860s' through the 'spread of plantation economies' that 'initially involved a large amount of kidnapping and coercive practices'.[46] In her study of the Australian-Pacific indentured labour trade,

Tracey Banivanua Mar argues that following the 'abolition of slavery, these laborers provided the essential cost-neutral, coercible, and colored labor that was deemed essential to the economic viability of white settlement in the tropical belt of Britain's Australian colonies'.[47] While 'A Basket of Bread-Fruit' is suggestive of the human trafficking that accompanied the Pacific labour trade – with the human heads replacing the commodity of the breadfruit – Becke nonetheless writes it as a story of survival against the odds.

Becke moves seamlessly from island loves to colonial loves in the story of two shipwreck victims, an unlikely setting for Becke's domestic title 'Enderby's Courtship'. Instead of the drawing rooms or dances we might expect from a typical nineteenth-century courtship tale, Becke presents us with two wretched specimens of humanity: 'The Thing that sat aft – for surely so grotesquely horrible a vison could not be a Man – pointed with hands like the talons of a bird of prey to the purple outline of the island in the west, and his black, blood-baked lips moved, opened and essayed to speak.'[48] The three victims include a ship's captain, his wife, and a passenger from Sydney, the titular Enderby. While this is the only story in the collection to contain entirely colonial characters, there is little difference between the status of white women in the islands and the islander women when it comes to trading themselves for a life of security. Mrs Langton marries the captain after her father states that 'Langton had made and was still making money in the island trade'.[49] This story, like so many of the other stories, points to the interrelation between exchange and exchangeability: the women in Becke's stories are versions of each other not so much because of their sexual loyalty or otherwise but because they are commodity objects within a more general island traffic of women, exchanged and positioned between men in various forms of sexual and economic subordination.

Enderby is charmed by the woman's beauty and angry at her husband's neglect. His rage comes to a head when they finally land on an island and Langton finds a nest of turtle eggs which he proceeds to devour rather than sharing with his weakened wife. In a fit of rage, Enderby smashes him in the head with a piece of coral. It is this brutal act that nonetheless shows Mrs Langton the difference between the two men. She convinces Enderby not to turn himself in for murder, as his act has delivered her from life with a selfish brute (a heroic rewriting of 'The Revenge of Macy O'Shea'). The two are married by a ship's captain and live a seemingly idyllic life on an island outpost. In this story, murder is no longer considered an unforgivable sin, but a means of redemption. The western notion of natural law is replaced with a more nuanced understanding of moral action – one in which one human life (and a wretched one at that) may be sacrificed to secure the happiness of others.

Apart from its violence, 'Enderby's Courtship' reads like any of a number of romantic stories, where a wife is saved from a terrible husband by a gentleman of her acquaintance. It is also in stark contrast to 'Long Charley's Good Little Wife', which presents one of the least romantic relationships in the collection. The story is simply a blunt description of a trader, Long Charley, bartering with an islander, Tibakwa (the Shark), for possession of his daughter. With characteristic honesty, Becke writes: 'In the South Seas, as in Australia and elsewhere, to get the girl of your heart is generally a mere matter of trade.'[50] In opposition to a western European philosophical tradition in which exchange and other forms of instrumentality are the modes of relation that love and friendship transcend, the calculative logic of Pacific cross-cultural relations is depicted as unable to accommodate any form of disinterested exchange:[51]

> Father willing to part, girl frightened – commenced to cry. The astute Charley brought out some new trade. Tirau's eye here displayed a faint interest. Charley threw her, with the air of a prince, a whole piece of turkey twill, 12 yards – value three dollars, cost about 2s. 3d. Tirau put out a little hand and drew it gingerly toward her. Tibakwa gave us an atrocious wink.[52]

Considered on its own, the story lacks any sense of moral direction. But appearing, as it does, within an archipelago of such stories, we inevitably compare it to other bargains, other loves. Is Charley's purchase any less of a travesty than 'Enderby's Courtship', where murder is the vehicle for the fulfillment of love? Is the security that Charley provides any more demeaning than Vaega selling herself to the highest bidder? Becke questions whether western sensitivities should be the ultimate determinant of moral action, especially given the fact that Europeans are frequently those engaged in making the bargains. He also problematises divisions between Indigenous economics of 'archaic' gift-exchange and 'capitalist commodity cultures' by showing the entanglement of Indigenous gift economies with endogenous systems of exchange.[53]

Reflecting this entanglement of Indigenous and European forms of exchange, 'The Methodical Mr. Burr of Majuro' asks what happens when one of these island trades goes wrong. Unlike other island men, Ned Burr seems uninterested in finding a wife, eventually choosing Le-jennabon, the daughter of the chief, whom he proceeds to woo with gifts despite warnings from the narrator about the frequency and ease of divorces among Marshall Islanders and his claim that 'your wife that died was a Manhikian – another kind. They don't breed that sort here in the Marshalls.'[54] Believing, as do all the men in the collection, that trading for a women's affections means having sole possession of the woman, Ned becomes suspicious of a young chief from a neighbouring island a few months after the marriage. As Bhattacharya argues, 'while island women's sexual freedom is an integral element of the colonial fantasy of the South Seas, Becke's male protagonists are often uncomfortable with the reality of women exercising sexual agency'.[55]

Appalled to discover that Le-jennabon has been receiving flower wreaths from the young man, Ned waits for 'his beauty' to meet the young man in the woods then shoots him with a rifle. His vengeance (and lesson) not complete, he saws off the man's head with a knife and has Le-jennabon carry it back to the village as a badge of shame. While the narrator seems unable to fully fathom Ned's savagery, Ned argues that it is this savagery that has won him the hearts of the people: 'It's just about the luckiest thing as could ha' happened. Ye see, it's given Le-jennabon a good idea of what may happen to her if she ain't mighty correct. An' it's riz me a lot in the esteem of the people generally as a man who hez business principles.'[56] As with Macy O'Shea, Ned's instance on getting what he paid for is seen as a virtue in the Pacific context, even while it appals the moral sensibilities of Becke's intended readers. This principle is also seen in the following story, 'A Truly Great Man', where a whaler turned trader shoots a native to protect his island trade and prove his reputation as a 'great man', earning him and his wife a position of respect in the village. Here violence, not peace, is the making of man.

Becke continues his interrogation of the alternative morality of the islands with 'The Doctor's Wife'. The subtitle of the story, 'Consanguinity – From a Polynesian Standpoint', addresses the main philosophical question of the collection: when two moral positions disagree, whose is correct? Drawing together the collection's ongoing interest in the universality versus the cultural specificity of moral law, the story concerns a doctor who offends the islanders when they learn he has married his cousin. He defends his choice by noting they are not siblings, but the islanders claim: 'It is the same; the same is the blood, the same is the bone. Even in our heathen days we pointed the finger at one who looked with the eye of love on the daughter of his father's brother or sister – for such did we let his blood out upon the sand.'[57] The doctor, as the narrator explains, has come to the islands to escape the restrictions of society and live a life of freedom. Yet his choice to marry his cousin brings shame upon him. It is only after his wife dies and he takes a native wife that the doctor is finally able to have healthy children. Here Becke implies that the islanders' morality makes more sense than colonial rules and that their superstition recognises the genetic consequences of incestuous relationships. Once again, Becke finds the social opprobrium of the island superior to western reliance on legal precedents.

The tension between romantic ideas of island loves and their commercial realities continues in the next story, 'The Fate of the *Alida*'. A white trader, Talpin, and his wife must sail on the *Alida*, whose supercargo is a disgusting womaniser (even by South Sea standards) who famously seduced the daughter of a friend only to abandon her in the streets of Honolulu (a tale that reads very much like ''Tis in the Blood' but without the woman's consent). Desperate to leave, Talpin takes passage on the *Alida* anyway, which 'turns turtle', according to rumour, lost in the islands. Five years later, the narrator finds Talipin's wife and daughter shipwrecked on a small island. The wife reveals that her husband was killed by the captain of the ship for defending her honour but that she was later able to avenge him. This horrible act marks her love for her husband as well as her tender care of their son, who is born on the islands. Yet even though the wife is willing to commit murder to protect the memory of her husband, she is still practical about her future. The story ends with her marrying the captain who rescues her from the islands. For the women of the islands, romance must be tempered by practicality (a lesson also seen in ''Tis in the Blood'). The anti-romance of 'The Fate of the *Alida*' seems both to confirm and destabilise the traditional notions of love codified in the imperial romance. While 'Enderby's Courtship' makes murder the prerequisite to a life of happiness, the murder of Talpin is only a prelude to a marriage of convenience.

'The Chilian Bluejacket' is the longest story in the collection and in many ways serves to aggregate the complications of the prior stories. Becke reflects on the impact white explorers and traders are having on the islands, setting the story on Easter Island, home of 'the survivors of a race doomed'.[58] The story concerns the white wife of a sea captain who disguises herself as a boy (a 'blue-jacket', or ordinary seaman) in order to discover the whereabouts of her husband, who has, unknown to her, taken a native wife on the island. Temeteri (the native woman) is also unaware of the 'other woman' and believes the captain will return for her, as he has formalised the marriage and fathered a son by her. Unconvinced, the native women urge Temeteri to marry a native man who offers her a golden coin. While many of the stories in the collection treat native marriage as a contractual relationship based on trade, here Becke has Temeteri refuse the deal, declining to become 'coinable'. Up to this point, stories involving men with two lovers have involved a faithful and an unfaithful woman. Yet here Becke presents a scenario where both wives, white and native, have a clear claim on the love of the captain. Both are courageous, both are faithful, and both bear him children. Unlike the previous stories in the collection, Becke does not indicate which woman is more wronged by the captain's behavior. Both women, white and native, suffer for his love to 'look upon strange lands'.[59] The end of the story reminds us again of the destruction of the people of Easter Island and connects these personal tragedies with the loss of entire peoples, suggesting that violent intimacies are small-scale echoes of the larger problem of cultural erasure in the Pacific.[60]

This two-woman problem (and its consequences), as well as the tension between island and colonial values, returns again for the final story of the collection. In 'Brantley of Vahitahi', the titular character makes a dreadful mistake, accidentally grounding a ship while sailing at night. In penance for his misdeed, he chooses to live out his life as a trader on the remote island. His only guiding light through the tragedy is the memory of his sister at home, Doris. While in the islands he 'married a young native girl – that is, taken her to wife in the Paumotuan fashion – and surely Doris, with her old-fashioned notions of right and wrong, would grieve bitterly if she knew it'.[61] Unlike Temeteri, who seems surprised by the captain's white wife, Luita quickly begins to suspect Brantley of loving a woman back home. Brantley is torn between the love of his sister (and the life he has left behind) and his new peace with Luita. Once again, the 'sentimental imperialist' is caught between two honourable obligations, and Becke is equally opaque about which woman has the greater claim.

The conflict comes to a head when Doris, suffering from consumption and near death, pays to find her brother, wishing to see him one last time. Unfortunately, she is taken to the house of Luita, who, upon assuming she is Brantley's lover, leaves the island with his child. Tragically, both women and the young child die and, unable to bear it, Brantley takes his own life. This ending is in direct contrast with the hopeful opening story. While 'Challis the Doubter' sets out the islands as a paradise where men can live free with native women, 'Brantley of Vahitahi' wonders if there can ever be peace between the world the European men have left and the new lives they make for themselves on the islands. Are these bold explorers finding new lives or are they harbingers of destruction for themselves and those they love? Seeing the collection as a whole foregrounds the continual tension throughout Becke's stories between ideas of new regenerative possibilities and late-nineteenth-century fears of cultural degeneration, with each story telling and retelling both the fantasy and its seemingly inevitable realities.

Navigating a new literary geography

In a world where 'free love' is more accurately viewed as a transaction, Becke's stories investigate the real costs of such loves. If we take 'Long Charley' as a litmus test for the commercial nature of island relationships, a baseline experiment to see if love can really be purchased, then the other stories work to show love as more than a financial transaction. These stories show lovers defending their relationships against moral judgement and sometimes killing their lovers for unfaithfulness. But all seem to argue that 'free' love, love without investment or attachment, is nothing more than a colonial fantasy. At the same time, Becke generally denies a sense of closure in individual tales, and he resists allowing a single interpretation or perspective to guide his collection: solutions to a problem that appear workable in one story can lead to disastrous outcomes in another, resulting in an 'unsettling experience' for the reader, who must make judgements either 'in the absence of a guide' or 'in the refusal of that guide to reassure us by taking any kind of lead'.[62]

As I have noted, the brevity of the tales allows Becke to paint a more comprehensive portrait of the islands as a whole and to draw implicit interconnections between them, rather than focusing on a single station or narrator. Yet it is also Becke's ability simultaneously to create and undermine paradisiacal discourse, showing the South Seas as a place of both innocence and rapacious colonial greed, that lends his tales the stamp of truth. As Victoria Warren neatly summarises, Becke 'appreciated how little it was possible for any of the players in that drama to grasp, more than partially, the significance of events which were irreversibly unfolding. In his writing, Becke innovated solutions to an enduring problem – how to narrate the advance of globalization.'[63]

Becke's complex, contradictory stories suggest that these islands, and their encroachment by various forms of western globalisation, cannot be narrated by a single colonial experience; they are too vast, too disparate, and too individual for any one story to claim itself as the definitive vision of the region. It is only by adjusting our expectations for narrative closure, by shifting between story and anthology, singular island and archipelago of experience, that we can begin to process Becke's work. The brevity of the tales, rather than being an aesthetic weak point, therefore allows us as critical readers a chance to aggregate a literary world, to view the tales in conversation both with each other and with the larger colonial perspective of the South Seas. Reading Becke's stories as a collection helps us get closer to Epeli Hau'ofa's idea of seeing the Pacific as a 'sea of islands', as 'a holistic perspective in which things are seen in the totality of their relationships'.[64] In literature, as in geography, we gain new insights when we refuse to see land masses as independent and unconnected, and rather observe the networks that can only be understood when placed in transoceanic contexts. Short stories, like islands, are interconnected, drawing richness from their variations, their points of comparison, and even their 'monotony', for it is in the repetition of the 'same' story that we begin to see the complexity of life and the impossibility of replicating the individual experience.

Notes

1 Louis Becke, *By Reef and Palm* (London: Unwin, 1894), p. 19.
2 Ann Lane Bradshaw, 'Joseph Conrad and Louis Becke', *English Studies*, 86:3 (2005), 212.
3 Bradshaw, 'Joseph Conrad and Louis Becke', 220.

4 Barbara Korte, *The Short Story in Britain: A Historical Sketch and Anthology* (Tübingen: A. Francke Verlag Tübingen und Basel, 2003), p. 20.

5 Harold Orel, *The Victorian Short Story: Development and Triumph of a Literary Genre* (Cambridge: Cambridge University Press, 1986), p. 184.

6 Clare Hanson, *Short Stories and Short Fictions 1880–1980* (London: Macmillan, 1985), p. 34.

7 Becke originally wrote stories for the Sydney *Bulletin*, fourteen of which were collected by the British publisher Unwin to be bound into *By Reef and Palm*. After signing with Unwin, Becke placed stories in British and American weekly magazines and/or literary journals (often simultaneously). Unwin distributed collections of previously published stories from the metropolitan magazines/papers to colonial markets (although some of the nonfiction does not follow this pattern), but Becke would also continue to write for multiple outlets, metropolitan and colonial.

8 A. Grove Day, 'By Reef and Tide: Louis Becke's Literary Reputation', *Australian Letters*, 6:1 (1963), 20.

9 See Bradshaw, 'Joseph Conrad and Louis Becke'; and J. H. Staple, 'Louis Becke's Gentleman Pirates and "Lord Jim"', *The Conradian*, 25:1 (2000), 72–82.

10 Eric Hayot, *On Literary Worlds* (Oxford: Oxford University Press, 2012), pp. 4, 6.

11 Chris Tiffin, 'Louis Becke, the *Bulletin* and *By Reef and Palm*', *Kunapipi*, 34:2 (2012), 163.

12 Ann Stoler, 'Tense and Tender Ties: The Politics of Comparison in North American History and (Post) Colonial Studies', *The Journal of American History*, 88:3 (2001), 263–84.

13 Sumangala Bhattacharya, '"The White Lady and the Brown Woman": Colonial Masculinity and Domesticity in Louis Becke's *By Reef and Palm* (1894)', in Richard D. Fulton and Peter H. Hoffenberg (eds), *Oceania and the Victorian Imagination: Where All Things Are Possible* (Burlington: Ashgate, 2013), p. 83.

14 Tiffin, 'Louis Becke, the *Bulletin* and *By Reef and Palm*', 163.

15 Becke, *By Reef and Palm*, p. 17.

16 Dani Redd, 'Towards an Archipelagraphic Literary Methodology: Reading the Archipelago in Julieta Campos' *The Fear of Losing Eurydice*', *Island Studies Journal*, 12:2 (2007), 315.

17 Elaine Stratford, 'The Idea of the Archipelago: Contemplating Island Relations', *Island Studies Journal*, 8.1 (2013), 4; Jonathan Pugh, 'Island Movements: Thinking with the Archipelago', *Island Studies Journal*, 8:1 (2013), 12. See also Elizabeth McMahon, 'Archipelagic Space and the Uncertain Future of National Literatures', *Journal of the Association for the Study of Australian Literature*, 13:2 (2013), https://pdfs.semanticscholar.org/fdfc/33c0c532d9a25ef0510dd1fd612f-13cba3b7.pdf (accessed 10 January 2020).

18 Becke, *By Reef and Palm*, pp. 24–5.

19 Vanessa Smith, *Intimate Strangers: Friendship, Exchange and Pacific Encounters* (Cambridge: Cambridge University Press, 2010), p. 160.

20 Becke, *By Reef and Palm*, p. 23.

21 Becke, *By Reef and Palm*, p. 31.

22 Lee Wallace, *Sexual Encounters, Pacific Texts, Modern Sexualities* (Ithaca: Cornell University Press, 2003), p. 11, cited in Smith, *Intimate Strangers*, p. 160.

23 Becke, *By Reef and Palm*, p. 37.

24 Becke, *By Reef and Palm*, p. 37.

25 Becke, *By Reef and Palm*, p. 35.

26 Becke, *By Reef and Palm*, p. 41.

27 Becke, *By Reef and Palm*, p. 42.

28 Becke, *By Reef and Palm*, p. 42. Becke's footnote defines 'papalagi' as 'foreign'.

29 On the idea of the island 'Venus', see Smith, *Intimate Strangers*, pp. 182–4.

30 Becke, *By Reef and Palm*, p. 44.

31 Becke, *By Reef and Palm*, p. 45.

32 Becke, *By Reef and Palm*, p. 46.

33 Becke, *By Reef and Palm*, p. 49.

34 Becke, *By Reef and Palm*, p. 50.

35 Becke, *By Reef and Palm*, p. 52.

36 See, e.g., Raeburn Lange, *Indigenous Ministers: Indigenous Leadership in Nineteenth-Century Pacific Islands* (Christchurch: Macmillan Brown Centre for Pacific Studies, University of Canterbury, 2005).

37 Becke, *By Reef and Palm*, p. 62.

38 Becke, *By Reef and Palm*, p. 62. Becke's footnote translates 'po uli uli' as 'Heathen, lit., "In the blackest night"'.

39 Becke, *By Reef and Palm*, pp. 66–7.

40 Becke, *By Reef and Palm*, p. 67.

41 Becke, *By Reef and Palm*, pp. 67–8.

42 Becke, *By Reef and Palm*, p. 68.

43 Becke, *By Reef and Palm*, p. 76.

44 Becke, *By Reef and Palm*, p. 79. Becke translates 'fa'a soma' as 'Samoan fashion', meaning to live with the girl without the European rites of marriage. I provide a reading of the violence in Becke's work and how it relates to codes of colonial civility in 'Terror in the South Seas: Violence, Relationships and the Works of Louis Becke', *Australasian Journal of Victorian Studies*, 20:2 (2015), 42–57.

45 Smith, *Intimate Strangers*, p. 241.

46 David Northrup, 'Migration from Asia, Africa and the South Pacific', in Andrew Porter (ed.), *The Oxford History of the British Empire Vol. 3: The Nineteenth Century* (Oxford: Oxford University Press, 2001), p. 94.

47 Tracey Banivanua Mar, *Violence and Colonial Dialogue: The Australian-Pacific Indentured Labor Trade* (Honolulu: University of Hawai'i Press, 2007), p. 1.

48 Becke, *By Reef and Palm*, p. 83.

49 Becke, *By Reef and Palm*, p. 89.

50 Becke, *By Reef and Palm*, p. 101.

51 Smith, *Intimate Strangers*, pp. 106–7.

52 Becke, *By Reef and Palm*, p. 103.

53 Smith, *Intimate Strangers*, p. 115.

54 Becke, *By Reef and Palm*, pp. 108–9.

55 Bhattacharya, 'The White Lady', p. 90.

56 Becke, *By Reef and Palm,* p. 115.

57 Becke, *By Reef and Palm,* p. 127.

58 Becke, *By Reef and Palm,* p. 163. Here Becke strongly prefigures the 'fatal impact' theory proposed by later historians.

59 Becke, *By Reef and Palm,* p. 187.

60 This emotion plays into many of our contemporary concerns about tourism to remote areas. Like Becke, we are drawn to their exoticism and difference but also fear our presence may cause irrevocable changes.

61 Becke, *By Reef and Palm,* p. 198.

62 Victoria Warren, 'Marlow's Older Brother: A Forgotten Australian, a Moral Morass, and the Last Free Islands of the South Pacific', *Margins,* 1 (2014), 18.

63 Warren, 'Marlow's Older Brother', 23.

64 Epeli Hau'ofa, *We Are the Ocean: Selected Works* (Honolulu: University of Hawai'i Press, 2008), p. 31.

Part III

Indigenous/Diasporic

13

'That's white fellow's talk you know, missis': wordlists, songs, and knowledge production on the colonial Australian frontier

Anna Johnston

Colonial linguistic studies are complex and intriguing textual sources that reveal much about everyday life and knowledge production under frontier conditions. Halfway through her Kamilaroi vocabulary, the Irish-Australian poet Eliza Hamilton Dunlop recorded the phrase: 'Yalla murrethoo gwalda[.] moorguia binna / Speak in your own language[.] I want to learn as I am stupid.'[1] Dunlop's self-positioning is clearly designed to put her Indigenous teachers at ease, setting the terms for her instruction. Yet as the phrase suggests, for Europeans in the Australian colonies, learning Indigenous languages could be an unsettling experience. Curious settlers placed themselves in awkward, dependent relationships with Indigenous people, whose motivations to engage with and teach settlers were various, but whose patience and precision were noted by those attempting to learn. So too their frustration and amusement: the missionary Lancelot Threlkeld described how Indigenous men such as his long-term collaborator Biraban 'shew the greatest readiness in pronouncing again and again not without laughing at my stupidity in not understanding quickly' when he attempted to learn the Awabakal language from Newcastle.[2] As David A. Roberts notes, this was 'a humbling experience, laden with rich, self-effacing moments that unsettled his cultural assumptions. ... At a time when much opinion was being aired about the supposed innate deficiency of the Aboriginal intellect, Threlkeld was moved to remark that his Aboriginal tutors thought him somewhat dim-witted in not being able to easily attain their native language'.[3]

This chapter uses the archival traces left by two colonial women to explore the relationship between language study and knowledge production, paying particular attention to linguistic texts that reveal traces of cross-cultural relationships and the Indigenous intermediaries who engaged in knowledge-making practices across the contact zone. In 1838, Eliza Hamilton Dunlop arrived from Ireland with her family: she was already a published poet with an acute ear for language and broad reading, having spent a privileged child-hood reading philosophical, historical, and classical texts in her father's library. Her interest in and use of Irish in her poetry prepared her for interest in Indigenous languages and forms of knowledge, and she had an acute polit-ical sense that was outraged by violence against Indigenous people. Her long residence at Wollombi, New South Wales enabled her to learn languages and to use Indigenous knowledge for poetic inspiration. Harriott Barlow's poli-tics were less clearly expressed than Dunlop's; however, her residence on the Queensland frontier exposed her to a variety of Indigenous people and their cultures. Between 1868 and 1874, she brought up her four children at her husband's sheep and cattle station, which failed to thrive in the harsh envi-ronment. Barlow was an intelligent, educated woman: when the family's finances declined and the bank foreclosed on the station, she established a highly regarded private girls' school in the nearby city of Toowoomba, which she ran for nearly twenty-five years. During her time on Warkon station, however, she worked with local people to make one of the first language studies of the region, and she sent it to London, where it was published in the leading anthropological journal. Gender made a difference to the kinds of language collected and the Indigenous knowledge to which settlers could become privy: women's collections were comparatively marginal at the time, and they were often missed among the large knowledge-aggregating projects of well-connected imperial collectors such as Sir George Grey and Sir Joseph Banks.[4] Gender also influenced the conditions of learning and exchange. These intimate forms of exchange on colonial frontiers reveal the imbrica-tion of language collection, knowledge production, Indigenous engagement, and settler advocacy, and determined in what forms these issues emerged from the colonial south to influence imperial print culture.

Linguistics and colonialism on the Australian frontier

Language studies, like other forms of knowledge collection and dissemina-tion, were inevitably bound up with the process of imperial expansion and colonial governmentality.[5] Colonised populations were marked, measured, and managed by their languages, even though many settler states sought to stamp out traditional languages and replace them with English, the lingua franca of commerce, education, labour, and the law across the British Empire. In Australia, James Cook's *Endeavour* journals provide the first hundred or so Indigenous words collected, in the Guugu Yimidhirr language of Cape York Peninsula. Early attempts to learn Australian Indigenous languages tended to be undertaken by individuals marked by a personal curiosity and, often, close relationships with particular Indigenous individuals or groups.

Yet because of the vast array and complexity of Indigenous Australian languages – estimated to be over 300 in the precolonial period – the task was difficult; the work was local and inchoate, and the effort made by some First Fleet officers to obtain the Sydney language beyond a purely functional exchange was soon abandoned, or else relegated to a personal interest pursued outside of official duties. On the colonial frontier, however, Indigenous people sought to communicate and sometimes to connect deeply with individual settlers, and some Europeans with a curiosity to learn recorded their findings.

The reciprocal relationship between the colonial officer and astronomer William Dawes and the Eora woman Patyegarang is perhaps the best known early example of linguistic knowledge production.[6] Arriving in 1788 with the First Fleet, Dawes was trained in scientific observation, and his employment at the Sydney Observatory joined together his independence of mind and interest in the natural world: a set of skills that made him open to a short but deep study of what the Indigenous linguist Jakelin Troy has defined as the 'Sydney language'. Although the late 1780s marked a 'brief "golden age" for language study', by the 1790s cultural contact between Indigenous and first settlers ensured that a nascent pidgin language was mostly used.[7] A range of Indigenous people are named in Dawes' account, including noted figures such as Bennelong. Dawes' language studies – two notebooks, containing around a thousand lexemes, approximately fifty sentences, and fourteen dialogues – are the fullest provided by any of the early colonial officials.[8] Troy notes that Dawes' informants were among the first Indigenous Australians to become familiar with the daily life of the English colonists, and that they were learning from Dawes reciprocally.

Patyegarang's engagements with Dawes are particularly notable for their interpersonal richness. As Ross Gibson suggests, accounts of Patyegarang's motivations for her connection with Dawes often bear the traces of authorial desires and speculations rather than definitive empirical evidence, but across the scholarship the young Eora woman is easily recognisable as an intelligent and energetic interlocutor, who provided Dawes not only with words and phrases but with close, physical, interpersonal opportunities to learn language and negotiate its meaning in context. Dawes' records reveal that Patyegarang was not averse to correcting his errors, and that pragmatic concerns such as access to food and resources were central to her purposes, as they were for other Indigenous people in Sydney.[9] Dawes' language learning was brief and intense: its scale was notable given his three short years of colonial residence.

Given the rapid changes and displacement (both linguistic and social) wrought by colonialism, few field studies of the Sydney language were produced until the late nineteenth century.[10] Gibson reads Dawes' language notebooks – only found in a London archive in 1972 – as prismatic and ever-expanding sources of insight into the momentous changes brought about by close and regular contact between English and Indigenous worlds in the early colonies. Like Troy, Smith, and Gibson, I argue that linguistic sources provide rich information that reveals much about intimate exchanges and attempts at communication under colonial conditions, even as aspects of the sources remain puzzling and resistant to elucidation, on both sides of the encounter. Dawes' studies reveal how his scientific training in observation affected his capacity to observe and learn from Patyegarang and other Eora people. Other colonists brought different motivations, but were no less reliant upon Indigenous knowledge and trusted guides. Indigenous motivations are harder to trace definitively, but we can make some conclusions drawing from textual evidence as well as from the gaps in the linguistic records.

For Lancelot Threlkeld at Lake Macquarie in the 1820s, language learning was central to his evangelical message and religious outreach to the Awabakal people.[11] Threlkeld had been trained by the London Missionary Society (LMS) at Gosford Academy, where the Rev. Samuel Greatheed collected information about Polynesian languages from returned LMS missionaries and other naval sources to train new recruits for the expanding Pacific mission field. Threlkeld was advantaged by his first posting in Rai'iatea, where he learned Polynesian languages and how to discern different dialects on neighbouring islands. Very early in his twenty-two years as a missionary in New South Wales, he met and developed a close relationship with Biraban, or Johny M'Gill: 'my black teacher', as Threlkeld first described him.[12] Threlkeld published his language studies assiduously between 1825 and 1859, sending them to colonial officials and others in a global imperial network of evangelists and language enthusiasts. From the 1830s, Threlkeld explicitly acknowledged his dependence upon Biraban, noting that '[a]n aboriginal of this part of the colony was my almost daily companion for many years, and to his intelligence I am principally indebted for much of my knowledge respecting the structure of the language'.[13] His publication *A Key to the Structure of the Aboriginal Language* (1850) bore a portrait of Biraban on the frontispiece as 'a tribute of respect to the departed worth of M'Gill, the intelligent aboriginal', and a brief account of his life.[14] This text was produced specifically for display at the Royal National Exhibition in London in 1851. Threlkeld's motivation for publication was political – to provide evidence to support his often controversial mission – and humanitarian: an 'anxiety to satisfy the friends of humanity, that our employment is not altogether without hope … and that success may ultimately be expected with the Divine aid'.[15] Threlkeld's studies were joined by other missionary linguistic studies, including those carried out by German missionaries at nearby Wellington Valley, but the relationship between Threlkeld and Biraban (like that of Dawes and Patyegarang) marked these foundational language studies as distinctive: indeed, as early examples of settler–Indigenous co-production of knowledge.[16]

Such examples of knowledge sharing and exchange between settler and Indigenous cultures have been identified individually and noted for their rich, interpersonal qualities. Yet the emergence of scholarship about Indigenous intermediaries requires a more comprehensive analysis that moves beyond the at times hagiographic accounts of unusually principled settlers and distinctive Indigenous celebrity figures.[17] Without losing the stories of intriguing individuals, situating linguistic encounters within a spectrum of interdependencies between visitors, settlers, and Indigenous guides of various kinds opens up the field for more complex mappings that allow extrapolation beyond individual cases. It also requires a subtle and complex reassessment – one that remains alert to the lure of settler apologetics – that sees frontier relations as marked both by violence and by intimacy, by dispossession and by curiosity. This demands an acknowledgement that the frontier, in Jan Critchett's memorable phrase, was sometimes as close as the body sharing your bed:

> The frontier was represented by the woman who lived near by and was shared by her Aboriginal partner with a European or Europeans. It was the group living down beside the creek or river. It was the 'boy' used as guide for exploring parties or for doing jobs now and then. The 'other side of the frontier' was just down the yard or as close as the bed shared with an Aboriginal woman.[18]

These messy, proximate intimacies between settlers and First Nations people did not make violence less likely: shockingly, as the latest work on colonial massacres reveals in repeated Australian cases, familiarity made victims more vulnerable to attack, because they were close by, less likely to flee or resist, and easy targets for settler vigilantes.[19] Yet intimacy also meant that communication, interdependence, and quotidian colonial life depended on workable relationships between settlers and Indigenous individuals, and that language learning was part of a complex array of mutually dependent and constitutive relationships.[20] This was particularly so for colonial women, often dependent upon Indigenous domestic labour to maintain households and family farms in remote locations. To this end, exploring linguistic studies carried out by two literate and educated women can provide an insight into this vector of colonial experience and its relationship to, and inclusion in, the wider print culture that underpinned Britain's second empire, as well as revealing European perceptions of Indigenous people both within and from outside settler colonial Australia.

Eliza Hamilton Dunlop and the linguistic frontier at Wollombi, 1839–80

In 1839, Eliza Hamilton Dunlop followed her police magistrate husband David Dunlop to his new posting at Wollombi, eight kilometres inland from the rough, thriving penal town of Newcastle, New South Wales. The small township was situated in a green, lush, and fertile valley, nestled below mountains and scattered with massive sandstone boulders and caves. It was Darkinyung country, rich with spiritual places, traditions, and stories, and a traditional meeting place between Darkinyung, Awabakal, and Wonnaruah people. The region was deeply influenced by the wave of change and often violent dispossession that swept up the northern frontier as pastoral holdings expanded, underpinned by convict labour.[21] The Upper Hunter valley police magistracy to which David Dunlop was appointed was amateur, self-interested, and resistant to the new Whig bureaucracy of Governor George Gipps, whose early initiatives added a new role of Aboriginal protection for police magistrates.[22] David Dunlop took his protection duties seriously, regularly petitioning the increasingly reluctant government for blankets to support Indigenous communities and encourage their participation in the colonial economy. He was well aware of their symbolic value, too, declaring to an 1845 inquiry that blankets functioned 'as a recognised tie between the ruler and the ruled'. They provided 'no sufficient recompense' for the loss of Aboriginal land, trees, and possums, but Aboriginal people 'accepted [them] from want'.[23]

Eliza Dunlop was equally concerned with Indigenous welfare, having published her striking poem 'The Aboriginal Mother' in response to the 1838 Myall Creek massacre of approximately thirty Wirrayaray and Kamilaroi women, children, and elderly men on the north-western frontier, which had been widely reported during divisive trials and judgements in the Dunlops' first year in the colony.[24] Dunlop's poem empathised with the Indigenous dead and the women and children survivors of the massacre, and it was published in the *Australian* newspaper only days before the perpetrators were publicly and controversially hanged: the most significant punishment of colonial violence against the Aboriginal population in the nineteenth century. The family's move to Wollombi provided the poet with personal connections to Indigenous communities, from whom she eagerly sought information about language, custom, and culture.

From the beginning of their Wollombi posting, Eliza and David Dunlop engaged with Indigenous people and interested local settlers to learn more about the different languages of the region. A table in Eliza Dunlop's papers records 'Different languages spoken in Seven of the Upper Districts', noting the information was gathered from an 1839 'Question and Answer between Mr Somerville, Mr Cox, and the Tribes'.[25] On the settler side, that meeting was witnessed by the Dunlops, most likely with Morris Townshend Somerville (a Hunter Valley landowner) and William Cox, junior (a pastoralist with stations very close to the site of the Myall Creek massacre). On the Indigenous side, it most likely included Boni (a senior man in the Wollombi clan of the Darkinyung people), other as yet unidentified members of the local Indigenous community (which likely included people displaced from Newcastle and the violent northwest frontier), and probably also visiting Aboriginal people, such as the noted songman Wulatji, who provided comparative information.[26]

The table maps four words against the different districts: water, fire, sun, and moon. The language names noted were improvisational, but they bear a phonetic relationship to the language groups that are now listed under the designated AIATSIS category Gamilaraay / Gamilaroi / Kamilaroi language (D23) (NSW SH55–12).[27] This archival source is a fair copy, made some time after the meeting, and it shows Dunlop's grasp of key aspects of Indigenous languages and places, such as noting how place names are formed from dialect names, how adoption practices worked on the death of a parent, and the importance of kinship terms, such as 'cousin or brother are often synonymous terms'. Two other brief comments link the local language-learning context to broader issues in settler society and global intellectual history: first, a note that a particular phrase means 'I am not telling a lie; it is true, should they use these words falsely a fight generally results'. This pertains to the intense public and legal debate throughout the 1830s and 40s about whether Indigenous witnesses should be allowed to give evidence in the colonial courts.[28] Second, the term 'Youroo' is noted as a term for God, though 'only known from white people'. Dunlop quotes Cicero – 'at inter homines gens nulla est tam fera quae not sciat Deum' – a well-known phrase used by moral philosophers and preachers of the period to argue for an innate, or natural, religion that cohered the human race, even if non-Christian nations were assumed to have not yet appreciated the proper (i.e. western) Christian mode of religion and civil society.[29] Dunlop's note questions this universalist assumption – asking, 'what shall we say of' Cicero's aphorism, in the light of Youroo being a recently acquired word – while other documents in her linguistic collection provide a detailed account of Indigenous 'Gods and Goddesses', describing named spiritual entities, their function, and their place within culture.

Dunlop's broad reading ensured that she contextualised her local, colonial experience within debates about religion, humanity, and race.[30] Ignorance of a deity was core to the exclusion of Indigenous people from full participation in court processes (even though they were subject to them, including death sentences); a presumed lack of Indigenous understanding of the consequences for perjury, along with a lack of translators, was used by many jurists to refuse Indigenous testimony. Settlers with knowledge of both language and culture argued strongly against this legal conundrum, especially Lancelot Threlkeld whom with Biraban translated many of the major cases of the 1830s. Such cases proliferated as violent conflict followed the pastoral frontier as it moved up the New South Wales central coast and interior.

Dunlop's acute awareness of the political aspects of knowledge about Indigenous languages was no doubt enhanced by her marriage to an officer of the courts. Other linguistic work related more to her own interpersonal and poetic engagements with Indigenous people in the region. One early, short study was titled 'Words of the Wollombi Tribe of Aboriginal Natives New South Wales'.[31] Lists of female and male names open the study, perhaps including those who spoke to her. Dunlop became aware of different kinds of knowledge that she could gain from different interlocutors, and that gender influenced both the knowledge made available to her and its transmission within the community. The predominance of recorded terms about food collection and distribution on an intimate, domestic level sketches out a process of linguistic collection that saw Dunlop undertaking local travels with Aboriginal women, collecting food, and naming the items and the means of subsistence.[32] These are the intimate spaces and experiences in which language learning took place: Dunlop moving among Aboriginal women and sharing their daily pursuits and domestic economies. She recorded variant terms showing her careful, phonetically acute response to the languages that surrounded her, aided by her poetic training, as well as the diverse language groups and the multilingual skills of her informants.[33]

Dunlop's longest vocabulary was 'Murree gwalda or Black's Language of Comileroi' (now Kamilaroi). Midway through this source, Dunlop noted the previously mentioned phrase that set the terms for her instruction: 'Yalla murrethoo gwalda[.] moorguia binna / Speak in your own language[.] I want to learn as I am stupid.'[34] Like most field vocabularies, the terms collected reveal the interpersonal conditions of language learning: parts of the body, which could only have been identified by the inquirer and the informer sitting very close, touching their own and each other's bodies. Relationships among families too could only be determined by personal knowledge of individuals and their interaction. Directive statements, questions, and phrases – 'Rub it', 'Bring them home', 'Did you eat enough?', 'Do you think it will rain?' – reveal how Indigenous people shared quotidian aspects of their lives with Dunlop to enhance communication. Importantly, the terms shared are not only traditional knowledge about the environment or practice, but also emerge from the contiguous colonial situation shared by the Dunlops and Kamilaroi-speaking people in Wollombi. Terms for Indigenous weapons, tools, and food preparation – including what materials were involved, how they were made, and what processes had to be undertaken – co-existed in Dunlop's wordlist alongside terms for European domestic and farm labour, from making the beds to milking.

Beyond the obvious quotidian advantages of having learned a variety of functioning Indigenous languages, Dunlop used her poetic and linguistic skills together to record Indigenous songs for posterity, to translate or 'versify' them for publication, and to provide inspiration for her own original poetry. Even before she had moved to Wollombi, in writing 'The Aboriginal Mother' Dunlop had used Indigenous words in her poetry to mark a sense of place and authenticity. In this, she participated in the widespread Romantic fascination with Indigenous and other exotic cultures.[35] Unusually, though, Dunlop's long residence in New South Wales meant that her knowledge deepened beyond what early correspondents in the vicious colonial press criticised as her 'cockney ... knowledge of the aboriginal natives ... acquired by reading the Last of the Mohicans'.[36] English poetry of the period was understood as being in a state of abeyance, if not decline, and 'slashing reviews' of a 'middle-class Cockney school' of liberal poets were common in British periodicals such as the *Quarterly Review* and *Blackwood's*.[37] Colonial writers, readers, and critics followed these debates closely and they influenced assessments of local writing, too. Yet when the sheet music of 'The Aboriginal Mother' was published in Sydney in 1842, the full lyrics were reproduced on the frontispiece, including a glossary of the Indigenous words and an extract from the legal case pertaining to the Myall Creek massacre. This set of authorising paratexts explicitly countered early press criticism, both gendered and racist, of Dunlop's poem.[38] Undaunted, Dunlop included Indigenous words, customs, and themes in several published poems in the 1840s, including 'The Eagle Chief' (1842), 'The Aboriginal Father' (1843), and 'Native Poetry: Nung-Ngnun' (1848). Dunlop's notes on her poems acknowledged her sources, including Boni, who both shared information with Dunlop about secret–sacred objects and provided advice about what information she could not access based on gender rules about cultural knowledge.[39] She had to abide by his polite but firm refusal to elucidate certain aspects that inspired 'The Eagle Chief'. 'Wallatu' was named by Dunlop as an Indigenous 'god of Poesy', a muse and source of inspiration for the 'Native Poetry'.[40] Within her lifetime Lancelot Threlkeld explained that Wallatu was likely a variation on the name Wulatji, a man in the Awabakal community who was revered as a songman and travelled the region to communicate his knowledge.[41] Wulatji was likely a living man transmitting traditional knowledge within colonial society, one who had inherited and was the custodian of a vital source of spiritual, intergenerational knowledge, as Jim Wafer suggests.[42]

Dunlop attempted a 'versification' of songs that Wulatji shared, despite her comments about the difficulties of translating Aboriginal songs. It is perhaps best considered an adaptation, and the first verse is:

> Our home, is the gibber-gunyah,
>   Where hill joins hill, on high;
> Where the Turruma, and berrambo,
>   Like twisted serpents lie!

And the rushing of wings, as the *Wangas* pass,
Sweeps the *Wallaby's* prints, from the glistening grass. (lines 1–6)[43]

The poetic themes are familiar from Dunlop's oeuvre – home places, local environments marked by hills and water, and gendered landscapes deep with history, mythology, and meaning – and distinguished by specific, rich linguistic terms. Here Indigenous words and ideas inflect Dunlop's colonial verse, so that the home is 'the gibber-gunyah', which she glosses for readers as a cave in a rock (distinctive features of Wollombi Valley). The sounds of Wanga (pigeon) fill the air; Makooroo / Makoro (fish) and Kanin (eel) glide in deep shady pools. This is a meaning-laden, self-sustaining human and animal landscape, inhabited by Indigenous people '[t]hat an *Amygest's* (whiteman's) track hath never been near'. On the one hand, we can read this poem as a settler fantasy: an appropriation of an autochthonous worldview akin to the prelapsarian Garden of Eden.[44] Yet, on the other, it falls within a minority Empire-wide tradition that considered Indigenous culture worth preserving and articulating for new audiences, especially settler colonial readers negotiating their own complex allegiances to place and nationality.[45]

Harriott Barlow on the Balonne River, 1868–74

Harriott Barlow compiled records of language groups from Aboriginal workers on Warkon Station in the Maranoa District south of Charleville, Queensland between 1868 and 1874. Indigenous people taught Barlow how to distinguish between eight different language groups, and how to talk about food collection, songs, gender and skin rules, and childcare. If Dunlop's motivation for engaging with Indigenous languages was interpersonal, political, and poetic, Barlow's intentions appear to have been both interpersonal and scholarly. She was brought to colonial Queensland by her older husband, Alexander, who had returned to England to marry. Alexander Barlow owned and traded pastoral property successfully in inland New South Wales in the 1840s and 50s, and bought Warkon Station in 1858, in the newly independent colony. The colonial frontier arrived late in Queensland, with much of violence carried out under the auspices of official bodies such as the Native Police, which had a fearsome reputation for violent dispossession of Indigenous communities.[46] In 1850, Yuleba River near Warkon Station had seen the violent dispersal of Mandandanji people as part of the preparation of pastoral leases for sale.[47] In 1861, the Culin-la-Ringo massacre had taken place 500 kilometres north of Warkon Station, part of a series of reprisals following the abduction of two young Aboriginal boys by visitors looking to secure a pastoral station.[48] In a violent escalation, seventeen members of the Wills family had been murdered; the Native Police then killed nearly seventy Indigenous people from the Comet and Dawson Rivers region, as widely reported in the colonial press: 'One of the blacks who was shot, cried out, "Me no kill white fellow!" showing plainly they well comprehended the proceeding.'[49] The *Sydney Morning Herald* ran a concerted campaign attempting to contextualise the Indigenous response, and condemning the disproportionate slaughter by the Native Police. The capacity and understanding of the Indigenous speaker of English was a point the paper made repeatedly: 'extermination' was not a policy that a British government should assist, 'inhabitants both black and white are subject to English law, and are equally entitled to its protection', and the reported declaration of innocence by the Indigenous man proved that justice and an 'appeal for quarter' should have prevailed.[50]

Harriott Barlow thus arrived into a violently disrupted frontier society. Her life on Warkon Station was rich with family and Indigenous society but isolated from other settler women: most of the nearby farms were 'bachelor stations'.[51] The climate was too harsh even for a regular fruit and vegetable garden, although the rivers were rich with fish, and both the Barlow children and the local Indigenous people caught large fish and game for the family's dinner table. Indigenous people clearly found Warkon Station under the Barlows a safe site: Harriott's son Frederick remembered a large number of family groups, up to eighty individuals, visiting and working on the site, although perhaps only thirty to forty people formed a consistent community. These groups would have included Aboriginal workers from several neighbouring language groups. Men worked on itinerant farm tasks as bark strippers, shepherds, and stockriders, while others hunted and women attended to the sheep. Aboriginal women helped his mother

> not so much in house-work ... but in such as sewing possum skins together to make a rug, while my Mother sat and made notes of aboriginal words and language and customs, from their information. She obtained a very good vocabulary of the language & dialects of different tribes in the district, by this means.[52]

Harriott Barlow learned Indigenous languages through the slow accretion of intimacy across needles in a possum-skin rug. Her manuscript provides detailed wordlists relating to eight Aboriginal groups.[53] These are among the earliest documentations of the Indigenous languages of South West Queensland. Barlow's notes accompanying the vocabulary provide precise information about groups and their relationship to particular boundaries based on river systems, kinship systems, medical and spiritual practices, and stories about particular named Indigenous people.

Although the vocabulary began ambitiously by mapping relationship terms, parts of the body, and time and place terms matched to the natural world across all eight dialects, Gungarri was the language to which Barlow had most access, and she noted it was the lingua franca for the diverse Indigenous groups in the region. Tellingly, given the conditions of her language collection, the term 'to sew' was named only in Gungarri, even though possum cloaks were named in six languages. Like Dunlop walking through the Wollombi valley, Barlow obviously shared food gathering and preparation tasks with Indigenous women. The edible roots, seeds, and stalks of the blue water lily were detailed along with other edible plants like water yams, orchids, and grass trees (xanhorrhoea). Three different kinds of grasses, located in precise environments (plains, sand ridges, and lagoons), were listed before terms for grinding slabs, grindstones, and phrases for 'Now it is ground', 'To bake or roast', and 'It is ready'.[54] Phrases useful for minding children were noted, such as how to comfort a child crying for its mother ('By and by she will come back', or 'Ka-boo ka nung a', a melodic phrase) and how to call a mother back to soothe a child; again, these were always in Gungarri, with only two other dialects known to Barlow on such intimate terms. The latter part of her vocabulary contains phrases predominantly in Gungarri, with some comparative data occasionally noted in other dialects. It was in Gungarri that Barlow learned to say 'I do not understand' and 'What do you mean?'. Her lists end with two columns of proper names, divided into gender. These lists include the names of a few Indigenous individuals whose stories emerge in her notes: Yehdell, a young man who communicated and translated corroboree songs for Barlow; and Yaboongoo and Boondidoo, Gungarri women who told Barlow stories about Yehdell's 'matrimonial troubles'.

Local Indigenous men such as Yehdell provided Barlow with some evidence about traditional songs, but also evidence about cross-cultural adaptation and linguistic borrowing, revealing a subtle and reflexive process of language exchange. Barlow was less intuitive than Dunlop. The poet had noted the use of repetition in Indigenous songs: 'The flights of the lyric Poets are marvellously short[:] perhaps the beauty of sentiment supplies the apparent deficiency – if not, repetition must – for all the aboriginal songs I have heard are frequently repeated.'[55] Barlow's ear was less trained, and her assessment was blunt: 'In singing all Corroboree songs the blacks keep repeating and transposing the words; apparently making utter nonsense for the sake of varying or preserving the rhythm, to suit their fancy or adapt it to the tune.'[56] Barlow fell back here on a long tradition of dismissing Indigenous languages in the Australian colonies. Threlkeld was incensed that settlers 'flatter themselves that they are of a higher order of created beings than the aborigines of this land, whom they represent as "mere baboons, having no language but that in common with the brutes!"'.[57] Refusing to recognise Indigenous linguistic skills and intellectual capacity was a key trait of those bent upon dispossession and dispersal, and part of a set of settler colonial practices that rendered Indigenous peoples as less than human and thus not entitled to rights, recognition, and sovereignty.

Despite Barlow's obvious difficulties in learning Indigenous languages and forms, she was also open to correction. The term for a fishing net made of kurrajong bark was 'birra'. Barlow noted: 'This word has a sound between "bizza" and "birra". I should prefer to write it bizza, but for the persistency with which the blacks corrected me.'[58] Such comments provide insight into the interplay between the scribe and the informer in linguistic encounters, for her informants were far from passive and naive interlocutors; rather, they were personally involved in both the transmission of knowledge and its most accurate written representation. It bears emphasising that this was the first time these languages were committed to writing, and that both the knowledge holder and the scribe were constructing an orthography as they proceeded. Three songs were recorded in a kind of running translation by Yehdell. Two are only brief. The 'Wugga-Wugga Song' (likely Wakka Wakka, AIATSIS code E28, from South East Queensland) is the longest:

> An old woman told me
> She think she hears 'mun ni nar'
> The splashing of water.[59]

Yehdell pointed out to Barlow that the Wakka Wakka version borrows words from English: '"Olg ooman" – that white fellow's talk you know missis, old woman!' He explained each phrase carefully, using his body to explain terms such as hearing, and explaining the meaning as well as the vocabulary, as part of a careful reciprocal negotiation of knowledge:

> old woman frightened, that cobon dark, she thinks she hears somebody bogie (bathing); 'gay-ro, gay-ro' – like it this way, beat the water, then it jump up – Splashing [Barlow inquires]? –
> Yes, that the way, hear him water splashing.[60]

Barlow's understanding of the nature of these songs – their meaning within local cultures, their allegorical function, and their status as knowledge invested with precedent and authority – was only partial. This was, in some significant and painful ways, salvage ethnography: data collected from individuals who were literally remnant populations, violently dispossessed of their lands and often, through massacre, disconnected from long-standing traditions of knowledge transmission based upon age, gender, and cultural authority.[61] Yet it also provides evidence of the deliberate and forward-thinking adaptations made by Indigenous individuals and communities to colonial modernity as it arrived in their country.

Barlow was in no doubt that Warkon Station sat on Indigenous country: her notes evidence what was painstakingly described to her as a dense landscape marked by environmental boundaries such as rivers, and linguistic boundaries that marked culture and society. For Indigenous Australians, 'country' has a multivalent meaning. Deborah Bird Rose defines it as 'a living entity with a yesterday, today and tomorrow, with a consciousness, and a will toward life'.[62] What might be understood as salvage linguistics was also a vital recording of ongoing knowledge traditions, shaped by the strategic choices made by individuals such as Yehdell to engage with new systems of epistemology and transmission.

Barlow made two important interventions in the preservation of the Indigenous knowledge she herself only partially understood. Her meticulous archival record was kept: unusually for colonial women's papers, her vocabulary was deposited in state archives. L. Schwenssen, a later owner of Warkon Station who was interested in its history, also transcribed her papers and enriched them by conducting interviews with Barlow's surviving sons in the 1950s. Second, Barlow sent her 'Vocabulary of Aboriginal Dialects of Queensland' to the Royal Anthropological Institute of Great Britain in 1871, where it was refereed, read at an Institute meeting in 1872, and published in 1873. It appeared in the newly merged Institute's second edition of their new journal, and was discussed by members at the meeting alongside a study of 'Names and their Origins' reflecting on Celtic languages and their influence on early Britain.[63] The surrounding discussion reflected the tension at the time between classical philology and comparative linguistics. Dr Richard Charnock deemed the preceding author's interpretations of Celtic naming traditions as 'far-fetched etymologies'. Of Barlow's paper, he confined his commentary to noting resemblances between sounds and meaning correspondences between the dialects.[64]

The reception of Barlow's work in the context of the Royal Anthropological Institute remains hazy, not least because of her gender.[65] Other colonial field collectors were made Fellows of the Institute for their contribution.[66] Barlow was not, as women were only admitted as such in 1875.[67] The cursory discussion that surrounds Barlow's paper is doubtless indicative of the imperial anthropological consumption of colonial data: the collateral intellectual benefits to the centre of violent, dispossessive colonialism. Governments used anthropological (including linguistic) knowledge of Indigenous populations to manage them: in the Australian context this included incarceration on reserves, removing children (particularly mixed-race) from families, and the complete regulation of Aboriginal lives (in Queensland under the Aboriginals Protection and Restriction of the Sale of Opium Act 1897), all of which were not only destructive of Indigenous culture, knowledge, and well-being, but which set up the conditions for multi-generational disadvantage that continues to plague contemporary communities. Yet, as this chapter has argued, it may be possible to keep both the dispossessive colonialism and the knowledge preservation in dual focus when approaching these southern archives of linguistic encounter.

Colonial archives and their afterlives

Colonial linguistic archives and textual sources provide compelling insights into both collectors and holders of traditional knowledge. Of course, they are not neutral spaces of unmediated sources, but highly constructed sites for preserving and creating knowledge. Nicholas Dirks identifies the 'archival structure of the conditions of historical knowledge', and notes the intersection of archives with 'the modern colonial state and its documentary apparatus'.[68] Linguistic sources are tainted by their imbrication with the power and racial privilege that adhered in settler colonial governance. Whose papers, whose donation, and who continues to undertake both the curation and the creation of knowledge from archives are acute (and politically significant) questions. Evidently, gender played a part in the proximity of particular linguistic sources to overt political structures, but also the status that these collections accrued in the colonial period and in posterity. Traces of Indigenous voices and agencies – including their knowledge and culturally specific modes of authority – have been deposited in linguistic texts and archives in the context of colonial interests, and in our current era these sources can appear tainted by their association with colonial-era ideologies. Yet the personal and political nature of the collaboration between Indigenous knowledge holders such as Patyegarang, Biraban, Boni, and Yehdell and their settler scribes complicates a reading of these sources as purely hegemonic. Reading along rather than against the grain of linguistic texts from the colonial field, we might hope to reconstruct not only the scientific, poetic, and scholarly motivations of scribes such as Dawes, Threlkeld, Dunlop, and Barlow, but also glimpses of how Indigenous knowledge holders engaged strategically and selectively with some settlers to communicate and continue their own long-standing knowledge traditions.

These sources remain open for new meanings and new interpretations by scholarly readers, future researchers, and Indigenous descendants and communities. Most powerfully, language reclamation and revitalisation projects are gaining momentum and critical mass in Indigenous communities across Australia. These colonial texts are put into action alongside community memories and oral histories to form an emerging renaissance of Indigenous languages, evident not only in the gradual increase of users of language, but also public interventions such as the State Library of New South Wales' Rediscovering Indigenous Languages website, a public source that is freely available to all users and which collects data and text corrections from communities in a dynamic fashion.[69] Related initiatives such as Indigenous 'Word of the Week' are often drawn from colonial texts, and now broadcast on national radio and social media, revoiced by Indigenous speakers who put the terms back into a cultural context for broad audiences.[70] Recent exhibitions such as the State Library of Queensland's *Spoken: Celebrating Queensland Languages* have displayed Barlow's manuscript alongside contemporary Indigenous communities' use of language sources: Central West Queensland communities describe how '[w]ords written on scraps of paper recorded by linguists … are now held in great esteem. [Communities use] collections and word lists to build and preserve their words for future generations'.[71] Such collateral and progressive uses of southern colonial print cultures suggest that new meanings will continue to be found and generated into the future.

Notes

1 [Eliza Hamilton Dunlop], 'Mrs. David Milson Kamilaroi Vocabulary and Aboriginal Songs, 1840', State Library of New South Wales, Sydney, A 1688.

2 Lancelot Threlkeld to Saxe Bannister, 27 September 1824, Council for World Mission (CWM), London, Australia Box 2.

3 David Andrew Roberts, '"Language to Save the Innocent": Reverend L. Threlkeld's Linguistic Mission', *Journal of the Royal Australian Historical Society*, 94:2 (2008), 107–25.

4 On George Grey's collection, see Lara Atkin, Sarah Comyn, Porscha Fermanis, and Nathan Garvey, *Early Public Libraries and Colonial Citizenship in the British Southern Hemisphere* (Cham: Springer International Publishing, 2019). On Banks' collection, see Vanessa Smith, 'Joseph Banks's Intermediaries: Rethinking Global Cultural Exchange', in Samuel Moyn and Andrew Sartori (eds), *Global Intellectual History* (New York: Columbia University Press, 2013), pp. 66–86; and John Gascoigne, 'Cross-Cultural Knowledge Exchange in the Age of the Enlightenment', in Shino Kinoshi, Maria Nugent, and Tiffany Shellam (eds), *Indigenous Intermediaries: New Perspectives on Exploration Archives* (Canberra: Australian National University Press, 2015), pp. 131–46.

5 Rachael Gilmour, *Grammars of Colonialism: Representing Languages in Colonial South Africa* (Basingstoke: Palgrave Macmillan, 2006); Johannes Fabian, *Language and Colonial Power: The Appropriation of Swahili in the Former Belgian Congo 1880–1938* (Cambridge: Cambridge University Press, 1986); Judith T. Irvine, 'The Family Romance of Colonial Linguistics: Gender and Family in Nineteenth-Century Representations of African Languages', *Pragmatics*, 5:2

(1995), 139–53; Alastair Pennycook, *English and the Discourse of Colonialism* (London and New York: Routledge, 1998); Christopher Herbert, 'Epilogue: Ethnography and Evolution', *Victorian Studies*, 41:3 (1998), 485–94.

6 See Jakelin Troy, 'The Sydney Language Notebooks and Responses to Language Contact in Early Colonial NSW', *Australian Journal of Linguistics*, 12:1 (1992), 145–70; Keith Smith, *Bennelong: The Coming in of the Eora, Sydney Cove 1788–1792* (East Roseville: Kangaroo Press, 2001); Deirdre Coleman, *Romantic Colonization and British Anti-Slavery* (New York: Cambridge University Press, 2005); Ross Gibson, 'Event-Grammar: The Language Notebooks of William Dawes', *Meanjin*, 68:2 (2009), n.p., and *26 Views of the Starburst World: William Dawes at Sydney Cove 1788–91* (Crawley: University of Western Australia Publishing, 2012); and Stephen Page, *Patyegarang* (San Francisco: Kanopy Streaming, 2015).

7 Troy, 'The Sydney Language Notebooks', 145–70.

8 David Collins, Watkin Tench, Philip Gidley King, and Governor Philip all recorded some language terms, but they acknowledged Dawes as the most sophisticated linguist, motivated by 'curiosity and philanthropy' to engage in a variety of projects related to better communication and more just relations across racial lines. Tench, quoted in Troy, 'The Sydney Language Notebooks', 149. See Coleman's *Romantic Colonization and British Anti-Slavery* on Dawes' subsequent career and anti-slavery activism in Sierra Leone.

9 Troy, 'The Sydney Language Notebooks', 145–70.

10 Troy notes: 'The later studies (Ridley and Rowley 1875; Mathews 1903) are very brief and incomplete. Therefore, the Sydney language notebooks stand unique as the only known substantial records of the language still extant' ('The Sydney Language Notebooks', 147).

11 A full account of Threlkeld's linguistic work can be read in chapter 2, Anna Johnston, *The Paper War: Morality, Print Culture, and Power in Colonial New South Wales* (Crawley: University of Western Australia Press, 2011). See also Hilary M. Carey, 'Lancelot Threlkeld and Missionary Linguistics in Australia to 1850', in Otto Zwartjes and Even Hovdhaugen (eds), *Missionary Linguistics / Lingüística Misionera: Selected Papers from the First International Conference on Missionary Linguistics, Oslo, March 13th–16th, 2003* (Amsterdam: John Benjamins, 2004), pp. 253–75; and Roberts, '"Language to Save the Innocent"', 107–25.

12 Lancelot Threlkeld, *Specimens of a Dialect of the Aborigines of New South Wales; Being the First Attempt to Form Their Speech into a Written Language* (Sydney: Arthur Hill, 1827).

13 Lancelot Threlkeld, *A Key to the Structure of the Aboriginal Language; Being an Analysis of the Particles Used as Affixes, to Form the Various Modifications of the Verbs; Shewing the Essential Powers, Abstract Roots, and Other Peculiarities of the Language Spoken by the Aborigines in the Vicinity of Hunter River, Lake Macquarie, Etc., New South Wales: Together with Comparisons of Polynesian and Other Dialects* (Sydney: Kemp and Fairfax, 1850).

14 Threlkeld, *A Key to the Structure of the Aboriginal Language*.

15 Threlkeld, *Specimens*.

16 Hilary M. Carey, 'Lancelot Threlkeld, Biraban, and the Colonial Bible in Australia', *Comparative Studies in Society and History*, 52:2 (2010), 447–78; 'Lancelot Threlkeld and Missionary Linguistics', 253–75.

17 Lynette Russell (ed.), *Colonial Frontiers: Indigenous–European Encounters in Settler Societies* (Manchester: Manchester University Press, 2001); Felix Driver and Lowri Jones, *Hidden Histories of Exploration: Researching the RGS–IBG Collections* (London: Royal Holloway, University of London, and Royal Geographical Society [with IBG], 2009); Rachel Standfield (ed.), *Indigenous Mobilities: Across and beyond the Antipodes* (Canberra: Australian National University Press, 2018); Tiffany Shellam, Maria Nugent, Shino Konishi, and Allison Cadzow (eds), *Brokers and Boundaries: Colonial Exploration in Indigenous Territory* (Canberra: Australian National University Press, 2016); Konishi et al. (eds), *Indigenous Intermediaries*.

18 Jan Critchett, *A 'Distant Field of Murder': Western Districts Frontiers, 1834–1848* (Melbourne: Melbourne University Press, 1990).

19 The Myall Creek massacre is a paradigmatic case: see Lyndall Ryan, 'Massacre in the Black War in Tasmania 1823–34: A Case Study of the Meander River Region, June 1827', *Journal of Genocide Research*, 10:4 (2008), 479–99; Philip G. Dwyer and Lyndall Ryan, 'Massacre in the Old and New Worlds, c.1780–1820', *Journal of Genocide Research*, 15:2 (2013), 111–5; and Jane Lydon and Lyndall Ryan (eds), *Remembering the Myall Creek Massacre* (Sydney: NewSouth, 2018). See also the University of Newcastle's Colonial Massacre Map, https://c21ch.newcastle.edu.au/colonialmassacres/map.php (accessed 10 January 2020).

20 Penelope Edmonds and Amanda Nettelbeck (eds), *Intimacies of Violence in the Settler Colony: Economies of Dispossession around the Pacific Rim* (New York: Palgrave Macmillan, 2018).

21 Lisa Ford and David A. Roberts, 'Expansion, 1820–1850', in Stuart Macintyre and Alison Bashford (eds), *The Cambridge History of Australia* (Melbourne: Cambridge University Press, 2011), pp. 121–48.

22 Hilary Golder, *High and Responsible Office: A History of the NSW Magistracy* (Sydney: Sydney University Press, 1991); Amanda Nettelbeck, *Indigenous Rights and Colonial Subjecthood: Protection and Reform in the Nineteenth-Century British Empire* (Cambridge: Cambridge University Press, 2019).

23 NSW Parliament Legislative Council, *Report from the Select Committee on the Condition of the Aborigines, with Appendix, Minutes of Evidence and Replies to a Circular Letter* (Sydney: Government Printing Office, 1845).

24 See Roger Milliss, *Waterloo Creek: The Australia Day Massacre of 1838, George Gipps and the British Conquest of New South Wales* (Ringwood: McPhee Gribble, 1992); Lydon and Ryan (eds), *Remembering the Myall Creek Massacre*; and Anna Johnston, '"The Aboriginal Mother": Poetry and Politics', in Lydon and Ryan (eds), *Remembering the Myall Creek Massacre*, pp. 68–84.

25 Although misleadingly titled and attributed, Dunlop's linguistic work is compiled in 'Mrs. David Milson Kamilaroi Vocabulary and Aboriginal Songs, 1840'.

26 Jim Wafer provides a rich, detailed account of the songman in 'Ghost-Writing for Wulatji: Incubation and Re-Dreaming as Song Revitalisation Practices', in Jim Wafer and Myfany Turpin (eds), *Recirculating Songs: Revitalising the Singing*

Practices of Indigenous Australia (Canberra: Asia-Pacific Linguistics Australian National University, 2017), pp. 193–256.

27 AIATSIS, 'Language Thesaurus', www1.aiatsis.gov.au/ (accessed 10 January 2020).

28 For an overview, including the role of Lancelot Threlkeld and Biraban in the colonial courts, see Johnston, *The Paper War*.

29 Thomas Moir glossed the phrase: 'There is no creature but man who has the least knowledge of God. But amongst men there is no nation so barbarous as not to know that they ought to believe in the existence of God; although they may be ignorant of the attributes proper to this Divine Being.' *A Treatise on the Existence of a Supreme Being, and Proofs of the Christian Religion* (London: Lackington & Company, 1819), p. 40.

30 See Anna Johnston and Elizabeth Webby (eds), *Eliza Hamilton Dunlop: Writing from the Colonial Frontier* (Sydney: Sydney University Press, 2021).

31 'Mrs. David Milson Kamilaroi Vocabulary and Aboriginal Songs, 1840'.

32 By corollary, Threlkeld writes about going fishing with Awabakal men on Lake Macquarie.

33 For a longer discussion of this source and 'The Eagle Chief', see Anna Johnston, 'Mrs Milson's Wordlist: Eliza Hamilton Dunlop and the Intimacy of Linguistic Work', in Penelope Edmonds and Amanda Nettelbeck (eds), *Intimacies of Violence in the Settler Colony: Economies of Dispossession around the Pacific Rim* (New York: Palgrave Macmillan, 2018), pp. 225–47.

34 'Mrs. David Milson Kamilaroi Vocabulary and Aboriginal Songs, 1840'.

35 Tim Fulford, *Romantic Indians: Native Americans, British Literature, and Transatlantic Culture 1756–1830* (Oxford: Oxford University Press, 2006); John O'Leary, *Savage Songs and Wild Romances: Settler Poetry and the Indigene, 1830–1880* (Amsterdam: Rodopi, 2011); Jason Rudy, *Imagined Homelands: British Poetry in the Colonies* (Baltimore: Johns Hopkins University Press, 2017).

36 'Domestic Intelligence: New Music', *Sydney Herald* (18 April 1842), p. 2.

37 Marilyn Butler, 'Culture's Medium: The Role of the Review', in Stuart Curran (ed.), *The Cambridge Companion to British Romanticism* (Cambridge: Cambridge University Press, 2010), pp. 127–52.

38 See Duncan Wu, '"A Vehicle of Private Malice": Eliza Hamilton Dunlop and the *Sydney Herald*', *The Review of English Studies*, 65:272 (2014), 888–903; and Johnston, '"The Aboriginal Mother"', pp. 68–84.

39 Deborah Bird Rose, 'Gendered Substances and Objects in Ritual: An Australian Aboriginal Study', *Material Religion*, 3:1 (2007), 34–46.

40 Eliza Hamilton Dunlop, 'Native Poetry: Nung-Ngnun', *Sydney Morning Herald* (11 October 1848), p. 3.

41 L. E. Threlkeld, 'Reminiscences. Aborigines – the Muses – Poetry', *Christian Herald, and Record of Missionary and Religious Intelligence* (11 November 1854), pp. 315–16.

42 Wafer, 'Ghost-Writing for Wulatji'.

43 Dunlop published the first version of this poem in 1848. This version is sourced from the new selected edition of Dunlop's poems; see Johnston and Webby (eds), *Eliza Hamilton Dunlop*.

44 See Terry Goldie, *Fear and Temptation: The Image of the Indigene in Canadian, Australian and New Zealand Literatures* (Kingston: McGill University Press, 1989); Patrick Brantlinger, *Dark Vanishings: Discourse on the Extinction of Primitive Races, 1800–1930* (Ithaca: Cornell University Press, 2003); and John O'Leary, 'Giving the Indigenous a Voice – Further Thoughts on the Poetry of Eliza Hamilton Dunlop', *Journal of Australian Studies*, 28:82 (2004), 92.

45 O'Leary, *Savage Songs and Wild Romances*; Jason Rudy, 'Floating Worlds: Émigré Poetry and British Culture', *ELH*, 81:1 (2014), 325–50, and *Imagined Homelands*.

46 Bob Reece, 'Review of Patrick Collins, *Goodbye Bussamarai: The Mandandji Land War, Southern Queensland 1842–1852* (2002)', *Bulletin (Australian Historical Association)*, 96 (2003), 78–82; Patrick Collins, *Goodbye Bussamarai: The Mandandanji Land War, Southern Queensland, 1842–1852* (St. Lucia: University of Queensland Press, 2002).

47 'Domestic Intelligence', *Moreton Bay Courier* (6 April 1850), p. 2.

48 See the *Colonial Frontiers Massacre Map*.

49 'The Nogoa Tragedy: Slaughter of Upwards of Sixty of the Supposed Murderers', *Sydney Morning Herald* (10 December 1861), p. 5.

50 *Sydney Morning Herald* (11 December 1861), p. 5.

51 F[red]. W. Barlow, 'Notes Regarding Warkon Station,' [1945], Fryer Library, The University of Queensland, Brisbane, F1733.

52 Barlow, 'Notes Regarding Warkon Station'.

53 Coongurrin (now Gungarri, AIATSIS Language Code D37); Wirri-Wirri (also Wirray-Wirray, AIATSIS code D66, a dialect of Gamilaraay spoken on the Balonne River); Ngoorie (Nguri, AIATSIS code D46, which extends along the Maranoa River); Yowalleri (Yuwaalaraay, AIATSIS code D27, connected to Gamilaraay and spoken from the Culgoa River north up the Balonne River); Cooinburri (Guyinbaraay, AIATSIS code D34, a dialect of Gamilaraay); Begumble (Bigambul, AIATSIS code 34, based on the Weir and Moonie Rivers south of Warkon); Cambooble (Gambuwal, AIATSIS code D29); and Parrumgoom (Barunggam, AIATSIS code D40). For this local historical knowledge, mapping on to the AIATSIS language codes, I am indebted to Desmond Crump's blogpost, Harriott Barlow Manuscript, ca. 1865, John Oxley Library-State Library of Queensland, http://blogs.slq.qld.gov.au/jol/2020/01/20/om91–69-harriet-barlow-manuscript-ca-1865/ (accessed 10 January 2020).

54 Barlow notes: 'The grasses were ground between two stones, and then made into a sort of damper. The Coongurri have no word for flour' ('Notes', 174).

55 'Mrs. David Milson Kamilaroi Vocabulary and Aboriginal Songs, 1840'.

56 H. Barlow, 'Vocabulary of Aboriginal Dialects of Queensland', *Journal of the Anthropological Institute of Great Britain and Ireland*, 2:2 (1872), 166. On song forms, see Jim Wafer and Myfany Turpin (eds), *Recirculating Songs: Revitalising the Singing Practices of Indigenous Australia* (Canberra: Australian National University Press, 2017).

57 Threlkeld, *Key to the Structure of the Aboriginal Language*, p. 4.

58 Barlow, 'Vocabulary of Aboriginal Dialects of Queensland', 166.

59 Barlow, 'Vocabulary of Aboriginal Dialects of Queensland', 166.

60 Barlow, 'Vocabulary of Aboriginal Dialects of Queensland', 166.

61 Jacob W. Gruber, 'Ethnographic Salvage and the Shaping of Anthropology', *American Anthropologist*, 72:6 (1970), 1289–99; James Clifford, 'The Others: Beyond the "Salvage" Paradigm', *Third Text*, 3:6 (1989), 73–8.

62 Rose, 'The Year Zero and the North Australian Frontier', in Rose and Anne Clarke (eds), *Tracking Knowledge in North Australian Landscapes: Studies in Indigenous and Settler Ecological Knowledge Systems* (Casuarina: North Australia Research Unit, Australian National University, 1997), pp. 19–36.

63 On the Institute, see George W. Stocking, Jnr, 'What's in a Name? The Origins of the Royal Anthropological Institute (1837–71)', *Man*, 6:3 (1971), 369–90.

64 Barlow, 'Vocabulary of Aboriginal Dialects of Queensland', 165–75. Classical philologists were primarily interested in languages and classical literary traditions; comparativists by contrast characterised their method as 'scientific', although they were barely interested in anthropological evidence, focusing instead on systematic comparisons of sound and meaning correspondences between related languages or dialects. Neither group considered the hundreds of synchronic grammatical studies, such as those produced by Dawes, Threlkeld, Dunlop, and Barlow, as particularly important work, although the comparativists needed it. Rather it was the synthetic, high-level work that mattered: at least until the widespread acceptance of Darwinian evolution changed this vibrant field from the 1870s onwards. See Frederick J. Newmeyer, *The Politics of Linguistics* (Chicago: University of Chicago Press, 1986); and Tomoko Masuzawa, *The Invention of World Religions: Or, How European Universalism Was Preserved in the Language of Pluralism* (Chicago: University of Chicago Press, 2005).

65 No correspondence has been found about how Barlow's manuscript was published by the Institute.

66 Threlkeld was made a Corresponding Fellow of the precursor organisation, the Ethnological Society, in 1854.

67 Many thanks to Royal Anthropology Institute Curator Sarah Walpole for this contextual information.

68 Nicholas B. Dirks, 'Annals of the Archive: Ethnographic Notes on the Sources of History', in Brian Keith Axel (ed.), *From the Margins: Historical Anthropology and Its Futures* (Durham: Duke University Press, 2002), p. 50.

69 State Library of New South Wales, https://indigenous.sl.nsw.gov.au/ (accessed 10 January 2020).

70 For an example drawn from Dunlop's wordlist, see Indigenous Services, State Library of New South Wales, Rediscovering Indigenous Languages: Word of the Week, https://indigenous-services-slnsw.tumblr.com/post/128317462709/our-word-of-the-week-is-batadee-according-to-mrs (accessed 10 January 2020).

71 *Spoken: Celebrating Queensland Languages*, Exhibition Text, State Library of Queensland, 21 November 2019–19 April 2020.

14

Kiro's thoughts about England: an unexpected text in an unexpected place

Michelle Elleray

On 16 May 1847, a Pacific Islander named Kiro landed in England, becoming one of the earliest recorded people to arrive there from Rarotonga, the most populous island in what are now the Cook Islands.[1] Pacific Islanders have a long history of global mobility, but this arrival was distinctive because Kiro had travelled from the South Pacific with Aaron Buzacott of the London Missionary Society (LMS) in order to help Buzacott with the translation of the Bible into Cook Islands Māori. Describing the missionary ship's arrival in later years, Kiro spoke of the water within the West India Docks as 'large rivers', compared the many ships' masts to 'an endless forest of leafless trees', and assumed the 'long and lofty buildings' were '*are bure* [pure]', or churches, only to learn they were instead '*are apinga*', or warehouses.[2] From a Rarotongan perspective, Kiro's substitution of churches for warehouses makes sense, since in Rarotonga any such buildings were tied to the LMS and consisted of churches and Takamoa Theological Institute. Christianity had been introduced to Rarotonga in 1823, and so Kiro, born around 1820, was part of the first generation to grow up with the new faith and its attendant technology of alphabetic literacy.[3]

Taken under Buzacott's wing, Kiro was aligned with the political power of the LMS mission in Rarotonga, and while on board the missionary ship that conveyed him to England he would have been understood as doing the Lord's work.[4] Indeed, the most senior member of the Cook Islands mission, Charles Pitman, had raised objections to Buzacott overseeing the final stage of the translation of the Bible in England on the grounds of an insufficient knowledge of Cook Islands Māori, and had only withdrawn these objections when Buzacott decided to take Kiro with him.[5] In later years, Buzacott told the British and Foreign Bible Society:

> I did not like to undertake [the translation of the Bible] without the assistance of a native. One was selected – a young man from the College, of good sound judgment; and during the two years he was with me in England he was of great assistance to me in translating, and correcting the portions already translated.[6]

The 1851 edition of *Te Bibilia Tapu*, published by the British and Foreign Bible Society, and the first to print the entire Bible in Cook Islands Māori, saw Kiro acting alongside Buzacott and others as a translator. Kiro was therefore integral to a major undertaking of the mission, and in England he would function for the LMS as living proof of missionary success in the South Pacific.

As Kiro prepared to disembark from the missionary ship on to the West India Docks, however, an altercation sees his status reframed:

> On being told to prepare for landing, he said he put together a few clothes in a bundle, but on coming upon deck, he was told by 'the Queen's officers' that he must leave his bundle behind; 'to this,' he said, 'I objected. I had no idea of leaving my clothes behind me, and especially my blanket, in which I expected to sleep at night. I was *maro* (obstinate) to take my bundle.[7] I knew it was my own, but the 'Queen's man' was *maro* too, and I had to yield.' This was a most unaccountable custom, to poor Kiro; he had no idea of being suspected of dishonesty.[8]

Kiro's status as a promising young man, a fellow Christian, and a person whose knowledge would facilitate the missionary cause is recognised in the Cook Islands and on board the missionary ship, but the limits of evangelical agency and status become apparent when he moves into the orbit of the West India Docks, a space that sees his social production as a (potential) thief, who is the focus of surveillance and suspicion. This moment, when Kiro is read in opposing ways from two different locations, resonates also for our readings of the texts Kiro authored or in which he features. I take Kiro's repositioning from missionary translator to common thief as he leaves the missionary ship for the West India Docks as a template for considering the challenges in reading the Christian Pacific Islander through British sites and archives. In doing so, I have kept as a guide the challenge issued by Tracey Banivanua Mar and Nadia Rhook in their article on Indigenous peoples within imperial networks 'to look harder in archives and actions for the unexpected, and to remain vigilant against assumptions about the ways power works through networks'.[9]

Networks, archives, and their traces

Forestalling the work of thieves had been integral to the formation of the West India Docks, which allowed shipping on the Thames to load and unload colonial goods. Formerly the West Indies merchants' ships had sailed further upriver to the Legal Quays between London Bridge and the Tower of London, but the inordinate time taken to berth and unload in the overcrowded waterways, as well as the significant attrition of goods through theft, saw a push to build new docks on the Isle of Dogs. The docks opened in 1802, and a significant feature was that the West India Dock Company sought and was granted permission to maintain a permanent military guard specifically to prevent thefts.[10] It is presumably one of these guards who is the Queen's officer mentioned by Kiro. Drawing on the Minute Books of the West India Dock Company, Walter Stern notes that theft was one of the 'besetting vices against which all dock administration waged a never ending struggle'; and while major thefts diminished, 'petty pilferage never completely stopped ... Nothing worried the directors of the Company more than this persistence of dishonesty. Every complaint was painstakingly investigated, a disproportionate amount of managerial time spent on discovering petty theft, and hardly a week passed without the summary dismissal of at least one dock labourer'.[11] Kiro thus finds himself inserted into a specific set of economic tensions between the opportunistic thief and the loss-fearing merchant.

As their name signals, moreover, the economics of the West India Docks are integrally tied to a colonial history. Invoking a key region of the British Empire, the West India Docks were predicated on economic relations with the Caribbean, and were built to secure the financial interests of planters and merchants who relied on the labour of enslaved Africans for their profits. The initiator of the West Indian Docks scheme was Robert Milligan, a West Indies merchant and owner of a plantation in Jamaica, and as Melissa Bennett and Kristy Warren note, some of the ships that left and arrived at the West India Docks shipped enslaved Africans to the Caribbean before loading their hold with plantation products for London.[12] The Caribbean context of the West India Docks saw people of colour designated as property rather than the possessors of property, and so the space reinforces a presumption that Kiro is not the owner of the clothes and blanket he carries. British merchants' relations with the Black Atlantic and Caribbean slavery are an anomalous frame for the Pacific Islander, and yet one that structures how Kiro is read when he arrives in England in 1847.

When the Queen's officer accosts Kiro as a thief, the insult is all the more dramatic because of the contrast with Kiro's location and status on board the LMS's missionary ship, the vessel of an institution that asserted the capacity of all, no matter their skin colour, to become Christian (even if their status within Christianity might be hierarchised). On board the ship, Kiro presumes the legitimacy of his voice in rejecting the Queen's officer's command – 'I objected', he recounts, and is obstinate in asserting his rights to the goods – but ultimately he is required to subordinate his understanding of the situation to the authority of the officer. Not only is Kiro socially produced as a potential threat to the financial interests of the British merchant class, he is also a threat in the assertion of his agency when he challenges the Queen's officer and stubbornly claims the right to choose what he carries.

But while in this episode the West India Docks reframe the status of the Pacific Islander Christian on the missionary ship, nineteenth-century evangelicalism likewise exerts its disciplinary imperatives on the Pacific Islander. Christianity might offer new opportunities with regard to social status, education, and (as in Kiro's case) geographic mobility, but it also came with norms and expectations by which the convert was expected to abide, and in light of which the validity of the convert's faith was assessed. Taking the insights gleaned from the episode at the West India Docks and applying them to Kiro's status within British evangelical circles, we need to ask how Kiro's textual production in missionary publications likewise shapes him to the LMS's ends, and where we might read Kiro as exceeding or challenging this disciplinary oversight.

We know of Kiro's arrival and reception in England because upon his return to the southern hemisphere he told his fellow Rarotongans about that moment, and a British missionary captured the account on paper. The narrative was then sent to the LMS Directors in London, who ensured its publication in the *Juvenile Missionary Magazine* (1844–87). This trajectory captures the simultaneous intimacy and distance of our textual relationship to Kiro: we hear his reaction to the sight of the Docks, and his assumption of his rights and agency in interacting with the officer, but we only have this record because a chain of British evangelicals deemed it of interest to British children. Our interest might lie in the perspective of the Pacific Islander, but our knowledge is dependent on his proximity and relevance to a British missionary network and its systems of print publication. The chance circumstances and fleeting record of Kiro's textual presence makes him a companion to the Māori and Pacific Islander travellers attended to by Alice Te Punga Somerville and Tracey Banivanua Mar, who delve into the challenges of historical investigation of these voyagers given the faintness of the traces they leave in the colonial archives. Writing of Kooley, for example, Te Punga Somerville describes this Māori girl as 'an almost imperceptible bump on archival pages', and her own scholarly task as 'looking for scraps of detail that may reveal something of [Kooley's] impact on her world and, in turn, on ours'.[13]

Kiro, however, is unusual in the extent to which he leaves behind an English-language textual record. Residing in England from 1847 to 1850, he wrote a travel journal intended for a Cook Islands readership, but that was instead published as a six-part series in the LMS's *Juvenile Missionary Magazine* – titled 'Kiro's Thoughts about England' (1850) – when he suddenly returned to the Pacific because of illness. Buzacott translated the journal, and the translation would also have undergone the editorial pen of Joseph John Freeman, the Home Secretary of the LMS and editor of the *Juvenile Missionary Magazine*. Since to my knowledge the original journal is no longer extant, we only have this abridged and highly mediated text.[14]

Kiro's writing about his time in England never made it back to his community; instead, an early example of Cook Islands writing published in English was preserved in a Victorian children's evangelical magazine.[15] In subtitling this chapter 'an unexpected text in an unexpected place', I reference my surprise at the location of Kiro's travel journal. But the wording is also a deliberate invocation of Banivanua Mar and Rhook's article, 'Counter Networks of Empires: Reading Unexpected People in Unexpected Places' (2018), which asks how 'Indigenous and subaltern people draw on, intervene in and place themselves in relation to imperial networks, for their own ends'.[16] In turn, Banivanua Mar and Rhook gesture to Philip Deloria's *Indians in Unexpected Places* (2004), a work that challenges settler assumptions that Indigenous engagements with modernity are somehow anomalous.[17] These issues of Indigenous agency and relations to modernity re-emerge as we consider the alphabetic literacy that arrived in the South Pacific with the missionaries, and writing on and by Kiro.

Missionary legibility and alphabetic literacy in the Pacific

In the fourth instalment of his account of England, Kiro tells us he has 'seen so much of this country' because he accompanies Buzacott when the latter is sent by the LMS to promote missionary work.[18] On these journeys, Buzacott was 'to tell what he has seen among the heathen', while Kiro served as a physical manifestation of what the mission had achieved overseas.[19] Kiro writes that in Buzacott's presentation, Christianity is the force that overcomes the anthropophagic practices of the Cook Islanders, and when people in Britain

> hear that our land, which *was* a heathen land, where men killed and ate one another, is now become Christian, and when they are told that some who *were* cannibals are now men of true piety, who believe and obey the commands of God, their rejoicing is great, because God has heard and answered the prayers of Christians of Baratane [Britain].[20]

By conflating the Cook Islander with the cannibal, a figure culturally positioned as the antithesis of humanity, Christianity is understood as a benevolent rescuing force, and the movement from 'heathen' to Christian is dramatised through polarity. In this framing, agency is accorded solely to the British who convert the Islanders. Whether these are missionaries or missionary supporters, Britons are the source of the Christian mission, as well as those whom 'God has heard' and whose prayers are now answered. Notably, agency is not accorded here to the Cook Islanders who chose to incorporate Christian belief and practices into their culture. In occluding the agency of Cook Islanders to reorient their religious practices, we see the British focus on what is recognisable to them as proper Christian practice, and fail to recognise Indigenous continuities and reworkings of traditional practices within the new faith. In the framing of these British Christians, Pacific Island communities are passive and static, only prompted to engage in change and reformation through the arrival of British missionaries, who are funded by metropolitan British evangelicals.

Cook Islands anthropophagy was slotted into pre-existing western constructions of the cannibal, which presented the practice as an all-consuming identity rather than situational and restricted. Maretu, a Cook Islander who undertook pastoral work for the LMS, gives a different account: 'No one ate human flesh during times of peace; it was only in times of war. ... Pigs, matured kava plants and fish poison were substituted for human sacrifices in times of peace, for to eat human flesh then was an offense against the rules of the ariki [ruler] and mataiapo [leader a rank below the ariki].'[21] Maretu was about eighteen years older than Kiro, but despite the rapid social change that accompanied the Rarotongans' shift to Christianity, we can assume Kiro also understood eating human flesh as a highly restricted practice, circumscribed to the martial arena. Nevertheless, Kiro positions himself within the evangelical binarism of cannibal and Christian when, on 14 September 1848, he accompanies Buzacott to Portsea. Kiro states that in front of the British congregation 'the minister of that town' asked him, 'What kind of people dwell in your country?' and Kiro replied, 'They were murderers and cannibals' who are now 'greatly changed. They have Missionaries amongst them, who have taught them, and told them about the good Word of God, and exhorted them to cast away their old customs.'[22] The conversation continues: '"And what did they do? ... Did they continue their old practices?" "No; they gave them up. They now keep holy the Sabbath, and learn the Word of God. ... now our land is filled with good books; murder is abandoned; cannibalism is abandoned."'[23] Here, Kiro makes himself legible as a Christian to his British evangelical audience by acquiescing to the construction of pre-Christian communities as the location of violence, and by asserting his distance from the cannibal. In doing so, he positions himself as not only a Christian but within a community now adept in the new technology of alphabetic literacy insofar as their 'land is filled with good books', and as evidenced by his writing of the travel journal itself.

The chapel in which the conversation between Kiro and the British pastor occurs was the former home of Charles Pitman, who had worked in Tahiti as an LMS missionary before establishing a church at Ngatangiia, a district in Rarotonga. Kiro's interlocutor introduces Pitman into the conversation when he asks whether Kiro is 'aware that Mr. Pitman lived here?' and whether the Rarotongans like Pitman and attend to his teachings. Kiro replies that:

'Our people have been much pleased with him and when he has exhorted them to cast away their sins and evil customs, very many have done so.'[24] While Pitman might exhort, he cannot compel, since to 'cast away ... sins and evil customs' in the name of Christianity has to be a choice of the convert. In Kiro's statement that 'very many have done so' is the unstated correlate that some have not, a reinforcement of Rarotongan agency in matters of faith. Rarotongan agency is present also in the phrasing of Kiro's assessment that '[o]ur people have been much pleased with him', which suggests that Pitman is subject to the Rarotongans' evaluation of his worth. While the British assumption is that Christianity is something bestowed by them on the Pacific Islander, through Kiro we can read conversion as co-produced by the Cook Islanders and the British missionary.

The British minister's questions nonetheless participate in a regular occurrence whereby the faith of the newly converted is tested and confirmed through public questioning, while the minister's belief that Christianity is something the British bestow on the Pacific Islanders is inherent in his assumption of the right to determine the adequacy of Kiro's statements, and his attention to Pitman's role in the conversion of Rarotongans generally. He then positions Kiro in alignment with Pitman, by asking him, 'When you return to Rarotonga, will you tell Mr. Pitman that you have been to his native town, and spoke from the same pulpit that he once preached in?'[25] The British minister thus calls forth a resonant symmetry: Pitman, the British missionary, is in the southern hemisphere preaching to the Cook Islanders, while the Rarotongan convert is in Pitman's former church in Britain, bearing witness to the power of Christianity. What is articulated as a process of transhemispheric mirroring, however, turns out to be asymmetrical: Pitman has power and authority in the Cook Islands, whereas Kiro's access to a privileged recognition is dependent on the appropriate performance of Christianity before the British congregation and his proximity to Pitman within missionary networks. Kiro can become a Christian and be celebrated as such in Britain, but he must constantly reassert his distance from the cannibal, understood by the British as the encapsulation of pre-Christian Cook Islands culture.

Moreover, the British minister's assumption that the key missionary dynamic to be attended to is that between the northern and southern hemispheres, or between metropole and (informal) colony, erases another integral factor in the conversion of the Cook Islanders to Christianity: the arrival and residence of Papehia, a Māʻohi from the Society Islands.[26] In 1823, Papehia was the first Christian missionary to land at Rarotonga, having already undertaken the task of conversion at Aitutaki, another of the Cook Islands. Four months later he was joined by a fellow Māʻohi missionary, and it was not until 1827 that the first British missionary, the aforementioned Pitman, took up residence on Rarotonga. Thus, when Kiro says the Cook Islanders are 'greatly changed' through the influence of the 'Missionaries amongst them', these emissaries of Christianity need to be understood as not simply Britons, but fellow Pacific Islanders. By shifting our perspective to witness Papehia's efforts as well as Pitman's, conversion to Christianity can be understood as an intra-Pacific as well as transhemispheric movement.

In the second instalment of 'Kiro's Thoughts about England', Kiro also positions himself in contrast to the non-Christian, only this time the figure is not the Pacific cannibal but instead the 'many coloured natives in this country, wandering about the streets, without house or home'.[27] Kiro does not read these fellow non-white residents sympathetically, since he understands their destitution to result from their failure to abide by Christian precepts and practices: 'It is their own fault if some natives get into trouble when they come here. They perhaps drink too much, or get into bad company, and then get taken up and punished; after this they wander about, like dogs in the street, and altogether forget God's care in bringing them to this country.'[28] Through his own care to conform to evangelical expectations, he declares his ethnicity to be subordinated to a shared faith with his British hosts, so that while 'My skin is dark, and theirs is white ... yet they do not despise me, but are greatly delighted to have me amongst them.'[29]

This precedence of affiliation through faith, rather than shared marginalisation on the basis of ethnicity, becomes more complicated if we turn back to Kiro's arrival at the West India Docks, a contextualising event that occurs chronologically earlier but is not described in the *Juvenile Missionary Magazine* until a year later. The lesson of that introductory episode was how rapidly Kiro can move from inclusion as a respected member of the Christian enterprise to being accosted as a thief by the 'Queen's man' – in other words, his affiliation through faith is in fact radically insecure and contingent. For the Pacific Islander in England, Christianity functions as not only faith but also as a means of survival, since although Kiro's journey from the southern hemisphere to the northern rests on his recognised value to the missionary project of translating the Bible, his relocation also leaves him reliant on British missionary networks for clothing, food, and housing. He might be welcomed by his British hosts, but only as long as he performs the role of the exemplary converted heathen that justifies their evangelical project. Kiro's rejection of the brown non-Christian, even if we would prefer another response, needs to be read in this context of precarity, which sees him reliant on British evangelical goodwill for sustenance in England and his voyage home to the South Pacific.

Indigenous conversion and Christian universality

For the mid-Victorian community within which Kiro circulates, he is an example of what *British* evangelicalism can achieve, and the generic

stereotype of the Pacific Islander is the cannibal against whom British evangelicals measure the value of their missionary enterprise. In this context, the
Pacific Islander Christian is an oxymoron, since 'Pacific Islander' encodes
cultural practices only understood as heathen, whereas 'Christian' is conflated with British cultural practices. We can see the required performance of
Britishness enacted visually in the portrait of Kiro that accompanies the first
instalment of 'Kiro's Thoughts about England' (Figure 14.1). While his body
is that of a Pacific Islander, as seen in the shading of his skin and the depiction of his facial features, the sartorial markers are emphatically British, and
his seated posture echoes portraits of prominent evangelical men found in
the widely read *Evangelical Magazine* (1793–1904). Kiro's portrait functions as a visual metaphor for how British evangelicalism wishes to understand Indigenous Christian converts from the Pacific: as appropriable to
metropolitan evangelical concerns, and with their Christianity indexed by
their ability to conform to British norms.

Within the disciplinary structures of Christianity, Kiro is required to dif-
ferentiate himself from the racialised non-Christian, but in an inverse move
(or logical extension) this also sees him conflate the white Christian with his
own subject position during a speech given at Exeter Hall. In a transcription
published in the *Juvenile Missionary Magazine*, Kiro initially introduces
himself in the expected mode as 'an individual that has come from the heathen country ... from the land of darkness'.[30] But Kiro's speech shifts direction when he uses his physical journey from the Cook Islands to England on
the missionary ship as a metaphor for the Christian's journey to heaven:

> The distance from my country, which I have had to traverse before coming
> here, is very great indeed, and the way is exceedingly dangerous; it could not
> be traversed except by a vessel, and that vessel has been provided. I am
> reminded, also, of another distant country, which is at a great distance from us,
> in consequence of sin; – it is the heavenly world. A ship has also been provided
> for it; that ship is the Lord Jesus Christ.[31]

While Kiro initially takes up the role of the exotic convert whose presence
on stage dramatises the movement from heathen darkness to Christian
enlightenment, he then shifts to position himself as a universal subject whose
experience encompasses that of his British audience. His transhemispheric
journey from Rarotonga to England might be singular, but turned into a
metaphor for the journey to heaven it speaks to all, and the description of
heaven as 'at a great distance from *us*' includes both Briton and Pacific
Islander (my emphasis). Kiro's physical journey across the ocean pivots
neatly into the Christian trope of Jesus as Pilot, with the soul as a boat that
needs guidance to its final harbour, Heaven. That is how Kiro's speech was
presumably received by his nineteenth-century British audience. For those

184   JUVENILE MISSIONARY MAGAZINE.

KIRO, A NATIVE OF RAROTONGA, NOW IN
ENGLAND.

KIRO was born about the year 1820, which was about two years before the introduction of the Word of God to his country. He is not of a noble or Chief family. His father was a tenant of Makea's, mentioned by Mr. Williams, and so was his grandfather, who was a diligent " tiller of the ground," and very clever at climbing the rocks, and catching the mountain birds, for which he was much respected by the Chiefs and principal people. In a time of war his grandfather was

Figure 14.1 'Kiro, a Native of Rarotonga, Now in England', 'Kiro's Thoughts about England', *Juvenile Missionary Magazine*, 7 (1850), 184

from the South Pacific, however, Kiro's physical journey corresponds not only to Christian images of the soul's journey to heaven, but also to accounts found throughout the Pacific Islands of the soul's journey home to 'Avaiki. In a final twist, while the British audience associates his home islands with a sinful darkness, Kiro reminds them that they are all sinners, and as such reliant on Christ and the Atonement to enter heaven. Rather than Kiro being appropriated to British norms, here Kiro's auditors are all appropriated to his journey and to the Christian journey more generally: the 'heathen country' and 'land of darkness' is as much England as the Cook Islands.

British late-eighteenth- to mid-nineteenth-century evangelicalism portrayed conversion as a moment of spiritual enlightenment that saw a rupture with the sinful past. This centring of rupture, however, introduces a misalignment with Cook Islands culture. The problem becomes apparent if we take the common Christian concept 'they will find their reward in *the next world*', which appears in the *Cook Islands Maori Dictionary*'s entry for 'muri' as "Ei *te ao ā muri* atu e kiteāi tō rātou tūtaki'.[32] In this translation heaven is 'te ao', the world, modified by 'muri', meaning something that will come later temporally. In a physical rather than temporal context, however, 'muri' means '(at) the back, behind'. In other words, while the English and Māori phrases share the sense of a spiritual journey and the passage from the present to a future world, the physical positioning of the person on the journey differs. In English we position ourselves as facing the future, understanding it to lie ahead of us and that our movement is away from the past, but in Māori the future lies behind you and you enter it backwards looking towards the past.[33] Thus for Cook Islanders, the past (tradition) and the future (modernity) are understood through continuity, not disjunction or removal. In this framing, Cook Islanders' adoption of Christianity certainly involved changes in cultural practice and belief, but insofar as the future can only be entered by looking to the past their culture emphasises relationality, not the rupture of nineteenth-century evangelicalism. While aspects of Pacific cultures were disavowed or suppressed in taking up the new faith, Christianity nevertheless became the dominant religion through Islanders' agency in suturing the new to the old in accordance with their own understanding of how one embraces the future. Rather than understanding the Pacific Islander Christian through disjuncture with the past, then, we might look for those moments in which Christianity is positioned in relation to pre-conversion culture.

We can see this at work in the third instalment of 'Kiro's Thoughts about England'. Initially, Kiro deploys conventional biblical imagery of famine and plenitude to express a person's relationship to God:

> I am often thinking now of those lands where the Gospel is not known, – where there is a famine of the Word of God. We [Cook Islanders] were once in that state, but now we have it. ... Let us not neglect our present privileges, nor think they will last for ever. It will not be harvest time always. Famines often follow plenty. Let us then diligently store our minds with the food of the good Word of God while we have it, lest a fearful time of famine should overtake us, when we could only lament our folly.[34]

These conventional words urging attention to faith are then followed by Kiro quoting a Cook Islands' chant that has no explicit Christian content, and may have been composed before the arrival of Christianity, since Kiro places its author (named in the *Juvenile Missionary Magazine* as 'Buku') in the past tense:

> While food and plenty stored our home,
> None e'er supposed the time might come
>   When famine might consume;
> But now, alas! without relief,
> Our land is filled with want and grief.
> Death preys on all. The child, the Chief,
>   Lament a common doom.[35]

Reading past Buzacott's Anglicisation of a Māori chant, we see Kiro use Buku to place Christian allegory in the context of Cook Islands oral culture and the traditional transmission of cultural memory and narratives through song. In Kiro's juxtaposition, Christianity is presented as an extension of already familiar Cook Islands precepts and practices rather than a rupture with traditional culture, while alphabetic literacy and the new technology of writing are integrated with an oral history conveyed through chant. Rather than accepting the nineteenth-century British framework of conversion as a movement away from the Indigenous past, Kiro's positioning of the present and future in relation to the past offers an understanding of Cook Islands history and culture as essential to the successful negotiation of modernity. The past is not the ossified preserve of a now superseded culture; instead traditional culture is positioned as dynamically engaged with the opportunities and lessons of the present.

While the British missionaries eschewed much of traditional Pacific culture and required a radical break with it, they nevertheless contributed to a blurring of the line between pre-Christian and Christian spirituality. Damon Salesa notes that in the nearby Samoan context, the British missionaries drew on local terms and concepts in explaining and naming Christianity.[36] In doing so, they presumably sought only to make western categories comprehensible, but nevertheless the effect was to establish continuities between Pacific religions and the new faith, even as Christianity was understood by the British as requiring the erasure of pre-Christian spirituality and attendant cultural practices. While LMS publications for a British readership drew a sharp line between a pre-Christian and post-Christian Pacific, the reality in the region was more complex.

The connection between the traditional and the new is evident also in the realm of writing, since one of the first uses Cook Islanders found for the alphabetic literacy introduced through missionaries was the recording of family genealogies that were integral to the intergenerational passage of land and hereditary titles.[37] Alphabetic literacy might be accessed through and facilitated by Christianity, but its use in the Pacific exceeded evangelical parameters and demonstrated new methods for pursuing local priorities. This indigenisation of alphabetic literacy can be read in its arrival on Rarotonga's shores: when Papehia landed on the beach at Avarua, evangelical accounts prominently record that he carried a Bible, and so Papehia's stature within Cook Islands Christianity positions alphabetic literacy as already incorporated into Pacific knowledge and practices, despite its foreign origin.[38] Whereas early western accounts of Pacific Islanders' first sight of writing often suggest the Islanders found it akin to magic, the Islanders' immediate apprehension of the possibilities of alphabetic literacy points instead to an insight, derived from their own extant signifying systems, into writing's capacity to transmit meaning over space and time. Thus, in his work on Indigenous appropriations of textuality in Hawai'i, David A. Chang conveys Pacific Islanders' relationship to the written word in terms of 'utility', rather than the western stress on the miraculous, and highlights the ways in which writing was a means to engage in the wider relationships and appurtenances of modernity.[39]

Mediated texts and Indigenous voices

Kiro's writing prompts us to consider how we are to read recovered literary texts by peoples disempowered through imperial processes, when those texts are only deemed worthy of publication and preservation through their conformity with the dominant structures of power, in this case the LMS and its British Protestant norms. Do we read the text's observance of evangelical expectations, whether these are expressed by Kiro or perhaps amplified through the process of translation and abridgement, as accommodation or consent? How do we wrest a Pacific Islander's account of his travels in England from the evangelical framework that enabled the text's publication? Kiro is both a person tied to dates, places, and events, and an interpretive challenge insofar as we learn of him through missionary texts. The LMS's archives yield historical information on Kiro, while textually shaping him into the exemplary convert required by them as evidence of the mission's success. Barring privately held knowledge or texts belonging to descendants, those of us operating with publicly available texts are therefore required to navigate the veil of evangelical priorities, assumptions, and blind spots.

Despite the preservation of Kiro's voice, however mediated, we are also left with a glaring absence. In their scholarship, Te Punga Somerville and Banivanua Mar have steered historical work on Māori and Pacific Islanders

to questions of Indigenous–Indigenous relations, in order to deflect a privileging of the westerner as the centre through which all colonial-era interactions pass.[40] Their scholarship prompts me to ask what Kiro had to say to
Mamoe and Mamoe Fafine, a Samoan couple who travelled to Britain with
Buzacott and Kiro in 1847. While the LMS publications and archives attend
to Mamoe and Mamoe Fafine on the one hand, and Kiro on the other, they
say little of their interactions. The exception is when Kiro arrives in England:
'On going into the [West India] docks he said to Mamoe, the Samoan native,
"Look at those long and lofty ranges of buildings; surely those are '*te an are
bure anga*'" [sic] – houses of prayer. But, to their surprise, they found they
were "*are apinga*" – storehouses.'[41] The one moment of recorded interaction
encapsulates a way of understanding Pacific history: the Pacific Islanders
expect Britain to be encountered through a shared faith, only to find instead
that the economics of colonial trade dominate.

It seems unlikely that Kiro would not further mention or reflect on the
Samoans in his travel journal. The three of them were the only recorded
Pacific Islanders on the vessel as it sailed to England, and they shared a common history of LMS missionary presence and the establishment of theological schools in their respective islands (Takamoa in Rarotonga, Malua in
Sāmoa). Additionally, the people of Avarua – the Rarotongan district where
Kiro had resided – traced their descent to Karika, a Samoan leader who
settled in Rarotonga in the thirteenth century.[42] Rarotongans and Samoans
also had overlapping vocabularies and cultural practices, particularly in
comparison to the British people the Islanders now found themselves among.
Not long after arrival in England the Samoans fell ill and by July were sent
to Brighton for their health; in October 1847 the LMS recorded their departure for the South Pacific, leaving Kiro alone in England.[43] 'Kiro's Thoughts
about England' tells us about England, as the title advertises, but did the
manuscript journal from which the excerpts were drawn widen this focus to
include Kiro's conversations with the Samoans? When the Samoans became
sick, Mamoe Fafine quite seriously, what was Kiro's response, and was their
illness on his mind when he too later sickened? What did Kiro think when
Mamoe and Mamoe Fafine returned to Sāmoa, leaving him the sole Pacific
Islander of the group in England? And what work is done by editing Kiro's
accounts to highlight Kiro's distinction between himself and the people of
colour on the streets, while erasing the lived relationship between Kiro,
Mamoe, and Mamoe Fafine?

The published and archival record of Kiro presents us with a fraught
opportunity: on the one hand, an opportunity, because we are able to access
this Cook Islander's writing and glimpse the possibilities and costs of his
journey to the northern hemisphere; but on the other hand, fraught, because
in their representation of the southern hemisphere the LMS's evangelical

and institutional investments see their publications obscure and conceal as well as reveal. Taking as our model the long history of Pacific Islanders' oceanic movements, extending far earlier than the arrival of westerners in the region, we therefore need our reading practices of Kiro's transhemispheric texts to be equally mobile and fluid.

Acknowledgements

My thanks to Jean Mason of the Cook Islands Library and Museum for discussions about Kiro. Thanks also to the Research Society for Victorian Periodicals for an Eileen Curran Award that enabled research on Kiro and the LMS at the School of Oriental and African Studies, University of London.

Notes

1 A Cook Islander sailor may have preceded Kiro, but the textual traces of such individuals are fainter, and their original Māori name and place of origin harder to determine. Rod Dixon and Michael Tavioni have tracked what appears to be an earlier Cook Islander arrival, Elizabeta Pitiman, named after her adoptive mother, Elizabeth Pitman (the wife of Charles Pitman), in 'The Mystery of Elizabeta Pitiman', *Cook Islands News* (25 August 2018), cookislandsnews.com/features/weekend/item/70531-the-mystery-of-elizabeta-pitiman (accessed 18 January 2020). The Cook Islands consist of fifteen inhabited islands in the South Pacific, of which Rarotonga is the largest. For much of the nineteenth century, the southern Cook Islands, which include Rarotonga, were known as the Hervey Islands; however, I have used the name by which the islands are currently known.

2 William Gill, 'Kiro's Return to Rarotonga', *Juvenile Missionary Magazine*, 8 (1851), 185.

3 British evangelicalism promoted alphabetic literacy among the poor at home and the so-called heathen overseas since it was understood as necessary for individual engagement with God's word.

4 The ship was the *John Williams*. For the history of its relationship to the South Pacific and the role of British children in fundraising for it, see Michelle Elleray, *Victorian Coral Islands of Empire, Mission, and the Boys' Adventure Novel* (New York: Routledge, 2020).

5 Much of Pitman's translation of the Bible had been lost in a hurricane and he wished to begin again, but Buzacott and a fellow missionary, William Gill, who both felt the translation had already been delayed enough, took charge of the project. Kiro is therefore part of a power play within Cook Islands mission politics. The LMS holdings of the Council for World Mission (CWM) archives are held at the School of Oriental and African Studies, University of London, UK; see

the years 1847–49 in CWM/LMS, Home, South Seas Committee Minutes, box 1, 1845–68, and the years 1847–48 in CWM/LMS, South Seas, Western Outgoing Letters, box 4, 1846–52.

6 'Report', *The Forty-Eighth Report of the British and Foreign Bible Society* (London: Richard Clay, 1852), p. cxxiii.

7 While the Cook Islands Māori word for 'obstinate' or 'stubborn' would now be spelled 'mārō', when quoting from nineteenth-century texts, which do not use macrons, I have left Māori words in their original form.

8 Gill, 'Kiro's Return', p. 185; italics in original.

9 Tracey Banivanua Mar and Nadia Rhook, 'Counter Networks of Empires: Reading Unexpected People in Unexpected Places', *Journal of Colonialism and Colonial History*, 19:2 (2018), n.p.

10 See Walter Stern, 'The First London Dock Boom and the Growth of the West India Docks', *Economica*, new series, 19:73 (1952), 62.

11 Stern, 'First London Dock Boom', 76.

12 On London involvement in the slave trade, including through the West India Docks, see Melissa Bennett and Kristy Warren's 'Looking Back and Facing Forwards: Ten Years of the London, Sugar & Slavery Gallery', *Journal of Historical Geography*, 63 (2019), 94–9 (esp. 94–5). Bennett and Warren describe Robert Milligan as 'involved in the business of slave factorage – the buying of enslaved people in bulk from slave ships for sale to clients on the island' of Jamaica (94).

13 Alice Te Punga Somerville, 'Living on New Zealand Street: Maori Presence in Parramatta', *Ethnohistory*, 61:4 (2014), 662; Tracey Banivanua Mar, 'Shadowing Imperial Networks: Indigenous Mobility and Australia's Pacific Past', *Australian Historical Studies*, 46:3 (2015), 340–55.

14 Buzacott appears to have been a supportive and sympathetic mentor of Kiro, and there is no basis to suggest any deliberate mistranslation of Kiro's journal. But Kiro was in England because of questions about the depths of Buzacott's familiarity with Cook Islands Māori, which raises the possibility of nuances Buzacott did not recognise and translate, and Buzacott reflects his culture and era in his dismissal of pre-Christian Rarotonga as a place of idolatry and violence.

15 In *Victorian Coral Islands*, I discuss how the shift in readership positions Kiro's journal as a disciplinary text for British children.

16 Banivanua Mar and Rhook, 'Counter Networks of Empire', n.p.

17 Philip Deloria, *Indians in Unexpected Places* (Lawrence: University Press of Kansas, 2004).

18 Kiro, 'Kiro's Thoughts about England', *Juvenile Missionary Magazine*, 7 (1850), 10–2, 34–7, 59–62, 77–9, 107–9, 127–30, 77.

19 Kiro, 'Thoughts', 78.

20 Kiro, 'Thoughts', 78; italics in original.

21 Maretu, *Cannibals and Converts: Radical Change in the Cook Islands*, trans. and ed. Marjorie Tua'inekore Crocombe (Suva: University of the South Pacific, 1983), p. 33.

22 Kiro, 'Thoughts', 78–9.

23 Kiro, 'Thoughts', 79.

24 Kiro, 'Thoughts', 79.

25 Kiro, 'Thoughts', 79.

26 Originally named Papeiha in the Society Islands, he became known as Papehia in the Cook Islands. For biographical details, see Taira Rere, *History of the Papehia Family* (Suva: Lotu Pasifika Productions, 1977); and Raeburn Lange, *Island Ministers: Indigenous Leadership in Nineteenth Century Pacific Islands Christianity* (Canberra: Pandanus Press, 2006).

27 Kiro, 'Thoughts', 36.

28 Kiro, 'Thoughts', 36–7.

29 Kiro, 'Thoughts', 36.

30 'Annual Services of the London Missionary Society', *Juvenile Missionary Magazine*, 6 (1849), 139.

31 'Annual Services', 139.

32 My emphasis. Jasper Buse and Raututi Taringa, *Cook Islands Maori Dictionary*, eds Bruce Biggs and Rangi Moeka'a (Rarotonga: The Ministry of Education, Government of the Cook Islands, and others, 1995).

33 Epeli Hau'ofa provides parallel examples of the relationship between spatial orientation and temporality in Hawaiian, Fijian, and Tongan languages, and we can see it also in the Māori saying from Aotearoa New Zealand, 'ka mua ka muri', which can be translated as looking to the past in order to move into the future; see 'Epilogue: Pasts to Remember', in Robert Borofsky (ed.), *Remembrance of Pacific Pasts: An Invitation to Remake History* (Honolulu: University of Hawai'i Press, 2000), pp. 459–60. Outside the Pacific, see Mark Rifkin's *Beyond Settler Time: Temporal Sovereignty and Indigenous Self-Determination* (Durham: Duke University Press, 2017), in which he discusses settler erasure of Indigenous temporal sovereignty.

34 Kiro, 'Thoughts', 59–60.

35 Kiro, 'Thoughts', 60. I have not been able to trace who Buku might be, but given that Kiro is the first generation to be raised within Christianity, and that he refers to Buku in the past tense as 'one of our countrymen … who used to lament and say …', it seems at most that Buku would have been alive during the transition towards a majority-Christian Rarotonga. See Kiro, 'Thoughts', 60.

36 Damon Ieremia Salesa, 'When the Waters Met: Some Shared Histories of Christianity and Ancestral Samoan Spirituality', in Tamasailau M. Suaalii-Sauni et al. (eds), *Whispers and Sanities: Samoan Indigenous Knowledge and Religion* (Wellington: Huia, 2014), pp. 146–7.

37 See Marjorie Tua'inekore Crocombe, 'Tata: Expression through the Written Word', in Ron Crocombe and Marjorie Tua'inekore Crocombe (eds), *Akono'anga Maori: Cook Islands Culture* (Suva: Institute of Pacific Studies, in association with the Cook Islands Extension Centre, University of the South Pacific / Rarotonga: Cook Islands Cultural and Historic Places Trust, and the Ministry of Cultural Development, 2003), p. 81.

38 David A. Chang notes that Māʻohi from the Society Islands were similarly foundational to the spread of alphabetic literacy among the Kānaka Maoli of Hawai'i. See 'The Good Written Word of Life: Native Hawaiian Appropriation of Textuality', *William and Mary Quarterly*, 75:2 (2018), 251–3.

39 Chang, 'Good Written Word', 251.

40 In addition to the works already mentioned, see Te Punga Somerville, *Once Were Pacific: Māori Connections to Oceania* (Minneapolis: University of Minnesota Press, 2012); and Banivanua Mar, 'Imperial Literacy and Indigenous Rights: Tracing Transoceanic Circuits of a Modern Discourse', *Aboriginal History*, 37 (2013), 1–28.

41 Gill, 'Kiro's Return', 185; italics in original.

42 See Ron Crocombe, 'Land Tenure in the Cook Islands' (PhD dissertation, Australian National University, 1961), pp. 13–17, 20, *New Zealand Electronic Text Collection: Te Pūhikotuhi o Aotearoa* (Victorian University of Wellington, 2016), nzetc.victoria.ac.nz/tm/scholarly/tei-CroLan.html (accessed 31 January 2020).

43 See CWM/LMS, Home, Incoming Correspondence, box 9, 1845–49, folder 5, jacket A, 7 July 1847, J. B. Stair, Brighton, to J. J. Freeman; and CWM/LMS, Home, Board Minutes, 1846–61, 4 July 1847, item 4, and 12 October 1847, item 1.

15

Mokena and Macaulay: cultural geographies of poetry in colonial Aotearoa

Nikki Hessell

In October 1926 the Māori-language periodical *Te Toa Takitini* featured some lines, in English, from *Horatius*, a poem in the English MP and writer Thomas Babington Macaulay's *Lays of Ancient Rome* (1842):

> To every man upon this earth
> Death cometh soon or late.
> And how can man die better
> Than facing fearful odds,
> For the ashes of his fathers,
> And the temples of his gods? (st. XXVII, lines 3–8)[1]

It was not unusual to see English poetry published in this particular Māori periodical. Regular readers of *Te Toa Takitini* would have been familiar with Rēweti Kōhere's series of essays 'He Kupu Tohunga' (Wise Sayings), which was designed to introduce English literature to Māori readers. Educated in English at the prestigious Māori boys' school Te Aute College, Kōhere produced writings throughout his career that were peppered with quotations from his favourite poets, including Burns and Shakespeare, which he almost always gave to readers in both English and Māori. It is likely that Kōhere encountered Macaulay's poem at Te Aute; *Horatius*, while not well known today, was a widely anthologised poem that formed a core part of the settler canon discussed in the introduction to this collection. The range of Kōhere's quotations is impressive; he rarely repeats himself, and instead produces new illustrative examples of apt English verse depending on the topic and argument of the essay in question. The exceptions to this pattern are the lines quoted above. Kōhere returned over and over again to Macaulay's lines in the course of a long and bitter negotiation with the New Zealand government over his traditional lands and the legacy of his grandfather, the renowned rangatira (chief) Mokena.

Macaulay was a suitable interlocutor for Kōhere not simply because he authored a poem that was well known in Aotearoa New Zealand in the nineteenth and early twentieth centuries. He had also produced one of the most memorable nineteenth-century images of New Zealand and its inhabitants in his famous formulation of a fallen London, in which 'some traveller from New Zealand shall, in the midst of a vast solitude, take his stand on a broken arch of London Bridge to sketch the ruins of St. Paul's'.[2] This image is often read as conjuring up a Pākehā New Zealander, a settler who has returned from the periphery to a fallen centre.[3] But in 1840, the year in which Macaulay composed these lines, the term 'New Zealander' referred not to all residents of the islands of New Zealand, but rather to Māori as the sovereign people of Aotearoa. This sovereignty was a topical question in 1840 New Zealand as well as 1840 Britain, since this was the year of the signing of the Treaty of Waitangi, the agreement between the British Crown and Māori chiefs that had led to British sovereignty in Aotearoa New Zealand. As a member of parliament, Macaulay might have been present in the House of Commons on 7 July 1840, when British MPs debated the nature of the new arrangements in the colony. His awareness of a Māori figure, of the sort he describes, would have emerged from within the political discourse around this new international treaty and the visits to Great Britain of various Māori intellectuals and leaders. Macaulay's Māori was mobile, traversing not only the geographic space between England and Aotearoa, and the temporal space between the flourishing Empire and its inevitable fall, but the cultural space between Indigenous and European art forms. He was able to articulate his thinking about past, present, and future via the idea of a mobile Māori, a character called into being in part by the recent political activity at Waitangi. But in Kōhere's appropriation of the lines from *Horatius*, it is Macaulay who is figured as mobile and exotic, his texts reaching Aotearoa and undergoing various translations, appropriations, and reinterpretations. Kōhere repurposes Macaulay's verse as a site to reimagine timescales, histories, languages, and geographies, just as Macaulay himself had done when he placed a 'New Zealander' at the centre of a reimagined metropolis.

The Treaty of Waitangi was a significant historical context for Kōhere's land grievance. It was, and is still, a deeply contested document, not least because the English and Māori versions do not say the same thing.[4] As Indigenous literary scholar Chadwick Allen has argued, the Treaty of Waitangi can act as:

> a 'silent second text' against which contemporary Maori works can be read as allegory. But because this silent second text speaks in two distinct, conflicting voices, the resultant allegory always explicitly rehearses the difficulty of reconciling the Treaty's divergent Maori- and English-language versions. However strongly a particular allegory might promote one version, it cannot suppress the other. Even in those works that never allude to treaty documents specifically,

tension between competing Maori and Pakeha versions of the 'truth' often is suggestive of treaty allegory. This effect is only enhanced in bilingual and dual-language texts.[5]

While Allen's framework is designed for the analysis of post-World War II creative writing by Māori, it is nevertheless a useful one for considering an earlier example like Kōhere's integration of English texts into his writing. The mobilisation of the two languages and their respective literary canons, ostensibly expressing the same sentiment but also operating in entirely different epistemological frameworks, mirrors the foundational diplomatic moment of the Treaty of Waitangi. To move between English and Māori in this way is always, as Allen suggests, to evoke the treaty and the partnership it both emerged from and encoded. 'Treaty allegory' is a productive way in which to read what Kōhere strives for when he cites Macaulay: a reminder of the Treaty of Waitangi and its complex linguistic and political status, and a reanimation of the relationships it envisaged.

This chapter, like others in this volume, challenges the periodisation implicit in the volume's title and picks up on Sarah Comyn and Porscha Fermanis' idea of 'necessary disorientations' in their introduction. While the texts I consider come from the early decades of the twentieth century, they are located within a literary and legal relationship formed in the nineteenth century. By repurposing Macaulay, Kōhere drew not just on a nineteenth-century British figure and his writings, but also on nineteenth-century New Zealand history and important tīpuna (ancestors) in his own family. The literary culture of the nineteenth century was still of great significance in the early twentieth century, and the textual and legal relationships between Māori and the government were infused with it.

Macaulay and Māori law

When Rēweti Kōhere quoted these lines from Macaulay, he was responding in part to a resonance between the cluster of literary ideas they express – ancestry, bravery, the defence of one's homeland, and the importance of remembering the past – and Māori conceptions of land and identity. Whakapapa (ancestry or genealogy) is central to Māori identity and provides one basis by which ownership of land might be confirmed. The significance of genealogy to identity is conveyed, to some extent, in the word iwi, which means both tribe and bones. Present-day affiliations are shaped by the metaphorical bones of one's ancestors. Another related concept in conversations about land tenure and ancestry is ahikaaroa (literally, long-burning fires), a word which indicates that long-term occupation of land – the occupation by one's ancestors as well as oneself, in other words – constitutes a legitimate indicator of ownership.[6] Macaulay's poetry was quintessentially English, but it sounded right in a Māori framework.

Kōhere's 1926 gloss on these lines emphasises not their foreign or English quality, but their obvious significance for his Māori readers. In the Māori prose that accompanies the poetic quotation in the 1926 article, Kōhere addresses his readers directly: 'Waihoki e te iwi whakaohongia nga toto tatou tipuna, kia mau ki o tatou morehu rangatira, ki nga tikanga rangatira'. (Kōhere himself provides no translation of these comments, since he was writing for a Māori-speaking audience, but in English they read: 'Also, to you all, awaken to the blood of your ancestors, hold on to the vestiges of our greatness, to the ways of greatness'.[7]) There was clearly something urgent about Macaulay's words that Kōhere wished to convey to his readers, something that went beyond a sense of similarity in underpinning cultural concepts. Kōhere's readers were being exhorted, in the present moment, to heed the lesson of these nineteenth-century poetic words. Kōhere speaks to his Māori readers of a collective vision of present-day activity that draws on past knowledge and successes.

For Kōhere, this context was especially topical in 1926, but dated back to nineteenth-century cross-cultural relationships. A 1913 ruling by the Native Land Court had vested ownership of the Marangairoa 1D Block of land in a rival claimant group, in contradiction to Rēweti Kōhere's testimony that his grandfather Mokena had secured the land for his descendants by helping the British forces in the New Zealand Wars of the 1860s.[8] There had been a further investigation of the title in 1919, which resulted in the Native Land Court ruling that the land should be subdivided into twenty freeholdings. Kōhere then began a long campaign of petitioning the government for the return of the land. He authored two petitions in 1920 and a further four in 1922, none of which led to the resolution for which he hoped.[9] By 1926, his persistent efforts at diplomatic engagement led the government to introduce the Native Land Amendment and Native Land Claims Adjustment Bill, which aimed, among other things, to clear up the question of ownership of the Marangairoa 1D Block. The bill was accompanied by the announcement of terms of reference for a Royal Commission on the confiscation of Māori land.[10]

It was at this point that Kōhere began the process of repeating Macaulay's lines. Parliament debated and passed the Native Land Amendment and Native Land Claims Adjustment Bill in the months leading up to October 1926 and Kōhere's first quotation from *Horatius*.[11] Late 1926 was thus a period of intense engagement between the Crown and Māori on the subject of land ownership and its history in New Zealand in general, but also a period of engagement that attended to the Marangairoa 1D Block specifically. The lines from Macaulay not only underscored Māori sophistication and cosmopolitanism, but also served as a blueprint for and a warning about how Māori might respond to legislation that interfered with their land rights, or to a Royal Commission's invitation to testify on confiscations. The bones of one's ancestors and the fires of ahikaaroa could be invoked and mobilised not only via Māori law, but also via English poetry.

Kōhere might have hoped that the legislative and administrative developments of 1926 would lead to the resolution of his grievance, but, unfortunately, the cycle of repetitive petition simply continued. The hearings into the Marangairoa 1D Block in 1927, prompted by the 1926 legislation, did not resolve the issue in his favour. For the rest of his life, Kōhere continued to petition parliament for redress and continued to draw on both the actual words in Macaulay's poem, and the cluster of values that those words suggested within a Māori epistemological framework, as the legal, moral, and emotional grounds for his case.[12]

Kōhere's petitions work within the standard formula for such documents. They outline his people's case and, as the body of evidence builds up through each new inquiry, they cite more and more material from earlier decisions, histories, and commentaries, bringing in the verbatim language of elders, judges, and parliamentarians. Kōhere's petitioning is thus always an exercise in citation, in the repetition of words that he believes constitute the agreement he has with the government about his people's legitimate title to the Marangairoa 1D Block. They come back, again and again, to the central points of ancestry and occupation, conveyed in Kōhere's prose by images of bones and fire. In a 1935 letter to the Prime Minister, Kōhere lamented the 1913 ruling by the Native Land Court: 'We, by it, lost three burial-grounds in one of which my own father rests – if it be rest. [...] In order to keep the matter alive or as a Maori would say, "To keep the fires burning on the land" we have lodged another petition praying for a further hearing of the Marangairoa 1D case.'[13] He would continue to repeat himself on these topics, commenting in a 1947 petition that, despite ongoing disappointments, 'we continued petitioning, not with any hope of success, but just to use a Maori phrase, "to keep our fires burning"'.[14] In some cases, he schooled his correspondents on the significance of these metaphors in terms of land tenure, telling the Minister of Māori Affairs: 'The Maori term for occupation is "ahikaroa" [sic], or the "long burning fire".'[15] In others, he testified to the significance of the burial sites, arguing that '[t]o hand over tribal burial-grounds, in one of which my own father was buried, is heinous and ghoulish,' and asking: 'Am I to be harassed and barred from recovering my father's bones? It is unthinkable.'[16] Through multiple official documents, Kōhere produces the same ideas: bones, fire, land, and law.

It is telling, then, that one of the cycles of repetition in these documents makes use of Macaulay's poem and the cluster of ideas that it suggests.

Throughout his communications with the government, Kōhere returns to Macaulay's lines, deploying them as part of an increasingly angry discourse. In his 1929 petition, for example, Kōhere asks: 'Who would have the heart to find fault with us for fighting and, maybe, for dying, for our heritage and for "the ashes of our fathers"?'[17] In an official letter of complaint to the Under-Secretary of the Native Department in 1946, Kōhere commented: 'All Courts in the past paid me respect for they recognised I was fighting for "the ashes of my fathers," and truth.'[18] His deployment of Macaulay in these instances, and the way in which he marks out the quotation in speech marks, suggests his desire to mobilise official Pākehā sympathy for his cause by linking it to a tradition of heroic action from within the European canon. But the lines from *Horatius* are also connected directly to the *legal* case that Kōhere wishes to mount, which is based on the combination of the presence of burial grounds on the disputed land and what he calls the 'fundamental fact of occupation'.[19] The ashes of his fathers are quite literally present on the land; so too are the ashes of ahikaaroa, the principal basis for claiming occupation and thus ownership. The fact that courts in the past had 'recognised' this suggests both the sense of formal legal recognition and an underlying human sympathy that poetry can help generate.

The ways in which Māori understandings can be inferred from Macaulay's poem are even more obvious in other engagements between Kōhere and the government. In a 1930 petition, for example, Kōhere wrote:

> We are absolutely certain our case has not been dealt with on its merits and we earnestly do not wish to appear to make a threat but it has been handed down from time immemorial that for a Maori to die for his land and in defence of "the ashes of his fathers" is to die a noble death. To expect us to desist is to expect us to play the coward.[20]

Here it is a traditional concept, one rooted in Māori history, which is laid out as the basis for the claim, but in order to convey the solemnity and longevity of this concept, Kōhere turns to a quotation that he expects his Pākehā interlocutors to comprehend immediately and to connect with the validity of his argument. Macaulay's lines are cited almost as if they are a whakataukī (proverb), the kind of rhetorical device that a Māori speaker might use in a speech or whaikōrero during a negotiation or encounter. The two cultures, and their different poetic, rhetorical, and political norms, are here fused into a single appeal to both sentiment and legality.

Kōhere's understanding of the potential of his quotations emerges from within the poem's own formulations of history and its uses. While the adoption of a classical subject might not seem inherently related to the British Empire, Meredith Martin has pointed out the ways in which the imperial periphery and its subjects were central to the conception of the *Lays* volume, which she reads 'as a bridge between late eighteenth- and early nineteenth-century romantic ideas of poetry, imagined primitive communities and fragmentary history, and later revivals of these ideas'.[21] In an instantiation of what Martin calls 'the ballad-theory of civilization', Macaulay's poems aim at a universal ballad history, woven into the fabric of all societies and thus feeding and shaping a comprehensive identity for the British Empire and its peoples. Martin specifically locates this universality in the same lines from *Horatius* that Kōhere chose to quote: of the character Horatius' declaration about 'the ashes of his fathers, / And the temples of his gods', Martin notes that the poem 'is now in the universal realm – about respecting the valor of any martial enemy, the purity of it, the beauty and simplicity of combat, what is seen as pure, primitive, and perfect about war and songs about war'.[22] When we read this universalising tendency from the perspective of a British author, it is natural to locate it within a wider imperial rhetoric that aims to romanticise a primitive past and eliminate cultural difference; as Catherine Hall has pointed out, it was these lines from *Horatius*, in particular, that were 'repeated by generation after generation of boys schooled in imperial patriotism' both in Britain and in countries like New Zealand.[23] The example of Rēweti Kōhere demonstrates the ways in which such universalising might be deployed by those targeted by British imperialism to productive ends, however. It is precisely the fact that Macaulay's lines *do* appear to suggest a universal human emotion that makes them suitable for his purposes.

Moreover, Macaulay's project is entirely invested in ideas of repetition. Martin locates in the *Lays* as a whole, and in *Horatius* in particular, a pattern of what she calls 'double and triple projections', in which Macaulay yokes together British India, the glory of the British military past, Roman military success and bravery, and, in *Horatius* itself, the invocation of an even more distant past and its martial traditions to which the Roman characters in the poem are being urged to respond by Horatius when he speaks.[24] Macaulay's own historical moment is being reframed by a series of past moments and the values they appear to encode. Kōhere's project aligns with Macaulay's aims here, although not, perhaps, in the way Macaulay might have envisaged. Kōhere places a series of new projections alongside Macaulay's own ones, adding nineteenth and twentieth-century New Zealand to the sites in which the values of *Horatius* make sense and can be invoked. Macaulay's project is all too successful, in this sense: it universalises emotions and values throughout the British world to the point where they not only become the property of citizens whom he largely discounted, but get used as a measure of the moral failings of the culture that encoded them in poetry.

Reimagining Mokena

Perhaps the most significant way in which Kōhere uses this poetry is to reconfigure the reception of a nineteenth-century life, that of his grandfather Mokena. One of the last publications of Kōhere's life brought together his battles over the land, his relationships with the government, his ancestors, and the importance of Macaulay's poem to his understanding of these issues. In *A Story of a Maori Chief* (1949), his biography of Mokena, Kōhere demonstrates the ways in which Aotearoa New Zealand's nineteenth-century cultural geographies continued to affect the present. The biography included a chapter entitled 'The Native Land Court: A Long Litigation'. The chapter begins in this way:

> It has been said that the history of Kautuku (or Marangairoa 1 D) is the history of Mokena Kohere, so it would not be out of place to say something of the case in which I have been a litigant for over 35 years and in which I mean to fight until I recover my people's ancestral home and sacred places.

> It is a well-known saying of the Maoris, 'He wahine, he whenua, ka ngaro te tangata' ('For women and land men perish'). And everybody is familiar with Macaulay's words:

> To every man upon this earth
> Death cometh soon or late;
> And how can man die better
> Than facing fearful odds,
> For the ashes of his fathers,
> And the temples of his gods![25]

This chapter contains a vast array of cited material: quotes from the judges in the various Native Land Court hearings, from people who knew Mokena, from traditional Māori stories, and from the reports of various experts inquiring into the land tenure at Marangairoa. It might seem somewhat unusual for a biography to move into events well beyond the lifespan of its subject, but, for Kōhere, this was the point of the exercise. Mokena's life was entirely bound up with questions of land: how one claimed it through one's ancestors, demonstrated ahikaaroa, and how connections to the land existed without interruption through past, present, and future.

Mokena himself was associated with fire and with land, both by his grand-son-biographer and by his tribe more generally. The *Encyclopedia of New Zealand* entry for Mokena (written by another of his descendants) makes this remark about his reputation and the way it is recorded in Ngāti Porou history:

> A Ngati Porou haka contains the line, 'But for Mokena, what then?' It commemorates Mokena's timely intervention to save captured Ngati Porou Hauhau from execution at Te Pito, near East Cape. While it relates to a specific

incident, the phrase may equally be applied to Mokena's service to the people throughout his lifetime. Some years after his death it was said: 'Mokena Kohere was the chief who enabled tribal fires to be rekindled, both in Waiapu and in Poverty Bay ... much of the heritage of his people might have been lost, but for Mokena.' (ellipsis in the original)[26]

Rēweti Kōhere, meanwhile, refers to his grandfather as a 'firebrand' and 'a fiery peacemaker'.[27] He cites comments made by Mokena and passed on to him by his grandfather's acquaintances, including a remark made while Mokena hoisted the Union Jack and ensured that Ngāti Porou remained loyal to the government and thus preserved their lands from confiscation:

> E hoki ia hapu, ia hapu, ki te tahu i tana ahi, i tana ahi (Let each sub-tribe return home to re-kindle its own fire).[28]

To talk about fire, ancestry, and land was thus not simply to evoke general Māori concepts, although they too were important. Instead, the nexus of fire, ancestry, and land particularly pertained, in Rēweti Kōhere's mind, to Mokena, to the piece of land, now known as the Marangairoa 1D Block, that he had fought to protect, and to the contentious modern history of that land. Mokena was the nineteenth-century sire, the 'father', whose ashes, literal and metaphorical, needed to be remembered and rekindled in the twentieth century. For his grandson Rēweti, he was a real-life model of the imagined or generic figures to whom Macaulay alluded.

The biography of Mokena was, in fact, another piece of diplomatic text, composed by Kōhere in the hope of engaging further with the government: at one point in the biography he comments, 'I hope [Native Land Court] Judges Harvey and Beechey will some day read this book'.[29] Macaulay's words are included here as part of the evidence, alongside a host of other documents including court reports, judgements, and first-hand testimonies, as part of the history of Kōhere and his people's ongoing engagement with the New Zealand government. They are a reminder of things said in petitions, in newspaper articles, and in letters of complaint over decades. But they are also, crucially, a reminder to judges, politicians, and other figures in Pākehā public life that their own culture, the culture imported to Aotearoa New Zealand in the late eighteenth and early nineteenth centuries and used as the basis for shaping the cultural geography of the country in the mid- to late-nineteenth century, had encoded the values of land, ancestry, and mana in verse, with the metaphor of fire binding those notions together.

The rhetoric and form of Māori political communication in the period in which Kōhere was writing is usefully illustrated by these examples. Engaging the attention of the state meant writing in English, either on one's own or via a lawyer, and adopting the terms and forms of the petition. This circumstance in part reveals the power dynamics at play: the New Zealand government controlled the process by which grievances could be heard, and could thus dictate the language and shape in which the grievance could be legitimately expressed. But it also reveals Māori dexterity at working both within and beyond the parameters of this engagement. A diverse array of cultural and historical information that might be brought to bear on a question of confiscation and reparation is curated; the right evidence is brought into the frame of the negotiation, in the language of one's interlocutors and in a form that they will appreciate and comprehend. This form frequently involves citing or repeating past promises in order to establish the evidential base for reparations.

But citation and repetition were also always factors in formal Māori communication, in particular the role of whaikōrero (speechmaking) in the deliberations. One important characteristic of whaikōrero is its strategic use of repetition. Speakers repeat chants, songs, proverbs, genealogies, formulaic expressions, and the words of previous speakers, as well as their own ideas. The cited material may be sourced from any moment from the very recent past (such as a previous speaker on the same occasion) to the beginning of creation.[30] As the historian Anne Salmond has noted, there is a dynamic relationship between repetition and originality in an effective whaikōrero:

> The central text of a *whaikōrero* is still highly stylised, but unlike the opening chants it is not completely predictable in wording. The orator cuts his cloth to fit the occasion, but weaves it out of a large set of phrases which are heard over and over again, in different arrangements. These phrases are poetic and mythological, providing a sort of verbal embroidery for the speech. Skilled orators use poetic sayings with an off-hand deftness, and it is these speakers who are most likely to abandon the well-worn repertoire for something more striking and original. They coin poetry of their own, or launch into vivid, witty prose, leaving aside the standard structures altogether.[31]

As well as inhabiting European forms of communication, then, Kōhere's use of Macaulay simultaneously inhabits the rhetorical world of whaikōrero. He draws together the timescales of the early decades of the nineteenth century, when these English poems were originally composed, and the political and judicial controversies around Māori land in the early decades of the twentieth century. As techniques, citation of poetry, repetition of the words of others, and an awareness of the very distant and the very recent past were all entirely conventional elements of Māori rhetoric. Macaulay, in other words, belonged to the Māori world too.

The citations of Macaulay have the potential to create quite different effects for different audiences. To an Anglophone Pākehā reader in early-twentieth-century Aotearoa New Zealand, these lines are conventional and their author relatively canonical. The verse reads as a familiar, perhaps even predictable, poetic flourish, but they are delivered in entirely unexpected forums and contexts: Māori periodicals, petitions, and formal letters to the government. To a Māori reader, the lines are operating in an almost diametrically opposed fashion, especially on the first occasion Kōhere uses them. They are new, unfamiliar, drawn from outside the conventional storehouse of verse, but the deployment of poetry itself is not unexpected, nor is the possibility that the speaker/author will introduce a striking literary example to illustrate their point. The citation of someone else's words marks the moment at which Kōhere seems, paradoxically, most original, as he deviates from both the Māori language and the conventional whakataukī (proverbs) of Māori poetry and oratory.

But if there is an electrifying effect when he first uses these lines, there is a different kind of energy harnessed when they are repeated across many years, many texts, and many genres. The lines of poetry take root in the rhetorical space of Māori law, and while they remain a feature of Kōhere's personal expression, they have simultaneously been offered as a contribution to the collective pool of poetic resources. They are beginning a potential journey towards becoming commonplace. To a Māori reader, they are more familiar with each iteration, helping to connect, via poetry, the contexts of Māori sovereignty, Pākehā government, and New Zealand history. To the Anglophone Pākehā reader, however, they are perhaps becoming *less* familiar with each repetition. The fact of their tentative socialisation within the various Māori-authored texts in which they appear unsettles the sense in which the lines can strictly be considered English poetry, as they come to seem connected to debates in the Māori world.

Robert Te Kotahi Mahuta writes about whaikōrero as collaborative endeavours between the orator and their audience, noting that there is a skill in listening to whaikōrero effectively that is partly shaped by the mixture of repetition and originality. As Mahuta comments, skilled listeners are not paying equal attention to every element; instead, '[a]ll they need to have attention for is the new or novel theme and the reference to contemporary affairs'.[32] To different readers, for different reasons, and on different occasions, Kōhere's citation of *Horatius* would have seemed new or novel, a moment to tune in and pay attention. To twenty-first century readers, his citations might demonstrate the ways in which history, land, law, fire, bones, and poetry are part of a shared cultural tradition in Aotearoa New Zealand today.

It is this complex hybrid model of law and legality that can be seen in Kōhere's use of Macaulay. As with all the examples in this book, the choice of English-language texts, especially poems by canonical authors, reveals a profound engagement with the norms and frames of reference of potential Anglophone interlocutors. It presents the case for a resurgent Māori identity from within a European tradition and aesthetic. Poetry here is construed as promise; Macaulay's construction of a history informed by one's ancestors is taken to signal a Pākehā understanding of historical continuity and gene-alogy as central to modern identities. The poetry participates in a process that New Zealand social anthropologist Raymond Firth described in an article published at almost exactly the same moment that Kōhere first quoted Macaulay. Firth's 1926 articles on 'Proverbs in Native Life' argued that the citation and repetition of proverbs in Māori rhetoric served as 'an enforce-ment of social conduct', in which 'the precise words' operated as 'a means of praise, reproach, and stimulation'.[33] In the case of Kōhere's use of Macaulay, it is also Pākehā social conduct that is being enforced. The poem makes sense within Māori epistemology, but citing it in the original English serves as a reminder to both Pākehā and Māori interlocutors that it is also European tradition that claims to value these aspirations.

The poetry thus acts as a compelling text to mediate between two peoples and as an example of Allen's notion of the 'treaty allegory'. Pākehā audi-ences are perhaps chastened by the reminder that their own literature has spoken authoritatively about cultural sovereignty; Māori audiences are per-haps emboldened by being armed with the language and forms in which Pākehā sympathies and understandings can be harnessed, in lines that closely echo their own intellectual grounds for identity and the transfer of knowledge. Like the formal constraints of the petition, the poetry can be read as both limiting Māori expression to the language and rhetoric of the colonisers, and, simultaneously, as opening up a space in which cross-cul-tural legal interactions can occur.

The historian Michael Belgrave has described courts and commissions of inquiry in New Zealand as 'points of friction' in which Indigenous and settler narratives are rehearsed and realigned.[34] Friction connotes conflict, of course, but also a means by which power and dynamism might be released, by which fires might be generated. This generative potential is significant in the face of the typical intentions of a court or commission of inquiry into Indigenous land in the settler colonies, including Aotearoa New Zealand. There are not many nouns that naturally take the verb 'to extinguish' in English, but 'fire' and 'native title' certainly do. The literary symbolism and legal ramifications of history's ashes could not be clearer for Indigenous peoples.

Notes

1 Rēweti Tūhorouta Kōhere, 'Nga Kupu Tohunga' [Wise Sayings], *Te Toa Takitini*, 62 (October 1926), 481. I have given the lines here as they are presented in *Te Toa Takitini,* a presentation which replaces the comma at the end of line 8 with a question mark in order to suggest a self-contained quote, and which does not capitalise 'Gods'. For an authorised version of the text, see Thomas Babington Macaulay, *The Life and Works of Lord Macaulay*, vol. 8 (London: Longmans,

Green and Co., 1897), pp. 466–84. Kōhere's Māori version reads: 'Ki ia tangata, ki ia tangata i tenei ao / He mate ano te mutunga a tona ra, / A he aha te mate tika atu mo te tangata / I te whawhai ki nga tino kaha / Mo nga koiwi o nga matua, / Mo nga ahurewa o ona atua?' This chapter uses modern diacritical marks for Māori-language texts, except in cases of quotation where the original source did not. It also uses Aotearoa, the Māori name for New Zealand, when appropriate.

2 Thomas Babington Macaulay, 'Von Ranke, *Edinburgh Review,* October 1840', in *Critical, Historical, and Miscellaneous Essays and Poems*, vol. 2 (Philadelphia: Porter and Coates, 1879), p. 466.

3 See, e.g., Robert Dingley, 'The Ruins of the Future: Macaulay's New Zealander and the Spirit of the Age', in Alan Sandison and Robert Dingley (eds), *Histories of the Future: Studies in Fact, Fantasy and Science Fiction* (Basingstoke: Palgrave Macmillan, 2000), pp. 15–33; and D. Skilton, 'Contemplating the Ruins of London: Macaulay's New Zealander and Others', *Literary London: Interdisciplinary Studies in the Representation of London,* 2:2 (2004), http://literarylondon.org/the-literary-london-journal/archive-of-the-literary-london-journal/issue-2-1/contemplating-the-ruins-of-london-macaulays-new-zealander-and-others/ (accessed 10 October 2019). Interestingly, there is an example of another Indigenous person reading Macaulay's New Zealander as probably Māori; in Adam Spry's discussion of the Anishinaabe periodical *The Progress*, he notes an article in which the contributor known as 'Wah-Boose' ('Rabbit') comments: 'Macauley [sic] says that history has a tendency to repeat itself; in his mind's eye he saw the New Zeelander [sic] gazing from the bridge upon the ruins of London! Pursue the analogy, and might not the future red man gaze upon the ruins of New York and Brooklyn from their great suspension bridge?' See Adam Spry, *Our War Paint Is Writers' Ink: Anishinaabe Literary Transnationalism* (Albany: SUNY Press, 2018), p. 40.

4 A detailed history of the signing of the Treaty of Waitangi can be found in C. Orange, *The Treaty of Waitangi,* 2nd edn (Wellington: Bridget Williams Books, 2011).

5 Chadwick Allen, *Blood Narrative: Indigenous Identity in American Indian and Maori Literary and Activist Texts* (Durham and London: Duke University Press, 2002), p. 20.

6 For information on ahikaaroa, see Hirini Moko Mead, *Tikanga Māori: Living by Māori Values* (Wellington: Huia Publishers, 2003), pp. 41–3, 359; and Mason Durie, *Te Mana, Te Kāwanatanga: The Politics of Māori Self-Determination* (Auckland: Oxford University Press, 1998), pp. 115–16.

7 Rēweti Tūhorouta Kōhere, 'Nga Kupu Tohunga', 481–2.

8 A very detailed history of the struggle over the Marangairoa Block, written by a member of the Kōhere family, can be found in Rarawa Kōhere, 'Tāwakewake: An Historical Case Study and Situational Analysis of Ngāti Ruawaipu Leadership' (PhD dissertation, Massey University, 2005). There is an especially clear and succinct appendix which outlines the history of the litigation (pp. 339–42).

9 These petitions can be found in the National Archives of New Zealand (hereafter NANZ) Wellington, MA1 Box 111, 112, and 113.

10 See the statement by Prime Minister and Native Affairs Minister Gordon Coates, which linked the introduction of the bill and the establishment of the Royal Commission, in *New Zealand Parliamentary Debates*, 208 (1925), 773–4. The full title of Commission was 'Royal Commission to Inquire into Confiscations of Native Lands and Other Grievances Alleged by Natives'.

11 The debate on the Native Land Amendment and Native Land Claims Adjustment Bill in the lower and upper houses of Parliament can be found in *New Zealand Parliamentary Debates*, 211 (1926), 285–95, 378–9. The section about Marangairoa 1D was not the subject of any comment in these debates, however. For more detail on the Royal Commission, see Bryan Gilling, 'Raupatu: The Punitive Confiscation of Maori Land in the 1860s', in Richard Boast and Richard S. Hill (eds), *Raupatu: The Confiscation of Maori Land* (Wellington: Victoria University Press, 2009), pp. 13–30; Mark Hickford, 'Strands from the Afterlife of Confiscation: Property Rights, Constitutional Histories and the Political Incorporation of Maori, 1920s', in Boast and Hill (eds), *Raupatu: The Confiscation of Maori Land*, pp. 169–204; and Richard S. Hill, *Enthroning 'Justice above Might'? The Sim Commission, Tainui and the Crown* (Wellington: Department of Justice, 1989). The Royal Commission's findings were published as *Confiscated Native Lands and Other Grievances. Report of the Royal Commission to Inquire into Confiscations of Native Lands and Other Grievances Alleged by Natives* (1928).

12 A detailed summary of the various hearings and decisions around the Marangairoa 1D Block up until the mid-1930s can be found in the 27 April 1936 memorandum in NANZ, Wellington, MA1 Box 112, Petition No. 286/32.

13 NANZ, Wellington, MA1 Box 112, letter by Rēweti Tūhorouta Kōhere, 12 February 1935.

14 NANZ, Wellington, MA1 Box 112, Petition No. 97/1947, p. 3, petition by Rēweti Tūhorouta Kōhere et al.

15 NANZ, Wellington, MA1 Box 113, p. 1, letter by Rēweti Tūhorouta Kōhere, 29 June 1953.

16 NANZ, Wellington, MA1 Box 112, p. 19, Rēweti Tūhorouta Kōhere, 'Charge of Bias against Judges J. Harvey and E. M. Beechey'; and NANZ, Wellington, MA1 Box 113, p. 1, letter by Rēweti Tūhorouta Kōhere, 3 June 1950.

17 NANZ, Wellington, MA1 Box 111, Petition No. 98/1929, p. 4, letter by Rēweti Tūhorouta Kōhere et al.

18 NANZ, Wellington, MA1 Box 112, p. 17, Rēweti Tūhorouta Kōhere, 'Charge of Bias against Judges J. Harvey and E. M. Beechey'.

19 NANZ, Wellington, MA1 Box 111, Petition No. 98/1929, p. 1, petition by Rēweti Tūhorouta Kōhere et al.

20 NANZ, Wellington, MA1 Box 111, Petition No. 87/1930, pp. 1–2, petition by Rēweti Tūhorouta Kōhere et al.

21 Meredith Martin, '"Imperfectly Civilized": Ballads, Nations, and Histories of Form', *ELH*, 82:2 (2015), 360.

22 Martin, '"Imperfectly Civilized": Ballads, Nations, and Histories of Form', 357.

23 Catherine Hall, 'Macaulay's Nation', *Victorian Studies*, 51:3 (2009), 518.

24 Martin, '"Imperfectly Civilized": Ballads, Nations, and Histories of Form', 355.

25 Rēweti Tūhorouta Kohere, *The Story of a Maori Chief* (Wellington: Reed, 1949), p. 86. He would again make reference to the whakatauki 'For women and land men perish' in a letter to the Minister of Māori Affairs about the Marangairoa 1D land block; see NANZ, Wellington, MA1 Box 113, p. 1, letter by Rēweti Tūhorouta Kōhere, 29 June 1953.
26 Rarawa Kōhere. 'Kohere, Mokena,' in *Dictionary of New Zealand Biography*, vol. 1, 1990, https://teara.govt.nz/en/biographies/1k15/kohere-mokena (accessed 2 October 2017).
27 Rēweti Tūhorouta Kohere, *The Story of a Maori Chief,* pp. 37, 45–6.
28 Rēweti Tūhorouta Kohere, *The Story of a Maori Chief,* p. 58.
29 Rēweti Tūhorouta Kohere, *The Story of a Maori* Chief, p. 87.
30 Poia Rewi, *Whaikōrero: The World of Māori Oratory* (Auckland: Auckland University Press, 2010), p. 19.
31 Anne Salmond, *Hui: A Study of Maori Ceremonial Gathering*, rev. edn (Auckland: Penguin, 2004), pp. 164–5. See also Rewi, *Whaikōrero: The World of Māori Oratory*.
32 Robert Te Kotahi Mahuta, 'Whaikoorero: A Study of Formal Maori Speech' (MA dissertation, University of Auckland, 1974), p. 7. See also Salmond, *Hui: A Study of Maori Ceremonial Gatherings,* p. 165.
33 Raymond Firth, 'Proverbs in Native Life, with Special Reference to those of the Maori, II (Continued)', *Folklore*, 37:3 (1926), 259, 261, 264.
34 Michael Belgrave, *Historical Frictions: Maori Claims & Reinvented Histories* (Auckland: Auckland University Press, 2005), p. 3.

16

Vigilance: petitions, politics, and the African Christian converts of the nineteenth century

Hlonipha Mokoena

It is not too much to say, that the intercourse of Europeans in general, without any exception in favour of the subjects of Great Britain, has been, unless when attended by missionary exertions, a source of many calamities to uncivilized nations. (Aborigines Protection Society [House of Commons], 1837, 3–4)

The demise of the word 'liberal', and the increasing opprobrium that is heaped upon it, is a consequence, in part, of its unchecked relationship to the history of colonialism. This failure of a political idea to take root in imperial outposts is, however, not a simple matter of hypocrisy, double-dealing, or inadequacy.[1] In the case of South Africa, the failure can be attributed to the fact that some of the country's earliest and most earnest 'liberals' were 'black', and the difficulty has often been in understanding how these black writers and thinkers contributed to the liberal tradition and why at some point they abandoned this tradition in favour of more radical and revolutionary ideas.[2] This forgotten history of liberalism and the liberal tradition means that almost by definition the word 'liberal' has come to mean 'a well-meaning white person' in South Africa. This chapter will trace the collapse of the liberal tradition in southern Africa through the instrument of the petition, which emerged as an important tool for marking sites of contestation and expressing the grievances of educated and converted African Christians (amakholwa), as well as of black professionals, black journalists, black clergy, and other marginalised groups in the nascent literary culture of nineteenth-century South Africa. The petitioners are almost always black/ African and their ideas about their relationship to the Empire and especially to Queen Victoria are what distinguishes their writing from any other type of political writing in South Africa. In their constant interaction with not just settlers but a variety of colonial and imperial officials, these petitioners often spoke the language of legal rights more consistently and more forcefully than would have been expected at the time.

The main endowment that made such a petition culture possible was the arrival of the printing press in southern Africa and the manner in which this technology changed the relationship between the state and its subjects. As a genre of political writing, the petition serves the function of not just delineating the political from the civil; it is also in itself a sign of the penetration of print culture into the consciousness and daily experiences of those who were by law British subjects but who were in practice excluded from the colonial privileges that accompanied subjugation. Even 'illiterate' African kings would occasionally appear as signatories to such petitions.[3] In choosing to use the printed word as an expression of political subjecthood, these men and women often invoked the notion of 'vigilance' as the raison d'etre of their actions. Their watchfulness over the actions and policies of successive colonial governments constitutes what I would call the 'major' tradition of liberal ideas in South Africa.

The distinction between 'minor' and 'major' traditions is important for understanding the fate of their ideas. As with other colonies, nearly all ideas in southern Africa arrived here 'second hand', and they were therefore always susceptible to failure and alteration.[4] At its inception, the liberal tradition was associated with missionaries and therein lay its future challenges. This constitutes a 'major' tradition in so far as these missionaries were themselves connected to other progressive movements in the imperial metropole, what became known as the 'Exeter Hall' social and philanthropic movements.[5] These interconnections and networks created the space for Indigenous and African proponents of liberal ideas to express their understanding of what such ideas might mean under the specific conditions of settler colonialism in South Africa. For a long while, these Africanised versions of liberal thought worked within the major tradition, until they could no longer subscribe to their 'tutelage' under the leadership of the missionary and/or were overtaken by the emergence of charismatic prophets and independent churches. By the end of the nineteenth century and the beginning of the twentieth, it became increasingly clear that the major liberal tradition would not deliver the promised political, economic, and civil rights to the African population. Thus, beginning in the 1930s, alternative ideas such as Garveyism, Ethiopianism, trade unionism, and Africanism began to splinter what had been previously an almost unanimous African politics into many 'minor' traditions – and liberalism became one of them. This chapter will therefore trace the manner in which the major liberal tradition failed to live up to its promise and thereby vacated the political ground that had been gained by the nineteenth-century African liberal advocates.

The alternation between Dutch and British rule in the Cape Colony has created an insurmountable challenge in tracing a single thread of liberal thought and political traditions from the colonial period to the present.[6] The importation of slaves, beginning in 1658, was the first instance of an illiberal policy that would initiate the liberal and 'enlightened' challenges to Dutch East India Company rule and later to slavery itself.[7] This is the foundation from which this chapter proposes to launch an argument about the history of protest literature in South Africa. Contrary to popular belief and perception, protest literature did not begin in the 1960s but is actually a long-standing tradition of South African letters; its provenance can be dated back to the beginning of the 'Anglicisation' of the Cape Colony and the attendant institutions and cultural assumptions that arrived with the British and the English language. What characterises this protest is not just that it was directed at the British Empire or the Queen of England, but that it was couched in the language of rights, citizenship, and subjecthood. This is what distinguishes it from the African Nationalism or Africanism that would define African politics from the 1960s to the end of apartheid. In the colonial era, protest was directed at the failure of the British Empire to recognise the black population as British subjects. This language of supplication may seem belaboured and ingratiating to our contemporary understanding, but in the colonial period it served the purpose of reinforcing the status and respectability of those who earnestly believed that British rule would be beneficent and uplifting.[8] Our retrospective understanding of the Empire's failures should not therefore interfere with the seriousness with which we read the writing and thought of these early black Victorians, who wished to be protected and recognised by the 'Great White Queen' presiding over the expansive British dominions.[9]

The major tradition: British rule and the ascendance of missionary discourse

The beginning of British rule in 1806 was not only about legal, commercial, political, and administrative reform; it was also the beginning of a long and contested tradition of Anglicisation that would affect the future of the Indigenous population of South Africa.[10] Initially, this Anglicisation involved no more than changed governorships, school curricula, and the arrival of missionaries, especially members of the London Missionary Society (LMS). The full impact of the Anglicisation of Cape discourse can perhaps be traced to the publication of the Scottish missionary Dr John Philip's *Researches in South Africa* (1828), which could be said to be the country's first anti-slavery text as well as its first 'minority' report. In the text, not only did Philip equate the treatment of the Indigenous Khoesan to slavery, but he also charged the settlers with general inhumanity towards their indentured servants and a denial of their rights as British subjects:

We have offered no particular directions about the machinery of government desirable in such a country. We have recommended no checks but such as are necessary to prevent one class of British subjects from oppressing and destroying another. In what we propose we suspend no weight upon the wheels of government. We ask nothing for the poor natives more than this, that they should have the protection the law affords to the colonists. There is nothing surely in these claims, against which the shadow of an objection can be urged.[11]

The importance of this text is not just its diagnostic quality but the fact that it generated a backlash response from the settlers who up to that point had never defended slavery or colonialism. This emergence of a settler historiography inaugurated the major tradition of 'separate but equal' and could therefore be linked to the emergence of Afrikaner nationalism and later apartheid.[12]

As a seminal point in the history of the liberal tradition in South Africa, Philip's *Researches* marks the beginning of what may be called the petition politics of African Christian converts. This nascent protest politics was epitomised by the 1836 delegation that went to London to present the case of the 'native' population of the colony to the Aborigines Protection Society (APS). There were many other such delegations to follow, but what marks this one as important was that it was a 'non-racial' or 'multi-racial' delegation consisting of men who were all the products of colonial encounter in one way or another. The term 'black' or 'African' is therefore already insufficient to capture the 'non-racial' character of the politics of protest that was symbolised by this 1836 delegation. This chapter will take this moment as the watershed moment of African liberalism and the nascent vigilance culture that would find better and more voluble articulation in subsequent decades.

Even before the evidence presented to the APS and the Select Committee of the House of Commons, the change in jurisdiction from the Dutch to the English had already had an impact on understandings of race, power, and citizenship. The decision of the Dutch East India Company, the Verenidge Oostindische Compagnie (VOC), to apportion land to free burghers, and thus allow for the farming, grazing, and ownership of land beyond the control of the Company, had already had a profound impact on the self-understanding of the settlers, who began to make claims not just against the Company but against Indigenes. This emergence of a language of rights would affect the structure and nature of British rule since the British would find that they were expected to simply endorse such rights as had been enjoyed under the VOC. Perhaps the only exception to this was in the case of accusations of corruption, where merchants and free burghers would accuse Company officials of corrupt practices.[13] The introduction of English common law was easily accepted by the free burghers; the introduction of the notion of equality before the law, less so. In terms of the impact of liberal ideas on this transformative period, it is no surprise that one of the areas of contention was the freedom of the press. Under Dutch rule, the only publications to emanate from the Cape were almanacs; there was no newspaper to speak of. Under the influence of the Scottish emigrés Thomas Pringle and John Fairbarn, the Cape denizens could read news reports in the *South African Commercial Advertiser* (established in 1824) and the *South African Journal* (also established in 1824 as Pringle's sole venture).[14] In the very same year that these publications were established, the two editors clashed with the then governor, Lord Charles Somerset, who accused the publications of opposing his government. This clash is often cited as the beginning of the struggle for the press in South Africa, since Somerset's position was that the press was an instrument at the disposal of the colonial government and should therefore be under its control. It was not until Ordinance 60 of 1829 that press freedom was recognised at the Cape as entailing the right of the press to dissent from government policy or opinion. It should also be added that this ordinance did not imply that African newspapers or those papers that were bilingual or published in Indigenous languages would automatically be granted the same freedom. This moment was almost exclusively about the liberal English-language press. The struggles for the autonomy of the black press were yet to come.

The change in rulership at the Cape should also be understood as the intensification of what have, in South African historiography, become known as the 'frontier wars', a term used to define a variety of conflicts that started around 1779 and ended in 1878. This is an important ingredient in the history of petitions and protest literature because, as is clear from the APS summation in the epigraph to this chapter, depredation stood in contrast to liberal ideas and added up to so many 'calamities'. There is already an extensive literature on these wars of dispossession, but what has often not been noted are the various roles played by 'intermediaries' who trafficked in both peace and war, and who would often be found translating the meanings of British annexations, boundaries, expropriations, and extortions. These intermediaries were often, but not always, men of colour, who would later give full or partial accounts of the role that they played in these conflicts and their conduct. In many instances their job descriptions in the colonial record are simply 'messengers' or 'frontier natives', and so their roles are often obscured. Missionaries were particularly invested in the identity of the 'frontier native':

> That the social effects which the liquor traffic is producing among the native people are equally to be deplored. Physically considered, the frontier natives of this country have few equals; but since they have had free access to intoxicating drink and acquired drinking habits, the effects is already seen in the shrivelled

and palsied forms, the cringing whining mien, the loss of all manliness and
self-respect; and if nothing be done to save them as a people they and their
children will sink to the level of Bushmen and degraded Hottentots.[15]

The quote above encapsulates two themes: first, that of the 'frontier native'
as a kind of barometer for the health and breadth of the 'civilising mission';
if the frontier native falls into a state of degradation and incapacitation then
that undermines the entirety of the colonial and mission projects. Second,
the United Missionary Conference presented these arguments as a memorial, and this hints at the ways in which the missionary and the mission
stations became the source of the language of supplication and entreaty. The
frontier native was therefore the first petitioner, as it were, since his or her
voice and point of view was ventriloquised by the missionaries to plead for
the prohibition of the sale of intoxicating drink to all Africans. The additional argument is obviously that to have a frontier native requires a frontier, and the implication is therefore that the frontier native was exactly that
African who was already a product of colonialism and mission intervention
and tutelage. This position as an intermediary was secured by the exemplary
role that he or she played in being an embodiment of the ideals of missionary endeavour. That is why it was so important for these intermediaries to
not fail or succumb to the allure of European vices.

The frontier wars are therefore important not just because of what they
tell us about the history of warfare and dispossession in South Africa but
also because of what they tell us about the communities and people who
were created by and emerged from this extended period of inconclusive
guerrilla warfare between the Indigenes and the British. In the face of the
Cape's new identity as a colony, therefore, the frontier wars shifted the
debate from the two metropoles of Cape Town and London to the extremities of the colonial territory and created what may be regarded as border-
lands. These open frontiers would play an important role in the emergence
of a literate and opinionated African elite whose sole function would be to
represent the position of the frontier native and to assuage missionary fears
that their efforts would be drowned in barrels of brandy.[16] It is therefore not
surprising that appended to the memorial of 1884 is 'native opinion' in the
form of quotes from the said frontier natives, who were opposed to the
opening of canteens and the sale of liquor to Africans.

The minor tradition: 'Hottentot nationalism' and the petition

John Philip's *Researches in South Africa* is important for another reason
and that is because it essentially presented the viewpoint of the people

whom the colonists had dubbed the 'Hottentots'. This terminology and identity has necessarily become complicated, since even the terms 'Khoe-san' or 'Khoekhoe' are continually debated.[17] The identity referred to is of the Indigenous communities who lived as hunter-gatherers and pastoralists across southern Africa. In colonial records and in the present they are identified as 'different' from the 'Bantu' physiologically, linguistically, socially, and culturally. These distinctions are only relevant for our argument to the extent that Philip used the term 'aborigines' to mean these communities, many of whom had congregated on mission stations, in part as a defence against a century of concerted genocide.[18] Thus, in political and philosophical terms, Philip was speaking and writing about a community or communities that were already relegated to the past tense and regarded as diminished in numbers from their previous multitude. This confluence between what may be termed missionary genocide studies and post-slavery discourses of freedom created the canvas on which Philip painted a picture of a community that was in search of a national identity and security of tenure. These two forces were later given the term 'Hottentot nationalism' by the historian Stanley Trapido.[19]

In Philip's terms, such national feeling and sentiment was still largely thought of as an expression of Hegelian self-determination, and there was therefore no 'actual' country or territory on to which this nationalism was mapped. This conception of a 'people without country' is articulated in Philip's statements about the Khoesan as a 'free people':

> Independent of printed statutes, there are certain rights which human beings possess, and of which they cannot be deprived but by manifest injustice. The wanderer in the desert has a right to his life, to his liberty, his wife, his children, and his property. The Hottentot has a right to a fair price for his labour; to an exemption from cruelty and oppression; to choose the place of his abode, and to enjoy the society of his children; and no one can deprive him of those rights without violating the laws of nature and of nations. If the perpetration of such outrages against the laws of nature and of nations is a crime, that crime is greatly aggravated when it is committed against the *lex loci*, against the written law of the land. The Hottentots, in addition to the unalienable rights conferred upon them by their Creator, have prescriptive rights in their favour; they are regarded by the British government as a free people; and the colonial law says, that they are to be treated in their persons, in their properties, and in their possessions, the same as other free people.[20]

The 'wanderer in the desert' was therefore not just meant to stand in for an actual hunter-gatherer but was also a response to the colonial and settler charge that because the 'Hottentots' did not cultivate the land, it could not belong to them and was thus *terra nullius*. By vacating such settler claims with the abstract notion of the 'wanderer in the desert', Philip was also dispensing with the colonial accusation that these communities (or remnants of these communities) were vagrants and should be expected to carry passes.

As a further expansion on the notion of 'free people', Philip then argued that it would in fact be in the interest of the colonists to give the 'Hottentots' the civil rights due to them, that their 'free labour' would be advantageous to the colony. Again, these arguments are not made in purely instrumental language but are drawn from discourses that had already been practised in anti-slavery movements:

> The remark of Tacitus, that 'there is nothing so sweet to man as the life of man,' is not more severe, as a reflection on human nature, than it is just, as respects its accordance with truth; and any system, which proposes to substitute free labour in the place of slave labour, is as great a bugbear to the generality of men accustomed to treat a particular class of their fellow creatures as slaves, as the representative system of Great Britain, or of Portugal, is to Ferdinand of Spain and his advisers and masters, who would rather see a country converted into a desert, than the inhabitants breathing the air of freedom.[21]

As a missionary, it is understandable why Philip supported the 'free labour' of his Khoesan converts, since it was only in such a state of freedom that these would-be acolytes could join mission stations and contribute to the furtherance of the Christian gospel. But self-interest is not the complete story. As with other missionaries in the field, Philip knew that he had to ventriloquise the thoughts and feelings of his converts since the power of the printing press was still mainly under missionary control. It is this control of printed media that makes his *Researches* an instalment in the minor tradition of missionary resistance, as the voices of his informants could only be heard from the vantage point of the mission station (and in some instances the British military).

In the history of missiology in South Africa, the names of mission stations – Bethelsdorp, Kat River, and Theopolis – have become synonymous not only with the missionary labours and failures of these cases of freedom but also with the rebellions that took place there.[22] It is in these rebellions that one hears the voices of the Africans who were petitioning the British government in their own words. However, before these can be considered it is important to highlight that the main achievement of the Exeter Hall campaigns in South Africa was the promulgation of Ordinance 50 of 1828, which has sometimes been pejoratively called the 'Hottentot Magna Carta'. This ordinance repealed the 1809 ordinance which had legalised the de facto enslavement of the Indigenous population while reinforcing the legality of passes as an instrument for controlling the labour of slaves and Indigenous people.

Ordinance 50 was therefore the main achievement of what might be termed the major tradition of liberalism in the Cape Colony.[23] This triumph could, however, also be said to have laid the foundation for the emergence of the minor tradition, since no sooner had the Khoesan been recognised as a 'free people' than the settlers began to find means to amend such rights: for example, by pressing for tighter vagrancy laws.

In the immediate aftermath of Ordinance 50 in 1829, the converts of Bethelsdorp and other mission stations drafted a memorial. In introducing their voices, the mission residents had to first express humility, even while using the indicative 'Sheweth'. This demonstrative and diagnostic finger-pointing would then extend to their own version of the history of depredation and dispossession. The tone of the memorial was to verbalise that despite the disadvantages and humiliation of being the dispossessed, the memorialists had nonetheless ticked the boxes of civilisation by acquiring property and livestock. Thus, beyond being an expression of supplication, the petition is also a reproduction of the ideological foundations of mission stations – the rewards of Christian sobriety and hard work; the negation of sloth and idleness through cultivation; and the usefulness of the communities to their settler neighbours. In their own words, the petitioners appealed not just for themselves but for their descendants:

> The Memorial of divers inhabitants of the district of Uitenhage, sprung principally from the Gona and other Hottentot tribes,
> Humbly Sheweth,
> That Memorialists have long been members of Bethelsdorp and can appeal confidently to their Missionaries and neighbours for testimony of their conduct as mechanics; and in their various pursuits.
> That hitherto want of land has checked the natural increase of their cattle, and deprived memorialists of the just reward of industry; nevertheless, under great disadvantages, some of them have acquired waggons, oxen, cows, goats, sheep and other property; and all possess competent skill in husbandry and as mechanics.
>
> That they wish to obtain grants upon certain tracts situated near the sea, between the Bosjesman and Sunday rivers, together with the Gora and lands adjacent in Uitenhage, at about half-way from Bethelsdorp to Theopolis and to settle there.
> That they have been informed of applications being recently made for the said lands; but they submit their own claims to be superior to those of any other persons whatever, and especially to the claims of individuals already possessing extensive farms.
> That memorialists know the value of instruction for their children, and of suitable means of religious communion for themselves; and trust to obtain the benefit of the provision recommended by His Majesty's Commissioners of

Inquiry in that behalf; to which they doubt not they may be able, hereafter, in a reasonable time to contribute.

That it may be right to impose certain conditions upon memorialists, in order to secure these grants to their children.[24]

As is evident, the memorialists had imbibed the idea that they were 'free' labourers whose industry and economy should have enabled them to enjoy the fruits of their efforts. This memorial therefore functions as an echo of Philip's exhortations that the 'free labour' ideology was the only ballast against settler oppression and that it was the function of the British government to ensure that the Khoesan were accorded the same rights as other British subjects. Thus, by 1829, the debate had already shifted away from the abstraction of land as the possession of the Indigenes to the idea that work and industry confer rights of occupation, ownership, and usage to those who have 'competent skill in husbandry and [work] as mechanics'.

This missionary moment and the ascendance of a minor liberal tradition can perhaps be best summed up by the testimony given by Andries Stoffels – who has been variously described as a Gonaqua, former Bethelsdorp resident, Kat River convert, and representative of the Khoekhoen – to the Select Committee on Aborigines in London in 1836. Stoffels travelled to England as part of a deputation that included John Philip, Jan Tshatshu, James Read Jr., and James Read Sr. The illustrated image of the five men itself speaks volumes about the nature and origins of both the minor and major liberal traditions in the Cape. Each man represented the zenith and nadir of each tradition (Figure 16.1).

When he appeared in front of the Select Committee in the House of Commons, Stoffels was cross-examined by the commissioners about his biography, and he replied, according to George McCall Theal, 'in accordance with their training':[25]

4938. *Chairman*: Are you a native of South Africa? – Yes.
4939. Do you belong to the Hottentots? – Yes.
4940. Were you one of the Kat River settlers? – Yes.
4941. Did you live for some years at Bethelsdorf before you went to the Kat River? – Yes, I lived at Bethelsdorf a long time.
4942. What is your age? – Between 50 and 60.
4943. Will you give the Committee a little outline of your life; where did you spend your early years? – We lived in the mountains till the missionaries, Vanderkemp and Read, came amongst us, then I came amongst human beings.
4944. How many years is it since you lived at Bethelsdorf? – I went to Bethelsdorf, when Dr. Vanderkemp left Graaff Reinet to come to Bethelsdorf; I then left Zuurveldt to come to the missionary station.
4945. You knew Dr. Vanderkemp? – Yes.

Figure 16.1 Richard Woodman, 'Jan or Dyani Tzatzoe (Tshatshu); Andries Stoffles; James Read Sr; James Read Jr; John Philip', published by Fisher Son & Co, after Henry Room, line and stipple engraving, 1844

4946. Was he a good man? – Yes.
4947. Did he labour hard for the benefit of the Hottentots? – Yes; it was after Dr. Vanderkemp and Mr. Read came among us that we put off our skins and put on clothes.

Although this is not a petition in the strict sense of the word, it does exhibit what Theal acerbically called 'training' since it is rhetorically aimed at giving the commissioners a sense of the massive physical and spiritual transformations that Andries Stoffels and other 'Hottentots' underwent in order to be 'amongst human beings'. The delegation was timed to coincide with the hearings of the Committee but also included an extensive 'humanitarian' tour of the United Kingdom. It was the first of many deputations by what one commentator referred to as the *rarae aves* of Africa, who had come to the metropole to petition the English monarch.[26] The importance of these moments was that their purpose was to present Africans as human beings who deserved to be treated justly even as they were being colonised. As with the other instruments of the major liberal tradition, the procession of African deputations would soon enough become obsolete.

Imbumba | ball of sinews: the making of protest politics in the 1880s

The last rebellion to take place on a mission station occurred on the Kat River Settlement, and in three years (1851–53) the world of the many adherents of the liberal tradition was irreversibly shattered. With the disbandment of the Kat River communities, the role played by missionaries in petitioning for Africans shifted since so many of their converts were dispersed. This also led to a geographical shift as various denominations began to compete and spread across the subcontinent. The decline of the LMS as the main mouthpiece for Africans should be seen not just as a collapse of the internal resources of the liberal tradition but also as an outcome of the arrival of other competing mission ideologies. Thus, by the 1880s, when eastern Cape Africans began establishing their own associations and organisations, there were already denominations of opinion and dissent among the black population. This denominationalism became the first hurdle to circumvent in the search for an 'African' voice, as expressed by S. N. Mvambo:

> Anyone looking at things as they are, could even go so far as to say it was a great mistake to bring so many church denominations to the Black people. For the Black man makes the fatal mistake of thinking that if he is an Anglican, he has nothing to do with anything suggested by a Wesleyan, and the Wesleyan also thinks so, and so does the Presbyterian. *Imbumba* must make sure that all these three are represented at the conference, for we must be united on political matters. In fighting for national rights, we must fight together. Although they look as if they belong to various churches, the White people are solidly united when it comes to matters of this nature. We Blacks think that these churches are hostile to one another, and in that way we lose our political rights.[27]

Also, unlike with the early 'Hottentot nationalism', the question of nationality and nationhood became hotly contested since many of these African converts were members of diverse 'ethnic' groups. Again, a note of caution should be added since the term 'ethnicity' comes loaded with the presumption of 'difference'. In reality, 'ethnicity' amounted mostly to an adherence to language, custom, and culture, and not to some inherent and intrinsic racial type. It was also on mission stations that such ethnic identities were negotiated, and sometimes elements of custom were abandoned in favour of an 'African' identity. Thus, as with the eighteenth- and early-nineteenth-century Khoesan Christian converts, the converts of the southeast coast found themselves a 'people without country', and the language of nationalism functioned as an imagined community to which these unmoored Africans could cling. The melting-pot culture of mission stations continued its function of moulding novel and sometimes unsettling identities, as a new group of Africans found its protest voice.[28] These 'new Africans' would also be much more in control of the printing press; their liberal and Victorian ideas were therefore more directly communicated, with the missionary playing less and less of a role as a spokesperson.[29]

The quintessential black liberal of this period was John Tengo Jabavu (1859–1921), who established the newspaper *Imvo Zabantsundu* ('The Black Opinion'), and his political views would dominate (both constructively and destructively) African opinion until the end of the century and the beginning of the Edwardian era.[30] The aspirations and achievements of this elite were represented in book form by T. D. Mweli Skota, who circa 1930 published *The African Yearly Register: Being an Illustrated National Biographical Dictionary (Who's Who) of Black Folks in Africa*.[31] Although intended to be an annual register, only one volume was published, and this fact epitomises the precarious and changing fortunes that this class of literati experienced in the twentieth century. The period between the creation of *Imbumba Yama Nyama* in 1882 and the victory of the National Party in 1948 could be said to have been the crucible of the liberal tradition, since those Africans who had voting rights in the Cape Colony (a right promulgated in 1854 and abrogated in 1936) continued to use this electoral instrument to impact parliamentary, colonial, and imperial politics, while those Africans who did not live in the colony continued to uphold its qualified electoral franchise as the desired political end of their activities.

The establishment of the South African Native National Congress (SANNC) in 1912 has created a retrospective historicisation in which it is assumed that, first, this was the first expression of the political ideology that would become known as African Nationalism and, second, that the evolution of SANNC into the African National Congress (ANC) in 1923 was a political fait accompli. In reality, the creation of SANNC was an outcome of already complex and competing egos and political ideas and positions. In 1912, apartheid was still a far-off reality, and the main concern of the men who met to create the organisation was not state racism; their main impetus was the exclusion of Africans from the deliberations concerning the unification of South Africa. The congregation of these men (for a long while women were present but excluded from officiating) was the culmination of a protest politics that had begun with the formation of organisations such as *Imbumba Yama Nyama* and, in 1884, the Native Education Association and the Native Electoral Association. All these organisations were concerned with uniting black Africans to contest the already existing electoral politics of the nascent country of South Africa; their goal was not 'autonomy' or 'self-determination'. The main weakness of these early organisations was that they met irregularly.

It is these movements that define the word 'vigilance'. Since many of these associations did not and could not directly challenge the existing political order created by the successive granting of responsible and representative government to the white minority, they could only engage in piecemeal and reformist parleys with white politicians and white capitalist interests. Even before the convening of SANNC, another intellectual of this period, Pixley ka Isaka Seme, penned an article and an invitation in 1911, published in John Tengo Jabavu's paper *Imvo Zabantsundu*, in which he wrote about 'Native Union'. Seme envisioned the purpose of a native congress as follows:

> The South African Native Congress is the voice in the wilderness bidding all the dark races of this sub-continent to come together once or twice a year in order to review the past and reject therein all those things which have retarded our progress, the things which poison the springs of our national life and virtue; to label and distinguish the sins of civilisation, and as members of one house-hold to talk and think loudly on our home problems and the solution of them.[32]

This was hardly a charter for radical politics or populist sentiment, and this would be the vein in which successive leaders of the Congress movement would think and articulate the concerns of the Africans.

While Africans were organising in their associations, white settler interests became more racially defined, especially after the Anglo-Boer War (South African War, 1899–1902), with Britain eager to conciliate the injured pride of Afrikaner republics by sacrificing the interests and welfare of the African population. Thus, where Ordinance 50 of 1828 was the apex of LMS agitation, the settlers began to whittle down the freedoms granted to Africans by challenging the non-racial franchise and also imposing restrictions on black people's right of movement. The Cape Colony, for example, passed a Vagrancy Act in 1889, and also the Glen Grey Act in 1894, which forced Africans to acquire individual land tenure while also making it impossible for them to use these tenure rights to register for the franchise. These increasing cramps in the political fabric of Cape liberalism were described by John Tengo Jabavu as 'Muzzling the Native' in an 1887 editorial in *Imvo Zabantsundu*. He wrote that the proposed voter-registration bill would increase the onus on prospective voters:

> Then, as if these stupendous difficulties were not enough to keep our countrymen from their rights as liege subjects of the Queen, the government proceeds to enact in clause 17 that 'No person shall be entitled to be registered as a voter by reason of his sharing in any communal or tribal occupation of lands, or place of residence.' Such are the provisions of a Bill whereby the aboriginal

inhabitants of this portion of her Majesty's dominion are to be deprived of the privileges they have enjoyed in common with their fellow-subjects, the Colonists, since British rule was set up.[33]

Again, this was hardly an incendiary renunciation, since it still depended so much on the notion of 'British subjects' as the central civil right at stake. Moreover, Jabavu's use of the word 'aboriginal' harked back to Philip's *Researches* and his particular conception of personhood and rights in terms of the 'wanderer in the desert'. Jabavu was not quite limning those kinds of philosophical depths, but he was nonetheless re-examining the liberal tradition in the face of its continual emasculation by settler claims.

Liberalism's 'Heartbreak House'[34]

The main paradox of liberal ideas in South Africa is that, despite the tradition's obvious failures and shortcomings, the end of apartheid witnessed the ascendance of one of its hallmarks, namely constitutional democracy. This chapter has attempted to show the longer history of liberalism and liberal ideas, and how the 1994 moment was not just a unique historical event but could be said to have been a culmination of an earlier tradition that had not borne fruit in the nineteenth century. Although in the contemporary period, the language is no longer one of 'British subjects' but of human rights, there is still the echo of the abrogated hopes and euphoria of the earlier period.

In its past incarnation, liberalism did not and could not rely on the present's secure institutional foundations. When LMS missionaries introduced their converts to the 'Word', they did not then fully realise the secular and political meanings to which Christian theology could be applied. It was only in the practice of missionary humanitarianism that the voices of the converted would seep through in protest against colonial dispossession and the denial of civil rights. When coupled with Exeter Hall politics, these voices of protest were often stifled by the missionary concern with metropolitan audiences and fundraising, even while they were being globalised by the long reach of these movements. Even with this reliance on the missionary, these voices remain important if we are to understand the 'non-racial' character of liberalism's foundations. Before the advent of competing ideas such as African Nationalism or Africanism, liberal ideas were the only game in town, and these early adherents spoke not only as British subjects but also as literates searching for the appropriate publics to whom their entreaties could be addressed. These assemblies of readers and petitioners would find their proper register only in the late nineteenth and early twentieth centuries, and the petition would remain the main instrument of vocalisation. The decline in missionary influence and the ascendance of various vigilance organisations was a first step towards this independent articulation, along with the liberation of the printing press from the stranglehold of the mission station. This confluence between the spread of denominations of black opinion and the ubiquity of local publications exposed liberalism's primary weakness, which was its dependence on the largesse of the missionary.

The main argument of the chapter has been about distinguishing between the minor and major liberal traditions in South Africa, and tracing the ways in which the major tradition failed to deliver on its promise and therefore led to the minimisation of liberalism in general. This trajectory was not just a consequence of colonial competition and the rise of settler demands but also the indeterminate ways in which liberalism depended on missionaries for its spread and justification. The African Christian convert was therefore almost always understood as a novice, and their version of liberal thought and politics was not given the same weight as that of the missionary. It is this history of ventriloquising that could be said to have limited liberalism's possible futures in South Africa.

Notes

1   In the case of South Africa, the most thoroughgoing history of liberalism is provided by Paul B. Rich, *Hope and Despair: English Speaking Intellectuals and South African Politics 1896–1976* (London: British Academic Press, 1993). In recent years, the debate has shifted towards the examination of liberal ideas within the universities and the attendant question of 'academic freedom'. See André Du Toit, 'Critic and Citizen: The Intellectual, Transformation and Academic Freedom', *Pretexts: Literary and Cultural Studies*, 9:1 (2000), 91–104; and Robert Bernaconi, 'The Paradox of Liberal Politics in the South African Context: Alfred Hoernlé's Critique of Liberalism's Pact with White Domination', *Critical Philosophy of Race*, 4:2 (2016), 163–81.

2   In this chapter, the words 'black' and 'African' are used to designate people of colour who under apartheid would have been designated as 'non-European'. The latter group includes the categories 'Bantu', 'Coloured', 'Indian', and 'Malay' that were variously used to classify so-called 'population groups'.

3   The spread of literacy in southern Africa was facilitated by the presence of missionaries and mission schools. For the purposes of this chapter, there are two important characteristics of mission education that need to be noted. The first is that it was often Indigenous rulers, who were in the main suspicious of literacy and the literate, who granted land to missionaries for the building of mission stations and schools. Their main logic was that the missionary would function as a 'witness' and scribe in times of crisis and would even occasionally be held hostage. The second characteristic was that many of these institutions were originally non-racial since even the children of the missionary would attend the same

lessons as the young black converts. For further reading, see Jeff Guy, 'Making Words Visible: Aspects of Orality, Literacy, Illiteracy and History in Southern Africa', *South African Historical Journal*, 31 (1994), 3–27; and Vivian Bickford-Smith, 'Words, Wars and World Views: The Coming of Literacy and Books to Southern Africa', *Bulletin du Bibliophile*, 1 (2003), 9–22.

4   There is obviously a bias here towards what may be called 'modern' ideas, meaning ideas that shaped and saturated Africa as a consequence of European contact. This is not to deny or ignore the presence of 'pre-modern' ideas about liberalism or human rights. For this latter discussion, see, e.g., Souleymane Bachir Diagne, 'Individual, Community, and Human Rights', *Transition*, 101 (2009), 8–15. For a general discussion of African philosophy, see P. H. Coetzee and A. P. J. Roux, *The African Philosophy Reader* (London: Taylor and Francis, 2004). One of the earliest attempts to problematise the peculiar nature of ideas in colonial 'dependencies' was presented by John X. Merriman to the subscribers of the South African Public Library. J. X. Merriman and South African Library, *Intellectual Life in the Colonies: A Lecture: Proceedings at the Fifty-eighth Anniversary Meeting of the Subscribers to the South African Public Library, Cape Town, Cape of Good Hope, Held on Saturday, the 7th May, 1887* (Cape Town: Townsend & Son, 1887).

5   In the case of southern Africa, the impact of this movement is contained in the history of the London Missionary Society (LMS) and its first superintendent, Dr John Philip. The first LMS missionary to establish a mission station was Dr Johannes Van der Kemp, who arrived in the Cape in 1799 and, after failure to convert the Xhosa, established a mission station in 1803, which was named Bethelsdorp and to which he hoped to attract converts from among the Khoesan. In 1820, John Philip was appointed as the Superintendent for the LMS in southern Africa and it was under his leadership that mission stations multiplied across the colony. For a fuller account of these early developments in LMS influence, see Robert Ross and Elizabeth Elbourne, 'Combatting Spiritual and Social Bondage: Early Missions in the Cape Colony', in Richard Elphick and Rodney Davenport (eds), *Christianity in South Africa: A Political, Social, and Cultural History* (Oxford and Cape Town: James Currey & David Philip, 1997), pp. 31–50.

6   For brief histories of the Dutch period and its impact on slavery and servitude, see Robert Ross, *Status and Respectability in the Cape Colony, 1750–1870: A Tragedy of Manners* (Cambridge: Cambridge University Press, 1999); Susan Newton-King, *Masters and Servants on the Cape Eastern Frontier, 1760–1803* (Cambridge: Cambridge University Press, 1999); Timothy Keegan, *Colonial South Africa and the Origins of the Racial Order* (Cape Town: David Philip, 1996); and Noel Mostert, *Frontiers: The Epic of South Africa's Creation and the Tragedy of Xhosa People* (New York: Knopf, 1992).

7   The constant desertion of company servants was another instance of illiberal VOC policy since those who were caught were often flogged and placed in stocks. The decision to allow free burghers to settle beyond company dominion was therefore the first step towards the creation of a colony since it was these free burghers who began to oppose what they perceived to be the tyrannical and

corrupt rule of the Company. These freed servants and employees of the VOC were the foundation of what became the settler population of the Cape Colony. And it is also these free burghers whom the British inherited when they took over the Cape Colony for the last time in 1806.

8 This phrase is borrowed from the title of Ross' book, *Status and Respectability*.

9 For a consideration of this history of southern African delegations to the 'Great White Queen', see Neil Parsons, *King Khama, Emperor Joe, and the Great White Queen: Victorian Britain through African Eyes* (Chicago: University of Chicago Press, 1998).

10 The documentary evidence for this shift in governance and politics is explored in André du Toit and Hermann Buhr Giliomee, *Afrikaner Political Thought: Volume One: 1780–1850* (Cape Town: David Philip, 1983).

11 John Philip, *Researches in South Africa; Illustrating the Civil, Moral, and Religious Condition of the Native Tribes: Including Journals of the Author's Travels in the Interior; Together with Detailed Accounts of the Progress of the Christian Missions, Exhibiting the Influence of Christianity in Promoting Civilization* (London: J. Duncan, 1828), p. xxvi.

12 This debate between John Philip and the settlers is explored in Andrew Bank, 'The Great Debate and the Origins of South African Historiography', *The Journal of African History*, 38:2 (1997), 261–81. The connection between these debates and the future of segregation and apartheid is a great leap and has been debated in South African historiography since the 1950s. The major figures of what became South Africa's liberal historiography are discussed in Christopher Saunders, *The Making of the South African Past: Major Historians on Race and Class* (Totowa: Barnes & Noble Books, 1988).

13 Stanley Trapido, 'From Paternalism to Liberalism: The Cape Colony, 1800–1834', *The International History Review*, 12:1 (1990), 76–104; Du Toit and Giliomee, *Afrikaner Political Thought*.

14 Kirsten McKenzie, '"Franklins of the Cape": The "South African Commercial Advertiser" and the Creation of a Colonial Public Sphere', *Kronos*, 25 (1998), 88–102.

15 John Harper, 'Memorandum of United Missionary Conference', in *Correspondence Respecting Cape Colony, 1883–6* (London: George E. B. Eyre & William Spottiswoode, 1884), pp. 38–9.

16 Martin Legassick, 'The Frontier Tradition in South African Historiography', *Collected Seminar Papers* (London: Institute of Commonwealth Studies, 1972).

17 See, e.g., the controversy regarding the exhibition at the South African National Gallery, titled 'Miscast'. Pippa Skotnes (ed.), *Miscast: Negotiating the Presence of the Bushmen* (Cape Town: University of Cape Town Press, 1996).

18 Mohamed Adhikari, *The Anatomy of a South African Genocide: The Extermination of the Cape San Peoples* (Athens: Ohio University Press, 2011).

19 Stanley Trapido, 'The Emergence of Liberalism and the Making of Hottentot Nationalism 1815–1834', *Collected Seminar Papers* (London: Institute of Commonwealth Studies, 1992).

20 Philip, *Researches in South Africa*, pp. xxvi–xxvii.

21 Philip, *Researches in South Africa*, p. 158.

22 Robert Ross, 'The Kat River Rebellion and Khoikhoi Nationalism: The Fate of an Ethnic Identification', *Kronos*, 24 (1997), 91–105.

23 Wayne Dooling, 'The Origins and Aftermath of the Cape Colony's "Hottentot Code" of 1809', *Kronos*, 31 (2005), 50–61.

24 Robert Ross, *These Oppressions Won't Cease: The Political Thought of the Cape Khoesan, 1777–1879: An Anthology* (Johannesburg: Witwatersrand University Press, 2017), pp. 6–15.

25 George McCall Theal, *History of South Africa since September 1795* (Cambridge: Cambridge University Press, 2010), p. 138.

26 This commentator is quoted in Parsons' book, *King Khama, Emperor Joe, and the Great White Queen*, p.110. The full statement reads:

> Black kings and princes are no longer the *rarae aves* that they were when his swarthy Majesty King Cetewayo first dawned upon an astounded London drawing room. Now an African of noble birth is to be met with at most fashionable receptions during the season, and black bishops talk theology with British deans at garden parties.
> All roads, even that from Africa, lead to London. Any day you can hardly walk down Piccadilly without rubbing shoulders with an Afghan, a Zulu, a Hottentot, or a foreigner of some kind.

27 Statement by S. N. Mvambo on the purpose of *Imbumba*, December 1883, cited in Thomas Karis and Gwendolen Carter, *From Protest to Challenge, Vol. 1: A Documentary History of African Politics in South Africa, 1882–1964: Protest and Hope, 1882–1934* (1972; Stanford: Hoover Institution Press, 2013), p. 12.

28 Norman Etherington, 'Mission Station Melting Pots as a Factor in the Rise of South African Black Nationalism', *The International Journal of African Historical Studies*, 9:4 (1976), 592–605.

29 David Attwell, 'Reprisals of Modernity in Black South African "Mission" Writing', *Journal of Southern African Studies*, 25:2 (1999), 267–85.

30 Les Switzer, 'The African Christian Community and Its Press in Victorian South Africa (La communauté chrétienne africaine et sa presse dans l'Afrique du Sud victorienne)', *Cahiers d'Études Africaines*, 24:96 (1984), 455–76.

31 T. D. Mewli Skota, *The African Yearly Register: Being an Illustrated National Biographical Dictionary (Who's Who) of Black Folks in Africa* (Johannesburg: R. L. Esson, 1939).

32 Karis and Carter, *From Protest to Challenge*, p. 72.

33 Karis and Carter, *From Protest to Challenge*, p. 13.

34 The term 'Heartbreak House', derived from George Bernard Shaw's 1920 play of the same name, has been used several times in South Africa's historiography to describe the failure of liberals to offer decisive leadership on the 'native question' and their real or imagined capitulation to white ethno-nationalism and Afrikaner nationalism. See Paul B. Rich, *Hope and Despair: English-Speaking Intellectuals and South African Politics 1896–1976* (London: British Academic Press, 1993).

17

Reading indigeneity in nineteenth-century British Guiana

Manu Samriti Chander

Innocence the magic charm is,
  Keeping sorrow's form at bay;
By its influence, every harm is
  Banished ruthlessly away;
Ill and danger fright her not,
  Happy is her simple lot.
          –E.M.[1]

'By the Lake: An Indian Eclogue' by 'E.M.' appeared in the British Guianese newspaper the *Colonist* in 1882 and was not, to my knowledge, ever republished. It did not really need to be. Its central trope – the Indigenous subject as innocent, childlike, and idle – is so often repeated in settler descriptions of native peoples, so unextraordinary, that the poem hardly bears multiple readings. Things get a bit more interesting, however, when we consider that its author was not a white settler but an Afro-Creole who would go on to be hailed as the first real British Guianese poet and, in the words of Arthur Schomburg, 'one of the greatest Negro poets in history'.[2] 'E.M.' was Egbert Martin, and, as I discuss below, his claim to represent British Guiana was founded precisely on the erasure of the Guianese native, or 'Amerindian'.[3]

This process of erasure, I argue, was not simply a consequence of a mode of poetic representation that figured the Amerindian as an object of knowledge. The rise of periodical culture in nineteenth-century British Guiana came to ground ideas of humanity in the capacity to read and thereby participate fully in the social life of the colony. Within this framework Indigenous peoples were understood as essentially illiterate, even as colonial missionaries sought to educate British Guianese Amerindians. As we see in the writings of a missionary such as John Henry Bernau, Christianisation was imagined to precede civilisation, which meant that converted Amerindians were always in danger of falling back into a pre-civilised state. Martin too failed to imagine the Amerindian as a fully literate, Christianised subject. The equation of a narrowly defined literacy with the category of the human, then, figures Indigenous peoples as always already 'read' – that is, as available for reading, and constitutively, non-reading.

The making of Guianese reading audiences

In 1881, the first daily newspaper produced in British Guiana, the *Demerara Daily Chronicle*, noted in its Prospectus that:

> As education has become more widely diffused among the people, the reading population has slowly but steadily increased, and to a much larger portion of the community than heretofore a daily paper has thus become a necessity. Hitherto, however, no attempt has been made to produce a daily journal at a price sufficiently moderate to bring it within reach of all the classes and sections of our Colonial Society. This want the CHRONICLE is intended to supply.[4]

The seemingly laudable efforts of a newspaper like the *Demerara Daily Chronicle* to reach 'all the classes and sections of our Colonial Society' must be read as part of an effort to outsell its less frequent weekly and monthly competitors and, at the same time, to shape the reading public into an ideologically coherent whole. Of course, the *Daily Chronicle*'s competitors were engaged in the very same project, which created a dynamic, conflictual, and continually shifting cultural field.

We can trace the emergence of a new phase of literary modernity to the rise of competing periodicals, which compels audiences, as Jon Klancher writes, 'to define themselves according to the interpretive mode they possess and the interpretive strategies thorough which that mode somehow allows them to "read" other audiences'.[5] It is precisely when readers begin to understand themselves in relation to discrete cultural groups possessed of discrete tastes and, at the very same time, a broader 'imagined community' that the promises of a unified nation become inextricably bound to literacy.[6] The modern nation coalesces, then, not despite a diversity of 'interpretive strategies', but because this diversity is understood to be a characteristic of the modern liberal democracy. Reasonable debate – no matter how contentious and conflictual – is not only tolerable but desirable. In the west this emergence is generally understood to be a late-eighteenth-century phenomenon.[7]

In British Guiana a newly dynamic public sphere starts to appear after emancipation in 1838. Nigel Westmaas offers a number of reasons for this development, including the appearance of the first Black newspaper (the *Freeman Sentinel*), technological advancements in printing in the colonies, and the rise of a new Black middle class, especially in the later decades of the nineteenth century.[8] Despite the fact that formal literacy remained the privilege of a small part of the population throughout the century, there were dozens of newspapers circulating during the period, many with short runs that, according to Westmaas, attest to the continually shifting and complexifying nature of the Guianese reading public.[9]

At the same time that the reading public was expanding beyond settler colonials to include a greater number of Creole readers, the status of the native Amerindian population was changing. Prior to emancipation, certain protections seemed to suggest that the Amerindian, while not quite human, had more innate value than the enslaved African within the British imagination.[10] In an 1811 letter concerning Governor Henry William Bentinck, who was accused of owning an enslaved Amerindian, the colonial officer John Daly decries such a transgression on the grounds that 'the aborigines of this Country ... are physically less able than Negroes, to undergo the hardships of Slavery'; as such, their enslavement is 'more repugnant to Humanity' than that of the African.[11] In 1817, Daly would praise the Amerindian's keen senses, which made them, he believed, invaluable for tracking down runaway enslaved Africans.[12] If the Black was understood as, in Calvin Warren's words, 'available equipment, equipment in human form', the Amerindian was a special kind of tool, delicate, and, in the wrong hands, breakable.[13]

After 1838, however, 'all other groups came to accord [the Amerindians] the lowest "racial" status in British Guiana ... on the grounds that they were uncivilized savages, lacking any culture of value'.[14] By 1892 it was therefore possible for one writer, reflecting on the 1891 census, to claim that Amerindians were of 'little or no social value and their early extinction must be looked upon as inevitable'.[15] Thus, as Black Creoles began to enter the cultural field and consequently became incorporated into the circuits of Guianese citizenship, Amerindians became increasingly dehumanised.

The making of Guianese reading audiences cannot be understood without attending to this process of exclusion, which I read in terms of two distinct conceptions of cultural tension, which Frank B. Wilderson III has called the 'rubric of conflict' and the 'rubric of antagonism'. The former refers to 'a rubric of problems that can be posed and conceptually solved', the latter to 'an irreconcilable struggle between entities, or positions, the resolution of which is not dialectical but entails the obliteration of one of the positions'.[16] In nineteenth-century British Guiana, multiple communities existed in conflictual relations which were often borne out in the periodical press. Underlying these conflicts, however, was an antagonism between the 'cultured' Guianese and the 'uncivilised' Amerindian, the cultural field's abject other. The Amerindian is effectively obliterated as a participant within the nineteenth-century Guianese public sphere; or rather, the public sphere is formed via the obliteration of the Amerindian.[17]

Consider, for example, an 1853 clash between the *Royal Gazette* and the *Colonist* – both state-sponsored periodicals – over how British law should handle the murder of one Amerindian by another. Where the editor of the *Colonist* advocated execution of the murderer as a means of deterring future incidences – 'the savage must be brought to dread the strong arm' – the editor of the *Royal Gazette* insisted that '[t]he moral obligation rests upon us to reclaim the untutored Indian, to bring him, if possible within those haunts where civilization may be found. Coax him, bribe him; we have taken possession of his heritage and we owe him this. But surely do not hang him.'[18] In the conflict between the editors, the Amerindian becomes a problem to be solved either rationally or morally. Yet the problem relies on the silence of the Amerindian, who has no voice in the debate, or whose voice remains inaudible within the structure of the cultural field. Indeed, I am suggesting, the field itself only coheres because of this silencing.

To put it differently: there was a colonial White press and a Creole Black press, but there was no Indigenous Red press. And over the course of the nineteenth century the mark of humanity would come to be tied to ownership of the means of cultural production and the capacity to disseminate cultural works – that is, the capacity to write and reach audiences whose humanity was defined by their literacy.

In offering up this argument I mean to supplement Shona Jackson's pathbreaking analysis of what she calls 'Creole indigeneity', whereby Creole claims to belonging erase those of Indigenous peoples. For Jackson, the primary means by which this erasure takes place is the elevation of labour as the mark of the human. Accepting the colonial capitalist association of labour with humanity, the Creole, Jackson argues, understands his belonging in terms of all he has done for the land, the work he has put into it. For Jackson, Amerindian labour has been rendered visible 'only as *cultural*, not the productive labor of economic development that allows the formerly enslaved and indentured to claim political belonging and right'.[19] To Jackson's discussion I would add that a second discourse, in addition to the discourse of human labour, has continually served to legitimise Creole belonging and displace Guianese Amerindians: literary labour. Where Jackson claims a 'relative cultural embrace and simultaneous political marginalization' of Amerindians, I wish to suggest that the long-standing association between literacy and cultural legitimacy means that the status of Amerindian culture in British Guiana has never actually risen to the level of 'culture' at all.[20]

That some Amerindians in the nineteenth century could read and write, thanks to missionary colonialism, did nothing to correct the belief that Indigenous peoples were *essentially* illiterate. The missionary John Henry Bernau, for example, includes in his 1847 *Missionary Labours in British Guiana* a number of letters written by his former Amerindian students that attest to their control of written English. These students' hard work and diligent, continued reading of the Bible suggests to Bernau that they are 'truly converted', where being Christianised is the precondition for becoming civilised.[21] Unlike the born Christian, however, the convert is always in danger of, in Bernau's words, 'relapsing again into a savage state'.[22] The 'savage' preliterate state is, according to this logic, the ontological condition of the Amerindian that haunts his existence as a literate subject.

The relationship between literacy and the rise of Creole indigeneity in the late nineteenth century is especially marked in the emergence of British Guiana's first national poet, Egbert Martin, best known to his readers as 'Leo'. Throughout the 1880s, before his death in 1890, Martin published two collections of poetry, a book of short stories, and numerous uncollected works in every major periodical in British Guiana. The *Guiana Herald* claimed he was 'far and away the first West Indian poet'.[23] About this characterisation A. J. Seymour writes, 'I presume the writer means first in quality', although, given what I have suggested above, the description does double duty, not only glorifying Martin but also granting him a historical priority that displaces all Indigenous cultural texts that preceded the emergence of the Guianese republic of letters.[24] As I discuss below, Martin was absolutely complicit in this act of erasure, which is particularly marked in his poems that sought to represent Amerindian peoples. In these poems it becomes clear how claiming a position as British Guiana's national (or proto-national) poet meant establishing oneself as its rightful native.

Egbert Martin's Creole indigeneity

Much of Martin's poetry is concerned with religious themes, but nowhere is the Protestant work ethic more visible than in the poem that closes his second volume. 'What Is the Good?' begins with the speaker expressing his doubt over his own poetic project, doubting whether one 'Can … ever hope to compass / Any great thing by rhyme' (lines 7–8).[25] He quells his own fears by reminding himself, and by extension his reader, that 'There is good in bare persistence', that literary labour, like any other form of labour, is its own reward:

> With the pen, or tool of labor,
>   Art or industry, – whate'er
> Comes into our lives as duty
>   Do it – heedless of the care. (lines 25–8)[26]

If, as Jackson argues, labour defines Creole belonging, Martin makes clear that the pen is one – and for him the primary – means by which belonging is enacted. And, consequently, it is a means by which the Amerindian is exiled.

If grounding humanity in literacy serves to expel from the category of the human Indigenous peoples understood as essentially illiterate, Creole writing about Indigenous peoples doubles this process. The forms of this second expulsion are diverse and reflect diverse forms of belonging, different ways of asserting oneself as the primary inhabitant of the land. Across Martin's short career, we see a shift in both the representation of the Amerindian and a shift in the terms by which he defines himself as an Emersonian 'representative man', the voice of British Guiana. These two shifts thoroughly inform one another.

Martin's first collection, *Leo's Poetical Works* (1883), sought to, in the words of its preface, 'reach the outward ears and sink deeply into the hearts of some of his fellow-pilgrims through this "*valley of tears*" carrying comfort to the sorrowful and oppressed; hope to the languid and desponding; strength to the weak and weary; light to those who sit in darkness; and cheerful encouragement to the "weary in well-doing"'.[27] Throughout the collection Martin employs this kind of religious rhetoric, where the bonds between Christian subjects allow for sympathetic understanding. Within this larger poetic project, the Amerindian functions to consolidate the Christian Creole community by virtue of its alterity.

'The Indian's Return', for example, describes a solitary Indian who returns after many years to a desolate village, cut off from the circuits of sympathy – 'His friends were gone, his kindred fled' (line 4) – and, worse, from the comfort that Christian faith provides the civilised Creole subject:

> Did he know the faith which a Christian knows?
>   Did he hope for a happier sphere?
> There would have been far less of sadness,
>   And more of trust, and more of gladness;
> But he only knew the pain which flows
>   From a deep and fixed despair. (lines 25–30)[28]

The companion to this piece, 'The Hammock Maker: An Indian Eclogue', presents Creole readers with another solitary Amerindian figure, an old hammock-maker who stands apart from the 'Younger braves' (line 15).[29] Like the figure in 'The Indian's Return', the hammock-maker suffers the pain of those outside the fold of Christianity: 'For his heart is constant sighing / In a superstitious dread; / Longing, longing to be dying, / Fearing, fearing to be dead' (lines 45–8).[30] If such figures elicit pity from Creole readers, they do not create the ties of fellow-feeling reserved for those 'fellow-pilgrims' whom Martin describes in his preface.

Martin's first collection was not as well received as he had hoped. In the preface to his follow-up collection, the 1886 volume *Leo's Local Lyrics*, he refers to criticisms of his earlier work, alluding to a particularly scathing review in *London's Saturday Review*, which read: '"Leo's" poems have not even the thinnest guise of poetry. They illustrate a strain of trite, and often silly reflection, and a sentiment of "goodiness" that is nauseating.'[31] As a consequence of this poor reception, Martin designed his second collection to appeal to a wider public, emphasising local British Guianese culture rather than the religious themes of his first book.[32] In doing so, he develops an alternative means of representing indigeneity and, in turn, authorising Creole belonging.

While much of Martin's biography, including what he read, remains a mystery, we know from an introductory note to his poem 'The Kaieteur Falls' that he had gained some knowledge of Amerindian peoples from Everard im Thurn's *Among the Indians of Guiana: Sketches Chiefly Anthropologic from the Interior of British Guiana* (1883).[33] Of particular interest to Martin seems to have been im Thurn's account of animism and especially his discussion of spirits dwelling within objects: 'To the Indians,' writes im Thurn, 'inanimate objects have spirits which differ not at all in kind from those of men.'[34] This section of im Thurn's study likely informed the first part of Martin's collection, titled 'Tropical Studies'. He writes in the preface to *Leo's Local Lyrics*:

> Anyone at all familiar with current Creole superstitions and the peculiar beliefs of Indian animism, must have noticed that a childishly simple credulity in the universal existence of spirits characterizes them all. Not only that, but the possible influences of these unseen existences on their lives, actions, dreams, etc., are all taken into account. As education advances, these beliefs, of course, give way, although they still exist to a very appreciable extent.[35]

'I have tried to weave this dim, far-off, intangible – call it – *spirituality* into a few of the tropical studies', Martin continues, and 'weave' is perhaps an appropriate verb. Martin structures many of his tropical studies as 'childishly simple' songs, weaving naivete into his form.[36] 'The Creek', for example, begins:

> Across the creek the midnight moonlight breaks,
> Along the creek the witching moonlight breaks,
> 'Tis like a soul that dreams but never wakes.
>
> The creek it hath a spirit in its breast,
> It hath a secret spirit in its breast,
> And oft it moves upon the water's crest.
>
> And oft it sings in dreadful notes and low,
> In thrilling, sighing, pining notes and low,
> That make you shudder as you hear them flow.

And that is why the village people find,
And that is why the simple people find
A something in the creek that's like the wind;

And that is why the little children flee,
And that is why the merry children flee,
From by its side when evening's dusk they see. (lines 1–15)[37]

Here and in other tropical studies, Martin offers heavy-handed anaphora and simple masculine rhymes that reproduce formally the innocence that he projects on to the natives, the 'simple people', as he puts it.

Tropical studies such as 'The Creek' move well beyond Martin's earlier representative strategy, whereby the Amerindian is situated outside the circuits of Christian sympathy, an object of pity but not a subject with whom feelings are shared. The later poems, while working to incorporate or 'weave' into his poems the Amerindian beliefs transmitted to him via the European im Thurm, effectively unincorporate the Indigenous subject, who no longer even rises to the level of object of knowledge. It thus becomes possible in other tropical studies for Martin to adopt the persona of one who subscribes to the animism that we know he dismissed as childish. In 'The Palm-Soul', for example, Martin presents a first-person narrator who embraces a palm tree and feels its spirit. The speaker then reflects: 'Nature feels / From mount to deep one sympathy, / One sense thro' all creation steals, / One sentiment of unity' (lines 12–15).[38] Read charitably, such poems represent an effort to reconcile Martin's cherished Christianity with the version of animism he ascribed to the Amerindian peoples. Yet such reconciliation, of course, can only take place on terms established by the Creole poet.

To be clear: in laying out this critique of Martin's poetic project, I do not wish to implicate Creole subjects alone for the displacement of the Guianese Amerindians; rather I want to show how such displacement is the consequence of colonial entanglements that begin with European imperialism. Here it must be remembered that Martin evacuates the native from his tropical studies 'in accordance … with public taste', where 'public' meant not only local Guianese Creoles but also representatives from the centre of literary and imperial power who had dismissed his first collection.[39] And, indeed, the strategy worked: the same journal that had derided *Leo's Poetical Works* praised the second collection's 'untutored frankness', suggesting that Leo had successfully inhabited the position of raw being he attributed to the Amerindian.[40] Thus, we need to understand Creole indigeneity as a form of appeal for recognition by Creole subjects to centres of imperial power. It is not just about Creole claims to belonging, but the acknowledgment of those claims by the wider, whiter world.

Decolonisation, then, involves refusing altogether recognition-based politics, where the Creole expects recognition from the Global North and offers recognition to Amerindian communities. To speak of 'recognition' in the context of Indigenous peoples is, of course, usually to speak of political recognition.[41] Yet, since at least the nineteenth century, the matter of cultural recognition – that is, how cultural products are legitimised within a national and transnational marketplace – has been powerful in delegitimising Indigenous claims to sovereignty. Culture, thus understood, is never merely superstructural. Rather, it informs all possible relationships between settler, Creole, and Indigenous peoples. What counts as culture must be radically rethought, then, beginning with the privileging of the written, which has long served as a mark of Creole belonging.

'[C]an't hear, can't see'

Writing, according to the late Lakota political activist Russell Means, has been 'one of the white world's ways of destroying the cultures of non-European peoples'.[42] Without bolstering what Adrien Delmas describes as '[t]he anthropological myth of native orality, generalised to all that was not European', it remains for the settler-scholar to acknowledge that a narrow conception of writing has served to authorise certain forms of belonging and delegitimise others.[43] Such an acknowledgment, however, should not be mistaken for unlearning writing in favour of learning to 'hear' or learning to 'see' Indigenous peoples. Reversing the process by which Indigenous peoples are deemed ontologically illiterate, Means deems the white world essentially incapable of approaching Indigenous cultures: 'I don't really care whether my words reach whites or not. They've already demonstrated through their history that they can't hear, can't see, they can only read.'[44]

If this seems an extreme position to take, we might consider how the effort to 'see' and 'hear' the Amerindian is woven into the history of nineteenth-century British Guiana. Im Thurn's volume, the same one that Martin drew upon for his tropical studies, includes over fifty plates and woodcuts depicting everything from 'A Macusi in Full Dancing Dress' to a 'Cobungru Woman, showing Leg-bands'. He provides readers with a table of 'Examples of the Chief Indian Languages of Guiana', presenting nine English words as they are spoken by seven different tribes. 'Unfortunately,' he writes, 'I have no Arecuna vocabulary at my disposal; but the language differs merely by very slight varieties of pronunciation from the Macusi.'[45] Readers are left to presume the unimportance of these 'very slight varieties'.

In addition to producing his ethnographic volume, im Thurn organised the British Guiana collection for the 1886 Colonial and Indian Exhibition in London. Millions of attendees were afforded the opportunity to gaze upon Indigenous artefacts from across the colony. Among those artefacts was a group of Amerindians, 'living ethnological displays' who built and then inhabited replica Amerindian villages.[46] The *Report of the Royal Commission for the Colonial and Indian Exhibition* (1886) provides some details about these 'Red Indians' of British Guiana, including their names, tribal affiliations, ages, and their roles within their respective communities; ten Amerindians in all, each 'baptized in the Church of England Mission'. Among the list are two entries who provide some indication of the ways that efforts to 'see' and 'hear' Indigenous peoples are limited by the history of articulating humanity in terms of literacy: Anthony Gordon, age 24, a 'Macoosi wood-cutter', and his cousin, Maria, age 8, 'Acowoio'. Anthony, we are told, 'reads and writes in English' and Maria 'reads and writes a little'.[47]

Notes

1 E.M. [Egbert Martin], 'By the Lake: An Indian Eclogue', *Colonist* (8 April 1882), n.p., lines 46–51.
2 The attribution of this praise to Schomburg comes from Eric D. Walrond's 'Visit to Arthur Schomburg's Library Brings out Wealth of Historical Information', which was first published in *Negro World* on 22 April 1922 and reprinted in Tony Martin (ed.), *African Fundamentalism: A Literary and Cultural Anthology of Garvey's Harlem Renaissance* (Dover: The Majority Press, 1991), p. 317.
3 The term 'Amerindian' is widely used in discussions of British Guiana as a means of distinguishing Indigenous peoples of the region from the Indians who were brought to the colony in large numbers by the British as indentured laborers in the post-emancipation era.
4 Prospectus, *Demerara Daily Chronicle* (10 November 1881), n.p.
5 Jon Klancher, *The Making of English Reading Audiences, 1790–1832* (Madison: University of Wisconsin Press, 1983), p. 46.
6 The phrase 'imagined community' comes, of course, from Benedict Anderson's *Imagined Communities: Reflections on the Origin and Spread of Nationalism* (London: Verso, 1983).
7 See, in addition to Klancher, Jared Gardner, *The Rise and Fall of Early American Magazine Culture* (Urbana: University of Illinois Press, 2012), especially p. 78: in America, Gardner writes, '[a]s the ideals of the Revolution quickly gave way to a rising tide of factionalism in the years following the ratification debate, the periodical would become invested with even greater hopes and fantasies as refuge, an asylum, where the best possibilities of the republic could be nourished'.
8 Nigel David Westmaas, 'A Mirror of Social and Political Ferment: The Newspaper Press of Guyana: 1838–1899' (PhD dissertation, Binghamton University, State University of New York, 2006), pp. 7–10.
9 Westmaas, 'A Mirror of Social and Political Ferment', p. 8.
10 See Mary Noel Menezes, *The Amerindians in Guyana, 1803–73: A Documentary History* (London: Frank Cass, 1979), p. 161: 'In 1793 a special Ordinance

prohibited the enslavement of Indians or the offspring of Indians.' This ordinance was honoured even after the British took control of the colonies in 1803.

11 Menezes, *The Amerindians in Guyana*, p. 164.

12 Menezes, *The Amerindians in Guyana*, p. 11.

13 Calvin L. Warren, *Ontological Terror: Blackness, Nihilism, and Emancipation* (Durham: Duke University Press, 2018), p. 28.

14 Andrew Sanders, 'British Colonial Policy and the Role of Amerindians in the Politics of the Nationalist Period in British Guiana, 1945–68', *Social and Economic Studies*, 36:3 (1987), 81. It should be noted that there was, prior to emancipation, a historically significant population of free Blacks in Guyana. See Adele Perry, *Colonial Relations: The Douglas-Connolly Family and the Nineteenth-Century Imperial World* (Cambridge: Cambridge University Press, 2015), pp. 56–7: 'between 1810 and 1830 the population of free people of color in Berbice, Demerara, and Essequibo grew by about 70 percent, and easily overtook the White population'.

15 E. D. Rowland, 'Census of British Guiana, 1891', *Timehri*, 6 (June 1892), 56, quoted in Mary Noel Menezes, *British Policy towards the Amerindians in British Guiana, 1803–1873* (Georgetown: Caribbean Press, 2011), p. 42.

16 Frank B. Wilderson III, *Red, White & Black: Cinema and the Structure of U. S. Antagonisms* (Durham: Duke University Press, 2010), p. 5.

17 For Wilderson, writing in the context of the United States, it is the Black American who exists in antagonistic relationship to the human, while '[t]he Red, Indigenous, or "Savage" position exists liminally as half-death and half-life between the Slave (Black) and the Human (White, or non-Black)' (*Red, White & Black*, p. 23). While a fuller discussion of this position lies beyond the scope of the present chapter, suffice it to say I do not believe that this schema holds up in the context of nineteenth-century British Guiana or modern-day Guyana. For a critique of Wilderson's understanding of indigeneity, see Iyko Day, 'Being or Nothingness: Indigeneity, Antiblackness, and Settler Colonial Critique', *Critical Ethnic Studies*, 1:2 (2015), 102–21.

18 Menezes, *British Policy towards the Amerindians in British Guiana*, pp. 172–3.

19 Shona N. Jackson, *Creole Indigeneity: Between Myth and Nation in the Colonial Caribbean* (Minneapolis: University of Minnesota Press, 2012), p. 10.

20 Jackson, *Creole Indigeneity*, p. 7.

21 John Henry Bernau, *Missionary Labours in British Guiana: With Remarks on the Manners, Customs, and Superstitious Rites of the Aborigines* (London: J. F. Shaw, 1847), p. 185: 'Christianize them first,' writes Bernau, 'and civilization, really deserving of the name, is sure to follow.'

22 Bernau, *Missionary Labours in British Guiana*, p. 215.

23 This and other praises were listed on the back page of Martin's second collection, *Leo's Local Lyrics* (Georgetown: Baldwin and Co., 1886), n.p.

24 A. J. Seymour, 'The Literary Tradition: The Poetry of Egbert Martin (Leo)', in *Kyk-Over-Al, Volume 1, Issues 1–3, December 1945-December 1946* (Georgetown: Caribbean Press, 2013), p. 199.

25 Leo [Egbert Martin], 'What Is the Good?', *Leo's Local Lyrics*, pp. 74–5.

26 Leo, 'What Is the Good?', *Leo's Local Lyrics*, pp. 74–5.

27 Leo, *Leo's Poetical Works* (London: W. H. and L. Collingridge, 1883), n.p.

28 Leo, 'The Indian's Return', *Leo's Poetical Works*, pp. 202–3.

29 Leo, 'The Hammock Maker: An Indian Eclogue', *Leo's Poetical Works*, pp. 204–5.

30 Leo, 'The Hammock Maker', *Leo's Poetical Works*, pp. 203–5.

31 [Anon.], 'Recent Poetry', *Saturday Review*, 57 (3 May 1884), p. 587.

32 For a fuller discussion of Martin's response to this criticism, see Manu Samriti Chander, *Brown Romantics: Poetry and Nationalism in the Global Nineteenth Century* (Lewisburg: Bucknell University Press, 2017), pp. 44–62.

33 Leo [Egbert Martin], 'The Kaieteur Falls', *Argosy* (5 July 1884), p. 2. Martin introduces his poem with a quotation from im Thurm's 'lately published, admirable work'.

34 Everard im Thurn, *Among the Indians of Guiana: Sketches Chiefly Anthropologic from the Interior of British Guiana* (London: Keegan, Paul, Trench, and Co., 1883), p. 349.

35 Leo, 'Preface', *Leo's Local Lyrics*, pp. v–vi.

36 Leo, 'Preface', *Leo's Local Lyrics*, pp. v–vi.

37 Leo, 'The Creek', *Leo's Local Lyrics*, pp. 3–8.

38 Leo, 'The Palm-Soul', *Leo's Local Lyrics*, pp. 18–19.

39 Leo, 'Preface', *Leo's Local Lyrics*, p. v.

40 [Anon.], 'New Books and Reprints', *Saturday Review* (6 November 1886), p. 635.

41 For an excellent discussion of the limits of the politics of recognition in Indigenous activist movements, see Glen Coulthard, *Red Skin, White Masks: Rejecting the Colonial Politics of Recognition* (Minneapolis: University of Minnesota Press, 2014), especially chapter 4.

42 Russell Means, 'The Same Old Song', in Ward Churchill (ed.), *Marxism and Native Americans* (Boston: South End Press, 1992), p. 19.

43 Adrien Delmas, 'Introduction: The Written Word and the World', in Adrien Delmas and Nigel Penn (eds), *Written Culture in a Colonial Context: Africa and the Americas 1500–1900* (Leiden: Brill, 2012), p. xxviii.

44 Means, 'The Same Old Song', p. 19.

45 Im Thurn, *Among the Indians of Guiana*, p. 166.

46 Sara Albuquerque, 'Glimpses of British Guiana at the Colonial and Indian Exhibition, 1886', *Culture and History Digital Journal*, 5:1 (2016), n.p., http://cultureandhistory.revistas.csic.es/index.php/cultureandhistory/article/view/97/333 (accessed 10 January 2020).

47 Albuquerque, 'Glimpses of British Guiana at the Colonial and Indian Exhibition, 1886', n.p.

18

'Some Genuine Chinese Authors': literary appreciation, comparatism, and universalism in the *Straits Chinese Magazine*

Porscha Fermanis

In 1897 Tan Teck Soon, the future manager of the Chinese-language newspaper *Thien Nan Shin Pao* ('The New Daily of the South'), complained that the Chinese residents of the Straits Settlements – from the 'half naked jinricksha puller' to the 'sleek merchant lolling in his well-equipped carriage' – were rarely associated with 'literature or literary achievements of any kind'.[1] Responding to British disparagements of contemporary Malay and Chinese literary cultures, Tan's three articles on 'Some Genuine Chinese Authors' in the *Straits Chinese Magazine* (1897–1907) are determined to prove otherwise, identifying Straits Chinese reading audiences, Chinese-language circulating libraries, translations of Chinese fiction into Romanised Malay, and professional Chinese storytellers and operatic troupes. If his own remit is to translate 'the best products of the Chinese mind' into 'English dress', Tan's argument for the variety and depth of contemporary Chinese culture counters the then prevailing view that literature was irrelevant to 'illiterate' Chinese communities in nineteenth-century Singapore, Malacca, and Penang, while simultaneously valorising popular forms of visual, oral, and aural entertainment alongside the revival of classical Chinese literature.[2]

Mark Ravinder Frost and Jan van der Putten have recently gone some way towards vindicating Tan Teck Soon's claims by demonstrating the existence of a small but significant Chinese and Malay middle class in the Straits Settlements from at least the mid-nineteenth century onwards, noting the extent to which commercial trading centres such as Singapore encouraged literacy, and arguing that the earliest Malay and Chinese publishers and literati were usually merchants, businessmen, and shopkeepers.[3] Extending his study to the imperial cities of the Indian Ocean rim, Frost has further sketched out a distinct public sphere that developed in Bombay, Rangoon, and Singapore after 1870, 'rooted in pan-religious movements' and reformist agendas, and 'sustained by the intelligentsias of intersecting diasporas', who were often

western-educated professionals, bi- or trilingual, and multi-ethnic in composition.[4] In South and Southeast Asia – wrongly imagined by 'Orientalists as
immobile and even timeless' – European colonial powers therefore encountered a highly connected and mobile society that moved between and within
Nanyang South Sea and Indian Ocean spaces, creating southern networks
that retained distinctive regional identities that long predated European
hegemony and western imperialism.[5] Although the size of the reading publics
associated with these various networks was relatively small, the last decade
of the nineteenth century saw the emergence of a distinctive multilingual
periodical culture with new progressive modes of pan-Asian addressivity.[6]

This chapter considers the relationship between language, literacy, and
literary appreciation in one of these culturally hybrid publications: the *Straits
Chinese Magazine*, a self-professed journal of 'Oriental and Occidental' culture modelled on the miscellany format of British monthly magazines. Edited
by Song Ong Siang, Lim Boon Keng, and later Wu Lien Teh, the magazine's
contributors were Chinese, Malay, and British, but its articles and original
fiction were primarily written in English with interlineal English-language
translations of Chinese and Malay source texts.[7] Registering an awareness
that the 'present chaotic state of public opinion' in the Straits Settlements was
partly the result of anxieties over the increasingly racialised regulation of
imperial citizenship, the editors used English-language literacy to 'negotiate a
place' for Southeast Asians in the Anglophone 'colonial public sphere', both
promoting Malay and Chinese cultural revivalism, and adopting 'foreign'
languages and cultural practices in order to do so.[8]

The aim of this chapter is not to provide an overview of the magazine's
revivalist project or its reformist politics, but rather to consider how its contributors navigate questions relating to cultural forms of knowledge, such as
linguistic standardisation, vernacular education, literary appreciation, and
canonicity.[9] English literature as a practice and discipline has always been
heavily implicated in the comparative cultural politics of nineteenth-century
philology whereby the 'quality of a society's language was the most telling
index of the quality of its personal and social life'.[10] My interest here is with
the ways in which Straits Chinese authors co-opt and/or negotiate the dual
epistemological commitment to comparatism and universalism that, as Uday
Singh Mehta argues, underpinned liberal justifications of empire and its deferral of self-determination for colonised subjects.[11] I consider, in particular,
how liberalism's unevenness informs the 'political stakes of relational thinking', a question that has permeated understandings of anticolonial and postcolonial nationalism ever since the recognition of comparison's origins in
racialised developmental categories.[12]

Three main schools of thought have emerged from debates surrounding
comparatism: the first involves an attempt to historicise comparative practises

by seeing them as a function of specific locations; the second aims to 'displace the problem of universality' by seeing colonialism as the meeting of incommensurable 'forms of particularity'; and the third reclaims universalism by understanding colonialism as 'a contestation of different universalisms'.[13] Drawing on Andrew Sartori and Manu Goswami's interventions in these debates, I read the strategic desire in the *Straits Chinese Magazine* to establish commensurability across cultural worlds – rather than 'to claim radical alterity' – as part of what Goswami has called a 'distinctively anticolonial project'.[14] While the *Straits Chinese Magazine* operated as a cultural broker for its elite Asian readership 'standing half-way between east and west', its confrontation with European (and especially British) culture also involved an intense engagement with the asymmetries of liberal thought.[15] My focus in this chapter is therefore on how the *Straits Chinese Magazine* was able to convene regional audiences and sensibilities in new and surprising ways, containing within it a 'subversive radicalising potential' that is often unacknowledged in studies of decolonisation in Southeast Asia.[16]

Arnoldian high culture and the politics of comparison

Conscious of the rise of racialised migration and labour policies across the Anglosphere, the editors of the *Straits Chinese Magazine* focused heavily on the accumulation of cultural capital for Chinese and (to a lesser extent) Malay populations in the Straits Settlements, giving literary culture a central role in its construction of a modern Asian identity.[17] As Philip Holden has noted, the magazine takes an Arnoldian view of high culture as the best way to chart both the external progress of a civilisation and the inner perfection of a 'best self', maintaining the view that culture is a 'privileged domain of expression' and noting '[t]he wonderful results of the arts and sciences for the characteristic features of modern European civilization'.[18] The view of literature upheld by the magazine, and promoted by influential nineteenth-century taste-makers such as Goethe, Arnold, and Ruskin, was the result of a gradual shift after 1700 from a rhetorical culture where reading was primarily seen as an instrument of social power to a new kind of cultural arrangement centred on literary appreciation, in particular on a close reading of literary 'classics' (western and non-western).[19] In this formulation, literature became the 'domain of a universalized, cosmopolitan discourse of the value of culture', which simultaneously sought to theorise culture as, in Arnold's words, 'the best that has been thought or said' and to see it trans-historically as 'the fruit of comparative analysis across time and societies'.[20]

Arnoldian echoes find expression in the *Straits Chinese Magazine* not only in the constant quotations from an emerging canon of 'classics' forged by common British education policies across colonial South Asia (especially from Shakespeare, Dryden, Milton, Keats, Shelley, Macaulay, Dickens, and Tennyson), but also in the related privileging of classical Chinese texts as the best representations of the 'spirit of the age' in which they were written, as both 'a powerful expression of natural feeling' and 'an insight into the political history of the period'.[21] If the 'literary language of China' is 'to all intents and purposes a *dead* language', it is nonetheless characterised by Lim Boon Keng as historically the most 'wonderful medium of written communication among the myriad inhabitants of the Far East from Corea [sic] and Japan in the Arctic North to the great Chinese settlements in the Malayan archipelago' – a language that has lived through and reflects 'generations, surviving all social cataclysms, and so many dynastic changes'.[22]

In adapting and applying Arnoldian views of high culture to a classical Chinese culture that both connects and acts metonymically for the achievements of various other eastern cultures, Lim is able to register classical Chinese and its written texts as serious rivals to the Latin and Greek classics, and to argue for the existence and longevity of an alternative eastern counter-culture to the western Judeo-Christian and Greco-Latin one. Even as he accepts the need for widespread political and educational reform in China, Lim's arguments are suggestive of the extent to which China considered itself to be an 'actively competing civilizational model' that could not easily be assimilated into 'progressivist, Eurocentric models of world history'.[23] While he adopts the comparative perspective of European philological discourses, noting that the position and status of classical Chinese can be 'fitly compared with that of Latin in the Middle Ages of Europe', his aim is to invert the comparatist paradigm by favourably comparing classical Chinese culture with the best that British culture has to offer.[24]

As the numerous book reviews of philological works in the *Straits Chinese Magazine* suggest, Lim, Tan, and their colleagues were well versed in the work of a community of European philologists such as William Jones and Friedrich Max Müller, who developed older rhetorical tropes of comparison and analogy derived from Christian and moral philosophy into a new scientific approach to the study of texts as 'historical specimens'.[25] To some extent, Lim and Tan see comparatism as a means of empowering Chinese civilisation within an increasingly racialised imperial world-system, crediting French, British, and Anglo-Chinese philologists with changing opinions regarding the 'utility of Chinese literature' and hence 'the capabilities of the Chinese race'.[26] Sinologists such as Herbert Giles, Paul Carter, and Ku Li Cheng are singled out for particular praise by Tan because their work indicates 'the true sympathetic spirit with which all such studies should be carried out'.[27] Yet while comparatism is seen as a potentially sympathetic mode of understanding difference, Lim and Tan are well aware that even sympathetic comparisons exist within a Eurocentric hierarchy of race relations that incorporates Asian difference into the model of the 'universal subject'.[28]

Concluding his review of Carter's *Buddhism and Its Christian Critics* (1897) with a call for a 'higher and scientific unity' which will 'transcend all racial distinctions', Tan sees Charles Darwin's evolutionary theories as critical for the development of more secular and racially aware forms of comparative understanding free from essentialist biologism and unwelcome Christian proselytising.[29] In his lengthy serialised article 'Chinese Problems', Tan embraces natural history models of variability and slow growth as a counterpoint both to '[h]asty views' of China by 'outsiders' that see it as immobile and despotic, and to the static and flattening tendencies of racial theory. Instead of analysing cultures and/or the relations between cultures 'entirely from *above-downwards*', Tan instead proposes a tree-shaped methodological model that argues for the functional interdependence of different parts of the cultural organism: '[Chinese civilization] is a *natural growth* and has its roots and branches in racial characteristics and national institutions, while the government is merely its leaves'.[30]

Capitalising on the evolutionary thrust of the 'tree of life' metaphor in *On the Origin of Species* (1859), Tan critiques those European comparatists who anachronistically extract Chinese manners and customs from their longer social, cultural, and historical contexts.[31] Indeed, the hastiness of foreign judgement towards China is a central theme of the magazine more generally.[32] In one of the many articles on the status of Chinese women, Lim Boon Keng (writing under the pseudonym Lim Ming Cheng) claims that '[f]oreigners recognise the secondary place Chinese women occupy without thinking of the complementary nature of their functions in the social economy. They … generalise from exceptions and abnormalities'. Lim's critique involves not just a reversal of the European comparative gaze by a hypothetical 'Chinese observer' in London and Paris (itself reminiscent of the infamous Chinese 'hypothetical mandarin'), but also an exposition of the defective use of Enlightenment methodologies by European comparatists: 'What a terrible picture of European life would be painted by a Chinese observer who made his observations among the inhabitants of the slums of London and Paris.'[33]

If Lim's defence of Chinese culture and society operates at the expense of a Chinese and Malay *lumpen proletariat* of '"cooks, coolies, carters"', it nonetheless usefully illuminates the ongoing tensions between indentured, free, and 'native' populations in the Straits. The elite 'orientalising' of 'social inferiors' as 'backward' was particularly prevalent in cosmopolitan port towns like Singapore where large diasporas and multi-imperial states produced various modernising projects based on the desire to figuratively and literally separate the 'modern' from the 'pre-modern' subject.[34] Actively encouraged by the Chinese Protectorate (est. 1877) to territorialise their own populations into ethno-environmental categories, the magazine's pan-Asiatic solidarities repeatedly break down in the face of 'backward-looking' Malay peasants and foreign-born 'sojourning' Chinese diasporas, who are portrayed in the magazine by G. T. Hare, the deputy Protector of Chinese, as unsettled, unhygienic, self-regulating entities without any permanent loyalty to the British regime.[35]

At the same time, a favourite tactic employed by the *Straits Chinese Magazine* is to point out how British interlocutors fall short of their own claims to neutrality and superior empirical knowledge systems: comparatists employ uneven and faulty grounds of comparison by comparing non-equivalent classes of people, while tourists and travelling correspondents 'express opinions not directly founded upon personal observation'.[36] Many of the critiques of British sinologists in the *Straits Chinese Magazine* similarly rest on their lack of methodological empiricism, Eurocentric comparative bias, and/or flawed generalisations.[37] Indeed, as Lim and Tan were only too aware, comparatism, in effect, made possible these kinds of generalities by subjugating the importance of direct lived experience to the creation of knowledge based on an 'abstract scale' of civilisational progress.[38]

A second key tactic used by the *Straits Chinese Magazine* is to attack attempts to essentialise or fetishise Chinese difference. A pseudonymous review by T. B. G. of Arthur Smith's *Chinese Characteristics* (1894) complains that the author (a missionary in China for over twenty years) has wilfully misunderstood Chinese society and culture, deliberately making 'things appear strange and peculiar'.[39] Employing a comparative perspective to critique western comparatist culture, T. B. G. co-opts a series of western proverbs to argue that 'the faults which form [the author's] long series of complaints are universal, and that "human nature is the same all the world over"'.[40] Other articles in the *Straits Chinese Magazine* similarly attempt to de-essentialise Chinese difference – in particular, claims of Chinese cruelty – by noting that supposedly 'Chinese' customs such as infanticide are not unknown in Europe and America, as well as comparing foot-binding to tight-lacing and piercings among Europeans.[41] An article by Wen Ching (another pseudonym of Lim Boon Keng) entitled 'Deformity as an Element of Beauty', for example, merges species and aesthetic discourses by explaining Chinese customs through the distinction between the beautiful and the sublime – itself a heavily racialised distinction in the Kantian tradition. If Lim follows 'Darwinian principles' in concluding that '[n]ature will win by exterminating ... rebellious races', his point is to show that all races use artificial disfigurements of the human body to 'realise certain vague conceptions of ideal beauty'.[42]

That comparison should end in this kind of universalism is not entirely surprising since comparison ultimately depends on the abandonment of radical difference. In this case, however, the use of comparative methodologies to assert the universality of human nature by Straits Chinese authors seems actively to draw on a western imperial epistemology which sought to 'align or educate the regnant forms of the unfamiliar with its own expectations'.[43] This strategy is perhaps most pronounced in the magazine's renditions of Malay and Chinese literary history, where a sense of Asian culture as Europe's degenerate shadow is most apparent, and where Malay and Chinese writers appear haunted by the prospect of civilisational stagnation or decline.[44] Increasingly focusing their attention on Chinese-language education and classical Chinese literature, Lim and Tan set out to rethink the place of Chinese culture in a multilingual imperial state, partly to prevent their 'national existence' from being 'swallowed up' by the Malay language and 'a local *patois* of English', and partly to prevent the creation of an imperial underclass of English-language literate Chinese clerks, who can quote Shakespeare, Milton, Johnson, and Macaulay but whose 'life-long drudgery at the counting desk' bears more than a passing resemblance to that of illiterate 'coolie' labourers.[45]

Utilitarian limits: Chinese and Malay literary history

Outlining both the classical and popular literary productions of the Han (206 BC–220 AD) and Tang (618–907 AD) dynasties from romances to encyclopedia, Tan Teck Soon argues in the third and concluding part of 'Some Genuine Chinese Authors' that 'in the poetry of the Tangs, the mental attainments of the Chinese reached their highest limit'. Although the Tang dynasty is generally considered to be one of the golden ages of ancient Chinese culture and history, Tan suggests that the 'unfitness of the Chinese mind to abstract reasoning' prevented the Tang Chinese from achieving the sublimity of Indian or Semitic poetry, instead producing a more prosaic, utilitarian version of poetic discourse. Even under the Sung dynasty (960–1279 AD), where there was a somewhat greater 'passion for speculative philosophy', Chinese intellectuals 'refused to be tempted to realms of abstract imagination' and instead produced predominantly practical treatises and tracts. In contrast to Malay literature, which is characterised by both Chinese and British authors as fanciful and hyperbolic, Tan sees Chinese literature's lack of 'enthusiasm' as its greatest defect, one which 'impairs' even its poetry and makes its philosophical works 'monotonous and uninspiring'.[46]

It quickly becomes clear, however, that the point of Tan's pan-Asian comparatism is to render Chinese literary culture compatible with developments in western literary culture, envisaging a return to a vernacular tradition of classic Chinese literature as consistent with a 'modern' cultural continuity:

Chinese literature 'has its analogue in the concrete tendency to which Western civilization itself is becoming more and more exposed, through its wealth of material details and its intense passion for scientific organization and visible uses'. Ultimately making a virtue of Chinese utilitarianism and concreteness, Tan argues for the proto-realism and proto-empiricism of Chinese literary culture, thereby subverting the orientalist stereotypes of European observers of China, and reducing his initial production of difference – the 'vast and complex civilization which appears to the stranger as belonging to a different planetary sphere' – to commensurability with a western 'passion for scientific organization'. If the belatedness of western empiricism is hinted at – both Tan and Lim believed that Confucianism had anticipated Enlightenment philosophy in its secular rationalism – there is nonetheless a clear attempt to reduce the unfamiliar to the commensurable: the 'different planetary' perspective of the east, which seemingly leaves it outside western universalism by implying, quite literally, the perspective of an entire planet, is shown to be just another version of the same thing, with Chinese culture and religion demonstrating the 'tolerant *spirit* of its civilization and ... its assimilative faculty'.[47]

In emphasising the assimilative faculties of Chinese culture, Tan is responding to the tendency of the west to dismiss the 'native imagination as the place of the fetish', rescuing ancient Chinese culture from accusations of mysticism and superstition.[48] Part of the goal of the *Straits Chinese Magazine* is to wean the Chinese community from what Sanjay Krishnan has called 'older ways of sense-making and being in the world', leaving behind those superstitions and 'silly tales' associated with 'pre-modern' forms of knowledge.[49] At the same time, there is also a serious attempt in the magazine to repatriate or recuperate Chinese and Malay folk tales.[50] Adopting a strategy that is part reversal and part assimilation, western comparative methodologies are therefore used against themselves in order to valorise Chinese culture as prior to European culture while simultaneously avowing and disavowing more traditional types of literary expression by seeing literary modernity as a dialectic between 'modern' and 'pre-modern' forms.[51]

The sense that the 'silly tales' of non-European literary traditions must be left behind is more pronounced in representations of Malay literary culture. That the Malays had little respect for their own literary history was a circulating theme among British and Chinese scholars of Malay literature. Whereas the Straits Chinese are said to have long had an 'unbounded confidence in the excellence of Chinese literature', the President of the Straits Branch of the Royal Asiatic Society, Archdeacon George F. Hose, argued in 1879 that Malays must be taught to 'value their own literature'.[52] Similarly, in a series of eleven articles published under the pseudonym 'Senex' and entitled 'Why Are the Malays Withering Away?' in the first Romanised

Malay newspaper *Bintang Timor* (est. 1894), founded by Song Ong Siang and Tan Boon Chin, it was pointed out, 'for the good of the Malays', that Malay economic and educational backwardness was due to their 'slavish adherence to outmoded custom'.[53] *Bintang Timor* received a heated response from the editors of the Malay newspaper *Jawi Peranakan* (est. 1876), but to some extent this paternalistic view of Malay culture as 'remnant' is echoed by Malay commentators in the *Straits Chinese Magazine* – for example, by Shaik Othman bin Sallim in his 1898 article on Malay *bangsawan* (opera). While the Malays have 'made more progress in the histrionic arts than the Chinese', Sallim concludes that the Malays are 'little known and still less understood' by an Anglophone reading audience, largely because they have taken little interest in preserving their own customs and folklore, which are fast disappearing 'before the path of European civilization'.[54]

Apart from Shaik Othman bin Sallim's article on Malay opera and two articles by Song Ong Siang on Abdullah bin Abdul al Kadir, who Song represents as the almost single-handed progenitor of Malay literary modernity, the only article-length examination of Malay literature in the magazine is an article entitled 'The Poetry of the Malays' (1897) by the British administrator and linguist R. J. Wilkinson, then Acting Inspector of Schools in Singapore.[55] Wilkinson attempts to undo some of the unfair stereotypes surrounding Malay peoples, including charges of illiteracy, but when sketching out the revival of popular Malay poetry he is mostly struck by the extent to which such poetry is 'not likely to be appreciated by Europeans'. The pantun, for example, is 'a most powerful form of poetry', yet when translated into English it 'loses the conciseness, mystery and force which endear it to the Malay'. Noting that many Europeans, from Victor Hugo to Hugh Clifford, have attempted but failed to render literal translations of the pantun, and that several Dutch experts, such as Baron von Hoevell and Dr van der Tuuk, have puzzled over the connection between its two halves, Wilkinson concludes that what is lost in translation is significant.[56]

Wilkinson's initial account of the apparent incommensurability of the pantun – and its resistance to translation into European languages based on deep grammatical and linguistic difference – leads him to a more general appreciation of Malay poetry, albeit one that is profoundly Eurocentric in its outlook and tone. Employing a universalising metric of global equivalence, Wilkinson takes the well-known lines from a popular Thomas Hood poem, 'The Bridge of Sighs' (1844), to give the reader 'some idea of Malay construction':

> One more unfortunate,
>   Weary of breath,
> Rashly importunate,
>   Gone to her death.

While many consider these lines 'elliptical', Wilkinson argues that, like the pantun, they nonetheless convey 'a definite meaning'. Similarly, he suggests that some lines from Canto II of Byron's *Childe Harold's Pilgrimage* (1812) allow us to see 'a succession of pictures all the more vividly because of the absence of auxiliary verbs, conjunctions, predicates and other portions of the mechanism of a sentence':

> The flying Mede, his shaftless broken bow;
>   The fiery Greek, his red pursuing spear;
> Mountains above; Earth's, Ocean's plain below;
>   Death in the van, Destruction in the rear

Malay, Wilkinson concludes, is 'impossible of adaptation to argument' but, like the poetry of Hood and Byron, it is 'brief and forcible when expressing a succession of simple ideas'.[57] The recalcitrant particularity of the pantun – its essential difference – is bridged by the apparent universality of poetic style.

Despite his admiration of some recent Malay publications which 'go far to acquit [the Malay] of the charge of being apathetic, illiterate and dull', Wilkinson's Eurocentric 'appreciation' of Malay poetry eventually collapses under the force of his insistence that the point of studying Malay literature does not lie in its intrinsic interest but rather in the way it enables an understanding of the 'native mind'. If Wilkinson's conclusion is that 'the Malay understands the European far better than the European understands the Malay', he nonetheless represents Malay literature as a naive mirror of Malay culture: 'There is not a veil of suspicion over his literature. It was not written to deceive the European. It is natural utterance and, if properly understood, represents a true picture of Malay life.' Wilkinson's reflections on the ways in which Malay poetry can help the European reader overcome various forms of deception and misrecognition suggest the extent to which his 'Malay' is an abstraction, represented through literary texts rather than through everyday life, conversation, or the experience of encounter: 'Great as is the power of personal relations, it must not be forgotten that the Malay in conversation is on his guard and represents himself not as he is but as he would like us to believe him.' In undermining the integrity of the encounter, Wilkinson confines the Malay-as-type to a symbolic expression of Malayness, to the 'embodiment of an abstract type' that is removed from a life world or way of being and becomes only a way of knowing.[58]

Summoning Shakespeare, Confucius, and Dickens

The same strategy of equivalence used by Wilkinson in his article on Malay poetry is, to some extent, adopted by Straits Chinese writers to accumulate the kind of cultural capital required for participation in the colonial public sphere. Quoting Shakespeare, Dryden, Byron, Keats, Shelley, Tennyson, and other writers that signified British learning, and modelling their essays and short stories on those by Dickens, Charles Lamb, and Wilkie Collins, this referencing of British culture made visible, as Holden has put it, 'the split between the pedagogic (the accumulated sense of British national identity) and the performative (the manner in which such identity is reinscribed, and rephrased in the colonies)'.[59] Yet amid the dazzling displays of knowledge, there are examples of a more critical position. If Shakespeare, Dickens, and others are meant to stand as placeholders for certain cultural values – and for the universalism of British culture more generally – the magazine can equally deflect the self-proclaimed universality of the western canon.

Two short case studies demonstrate the ways in which British universality is undermined by both Straits Chinese and British writers. The first is a colloquy written by the Reverend Archibald Lamont, a Scottish Presbyterian missionary from Glasgow, who founded the Singapore Chinese Educational Institute in 1892 to educate Chinese men for leadership roles.[60] The second, a short story modelled on Dickens' *A Christmas Carol* (1843), was published anonymously by Lim Boon Keng.[61] In Lamont's colloquy, 'Two Real Ghosts', the aptly named Mr Yew Go Back and Mr Wo Wo Bee meet to discuss the possibility of a séance as part of their newly formed Spiritualist Society. They are subsequently joined by a friend, Mr Wee Tin Tack, and three Europeans: Mr Flabbyton, who is well liked by the Chinese community; Mr Wingwye, who has attended on the condition that he be allowed to say what he thinks; and Mr Carson, who is 'fresh from Europe'. During the séance, the ghost of Shakespeare is called upon and he too is 'fresh from Europe' or, in other words, unacculturated in the ways of eastern culture. After criticising the 'Chinaman's English' and their '"jip" tones', Shakespeare characterises his own genius as being able to 'see human nature and paint it true. My watchword is character.'[62]

Satirising both popular accounts of the universality of Shakespearean character types and the idea of Renaissance humanism as something that could be used to 'civilise' native populations, Lamont's Shakespeare goes on to argue that the Straits Chinese character is degenerate: 'Be Chinese civilization what it may – let the fluid West be transparent with the faults of hell – the civilization of the Straits Chinese spells failure.'[63] His pronouncements on Asian degeneracy trigger a disagreement among the Europeans along Anglicist and Orientalist lines. Mr Wingwye sees Shakespeare's comments as a confirmation that 'it's no good educating the Chinese on our lines', whereas the more sympathetic Mr Flabbyton characterises Shakespeare as a symbol for western cultural values that make no sense in an eastern context: 'I'm glad he's gone. Had Shakespeare lived twenty years in the East as I've done, he'd be more charitable.'[64]

If Shakespeare stands as a symbol for ethnocentrism on a grand scale, as well as for the ways in which western literary classics lose their meaning and value outside of a European context, Confucius fares little better. The Chinese gentlemen summon Confucius as representative of their position, although they are ironically unable to speak to him in Chinese (speaking only a colloquial Straits Malay patois) and are worried about the fact that they have not registered their society under the Societies Ordinance and could therefore occasion his deportation – a position that echoes Lamont's ongoing concern with British attempts to circumscribe the free movement of Chinese immigrants. Reflecting Lamont's Presbyterian background, Confucius denies Confucianism's status as a religion: 'Have I ever claimed to be a religious teacher? Never. I taught ethics and politics to an ungrateful generation.'[65] Concluding that his teachings have been obfuscated by mysticism and that '[y]ou revere me not for my own sake nor for the sake of my teaching, but simply that you may shirk the obligations of your time' [i.e. reform], the story ends without any sense of agreement between the Straits Chinese and their British friends, pointing to the incommensurability of their religious beliefs and their positions as coloniser and colonised, as well as to the failure of either Shakespeare or Confucius, as representative figures of a western and eastern canon, to adequately speak to or reconcile those positions.

The failure of universalism also figures in the short story 'A Vision of Bong Khiam Siap'. Like Ebenezer Scrooge, Bong Khiam Siap, which means salty or rubbery in Hokkien, is a miserly self-made man.[66] Having come to Singapore at the age of eighteen to work as a cook's assistant in a Chinese business house, he eventually runs the firm through a combination of hard work and blatant self-interest. Now one of the conservative elite and a staunch opponent of the Straits Chinese reform party, Bong proposes a donation to a Diamond Jubilee Memorial Hall in honour of Queen Victoria, but refuses to support an alternative proposal – a local institution for the education of girls – on the basis that female education 'is like throwing money into a pool of dirty water'.[67] Following the logic of Dickens' original story, Bong has a visionary dream sequence triggered by the celebrations surrounding Queen Victoria's Jubilee in which he is twenty-five years older. The Straits Chinese population in Singapore has increased but women vastly outnumber the men. This, we are told, is directly related to Bong's own lack of support for local education: the influx of highly trained foreign wage earners has meant that the Straits Chinese men have been forced to emigrate elsewhere.

The story uses Dickens' visionary conceit to travel to a Chinese women's prison where uneducated women are caught in a cycle of gaming, debt, addiction, and ruin; a Chinese club frequented by high-class Chinese prostitutes; a children's hospital with female Chinese nurses; and a domestic household where a young literate Chinese girl provides for her family by painting candles. These dream visions gather together some intersecting themes that run throughout the various issues of the *Straits Chinese Magazine* including Chinese reform and the nature it should take; the education of Straits Chinese communities and its economic benefit to Britain; the position and education of Straits Chinese women as an index of Chinese civilisation; and Queen Victoria's Golden Jubilee celebration and the best way for loyalist Straits Chinese to mark the occasion.[68] Yet despite his remarkable dream and the lessons it potentially entails, we are told that Bong's view of reform did not change at all and that he has failed to redeem himself in any meaningful way: 'Bong Khiam Siap died as he had lived – a stern and uncompromising opponent of any form of education for Straits Chinese women, and a bitter enemy of the reform party.'[69]

The failure of Dickens' moral-conversion narrative echoes an accompanying article in the same volume on 'Straits Chinese Hedonism' by W. C. Lin (another of Lim Boon Keng's pseudonyms). The article is ostensibly about Straits Chinese dandies but it also depicts the character of the 'Baba miser' who loves the 'Almighty Dollar' and 'chooses to inhabit filthy premises, to eat coarse food, and to dress in rags'.[70] While the Baba Miser's stinginess hints – like Scrooge's lonely and unhappy childhood – at a traumatic history of hardship, Lim argues that educated reformists must rise up against the self-made man who has not taken the opportunity to educate himself or others: 'We must begin the campaign in our own homes, then try to carry it through in the *kampong* and finally assail the strongest positions held by the hereditary enemies of progress – the wealthy conservatives.'[71] Lacking the capacity for change and personal emancipation, these miserly conservatives are, for Lim, comparable to their consumptive opposites, the dandies: both are selfish capitalists and slaves of a foreign imperial system that simultaneously guarantees their economic prosperity and defers their entitlement to universal rights.

Lim's emphasis on the repudiation of material self-interest makes itself felt throughout the magazine in what Holden has called its disciplinary 'body project'; that is, a project rooted in the idea that self-discipline, self-improvement, and a kind of muscular Confucianism would lead to an autonomous Chinese society free from colonial governance and paternalistic protective measures.[72] Here the Arnoldian consciousness of a 'best self' is entangled with the political project of using 'disinterested self-cultivation' to construct an extra-economic space 'homologous with the universal collective interest'.[73] As this article suggests, Dickens' story is not being used in the magazine in the familiar or straightforward sense of mimicry or cultural transmission but rather in the service of a politically charged campaign against wealthy Chinese conservatives opposed to widespread economic and political reform – one that might be extended to and carried through proletariat kampongs (villages). It is, of course, possible to read this article in a Gramscian sense as the attempt of an emergent bourgeoisie elite to assert 'moral-intellectual leadership' over a labouring peasantry, but it also demonstrates the ways in which the language of culture is used to position an emerging national or collective life as a force working against the capitalist 'determinations of petty self-interest'.[74]

Ethnic nationalism in Southeast Asia

Representations of literary culture in the *Straits Chinese Magazine* register the claims of two influential sets of ideas: the first is the set of ideas surrounding comparatism and related forms of civilisational and cultural development; the second is the set of ideas surrounding liberal universalism. Elucidating the ways in which these two discourses work together to produce 'modernity's dream of a universal subject' has been one of the key aims of this chapter.[75] The tactic of universal equivalence is used by Lim Boon Keng, Tan Teck Soon, and other Straits Chinese contributors to minimise the fetishisation of Chinese difference, to taxonomise and transcode Chinese customs and creative expressions within well-established European comparatist frameworks, and to produce an 'equivalence of judgement' from which to assess their own culture.[76]

For all these reasons, the magazine is conventionally read as an apology for both British and Chinese imperialism, occupying an 'awkward place in the historiography of the decolonial order', and inhabiting the uneasy space of bourgeois politics and writing in English in a moment of emerging Malay anticolonial nationalism.[77] As Neil Khor has pointed out, Straits Chinese reform sat in particular tension with the development of ethnic nationalism in Malaya, where Malays rejected the Straits Chinese claim to a 'homeland', indigeneity, and/or settled status, and shifted to writing in Malaysian rather than English.[78] Elite Anglophone literary societies and periodicals in the Straits Settlements are therefore often associated with a kind of 'performed Englishness', whereby loyalism and participation in the colonial public sphere is seen as false consciousness, at odds with the more authentic forms of radicalism associated with workers and peasants in the kampongs.[79] In particular, the aspiration of universality is perceived as a racialised project trapped within a colonial ethnographic logic, while pan-Asian internationalism is seen as the 'failed negation of nationalism'.[80]

Yet such narratives, as Peter Hill has pointed out, are in danger of retroactively 'direct[ing] our attention ... to the *provenance* of ideas and cultural practices' as 'western versus eastern' or 'traditional-inherited' versus 'modern-imported' rather than to their (then) contemporary resonances and meanings.[81] The *Straits Chinese Magazine*'s ideological and representational structures are certainly informed by the 'universal value form' inculcated by English-language education, but Straits Chinese writers by no means simply reproduce the discourse of the universal equivalent, instead consciously and unconsciously bringing into play supressed Sinocentric and Islamocentric perspectives.[82] There is a strong sense in the magazine, for example, that comparatism retains and naturalises Eurocentric racial distinctions, and that there are good and bad forms of comparison.[83] Similarly, the magazine's explicit flirtations with British literary authors and texts often work to render them unfamiliar rather than familiar, suggesting the ways in which Anglophone styles, forms, and plots were used to point to the false universalism of western norms in a Southeast Asian context. Certainly, the Straits Chinese community never simply self-identified as non-white 'Britishers', asserting their own modernity and cultural particularity, as well as an autonomous inner domain or 'spirit' separate from the universalising claims of imperial liberalism: 'the reform must be a real reform within and without, not a mere adoption of a European external covering to hide the old sores of an inner life'.[84]

Mark Frost, Saul Dubow, Daniel Goh, and others have recently argued for the importance of reformist and petit-bourgeois nationalists who used 'the language of late-nineteenth-century liberalism to call the British Empire to account', noting that 'assertions of Britishness or Englishness could run counter to the declared interests of the British state'.[85] It is therefore possible to understand the *Straits Chinese Magazine* as an attempt to think and agitate pluricentrically for 'contending political futures' rather than as crudely nationalist or anti-nationalist or as a minor episode in an inevitable teleology towards future or emergent nationhoods.[86] The plural forms of cultural nationalism in the *Straits Chinese Magazine* point to the importance of English-language periodical culture in the emergence of Southeast Asian nationalisms and to the extent to which ethnic nationalisms could emerge from apparently loyalist periodicals. If by 1907 the *Straits Chinese Magazine* was abandoned because of a lack of support among its intended reading audience of elite Malay and Chinese communities, its reformist agenda and belief in the importance of culture for Chinese identity was later mobilised by Sun Yat-sen in the service of a more aggressive kind of cultural nationalism and sinification – one that rested on a revitalised Confucianism as a distinctive form of religious modernity, and saw Chinese-language education both as a source of national strength and an effective response to the ongoing threat of western imperialism.[87]

Acknowledgements

This research was funded by the European Research Council under the Horizon 2020 research and innovation programme (grant agreement no.

679436). My thanks go to Gracie Lee, Special Collections, National Library of Singapore, for her assistance with sources for this chapter, and to Hussein Omar for his insightful suggestions and comments.

Notes

1 *Straits Chinese Magazine (SCM)*, 1:2 (June 1897), 63. See also *SCM*, 1:3 (September 1897), 95–9, and *SCM*, 1:4 (December 1897), 136–41.

2 *SCM*, 1:2 (June 1897), 64–5.

3 Mark Ravinder Frost, '*Emporium in imperio*: Nanyang Networks and the Straits Chinese in Singapore, 1819–1914', *Journal of Southeast Asian Studies*, 36 (2005), 29–36; Jan Van de Putten, 'Abdullah Munsyi and the Missionaries', *Bijdragen tot de Taal-, Land-en Volkenkunde (BKI)*, 162:4 (2006), 407–40.

4 Mark Frost, '"Wider Opportunities": Religious Revival, Nationalist Awakening and the Global Dimension in Colombo, 1870–1920', *Modern Asian Studies*, 36:4 (2002), 937–67; Isabel Hofmeyr, 'The Black Atlantic Meets the Indian Ocean: Forging New Paradigms of Transnationalism for the Global South – Literary and Cultural Perspectives', *Social Dynamics: A Journal of African Studies*, 33:7 (2007), 7.

5 Tony Ballantyne, 'Mobility, Empire, Colonisation', *History Australia*, 11:2 (2014), 25. See also Janet L. Abu-Lughod, *Before European Hegemony: The World System A. D. 1250–1350* (Oxford: Oxford University Press, 1989); John M. Hobson, *The Eastern Origins of Western Civilisation* (Cambridge: Cambridge University Press, 2004).

6 Frost, '"Wider Opportunities"', 940.

7 See also *SCM*, 1:2 (June 1897), 64–7, *SCM*, 2:5 (March 1898), 18, and *SCM*, 5:19 (September 1901), 96. Song and Lim were educated at the elite Raffles Institution in Singapore and subsequently as Queen's Scholars at Cambridge and Edinburgh Universities, where Song studied law and Lim studied medicine.

8 *SCM*, 1:1 (March 1897), 2, 20; Philip Holden, 'Communities and Conceptual Limits: Exploring Malaysian Literature in English', *Asiatic*, 3:2 (2009), 58.

9 For a general overview, see Bonny Tan, *The Straits Chinese Magazine*: A Malayan Voice', *BiblioAsia*, 7:2 (2011), 30–5.

10 Terry Eagleton, *Literary Theory: An Introduction* (Oxford: Blackwell, 1983), p. 56.

11 Uday Singh Mehta, *Liberalism and Empire: A Study in Nineteenth-Century British Liberal Thought* (Chicago: University of Chicago Press, 1999), pp. 18, 20.

12 Rita Felski and Susan Stanford Friedman, 'Introduction', in Rita Felski and Susan Stanford Friedman (eds), *Comparison: Theories, Approaches, Uses* (Baltimore: Johns Hopkins University Press, 2013), p. 2. On the Eurocentrism of comparison, see, e.g., Ann Laura Stoler, 'Tense and Tender Ties: The Politics of Comparison in North American History and (Post) Colonial Studies', *The Journal of American History*, 88:3 (2001), 829–65 (esp. 863–4); and Johannes Fabian, *Time and the Other: How Anthropology Makes Its Object*, foreword Matti Bunzl (1983; New York: Columbia University Press, 2002).

13 Andrew Sartori, *Bengal in Global Concept History: Culturalism in the Age of Capital* (Chicago: University of Chicago Press, 2008), p. 9; Hofmeyr, 'Black Atlantic', 7–8. On European claims to universality, see Dipesh Chakrabarty, *Provincializing Europe: Postcolonial Thought and Historical Difference* (Princeton: Princeton University Press, 2000).

14 Manu Goswami, 'Imaginary Futures and Colonial Internationalisms', *The American Historical Review*, 117:5 (2012), 1471–2, and 'Autonomy and Comparability: Notes on the Anticolonial and the Postcolonial', *boundary 2*, 32:2 (2005), 204, 205. See also Sartori, *Bengal in Global Concept History*, esp. pp. 5, 19, 22.

15 Chinese authority structures in the Straits were regarded by the British as something like a parallel *imperium in imperio*. See, e.g., *SCM*, 2:5 (March 1898), 1–2.

16 Mark Frost, 'Imperial Citizenship or Else: Liberal Ideals and the Indian Unmasking of Empire, 1890–1919', *The Journal of Imperial and Commonwealth History*, 46:5 (2018), 866.

17 See, e.g., *SCM*, 3:10 (June 1899), 61–7, and *SCM*, 3:11 (September 1899), 106–12; Holden, 'Communities and Conceptual Limits', 58.

18 Philip Holden, 'Colonial Fiction, Hybrid Lives: Early Singaporean Fiction in *The Straits Chinese Magazine*', *Journal of Commonwealth Literature*, 33:1 (1998), 87; *SCM*, 2:7 (September 1898), 90.

19 Trevor Ross, *The Making of the English Literary Canon: From the Middle Ages to the Late Eighteenth Century* (Montreal and Kingston: McGill-Queen's University Press, 1998), p. 228.

20 Michael Allan, 'Reading with One Eye, Speaking with One Tongue: On the Problem of Address in World Literature', *Comparative Literature*, 44:1–2 (2007), 15. For a direct reference to Arnold, see *SCM*, 6:21 (March 1902), 97.

21 *SCM*, 1:3 (September 1897), 96. On colonial literary education, see Gauri Viswanathan, *Masks of Conquest: Literary Studies and British Rule in India* (New York: Columbia University Press, 1989); and Daniel Goh, 'Elite Schools, Postcolonial Chineseness and Hegemonic Masculinities in Singapore', *British Journal of Sociology of Education*, 36:1 (2005), 137–55.

22 *SCM*, 5:18 (June 1901), 66. See also *SCM*, 6:21 (March 1902), 30.

23 Eric Hayot, *The Hypothetical Mandarin: Sympathy, Modernity, and Chinese Pain* (Oxford: Oxford University Press, 2009), p. 9. See, e.g., *SCM*, 5:19 (September 1901), 108.

24 *SCM*, 5:19 (June 1901), 96. See also Ah Sing's argument that '[n]o one nation contains all the best that has been thought and said in the world', in *SCM*, 6:21 (March 1902), 97.

25 Devin Griffiths, *The Age of Analogy: Science and Literature between the Darwins* (Baltimore: Johns Hopkins University Press, 2016), p. 14.

26 See, e.g., *SCM*, 2:5 (March 1898), 31. On European sinologists, see *SCM*, 1:2 (June 1897), 64. Müller is called a 'champion of the cause of the misunderstood Asiatics' in *SCM*, 5:17 (March 1901), 10.

27 *SCM*, 2:5 (March 1898), 31.

28 See Sanjay Krishnan's 'History and the Work of Literature in the Periphery', *Novel: A Forum on Fiction*, 42 (2009), 483–9 (esp. 485), and 'Reading Globalization from the Margin: The Case of Abdullah Munshi', *Representations*, 99 (2007), 40–73 (esp. 51).

29 *SCM*, 5:19 (September 1901), 83. See also *SCM*, 1:1 (March 1897), 26.

30 *SCM*, 2:8 (December 1898), 132.

31 Charles Darwin, *On the Origin of Species* (London: John Murray, 1859), p. 129. See also Lim's rejection of an immediate reform of Chinese customs in favour of 'first shaping public opinion' and his pen name 'Historicus', *SCM*, 1:3 (September 1897), 110, and *SCM*, 5:18 (June 1901), 51.

32 See, e.g., *SCM*, 1:1 (March 1897), 16, and *SCM*, 1:4 (December 1897), 158. On the 'self-conceit and egotism' of Europeans in the east, see *SCM*, 7:3 (September 1903), 101.

33 *SCM*, 1:4 (December 1897), 158. See also *SCM*, 5:19 (September 1901), 154.

34 *SCM*, 2:7 (September 1898), 117. On the elite 'orientalising' of social inferiors in the Egyptian context, see Hussein Omar, 'Arabic Thought in the Liberal Cage', in Faisal Devji and Zaheer Kazmi (eds), *Islam after Liberalism* (Oxford: Oxford University Press, 2005), p. 19.

35 *SCM*, 1:1 (March 1897), 3–8.

36 *SCM*, 2:8 (December 1898), 154.

37 See, e.g., *SCM*, 2:5 (March 1898), 29, and *SCM*, 1:4 (December 1897), 182.

38 Mehta, *Liberalism and Empire*, pp. 20–1.

39 *SCM*, 2:7 (September 1898), 116.

40 *SCM*, 2:7 (September 1898), 117.

41 *SCM*, 1:2 (March 1897), 55–6. On European cruelty in war, see, *SCM*, 5:19 (September 1901), 127.

42 *SCM*, 1:4 (December 1897), 164, 165.

43 Mehta, *Liberalism and Empire*, p. 18.

44 On the loss of the Chinese language, see *SCM*, 3:9 (March 1899), 11–15, and *SCM*, 11:4 (December 1907), 141–2.

45 *SCM*, 1:1 (March 1897), 7; *SCM*, 1:2 (June 1897), 54.

46 *SCM*, 1:4 (December 1897), 140, 141. See also the pan-Asian comparison in Tan's article on 'Chinese Problems', *SCM*, 2:5 (March 1898) 1–2.

47 *SCM*, 1:4 (December 1897), 141; *SCM*, 2:7 (September 1898), 89; *SCM*, 3:10 (June 1899), 70. On Confucianism and Enlightenment, see Christine Doran, 'Singapore', in Benjamin Isakhan and Stephen Stockwell (eds), *The Edinburgh Companion to the History of Democracy* (Edinburgh: Edinburgh University Press, 2012), pp. 258, 261.

48 Krishnan, 'Literature in the Periphery', 383. There is a strong sense throughout the magazine of writing back to British authors like Hugh Clifford. See, e.g., *SCM*, 2:5 (March 1898), 38, *SCM*, 5:19 (September 1901), 116, and *SCM*, 9:2 (June 1905), 41.

49 Krishnan, 'Literature in the Periphery', 484.

50 See, e.g. *SCM*, 1:1 (March 1897), 12–14, and *SCM*, 8:3 (June 1904), 91–3.

51 Javed Majeed, 'Literary Modernity in South Asia', in Douglas Peers and Nandini Gooptu (eds), *India and the British Empire* (Oxford: Oxford University Press, 2012), pp. 265, 263; Mehta, *Liberalism and Empire*, pp. 18, 20

52 *SCM*, 1:2 (June 1897), 54; *Journal of the Malaysian Branch of the Royal Asiatic Society (JMBRAS)*, 4 (1879), xxi.

53 William R. Roff, *The Origins of Malay Nationalism* (Singapore: Oxford University Press, 1994), p. 54.

54 *SCM*, 2:8 (December 1898), 129, 131, 128.

55 On Abdullah Munshi, see *SCM*, 8:4 (December 1904), 190–202, and *SCM*, 9:3 (September 1905), 96.

56 *SCM*, 1:2 (June 1897), 39, 41, 47, 45, 47.

57 *SCM*, 1:2 (June 1897), 47.

58 *SCM*, 1:2 (June 1897), 47; Mehta, *Liberalism and Empire*, p. 25.

59 Philip Holden, 'China Men: Writing the British Nation in Malaya', *SPAN*, 38 (1994), 70–1. See, e.g., *SCM*, 1:1. March (1897), 16, 23, *SCM*, 1:2 (June 1897), 52, 53, and *SCM*, 1:4 (December 1897), 124

60 Lamont had close ties with Tan Teck Soon, with whom he purchased the *Daily Advertiser* in 1890, co-ran the Chinese Educational Institute, and collaborated on a novel, *Bright Celestials* (1894).

61 Khor, 'Imperial Cosmopolitan Malaya', 42.

62 *SCM*, 1:3 (September 1897), 100, 101.

63 *SCM*, 1:3 (September 1897), 100. For fears of degeneracy and/or stagnancy, see *SCM*, 2:7 (September 1898), 92; and *SCM*, 3:10 (June 1899), 59.

64 *SCM*, 1:3 (September 1897), 101.

65 On Confucianism as religion, see, e.g., *SCM*, 1:2 (June 1897), 58, and *SCM*, 3:12 (December 1899), 163–6. For Lim's fierce debate with William Murray over the superiority of Confucian 'universal truths', see *SCM*, 8:3 (September 1904), 128–30, *SCM*, 9:2 (June 1905), 73–8, and *SCM*, 9:3 (September 1905), 106–8.

66 Neil Khor, 'Imperial Cosmopolitan Malaya: A Study of Realist Fiction in the *Straits Chinese Magazine*', *JMBRAS*, 1 (2008), 37.

67 *SCM*, 4:15 (September 1900), 103, 103–4.

68 On 'native education', see *SCM*, 1:1 (March 1897), 27, *SCM*, 1:2 (June 1897), 71, *SCM*, 1:4 (December 1897), 174, and *SCM*, 4:15 (September 1900), 94. On Chinese women, see, e.g., *SCM*, 1:1 (March 1897), 16–23, and *SCM*, 5:19 (September 1901), 154–7.

69 *SCM*, 4:15 (September 1900), 108.

70 *SCM*, 4:15 (September 1900), 109.

71 *SCM*, 4:15 (September 1900), 111. See also *SCM*, 7:4 (December 1903), 130.

72 Philip Holden, 'The Beginnings of "Asian Modernity" in Singapore: A Straits Chinese Body Project', *Common/Plural*, 7:1 (1999), 59–78.

73 Andrew Sartori, 'The Resonance of "Culture": Framing a Problem in Global Concept-History', *Comparative Studies in Society and History*, 47:4 (2005), 682.

74 Sartori, *Bengal in Global Concept History*, p. 12, and 'The Resonance of "Culture"', 682, 683; Goswami, 'Autonomy and Comparability', 217. On the need for an 'Asiatic daily' that would be 'in touch with the Asiatic proletariat', see *SCM*, 9:2 (June 1905), 41.

75 Hayot, *The Hypothetical Mandarin*, p. 6.

76 See, e.g., *SCM*, 2:7 (September 1898), 92; and Krishnan, 'Reading Globalization', 54.

77 Mohd Noordin Sopiee, *From Malayan Union to Singapore Separation: Political Unification in the Malaysia Region, 1945–65* (Kuala Lumpur: University of Malaya Press, 1974), p. 75; Philip Holden, 'Dissonant Voices: Straits Chinese and the Appropriation of Travel Writing', *Studies in Travel Writing*, 2:1 (1998), 183; Daniel Goh, 'Unofficial Contentions: The Postcoloniality of Straits Chinese Political Discourse in the Straits Chinese Legislative Council', *Journal of Southeast Asian Studies*, 41:3 (2010), 484.

78 Neil Khor, 'Malacca's Straits Chinese Anglophone Poets and their Experience of Malaysian Nationalism', *Archipel*, 76 (2008), 127–49.

79 Philip Holden, 'The Littoral and the Literary: Making Moral Communities in the Straits Settlements and the Gold Coast in the Late Nineteenth and Early Twentieth Centuries', in Derek Heng and Syed Muhd Khairudin Aljunied (eds), *Singapore in Global Context* (Amsterdam: Amsterdam University Press, 2011), p. 93.

80 Denise Ferreira da Silva, *Toward a Global Idea of Race* (Minneapolis: University of Minnesota Press, 2007), p. 169; Goswami, 'Imaginary Futures', 1461.

81 Peter Hill, *Utopia and Civilisation in the Arab Nahda* (Cambridge: Cambridge University Press, 2020), pp. 9–10. See also Omar, 'Arabic Thought in the Liberal Cage', pp. 20, 21.

82 Krishnan, 'Reading Globalization', 59.

83 Griffiths, *Age of Analogy*, p. 17. On the 'haunting' legacies of bad or difficult comparison, see Benedict Anderson, *The Spectre of Comparisons: Nationalism, Southeast Asia and the World* (London: Verso, 1998).

84 *SCM*, 2:5 (March 1898), 25. See also Lim Boon Keng's *The Chinese Crisis from Within* (1901). On the fear of becoming 'Malayanised or Europeanised', see *SCM*, 3:10 (June 1899), 59.

85 Saul Dubow, 'How British Was the British World? The Case of South Africa', *The Journal of Imperial and Commonwealth History*, 37:1 (2009), 18.

86 Goswami, 'Imaginary Futures', 1462.

87 C. M. Turnbull, *A History of Modern Singapore, 1819–2005* (Singapore: National University of Singapore Press, 2009), p. 21.

The south in the world

Elleke Boehmer

In Herman Melville's huge and perennially remarkable novel *Moby-Dick* (1851), the fateful *Pequod* with Captain Ahab at the helm pursues his nemesis the eponymous white whale from the Atlantic through the Southern Ocean and the Indonesian archipelago into the South Seas. As it does so, its heterogeneous crew crosses paths with a number of other whalers, including the *Goney* (or the *Albatross*) and the *Rachel*. These are fortuitous crossings in those weltering immensities, yet each whaler is met with a sense of fateful inevitability and each encounter is heavy with inarticulate surmise and expectation. The crews as they pass one another have the impression that these vast southern immensities throw up north–south conjunctions. However, as profound is the feeling that the far extremities of the great oceans defy attempts to circumscribe and understand their immensity, especially those pitched from the north, represented here by Ahab. The narrator Ishmael's friend Queequeg, the tattooed Fijian, by contrast, is in his element for much of the *Pequod*'s journey. Yet he too, idol-worshipping and superstitious, is typecast according to northern conventions.[1]

As *Worlding the South* explores, southern hemisphere histories are threaded through with many tenuous and yet still tenacious human conjunctions like the *Pequod*'s – conjunctions often realised in or crystallised through maps, books, letters, panoramas, and other kinds of inscription and installation. These verbal, textual, and cartographic networks the book's contributors study in abundant, fascinating detail. As against the monolithic constructs of empire and nation of much nineteenth- and twentieth-century colonial history, the editors Sarah Comyn and Porscha Fermanis offer this transnational, transactional, and latitudinal south-centred project – one that zigzags through and across the nineteenth-century British world, but without at any point reifying it as a construct. The book puts in place a critical exercise of worlding, or, more properly, *re-worlding*, which is conceived as a double movement *both* of showing how the south was made into a knowable global object *and* of unravelling the representational strategies and entangled histories that made the south conceivable in this way. This endeavour allows the editors and contributors to deprioritise imperial orientations and identities in favour of southern perspectives, bringing in different circuits of production and alternative temporalities, including from Black and Indigenous worlds. Worlding as a methodology thus encourages the contributors critically to probe and re-examine how the world has been naturalised historically and invites contrapuntal, southern perspectives to come to the fore.

Each one of the book's eighteen detailed case studies contributes from its particular regional and methodological vantage point to this series of double movements, tracing from multiple different perspectives the gradual knitting of the lands, islands, and oceans of the British-governed southern hemisphere into the institutions of colonial modernity. From the late eighteenth century and the arrival in 1788 of the First Fleet on the east coast of the Australian continent, we see the widely separated spaces of the south stochastically folded into what Immanuel Wallerstein described as the one but uneven capitalist world, and we observe how local Black and Indigenous knowledge is often occluded, mistaken, overwritten, and erased as a result.[2] At the same time, we track the funnelling of human populations and communities through and around the shapes and contours of the southern hemisphere's main land masses and archipelagos – an important, age-old process, as Barry Lopez highlights in *Arctic Dreams* (1986): 'the way landscape funnels human movement, such that encounters with strangers are half expected', as they are on the *Pequod*.[3] The essays further trace the long-distance journeys not only of commodities and newspapers, but also of fads and fashions that refract from the metropolis to the Antipodes and then sometimes bounce from the colonies back to London, as wittily narrated, for example, in Clara Tuite's study of the Regency yet also antipodean cult of the dandy.

Worlding the South critically analyses from its range of regional, historical, and theoretical vantage points the combination of forces including trade, commerce, emigration, and travel through which the south was worlded – an external, objectifying process. But it also considers how the south might be reimagined from within. We focus on southern subjectivities, orientations, and perspectives – in short, worldings – and use these to attempt to rethink British or metropolitan hegemonies. We see how southern worlds emerge piece by piece from these different processes of knowledge-gathering and exchange, and then how critical re-reading might undo these Eurocentric and often imperial inscriptions.

Responding to the double movement that the book encourages, it is worth interchanging its core titular terms for a moment, or, as it were, spinning its poles, to ask what 'the south' *was* that was 'worlded' in these ways? What did and does this south comprise? How was and is it in actual fact lived and perceived? This may be a more provocative question – one that is probably too far-reaching to address satisfactorily in a book-ending chapter.[4] How the worlds of the south might themselves be set up epistemologically, what southern experience might entail, and how it is understood is dealt with more implicitly in these pages, perhaps unavoidably so, in what is a literary historical project first and foremost.

Indeed, I would venture to say, there is something about the study of southern worlds that might by definition have to remain always beyond our analytic reach. For the south ultimately far eludes the indices of otherness that scholars of different global souths have instated as compensatory short-hand for the southern hemisphere's alternative temporalities, as Comyn and Fermanis write. This chapter, 'The south in the world', tries to give a few tentative answers of its own to those questions of southness by offering a meditation in closing on some of the more elusive meanings of the south that the collection calls up, inspired by the same critical orientations that it explores. For reasons that I clarify further in later sections of the chapter, I begin by turning first to a cluster of literary writings from the south and, in particular, to the implications and glimmerings of alternative worlds they open to the reader. Without in any sense reinstating institutions of literature that have been largely northern in provenance and repressive in application, I contend that it is through the border-traversing, world-opening capacities of southern writing and reading that new perspectives on the south may be sparked.[5] In a word, re-worlding crucially begins with the insights of imaginative writing.

The south as 'sea country'

The southern-hemisphere novelist J. M. Coetzee, South African-born, now Australian, has audaciously suggested in recent years that there is only 'one south', a 'unique world' that seems, from his perspective, to circle the southern subtropics. In these spaces, he has evocatively yet cryptically written, 'the winds blow in a certain way and the leaves fall in a certain way and the sun beats down in a certain way that is instantly recognisable from one part of the South to another'.[6] As in his *Jesus* novel trilogy (2013–19), set in a fictional Southern Cone or Chile-like country, this south is remote, provincial, derivative, and Spanish-speaking. The region forms the final destination on a complicated but undisclosed migration route across the ocean that appears to strip migrant characters of any memory of their former homelands.[7] Key features such as climate manifest laterally in this cross-continental world, uniting its inhabitants through a framework of mutual recognition. (Indeed, the southern subtropical zone Coetzee appears to outline in actuality forms the most inhabited part of the hemisphere.) We notice, however, the extent to which this 'one south' defies expression, even for a writer as magisterially fluent as Coetzee. It can only be designated in so many unspecific phrases: 'in a certain way ... in a certain way ... in a certain way'.

For Indigenous Australian writer Alexis Wright in her phantasmagoric epic *Carpentaria* (2006), set in the Gulf country of north-western Queensland, the south is at times the place from which corrupt and out-of-touch Canberra politicians and their edicts issue. At a significant point in the novel, bushfires enflame the southern horizon, confirming it as a hostile zone.[8] Mostly, though, visions of 'seas of oceans' shared by elders, like Norm Phantom, and their heirs erase north–south as well as past–future divides. Country including 'sea country' subsumes such distinctions, as another elder, Joseph Midnight, openly recognises, while he at the same time interestingly denies the existence of a present-day or 'contemporary world'. To him, future and past are co-present: 'It's the same world as I live in, and before that, and before that. No such thing as a contemporary world.' Song and performances co-exist within and call up this continuous and living space–time though only if 'remembered in the right sequence where the sea was alive, waves were alive, currents alive, even the clouds'.[9] As a caution to all northern travellers and presumably scholars, too, this is country that will only allow us to move through it where it 'lets' us through.

In contrast to Wright's borderless vision of a tropical 'sea country', the Western Australian writer Tim Winton for his part tends to see the southern lands, seas, and skies he hymns in his fiction through a determinedly regional, specifically Western Australian, lens. Yet many of his enthused observations of these desert landscapes and ocean views are, at the same time, distinctively southern in a far broader and more ecumenical sense. As he writes in *Island Home* (2015): 'The white southern beaches won me over. They were the purest, the least trammelled and the loveliest I'd ever seen. And there were so many of them.'[10] Yet, we might immediately observe, many littorals of the southern oceans feature such beaches. They are not exclusive to his continent. From Winton's impassioned descriptions of what he sees as his country a strong sense of the south in the world thus arises obliquely, as if through cracks in the lens, as again in the following:

> In Australia the sky is not the safe enclosing canopy it appears to be elsewhere. It's the scantiest membrane imaginable, barely sufficient as a barrier between earthbound creatures and eternity. Standing alone at dawn on the Nullarbor, or out on a saltpan the size of a small country, you feel a twinge of terror because the sky seems to go on forever. It has perilous depths and oceanic movements. In our hemisphere the sky stops you in your tracks, derails your thoughts, unmoors you from where you were going before it got you by the collar.[11]

Notice how the description modulates from claiming such skies for Australia to allowing them to widen across 'our hemisphere'. *Yes, and* ... the southern reader of this passage would want to observe, feeling the impact of the evocation, recognising that depth of sky Winton is talking about, yet doing so from any number of possible vantage points across the south: not only the Nullarbor but also the Atacama, the Karoo, the Namib desert (all notable dark-sky sites across the hemisphere). Incidentally, the word *saltpan*, from Dutch through Afrikaans, nicely clinches the point. Winton needs to borrow a word from another southern world to describe a southern feature that forms a fundamental part of his sensory experience of the south.

Turning to my own fictional maps of the south for a moment, my 2019 short-story collection *To the Volcano* tries to capture from a range of different viewpoints similar latitudinal moments of southern awareness.[12] Stories set across the south – in Australia, South Africa, Zimbabwe, Botswana, and Argentina – reflect upon a distinctive southern sensorium while also registering aslant the south's histories of violence and dispossession. These moments of awareness – of distance, transit, haunting, ice-blue light, and 'seething' lands that elude naming – are spaced out across the south, and across the collection. Yet they remain horizontally connected, mapping intersecting contours of southern affinity. This project of navigation through story is supported at a formal level by the shape of the short-story collection itself – its pluricentredness permits effects of both dispersal and collocation, as also in the writing of Louis Becke, discussed in these pages, and indeed of his near contemporary the New Zealand-born Katherine Mansfield. The metaphor of the archipelago will unsurprisingly return later in this chapter via Epeli Hau'ofa as a particularly suggestive vehicle of southern understanding.

As I have demonstrated here by literary example, exploring the south in or of the world means registering an important caveat. To understand southern worlds, we need to tune into southern languages, notations, and perceptions. Conversely, properly conceiving of the southern hemisphere using northern conceptual tools may be challenging, not to say impossible, without extensive linguistic and anthropological work, all of it latitudinal, translational, and comparative – probably more thoroughgoing work than any one book can deliver. To date, geo-epistemological questions setting the south in relation to the rest of the world have almost invariably been northern or north-centred, in the sense that they are not only constructs of northern imaginations but also assume an interpretive perspective directed from that hemisphere, as we will see again. It is no accident that the southern writers I have cited in illustration all use versions of global literary English to evoke their southern contexts. Though they may speak first to southern readers, they all also have in mind global audiences who tend to see the world through northern frameworks.

Southern spaces, northern frameworks

Geographies ceaselessly shape human history. In the southern hemisphere, the dominant, history-moulding land masses comprise the two great continents running north–south of South America and Africa, the island-continent of Australia, with the until recently uninhabited, slightly larger island-continent Antarctica to the south, at the Pole, and in the Pacific, and to a lesser extent the Indian Ocean, various larger and smaller island clusters. Some geographers hold that there is a fifth southern continent, Zealandia, or Tasmantis, a submerged continental crust of which the islands of New Zealand form a central spine. All of these land masses together (as well as India) formed part of the great southern continent, Gondwanaland, which broke up about 80 million years ago: they still bear signs of having undergone similar processes of glaciation. Vegetation in one remote part is often related to that in another part, as we find with the Kerguelen cabbage, for example, that grows on the Indian Ocean island of that name and is also found in the higher latitudes of South America.[13]

Sketching these spaces in our minds or on the world map, we immediately notice that the southern hemisphere lacks its northern counterpart's great east–west land bridge of Eurasia, with the further possibilities for cross-continental movement into the Americas of the once frozen Bering Sea, which narrowly separates Asia and Alaska. In the southern hemisphere, all traffic between the continents and islands is necessarily across oceans; all migration was traditionally by sea. Lopez's funnelling of populations through and across land masses always tends to operate north–south. Till the age of jet travel and even beyond, the southern journeys of rafts, canoes, and ships were often both isolating and precarious, as the *Pequod*'s crew many times discovers. Yet, despite these very different southern arrangements, it is according to northern processes and paradigms that the south is predominantly understood.

Most of the contributors to this book to a greater or lesser extent share these northern perspectives, willy-nilly, including the writer of this chapter, southern-born though many of us are. Symptomatically, the editors' introduction draws in the main on northern literary-critical discourses to set up its theoretical scaffolding. And how could it not? It is almost impossible, or, better said, conceptually intractable, for any research largely located in western or northern institutions of learning entirely or even substantially to unthink or dismantle this inflection. This needs to be properly recognised if our researches on the south are to be true – even if tangentially – to the south's Indigenous and Black realities, as well as respectful of its epistemological elusiveness.

To expand on this further, seeing the south in the world necessarily means viewing it through the lenses of the northern academy, located in educational institutions and pedagogic traditions that have developed in the north. Southern worlds, including the world that is the Global South – a development designation with a similar valence to the now outmoded 'Third World' – have generally been explained using northern analytical tools. It was and still is in the northern hemisphere, across its temperate zones, that many of the centres and archives of authoritative knowledge about the world (including the south) lie. It is in the north that the greatest number of professional scholars remains concentrated. The dominant technologies through which the south is studied are northern in provenance – they have been so since the late 1400s, and further back even than that, if China and India are deemed northern also (which they are, of course, in hemispheric terms). Even north–south global divides are northern constructs. As the editors remind us, far from being 'a pre-defined ... conceptual category', the south began as a European discursive production.

In short, for at least six centuries, since Vasco Da Gama rounded the Cape of Good Hope to reach India in 1497–98, and the Ferdinand Magellan and Juan Sebastián Elcano expedition circumnavigated the globe in 1521–22, the world as a whole, including the southern hemisphere, has generally been understood from the vantage point of the north. This is not to say, of course, that southern spaces have not produced great thinkers, navigators, discoverers, and scholars across those centuries and before. It is rather that in the annals of world history their names do not carry value. They do not feature prominently, if at all, in part because of the complex and destructive effects of the different waves of empire that have swept across the world from the north, in part because, as a result, those annals have been produced there. Happily, this emphasis may now be shifting with renewed attention being given, for example, to the crucial navigational expertise of the Tahitians Tupaia and Mai, who travelled with Captain James Cook on his first, and second and third voyages respectively, or to the role of Indigenous and Black petitioners and translators in nineteenth-century rights campaigns, such as the South African Gonaqua Andries Stoffels, among those named in Hlonipha Mokoena's essay.[14]

Indicatively, the world as first seen from space showed the South Pole 'at the top', but the image was inverted when it was first published. To have the north uppermost and dominant is the accepted view, concurring with normative world maps. Northerners, who as we already know make up most of the world's population, rarely have reason to view the south in any other way. This would apply especially to those northerners who have not visited the south, a significant majority within that majority. The relativising antipodean perspectives aired in Australian newspapers and periodicals that Comyn discusses in Chapter 2 infrequently constituted a northern pastime.

From the time of Bartolomeu Dias and Vasco Da Gama, northerners have been indifferent to the south unless it offered promises of wealth to be exploited, as did mining or whaling. Hence the importance of a collection such as this, which insists on dislodging such entrenched lines of sight by contemplating the world from the various perspectives and orientations of its different southerly regions and their histories. The project is extremely ambitious, even within the geo-political delimitations of the category signalled in the subtitle, the 'southern settler colonies'.

From this recognition of what might be termed southern heuristics the question arises, how then practically speaking do we go about studying the south? If the south cannot be perceived outside of northern terminologies, does this not effectively set 'the real south' and its far peripheries at a remove from analytic understanding, at a remove even from a collection of case studies on the south?[15] As we see, for example, in the several chapters investigating efforts by southerners over time to convey and explain something of their southern environments to northerners, such as Kiro or Kōhere (or, I would add, in respect of South America, Jeremy Button of Tierra del Fuego on board the *Beagle*), is it necessary to translate and thereby inevitably filter and adapt ideas of the past and future, history and geography, through northern languages and allegorical models to do so?

Even eloquently transmigrated texts, such as the Māori writer and petitioner Kōhere's allegorical inflection through Thomas Babington Macaulay of Māori land claims, speak in 'distinct, conflicting voices', as Nikki Hessell observes. Efforts to 're-territorialise' global intellectual production are ethically all very well and to be encouraged. However, the project of undoing the legacies of colonial knowledge making and 'related understandings of southness', as the editors write, represents a significant philosophical challenge, further complicated by economic and infrastructural inequalities, given the relative material poverty of many countries in the south. This impelled my turn above to literary writing with its suggestive metaphorical and rhythmic effects to capture something of the south. Put simply, critical theory that is necessarily predicated on dominant northern constructs cannot get us there.

On northern self-construction, it is also important to recognise that the south is not just another version of the Orient, a projection by metropolitan cultures on to the lands beyond the equator. In that sense it entirely escapes the category of 'uncanny temporal figure' the editors cite, alluding to the Comaroffs, Harry Harootunian, and others. It does not bear analogy with the fabulous east, at once desired and feared by a rapacious west, within that polarised imperial dynamic that Edward Said famously defined.[16] If, according to the timelines of the north or west, the east was degenerate and Africa backward, if the former lagged behind and the latter had not yet mounted the scale of civilisation, the south, by contrast, was nowhere on or near this scale. Far distant geographically, it was also seen as far distant in time, lying entirely outside the chronologies of the north. If the north had temporality, the south was anthropology, to adapt from Johannes Fabian's *Time and the Other* (1983).[17] The south was always the raw to the north's cooked.

As a further illustration of this conceptual and historical remoteness, we might remember the number of times in this collection that individuals, products, and papers reach the north and gain recognition and comprehensibility only through this process of arrival. Before, they formed part of a story or a myth; now they became verifiable fact. The artist-explorer Thomas Baines, discussed by Lindy Stiebel in Chapter 10, for instance, took pains to present his finished coronation map of Zululand to the Royal Geographical Society in London in 1874, and this duly secured his election to the Society as Honorary Fellow for life. Though his mapmaking and prospecting journeys took in much of southern Africa and included a trip to northern Australia, the professional recognition for his work in and across the south had to come from the centre. So, too, as Manu Samriti Chander observes in his study of Guianese reading publics, educational recognition for Creole elites in British Guiana could be bestowed only by London. Meanwhile, within the imperial hierarchical scale, as he also writes, the Indigenous peoples of the colony were deemed 'ontologically illiterate'.

The clustered and multi-textured south

In their wide-ranging and comprehensive introduction, Comyn and Fermanis approach the south as an assemblage of the southern colonies of the British world that together provide occasion for developing overarching synthesising frameworks from worlding through to hemispheric analysis. But this is not all. The southern spaces they draw together, they further interconnect historically and thematically, first, through investigating the experiences of 'imperialism, settler and mercantile colonialism' that have linked these spaces, and, second, through exploring a 'set of shared thematic concerns, literary forms and tropes' that may be said to be 'distinctive (although not always exclusive) to the region', and that demonstrate plasticity across it. In these ways, they open roads to re-worlding. In the case studies collected here, these forms and motifs include the female testimonial, the letter, the short story, documents of settlement and enclosure, and tropes of antipodal inversion – this last curiously more prevalent in Australian writing than, say, in South African or New Zealand.

Broadly speaking, then, the editors' south forms an overarching analytic construct validated by colonial history and seemingly corroborated in shared and overlapping cultural and aesthetic practices, traced in more detail in some of the chapters. It is by building transnational and transoceanic frameworks while at the same time addressing local, fluid, and peripheral perceptions that their project endeavours to resist, on the one hand, the exclusive 'metropolitan-dominated' tendencies of settler colony studies and, on the other, the nation-centred focus of literary histories. At moments, it is true, the enterprise of theorising the south by a layering on of hypotheses can appear to be at disciplinary or methodological cross-purposes, though the vigilant critical project of worlding and re-worlding (and re-wording) mitigates the 'supra-planetary' nature of the endeavour. Southness will per-haps always elude northern analysis to some degree, its local and Indigenous detail always slipping just beyond the frame. This is particularly the case, once again, when historiographies of the south operate across sharp hierar-chical gradients. Top-down global southern analysis is inimical to doing lateral or south–south comparative work.

How do the eighteen chapters that make up *Worlding the South* see the south in the world? The southern hemisphere that the case studies map is geographically multi-textured, the lands, regions, and islands within its four (or five) continents and their surrounding oceans drawn into a loosely con-nected and dynamic British world network stretching from Guyana to Malaysia and the South Pacific. Each chapter explores a corner, cluster, centre, or connection within this fluid hemisphere, tracing how it was brought into global structures of knowledge that include the panorama, the coronation map, and the printing office. Fariha Shaikh and Michelle Elleray, for exam-ple, observing how mobile imperial subjectivities shifted between Britain and Australia, and the Cook Islands and Britain, respectively, examine the technologies of newspaper production and bible translation that were 'actively involved' in their production.

Intriguing entanglements, switchbacks, and lateral connections emerge from many of the readings, such as when Louis Becke's stories in Jennifer Fuller's study can be seen to mobilise an understanding of Pacific islands as at once totality and network, following Epeli Hau'ofa. Stretching these con-nections latitudinally across other chapters, emigrant ships to Australia are found to be built of Burmese teak, as in Shaikh, while, in Elleray's account, the Cook Islander Kiro helps London Missionary Society members *in London* with translating the Bible into Cook Islands Māori.

Ingrid Horrocks on the peripatetic artist Augustus Earle in New Zealand further develops this central model of mobility. She persuasively points out that when contact or encounter such as between Māori and Pākehā is framed as fluid and interactive rather than conflictual and binary, both sides to the encounter become contemporary to each other. We move away from the view that one party is frozen in time in relation to the other, as if 'waiting to be visited, observed, and eventually colonised' by the 'traveller-artist-anthropol-ogist-colonist'. Jason Rudy *et al.* extend such lateral southern connections in their study of the remarkable expatriate and utopian Australian community of Colonia Cosme in 1890s Paraguay. In this case, once again, the *Cosme Monthly* with its insets of poetry and song worked as a technology that gave shape and expression to this transplanted southern colony.

For many contributors, interestingly, the nation, or, more precisely, the nation in formation, remains a prevalent category of analysis, even in spite of the editors' transnational emphases. Especially where countries of the south remained peripheral to imperial and neo-imperial global markets, the nation continued to be an important site of economic planning and cultural mobilisation. Jane Stafford, for example, explores how Defoe's *Robinson Crusoe* was read as a settler parable for colonial New Zealand, and not only by Pākehā. Ken Gelder and Rachael Weaver in 'The Transnational Kangaroo Hunt' discuss kangaroos as objects, specimens, and actual animals that disseminated a certain idea of Australian and antipodean typicality abroad. Many of the mobile documents discussed in these pages, including newspapers, maps, and translated bibles, played a role in embedding and concretising the shape of the nation in different colonial spaces. As Lindy Stiebel finds, Thomas Baines' coronation map of Zululand entrenched the idea of the Zulu nation to the degree that when the Anglo-Zulu War broke out in 1879, there was for the British 'a visible country to be conquered'.

Overall, the south in this collection emerges more in the breach than from direct observation, more from looking past than looking at – as might stand to reason. For Fermanis and Comyn, the perceptual south grows out of and yet evades a predictive 'vertical hierarchy' of 'above and below'. It gleams from between the lines, as in the literary examples cited earlier. Similarly, new critical understanding shines out fitfully from between the Indigenous words and glosses in Eliza Dunlop's far-sighted 1838 poem 'The Aboriginal Mother', as Anna Johnston demonstrates.

Many of the chapters draw out southern viewpoints by bearing down on local and specific detail, to avoid the risk to their heuristic focus that more comparative but inevitably also more homogenising work across southern spaces might bring. Such close involvement, as demonstrated in Grace Moore's study of the nineteenth-century botanist and fiction-writer Louisa Atkinson, for instance, allows a fuller understanding of, in this case, Atkinson's complicated respect for the bush to emerge. Atkinson in Moore's description learns, even if only partially, to see the land as a formative space for *all* of its inhabitants. An equally conflicted sympathy comes through in the English naturalist William Burchell's travel writing, discussed in Matthew Shum's chapter, such as when Burchell sitting down with local Khoisan people observes that: even 'in the midst of this horde ... I had been one of them'.

To see the south in the world means looking to the side, beyond 'centres in modernity', towards 'composite and overlapping' Black and Indigenous realities – or 'the more fluid worlds of the southern hemisphere', to quote Peter Otto in his chapter on the Sydney panorama. Working within such southern interstices we evade to some extent the static ontological binaries of twentieth-century colonial theory, and so challenge the hegemony of 'literary worlds' framed in terms of copies and originals, as discussed in Eric Hayot's compelling analysis.[18] Off-beam, oblique, and liquid southern perspectives transform embedded views of the colonial encounter cast as mobile Europeans meeting sedentary Indigenous people caught in the waiting-room of history, to refer once again to Horrocks via Dipesh Chakrabarty.[19] The recognition that then emerges, of the 'radical contemporaneity' of 'coeval others' across the south and the 'co-presence of [their] simultaneous diverging narratives', is perhaps one of the most distinctive and heuristically powerful of the southern perspectives and re-worldings explored in these pages.

Criss-crossed navigational routes, career pathways, lines of knowledge making, and newspaper dissemination – southern networks in *Worlding the South* are almost by definition partial and patchy. Missing connections and fortuitous link-ups are part of their looseness and contingency. But this looseness also means that they thereby allow creative adaptation and reappropriation. Though ideas often arrived in the south second-hand, as Mokoena observes, at the same time they were susceptible to alteration and regeneration, especially at those places of looseness and rupture. Tracey Banivanua Mar, Nadia Rhook, and others influentially demonstrate in their research that resistance emerges out of the structural flaws, gaps, broken links, and ellipses that are endemic to any colonial-type assertion of planetary consciousness. Or, as Mokoena goes on to say: 'It is in these rebellions that one hears the voices of the Africans who were petitioning the British government in their own words.'

The south in these pages manifests again and again as an assemblage of heterogeneous spaces and locales – ships' decks and hills of green stones and arid interiors and rocky atolls and caves in rocks and the 'boundless aerial spaces' that Burchell observes on his travels (I pick and cite at random) – spaces that are interconnected across vast distances and at many levels by mobile subjects of all kinds.[20] This south both invites and makes possible archipelagic reading: the kind of approach that Fuller recommends for Becke's Pacific short stories can be expanded to the entire constellated collection. Holistic archipelagic reading, as the Pacific islands theorist Epeli Hau'ofa observes, respects the character of the south by channelling how its oceanic energies interact with and sweep around its land-masses. It invites us to think 'pluricentrically', to quote Fermanis in her study of the *Straits Chinese Magazine*. It sheds light on interlaced oceans, lands, and islands 'in the totality of their relationships'.[21]

It may be, then, that the idea of the archipelago finally brings us closer than any other heuristic device to the 'certain something' of the south. Or, at least, it allows us to perceive the south in ways that are truly southern (at least to the extent that we can tell), that resonate with its uneven and inter-twined spatial, atmospheric, and political arrangements, that can properly be termed 'epistemologies of the south', in Boaventura de Sousa Santos' term. Archipelagic heuristics support this book's task of re-angling the literary lenses of the nineteenth-century British literary world in order properly to bring in the stories, interpretations, and agency of the southern colonies and their peoples. The archipelago invites us to think connectively and fluidly through and across the spaces of the south, following and retracing as we do so the many mazy lines that the chapters in this collection have made available to us. The archipelagic view also resists the centre–periphery models that have always been inflicted on the south; it explodes restrictive concentric arrangements of original and copy.

In imagination, reading the south in clustered and multicentred ways tunes us into the hemisphere's vast 'sea country' and its scattered lands and meandering coastlines, echoing and funnelling their particular shapes, flows, and densities – shapes that in turn might be said to mirror the brilliant constellations of its radiant night skies, the Milky Way's 'fierce field of light'.[22] An archipelagic perspective allows us to envision the scattered lands and islands of the south once again as dispersed fragments of the ancient great mass of Gondwanaland, puzzle pieces of the continent, sea-washed parts of the main. By thinking different spaces within the one metaphoric frame of the archipelago we plot virtual connection in a resonant, multi-axial, defiantly southern way, gathering singularities into clustered patterns that militate against any idea of a world imposed from above.

Notes

1 See Herman Melville, *Moby-Dick*, ed. H. Beaver (London: Penguin, 1986). Indeed, it is factually true that the southern hemisphere across history and into the present day is less inhabited, bearing only 11% of the world's 7.3 billion people. The antipodean hemisphere is also significantly more fluid and bluer, holding 80% of ocean to the north's 60%.

2 Immanuel Wallerstein, *Historical Capitalism with Capitalist Civilization* (London: Verso, 1996).

3 Barry Lopez, *Arctic Dreams* (1986; London: Vintage, 2014), p. 258. See also the more recent *Horizon* (2019) with its further speculations about travel across great distances.

4 I try to answer it at greater length in a new study, a literary and cultural history of responses to the southern hemisphere, with the working title *Southern Imagining* (forthcoming). See also my discussion of southness in Elleke Boehmer, *The Shouting in the Dark and Other Southern Writing* (Crawley: UWA Publishing, 2019), pp. 241–92.

5 See the discussions of reading for relevance and the capacity of literature to keep refreshing how we understand the world in Elleke Boehmer, *Postcolonial Poetics: 21st-Century Critical Readings* (Basingstoke: Palgrave Macmillan, 2018).

6 James Halford, 'Southern Conversations: J. M. Coetzee in Buenos Aires', *Sydney Review of Books* (28 February 2017), n.p., https://sydneyreviewofbooks.com/essay/southern-conversations-j-m-coetzee-in-buenos-aires/ (accessed 1 May 2020).

7 See J. M. Coetzee, *The Childhood of Jesus, The Schooldays of Jesus, The Death of Jesus* (London: Harvill Secker, 2013, 2016, 2019).

8 Alexis Wright, *Carpentaria* (Sydney: Giramondo Press, 2006), pp. 375–82.

9 Wright, *Carpentaria*, pp. 375–8.

10 Tim Winton, *Island Home* (Sydney: Penguin Random House Australia, 2015), p. 173.

11 Winton, *Island Home*, p. 18.

12 Elleke Boehmer, *To the Volcano* (Brighton: Myriad Editions, 2019), esp. pp. 28, 41.

13 Kate Teltscher, *Palace of Palms: Tropical Dreams and the Making of Kew* (London: Picador, 2020), p. 84. See also Nicholas Shakespeare, *In Tasmania* (New York: Overlook Press, 2004).

14 Kate Fullagar, *The Warrior, the Voyager and the Artist: Three Lives in an Age of Empire* (Yale: Yale University Press, 2020).

15 Elleke Boehmer, *Colonial and Postcolonial Literature: Migrant Metaphors* (Oxford: Oxford University Press, 2005), chapter 1. See also my efforts to interrogate centre–periphery models of empire by working laterally in *Empire, the National, and the Postcolonial: Resistance in Interaction* (Oxford and New York: Oxford University Press, 2002).

16 Edward Said, *Orientalism* (London: Pantheon, 1978).

17 Johannes Fabian, *Time and the Other: How Anthropology Makes Its Object*, foreword Matti Bunzl (New York: Columbia University Press, 2002).

18 Eric Hayot, *On Literary Worlds* (Oxford: Oxford University Press, 2012).

19 Dipesh Chakrabarty, *Provincializing Europe* (Princeton: Princeton University Press, 2000).

20 See Antoinette Burton and Isabel Hofmeyr, 'Introduction', in Antoinette Burton and Isabel Hofmeyr (eds), *Ten Books That Shaped the British Empire: Creating an Imperial Commons* (Durham: Duke University Press, 2014), p. 1.

21 Epeli Hauʻofa, *We Are the Ocean: Selected Works* (Honolulu: University of Hawaiʻi Press, 2008), p. 31.

22 Wright, *Carpentaria*, pp. 378–80; Tim Winton, *The Boy behind the Curtain* (Sydney: Penguin Random House Australia, 2016), p. 75.

Bibliography of secondary sources

Abu-Lughod, Janet L., *Before European Hegemony: The World System A.D. 1250–1350* (Oxford: Oxford University Press, 1989)

Adhikari, Mohamed, *The Anatomy of a South African Genocide: The Extermination of the Cape San Peoples* (Athens: Ohio University Press, 2011)

Agathocleous, Tanya, 'Imperial, Anglophone, Geopolitical, Worldly: Evaluating The "Global" in Victorian Studies', *Victorian Literature and Culture*, 43 (2015), 651–8

— and Jason R. Rudy, 'Victorian Cosmopolitanisms', *Victorian Literature and Culture*, 38 (2010), 389–97

Albuquerque, Sara, 'Glimpses of British Guiana at the Colonial and Indian Exhibition, 1886', *Culture and History Digital Journal*, 5.1 (2016), n.p., http://cultureandhistory.revistas.csic.es/index.php/cultureandhistory/article/view/97/333 (accessed 1 February 2020)

ALICE, http://alice.ces.uc.pt/en/ (accessed 26 June 2019)

Allam, Lorena, and Carly Earl, 'For Centuries the Rivers Sustained Aboriginal Culture. Now They Are Dry, Elders Despair' (21 January 2019), n.p., www.theguardian.com/australia-news/2019/jan/22/murray-darling-river-aboriginal-culture-dry-elders-despair-walgett (accessed 10 November 2019)

Allan, Michael, 'Reading with One Eye, Speaking with One Tongue: On the Problem of Address in World Literature', *Comparative Literature*, 44.1–2 (2007), 1–19

Allen, Chadwick, *Blood Narrative: Indigenous Identity in American Indian and Maori Literary and Activist Texts* (Durham and London: Duke University Press, 2002)

— 'Decolonizing Comparison: Toward a Literary Studies', in *The Oxford Handbook of Indigenous American Literature*, ed. by James H. Cox and Daniel Heath Justice (Oxford: Oxford University Press, 2014), 377–94

— *Trans-Indigenous: Methodologies for Global Native Literary Studies* (Minneapolis: University of Minnesota Press, 2012)

— 'A Trans*national* Native American Studies?', n.p., https://escholarship.org/uc/item/82m5j3f5 (accessed 26 June 2019)

Anderson, Benedict, *Imagined Communities: Reflections on the Origin and Spread of Nationalism* (London: Verso, 1983)

— *The Spectre of Comparisons: Nationalism, Southeast Asia and the World* (London: Verso, 1998)

Anderson, Margaret, 'Mrs. Charles Clacy, Lola Montez, and Poll the Grogseller: Glimpses of Women on the Early Victorian Goldfields', in *Gold: Forgotten Histories and Lost Objects of Australia*, ed. by Iain McCalman, Alexander Cook, and Andrew Reeves (Cambridge and New York: Cambridge University Press, 2001), pp. 225–49

Anderson, Warwick, 'Racial Conceptions in the Global South', *ISIS*, 15.4 (2014), 782–92

Appadurai, Arjun, 'Disjuncture and Difference in the Global Cultural Economy', in *The Phantom Public Sphere*, ed. by Bruce Robbins (Minneapolis: University of Minnesota Press, 1993), pp. 269–96

Araluen, Evelyn, 'Resisting the Institution', *Overland*, 227 (2017), n.p., https://overland. org.au/previous-issues/issue-227/feature-evelyn-araluen/ (accessed 26 June 2019)

Archibald, Jo-Ann, Jenny Lee-Morgan, and Jason De Santolo, eds, *Decolonizing Research: Indigenous Storywork as Methodology* (London: Zed, 2019)

Armitage, David, Alison Bashford, and Sujit Sivasundaram, 'Introduction: Writing World Oceanic Histories', in *Oceanic Histories*, ed. by David Armitage, Alison Bashford, and Sujit Sivasundaram (Cambridge: Cambridge University Press, 2018), pp. 1–28

Atkin, Lara, 'The South African "Children of the Mist": The Bushman, the Highlander and the Making of Colonial Identities in Thomas Pringle's South African Poetry (1825–1834)', *The Yearbook of English Studies*, 48 (2018), 199–215

— Sarah Comyn, Porscha Fermanis, and Nathan Garvey, *Early Public Libraries and Colonial Citizenship in the British Southern Hemisphere* (Cham: Springer International Publishing, 2019)

Atkinson, Alan, *The Europeans in Australia: A History, Vol. 1, The Beginning* (Oxford: Oxford University Press, 1997)

Attwell, David, 'Reprisals of Modernity in Black South African "Mission" Writing', *Journal of Southern African Studies*, 25.2 (1999), 267–85

— and Derek Attridge, eds, *The Cambridge History of South African Literature* (Cambridge: Cambridge University Press, 2012)

Atwood, Bain, *Possession: Batman's Treaty and the Matter of History* (Melbourne: Melbourne University Press, 2009)

Auerbach, Jeffrey, *Imperial Boredom: Monotony and the British Empire* (Oxford: Oxford University Press, 2018)

Ballantyne, Tony, 'Christianity, Commerce, and the Remaking of the Māori World', in *Facing Empire: Indigenous Experience in a Revolutionary Age*, ed. by Kate Fullagar and Michael McDonnell (Baltimore: Johns Hopkins Press, 2018), pp. 192–213

— 'Mobility, Empire, Colonisation', *History Australia*, 11.2 (2014), 7–37

— 'Putting the Nation in its Place? World History and C. A. Bayly's *The Birth of the Modern World*', in *Connected Worlds: History in Transnational Perspective*, ed. by Anne Curthoys and Marilyn Lake (Canberra: ANU Press, 2005), pp. 23–44

— 'Strategic Intimacies: Knowledge and Colonization in Southern New Zealand', *Journal of New Zealand Studies*, 14 (2013), 4–18

Ballard, Charles, *John Dunn: The White Chief of Zululand* (Johannesburg: Ad Donker, 1985)

Banivanua Mar, Tracey, *Decolonisation and the Pacific: Indigenous Globalisation and the Ends of Empire* (New York: Cambridge University Press, 2016)

— 'Imperial Literacy and Indigenous Rights: Tracing Transoceanic Circuits of a Modern Discourse', *Aboriginal History*, 37 (2013), 1–28

— 'Shadowing Imperial Networks: Indigenous Mobility and Australia's Pacific Past', *Australian Historical Studies*, 46.3 (2015), 340–55

— *Violence and Colonial Dialogue: The Australian-Pacific Indentured Labor Trade* (Honolulu: University of Hawai'i Press, 2007)

— and Nadia Rhook, 'Counter Networks of Empires: Reading Unexpected People in Unexpected Places', *Journal of Colonialism and Colonial History*, 19.2 (Summer 2018), n.p., https://muse.jhu.edu/article/700162 (accessed 26 June 2019)

Bank, Andrew, 'The Great Debate and the Origins of South African Historiography', *The Journal of African History*, 38.2 (1997), 261–81

Barrell, John, *English Literature in History, 1730–80: An Equal, Wide Survey* (London: Hutchinson, 1983)

Bauer, Ralph, 'Hemispheric Studies', *PMLA*, 124.1 (2009), 234–50

Bayly, C. A., Sven Beckert, Matthew Connelly, Isabel Hofmeyr, Wendy Kozol, Patricia Seed, 'AHR Conversation: On Transnational History', *The American Historical Review*, 111.5 (2006), 1441–64

Beckett, Gorden, *The Colonial Economy of NSW: A Retrospective between 1788 and 1835* (Singapore: Trafford, 2012)

Belgrave, Michael, *Historical Frictions: Maori Claims & Reinvented Histories* (Auckland: Auckland University Press, 2005)

Belich, James, *Replenishing the Earth: The Settler Revolution and the Rise of the Anglo-World, 1783–1939* (New York and Oxford: Oxford University Press, 2009)

Bell, Bill, 'Bound for Australia: Shipboard Reading in the Nineteenth Century', *Journal of Australian Studies*, 25 (2001), 5–18

—— 'Crusoe's Books: The Scottish Emigrant Reader in the Nineteenth Century', in *Across Boundaries: The Book in Culture and Commerce*, ed. by Bill Bell, Philip Bennett, and Jonquil Bevan (Winchester: Oak Knoll Press, 2000), pp. 116–29

Bell, Leonard, 'Augustus Earle's *The Meeting of the Artist and the Wounded Chief Hongi, Bay of Islands, New Zealand, 1827*, and His Depictions of Other New Zealand Encounters', in *Voyages and Beaches: Pacific Encounters, 1769–1840*, ed. by Alex Calder, Jonathan Lamb, and Bridget Orr (Honolulu: University of Hawai'i Press, 1999), pp. 241–63

—— 'Not Quite Darwin's Artist: The Travel Art of Augustus Earle', *Journal of Historical Geography*, 43 (2014), 60–70

—— 'To See or Not to See: Conflicting Eyes in the Travel Art of Augustus Earle', in *Orientalism Transposed; the Impacts of the Colonies on British Culture*, ed. by Julie F. Codell and Dianne Sachko Macleod (Aldershot and Brookfield: Ashgate, 1998), pp. 117–39

Benjamin, Walter, *Illuminations*, trans. by Harry Zorn, ed. by Hannah Arendt (London: Pimlico, 1999)

Bennett, Bruce, 'The Trader's Eye: Louis Becke's Oceania', *SPAN*, 48–9 (1999), 150–8

Bennett, Melissa, and Kristy Warren, 'Looking Back and Facing Forwards: Ten Years of the London, Sugar & Slavery Gallery', *Journal of Historical Geography*, 63 (2019), 94–9

Bentley, Trevor, *Pakeha Maori: The Extraordinary Story of the Europeans who Lived as Maori in Early New Zealand* (Auckland: Penguin, 1999)

Bernasconi, Robert, 'The Paradox of Liberal Politics in the South African Context: Alfred Hoernlé's Critique of Liberalism's Pact with White Domination', *Critical Philosophy of Race*, 4.2 (2016), 163–81

Bewell, Alan, *Natures in Translation: Romanticism and Colonial Natural History* (Baltimore and London: Johns Hopkins University Press, 2017)

—— *Romanticism and Colonial Disease* (Baltimore and London: Johns Hopkins University Press, 2003)

Bhabha, Homi K., 'Introduction', in *Nation and Narration*, ed. by Homi K. Bhabha (London and New York: Routledge 1990), pp. 1–7

Bhattacharya, Sumangala, '"The White Lady and the Brown Woman": Colonial Masculinity and Domesticity in Louis Becke's By Reef and Palm (1894)', in *Oceania and the Victorian Imagination: Where All Things Are Possible*, ed. by Richard D. Fulton and Peter H. Hoffenberg (Farnham: Ashgate, 2013), pp. 79–92

Binney, Judith, 'Tuki's Universe', *New Zealand Journal of History*, 38.2 (2004), 215–32

— with Vincent O'Malley and Alan Ward, *Te Ao Hou: The New World, 1820–1920* (Wellington: Bridget Williams Books, 2018)

Blaser, Mario, 'Ontology and Indigeneity: On the Political Ontology of Heterogeneous Assemblages', *Cultural Geographies*, 2.1 (2014), 49–58

Bode, Katherine, 'Fictional Systems: Mass-Digitization, Network Analysis, and Nineteenth-Century Australian Newspapers', *Victorian Periodicals Review*, 50.1 (2017), 100–38

— *Reading by Numbers: Recalibrating the Literary Field* (London: Anthem Press, 2012)

— '"Sidelines" and Trade Lines: Publishing the Australian Novel, 1860–1899', *Book History*, 15 (2012), 93–122

— 'Thousands of Titles Without Authors: Digitized Newspapers, Serial Fiction, and the Challenges of Anonymity', *Book History*, 19 (2016), 284–316

Boehmer, Elleke, *Colonial and Postcolonial Literature: Migrant Metaphors* (Oxford: Oxford University Press 1995)

— *Empire, the National and the Postcolonial: Resistance in Interaction* (Oxford: Oxford University Press, 2002)

— *Postcolonial Poetics: 21st-Century Critical Readings* (Basingstoke: Palgrave Macmillan, 2018)

Bonyhady, Tim, *Images in Opposition: Australian Landscape Painting, 1801–1890* (Oxford: Oxford University Press, 1984)

Bose, Sugata, *A Hundred Horizons: The Indian Ocean in the Age of Global Empire* (Cambridge, MA: Harvard University Press, 2006)

Boult, Trevor, *St Helena: A Maritime History* (Stroud: Amberley, 2016)

Bradshaw, Ann Lane, 'Joseph Conrad and Louis Becke', *English Studies*, 86.3 (2005), 206–25

Brantlinger, Patrick, *Dark Vanishings: Discourse on the Extinction of Primitive Races, 1800-1930* (Ithaca: Cornell University Press, 2003)

— *Taming Cannibals: Victorians and Race* (Cornell: Cornell University Press, 2011)

Brett, André, 'Colonial and Provincial Separation Movements in Australia and New Zealand, 1856–1865', *The Journal of Imperial and Commonwealth History*, 47.1 (2019), 51–75

Breward, Christopher, *Fashioning London: Clothing and the Modern Metropolis* (Oxford: Berg, 2004)

Buchanan, Susan Locher, *Burchell's Travels: The Life, Art and Journeys of William John Burchell* (Cape Town: Penguin Books, 2015)

Burton, Antoinette, and Isabel Hofmeyr, 'Introduction', in *Ten Books That Shaped the British Empire: Creating an Imperial Commons*, ed. by Antoinette Burton and Isabel Hofmeyr (Durham: Duke University Press, 2014), pp. 1–28

Buse, Jasper, and Raututi Taringa, *Cook Islands Maori Dictionary*, ed. by Bruce Biggs and Rangi Moeka'a (Rarotonga: The Ministry of Education, Government of the Cook Islands / London: School of Oriental and African Studies, University of London / Suva: Institute of Pacific Studies, University of the South Pacific /

Auckland: Centre for Pacific Studies, University of Auckland / Canberra: Pacific Linguistics, Research School of Pacific and Asian Studies, Australian National University, 1995)

Butler, Marilyn, *Mapping Mythologies: Counter-Currents in Eighteenth-Century British Poetry and Cultural History* (Cambridge: Cambridge University Press, 2015)

Calder, Alex, *The Settler's Plot: How Stories Take Place in New Zealand* (Auckland: Auckland University Press, 2011)

Carey, Hilary M., 'Lancelot Threlkeld and Missionary Linguistics in Australia to 1850', in *Missionary Linguistics / Lingüística Misionera: Selected Papers from the First International Conference on Missionary Linguistics, Oslo, March 13th–16th, 2003*, ed. by Otto Zwartjes and Even Hovdhaugen (Amsterdam: John Benjamins, 2004), pp. 253–75

— 'Lancelot Threlkeld, Biraban, and the Colonial Bible in Australia', *Comparative Studies in Society and History*, 52.2 (2010), 447–78

Carruthers, Jane, and Marion Arnold, *The Life and Work of Thomas Baines* (Cape Town: Fernwood Press, 1995)

Carter, David, 'After Postcolonialism', *Meanjin*, 66.2 (2007), 114–9

Carter, Paul, 'Australindia: The Geography of Imperial Desire', *Postcolonial Studies*, 18 (2015), 222–33.

— *The Road to Botany Bay* (London: Faber, 1987)

Cassano, Franco, *Southern Thought and other Essays on the Mediterranean*, trans. and ed. by Norma Bouchard and Valerio Ferme (New York: Fordham University Press, 2012)

Castellanos, Bianet, Lourdes Gutiérrez Nájera, and Arturo Aldama, eds, *Comparative Indigeneities of the Américas: Toward a Hemispheric Approach* (Tucson: University of Arizona Press, 2012)

Chakrabarty, Dipesh, *Provincializing Europe: Postcolonial Thought and Historical Difference* (Princeton: Princeton University Press, 2000)

Chander, Manu Samriti, *Brown Romantics: Poetry and Nationalism in the Global Nineteenth Century* (Lewisburg: Bucknell University Press, 2017)

Chandler, David, and Julian Reid, '"Being in Being": Contesting the Ontopolitics of Indigeneity', *The European Legacy*, 23.3 (2018), 251–68

Chang, David A., 'The Good Written Word of Life: Native Hawaiian Appropriation of Textuality', *William and Mary Quarterly*, 75.2 (2018), n.p.

Clarke, Patricia, *Pioneer Writer: The Life of Louisa Atkinson: Novelist, Journalist, Naturalist* (Sydney: Allen & Unwin, 1990)

Clifford, James, 'Indigenous Articulations', in *The Worlding Project: Doing Cultural Studies in the Era of Globalization*, ed. by Rob Wilson and Christopher Leigh Connery (Berkeley: New Pacific Press, 2007), pp. 13–39

— 'Notes on Travel and Theory', *Centre for Cultural Studies Inscriptions*, 5 (1989), n.p., https://culturalstudies.ucsc.edu/inscriptions/volume-5/james-clifford/ (accessed 5 July 2019)

— 'The Others: Beyond the "Salvage" Paradigm', *Third Text*, 3.6 (1989), 73–8

— *Returns: Becoming Indigenous in the Twenty-First Century* (Cambridge, MA: Harvard University Press, 2013)

Codell, Julie F., 'Introduction: Imperial Co-histories and the British and Colonial Press', in *Imperial Co-histories: National Identities and the British and Colonial Press*, ed. by Julie F. Codell (Danvers: Rosemount, 2003), pp. 15–28

Coetzee, J. M., 'Farm Novel and "Plaasroman" in South Africa', *English in Africa*, 13.2 (1986), 1–19.

— *White Writing: On the Culture of Letters in South Africa* (Sandton: Radix, 1988)

Coetzee, P. H., and A. P. J. Roux, *The African Philosophy Reader* (London and New York: Taylor & Francis, 2004)

Coleman, Deirdre, *Romantic Colonization and British Anti-Slavery* (Cambridge: Cambridge University Press, 2005)

Coleman, Julie, *A History of Cant and Slang Dictionaries: Volume 2: 1785–1858* (Oxford: Oxford University Press, 2004)

Colley, Linda, *Britons: Forging the Nation 1707–1837* (New Haven: Yale University Press, 1992)

Collins, Patrick, *Goodbye Bussamarai: The Mandandanji Land War, Southern Queensland, 1842–1852* (St. Lucia: University of Queensland Press, 2002)

Collis-Buthelezi, Victoria, 'Caribbean Regionalism, South Africa, and Mapping New World Studies', *Small Axe*, 19.1 (2015), 37–54

— 'Under the Aegis of Empire: Cape Town, Victorianism, and Early-Twentieth-Century Black Thought', *Callaloo*, 39.1 (2016), 115–32

Comaroff, Jean, and John Comaroff, 'Theory from the South: A Rejoinder', *Cultural Anthropology Online*, 25 February 2012, n.p., https://culanth.org/fieldsights/theory-from-the-south-a-rejoinder (accessed 24 June 2019)

— *Theory from the South: Or, How Euro-America Is Evolving Toward Africa* (Boulder: Paradigm Publishers, 2011)

Comment, Bernard, *The Panorama* (London: Reaktion Books, 1999)

Comyn, Sarah, and Porscha Fermanis, 'Rethinking Nineteenth-Century Literary Culture: British Worlds, Southern Latitudes and Hemispheric Methods', *Journal of Commonwealth Literature* (2021), n.p., https://doi.org/10.1177/0021989420982013 (accessed 1 February 2021)

Connell, Raewyn, *Southern Theory: The Global Dynamics of Knowledge in Social Science* (Sydney: Allen & Unwin, 2007)

Cooppan, Vilashini, 'The Corpus of a Continent: Embodiments of Australia in World Literature', *JASAL: Journal of the Association for the Study of Australian Literature*, 15.3 (2015), 1–19

Coulthard, Glen, *Red Skin, White Masks: Rejecting the Colonial Politics of Recognition* (Minneapolis: University of Minnesota Press, 2014)

Cranston, C. A., and Charles Dawson, 'Climate and Culture in Australia and New Zealand', in *A Global History of Literature and the Environment*, ed. by John Parham and Louise Westling (Cambridge: Cambridge University Press, 2016), pp. 239–53

Critchett, Jan, '*A Distant Field of Murder*': Western Districts Frontiers, 1834–1848* (Melbourne: Melbourne University Press, 1990)

Crocombe, Marjorie Tua'inekore, 'Tata: Expression Through the Written Word', in *Akono'anga Maori: Cook Islands Culture*, ed. by Ron Crocombe and Marjorie Tua'inekore Crocombe (Suva: Institute of Pacific Studies, in association with the Cook Islands Extension Centre, University of the South Pacific / Rarotonga: Cook Islands Cultural and Historic Places Trust, and the Ministry of Cultural Development, 2003), pp. 81–91

Crocombe, Ron G., 'Land Tenure in the Cook Islands' (unpublished doctoral thesis, Australian National University, 1961), *New Zealand Electronic Text Collection: Te Pūhikotuhi o Aotearoa* (Victorian University of Wellington, 2016), n.p., nzetc. victoria.ac.nz/tm/scholarly/tei-CroLan.html (accessed 31 January 2020)

Crosby, Alfred, *Ecological Imperialism: The Biological Expansion of Europe, 900–1900* (Cambridge: Cambridge University Press, 1986)

Crouch, David, *Colonial Psychosocial: Reading William Lane* (Newcastle upon Tyne: Cambridge Scholars Publishing, 2015)

Curless, Gareth, Stacey Hynd, Temilola Alanamu, and Katherine Roscoe, 'Editor's Introduction: Networks in Imperial History', *Journal of World History*, 26.4 (2016), 705–32

Curling, Jonathan, *Janus Weathercock: The Life of Thomas Griffiths Wainewright* (London: Nelson, 1938)

Currey, C. H., 'Field, Barron (1786–1846)', *Australian Dictionary of National Biography*, n.p., https://adb.anu.edu.au/biography/field-barron-2041/text2523 (accessed 12 February 2020)

Dainotto, Roberto M., *Europe (In Theory)* (Durham: Duke University Press, 2007)

Daniels, Kay, 'Feminism and Social History', *Australian Feminist Studies*, 1 (1985), 27–40

Dart, Gregory, 'Flash Style: Pierce Egan and the Literary Culture of the 1820s', *History Workshop Journal*, 51 (2001), 181–205

Dassow Walls, Laura, *The Passage to Cosmos: Alexander Humboldt and the Shaping of America* (Chicago: Chicago University Press, 2009)

Davidson, Graeme, *City Dreamers: The Urban Imagination in Australia* (Sydney: NewSouth Publishing, 2016)

Davies, Dominic, *Imperial Infrastructure and Spatial Resistance in Colonial Literature, 1880–1930* (Oxford: Peter Lang, 2017)

Day, A. Grove, 'By Reef and Tide: Louis Becke's Literary Reputation', *Australian Letters*, 6.1 (1963), 17–26

Day, Iyko, 'Being or Nothingness: Indigeneity, Antiblackness, and Settler Colonial Critique', *Critical Ethnic Studies*, 1.2 (2015), 102–21

Deb, Nilanjana, '(Re)moving Bodies: People, Ships and Other Commodities in the Coolie Trade from Calcutta', in *Commodities and Culture in the Colonial World*, ed. by Supriya Chaudhuri, Josephine McDonagh, Bryan Murray, and Rajeswari Rajan (London: Routledge, 2018), pp. 115–28

Delmas, Adrien, 'Introduction: The Written Word and the World', in *Written Culture in a Colonial Context: Africa and the Americas 1500–1900*, ed. by Adrien Delmas and Nigel Penn (Leiden: Brill, 2012), pp. 95–122

Deloria, Philip, *Indians in Unexpected Places* (Lawrence: University Press of Kansas, 2004)

DeLoughrey, Elizabeth, *Routes and Roots: Navigating Caribbean and Pacific Island Literatures* (Honolulu: University of Hawai'i Press, 2010)

— Jill Didur, and Anthony Carrigan, 'Introduction: A Postcolonial Environmental Humanities', in *Global Ecologies and the Environmental Humanities*, ed. by Elizabeth DeLoughrey, Jill Didur, and Anthony Carrigan (London and New York: Routledge, 2015), pp. 1–32

Dening, Greg, *Mr Bligh's Bad Language: Passion, Power, and Theatre on the Bounty* (Cambridge: Cambridge University Press, 1992)

De Schmidt, Johanna, '"This Strange Little Floating World of Ours": Shipboard Periodicals and Community-Building in the "Global" Nineteenth Century', *Journal of Global History*, 11 (2016), 229–50

Diagne, Souleymane Bachir, 'Individual, Community, and Human Rights', *Transition*, 101 (2009), 8–15

Dias, Vicente M., and J. Kehaulani Kauanui, 'Native Pacific Cultural Studies on the Edge', *The Contemporary Pacific*, 13.2 (2001), 315–42

Dick, Archie L., *The Hidden History of South Africa's Book and Reading Cultures* (Toronto and London: University of Toronto Press, 2012)

Dine, Philip, 'Horse Racing in Early Colonial Algeria: From Anglophilia to Araboma-nia', in *Sporting Cultures, 1650–1850*, ed. by Daniel O'Quinn and Alexis Tadié (Toronto: University of Toronto Press, 2018), pp. 136–60

Dingley, Robert, 'The Ruins of the Future: Macaulay's New Zealander and the Spirit of the Age', in *Histories of the Future: Studies in Fact, Fantasy and Science Fiction*, ed. by A. Sandison and R. Dingley (Basingstoke: Palgrave, 2000), pp. 15–33

Dixon, Robert, 'Australian Literature–International Contexts', *Southerly*, 67.1/2 (2007), 15–27

Dominy, Graham, 'Thomas Baines and the Langalibalele Rebellion: A Critique of an Unrecorded Sketch of the Action at "Bushman's Pass", 1873', *Natal Museum Journal of Humanities*, 3 (1991), 41–55

— 'Thomas Baines: The McGonagall of Shepstone's 1873 Zululand Expedition?', *Natalia*, 21 (1991), 75–9

Donaldson, Mike, 'The End of Time? Aboriginal Temporality and the British Inva-sion of Australia', *Time and Society*, 5.2 (1996), 187–207

Dooling, Wayne, 'The Origins and Aftermath of the Cape Colony's "Hottentot Code" of 1809', *Kronos*, 31 (2005), 50–61

Doran, Christine, 'Singapore', in *The Edinburgh Companion to the History of Democracy*, ed. by Benjamin Isakhan and Stephen Stockwell (Edinburgh: Edin-burgh University Press, 2012) pp. 257–70

Douglas, Bronwen, 'Foreign Bodies in Oceania', in *Foreign Bodies: Oceania and the Science of Race, 1750–1940*, ed. by Bronwen Douglas and Chris Ballard (Canberra: Australian National University Press, 2008), pp. 3–32

Driver, Felix, and Lowri Jones, *Hidden Histories of Exploration: Researching the RGS–IBG Collections* (London: Royal Holloway, University of London, with the Royal Geographical Society, 2009)

Driver-Burgess, Frith, 'Korero Pukapuka, Talking Books: Reading in Reo Māori in the Long Nineteenth Century' (unpublished master's thesis, Victoria University of Wellington, 2015)

Dubow, Saul, 'How British was the British World? The Case of South Africa', *The Journal of Imperial and Commonwealth History*, 37.1 (2009), 1–27

— *Scientific Racism in Modern South Africa* (Cambridge: Cambridge University Press, 1995)

Dunk, Jonathan, 'Reading the Tracker: The Antimonies of Aboriginal Ventrilo-quism', *JASAL: Journal of the Association for the Study of Australian Literature*, 17.1 (2017), 1–12

Durie, Mason, *Te Mana, Te Kāwanatanga: The Politics of Māori Self-Determination* (Auckland: Oxford University Press, 1998)

Dusinberre, Martin, and Roland Wenzlhuemer, 'Editorial – Being in Transit: Ships and Global Incompatibilities', *Journal of Global History*, 11.2 (2016), 155–62

Du Toit, André, 'Critic and Citizen: The Intellectual, Transformation and Academic Freedom', *Pretexts: Literary and Cultural Studies*, 9.1 (2000), 91–104

— 'The Legacy of Daantjie Oosthuizen: Revisiting the Liberal Defence of Academic Freedom', *African Sociological Review / Revue Africaine de Sociologie*, 9.1 (2005), 40–61

— and Hermann Buhr Giliomee, *Afrikaner Political Thought: Volume One: 1780–1850* (Claremont: David Philip, 1983)

Dwyer, Philip G, and Lyndall Ryan, 'Massacre in the Old and New Worlds, c.1780–1820', *Journal of Genocide Research*, 15.2 (2013), 111–15

Eagleton, Terry, *Literary Theory: An Introduction* (Oxford: Blackwell, 1983)

Edmonds, Penelope, '"I followed England round the world": The Rise of Trans-Imperial Anglo-Saxon Exceptionalism and the Spatial Narratives of Nineteenth-Century British Settler Colonies of the Pacific Rim', in *Reorienting Whiteness*, ed. by Leigh Boucher, Jane Carey, and Katherine Ellinghaus (Basingstoke: Palgrave Macmillan, 2009), pp. 99–115

— and Amanda Nettelbeck, 'Precarious Intimacies: Cross-Cultural Violence and Proximity in Settler Colonial Economies of the Pacific Rim', in *Intimacies of Violence in the Settler Colony: Economies of Dispossession around the Pacific Rim*, ed. by Penelope Edmonds and Amanda Nettelbeck (New York: Palgrave Macmillan, 2018), pp. 1–21

Eisler, William, *The Furthest Shore: Images of Terra Australis from the Middle Ages to Captain Cook* (Cambridge: Cambridge University Press, 1995)

Elleray, Michelle, *Victorian Coral Islands of Empire, Mission, and the Boys' Adventure Novel* (New York: Routledge, 2020)

Elliott, Jane, 'Was There a Convict Dandy? Convict Consumer Interests in Sydney, 1788–1815', *Australian Historical Studies*, 26 (1994), 373–92

Ellis, Markman, '"That Singular and Wonderful Quadruped": The Kangaroo as Historical Intangible Natural Heritage in the Eighteenth Century', in *Intangible Natural Heritage: New Perspectives on Natural Objects*, ed. by Eric Dorfman (New York: Routledge, 2012), pp. 56–87

Eperjesi, John, *The Imperialist Imaginary: Visions of Asia and the Pacific in American Culture* (Hanover: University Press of New England, 2005)

Erle, Sibylle, Laurie Garrison, Verity Hunt, and Phoebe Putnam, eds, *Panoramas, 1787–1900: Texts and Contexts*, 5 vols (London: Pickering and Chatto, 2013)

Etherington, Norman, 'Mission Station Melting Pots as a Factor in the Rise of South African Black Nationalism', *The International Journal of African Historical Studies*, 9.4 (1976), 592–605

Evans, Tanya, *Fractured Families: Life on the Margins in Colonial New South Wales* (Sydney: UNSW Press, 2015)

Fabian, Johannes, *Language and Colonial Power: The Appropriation of Swahili in the Former Belgian Congo 1880–1938* (Cambridge: Cambridge University Press, 1986)

— *Time and the Other: How Anthropology Makes Its Object*, foreword Matti Bunzl (1983; repr. New York: Columbia University Press, 2002)

Farrell, Michael, 'The Colonial Baroque in Australia: On Drover Boab Texts, Wiradjuri Clubs, and Charlie Flannigan's Drawings', *Criticism*, 58.3 (2016), 409–31

— *Writing Australian Unsettlement: Modes of Poetic Invention 1796–1945* (New York: Palgrave Macmillan, 2015)

Faulconbridge, James, and Allison Hui, 'Traces of a Mobile Field: Ten Years of Mobilities Research', *Mobilities*, 11.1 (2016), 1–14

Feldman, Jessica R., *Gender on the Divide: The Dandy in Modernist Literature* (Ithaca, NY: Cornell University Press, 1993)

Felski, Rita and Susan Stanford Friedman, 'Introduction', in *Comparison: Theories, Approaches, Uses*, ed. by Rita Felski and Susan Stanford Friedman (Baltimore: Johns Hopkins University Press, 2013), pp. 1–14

Festa, Lynn, *Sentimental Figures of Empire in Eighteenth-Century Britain and France* (Baltimore: Johns Hopkins University Press, 2006)

Fiddian-Qasmiyeh, Elena, and Patricia Daley, eds, *Handbook of South-South Relations* (Oxford: Routledge, 2018)

Findlay, Elisabeth, 'Peddling Prejudice: A Series of Twelve Profile Portraits', *Postcolonial Studies*, 16.1 (2013), 2–27

Firmat, Gustavo Pérez, ed., *Do the Americas Have a Common Literature?* (Durham: Duke University Press, 1990)

Firth, Raymond, 'Proverbs in Native Life, with Special Reference to those of the Maori, II (Continued)', *Folklore*, 37.3 (1926), 245–70

Fletcher, B. H., 'Grose, Francis (1758–1814)', *Australian Dictionary of National Biography*, n.p., https://adb.anu.edu.au/biography/grose-francis-2130/text2701 (accessed 12 February 2020)

Ford, Lisa, and David A. Roberts, 'Expansion, 1820–1850', in *The Cambridge History of Australia*, ed. by Stuart Macintyre and Alison Bashford (Melbourne: Cambridge University Press, 2011), pp. 121–48

Ford, Thomas H., and Justin Clemens, 'Barron Field's *Terra Nullius* Operation', *Australian Humanities Review*, 65 (November 2019), 1–19

Forsdick, Charles, and Jennifer Yee, 'Towards a Postcolonial Nineteenth-Century', *French Studies*, 72.2 (2018), 161–75

Foster, Tol, 'Of One Blood: An Argument for Relations and Regionality in Native American Literary Studies', in *Reasoning Together: The Native Critical Collective*, ed. by Janice Acoose, Daniel Heath Justice, Christopher B. Teuton, and Craig Womack (Norman: University of Oklahoma Press, 2008), pp. 265–302

Fraser, Hilary, Stephanie Green, and Judith Johnston, *Gender and the Victorian Periodical* (Cambridge: Cambridge University Press, 2003)

Frost, Mark Ravinder, '*Emporium in imperio*: Nanyang Networks and the Straits Chinese in Singapore, 1819–1914', *Journal of Southeast Asian Studies*, 36 (2005), 29–36

—— 'Imperial Citizenship or Else: Liberal Ideals and the Indian Unmasking of Empire, 1890–1919', *The Journal of Imperial and Commonwealth History*, 46.5 (2018), 845–73

—— '"Wider Opportunities": Religious Revival, Nationalist Awakening and the Global Dimension in Colombo, 1870–1920', *Modern Asian Studies*, 36.4 (2002), 937–67

Fulford, Tim, *Romantic Indians: Native Americans, British Literature, and Transatlantic Culture 1756–1830* (Oxford: Oxford University Press, 2006)

—— Debbie Lee, and Peter J. Kitson, eds, *Literature, Science and Exploration in the Romantic Era* (Cambridge: Cambridge University Press, 2004)

Fullagar, Kate, 'Introduction: The Atlantic World in the Antipodes', in *The Atlantic World in the Antipodes: Effects and Transformations since the Eighteenth Century*, ed. by Kate Fullagar (Newcastle upon Tyne: Cambridge Scholars Publishing, 2012), pp. xiii–xx

—— *The Warrior, the Voyager and the Artist: Three Lives in an Age of Empire* (Yale: Yale University Press, 2020)

Fuller, Jennifer, 'Terror in the South Seas: Violence, Relationships, and the Works of Louis Becke', *Australasian Journal of Victorian Studies*, 20.2 (2015), 42–57

Gammage, Bill, *The Biggest Estate on Earth: How Aborigines Made Australia* (Sydney: Allen and Unwin, 2011)

Gardner, Jared, *The Rise and Fall of Early American Magazine Culture* (Urbana: University of Illinois Press, 2012)

Garvey, Nathan, *The Celebrated George Barrington: A Spurious Author, the Book Trade, and Botany Bay* (Potts Point: Hordern House, 2008)

Gascoigne, John, 'Cross-Cultural Knowledge Exchange in the Age of the Enlightenment', in *Indigenous Intermediaries*, ed. by Shino Konishi, Maria Nugent, and Tiffany Shellam (Canberra: Australian National University Press, 2015), pp. 131–46

Gelder, Ken, 'The Postcolonial Gothic', in *The Cambridge Companion to the Modern Gothic*, ed. by Jerrold E. Hogle (Cambridge: Cambridge University Press, 2014), pp. 191–207

Gibson, Ross, 'Event-Grammar: The Language Notebooks of William Dawes', *Meanjin*, 68.2 (2009), n.p., https://meanjin.com.au/essays/event-grammar-the-language-notebooks-of-william-dawes/ (accessed 1 February 2020)

— *26 Views of the Starburst World: William Dawes at Sydney Cove 1788–91* (Crawley: University of Western Australia Publishing, 2012)

Gikandi, Simon, *Maps of Englishness: Writing Identity in the Culture of Colonialism* (New York: Columbia University Press, 1996)

— 'Realism, Romance, and the Problem of African Literature', *Modern Language Quarterly*, 73.3 (2012), 309–29

— *Slavery and the Culture of Taste* (Princeton: Princeton University Press, 2011)

Giles, Paul, *Antipodean America: Australasia and the Constitution of U. S. Literature* (Oxford: Oxford University Press, 2013)

— *Virtual Americas: Transnational Fictions and the Transatlantic Imaginary* (Durham and London: Duke University Press, 2002)

Gilling, Bryan, 'Raupatu: the Punitive Confiscation of Maori Land in the 1860s', in *Raupatu: The Confiscation of Maori Land*, ed. by Richard Boast and Richard S. Hill (Wellington: Victoria University Press, 2009), pp. 13–30

Gillis, John R., 'The Blue Humanities', *Humanities*, 34.3 (2013), n.p., www.neh.gov/humanities/2013/mayjune/feature/the-blue-humanities (accessed 1 February 2020)

Gilmour, Joanna, *Elegance in Exile: Portrait Drawings from Colonial Australia* (Canberra: National Portrait Gallery, 2012)

Gilmour, Rachael, *Grammars of Colonialism: Representing Languages in Colonial South Africa* (Basingstoke: Palgrave Macmillan, 2006)

Gilroy, Paul, *The Black Atlantic: Modernity and Double Consciousness* (Cambridge, MA: Harvard University Press, 1993)

Gissibl, Bernhard, 'The Conservation of Luxury: Safari Hunting and the Consumption of Wildlife in Twentieth-Century East Africa', in *Luxury in Global Perspective: Objects and Practices, 1600–2000*, ed. by Bernd-Stefan Grewe and Karin Hofmeester (Cambridge: Cambridge University Press, 2016)

Goh, Daniel, 'Elite Schools, Postcolonial Chineseness and Hegemonic Masculinities in Singapore', *British Journal of Sociology of Education*, 36.1 (2005), 137–55

— 'Unofficial Contentions: The Postcoloniality of Straits Chinese Political Discourse in the Straits Chinese Legislative Council', *Journal of Southeast Asian Studies*, 41.3 (2010), 483–507

Golder, Hilary, *High and Responsible Office: A History of the NSW Magistracy* (Sydney: Sydney University Press, 1991)

Goldie, Matthew Boyd, *The Idea of the Antipodes: Place, People and Voices* (London and New York: Routledge, 2010)

Goldie, Terry, *Fear and Temptation: The Image of the Indigene in Canadian, Australian, and New Zealand Literatures* (Montreal and Kingston: McGill-Queens University Press, 1989)

González, Natalicio, 'The Paraguayan People and Their Natural Tendencies', in *The Paraguay Reader: History, Culture, Politics*, ed. by Peter Lambert and Andrew Nickson (Durham: Duke University Press, 2013), pp. 178–83

Goodlad, Lauren M. E., 'Cosmopolitanism's Actually Existing Beyond; Toward A Victorian Geopolitical Aesthetic', *Victorian Literature and Culture*, 38 (2010), 399–411

— *The Victorian Geopolitical Aesthetic* (Oxford: Oxford University Press, 2015)

Goswami, Manu, 'Autonomy and Comparability: Notes on the Anticolonial and the Postcolonial', *boundary 2*, 32.2 (2005), 201–25

— 'Imaginary Futures and Colonial Internationalisms', *The American Historical Review*, 117.5 (2012), 1461–85

Gottlieb, Evan, *Romantic Globalism: British Literature and the Modern World Order, 1750–1830* (Columbus: Ohio State University Press, 2014)

Graham, Mary, 'Some Thoughts about the Philosophical Underpinnings of Aboriginal Worldviews', *Australian Humanities Review*, 45 (2008), 181–94

Griffiths, Devin, *The Age of Analogy: Science and Literature Between the Darwins* (Baltimore: Johns Hopkins University Press, 2016)

— and Deanna Kriesel, 'Introduction: Open Ecologies', *Victorian Literature and Culture*, 48.1 (2020), 1–28

Griffiths, Phil, '"This is a British Colony": The Ruling-Class Politics of the Seafarer's Strike, 1878–79', *Labour History*, 105 (2013), 131–51

Griffiths, Tom, 'Remembering', in Christine Hansen and Tom Griffiths, *Living With Fire: People, Nature and History in Steels Creek* (Collingwood: CSIRO Publishing, 2012), pp. 159–85

Grimshaw, Patricia, Marilyn Lake, Ann McGrath, and Marian Quartly, *Creating a Nation, 1788–1900* (Ringwood: Penguin Book Australia, 1994)

Groth, Helen, 'Mediating Popular Fictions: From the Magic Lantern to the Cinematograph', in *New Directions in Popular Fiction: Genre, Distribution, Reproduction*, ed. by Ken Gelder (London: Palgrave Macmillan, 2016), pp. 287–308

Gruber, Jacob W., 'Ethnographic Salvage and the Shaping of Anthropology', *American Anthropologist*, 72.6 (1970), 1289–99

Guy, Jeff, *Theophilus Shepstone and the Forging of Natal* (Pietermaritzburg: University of KwaZulu-Natal Press, 2013)

Hackforth-Jones, Jocelyn, *Augustus Earle: Travel Artist* (Canberra: National Library of Australia, 1980)

— *Augustus Earle: Travel Artist: Paintings and Drawings in the Rex Nan Kivell Collection National Library of Australia* (Martinborough: Alister Taylor, 1980)

Hadot, Pierre, *The Veil of Isis: An Essay on the History of the Idea of Nature* (Cambridge, MA: The Belknap Press, 2006)

Halford, James, 'Southern Conversations: J. M. Coetzee in Buenos Aires', *Sydney Review of Books* (28 February 2017), n.p., https://sydneyreviewofbooks.com/essay/southern-conversations-j-m-coetzee-in-buenos-aires/ (accessed 1 May 2020)

Hall, Catherine, 'Macaulay's Nation,' *Victorian Studies*, 51.3 (2009), 505–23

Hall, Stuart, 'Gramsci's Relevance for the Study of Race and Ethnicity', *Journal of Communication Inquiry*, 10.2 (1986), 5–27

Hannabuss, Stuart, 'Islands as Metaphors', *Universities Quarterly*, 38.1 (1983/4), 70–82

Hansen, David, '"Another man's understanding": Settler Images of Aboriginal People', in *Colony: Australia 1770–1861 / Frontier Wars*, ed. by Cathy Leahy and Judith Ryan (Melbourne: National Gallery of Victoria, 2018), pp. 108–19

Hanson, Clare, *Short Stories and Short Fiction 1880–1945* (London: Macmillan, 1985)

Harootunian, Harry, 'Remembering the Historical Present', *Critical Inquiry*, 33.3 (2007), 471–94

Harris, Margaret, 'The Antipodean Anatomy of Victorian Studies', *AUMLA: Journal of the Australasian Universities Modern Language Association*, 100 (2003), 61–72

Harris, Wendell V., *British Short Fiction in the Nineteenth Century* (Detroit: Wayne State University Press, 1979)

Harrison, Robert Pogue, *Forests: The Shadow of Civilization* (Chicago: University of Chicago Press, 1992)

Harter, Eugene C., *The Lost Colony of the Confederacy* (Oxford, MS: University of Mississippi Press, 1985)

Hau'ofa, Epeli, 'Epilogue: Pasts to Remember', in *Remembrance of Pacific Pasts: An Invitation to Remake History*, ed. by Robert Borofsky (Honolulu: University of Hawai'i Press, 2000), pp. 453–71

— 'Our Sea of Islands', in *A New Oceania: Rediscovering Our Sea of Islands*, ed. by Eric Waddell, Vijay Naidu, and Epeli Hau'ofa (Suva: University of the South Pacific, 1993), pp. 2–17

— *We Are the Ocean* (Honolulu: University of Hawai'i Press, 2008)

Hayot, Eric, *The Hypothetical Mandarin: Sympathy, Modernity, and Chinese Pain* (Oxford: Oxford University Press, 2009)

— *On Literary Worlds* (Oxford: Oxford University Press, 2012)

Heidegger, Martin, 'The Age of the World Picture', in *Off the Beaten Track*, trans. and ed. by Julian Young and Kenneth Hayes (Cambridge: Cambridge University Press, 2002), pp. 1–56

— 'On the Origin of the Work of Art', in *Basic Writings*, ed. by David Farrell Krell (New York: Harper Collins, 2008), pp. 143–212

Herbert, Christopher, 'Epilogue: Ethnography and Evolution', *Victorian Studies*, 41.3 (1998), 485–94

Hessell, Nikki, *Romantic Literature and the Colonised World: Lessons from Indigenous Translations* (Basingstoke: Palgrave Macmillan, 2018)

Hewett, Dorothy, 'The Journey of Henry Lawson', *Australian Left Review*, 7 (1967), 28–34

Hiatt, Alfred, '*Terra Australis* and the Idea of the Antipodes', in *European Perceptions of Terra Australis*, ed. by Anne M. Scott, Alfred Hiatt, Claire McIlroy, and Christopher Wortham (London and New York: Routledge, 2016), pp. 9–44

— *Terra Incognita: Mapping the Antipodes Before 1600* (Chicago: University of Chicago Press, 2008)

Hickford, Mark, 'Strands from the Afterlife of Confiscation: Property Rights, Constitutional Histories and the Political Incorporation of Maori, 1920s', in *Raupatu: The Confiscation of Maori Land*, ed. by Richard Boast and Richard S. Hill (Wellington: Victoria University Press, 2009), pp. 169–204

Higgins, David, 'Writing to Colonial Australia: Barron Field and Charles Lamb', *Nineteenth-Century Contexts*, 32.3 (2010), 219–33

Hill, Peter, *Utopia and Civilisation in the Arab Nahda* (Cambridge: Cambridge University Press, 2020)

Hill, Richard S., *Enthroning 'Justice Above Might'? The Sim Commission, Tainui and the Crown* (Wellington: Department of Justice, 1989)

— *Maori and the State: Crown-Maori Relations in New Zealand/ Aotearoa, 1950–2000* (Wellington: Victoria University Press, 2009)

Hitchcock, Peter, *The Long Space: Transnationalism and Postcolonial Form* (Stanford: Stanford University Press, 2010)

Hoagwood, Terence Allan and Kathryn Ledbetter, *'Colour'd Shadows': Contexts in Publishing, Printing, and Reading Nineteenth-Century British Women Writers* (Basingstoke: Palgrave Macmillan, 2005)

Hobson, John M., *The Eastern Origins of Western Civilisation* (Cambridge: Cambridge University Press, 2004)

Hofmeyr, Isabel, 'The Black Atlantic Meets the Indian Ocean: Forging New Paradigms of Transnationalism for the Global South – Literary and Cultural Perspectives', *Social Dynamics: A Journal of African Studies*, 33.7 (2007), 3–32

— *Gandhi's Printing Press: Experiments in Slow Reading* (Cambridge, MA: Harvard University Press, 2013)

— *The Portable Bunyan: A Transnational History of The Pilgrim's Progress* (Princeton: Princeton University Press, 2004)

— 'Southern by Degrees: Islands and Empires in the South Atlantic, the Indian Ocean, and the Subantartic World', in *The Global South Atlantic*, ed. by Kerry Bystrom and Joseph R. Slaughter (New York: Fordham University Press, 2018), pp. 81–96

— 'Universalizing the Indian Ocean', *PMLA*, 125.3 (2010), 721–9

Holden, Philip, 'The Beginnings of "Asian Modernity" in Singapore: A Straits Chinese Body Project', *Common/Plural*, 7.1 (1999), 59–78

— 'Between Modernization and Modernism: Community and Contradiction in the Paracolonial Short Story', *Philippine Studies*, 55.3 (2007), 319–43

— 'China Men: Writing the British Nation in Malaya', *SPAN*, 38 (1994), 75–85

— 'Colonial Fiction, Hybrid Lives: Early Singaporean Fiction in *The Straits Chinese Magazine*', *Journal of Commonwealth Literature*, 33.1 (1998), 85–97

— 'Communities and Conceptual Limits: Exploring Malaysian Literature in English', *Asiatic*, 3.2 (2009), 54–68

— 'Dissonant Voices: Straits Chinese and the Appropriation of Travel Writing', *Studies in Travel Writing*, 2.1 (1998), 181–9

— 'The Littoral and the Literary: Making Moral Communities in the Straits Settlements and the Gold Coast in the Late Nineteenth and Early Twentieth Centuries', in *Singapore in Global Context*, ed. by Derek Heng and Syed Muhd Khairudin Aljunied (Amsterdam: Amsterdam University Press, 2011), pp. 89–110

Holmes, Richard, *The Age of Wonder: How the Romantic Generation Discovered the Beauty and Terror of Science* (London: Harper Press, 2009)

Horrocks, Ingrid, 'A World of Waters: Imagining, Voyaging, Entanglement', in *A History of New Zealand Literature*, ed. by Mark Williams (Cambridge: Cambridge University Press, 2016), pp. 17–30

Hunter, Lani Kavika, 'Spirits of New Zealand: Early Pakeha Writers on Maori' (unpublished doctoral thesis, Auckland University, 2004)

Huston, James L., *The Panic of 1857 and The Coming of the Civil War* (Baton Rouge: Louisiana State University Press, 1987)

Iqani, Mehita, and Fernando Resende, *Media and the Global South: Narrative Territorialities, Cross-Cultural Currents* (London: Routledge, 2019)

Irvine, Judith T., 'The Family Romance of Colonial Linguistics: Gender and Family in Nineteenth-Century Representations of African Languages', *Pragmatics*, 5.2 (1995), 139–53

Ivison, Duncan, 'Non-Cosmopolitan Universalism: On Armitage's Foundations of International Political Thought', *History of European Ideas*, 41.1 (2015), 78–88

Jackson, Shona N., *Creole Indigeneity: Between Myth and Nation in the Colonial Caribbean* (Minneapolis: University of Minnesota Press, 2012)

Jacob, Christian, *The Sovereign Map: Theoretical Approaches in Cartography throughout History*, trans. by Tom Conley (Chicago: University of Chicago Press, 2006)

Jaffer, Aaron, *Lascars and Indian Ocean Seafaring, 1780–1860: Shipboard Life, Unrest and Mutiny* (Woodbridge: Boydell, 2015)

Johannesburg Workshop in Theory and Criticism, n.p., www.jwtc.org.za (accessed 26 June 2019)

Johnston, Anna, '"The Aboriginal Mother": Poetry and Politics', in *Remembering the Myall Creek Massacre*, ed. by Jane Lydon and Lyndall Ryan (Sydney: NewSouth, 2018), pp. 68–84

— *Missionary Writing and Empire, 1800–1860* (Cambridge: Cambridge University Press, 2003)

— 'Mrs Milson's Wordlist: Eliza Hamilton Dunlop and the Intimacy of Linguistic Work', in *Intimacies of Violence in the Settler Colony: Economies of Dispossession around the Pacific Rim*, ed. by Penelope Edmonds and Amanda Nettelbeck (Cham: Palgrave Macmillan, 2018), pp. 225–47

— *The Paper War: Morality, Print Culture, and Power in Colonial New South Wales* (Crawley: University of Western Australia Press, 2011)

— and Elizabeth Webby, eds, *Eliza Hamilton Dunlop: Writing from the Colonial Frontier* (Sydney: Sydney University Press, 2021)

Jolly, Margaret, 'Imagining Oceania: Indigenous and Foreign Representations of a Sea of Islands', *The Contemporary Pacific*, 19.2 (2007), 508–45

— 'The South in Southern Theory: Antipodean Reflections on the Pacific', *Australian Humanities Review*, 44 (2008), n.p., http://australianhumanitiesreview.org/2008/03/01/the-south-in-southern-theory-antipodean-reflections-on-the-pacific/ (accessed 26 June 2019)

Jose, Nicholas, 'Introduction', in *Macquarie PEN Anthology of Australian Literature*, ed. by Nicholas Jose (Sydney: Allen & Unwin, 2009), pp. 1–2

Joyce, Patrick D., *The Rule of Freedom: Liberalism and the Modern City* (London and New York: Verso, 2003)

Karis, Thomas, and Gwendolen Carter, eds, *From Protest to Challenge, Vol. 1: A Documentary History of African Politics in South Africa, 1882–1964: Protest and Hope, 1882–1934* (1972; repr. Stanford: Hoover Institution Press, 2003)

Karskens, Grace, *The Colony: A History of Early Sydney* (Sydney: Allen & Unwin, 2009)

— 'Red Coat, Blue Jacket, Black Skin: Aboriginal Men and Clothing in early New South Wales', *Aboriginal History*, 35 (2011), 1–36

Kaul, Chandrika, *Reporting the Raj: The British Press and India, c. 1880–1922* (Manchester: Manchester University Press, 2003)

Keegan, Timothy, *Colonial South Africa and the Origins of the Racial Order* (Cape Town: David Philip, 1996)

Keneally, Thomas, *Australians: Eureka to the Diggers* (Sydney: Allen & Unwin, 2011)

Keynes, Richard, *The Beagle Record* (Cambridge: Cambridge University Press, 2012)

Khor, Neil, 'Imperial Cosmopolitan Malaya: A Study of Realist Fiction in the *Straits Chinese Magazine*', *JMBRAS*, 81.1 (2008), 27–47

— 'Malacca's Straits Chinese Anglophone Poets and their Experience of Malaysian Nationalism', *Archipel*, 76 (2008), 127–49

Klancher, Jon, *The Making of English Reading Audiences, 1790–1832* (Madison: University of Wisconsin Press, 1983)

Kleinpenning, Jan M. G., *Rural Paraguay, 1870–1963: A Geography of Progress, Plunder and Poverty*, 2 vols (Madrid: Iberoamericana Vervuert, 2009)

Koditschek, Theodore, *Liberalism, Imperialism, and the Historical Imagination: Nineteenth-Century Visions of a Greater Britain* (Cambridge: Cambridge University Press, 2011)

Kōhere, Rarawa, 'Kohere, Mokena', in *Dictionary of New Zealand Biography*, 5 vols (1990–2000) I (1990), n.p., https://teara.govt.nz/en/biographies/1k15/kohere-mokena (accessed 2 October 2017)

— 'Tāwakewake: An Historical Case Study and Situational Analysis of Ngāti Ruawaipu Leadership' (unpublished doctoral thesis, Massey University, 2005)

Konishi, Shino, 'First Nations Scholars, Settler Colonial Studies, and Indigenous History', *Australian Historical Studies*, 50 (2019), 1–20

— Maria Nugent, and Tiffany Shellam, eds, *Indigenous Intermediaries: New Perspectives on Exploration Archives* (Canberra: Australian National University Press, 2015)

Korte, Barbara, *The Short Story in Britain: A Historical Sketch and Anthology* (Tübingen: A. Francke Verlag Tübingen und Basel, 2003)

Kranidis, Rita S., *The Victorian Spinster and Colonial Emigration: Contested Subjects* (Basingstoke: Macmillan, 1999)

Krishnan, Sanjay, 'History and the Work of Literature in the Periphery', *Novel: A Forum on Fiction*, 42 (2009), 483–9

— 'Reading Globalization from the Margin: The Case of Abdullah Munshi', *Representations*, 99.1 (2007), 40–73

Kyle, Noeline J., '"Delicate health … interesting condition …": Eliza Darling, Pregnancy and Philanthropy in Early New South Wales', *History of Education*, 24 (1995), 25–43.

Laband, John, *The Eight Zulu Kings* (Johannesburg: Jonathan Ball, 2018)

— and John Wright, *King Cetshwayo kaMpande* (Durban and Ulundi: Shuter and Shooter, KwaZulu Monuments Council, 1980)

Lake, Marilyn, 'White Man's Country: The Transnational History of a National Project', *Australian Historical Studies*, 34.122 (2003), 346–63

Lamb, Jonathan, Vanessa Smith, and Nicholas Thomas, 'Introduction', in *Exploration and Exchange: A South Seas Anthology, 1680–1900*, ed. by Jonathan Lamb, Vanessa Smith, and Nicholas Thomas (Chicago: University of Chicago Press, 2000), pp. xiii–xxv

Lange, Raeburn, *Island Ministers: Indigenous Leadership in Nineteenth Century Pacific Islands Christianity* (Canberra: Pandanus Press, 2006)

Langton, Marcia, *Well, I Heard it on the Radio and Saw it on the Television* (North Sydney: Australian Film Commission, 1993)

Law, Graham, 'Savouring of the Australian Soil? On the Sources and Affiliations of Colonial Newspaper Fiction', *Victorian Periodicals Review*, 37.4 (2004), 75–97

Lawson, Elizabeth, 'Louisa Atkinson: The Distant Sound of Native Voices', Occasional Paper No. 15 (English Department University College, Australian Defence Force Academy, Canberra, 1989)

— 'Louisa Atkinson: Writings on Aboriginal Land Ownership', *Margin*, 21 (1989), 15–20.

— *The Natural Art of Louisa Atkinson* (Sydney: State Library of New South Wales Press, 1995)

Lazarus, Neil, *The Postcolonial Unconscious* (Cambridge: Cambridge University Press, 2011)

Legassick, Martin, 'The Frontier Tradition in South African Historiography', *Collected Seminar Papers, Institute of Commonwealth Studies*, 12 (1972), 1–33

Levander, Caroline, and Walter Mignolo, 'Introduction: The Global South and World Dis/Order', *The Global South*, 5.1 (2011), 1–11

Lifshey, Adam, *Specters of Conquest: Indigenous Absence in Transatlantic Literatures* (New York: Fordham University Press, 2010)

Lineham, Peter, *Sunday Best: How the Church Shaped New Zealand and New Zealand Shaped the Church* (Auckland: Massey University Press, 2017)

Lionnet, François, and Shu-mei Shih, eds, *Minor Transnationalism* (Durham: Duke University Press, 2005)

Loader, Arini, 'Early Māori Literature: The Writing of Hajaraia Kiharoa', in *A History of New Zealand Literature*, ed. by Mark Williams (Cambridge: Cambridge University Press, 2016), pp. 31–43

Lootens, Tricia, 'Hemans and Home: Victorianism, Feminine "Internal Enemies", and the Domestication of National Identity', *PMLA*, 109.2 (1994), 238–53

Lopez, Barry, *Arctic Dreams* (1986; repr. London: Vintage, 2014)

Lott, Eric, *Love and Theft: Blackface Minstrelsy and the American Working Class* (1993; repr. Oxford: Oxford University Press, 2013)

Lowe, Gail, 'Book History', in *The Oxford History of the Novel in English, Volume 9: The World Novel to 1950*, ed. by Ralph Crane, Jane Stafford, and Mark Williams (Oxford: Oxford University Press, 2016), pp. 11–28

Lydon, Jane, and Lyndall Ryan, eds, *Remembering the Myall Creek Massacre* (Sydney: NewSouth Publishing, 2018)

Macdonald, Charlotte, 'Beyond the Realm: The Loss of Culture as the Colonial Condition', *Journal of New Zealand Studies*, 12 (2011), 1–12

Mackenzie, John M., 'Lakes, Rivers and Oceans: Technology, Ethnicity and the Shipping of Empire in the Late Nineteenth Century', in *Maritime Empires: British Imperial Maritime Trade in the Nineteenth Century*, ed. by David Killingray, Margarette Lincoln, and Nigel Rigby (Woodbridge: Boydell in association with National Maritime Museum, 2004), pp. 111–27

Macoun, Alissa, and Elizabeth Strakosch, 'The Ethical Demands of Settler Colonial Theory', *Settler Colonial Studies*, 3.4 (2013), 426–43

Macqueen, Ian M., *Black Consciousness and Progressive Movements under Apartheid* (Pietermaritzburg: University of KwaZulu-Natal Press, 2018)

Mahuta, Robert Te Kotahi, 'Whaikoorero: A Study of Formal Maori Speech' (unpublished master's thesis, University of Auckland, 1974)

Majeed, Javed, 'Literary Modernity in South Asia', in *India and the British Empire*, ed. by Douglas Peers and Nandini Gooptu (Oxford: Oxford University Press, 2012), pp. 262–83

Mandler, Peter, 'The Problem with Cultural History', *Cultural and Social History*, 1 (2004), 94–117

Marcus, Sharon, 'Same Difference? Transnationalism, Comparative Literature, and Victorian Studies', *Victorian Studies*, 45.4 (2003), 677–86

Maretu, *Cannibals and Converts: Radical Change in the Cook Islands*, trans. and ed. by Marjorie Tua'inekore Crocombe (Suva: University of the South Pacific, 1983)

Martin, Meredith, '"Imperfectly Civilized": Ballads, Nations, and Histories of Form', *ELH*, 82.2 (2015), 345–63

Martin, Susan K., '"Tragic ring-barked forests" and the "Wicked Wood": Haunting Environmental Anxiety in Late Nineteenth-Century Australian Literature', in *Victorian Environmental Nightmares*, ed. by Laurence W. Mazzeno and Ronald D. Morrison (London: Palgrave Macmillan, 2019), pp. 121–43

Martin, Tony, ed., *African Fundamentalism: A Literary and Cultural Anthology of Garvey's Harlem Renaissance* (Dover: The Majority Press, 1991)

Masilela, Ntongela, 'Vernacular Press', in *Encyclopedia of African Literature*, ed. by Simon Gikandi (London: Routledge, 2003), pp. 547–54

Massey, Doreen, *For Space* (London: Sage, 2005)

Masuzawa, Tomoko, *The Invention of World Religions: Or, How European Universalism Was Preserved in the Language of Pluralism* (Chicago: University of Chicago Press, 2005)

Matsuda, Matt K., *Pacific Worlds: A History of Seas, Peoples, and Cultures* (Cambridge: Cambridge University Press, 2012)

Maynard, Margaret, *Fashioned from Penury: Dress as Cultural Practice in Colonial Australia* (Cambridge: Cambridge University Press, 1994)

McCann, Andrew, 'Romanticism, Nationalism and the Myth of the Popular in William Lane's *The Workingman's Paradise*', *Journal of Australian Studies*, 25.70 (2001), 1–12

McCormick, E. H., 'Introduction', in *Narrative of a Residence in New Zealand; Journal of a Residence in Tristan Da Cunha*, ed. by E. H. McCormick (1832; repr. Oxford: Clarendon, 1966), pp. 1–46

McKenzie, Kirsten, '"Franklins of the Cape": The "South African Commercial Advertiser" and the Creation of a Colonial Public Sphere, 1824–1854', *Kronos*, 25 (1998), 88–102

McLachlan, Noel, 'Introduction', in James Hardy Vaux, *The Memoirs of James Hardy Vaux*, ed. by Noel McLachlan (London: Heinemann, 1964), pp. xv–lxxxii

McQueen, Humphrey, *A New Britannia: An Argument Concerning the Social Origins of Australian Radicalism and Nationalism* (1970; repr. New York: Penguin, 1980)

Mead, Hirini Moko, *Tikanga Māori: Living By Māori Values* (Wellington: Huia Publishers, 2003)

Mead, Philip, 'Nation, Literature, Location', in *The Cambridge History of Australian Literature*, ed. by Peter Pierce (Cambridge: Cambridge University Press, 2011), pp. 549–67

Means, Russell, 'The Same Old Song', in *Marxism and Native Americans*, ed. by Ward Churchill (Boston: South End Press, 1992), pp. 19–34

Mehta, Uday Singh, *Liberalism and Empire: A Study in Nineteenth-Century British Liberal Thought* (Chicago: University of Chicago Press, 1999)

Menezes, Mary Noel, *The Amerindians in Guyana, 1803–73: A Documentary History* (London: Frank Cass, 1979)

— *British Policy towards the Amerindians in British Guiana, 1803–1873* (Georgetown: Caribbean Press, 2011)

Merleau-Ponty, Maurice, *Phenomenology of Perception*, trans. by Colin Smith (London: Routledge and Kegan Paul, 1962)

Mignolo, Walter D., 'The Global South And World Dis/order', *Journal of Anthropological Research*, 67 (2011), 165–88

—— *Local Histories/Global Designs: Coloniality, Subaltern Knowledges, and Border Designs* (Princeton: Princeton University Press, 2000)

—— 'On Comparison: Who is Comparing What and Why?', in *Comparison: Theories, Approaches, Uses*, ed. by Rita Felski and Susan Stanford Friedman (Baltimore: Johns Hopkins University Press, 2013), pp. 99–119

Milliss, Roger, *Waterloo Creek: The Australia Day Massacre of 1838, George Gipps and the British Conquest of New South Wales* (Ringwood: McPhee Gribble, 1992)

Mitchell, W. J. T., 'Imperial Landscapes', in *Landscape and Power*, 2nd edn (Chicago: University of Chicago Press, 2002), pp. 5–34

Mkhize, Khwezi, 'Empire Unbound: Imperial Liberalism, Race and Diaspora in the Making of South Africa' (unpublished doctoral thesis, University of Pennsylvania, 2015)

Monin, Paul, 'Maori Encounters and Colonial Capitalism', in *The New Oxford History of New Zealand*, ed. by Giselle Byrnes (Melbourne: Oxford University Press, 2009), pp. 125–46

Moore, Grace, '"Raising high its thousand forked tongues": Campfires, Bushfires, and Portable Domesticity in Nineteenth-Century Australia', *19: Interdisciplinary Studies in the Long Nineteenth Century*, 26 (2018), n.p., https://doi.org/10.16995/ntn.807 (accessed 19 November 2019)

—— 'Surviving Black Thursday: The Great Bushfire of 1851', in *Victorian Settler Narratives: Emigrants, Cosmopolitans and Returnees in Nineteenth-Century Literature*, ed. by Tamara S. Wagner (London and New York: Routledge, 2016), pp. 129–39

Moraru, Christian, '"World", "Globe", "Planet": Comparative Literature, Planetary Studies, and Cultural Debt after the Global Turn', n.p., https://stateofthediscipline.acla.org/entry/"world"-"globe"-"planet"-comparative-literature-planetary-studies-and-cultural-debt-after (accessed 2 March 2020)

Moreton-Robinson, Aileen, ed., *Critical Indigenous Studies: Engagements in First World Locations* (Tucson: University of Arizona Press, 2016)

Moretti, Franco, 'Conjectures on World Literature', *New Left Review*, 1 (2000), 54–68

Morieux, Renaud, Clare Anderson, Jonathan Lamb, David Armitage, Alison Bashford, and Sujit Sivasundaram, 'Oceanic Histories: A Roundtable', *Journal of Colonialism and Colonial History*, 19.2 (2018), n.p., https://muse.jhu.edu/article/700167 (accessed 1 February 2020)

Mosquera, Geraldo, 'Some Problems in Transcultural Curating', in *Global Visions: Towards a New Internationalism in the Visual Arts*, ed. by Jean Fisher (London: Kala Press, 1994), pp. 133–9

Mostert, Noel, *Frontiers: The Epic of South Africa's Creation and the Tragedy of the Xhosa People* (New York: Knopf, 1992)

Motion, Andrew, *Wainewright the Poisoner* (New York: Alfred A. Knopf, 2000)

Moura, Sabrina, ed., *Southern Panoramas: Perspectives for Other Geographies of Thought* (Rio de Janeiro: Videobrasil, 2015)

Muckerjee, Upamanyu Pablo, 'Introduction: Victorian World Literature', *The Yearbook of English Studies*, 41.2 (2011), 1–19

Muecke, Stephen, 'Cultural Studies' Networking Strategies in the South', *Australian Humanities Review*, 44 (2008), 39–51

Müller, Gesine, Jorge J. Locane, and Benjamin Loy, 'Introduction', in *Re-Mapping World Literature: Writing, Book Markets and Epistemologies between Latin America and the Global South*, ed. by Gesine Müller, Jorge J. Locane, and Benjamin Loy (Boston: De Gruyter, 2018), pp. 1–12

Murphy, Kevin, and Sally O'Driscoll, *Studies in Ephemera: Text and Image in Eighteenth-Century Print* (Lewisburg: Bucknell University Press, 2013)

Murray, Kevin, 'Keys to the South', *Australian Humanities Review*, 44 (2008), 23–38

Murray-Oliver, Anthony, *Augustus Earle in New Zealand* (Christchurch: Whitcombe & Tombs, 1968)

Muthyala, John, *Reworlding America: Myth, History and Narrative* (Athens: Ohio University Press, 2006)

Myers, Janet C., *Antipodal England: Emigration and Portable Domesticity in the Victorian Imagination* (New York: State University of New York Press, 2009)

Mzamane, Mbulelo Vizikhungo, 'Colonial and Imperial Themes in South African Literature, 1820–1930', *The Yearbook of English Studies*, 13 (1983), 181–95

Naidu, Sam, 'The Emergence of the South African Farm Crime Novel: Socio-Historical Crimes, Personal Crimes, and the Figure of the Dog', *English in Africa*, 43.2 (2016), 9–38

Nathan, Hans, *Dan Emmett and the Rise of Early Negro Minstrelsy* (Norman: University of Oklahoma Press, 1962)

Nettelbeck, Amanda, *Indigenous Rights and Colonial Subjecthood: Protection and Reform in the Nineteenth-Century British Empire* (Cambridge: Cambridge University Press, 2019)

Neville, Richard, *Mr J.W. Lewin, Painter and Naturalist* (Sydney: NewSouth Publishing and National Library of Australia, 2012)

Newmeyer, Frederick J., *The Politics of Linguistics* (Chicago: University of Chicago Press, 1986)

Newton-King, Susan, *Masters and Servants on the Cape Eastern Frontier, 1760–1803* (Cambridge: Cambridge University Press, 1999)

Nicholson, Ian Hawkins, *Log of Logs: A Catalogue of Logs, Journals, Shipboard Diaries, Letters, and All Forms of Voyage Narratives, 1788 to 1988, for Australia and New Zealand and Surrounding Oceans* (Nambour: The Author jointly with the Australian Association for Maritime History, 1990)

Nishime, Leilani, and Kim D. Hester Williams, 'Introduction: Why Racial Ecologies', in *Racial Ecologies*, ed. by Leilani Nishime and Kim D. Hester Williams (Washington: University of Washington Press, 2018), pp. 3–18

Nixon, Rob, *Slow Violence and the Environmentalism of the Poor* (Cambridge, MA: Harvard University Press, 2011)

Nugent, Maria, 'Jacky Jacky and the Politics of Aboriginal Testimony', in *Indigenous Intermediaries*, ed. by Shino Konishi, Maria Nugent, and Tiffany Shelam (Canberra: Australian National University Press, 2015), pp. 67–84

Ogburn, Miles, *Indian Ink: Script and Print in the Making of the East India Company* (Chicago: Chicago University Press, 2007)

O'Leary, John, *Savage Songs and Wild Romances: Settler Poetry and the Indigene, 1830–1880* (Amsterdam: Rodopi, 2011)

Olsen, Penny, *Louisa Atkinson's Nature Notes* (Canberra: National Library of Australia, 2015)

O'Malley, Vincent, *The Meeting Place: Māori and Pākehā Encounters, 1642–1840* (Auckland: Auckland University Press, 2012)

Omar, Hussein, 'Arabic Thought in the Liberal Cage', in *Islam After Liberalism*, ed. by Faisal Devji and Zaheer Kazmi (Oxford: Oxford University Press, 2005), pp. 17–45

Opland, Jeff, 'Nineteenth-Century Xhosa Literature', *Kronos*, 30 (2004), 22–46

Orange, Claudia, *The Treaty of Waitangi*, 2nd edn (Wellington: Bridget Williams Books, 2011)

Orel, Harold, *The Victorian Short Story: Development and Triumph of a Literary Genre* (Cambridge: Cambridge University Press, 1986)

Otto, Peter, *Multiplying Worlds: Romanticism, Modernity, and the Emergence of Virtual Reality* (Oxford: Oxford University Press, 2011)

Page, Stephen, *Patyegarang* (San Francisco: Kanopy Streaming, 2015)

Parr, C. J., 'A Missionary Library: Printed Attempts to Instruct the Maori, 1815–1845', *Journal of the Polynesian Society*, 70 (1961), 436–40

Parsons, Neil, *King Khama, Emperor Joe, and the Great White Queen: Victorian Britain through African Eyes* (Chicago and London: University of Chicago Press, 1998)

Paterson, Lachy, *Colonial Discourses: Niupepa Māori, 1855–1863* (Dunedin: Otago University Press, 2006)

Pawson, Eric, and Tom Brooking, eds, *Making a New Land: Environmental Histories of New Zealand*, new edn (Dunedin: Otago University Press, 2013)

Peach, Annette, *Portraits of Byron* (London: The Walpole Society, 2000)

— 'Wainewright, Thomas Griffiths [pseuds. Janus Weathercock, Cornelius van Vinkbooms]', *Oxford Dictionary of National Biography*, n.p., https://doi.org/10.1093/ref:odnb/28403 (accessed 1 February 2020)

Pennycook, Alastair, *English and the Discourse of Colonialism* (London and New York: Routledge, 1998)

Perkins, T. M., 'Atkinson, James: 1795–1834', *The Australian Dictionary of National Biography*, n.p., http://adb.anu.edu.au/biography/atkinson-james-1726 (accessed 30 November 2019)

Perry, Adele, *Colonial Relations: The Douglas-Connolly Family and the Nineteenth-Century Imperial World* (Cambridge: Cambridge University Press, 2015)

Piesse, Jude, *British Settler Emigration in Print, 1832–1877* (Oxford: Oxford University Press, 2016)

Pierce, Peter, ed., *The Cambridge History of Australian Literature* (Cambridge: Cambridge University Press, 2009)

Plumb, Christopher, *The Georgian Menagerie: Exotic Animals in Eighteenth-Century London* (London: I. B. Tauris & Co. Ltd., 2015)

Pope, Alexander, *Alexander Pope: The Major Works*, ed. by Pat Rodgers (Oxford: Oxford University Press, 2008)

Poulton, Edward B., *William John Burchell* (London: Spottiswood & Co Ltd, 1907)

Pound, Francis, 'Spectator Figures in Some New Zealand Paintings & Prints', *Art New Zealand*, 23 (1982), 40–5

Pratt, Mary Louise, 'Fieldwork in Common Places', in *Writing Culture: The Poetics and Politics of Ethnography*, ed. by James Clifford and George E. Marcus (Berkeley: University of Berkeley Press, 1986)

— *Imperial Eyes: Travel Writing and Transculturation* (London: Routledge, 1992)

— *Imperial Eyes: Travel Writing and Transculturation*, 2nd edn (New York: Routledge, 2008)

Pulte, Helmut and Scott Mandelbrote, eds, *The Reception of Isaac Newton in Europe*, 3 vols (London: Bloomsbury Academic, 2019)

Putten, Jan van der, 'Abdullah Munsyi and the Missionaries', *Bijdragen tot de Taal-, Land-en Volkenkunde (BKI)*, 162.4 (2006), 407–40

Radhakrishnan, R., *Theory in an Uneven World* (Malden: Blackwell, 2003)

Raine, Philip, *Paraguay* (New Brunswick: Scarecrow Press, 1956)

Ramazani, Jahan, *A Transnational Poetics* (Chicago: Chicago University Press, 2009)

Reece, Bob, 'Rev, of Patrick Collins, Goodbye Bussamarai: The Mandandji Land War, Southern Queensland 1842–1852 (2002)', *Bulletin (Australian Historical Association)*, 96 (2003), 78–82

Reeder, Jessie, *The Forms of Informal Empire* (Baltimore: Johns Hopkins University Press, 2020)

Reimer, Mavis, Clare Bradford, and Heather Snell, 'Juvenile Fiction', in *The Oxford History of the Novel in English, Volume 9: The World Novel to 1950*, ed. by Ralph Crane, Jane Stafford, and Mark Williams (Oxford: Oxford University Press, 2016), pp. 280–99

Rere, Taira, *History of the Papehia Family* (Suva: Lotu Pasifika Productions, 1977)

Rewi, Poia, *Whaikōrero: The World of Māori Oratory* (Auckland: Auckland University Press, 2010)

Rich, Paul B., *Hope and Despair: English-Speaking Intellectuals and South African Politics, 1896–1976* (London: British Academic Press, 1993)

Rifkin, Mark, *Beyond Settler Time: Temporal Sovereignty and Indigenous Self-Determination* (Durham: Duke University Press, 2017)

Roberts, David Andrew, '"Language to Save the Innocent": Reverend L. Threlkeld's Linguistic Mission', *Journal of the Royal Australian Historical Society*, 94.2 (2008), 107–25

Roberts, Jane, *Royal Landscape: The Gardens and Parks of Windsor* (New Haven and London: Yale University Press, 1997)

Roediger, David R., *The Wages of Whiteness: Race and the Making of the American Working Class*, revised edn (1991; repr. London: Verso, 2007)

Roff, William R., *The Origins of Malay Nationalism* (Singapore: Oxford University Press, 1994)

Rogers, Shef, 'Crusoe among the Maori: Translation and Colonial Acculturation in Victorian New Zealand', *Book History*, 1 (1998), 182–95

Rose, Deborah Bird, 'Gendered Substances and Objects in Ritual: An Australian Aboriginal Study', *Material Religion*, 3.1 (2007), 34–46

— 'An Indigenous Philosophical Ecology: Situating the Human', *The Australian Journal of Anthropology*, 16.3 (2005), 294–305

— *Nourishing Terrains: Australian Aboriginal Views of Landscape and Wilderness* (Canberra: Australian Heritage Commission, 1996)

— 'The Year Zero and the North Australian Frontier', in *Tracking Knowledge in North Australian Landscapes: Studies in Indigenous and Settler Ecological Knowledge Systems*, ed. by Deborah Rose and Anne Clarke (Casuarina: North Australia Research Unit, Australian National University, 1997), pp. 19–36

Rose, Jonathan, *The Intellectual Life of the British Working Class* (New Haven: Yale, 2001)

Ross, Lloyd, *William Lane and the Australian Labor Movement* (1935; repr. Sydney: Hale & Iremonger, 1980)

Ross, Robert, 'The Kat River Rebellion and Khoikhoi Nationalism: The Fate of an Ethnic Identification', *Kronos*, 24 (1997), 91–105

— *Status and Respectability in the Cape Colony, 1750–1870: A Tragedy of Manners* (Cambridge: Cambridge University Press, 1999)

— *These Oppressions Won't Cease: The Political Thought of the Cape Khoesan, 1777–1879: An Anthology* (Johannesburg: Witwatersrand University Press, 2017)

Ross, Trevor, *The Making of the English Literary Canon: From the Middle Ages to the Late Eighteenth Century* (Montreal and Kingston: McGill-Queen's University Press, 1998)

Rowse, Tim 'The Indigenous Redemption of Liberal Universalism', *Modern Intellectual History*, 12.3 (2015), 579–60

Rudy, Jason R., *Imagined Homelands: British Poetry in the Colonies* (Baltimore: Johns Hopkins University Press, 2017)

Russell, Lynette, ed., *Colonial Frontiers: Indigenous-European Encounters in Settler Societies* (Manchester: Manchester University Press, 2001)

— *Roving Mariners: Australian Aboriginal Whalers and Sealers in the Southern Oceans, 1790–1870* (New York: State University of New York Press, 2012)

Ryan, Lyndall, 'Massacre in the Black War in Tasmania 1823–34: A Case Study of the Meander River Region, June 1827', *Journal of Genocide Research*, 10.4 (2008), 479–99

Ryan, Simon, *The Cartographic Eye: How Explorers Saw Australia* (Cambridge: Cambridge University Press, 1996)

Sadleir, Michael, *Blessington-D'Orsay: A Masquerade* (London: Constable, 1947)

Saha, Jonathan, 'No, You're Peripheral', 18 July 2013, n.p., https://colonizinganimals.blog/2013/07/18/no-youre-peripheral/ (accessed 5 April 2019)

Said, Edward, *Orientalism* (London: Pantheon, 1978)

— *The World, the Text, and the Critic* (Cambridge, MA: Harvard University Press, 1984)

Salesa, Damon Ieremia, 'The Pacific in Indigenous Time', in *Pacific Histories: Ocean, Land, Peoples*, ed. by David Armitage and Alison Bashford (Basingstoke: Palgrave Macmillan, 2014), pp. 31–52

— *Racial Crossings: Race, Intermarriage, and the Victorian British Empire* (Oxford: Oxford University Press, 2011)

Salmond, Anne, *Hui: A Study of Maori Ceremonial Gatherings*, revised edn (Auckland: Penguin, 2004)

— *Tears of Rangi: Experiments across Worlds* (Auckland: Auckland University Press, 2017)

— *Two Worlds: First Meetings between Maori and Europeans, 1642–1772* (Auckland: Viking, 1991)

Samuelson, Meg, 'Rendering the Cape-as-Port: Sea-Mountain, Cape of Storms/Good Hope, Adamastor and Local-World Literary Formations', *Journal of South African Studies*, 42.3 (2016), 523–37

— and Charne Lavery, 'The Oceanic South', *English Language Notes*, 57.1 (2019), 37–50

Sanders, Andrew, 'British Colonial Policy and the Role of Amerindians in the Politics of the Nationalist Period in British Guiana, 1945–68', *Social and Economic Studies*, 36.3 (1987), 77–98

Santos, Boaventura de Sousa, *Another Knowledge Is Possible: Beyond Northern Epistemologies* (London and New York: Verso, 2008)

— *The End of the Cognitive Empire: The Coming of Age of Epistemologies of the South* (Durham: Duke University Press, 2018)

Sartori, Andrew, *Bengal in Global Concept History: Culturalism in the Age of Capital* (Chicago: Chicago University Press, 2008)

— 'The Resonance of "Culture": Framing a Problem in Global Concept-History', *Comparative Studies in Society and History*, 47.4 (2005), 676–99

Saunders, Christopher, *The Making of the South African Past: Major Historians on Race and Class* (Totowa: Barnes & Noble Books, 1988)

Sax, Boria, *Imaginary Animals: The Monstrous, the Wondrous and the Human* (London: Reaktion, 2013)

Scates, Bruce, 'Gender, Household and Community Politics: The 1890 Maritime Strike in Australia and New Zealand', *Labour History*, 61 (1991), 70–87

Schaffer, Kay, *In the Wake of First Contact: The Eliza Fraser Stories* (Cambridge: Cambridge University Press, 1995)

Scully, Richard, 'Britain in the *Melbourne Punch*', *Visual Culture in Britain*, 20.2 (2019), 152–71

Sedgwick, Eve Kosofsky, *Touching Feeling: Affect, Pedagogy, Performativity* (Durham and London: Duke University Press, 2003)

Selzer, Anita, *Governors' Wives in Colonial Australia* (Canberra: National Library of Canberra, 2002)

Serres, Michel, *The Parasite*, trans. Lawrence R. Schehr (Baltimore: Johns Hopkins University Press, 1982)

Seymour, A. J., 'The Literary Tradition: The Poetry of Egbert Martin (Leo)', in *Kyk-Over-Al, Volume 1, Issues 1–3, December 1945–December 1946* (Georgetown: Caribbean Press, 2013)

Shaikh, Fariha, *Nineteenth-Century Settler Emigration in British Literature and Art* (Edinburgh: Edinburgh University Press, 2018)

Shakespeare, Nicholas, *In Tasmania* (New York: Overlook Press, 2004)

Shapiro, Stephen, *The Culture and Commerce of the Early American Novel: Reading the Atlantic World-System* (University Park: Penn State University Press, 2008)

Shellam, Tiffany, Maria Nugent, Shino Konishi, and Alison Cadzow, eds, *Brokers and Boundaries Colonial Exploration in Indigenous Territory* (Canberra: Australian National University Press, 2016)

Silva, Denise Ferreira da, *Toward a Global Idea of Race* (Minneapolis: University of Minnesota Press, 2007)

Simons, John, *Kangaroo* (London: Reaktion, 2013)

Simpson, Kathryn, 'H. Rider Haggard, Theophilus Shepstone and the Zikali Trilogy: A Revisionist Approach to Haggard's African Fiction' (unpublished doctoral thesis, Edinburgh Napier University, 2016)

Sithole, Tendayi, *Steve Biko: Decolonial Meditations of Black Consciousness* (Lanham: Lexington Books, 2016)

Skilton, David, 'Contemplating the Ruins of London: Macaulay's New Zealander and Others', *Literary London: Interdisciplinary Studies in the Representation of London*, 2.2 (2004), n.p., http://literarylondon.org/the-literary-london-journal/archive-of-the-literary-london-journal/issue-2-1/contemplating-the-ruins-of-london-macaulays-new-zealander-and-others/ (accessed 1 February 2020)

Skota, T. D. Mweli, *The African Yearly Register: Being an Illustrated National Biographical Dictionary (Who's Who) of Black Folks in Africa* (Johannesburg: R. L. Esson, 1939)

Skotnes, Pippa, ed., *Miscast: Negotiating the Presence of the Bushmen* (Cape Town: University of Cape Town Press, 1996)

Slater, David, *Geopolitics and the Post-Colonial: Rethinking North-South Relations* (Oxford: Blackwell, 2004)

Sleight, Simon, 'Wavering between Virtue and Vice: Constructions of Youth in Australian Cartoons of the Late-Victorian Era', in *Drawing the Line: Using Cartoons as Historical Evidence*, ed. by Richard Scully and Marian Quartly (Clayton: Monash University ePress, 2009), pp. 194–239

Slezak, Michael, 'The Destruction of Australia's Landscape', *Guardian* (7 March 2018), n.p., www.theguardian.com/environment/2018/mar/07/scorched-country-the-destruction-of-australias-native-landscape (accessed 10 November 2019)

Sloterdijk, Peter, *In the World Interior of Capital: Towards a Philosophical Theory of Globalization*, trans. by Wieland Hoban (Cambridge: Polity, 2013)

Smith, Bernard, *Modernism's History: A Study in Twentieth-Century Art and Ideas* (Sydney: University of New South Wales Press, 1998)

Smith, Keith, *Bennelong: The Coming in of the Eora, Sydney Cove 1788–1792* (East Roseville: Kangaroo Press, 2001)

Smith, Vanessa, 'Crusoe in the South Seas: Beachcombers, Missionaries and the Myth of the Castaway', in *Robinson Crusoe: Myths and Metamorphoses*, ed. by Lieve Spaas and Brian Stimpson (London: Macmillan, 1996), pp. 62–77

— *Intimate Strangers: Friendship, Exchange and Pacific Encounters* (Cambridge: Cambridge University Press, 2010)

— 'Joseph Banks's Intermediaries: Rethinking Global Cultural Exchange', in *Global Intellectual History*, ed. by Samuel Moyn and Andrew Sartori (New York: Columbia University Press, 2013), pp. 66–86

— *Literary Culture and the Pacific: Nineteenth-Century Textual Encounters* (Cambridge: Cambridge University Press, 1998)

Sopiee, Mohd Noordin, *From Malayan Union to Singapore Separation: Political Unification in the Malaysia Region, 1945–65* (Kuala Lumpur: University of Malaya Press, 1974)

Southern Conceptualisms Network, n.p., www.museoreinasofia.es/en/southern-conceptualisms-network (accessed 26 June 2019)

Sparke, Matthew, 'Everywhere but Always Somewhere: Critical Geographies of the Global South', *The Global South*, 1.1 (2007), 117–26

Spender, Dale, *Writing a New World: Two Centuries of Australian Women Writers* (London and New York: Pandora, 1988)

Spitta, Silvia, *Between Two Waters: Narratives of Transculturation in Latin America* (Houston: Rice University Press, 1995)

Spivak, Gayatri Chakravorty, *Death of a Discipline* (New York: Columbia University Press, 2003)

— 'The Rani of Sirmur: An Essay in Reading the Archives', *History and Theory*, 24.3 (1985), 247–72

— 'Three Women's Texts and a Critique of Imperialism', *Critical Inquiry*, 12.1 (1985), 243–61

Spry, Adam, *Our War Paint Is Writers' Ink: Anishinaabe Literary Transnationalism* (Albany: SUNY Press, 2018)

Stallard, Avan Judd, *Antipodes: In Search of the Southern Continent* (Melbourne: Monash University Publishing, 2016)

Stampp, Kenneth, *America in 1857: A Nation on the Brink* (Oxford: Oxford University Press, 1990)

Standfield, Rachel, ed., *Indigenous Mobilities: Across and Beyond the Antipodes* (Canberra: Australian National University Press, 2018)

Staple, J. H., 'Louis Becke's Gentleman Pirates and *Lord Jim*', *The Conradian*, 25.1 (2000), 72–82

Steer, Philip, 'The Historians, the Literary Critics, and the Victorian Settler Empire', *Literature Compass*, 15.5 (2018), 1–8

— *Settler Colonialism in Victorian Literature: Economics and Political Identity in the Networks of Empire* (Cambridge: Cambridge University Press, 2020)

Steinberg, Philip E., *The Social Construction of the Ocean* (Cambridge: Cambridge University Press, 2001)

Stern, Walter, 'The First London Dock Boom and the Growth of the West India Docks', *Economica*, new series, 19.73 (1952), 59–77

Stiebel, Lindy, *Imagining Africa: Landscape in H. Rider Haggard's African Romances* (Westport: Greenwood Press, 2001)

— 'A Map to Treasure: The Literary Significance of Thomas Baines's "Map of the Gold Fields of South Eastern Africa" (1875)', *South African Historical Journal*, 39 (1998), 64–9

— and Jane Carruthers, '"The Last Hurrah": Thomas Baines and the Expedition to the Coronation of Cetshwayo kaMpande, Zululand, 1873', *Southern African Humanities*, 32 (2019), 57–82

— and Jane Carruthers, eds, *Thomas Baines: Exploring Tropical Australia, 1855 to 1857* (Canberra: National Museum of Australia, 2012)

— and Jane Carruthers, Vivian Forbes, and Norman Etherington, *Thomas Baines: The Great Map* (Durban: Campbell Collections of the University of Natal, 2001), CD

Stocking, Jnr, George W., 'What's in a Name? The Origins of the Royal Anthropological Institute (1837–71)', *Man: Journal of the Royal Anthropological Institute*, new series, 6.3 (1971), 369–90

Stoler, Ann Laura, 'Tense and Tender Ties: The Politics of Comparison in North American History and (Post) Colonial Studies', *The Journal of American History*, 88.3 (2001), 829–65

Stone, Jeffery, 'The Cartography of Thomas Baines', in *Thomas Baines: Artist in Service of Science*, ed. by Michael Stevenson (London: Christie's, 1999), pp. 118–29

Sturma, Michael, 'By Reef and Palm: Sexual Politics and South Seas Tales', *Journal of Australian Studies*, 21.53 (2009), 108–19

Sweeney, Amin, *A Full Hearing: Orality and Literacy in the Malay World* (Berkeley: University of California Press, 1987)

Switzer, Les, 'The African Christian Community and Its Press in Victorian South Africa (La communauté chrétienne africaine et sa presse dans l'Afrique du Sud victorienne)', *Cahiers d'Études Africaines*, 24.96 (1984), 455–76

Tacey, Ivan, 'Tropes of Fear: The Impact of Globalization on Batek Religious Landscapes', *Religions*, 4 (2013), 240–66

Tally, Robert T., Jr, *The Routledge Handbook of Literature and Space* (London: Taylor & Francis, 2017)

Tan, Bonny, '*The Straits Chinese Magazine*: A Malayan Voice', *BiblioAsia*, 7.2 (2011), 30–5

Teltscher, Kate, *Palace of Palms: Tropical Dreams and the Making of Kew* (London: Picador, 2020)

Te Punga Somerville, Alice, 'Canons: Damned If You Do and Damned If You Don't: A Response to Adam Kostsko', *Australian Humanities Review*, 60 (2016), 186–90

— 'The Lingering War Captain: Maori Texts, Indigenous Contexts', *Journal of New Zealand Literature*, 24.2, Special Issue: Comparative Approaches to Indigenous Literary Studies (2007), 20–43

— 'Living on New Zealand Street: Maori Presence in Parramatta', *Ethnohistory*, 61.4 (2014), 655–9

— *Once Were Pacific: Māori Connections to Oceania* (Minneapolis: University of Minnesota Press, 2012)

Theal, George McCall, *History of South Africa Since September 1795* (Cambridge: Cambridge University Press, 2010)

Thomas, Nicholas, 'Liberty and License: The Forsters' Accounts of New Zealand Sociality', in *Voyages and Beaches: Pacific Encounters, 1769–1840*, ed. by Alex Calder, Jonathan Lamb, and Bridget Orr (Honolulu: University of Hawai'i Press, 1999), pp. 132–55

Thomas, Sue, *Imperialism, Reform, and the Making of Englishness in Jane Eyre* (Basingstoke: Palgrave Macmillan, 2008)

Tiffin, Chris, 'Louis Becke, the *Bulletin* and *By Reef and Palm*', *Kunapipi*, 34.2 (2012), 163–9

Tonkin, Maggie, Mandy Treagus, Madeleine Seys, and Sharon Crozier-De Rosa, 'Re-visiting the Victorian Subject', in *Changing the Victorian Subject*, ed. by Maggie Tonkin, Mandy Treagus, Madeleine Seys, and Sharon Crozier-De Rosa (Adelaide: University of Adelaide Press, 2014), pp. 1–20

Trapido, Stanley, 'The Emergence of Liberalism and the Making of Hottentot Nationalism 1815–1834', *Collected Seminar Papers. Institute of Commonwealth Studies*, 42 (1992), 34–60

— 'From Paternalism to Liberalism: The Cape Colony, 1800–1834', *The International History Review*, 12.1 (1990), 76–104

Treagus, Mandy, 'Crossing "The Beach": Samoa, Stevenson and the "Beach at Falesä"', *Literature Compass*, 11.5 (2014), 312–20

— *Empire Girls: The Colonial Heroine Comes of Age* (Adelaide: University of Adelaide Press, 2014)

Troy, Jakelin, 'The Sydney Language Notebooks and Responses to Language Contact in Early Colonial NSW', *Australian Journal of Linguistics*, 12.1 (1992), 145–70

Tsing, Anna, *Friction: An Ethnography of Global Connection* (Princeton: Princeton University Press, 2004)

Tuck, Eve, and K. Wayne Yang, 'Decolonization is not a Metaphor', *Decolonization: Indigeneity, Education & Society*, 1.1 (2012), 1–40

Tuhiwai Smith, Linda, *Decolonizing Methodologies: Research and Indigenous Peoples* (Auckland: Zed, 1999)

Turnbull, C. M., *A History of Modern Singapore, 1819–2005* (Singapore: National University of Singapore Press, 2009)

Tusan, Michelle, 'Empire and the Periodical Press', in *The Routledge Handbook to Nineteenth-Century British Periodicals and Newspapers*, ed. by Andrew King, Alexis Easley, and John Morton (London: Routledge, 2016), pp. 153–74

Vann, J. Don, and Rosemary T. VanArsdel, eds, *Periodicals of Queen Victoria's Empire: An Exploration* (Toronto: University of Toronto Press, 1996)

Van Toorn, Penny, *Writing Never Arrives Naked* (Canberra: Aboriginal Studies Press, 2006)

Veracini, Lorenzo, 'Introducing Settler Colonial Studies', *Settler Colonial Studies*, 1.1 (2011), 1–12

Viswanathan, Gauri, *Masks of Conquest: Literary Study and British Rule in India* (New York: Columbia University Press, 1989)

Wafer, Jim, 'Ghost-Writing for Wulatji: Incubation and Re-Dreaming as Song Revitalisation Practices', in *Recirculating Songs*, ed. by Jim Wafer and Myfany Turpin (Canberra: Australian National University Press, 2017), pp. 193–256

— and Myfany Turpin, eds, *Recirculating Songs: Revitalising the Singing Practices of Indigenous Australia* (Canberra: Australian National University Press, 2017)

Wagner, Tamara S., 'Introduction: Narrating Domestic Portability: Emigration, Domesticity, and Genre Formation', in *Victorian Settler Narratives: Emigrants, Cosmopolitans and Returnees in Nineteenth-Century Literature*, ed. by Tamara S. Wagner (London: Pickering & Chatto, 2011), pp. 1–22

Wallerstein, Immanuel, *Historical Capitalism with Capitalist Civilization* (London: Verso, 1996)

— *The Modern World-System* (New York: Academic Press, 1964)

Wallis, J. P. R., *Thomas Baines: His Life and Explorations in South Africa, Rhodesia and Australia, 1820–1875*, 2nd edn (Cape Town: A. A. Balkema, 1976)

Warren, Calvin L., *Ontological Terror: Blackness, Nihilism, and Emancipation* (Durham: Duke University Press, 2018)

Warren, Victoria, 'Marlowe's Older Brother: A Forgotten Australian, a Moral Morass, and the Last Free Islands of the South Pacific', *Margins*, 1 (2014), 16–24

Waterhouse, Richard, 'The Minstrel Show and Australian Culture', *Journal of Popular Culture*, 24 (1990), 147–66

Watson, Alex and Laurence Williams, 'British Romanticism in Asia, 1820–1950: Modernity, Tradition, and Transformation in India and East Asia', in *British Romanticism in Asia: The Reception, Translation, and Transformation of Romantic Literature in India and East Asia*, ed. by Alex Watson and Laurence Williams (Basingstoke: Palgrave Macmillan, 2019), pp. 1–38

Webby, Elizabeth, 'Australia', in *Periodicals of Queen Victoria's Empire: An Exploration*, ed. by J. Don Vann and Rosemary T. VanArsdel (Toronto: University of Toronto Press, 1996), pp. 19–60

Wenzlhuemer, Roland, 'The Ship, the Media, and the World: Conceptualizing Connections in Global History', *Journal of Global History*, 11.2 (2016), 163–86

Westmaas, Nigel David, 'A Mirror of Social and Political Ferment: The Newspaper Press of Guyana: 1838–1899' (unpublished doctoral thesis, Binghamton University, State University of New York, 2006)

Wevers, Lydia, *Country of Writing: Travel Writing and New Zealand 1809–1900* (Auckland: Auckland University Press, 2002)

Wilderson III, Frank B., *Red, White & Black: Cinema and the Structure of U. S. Antagonisms* (Durham: Duke University Press, 2010)

Wilentz, Sean, *Chants Democratic: New York City and the Rise of the American Working Class, 1788–1850*, 20th anniversary edn (Oxford: Oxford University Press, 2004)

Willan, Brian, 'What "Other Devils"? The Texts of Sol T. Plaatje's *Mhudi* Revisited', *Journal of Southern African Studies*, 41.6 (2015), 1331–47

Williams, John, 'Isidore, Orosius and the Beatus Map', *Imago Mundi*, 49 (1997), 7–32

Williams, Mark, ed., *A History of New Zealand Literature* (Cambridge: Cambridge University Press, 2016)

Wolfe, Patrick, 'Settler Colonialism and the Elimination of the Native', *Journal of Genocide Research*, 8.4 (2006), 387–409

— *Settler Colonialism and the Transformation of Anthropology: The Politics and Poetics of an Ethnographic Event* (London and New York: Cassell, 1998)

Wong, Edlie L., *Racial Reconstruction: Black Inclusion, Chinese Exclusion, and the Fictions of Citizenship* (New York: New York University Press, 2015)

Wright, Christine, *Wellington's Men in Australia: Peninsular War Veterans and the Making of Empire c. 1820–40* (Basingstoke: Palgrave Macmillan, 2011)

Wu, Duncan, '"A Vehicle of Private Malice": Eliza Hamilton Dunlop and the *Sydney Herald*', *The Review of English Studies*, 65.272 (2014), 888–903

Yan, Shu-Chuan, '"Kangaroo Politics, Kangaroo Ideas, and Kangaroo Society": The Early Years of Melbourne Punch in Colonial Australia', *Victorian Periodicals Review*, 52.1 (2019), 80–102

Young, Sally, *Paper Emperors: The Rise of Australia's Newspaper Empires* (Sydney: University of New South Wales Press, 2019)

Zhan, Mei, *Other-Worldly: Making Chinese Medicine through Transnational Frames* (Durham: Duke University Press: 2009)

Index

Abdul Kadir, Abdullah 366
Aboriginal (Australian) 7, 49, 50, 51,
    114, 177, 180
  languages 24, 197, 273–88
  people 16, 21, 22, 45, 49, 50,
    51, 93, 94, 111–12, 129, 141–2,
    182, 183, 186, 187, 188, 207,
    208, 228, 273–5, 277–88,
    293n.64
  protection 278, 286
  stolen generations 14
  see also dispossession; protectionism
Aborigines Protection Society 327, 330
  see also protectionism
acclimatisation 21, 179–81, 196, 200,
    206
  see also natural history
acculturation 6, 18, 20, 21
African
  activism 328, 329, 341
  liberalism 327, 328, 330, 335, 340,
    341–2, 343n.4
  National Congress 339
  nationalism 2, 329, 339, 341
  see also Black Consciousness; protest
Allen, Chadwick 8, 313–14, 323
American South 17, 150, 152
Amerindian peoples 25, 346, 348, 349,
    350, 351, 352, 353, 354, 355,
    355n.3
Anglosphere 4, 360
  see also British world studies
Anglo-Zulu War 223, 229, 388
Angus, George French 125, 129,
    137n.30
  Savage Life and Scenes in Australia
    and New Zealand 129, 137n.30

animism 352, 353
Anti-Chinese League 140
  see also Sinophobia
Antipodes 19, 39, 59–65, 67, 69, 70,
    71, 74n.4, 75n.14, 82, 103, 106,
    108, 129, 379
  antipodal inversion 59, 61–3, 65, 68,
    70, 71, 72, 75n.14, 386
  antipodean imagination 19, 58, 59,
    60, 68, 72, 384, 388
anti-racism movements 1
anti-slavery 21, 180, 289n.8, 329, 334
  see also slavery
Aotearoa 24, 120, 121, 122, 172, 312,
    313, 319, 320, 321, 322, 323
  see also New Zealand
apartheid 25, 329, 330, 339, 341,
    342n.2, 344n.12
Appadurai, Arjun 96
Araluen, Evelyn 8
archipelagic 256, 263, 267, 389, 390
Arnold, Matthew 360–1, 370
Atkinson, Louisa 21–2, 196–210,
    213n.56, 388
  'After Shells in the Limestone'
    209–10
  Gertrude the Emigrant 196, 203–6
  Tom Hellicar's Children 203, 204,
    206–7
  Tressa's Resolve 206–7
  see also journalism; natural history
Australia 1, 2, 4, 7, 13, 14, 15, 16,
    17, 19, 20, 23, 47, 48, 60, 62,
    63, 65, 66, 67, 68, 70, 81, 83, 88,
    89, 92, 94, 103, 104, 105, 106–7,
    109, 112, 120, 139–41, 142, 143,
    147, 149, 150, 153, 154, 178, 179,

180, 181–4, 186, 187, 189, 190,
191, 197, 199, 201, 202, 203, 206,
225, 263, 274, 277, 287, 381, 382,
383, 387
colonisation of 16, 24, 45, 49, 58–9,
74n.7, 85, 111, 142,
exploration of 48, 187, 188, 215,
228, 231, 386
landscape of 16, 21, 22, 45, 48, 63,
90, 92, 129, 196, 197, 199, 202,
206, 208, 209
see also Aboriginal (Australian)
Australian Constitutions Act 59
Awabakal people 24, 276, 278, 281,
291n.32

Bachapin (Tswana) people 244
Baines, Thomas 22, 215–32, 386, 388
Ballantyne, Tony 168
Banivanua Mar, Tracey 17, 262, 295,
297, 298, 306, 389
Banks, Joseph 48, 122, 178, 274
Barlow, Harriott 24, 274, 282–7, 288,
293n.64
'Vocabulary of Aboriginal Dialects of
Queensland' 286
see also linguistic studies
Barrow, John 239
Beauvoir, (Count) Ludovic de 184–6
Becke, Louis 23, 253–67, 268n.7, 382,
387, 389
By Reef and Palm 23, 253, 254,
255, 257
Bennelong 178, 180, 275
Bernau, John Henry 346, 349, 350
*Missionary Labours in British
Guiana* 349
see also Christianity; conversion;
missionary
Bhabha, Homi K. 11, 141
Bible 161–2, 169, 171–2, 294–5, 301,
306, 308n.6, 349, 387, 388
Te Bibilia Tapu 295
te reo 171
bildungsroman 17
Bintang Timor 366
Biraban (Johny M'Gill) 273, 276,
279, 287
blackbirding 261
Black Consciousness 1, 2, 27n.27

Blessington, (Countess) Marguerite
Gardiner 78, 79, 90
circus 78–9, 84
Conversations of Lord Byron 79
Blessington, (Lady) Harriet Gardiner
78, 79, 97
The Idler in France 84, 97
The Idler in Italy 84
blue humanities 20, 103, 116n.1
see also oceanic studies
Boehmer, Elleke 4, 8
To the Volcano 382
Boer people 8, 216, 231
Boer South African Republic 223
Boongaree/Bungaree 45, 50, 55,
101n.54
Botany Bay 45, 46, 49, 54, 66, 82, 83,
89, 98, 100n.37, 178, 180
British and Foreign Bible Society 294–5
see also Bible
British Guiana 2, 25, 346–52, 354, 355,
355n.3, 356n.14, 356n.17, 386
British world studies 2, 3, 4–5, 7
see also Anglosphere
Bulletin 147, 148, 255, 268n.7
Bunyan, John 169, 172
Pilgrim's Progress 169–71
Burchell, William 22, 236–50
*Travels in the Interior of Southern
Africa* 22, 236
see also natural history; travel writing
Burford, Robert 39, 41, 43, 44, 46, 47,
48, 49, 51, 52
'A View of the Town of Sydney' 20,
39, 43, 53, 46, 47, 48, 51, 53,
54, 55
*Description of a View of the Town of
Sydney* 43, 45–6
'Panorama of Sydney N.S.W.' 43, 44
see also panoramas
Buzacott, Aaron 294, 295, 297, 298,
299, 305, 307, 308n.5, 309n.14
see also London Missionary Society
(LMS); missionary
Byron, (Lord) George Gordon 78, 79,
82, 84, 88, 89, 90, 96, 97, 162,
166, 367, 368
Childe Harold's Pilgrimage 367
Don Juan 82, 84, 85, 89, 90
Hours of Idleness 83

cannibalism 114, 149, 260, 299
canonicity 1, 3, 4, 15, 16, 17, 21, 78,
    253, 254, 255, 312, 314, 317, 321,
    322, 359, 360, 368, 369
Cape Colony 18, 215, 236, 237, 328,
    329, 335, 339, 340, 343n.7
Cape Muslims 18
Cape Town 4, 225, 236, 237, 247, 248,
    249, 332
Carlyle, Thomas 58, 96
cartography 5, 18, 42, 59–61, 75n.13,
    217, 231, 256
    see also mapping
Cetshwayo kaMpande 22, 215, 216,
    219, 221, 226, 227, 231
Chakrabarty, Dipesh 11, 389
Chinese 2, 7, 25–6, 48, 140, 141, 188,
    359, 361, 362, 363, 364, 365, 366,
    369, 370, 371
    cultural revivalism 358, 359, 365–6
    diasporas 2, 25, 140, 362
    language 361, 364, 369, 372
    Protectorate 362, 363
    Straits 25–6, 358, 359, 364, 365, 367,
        368, 369, 370, 371, 372
Christianity 24, 137n.29, 294, 296–
    302, 304–6, 310n.36, 351, 353
    see also conversion; London
    Missionary Society (LMS);
    missionary
class 19, 20, 52, 65, 66, 70, 82, 86, 90,
    96, 105, 139, 140, 141, 142, 146,
    147, 149–51, 153, 154, 155n.23,
    169, 172, 197, 202, 250, 281,
    296, 330, 334, 339, 347, 358, 363,
    364, 369
    see also labour
Clacy, Ellen 198, 202, 204, 205,
    212n.28
    'The Bush Fire' 202, 212n.32
Clifford, Hugh 366, 375n.48
Clifford, James 6, 8, 18
Coetzee, J. M. 241, 380–1
    Jesus trilogy 380
Collins, David 69, 289n.8
    *An Account of the English Colony in
    New South Wales* 69
Collins, Wilkie 368
colonialism 1, 3, 5, 8, 9, 15, 17, 19, 21,
    24, 25, 98, 103, 107, 110, 111,

134, 223, 242, 246, 274, 275, 286,
    287, 327, 328, 330, 332, 349,
    360, 386
    see also dispossession; settlement
Colonist 346, 348, 349
communism 145, 148, 156n.34
comparatism 25–6, 359, 361, 363, 364,
    371, 372
Confucianism 365, 369, 370, 372
Conrad, Joseph 254, 255, 256,
conversion 300, 301, 304, 305
    see also Christianity; London
    Missionary Society (LMS);
    missionary
convictism 19, 47, 49, 51, 52, 65–6,
    76n.34, 81–4, 85, 86, 88, 89, 95,
    96–8, 106, 122, 278
    see also transportation
Cook, (Captain) James 122, 136n.9,
    178, 260
    Endeavour journals 122, 274,
Cook Islands 24, 294–5, 297, 298,
    299, 300, 302, 304, 305,
    308n.2, 387
Copernicus, Nicolaus 41
    *On the Revolutions of the Heavenly
    Spheres* 41
Cosme 139, 142, 143, 145–54
    see also Nueva Australia
Cosme Evening Notes 143, 145,
    146, 148
Cosme Monthly 20, 139, 143, 144, 145,
    146, 147, 149, 152, 153, 154
cosmopolitanism 13, 23, 316
Creole 23, 25, 346, 348, 349, 350, 351,
    353, 354, 386
    indigeneity 25, 349, 350, 352,
    353, 354
cultural geography 5–6, 319, 320

dandyism 79, 81–2, 83, 84, 86, 90, 92,
    95, 96, 98, 379
    see also fashion/fashionability
Darkinyung people 23, 24, 278
Darling, (Governor) Ralph 45, 50, 55,
    93, 180
Darling, Eliza 50
Darug/Dharug nation 197
Darwin, Charles 122, 124, 186, 362
    On the Origin of Species 362

Darwin, Erasmus 46
Dawes, William 275, 276, 287, 289n.8, 293n.64
Dawson, Robert 187
decolonialisation 8, 9, 11, 14, 17, 353, 360
Defoe, Daniel 21, 162, 163, 164, 166, 169, 172, 388
    Robinson Crusoe 21, 161–7, 169, 170, 171, 172, 173, 388
DeLoughrey, Elizabeth 123, 137n.23
Demerara Daily Chronicle 347
Dening, Greg 123
Dickens, Charles 58, 71, 97, 361, 368–9, 370
    A Christmas Carol, 368
    A Tale of Two Cities, 71
dispossession 5, 18, 21, 22, 24, 49, 50, 110, 122, 180, 182, 210, 277, 278, 282, 285, 331, 332, 335, 341, 382
    see also colonialism; settlement; settler colonial studies
D'Orsay, (Count) Alfred 78, 79, 82, 90, 92, 97
Dube, John Langalibalele 18
Dumaresq, (Colonel) Henry 39, 43, 45, 50, 55
Dunlop, Eliza Hamilton 15, 23, 273, 274, 277–82, 284, 287, 291n.43, 293n.64, 293n.70, 388
    'The Aboriginal Mother' 278, 281, 388
    see also linguistic studies
Dutch East India Company (VOC) 329, 330

Earle, Augustus 20, 39, 120–35, 135n.3, 136n.8, 137n.40, 186, 387
    A Bivouac of Travellers in Australia 186, 187
    A Narrative of a Nine Months' Residence in New Zealand 20, 120, 122, 124–9, 135n.2, 137n.37
    see also travel writing
ecocriticism 20, 21, 22, 120, 121, 122, 134, 136n.18, 199, 205, 210
Egan, Pierce 86, 89
    Life in London 86, 89

emigration 5, 20, 65, 66, 68, 69, 88, 104–7, 115, 140, 162, 163, 188, 189, 199, 201, 369, 379
encounter narratives 3, 18, 20, 21, 47, 61, 105, 111, 112, 115, 121, 123–5, 127, 131–2, 167, 243–6, 250, 276–7, 285, 287, 317, 330, 367, 387, 389
Enlightenment 26, 43, 51, 125, 241, 362, 365
    Scottish 241
Eora people 178, 189, 275, 276
ethnocentrism 369
Eurocentrism 5, 9, 11, 12, 14, 18, 19, 23, 26, 59, 62, 72, 255, 361, 362, 363, 366, 367, 372, 379
Evangelical Magazine 302
evangelicalism 169, 276, 297, 299, 301, 302, 304, 306, 307, 308n.3
    see also Christianity; London Missionary Society (LMS); missionary
Exeter Hall 302, 328, 334, 341
exoticism 24, 69, 255, 270n.60, 302, 313

Fabian, Johannes 386
Fairbarn, John 331
fashion/fashionability 19, 63, 79, 82–3, 85, 86, 95, 96, 100n.40, 379
    see also dandyism
Fernyhough, William 92, 93, 94
Field, Barron 16, 88, 100n.38
    First Fruits of Australian Poetry 16, 88
First Nations people 277
    see also Aboriginal (Australian); Māori
flash culture 19, 82, 83, 85, 86, 87, 88, 89, 98, 99n.7
Foster, George 240
Freeman, Joseph John 297
Freeman Sentinel 347
Friedrich, Caspar David 132

Galmarra ('Jacky') 16
Gamilaraay people 210, 279, 292n.53
Gikandi, Simon 15, 145–6
Gipps, (Governor) George 278

globalisation 1, 8, 9, 10, 13, 18, 23, 179, 267
Global South 1, 5, 9, 28n.18, 103, 115, 384
  critique of 26n.3
globes 40, 41, 42
Goethe, Johann Wolfgang von 240, 360
Govett, William Romaine 90–2
Grey, George 168, 169, 172, 274, 288n.4
Grose, Francis 82, 83, 85, 86, 87
  Classical Dictionary of the Vulgar Tongue 82, 83, 84, 86
Guaraní 20, 145, 146, 149, 150, 152, 153, 154
Guiana Herald 350
Gungarri 284
Guugu Yimidhirr 274
Guyana 356n.17, 387
  see also British Guiana

Hadot, Pierre 22, 240, 242
Haggard, H. Rider 17
  King Solomon's Mines 17
  see also imperial, romance
Haller, Albrecht von 41, 42
Harootunian, Harry 1, 125, 385
Harpur, Charles 15, 16, 207
Hau'ofa, Epeli 12, 267, 310n.33, 382, 387, 389
Hawai'i 14
Heath, William 54
Heidegger, Martin 10, 11
Hemans, Felicia 146, 147, 148
hemispheric studies 3, 4, 7, 11, 386
Hocken, Thomas 171
Hofmeyr, Isabel 7, 27n.9, 169, 171
Horne, R. H. 58
Hotten, James Camden 87
  Dictionary of Modern Slang, Cant, and Vulgar Words 87–8
Humboldt, Alexander von 240, 241
  Views of Nature 240
  see also natural history
Hunter, John 177, 186

imperial
  cartographies 1, 5, 12, 22, 231–2
  desire 1, 105, 257

imaginaries 6, 26n.4, 40, 59, 115
  geographies 1, 18, 55, 59, 125, 221
  literacy 23, 24, 306
  networks 15–16, 21, 47, 162, 168, 257, 267, 295, 298, 300, 378
  romance 17, 265
imperialism 3, 5, 10, 11, 18, 122, 123, 134, 142, 189, 258, 318, 353, 359, 371, 372, 386
Im Thurn, Everard 352, 354
India 14, 96, 104, 107, 120, 198, 318, 383, 384
Indian diaspora 2
indigeneity 21, 352, 356n.17, 371
Indigenous
  activism 1, 5, 21
  cartographies 12
  ontologies 6
  studies 2, 4, 8, 9
interregionalism 6, 7
  see also regionalism
intimacy 277, 283, 297
  interracial 23, 255
Ireland 19, 78, 90, 273
Islamocentric 26, 372
island studies 12, 123, 137n.23, 256–7
Italy 78

Jabavu, John Tengo 339, 340–1
  Imvo Zabantsundu 340–1
Jawi Peranakan 366
Jones, William 361
journalism 203, 208–10, 225
  see also periodicals
Juvenile Missionary Magazine 297, 301, 302–5

Kamilaroi
  language 273, 279, 280
  people 278, 280
kangaroo 21, 49, 51, 53, 90, 178–81, 388
  hunting 21, 177–92
Karoo, the 241, 242, 382
Khoisan/Khoesan people 8, 17, 236, 243, 247–8, 329, 333–6, 338, 388
Kiro 24, 294–308
  'Kiro's Thoughts about England' 24, 297–308

Kōhere, Mokena 24, 312, 315, 319–20
Kōhere, Rēweti 24, 312–23, 323–4n.1, 324n.8, 385
A Story of a Maori Chief 319
Krishnan, Sanjay 10, 11, 365

labour 3, 17, 20, 66, 84, 95–6, 107, 134, 139–40, 149, 151–4, 206, 216, 296, 333–7, 349, 350, 360, 371
  convict 83, 85, 278
  coolie 141, 364
  domestic 112, 277, 280
  indentured 17, 261–2, 329, 349, 355n.3, 362
  movements/unions 139–42, 146
  see also class
lag fever 19, 82–3, 88, 98
Lamb, Charles 96, 368
Lamont, Archibald 368–9
Landor, Edward Wilson 188–9
Lane, William 20, 139–54
  Boomerang 139, 140, 148, 153
  Cosme Monthly 20, 139, 143–8, 149–54
  White or Yellow 140
  Worker 140–2, 153, 155n.8
  The Workingman's Paradise 16
  see also labour; utopianism
languaging 14
Lawson, Henry 15, 16, 148–9, 150
Lee, Sarah Bowdich 181, 183, 191
  Adventures in Australia 182
  The African Wanderers 182
liberalism 23, 25, 26, 327, 328, 330, 335, 341–2, 342n.1, 359, 372
Lim, Boon Keng 359, 361, 362–3, 368, 370, 371
linguistic studies 3, 9, 19, 23–4, 88, 273–88, 382
  see also philology
literacy 14, 17, 18, 24, 25, 171, 294, 298–9, 305–6, 328, 342–3n.3, 346–7, 347–9, 350, 351, 354–5, 358, 359, 366, 367, 386
London Missionary Society (LMS) 259, 276, 294–5, 296, 297, 298, 299, 305, 306, 307, 308n.5, 329, 338, 340, 341, 343n.5, 387

see also Christianity; evangelicalism; missionary
Longfellow, Henry Wadsworth 58

Macaulay, Thomas Babington 24, 58, 312–13, 314–16, 316–17, 318, 319, 320, 321, 322–3, 361, 364, 385
  Horatius 312, 313, 315, 317, 318, 322
  Lays of Ancient Rome 312, 318
Maclise, Daniel 78–9, 90, 91
Macquarie, (Governor) Lachlan 45
Malay
  culture/literature 358, 359, 365–7
  language 364, 369
  people 2, 25, 358, 360, 362–3, 367
  nationalism 371–2
Malay Archipelago 6, 361
  see also Straits Settlements
Malaysia 387
Mamoe/Mamoe Fafine 307
Mandandanji people 24, 282,
Māori 7, 8, 12, 14, 20, 24, 122, 128, 131–2, 170, 171, 172, 312, 314, 315, 316, 317, 319, 320, 321, 322
  Cook Islands 294, 295, 304, 387
  land claims 25, 315, 315–16, 320, 324n.8
  people 12, 24, 120, 121, 122, 125, 126, 127, 128, 129, 130, 134, 166, 167–8, 171, 172, 173, 313, 314, 319, 387
  te reo 21, 169, 170, 171
  Treaty of Waitangi 13, 129, 313–14
  see also dispossession; First Nations people
mapping 12, 50, 132, 217, 221, 230, 284, 382
Maretu 299
Marsh, Selina Tusitala 6
Martin, Egbert 25, 346, 350–4
  Leo's Local Lyrics 351–3
  Leo's Poetical Works 351, 353
Marx, Karl 139, 154
Maslen, Thomas J. 5
Melbourne 71, 72, 106, 141
Melbourne Punch 58, 62, 66–7, 68, 70, 71–2, 73
Melville, Herman 378

Moby Dick 378
Mignolo, Walter 14
minstrelsy 20, 139, 146, 149–54
  see also American South; racism
missionary 24, 122, 171, 218, 247, 260,
    273, 276, 294–5, 296–7, 298,
    299–300, 301, 302, 306, 327–8,
    329, 332, 334, 336, 341–2
  humanitarianism 341
  presses 15, 25, 297
  see also Christianity; evangelicalism;
    London Missionary Society (LMS)
Mitchell, Thomas 91, 92–3, 94, 95
  Expeditions into the Interior 94
mobilities studies 20, 120, 128, 132,
    134–5, 257
mondialisation 10, 18
Mount Dispersion massacre 93–4
Mueller, Ferdinand von 196, 200
Müller, Friedrich Max 361, 374n.26
Murray, John 88, 89–90, 100n.38
Myall Creek massacre 278, 281,
    290n.19

Nanyang 25, 359
Napoleon 78, 92
  Napoleonic Wars 92, 94
Natal 215, 216, 219, 224, 228, 229,
    230, 231
  Land and Colonisation Company
    216
  Volunteer Escort 216, 219, 220, 222
Natal Mercury 22, 217, 221, 224,
    225–6, 228, 229, 230
nationalism 16, 25, 333, 338–9
  Afrikaner 330, 339, 345n.34
  anticolonial 359, 371
  Australian 147, 256
  cultural 372
  ethnic 25, 371–3
  postcolonial 359
Native Land Court 315, 316, 319, 320
natural history 111, 124, 184, 189,
    196–7, 208–9, 238–9, 262
  see also acclimatisation
New South Wales 23, 43, 48, 49, 53,
    63–4, 74n.7, 82, 83, 85, 86, 88,
    139, 140, 177, 182, 187, 196–8,
    201, 203, 209, 210, 274, 276,
    278–81, 282

New Zealand 1, 2, 4, 7, 13, 17, 21, 60,
    120, 121–3, 124, 126–9, 131–2,
    139, 143, 161–3, 165, 183,
    312–13, 315, 318–20, 321–3, 383,
    386, 387, 388
  see also Aotearoa
New Zealand Wars 315
Newton, Isaac 41–3, 46
  *Philosophiae Naturalis Principia
    Mathematica* 41
Ngāti Porou 24, 319–20
Norris, Emilia Marryat 183, 191
  Jack Stanley 183
Nueva Australia 20, 142–3, 154
  see also Cosme; Lane, William

Oceania 6, 12, 60, 259
oceanic studies 3, 32n.67, 104
  see also blue humanities
oceans 12, 20, 40, 55, 66, 103, 107,
    109, 110, 111, 302, 378, 379, 380,
    381, 383, 387, 389, 390n.1
  Indian Ocean 2, 6, 25, 358,
    359, 383
  Pacific Ocean 45
  South Atlantic Ocean 2
  Southern Ocean 2, 3, 106, 116n.5,
    378
  South Pacific Ocean 2
ontopolitics 6, 29n.30
orality 14, 18, 254, 287, 305, 354, 358

Pacific Islands 2, 6, 7, 253–67, 294,
    303, 306
  see also Cook Islands; Samoa
Pākehā 20, 121, 128, 167, 168,
    169, 170, 171, 172, 173, 313,
    314, 317, 320, 321, 322, 323,
    387, 388
panoramas 18–19, 39, 40–1, 43, 120,
    241, 378, 387, 389
  as exhibition 52, 53, 54
  as fiction 49, 50, 51
  panoramic realism 43, 45, 46
  as regeneration 46, 47, 48
  see also Burford, Robert
Paraguay 20, 139, 142–4, 146–8, 149,
    150, 153–4
Pasifika 7
pastoralism 198–202

Paterson, Banjo 147, 148
Patyegarang 275–6, 287
periodicals 15–16, 20, 23, 25, 104–5,
    254–5, 281, 322, 347–9, 359, 371,
    372, 384
    see also journalism
periodicity 2, 4, 13–14, 314
    trans-periodising 13
petitions 14, 23, 24, 25, 278, 315–17,
    320, 322, 323, 327–8, 330, 331,
    332, 334, 335–7, 338, 341, 384,
    385, 389
    see also protest
Philip, John 329, 332–4, 336, 337, 341,
    343n.5
    Researches in South Africa 329, 330,
    332–4
    see also London Missionary Society
    (LMS); missionary
Phillip, (Governor) Arthur 43, 46, 85,
    178, 180
Phillips, Thomas 96–7
philology 286, 359, 293n.64
    see also linguistic studies
picturesque 129, 132, 188, 197, 241
Piper, John 92–4, 95
Pitman, Charles 294, 299–300, 301
plaasroman 17
Plaatjie, Sol 17
    Mhudi 17
Pope, Alexander 42
    Essay on Man 42
Port Jackson 39, 43, 45, 47, 69, 177
Power, (Major) Robert 97
Pratt, Mary Louise 121, 123, 128, 132,
    239
    Imperial Eyes 121, 239
Pringle, Thomas 331
prospect view 19, 20, 40, 53, 121, 126,
    131–2, 134
    see also panoramas; travel writing
protectionism
    economic 65
    legal 278, 286, 330, 348, 362–3
        see also Aboriginal (Australian);
        Aborigines Protection Society;
        Chinese, Protectorate
protest
    literature 25, 329, 331
    politics 330, 339, 341

see also African, activism; petitions
Queensland 24, 74n.6, 139–40, 141,
    197, 207, 274, 282, 283, 285, 286,
    288, 381

racism 20, 114, 140, 146, 150–1, 187,
    197, 201, 339
    see also Sinophobia;
    White Australia
realism 42, 48, 253, 254, 256, 365
Regency 19, 78, 82, 83, 85, 88, 90, 92,
    97, 98
regionalism 4, 5, 6, 7, 16, 359, 360,
    279, 381
    see also interregionalism
responsible government 59, 67, 74n.6
Romanticism 16, 239
    global 12–13, 14
Romantic movement/period 2, 4, 16,
    43, 83, 186, 239–40, 241, 281
Rose, Deborah Bird 6, 197, 199, 206,
    286
Royal Anthropological Institute 286
Royal Gazette 348–9
Royal Geographical Society (RGS) 217,
    219, 221, 223, 228, 231, 386

Said, Edward 11, 385
Samoa 261, 305
    people of 258, 307
San people 238, 243–7, 247–8, 249,
    250n.2
Santos, Boaventura de Sousa 5
sea voyages 104, 105, 110, 112, 114,
    122, 136n.8, 234n.61, 240, 259,
    297, 301, 384
    between Britain and Australia 103,
    106, 107, 180, 212n.27
sentimentalism 147, 244, 246,
    257, 258
settlement 16, 18, 20, 21, 40, 45, 48,
    49, 51, 114, 142, 153–4, 162, 177,
    187, 196, 209, 237
    see also colonialism; dispossession
settler colonial studies 3, 8, 103
    critiques of 8
Shakespeare, William 84–5, 254, 312,
    361, 364, 368–9
Shepstone, Theophilus 215, 216, 217,
    218, 221, 224

shipboard writing
  diaries/journals 105, 177, 178,
    184, 187
  fiction 124, 134
  periodicals 103, 104–5, 105–7,
    108–9, 117n.22
  short story 15, 23, 70, 111, 200, 202,
    253–5, 368, 369, 382, 386
Singapore 25, 258, 362, 366, 369
  see also Straits Settlements
Sinocentrism 26, 372
Sinophobia 141
  see also racism; White Australia
Skota, T. D. Mweli 339
  African Yearly Register 339
slavery 145, 151, 153, 154,
    180, 262, 296, 309n.12,
    329, 330, 334, 348
  see also anti-slavery
Sloterdijk, Peter 39, 40
  Spheres: Plural Spherology 39
Smith, Linda Tuhiwai 9
sociability 19, 40, 48, 103, 114, 115
Song, Ong Siang 359, 366
South Africa 1, 2, 4, 7, 13, 17, 215, 327,
    328, 329, 330, 331, 332, 334, 339,
    341, 342, 382
South African Gold Fields Exploration
    Company 216
South African Native National
    Congress (SANNC) 25, 339, 340
  see also African, activism; protest
South African War 340
South America 2, 7, 20, 88, 124, 139,
    141, 142, 154, 186, 383, 385
southern
  continent 58, 59, 60–1, 142, 154
  epistemologies 5, 390
  hemisphere 1, 2, 4, 14, 19, 20, 23, 39,
    41, 55, 58, 67, 72, 103, 105, 106,
    107, 121, 154, 297, 300, 307, 378,
    379, 380, 382, 383, 384, 387
  latitudinal studies 7
  perspectives 3, 4, 7, 8, 12, 13, 379,
    388, 389
  theory 115, 385
  topographies 1, 5–6, 383
South Seas 25, 253, 254, 255, 256, 263,
    264, 267, 378
  see also Pacific Islands

sovereignty 8, 285, 313, 322, 323, 354
spatialisation 10, 18, 19, 40, 103,
    105, 115
Spivak, Gayatri Chakravorty 9, 11, 15
Stevenson, Robert Louis 254, 256
Stoffels, Andries 336, 337, 384
Straits Chinese Magazine 25–6, 358–72
Straits Settlements 2, 358, 359,
    360, 371
  see also Malay Archipelago;
    Singapore
sublime 52, 127, 137n.38, 197, 240–1,
    242, 363
  see also travel writing
Sydney 39, 43, 45, 46, 47, 48, 49, 50,
    51, 52, 53, 54, 90, 129, 141, 148,
    177, 186, 187, 197, 275, 281
Sydney Morning Herald 196, 199,
    209, 283
Sydney Punch 63, 68, 69, 70

Tan, Teck Soon 358, 361, 362, 363,
    364–5, 371
Tennyson, Alfred 58, 361, 368
Te Punga Somerville, Alice 13, 16,
    297, 306
Terra Australis 58, 59, 74n.4
terra nullius 16, 67, 333
Te Toa Takitini 312
Te Wherowhero 168
Threlkeld, Lancelot 274, 276, 279,
    281, 284, 287
  *A Key to the Structure of the
    Aboriginal Language* 276
  see also linguistic studies; missionary
tourism 82, 270n.60
transculturation 6, 21
trans-Indigenous 8
translation 14, 21, 24, 169–72, 285,
    294–5, 297, 304, 306, 308n.5,
    309n.14, 313, 359, 366, 387
transnationalism 3, 4, 13, 82,
    178, 182
transportation 19, 65–6, 76n.33, 82–4,
    85, 86, 88, 89, 96
  see also convictism
travel writing 18, 20, 120, 121, 123,
    127, 128, 182, 184, 187–9, 189–91
Treaty of Waitangi 13, 129, 313–14
Troy, Jakelin 275, 289n.10

Tuck, Eve 9
Tuki Tahua 12

universalism 23, 24, 25, 359, 360, 363,
     365, 368, 369, 371, 372
unsettlement 16, 17, 40
utopianism 20, 124, 139, 140, 149, 154

Van Diemen's Land 82, 88, 96, 97, 98
Vaux, James Hardy 82, 86–7, 88, 89–90
     Memoirs 86–7, 88, 90, 100n.38
     Vocabulary of the Flash Language
     82, 86
vernacular presses 15, 23
Vetch, James 5
Victoria
     colony of 58, 67, 74n.6, 184, 189,
     202
     Queen 327, 369, 370
Victorian studies 2, 4
     global 12–13
Vidal, Mary Theresa 200, 201
     'The Cabramatta Store' 200

Wakefield, Edward Gibbon 5
     A Letter from Sydney 5
Wainewright, Thomas Griffiths 96–7, 98
Wallerstein, Immanuel 379
Weekes, Henry 161, 163, 166–8
Wentworth, William Charles 16

West India Dock Company 296
Wheelwright, Horace 189–92
     Bush Wanderings of a Naturalist
     189, 190
White Australia 16, 150
     policy 141
     see also racism; Sinophobia
Wilkinson, R. J. 366–7
Winton, Tim 381–2
     Island Home 381
Wonnaruah people 24, 278
worlding 3, 4, 10–11, 20, 120, 378–9,
     386, 387
world-systems theory 11, 32n.55
Wright, Alexis 381
     Carpentaria 381
Wulatji 279, 281

Xhosa
     culture 14
     people 343n.5

Yang, K. Wayne 9
Yehdell 284, 285, 286, 287
Yemmerrawanne 178
Yuwalaraay people 210

Zululand 22, 215, 216, 223, 224, 229,
     231, 388
Zulu people 17, 22, 216, 224, 226–8, 229

CPSIA information can be obtained
at www.ICGtesting.com
Printed in the USA
LVHW071608110322
713244LV00006B/52

9 781526 152886

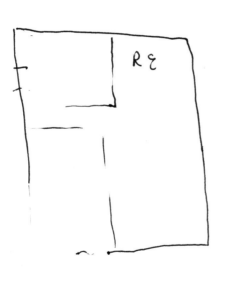

RA | 1 | 5 | Sw
        | 6 | RE

>Sw | 2 |
T2 | 3 |
KKG | 4 | Lw | 7 MA
             | 8 | ☐ 10
        9

Budget / Personell - AP ?
Alumni

RE